DATE DUE

Brodart Co.   Cat. # 55 137 001   Printed in USA

INTERNATIONAL HANDBOOK OF ENTREPRENEURSHIP AND HRM

International Handbook of Entrepreneurship and HRM

Edited by

Rowena Barrett

Department of Human Resource Management, Leicester Business School, De Montfort University, UK

and

Susan Mayson

Department of Management, Monash University, Australia

Edward Elgar
Cheltenham, UK • Northampton, MA, USA

Published by
Edward Elgar Publishing Limited
Glensanda House
Montpellier Parade
Cheltenham
Glos GL50 1UA
UK

Edward Elgar Publishing, Inc.
William Pratt House
9 Dewey Court
Northampton
Massachusetts 01060
USA

A catalogue record for this book
is available from the British Library

Library of Congress Control Number: 2008926561

ISBN 978 1 84542 926 3 (cased)

Printed and bound in Great Britain by MPG Books Ltd, Bodmin, Cornwall

Contents

v

Contributors

David Audretsch, Max Planck Institute of Economics, Germany

Rowena Barrett, De Montfort University, UK

Robert Blackburn, Kingston University, UK

Deborah Blackman, University of Canberra, Australia

Grahame Boocock, Loughborough University, UK

S. Michael Camp, The Ohio State University, USA

Melissa S. Cardon, Pace University, USA

Charlotte Carey, Birmingham City University, UK

Catherine Cassell, University of Manchester, UK

Elizabeth Chell, Kingston University, UK

Li Xue Cunningham, City University, UK

Cinzia Dal Zotto, Jönköping University, Sweden

Kevin Daniels, Loughborough University, UK

Hefin David, University of Wales Institute, Cardiff, UK

David Devins, Leeds Metropolitan University, UK

Jane Glover, Loughborough University, UK

James D. Grant, Saint Mary's University, Canada

Veronica Gustafsson, Jönköping University, Sweden

Richard Harris, University of Glasgow, UK

Robert L. Heneman, The Ohio State University, USA

Kevin Hindle, Swinburne University, Australia

Julie Holland, Loughborough University, UK

Jeff Hyman, University of Aberdeen, UK

Sarah Jack, Lancaster University, UK

Shaheena Janjuha-Jivraj, University of Reading, UK

David M. Kaplan, Saint Louis University, USA

Jerome A. Katz, Saint Louis University, USA

Susan Marlow, De Montfort University, UK

Lynn M. Martin, Birmingham City University, UK

Susan Mayson, Monash University, Australia

Jonathan Michie, University of Birmingham, UK

Erik Monsen, Max Planck Institute of Economics, Germany

Sara Nadin, University of Bradford, UK

Fraser Osborne, University of Aberdeen, UK

Srikanth Sursani Reddy, Birmingham City University, UK

Renee Reid, Glasgow Caledonian University, UK

Jeffrey Robinson, New York University, USA

Chris Rowley, City University, UK

Maura Sheehan, University of Dallas, USA

David Smallbone, Kingston University, UK

Judith W. Tansky, The Ohio State University, USA

Ibraiz Tarique, Pace University, USA

Scott Taylor, University of Essex, UK

Amanda Thompson, De Montfort University, UK

Terry H. Wagar, Saint Mary's University, Canada

Niel Warriner, Monash University, Australia

Gerald Watts, University of Gloucestershire, UK

Ian Williamson, Melbourne Business School, Australia

Acknowledgements

This book is a joint effort and through its production we have been sustained by our friendship which extends beyond our relationship as colleagues. We would like to acknowledge the assistance Sharon Fowler and Emily Severn provided us with chasing authors and editing chapters. We also want to acknowledge the contribution of those who joined us in Hawaii in August 2005 and in Prato in July 2006 to discuss many of the chapters that appear in the book. Finally, family is also important – thanks Al and Scott!

Every effort has been made to trace all the copyright holders but if any have been inadvertently overlooked the publishers will be pleased to make the necessary arrangements at the first opportunity.

1 Introduction: at the intersection of entrepreneurship and human resource management

Rowena Barrett and Susan Mayson

Is there anything left to say?

In recent years there has been a growing literature on human resource management (HRM) and smaller firms which has also encompassed firms that are growing and entrepreneurial. For example we have seen a special edition of *Entrepreneurship Theory and Practice* (Katz et al., 2000), two of *Human Resource Management Review* (Baron, 2003; Barrett and Mayson, 2006) and one of *Human Resource Management* (Huselid, 2003; Tansky and Heneman, 2003), with another of *Human Resource Management* (to be edited by Ribeiro, Roig and Tansky) scheduled for publication in 2010. In addition, symposia on the topic have been undertaken at the Academy of Management in 2005 (organized by Mayson) and in 2004 (organized by Hayton). Papers dealing with issues of HRM for new, small, growing and/or entrepreneurial firms have been presented at a range of different conferences, whether they are management oriented such as the Academy of Management (AoM) and its regional variants (for example, the British Academy of Management (BAM) or the Australian and New Zealand Academy of Management (ANZAM)), entrepreneurially focused ones like the Babson College Entrepreneurship Research conference or ones focused specifically on smaller firms such as the conferences of the Institute for Small Business and Entrepreneurship (ISBE) in the UK or the International Council for Small Business (ICSB) and its regional affiliates.

With all these papers and all this discussion is there anything left to say? Well yes, we think there is and we are glad Edward Elgar agree with us! We believe there is much to say about the contribution of HRM to small and entrepreneurial firms.

What has been said recently . . .

In preparing this introduction, we updated our knowledge of the current literature including recent special issues to see if calls for more research at the intersection of human resource management and entrepreneurship had been taken up by scholars in the areas of HRM and entrepreneurship.

On the HRM side, Tansky and Heneman's (2006) edited volume is premised on the view that HRM is important to the success or failure of high-growth entrepreneurial firms. Chapters in their volume survey a range of HRM-related issues and highlight the specific HRM context and needs of entrepreneurial firms. The final chapter by Klaas and Klimchak (2006) points to key areas of future research that should be enough to whet the appetite of any scholar interested in this field. As they argue, there is still much to understand about how entrepreneurial firms can benefit from investing in HR and what kind of HRM practices and programmes are most likely to be critical for their success.

Similarly, we looked at Kuratko's (2006) tribute for the 50th anniversary of the ICSB conference, in a special issue of the *Journal of Small Business Management* (April, 2006). He identifies HRM (along with venture financing, small firm performance and entrepreneurial ethics, to name a few) as an emerging theme in entrepreneurship research. Papers published in the special issue were chosen as they were considered 'the very best' of research presented at the June 2005 conference in Washington DC. Written by scholars from the US, Canada, Europe, Australia, New Zealand and Ireland, the selected articles focus on a broad array of issues including organizational growth and performance. Most importantly for us a few of these papers do address various human resource implications in this context, namely succession planning (Bruce and Picard, 2006), the attraction and recruitment of key staff (Audretsch and Lehmann, 2006), corporate governance (Bartholomeusz and Tanewski, 2006) and work–family conflict (Shelton, 2006).

On the entrepreneurship side of the ledger, less has been said about the contribution of HRM to the understanding of entrepreneurial firm performance and growth. This may be explained by Gartner et al.'s (2006) introduction to a special edition of *Entrepreneurship: Theory and Practice* devoted to understanding linkages among published entrepreneurship scholars. In this edition authors use bibliometric techniques to map the pattern of networks and linkages among published entrepreneurship authors (see Grégoire et al., 2006; Schildt et al., 2006; Reader and Watkins, 2006). Drawing on Pearce's (2003) data about the divisional co-membership of AoM members, Gartner et al. (2006) show two distinct nodes of membership which are centred on organizational behaviour (OB) and business strategy (BPS). HRM scholars belong in the OB node while entrepreneurship scholars are found in the BPS node. There is no overlap in the membership of the entrepreneurship and HRM divisions of the AoM (where a minimum of 27 per cent of members need to overlap for this to occur). Such evidence underpins the argument that entrepreneurship scholars typically stay loyal to their 'home' discipline and they are 'primarily oriented to core issues embedded in other disciplines' (Gartner et al., 2006: p. 324). Moreover, the home discipline for many entrepreneurship scholars is likely to be strategy or strategic management and this explains why many scholars may prefer to focus on the 'harder' economic and strategy factors that contribute to firm success and failure rather than the so-called 'softer' people and relationship issues.

So unsurprisingly when HRM is addressed by entrepreneurship scholars it is generally in the language of 'resources' and as just one of many resources that can be utilized in the development of entrepreneurial ventures. And this can be seen in Kuratko's description of entrepreneurship today being 'a complex phenomenon involving multiple stakeholders, an array of inputs that can be combined in innumerable ways' (2006, p. 485).

The state of play in the entrepreneurship discipline can also explain why we see relatively little work on HRM issues. For example it may be as a result of the persistence of thinking about the entrepreneur as a heroic individual. This sort of thinking, Drakopoulou Dodd and Anderson (2007) argue, perseveres for a range of reasons but includes the extent of the use of positivist methods in the field. A functionalist paradigm has been found to dominate the field (Grant and Perren, 2002). And with this in mind Zahra's (2007) lament that a lack of attention has been paid to the context in which entrepreneurship research is conducted, can be interpreted as perhaps a plea for more 'interesting' research (see Barley, 2006) rather than more 'solid' research. Zahra argues that in 'reading recent entrepreneurship papers, however, one rarely gets a sense of the substance, magnitude or dynamics of the research context' (2007, p. 445).

Theory building requires attention to detail as well as creativity and innovation and will be greatly enhanced by paying attention to the 'complexity, uniqueness and richness' (Zahra, 2007: p. 444) of entrepreneurial phenomena (see also Alvarez and Molloy, 2006). All of this is important in understanding HRM in small, growing and entrepreneurial firms. Clearly in both fields there is a willingness to look at new questions in new ways. We can see this in the HRM field when Ferris et al. state:

> For HRM scholars, there are multitudes of interesting questions to ask and research streams to develop and pursue . . . We have perhaps never witnessed more intellectually stimulating times in this field . . . and it encourages (no, demands!) creative, innovative, uninhibited and nonlinear thinking if we are to make significant contributions to new knowledge, and truly develop a more informed understanding of HRM (1999: p. 408).

It can also be seen in the entrepreneurship field when Kuratko writes, 'I believe we are at a point in time when the gap between what can be imagined and what can be accomplished has never been smaller' (2006: p. 490).

While we are still at the early stages of developing theory in the area of HRM in small and entrepreneurial firms and have very 'limited knowledge about the extent to which existing HRM theories extend to smaller entrepreneurial firms' (Tansky and Heneman, 2006: p. xiii), this handbook is our contribution to closing the gap.

This handbook . . .

As such, this handbook is a direct response to a growing recognition that too little is known about the intersection of the disciplines of HRM and entrepreneurship. Underpinning a call for more research at the intersection of HRM and entrepreneurship is the understanding that business growth is the key to economic development. Entrepreneurship generates economic growth (Schumpeter, 1934) and this occurs by combining resources in new ways to create and exploit new opportunities (Shane and Venkataraman, 2000; Shane et al., 2003; Stevenson and Jarillo, 1990; Venkataraman, 1997). While much of the literature focuses on new and emergent firms or start-ups as the places in which entrepreneurship occurs, the above definition does not limit entrepreneurial activity in such a manner (Shane et al., 2003).

It is important to understand the role of HRM in developing sustainable entrepreneurship and entrepreneurial ventures as well as how HRM practices and procedures can be used to help navigate or indeed drive the changing landscape in small and entrepreneurial firms. As Baron argues, 'growing evidence suggests that an inability on the part of some founders of new ventures to successfully manage HRM issues is an important factor in their ultimate failure' (2003: p. 253). Therefore it is also important to understand the contribution and roles individuals, other than the individual entrepreneur or entrepreneurial team, play in the success (or otherwise) of the entrepreneurial venture and whether this changes at different stages in the venture's growth.

So for this handbook we sought theoretical and empirical contributions and hoped potential contributors might address a range of questions and draw on a variety of theoretical and methodological approaches. Some of the questions we posed included: how do new or growing firms deal with the problems caused by the complexity associated with resource (including human resource) acquisition, allocation and development? What is the relationship between the implementation of various HRM policies and procedures on the speed and direction of growth in entrepreneurial firms? How do we theorize the complexity of HRM in new, growing or emergent ventures? What effect do different contexts (national, business, labour market, product market, organizational type amongst others) have on the capacity to develop and manage new entrepreneurial firms? Do theories of HRM apply in new ventures? What can entrepreneurs do to manage human resources to maximize the value of people to the organization? These questions of course do not represent the totality of what can be fruitfully explored at the intersection of HRM and entrepreneurship.

We are thrilled that others are also interested in closer ties between HRM and entrepreneurship, particularly given Gartner et al.'s argument that 'it may be too much to expect scholars to pay attention to other scholarship beyond their immediate circle' (2006: p. 327). We are excited by the breadth of questions our colleagues are interested in researching in order to achieve these closer ties. However, we do observe that often this is from the perspective of HRM or management fields rather than entrepreneurship and the only danger there is that we can 'focus on HRM in small firms, *per se*, rather than look at the field of entrepreneurship' (Barrett and Mayson, 2006: p. 444). Few would disagree with Cardon and Stevens when they write 'while virtually all emerging firms are small at inception, not all small firms are emerging' (2004: p. 279). Researchers do not necessarily equate all small firm activity with entrepreneurial activity. And so rather than join the 'many papers [that] do not distinguish whether they are talking about small or large firms, emerging or established firms or even small or medium sized enterprises' (Cardon and Stevens, 2004: p. 299), all we want to do is acknowledge that in a number of these chapters the focus is on smaller firms (small or small and medium-sized ones). This does not, however, diminish any potential or actual contribution these chapters make to theory or practice.

The chapters we have selected bring different theoretical and empirical observations from research conducted by new and established scholars based in the US, UK, Canada, Australia and Europe. We have organized this book into three parts. The three chapters that make up Part I address 'big' issues around theory and methodology. In Part II, ten chapters focus on HRM and entrepreneurship and the nature of HRM in smaller, newer, growing and/or entrepreneurial firms, while in Part III another ten chapters address more specific HRM issues in the context of entrepreneurial and smaller firms.

Contents of Part I
The first chapter in Part I is written by Elizabeth Chell (Chapter 2) who provides an excellent review and overview of the various approaches that have been used to explore entrepreneurs and entrepreneurship. Her focus is on nascent entrepreneurs and she considers the HRM issues that become apparent as the venture emerges and develops. As we argued earlier, all too often it seems that the only way HRM is addressed in the discussions of entrepreneurship is in term of resources – and there is often no privileging of human resources over others. In examining three models of

entrepreneurship – where the models focus on (1) traits, (2) cognitive-based behaviour and (3) human and social capital – Chell identifies the implications for human capital, HRM and human resource development. She argues that in the creation, development and sustainability of new ventures human resources play a critical role, and without their development or recognition of this importance the future of the new enterprise is somewhat precarious.

David Audretsch and Eric Monsen (Chapter 3) similarly contribute an excellent review of a different part of the entrepreneurship literature focusing on the concept of 'entrepreneurship capital'. This they define as 'a subset of social capital and refer to those social and relational factors, forces and processes that promote or hinder the interaction of various economic agents and their ability to employ, integrate and exploit physical, human and knowledge capital for entrepreneurial ends'. They use this to explain the 'economic and entrepreneurial performance of a region's or firm's human resources'. Aside from having the longest reference list of any chapter in the book, in considering entrepreneurship capital at the level of the region, and industry, firm, team and individual they not only highlight gaps and areas for further study but also ways in which these gaps can be filled.

We finish Part I by moving from theory to research with a chapter (Chapter 4) by Catherine Cassell and Sara Nadin. They question the dominance of a functionalist methodological paradigm in the entrepreneurship (and HRM) fields and suggest reasons for this dominance despite the use of other approaches. They explore the value that using interpretivist approaches would, and can, bring to the theoretical and methodological development of the discipline and use examples from various studies to show the potential value of such approaches and how some of the challenges might be overcome. This chapter provides a good base for understanding the different approaches used in empirical pieces in Parts II and III of the handbook. There is neither an overwhelming positivist nor interpretivist approach taken in chapters in this handbook – although there is some evidence of the different training in research techniques that academics receive in different countries. We would not be wrong to say methodological pluralism characterizes the chapters.

Contents of Part II
Part I of the handbook provides some of the theoretical and methodological groundwork for Part II, which encompasses chapters 5 to 14. In this part the focus is firmly on HRM and entrepreneurship and the nature of HRM in smaller, newer, growing and/or entrepreneurial firms. Questions about the formality of HRM in these firms are addressed in a number of

the chapters while context, such as the ownership context or where the firm is located, is also covered in some of the chapters.

We open Part II with a chapter (Chapter 5) by Cinzia Dal Zotto and Veronica Gustafsson who seek to examine the role of HRM as an entrepreneurial tool in both new and established firms (intrapreneurship). They argue that those involved in starting up a new firm or launching a new product or market need to be selected, empowered, developed, motivated and supported. It is therefore through various HRM practices that growth can be fostered in new and young firms and the entrepreneurial spirit stimulated in more established firms. They conduct two case studies in the Scandinavian media industry to show what this means in practice and the way various practices can be used to leverage innovative capabilities for entrepreneurship and intrapreneurship.

In Chapter 6 we (Rowena Barrett and Susan Mayson) take up the issue of formality and informality in HRM practice in small firms which is an issue explored in a number of other chapters. We report data from interviews with 11 small business owners to explore what small business owners mean when they say they have particular HRM practices in place, why they have them and how they are used. While most would argue that HRM in small firms is characterized by informality and it is fairly well accepted that HRM practices become more formalized as firms grow, our purpose in this chapter is to explore the logic of the formalizing practices. Drawing on older ideas about the nature of bureaucracy and 'good' and 'bad' rules enables us to argue that formal and informal HRM practices can co-exist within firms. The logic of formalization can be enabling or constraining and therefore formality and informality are not either ends of a continuum.

In Chapter 7, Jonathan Michie and Maura Sheehan have a slightly different take on the issue of formality and seek to explore the relationship between formal HRM practices and organizational performance. While this relationship has been the subject of considerable research in the US, UK and elsewhere, infrequently the focus has been on smaller firms. This omission is problematic and while the research on the HRM–performance linkage is not necessarily conclusive it does raise the question about whether HRM theories do apply to smaller firms. In a matched sample of US and UK smaller firms in specific manufacturing and service industry sectors, Michie and Sheehan investigate the contribution HRM practices make to objective and subjective measures of performance. Their investigation is located in the literature, which suggests bundles of HRM practices can be a resource offering the firm a source of competitive advantage (for example Barney, 1991; Becker and Huselid, 1998; MacDuffie, 1995). Their results suggest that the generally positive HRM–performance relationship found in other studies is also found in smaller firms. Moreover while the liabilities of smallness mean that the cost of implementing HRM practices can be high, their analysis suggests that generally 'HRM practices do appear to pay'. The processes by which this occurs are clearly an area for further work.

While Michie and Sheehan looked at the relationship between HRM and performance generally, in Chapter 8 Robert Heneman, Judith Tansky and Michael Camp specifically explore the relationship between HRM and organizational growth. Their chapter is underpinned by similar literature but data is incorporated from a range of different sources to examine the process and philosophy of HRM in high- and low-growth firms. The data includes a survey of, and focus groups with, a small group of CEOs of high- (N=16) and low- (N=21) growth entrepreneurial firms as well as analysis of 672 responses from the 1998 survey of Entrepreneur of the Year® Institute (EOYI) members and a case study of a high-growth firm in the US Midwest. The array of data enables Heneman et al. to explore the 'what' and 'how' in relation to HRM strategies in high-growth firms. 'Visionary' and 'contemporary' is how they describe HRM strategies in high-growth firms and this is systematically different to that applied within low-growth firms.

A similar conclusion can be drawn from the survey data in Chapter 9 which we (Rowena Barrett and Susan Mayson) produced with Niel Warriner. The purpose of our survey of 2500 small but growing Australian firms was to explore how HRM could contribute to growth and therefore whether growing firms would use more formal HRM practices. We proposed that in small firms where there was evidence of planning and/or where the owner delegated some or all of their responsibility for management there would be formal HRM practices. Acknowledging that firms grow in different ways, we use three different growth measures dealing with the firm's future growth orientation as well as past growth in sales and employees. Our findings are consistent with the idea that unless owners recognize the need to plan, which will also most likely entail delegating some responsibilities for direct supervision to other managers, then they are unlikely to succeed in using formal HRM practices.

The message from Chapters 7, 8 and 9 is that HRM matters. Although the causal ordering of the relationship between HRM and competitive success and growth is not addressed, these chapters help us to understand whether more formal organizational systems and routines are more likely to be used to nurture human capital in entrepreneurial firms. Some may argue that this formalization can be problematic and so in Chapter 10 Lynn Martin, Shaheena Janjuha-Jivraj, Charlotte Carey and Srikanth Sursani Reddy explore the effects of formalization on the psychological contract in 30 new entrepreneurial teams over a six-year period. While these firms started out with a team based on friendship, family ties or shared values, as they developed, grew, faced crises and sometimes disappeared (only 21 remained at the end of the six-year period), these relationships needed to be re-negotiated. Martin et al. chart how the language used to describe these relationships changed, as well as how team members perceive change in their psychological contract with the organization. Formalization may lead to firms 'being more professional' but for team members who became 'employees' this was a negative, and explained as 'we work here but we don't belong here'. The study reported in this chapter provides insights into the human dynamics accompanying business growth and development. It also reminds us of the need to consider a range of views and opinions in our research in order to capture the ways different participants perceive, experience and respond to attempts to formalize practices. Attention to this may help us to understand why formal and informal HRM practices can and do co-exist.

In Chapter 11 Susan Marlow and Amanda Thompson push the growth angle further and look at the HRM practices in six firms that employ enough people to be termed 'medium-sized' in the UK. Increasing numbers of people at the workplace makes the management task more complex and their argument is that we should see formal HRM practices in place. From interviews with managers and employees in these firms they show that developing a formal practice to deal with some aspect of labour management was often a response to certain 'critical incidents' and not an inevitable result of growth. However, they do show that developing a strategy to deal with an HR issue does not always mean it is then embedded into practice. As such they highlight the deficiencies of research that relies on surveys of whether or not something exists, and argue for more in-depth qualitative research looking at reasons why employers and employees embrace or resist formalization.

To some degree in Chapter 12 Jeff Hyman, Fraser Osborne and Sarah Jack undertake this task by reviewing paternalism as a managerial approach and the effects of the culture of organizations dominated by owners (or founders) on HRM. While paternalism can have negative connotations, being associated with the dominance and control of owners, in their chapter Hyman et al. report on a case study of 'benevolent paternalism' and suggest that the positive behaviour reciprocated by employees means under some conditions this may indeed offer some insights into effective management. Their study, like those reported in Chapters 10 and 11, also incorporates the voice of employees and therefore ensures that their attitudes and behavioural orientations, which contribute to organizational culture, are not overlooked. The culture of benevolent paternalism in the case study firm engendered cohesion and a shared idea of the firm as a family. Employees were committed and empowered, while various formal and informal communication modes underpinned the development of trust. Hyman et al. do raise the question of the sustainability of this approach with further growth and like the two foregoing chapters recommend further in-depth qualitative analysis to chart the effect of change over time.

The importance of context has been implicit in many of the chapters in this part of the handbook and so to conclude Part II we have two chapters that explore the effect of context on the intersection of HRM and entrepreneurship more explicitly. In Chapter 13, written by Richard Harris and Renee Reid, the context is family ownership. In an analysis of the 2004 UK WERS data Harris and Reid explore barriers to growth in small family businesses. The question driving this analysis is whether family firms are different. Their evidence is mixed as to whether the economic performance of these firms is different although their analysis of earlier WERS data points to employee involvement practices playing a contributory role. Their analysis of the 2004 WERS data focuses on employee involvement and HRM strategies and by and large their findings suggest family firms do use different practices. Their findings point to a culture of (sophisticated) paternalism operating in family businesses and that this culture is the key to understanding the use of best practice HRM practices in small family firms.

In Li Xue Cunningham and Chris Rowley's chapter (Chapter 14) the context is China. While the research in other chapters has generally been conducted in specific geographical areas – Australia, US, UK, Canada and Scandinavia for example – the authors have generally underplayed this context in favour of dealing with other questions. In China smaller firms play a key role in structural reform and in the area Cunningham and Rowley conduct their research – Jiangsu – private industry and smaller firms account for over 90 per cent of the province's total industrial output. However, this is also a region with significant amounts of foreign direct investment and the advent of foreign-owned companies places considerable pressure on smaller firms to compete. The question of convergence drives this study and through 114 responses to a survey and interviews with various managers, employees and trade union representatives in 13 firms, Cunningham and Rowley explore the transfer and adoption of HRM practices in smaller firms. Their results suggest change is occurring but that it is partial and slow, such that 'Westernized' HRM practices can be found sitting alongside more traditional ways of managing in these small Chinese firms.

Contents of Part III
In the third part of the handbook the focus shifts from overviews to more specific HRM practices or issues and what they mean or how they appear

in the context of smaller and entrepreneurial firms. However, in opening this part we look at the effect of regulation on smaller firms with a chapter (Chapter 15) by Rob Blackburn and David Smallbone. In the developed world the state frequently takes an interventionist stance on matters around employing and employment. In this chapter Blackburn and Smallbone investigate the effect of intervention on the strategy and practices in smaller firms. They argue that interventions are more often met with resistance rather than acceptance and suggest that when you take into account the 'real world' of business owners you get a 'strategic stickiness' – that is a drive for stability rather than change as a response to regulation and intervention. That is not to say all small firms' owner–managers respond in this way as other internal and external factors also influence how they respond. Blackburn and Smallbone illustrate their argument by re-examining data collected to investigate the effect on health and safety regulations and employment legislation on smaller firms in the UK. In doing so, they not only explore common themes in relation to business responses to regulation but also identify the relative merits of different methodologies in examining the effects on owner–manager strategies.

In Chapter 16, Hefin David and Gerald Watts explore the decision to become an employer. This is a significant step in the life of a small business and in the life of the individual entrepreneur and one which may affect their self-concept. David and Watts use the notion of the first employment decision as a learning process to frame and inform case studies of five small business owners. While it is recognized that small business employers can face difficulties in recruitment, all too often the focus is on the barriers to employment or the 'red tape' around employment. In this chapter, however, the importance of individuals' experiential history is acknowledged and in interviews five small business owners recall the experience of employing someone for the first time and then reflect on the ways in which their experience informed their emergent employment strategy. The analysis of the results leads to the development of a conceptual framework capturing some key aspects of the decision to become an employer and the learning process following this decision. In looking at the personal rather than structural or procedural barriers to employing, the authors throw some light on what can be done to assist and support the transition of individuals from being self-employed to becoming an employer.

Melissa Cardon and Ibraiz Tarique, in Chapter 17, also deal with recruitment issues but from the perspective of questioning how attractive smaller organizations are to potential recruits. Their study examines the potential applicant perceptions of organizational attractiveness and how these are influenced by the size and age of the firm, as well as by the extraversion and risk-taking propensity of the applicant. As such, Cardon and Tarique explore whether 'smallness' and 'newness' are liabilities in attracting new recruits. To investigate this they distribute nine organizational descriptions (based on three different firm sizes and firm ages) to a sample of under-graduate students, gathering data in two surveys four weeks apart. Their findings highlight that not all small firms are the same and suggest that treating 'small' firms as a homogeneous group is problematic. This is the case as specific sizes and ages of firms can be seen as liabilities for some rather than 'smallness' and 'newness' being liabilities for all small firms.

In Chapter 18, Ian Williamson and Jeffrey Robinson also deal with the issue of recruitment but this time the purpose is to consider how small firms locate and hire new employees. They explore the relationship between the practices small firms use to recruit and then the effectiveness of those prac-tices, specifically the number of applicants attracted and the time taken to fill positions. In terms of the practices used to recruit, Williamson and Robinson distinguish between informal practices, which rely on social net-works to attract applicants, and formal practices, which rely on asocial means and brokers such as institutions or organizations that assist small firms by identifying potential employees. As their study draws on data from 2521 US small firms (defined as firms with less than 500 employees) they are able to examine how firm size shapes the effectiveness of recruitment practice portfolios. Like many of the other studies in this handbook, this chapter reinforces the message that not all small firms are the same, as the authors found that the effectiveness of recruitment methods is contingent on the size of the firm. They argue that HRM in small firms is dynamic and cannot be portrayed by standardized descriptions.

Deborah Blackman and Kevin Hindle also deal with the issue of recruit-ment in Chapter 19 but this time using ideas about the psychological contact to explore the mismatch between entrepreneurial business owners' and their employees' expectations. They argue that relationships are critical for successful entrepreneurship but they are largely absent from a range of models of the entrepreneurial development process. The purpose of this chapter is to show where this absence can be found, highlight the conse-quences of poor psychological contracts and to propose ways of imple-menting successful entrepreneurial relationships through the application of the psychological contract. As they argue, 'at the very least, conscious and overt inclusion of the employment decision into any stage-model of the entrepreneurial development process will reflect the stages of growth more realistically'.

Growth through innovation and the ways HRM can address strategic and structural concerns from the early stages of a firm's development is the focus of the next chapter (Chapter 20) by Grahame Boocock, Kevin Daniels, Jane Glover and Julie Holland. Specifically their concern is with the creation of the right environment for individual and group problem solving. Boocock et al. explore whether the Job Demands-Control (-Support) [JDC(S)] model (Karasek and Theorell, 1990) can be applied to small firms. This model proposes that support and control promotes effective problem solving enabling employees to cope with work demands. As such, their focus is on job design, which is infrequently discussed in the context of smaller firms. After considering issues around learning in small firms as well as specific characteristics of small firms, they report results from their study of learning and innovation activities of over 115 employees in 15 UK firms. Their conclusion is that with relatively modest adjustments in job design, the well-being, learning, motivation and performance of employees in smaller firms could be enhanced. Boocock et al. close with a list of seven areas where work design and problem-solving processes could be improved.

The theme of learning is taken up in Chapter 21 by David Devins when he case studies two publicly funded skill development programmes in the UK. The People and Technology Project (PAT) sought to widen workforce learning while the focus of Developing Manager Skills Project (DMS) was on supporting problem solving, business planning and associated skills development for small business managers. Through analysis of the content and the process of delivering the different programmes, Devins argues that the experience of participating encouraged some changes in the HRM and skills acquisition practices within the participating firms. A critical element in the success of the programmes was the role played by the coach (in the DMS) and animateur (in the PAT). Devins' analysis suggests that if learning is to be encouraged then it is important that a proactive and targeted approach is taken to skill development. Moreover, trusting relationships need to be built by those supplying the training with those receiving it if small business managers and employees are to invest time in participating.

In Chapter 22 Scott Taylor reviews the evidence of and theory underpinning training and development in small firms. He argues that the majority of literature in this area either assesses funded programmes or deals with entrepreneurship education. He argues that underpinning both of these streams of literature is the assumption that engagement with training and development must be founded on the pursuit of organizational success. This he questions, and in reviewing some of the key literature from each of these streams he suggests ways that future research might be more nuanced and contextualized. Taylor's call is for concepts such as 'size' and 'entrepreneurship' to be reconsidered and the implications of the embeddedness of small and entrepreneurial firm to be explored in more detail. This would, Taylor suggests, lead to more robust theoretical frameworks to underpin empirically informed analysis of training and development in smaller and entrepreneurial firms.

By and large the chapters to this point in this part of the handbook have focused on various issues related to the management of employees in smaller and entrepreneurial firms. In Chapter 23 David Kaplan and Jerome Katz take a different approach and seek to explain the career path of entrepreneurs. While organizational influences act on the entrepreneur's career they do so differently from how they might impact on traditional careers: the entrepreneur is responsible from the very beginning for the success or failure of the enterprise which is very different from what most people experience on their first day at work. Career theory does not adequately explain this situation. By building on work looking at the different types of entrepreneurs and the career paths they follow, Kaplan and Katz consider how the emerging organization might shape an entrepreneur's career to develop a flexible framework of entrepreneurial careers. Actionable ideas about how researchers may 'test' their four-stage model are offered while the importance of doing so, particularly in terms of advising and counselling potential and practising entrepreneurs, is outlined. This chapter, like many of the others, is a great example of how ideas from different literatures can be brought together to further our understanding of entrepreneurship and HRM.

In the final chapter (Chapter 24) Terry Wagar and James Grant look at the intention for managers and professionals in small business to (voluntarily) quit their job. While turnover has been researched extensively and there is an acceptance that management practices play a part in making firms more (or less) attractive places for individuals to work, few studies have focused on smaller firms. Wagar and Grant specifically examine high commitment/involvement HRM practices, employee voice and organizational cost-cutting measures on the intention to quit with a sample of 351 of their university's alumni working in smaller Canadian firms. Of these, around 28 per cent said they intended to quit their job in the next two years and the negative effect of high commitment/involvement HRM practices on quit rates found generally in the literature is also shown by Wagar and Grant to operate in these smaller firms. One of the key findings of this chapter is that investment in people is very important – this may be through a high-involvement HRM strategy or by creating a workplace climate which is attractive to employees. As we know from earlier chapters, attracting new employees can be difficult; here we have some evidence of what is important to retain them.

In summary . . .
So, these are the 24 chapters that make up this *Handbook of Entrepreneurship and HRM*. Clearly a lot of ground has been covered in these chapters and through them we gain greater insight into what goes on – theoretically and/or empirically – in terms of managing people in smaller and entrepreneurial firms. Human relationships play an extremely important role in the success

of small firms and entrepreneurial ventures. And through this collection we hope that this point has been well made.

However, as with all research, as many new questions arise as old ones are answered. By no means do we think the intersection of the entrepreneurship and HRM fields has been comprehensively mapped. Just today an email came about a report from Grant Thornton (Australia) showing that only 2 per cent of the 250 business owners employing between 20 and 400 people they surveyed said they used competitive remuneration strategies to attract high calibre staff (http://www.smartcompany.com.au/Growth-Resources/Managing-People.html). Why so few? What are they doing instead? Don't they know there is a 'war for talent' going on? Compensation 'significantly affects recruiting and retention efforts of small firms; if they cannot pay applicants enough, then they cannot recruit or retain critical skills or knowledge they need to operate effectively' (Cardon and Stevens, 2004: p. 304). However, it is unfortunate that we were unable to include a chapter on pay, rewards and compensation.

A range of other areas could also have been addressed. The effect of different institutional contexts on the way new ventures emerge and develop could be explored in more detail. Similarly, work on issues relating to employment flexibilities and work–life balance in small, growing and entrepreneurial firms is notably absent from this volume (for a very recent example see Jennings and McDougald, 2007). Other functional aspects of HRM in entrepreneurial firms could have been explored. For example, how can employees develop a career in a smaller firm where there is limited or no hierarchy? There are many interesting issues around performance management that could have been examined, while organizational change in entrepreneurial ventures is another area of research worthy of further study. Issues around managing diversity, whether that comes from gender, ethnicity, religious beliefs, age or sexuality for example, are notably absent from this collection, although certainly not by design. Quite clearly there is more work to be done, not only on the topics we have covered but also on those which were not addressed. Our fervent hope is that we inspire a few more researchers to take up the challenge of exploring the intersection of the fields of entrepreneurship and HRM.

Having said that, it has been a pleasure working with all the authors of these chapters to produce this handbook. We have learned a lot (some of which has nothing to do with HRM and entrepreneurship but more to do with academic workloads!). We feel quite privileged to have taken on the role of co-editors. We thank all authors for their commitment to and support for this venture. We also thank Edward Elgar for their willingness to commission such a work.

Happy reading!

References

Alvarez, S.A. and J.C. Molloy (2006), 'Why human resource management differs in entrepreneurial and established firms: Theoretical foundations', in J.W. Tansky and R.L. Heneman (eds), *Human Resource Strategies for the High Growth Entrepreneurial Firm*, Greenwich, CT: Information Age Publishing, pp. 1–12.

Audretsch, D.B. and E. Lehmann (2006), 'Entrepreneurial access and absorption of knowledge spillovers: Strategic board and managerial composition for competitive advantage', *Journal of Small Business Management*, **44**, 155–66.

Barley, S. (2006), 'When I write my masterpiece: Thoughts on what makes a paper interesting', *Academy of Management Journal*, **49**, 16–20.

Barney, J.B. (1991), 'Firm resources and sustained competitive advantage', *Journal of Management*, **17**(1), 99–120.

Baron, R. (2003), 'Editorial: Human resource management and entrepreneurship: Some reciprocal benefits of closer links', *Human Resource Management Review*, **13**, 253–56.

Barrett, R. and S. Mayson (2006), 'Exploring the intersection of HRM and entrepreneurship. Guest editors' introduction to the special edition on HRM and entrepreneurship', *Human Resource Management Review*, **16**, 443–44.

Bartholomeusz, S. and G.A. Tanewski (2006), 'The relationship between family firms and corporate governance', *Journal of Small Business Management*, **44**, 245–67.

Becker, B.E. and M.A. Huselid (1998), 'High performance work systems and firm performance: A synthesis of research and managerial implications', in G.R. Feffis (ed.), *Research in Personnel and Human Resources*, Vol. 16, Stanford, CT: JAI Press, pp. 53–101.

Bruce, D. and D. Picard (2006), 'Making succession a success: Perspectives from Canadian small and medium sized enterprises', *Journal of Small Business Management*, **44**, 306–309.

Cardon, M. and C. Stevens (2004), 'Managing human resources in small organizations: What do we know?', *Human Resource Management Review*, **14**, 295–323.

Drakopoulou Dodd, S. and A. Anderson (2007), 'Mumpsimus and the myth of the individualistic entrepreneur', *International Small Business Journal*, **25**, 341–60.

Ferris, G.R., W.A. Hochwarter, M.R. Buckley, G. Harrell-Cook and D.D. Frink (1999), 'Human resources management: Some new directions', *Journal of Management*, **25**, 385–415.

Gartner, W.B., P. Davidsson and S.A. Zahra (2006), 'Are you talking to me? The nature of community in entrepreneurship scholarship', *Entrepreneurship: Theory and Practice*, **30**, 321–31.

Grant, P. and L. Perren (2002), 'Small business and entrepreneurial research: Meta-theories, paradigms and prejudices', *International Small Business Journal*, **20**, 185–211.

Grégoire, D.A., M.X. Noël, R. Déry and J-P. Béchard (2006), 'Is there conceptual convergence in entrepreneurship research? A co-citation analysis of *Frontiers of Entrepreneurship Research*, 1981–2004', *Entrepreneurship: Theory and Practice*, **30**, 333–73.

Huselid, M. (2003), 'Editor's note: Special issue on small and medium-sized enterprises: A call for more research', *Human Resource Management*, **42**, p. 297.

Jennings, J.E. and M.S. McDougald (2007), 'Work–family interface experiences and coping strategies: Implications for entrepreneurship research and practice', *Academy of Management Review*, **32**, 747–60.

Karasek, R.A. and T. Theorell (1990), *Healthy Work*, New York: Basic Books.

Katz, J.A., H.E. Aldrich, T.M. Welbourne and P. Williams (2000), 'Guest editors' comments. Special issue on human resource management and the SME: Towards a new synthesis', *Entrepreneurship: Theory and Practice*, **25**, 7–10.

Klaas, B. and M. Klimchack (2006), 'Entrepreneurship and human resources: Directions for future research', in J.W. Tansky and R.L. Heneman (eds), *Human Resource Strategies for the High Growth Entrepreneurial Firm*, Greenwich, CT: Information Age Publishing, pp. 245–58.

Kuratko, D. (2006), 'A tribute to 50 years of excellence in entrepreneurship and small business', *Journal of Small Business Management*, **44**, 483–92.

MacDuffie, J. (1995), 'Human resource bundles and manufacturing performance: Organizational logic and flexible production systems in the world auto industry', *Industrial and Labour Relations Review*, **48**, 197–221.

Pearce, J. (2003), 'President's message: A bifurcated academy?', *The Academy of Management News*, **34**(1), 1–2.

Reader, D. and D. Watkins (2006), 'The social and collaborative nature of entrepreneurship scholarship: A co-citation and perceptual analysis', *Entrepreneurship: Theory and Practice*, **30**, 417–41.

Schildt, H.A., S. Zahra, and A. Sillanpää (2006), 'Scholarly communities in entrepreneurship research: A co-citation analysis', *Entrepreneurship: Theory and Practice*, **30**, 399–415.

Schumpeter, J. (1934), *The Theory of Economic Development*, Cambridge, Mass.: Harvard University Press.

Shane, S., E.A. Locke and C.J. Collins (2003), 'Entrepreneurial motivation', *Human Resource Management Review*, **13**, 257–79.

Shane, S. and S. Venkataraman (2000), 'The promise of entrepreneurship as a field of research', *Academy of Management Review*, **25**, 217–26.

Shelton, L.M. (2006), 'Female entrepreneurs, work–family conflict, and venture performance: New insights into the work–family interface', *Journal of Small Business Management*, **44**, 285–97.

Stevenson, H. and J. Jarillo (1990), 'A paradigm of entrepreneurship: Entrepreneurial management', *Strategic Management Journal*, **11**, 17–27.

Tansky, J.W. and R.L. Heneman (2003), 'Guest editors' note: Introduction to the special issue on human resource management in SMEs: A call for more research', *Human Resource Management*, **42**, 299–302.

Tansky, J.W. and R.L. Heneman (2006), 'HR in high growth entrepreneurial firms', in J.W. Tansky and R.L. Heneman (eds), *Human Resource Strategies for the High Growth Entrepreneurial Firm*, Greenwich, CT: Information Age Publishing, pp. xi–xx.

Venkataraman, S. (1997), 'The distinctive domain of entrepreneurship research: An Editor's perspective', in J.A. Katz and J. Brockhaus (eds), *Advances in Entrepreneurship, Firm Emergence and Growth*, JAI Press, Greenwich, CT, pp. 119–38.

Zahra, S.A. (2007), 'Contextualizing theory building in entrepreneurship research', *Journal of Business Venturing*, **22**, 443–52.

PART I

THEORY AND RESEARCH METHODS

2 The nascent entrepreneur, business development and the role of human resources
Elizabeth Chell

Introduction

The activity of entrepreneurship is not a new phenomenon as testified by eighteenth-century economists in Europe and America (Chell et al., 1991; Hébert and Link, 1988). Entrepreneurship has become important from practical and policy perspectives for governments around the globe and it is therefore incumbent on theoreticians to develop sound, evidence-based models of the entrepreneur and entrepreneurial process. To date entrepreneurship is under-theorized and under-researched (Shane, 2003). There is no consensus on defining the terms 'entrepreneurship' or 'entrepreneur' although we are beginning to see convergence.

In this chapter the focus is on nascent entrepreneurship, while '[a] nascent entrepreneur is defined as someone who initiates serious activities that are intended to culminate in a viable business startup' (Aldrich, 1999: p. 77). Thus, nascent entrepreneurs have a serious intention to found a business venture and they are at the very early stages of garnering resources, learning heuristically how to go about the act of founding, and as such they are in the throes of testing out and developing their ideas, seeking to realize opportunities and indulging in impression management. Human resource management (HRM) issues become evident as the nascent entrepreneurial venture develops. Thus the objective of this chapter is to explore current theory and evidence on the nature and process of nascent entrepreneurship in order to consider various HRM implications.

The chapter is organized in the following way. First the various approaches taken to understanding the nature of the entrepreneur, the entrepreneurial process and the key nexus of entrepreneurship and innovation – opportunity recognition – are considered. A further consideration of the trait approach is undertaken in this section and it commences with an examination of research evidence around the idea that a single trait characterizes the entrepreneur, thus placing the individual entrepreneur at the nexus of innovation and discovery. An examination of research evidence looking at a constellation of traits and also new traits that have more recently been investigated is also undertaken. In the next section the entrepreneurial process is considered from a cognitive perspective and the research underpinning 'opportunity recognition' is discussed in some detail. We then turn to consider the entrepreneurial process from a human and social capital perspective, highlighting resource-based theory and networking approaches. Finally, the implications for HRM are drawn out and discussed.

Models of entrepreneurs and entrepreneurship

The trait approach has been heavily criticized in the past (see for example, Chell, 1985; Gartner, 1988). How personality is defined is problematic, for example, is it 'hard-wired' into an individual's genetic profile or does social learning play a role? If there is a social learning basis then it suggests personality is comprised of attitudes, beliefs, values, competencies, planning strategies and so forth that equip the individual to manage particular situations and steer a path through their life course (Bandura, 1977; Mischel, 1973). It also suggests that various characteristics may be learnt, and for entrepreneurs there may be typical situations they encounter which would contribute to 'shaping' their behaviour. Psychologists would term this 'interactionism' (Chell, 1985; Matthews et al., 2003).

In the specific case of the entrepreneur various economists have put forward theories concerning the entrepreneurial process and the entrepreneurial firm from which specific person characteristics have been deduced (for example Casson, 1982; 2005; Kirzner, 1973; Knight, 1921; Schumpeter, 1934; Shackle, 1972; 1979). Current thinking is that the entrepreneurial process comprises recognition, development and exploitation of opportunities. Different aspects of behaviour and context operate differentially in these different phases of opportunity development. This raises the question whether it is idiosyncratic knowledge and information that individuals have which enables them to exploit a perceived opportunity successfully and/or whether there are particular capabilities that entrepreneurs possess to facilitate this process.

From a social learning approach the attribution of person labels can be accommodated where there is perceived consistency in behaviour. From an economic development perspective there is a requirement for specific human capital in order to found sustainable enterprises and this is an important consideration. Furthermore, to be able to assume that such capital can be developed experientially, and through social learning processes, is important for HRM policy, as it presupposes interaction with the environment and situations to facilitate learning. These issues will be explored below when we move through the various trait approaches to measuring the entrepreneurial persona.

The entrepreneur model 1: the trait approach

As in the case of leadership research, initially, there was a quest to discover the trait or set of traits distinguishing entrepreneurs from non-entrepreneurs and/or managers (Brockhaus, 1980). Three key traits have been attributed to entrepreneurs and extensively researched, which are termed 'the Big Three' (Chell, 2008): need for achievement (NAch); locus of control (LOC); and risk-taking propensity. Intuitively, these traits are appealing. The challenges nascent entrepreneurs face suggest: they should be strongly motivated to overcome obstacles and to achieve, as originally described by McClelland (1961); they should feel a great sense of personal control over outcomes (Rotter, 1966); and, given the uncertain nature of the context in which entrepreneurial activity is engaged, they appear to need to manage risk (Knight, 1921).

What evidence supports entrepreneurs having or developing these three characteristics? NAch has been strongly criticized by Fineman (1977); however, Johnson (1990) found a positive relationship between achievement motivation and entrepreneurship in 20 out of 23 studies. Later evidence, such as Sagie and Elizur's (1999), showed achievement motive to be multi-dimensional and revealed some encouraging results. Stewart et al. (1999) showed entrepreneurs to have higher achievement motivation and risk-taking propensity than corporate managers or small business owners. Utsch et al. (1999) showed achievement motivation, autonomy, innovativeness and competitive aggression discriminated between entrepreneurs and managers. Lee and Tsang (2001) demonstrated NAch to be associated with venture growth amongst Chinese entrepreneurs. However, they stated that personality traits were not important predictors of venture growth, and experience was important, while attention should be placed on venture skills. Later studies have been designed to incorporate complex configurations of variables (for example Korunka et al., 2003) such as personality, resources, environment and organizing activities in the context of the business start-up process. Different patterns emerge as a consequence of heterogeneous start-up conditions and they concluded it was inappropriate to investigate the personality characteristics of nascent entrepreneurs and new business owner–managers in isolation from their wider context. Hansemark (2003) carried out a longitudinal, before-and-after study to obviate criticisms levelled at previous studies that they had measured the characteristics of established business owners and therefore could not provide a basis for prediction of future entrepreneurial activity (Thornton, 1999). Their study showed no significant results for NAch, although LOC appeared to predict business founding in male subjects. Baum and Locke (2004) following Carsrud and Krueger (1995) suggested NAch, risk-taking propensity and internal locus of control (ILOC) were the wrong traits for empirical study. Finally, Collins et al. (2004) found that NAch was a better predictor of entrepreneurial performance than of career choice. They also made the point that this personality construct did not necessarily have a single influence on behaviour, but its effects may be cumulative over time.

Turning specifically to research examining whether entrepreneurs have a strong ILOC we see mixed evidence in the 1980s (see, for example, Begley and Boyd, 1986; Brockhaus, 1982; Chell and Burrows, 1991 and Chell et al., 1991 for an overview). Bonnett and Furnham (1991) found that a group of young entrepreneurs could be distinguished from a control group on both the Protestant Work Ethic and the Economic LOC scales. Engle et al. (1997) revealed no significant difference between intrapreneurs (entrepreneurs employed in companies) and employees on LOC. Mueller and Thomas (2000) found some evidence to suggest that LOC, combined with innovativeness, was more prevalent in countries with individualistic cultures. Lee and Tsang (2001) demonstrated that owner–managers (entrepreneurs) of large firms with high growth rates exhibit ILOC compared with owner–managers of small firms, while Hansemark (2003) showed that ILOC had predictive power for male entrepreneurs. There have been some issues raised around the measurement of LOC (for example Engle et al., 1997) and so some studies have used combined measures of several personality traits, including LOC.

With the evidence for LOC as a predictor of entrepreneurship not being strong, does risk-taking propensity fare any better? The measurement of risk-taking has been confounded by definitional and measurement problems (see for example, Meredith et al., 1982; Carland et al., 1984; Timmons et al., 1985). Research has attempted to address different approaches to risk. For example, Palich and Bagby (1995) suggest entrepreneurs do not see themselves as being more likely to take risks than managers of large corporations (but they may perceive less risk). Sarasvathy et al. (1998) compared entrepreneurs with bankers in their perception and management of a variety of risks and found entrepreneurs and bankers constructed risk differently, adopted different strategies and tactics toward risk management and took a different view of responsibility for outcomes. Stewart et al. (1999) found entrepreneurs were driven to succeed and had a high propensity for risk-taking, whereas small business owners were less risk-oriented. Stewart and Roth's (2001) analysis confirmed the theory that entrepreneurs are more inclined to take risks than managers because the 'entrepreneurial function entails coping with a less structured, more uncertain set of possibilities' (p. 146). Miner and Raju (2004) contested this conclusion as they found entrepreneurs were less likely to take risks than managers and instead suggested entrepreneurs were risk avoidant. They argue that managers exerted 'post-decisional control' over risk whereas entrepreneurs exercised 'pre-decisional control'. It would appear that a great deal more research could be carried out to understand decision making in the context of perceived risk and to measure it in different target populations.

Given such mixed evidence, unsurprisingly researchers have turned to consider other traits. To do this does, however, require a strong and convincing theoretical basis for the selection and measurement of a trait in a population. Therefore, of the alternative traits more recently identified by entrepreneurship scholars, what arguments and evidence have been adduced?

The measurement of a constellation of traits
There have been several attempts to identify and measure psychometrically a constellation of traits to predict entrepreneurship. Caird (1991; 1992) constructed the General Enterprising Tendency (GET) test to assess people with 'enterprising characteristics'. However, small sample size, construct validity and measurement issues made this work problematic. Robinson et al. (1991) argued that a measure of attitude held great promise and developed the Entrepreneurial Attitude Orientation (EAO) measure with four scales: achievement; innovation; personal control; and self-esteem. An attractive feature of the measure was the inclusion of affect (feelings and emotions), cognition (beliefs) and conation (desire and volition). Using this measure they were able to discriminate between entrepreneurs and non-entrepreneurs.

Huefner, Hunt and Robinson (1996) used the EAO adding three further items – the entrepreneurial quotient (EQ), Myers–Briggs Type Indicator (MBTI), and Herrmann Brain Dominance Instrument (HBDI) – to discriminate between entrepreneurs and non-entrepreneurs and to test whether this would increase the measure's predictive power. In general they were able to differentiate between entrepreneurs, non-entrepreneurs and owner–managers. They also found some gender differences in which the male participants had a higher EQ than the female. EQ gave the best overall result, and the best combination of tests proved to be the EQ/EAO/MBTI. Nonetheless the team reported some 30 per cent were misclassifications.

Reynierse (1997) also worked with the MBTI to evaluate the prior work of Carland et al. (1988), who concluded entrepreneurs were intuitive thinkers and small business owners were sensory-judgement types. His work showed entrepreneurs to be intuitive-thinking-perceiving types and as such he was able to differentiate them from lower level managers. Compared with the latter group, entrepreneurs were also more likely to be extroverted (outgoing), intuitive (follow their hunches) and perceiving (spontaneous and open to change). A further comparison between entrepreneurs and executives showed entrepreneurs to be more perceiving than executives who were more judging (organized, close-minded, controlling types). Small firm owner–managers were revealed to be more feeling types, suggesting warmth, loyalty and commitment to values and being consistent with family-oriented, lifestyle business. Indeed, the evidence appeared to support the view that small business owner–managers could be differentiated both from entrepreneurs and managers using this measure. The mindset of entrepreneurs and bureaucrats, Reynierse (1997) suggested, was, moreover, fundamentally different: the former being perceiving types and the latter judging. Some further support has been given to this approach by Muller and Gappisch (2005).

In the quest to determine personality structure, the 'Big Five' with the dimensions of Neuroticism (N), Extraversion (E), Openness (O), Agreeableness (A) and Conscientiousness (C) has been promulgated. Several studies have examined the entrepreneur's personality structure using the Big Five as a predictor of the business venture's long-term survival. In sum, Amit et al. (1993) found a negative relationship between O and long-term venture survival. Envick and Langford (2000) found no significant differences between a sample of managers and entrepreneurs on N, E or O but did on C and A. This suggested managers were more cautious, organized and planned than entrepreneurs but they were more team-oriented and considerate. Ciavarella et al. (2004) found E, N and A were not predictive of long-term venture survival, but C was.

Research such as this can be problematic in respect of design. The entrepreneurial act of business creation or innovation is a process of a given duration, beyond which more management is needed to establish the business, develop its markets and ensure profitability and survival. The original entrepreneurs could in the long term have either moved on (as in the case of serial entrepreneurs) or could be engaged in more managerial practices. This could confound results unless the research design was longitudinal. Yet we know too few studies use longitudinal designs (Furnham, 2007).

Other entrepreneurial traits
Whilst a number of possible entrepreneurial traits have been investigated, the following were selected for theoretical location. Proactivity, for example, has a lengthy pedigree, with Schumpeter (1934) suggesting entrepreneurs to be a dynamic and proactive force – a view supported by Leavitt (1988) and Chell et al. (1991). Bateman and Crant (1993) suggested that proactive behaviour changes environments as the proactive person scans the environment for opportunities, takes initiative, acts and perseveres. Crant (1996) also investigated whether proactivity was associated with entrepreneurial intentions. Using a sample of 181 students he showed that

entrepreneurial intentions were associated with being male, having an education, an entrepreneurial parent and a proactive personality. Becherer and Maurer (1999) investigated further the link between proactivity and entrepreneurial behaviour in 215 small company executives and the impact on these executives' firm performance. They found proactivity was significantly correlated with the entrepreneurial posture of the firm, increased sales and the number of firms founded by these executives. They also found that the higher the proactive disposition the more likely the business was to be founded rather than purchased. Kickul and Gundry (2002) also examined small firm owner–managers' proactive personality, this time in relation to strategic orientation and innovation. Using a sample of 107 small firm owner–managers they found that the prospector strategy orientation mediated the relationship between proactive personality and three types of innovations: innovative targeting processes, innovative organizational systems, and innovative boundary supports.

It has been argued that despite entrepreneurs operating in uncertain environments, they are less affected by stress than non-entrepreneurs. Begley and Boyd (1986) found no difference between founders and non-founders on a measure of Type A behaviour. However Buttner (1992) found entrepreneurs experience higher levels of stress due to role ambiguity. Entrepreneurs had more health problems, were less able to relieve work-related tensions and were less satisfied with their work than managers. How stress has been measured has not been unproblematic. Harris et al. (1999) attempted to evaluate job stress in a sample of entrepreneurs. They administered a modified Job Stress Questionnaire (JSQ) to 169 male and 56 female entrepreneurs. Entrepreneurs were compared with three other occupational groups – white and blue collar workers and professionals. Entrepreneurs scored significantly higher than the other three groups on workload, but significantly lower on role ambiguity and skills' utilization. The results suggested that workload was the greater source of stress for entrepreneurs, who spent on average 56 hours per week on work-related activities. The other occupational groups tended to work set hours per week. Entrepreneurs experienced less stress from 'under utilization of skills' than the other occupational groups, likewise they suffered lower levels of stress from role ambiguity.

Related work on 'tolerance of ambiguity' (Sexton and Bowman, 1984) suggested that entrepreneurs were more able to manage stress arising from ambiguity than managers, whereas Schere (1987) has suggested that entrepreneurs have a high tolerance for ambiguity and a low aversion to uncertainty. Gooding (1989 in Park, 2005: p. 743) demonstrated that when entrepreneurs and managers were presented with unequivocal (unambiguous) data, they processed it in the same way, although entrepreneurs viewed equivocal data more positively than managers. As was reported above, entrepreneurs experienced lower levels of stress from role ambiguity than did blue or white collar workers (Harris et al., 1999).

Summary
The search for entrepreneurial traits continues to be problematic. There is some support for NAch and mixed support for ILOC. The evidence points to including such measures with a complex configuration of others. Pursuing opportunities on the face of it is risky, but again the research evidence in respect of measures of risk-taking propensity shows no clear pattern. However, what emerges is the difference between risk perception and management. More carefully constructed measures of the cognitive and affective dimensions of risk as they affect different groups – entrepreneurs, venture capitalists, bankers and so forth – should yield some interesting and potentially useful findings.

Furthermore, these so-called traits – NAch, ILOC and risk-taking propensity – could have important implications for HRM. For example: how do such behavioural expression impacts on others? How does the entrepreneur manage issues of work load? What level of goals does s/he set for her/himself and others? How does the perception of risk and judgements about the pursuit of perceived risky opportunities impact on others? How do these factors affect ways of working, morale and motivation? Whilst the entrepreneur may be able to manage ambiguity and uncertainty, what of his/her co-workers? More evidence is needed to answer these questions and from research designed to examine management style and management behaviour in nascent and established enterprises.

An effective attempt to measure the entrepreneurial profile focused on affect, cognition and conation (Robinson et al., 1991). Evidence based on the MBTI also suggests that entrepreneurs think differently from non-entrepreneurs, for example that they are intuitive and open to change. Others have also supported this conclusion (Allinson et al., 2000; Chell et al., 1991; Mitchell et al., 2005). The implication is that a different cognitive style would be associated with entrepreneurs. Evidence of such different cognitive styles was found by Kirton (1980) who identified 'adaptive and innovative types' in organizations. The identification of two styles of thinking can be reconciled with thinking that contrasts routine and incremental change and innovation with disruptive and radical approaches. Such contrasting styles have profound implications for the management of change and innovation, in which HRM has a major role to play.

Finally from other single trait measures there is support for proactivity, which along with entrepreneurial intentions, suggests that entrepreneurs scan the environment for opportunities, take initiative and persevere.

Entrepreneurs who are focused on change, development and growth of their nascent enterprise will expect their associates to respond accordingly. Entrepreneurs who take for granted others' support may be disappointed. For HRM the implications are that entrepreneurs should be trained in the management of this process in order to exercise leadership and carry others along with them (Witt, 1998). Work lending support to this view will be discussed in the next section.

The entrepreneurial process model 2: the cognitive approach
In the 1970s trait theory was severely criticized and a search for alternatives ensued (Hampson, 1982; Mischel, 1973). The problem with traits as explanatory variables of behaviour was extended to an examination of the entrepreneurial persona (Chell, 1985; Gartner, 1988). Mischel (1973) put forward a set of 'cognitive social learning person variables' to substitute for traits, whilst Hampson (1982; 1988) suggested personality was constructed from expert, lay and self perspectives (Chell et al., 1991).

In the 1990s Mischel and colleagues developed the Cognitive Affective Personality System (CAPS) model (Mischel and Shoda, 1995). The CAPS model was an attempt to reconcile the observation of personality being stable and invariant across situations with research that has found inconsistencies in people's behaviour across situations. Mischel and Shoda (1995) proposed that individuals have a unique behavioural signature arising from dynamic social interaction, social learning, socialization and their biology. Distinctive behavioural patterns result over time but are modified to suit the particularities of the situation. For example an individual may not characteristically behave in an anxious manner, but given a serious medical prognosis they may well exhibit signs of anxiety. This theorizing attempts to link the biological basis of personality, perception and interpretation of situations with a behavioural response, which is contingent on past experience, cultural, historical and learnt behaviours. This 'if-then' behavioural response was termed the individual's behavioural signature which tends to be characteristic of the individual and shows behavioural consistency. It has both interpersonal dynamic and social learning elements that enable adaptability and responsiveness to changes in circumstances to be explained (Shoda et al., 2002). While the CAPS model has not yet been applied in the entrepreneurship context, its usefulness in explaining entrepreneurial alertness, responsiveness to change and ability to cope with ambiguity is evident.

Opportunity recognition
Opportunity recognition or not insignificantly, opportunity creation, is an essential element of entrepreneurial behaviour (Chell et al., 1991; Gaglio

and Katz, 2001; Kaish and Gilad, 1991; Kirzner, 1979; Shane, 2000; 2003; Stevenson and Jarillo, 1990). There are two contrasting ontological positions in respect of the status of opportunities. The first suggests that opportunities exist to be identified by the alert entrepreneur, which is a realist or positivist position. The second suggests that opportunities emerge (Bouchikhi, 1993) through a process of tacit knowledge and insight.

Gaglio and Katz (2001) differentiated between alert and non-alert individuals in the marketplace on the basis of the former having capability for 'veridical perception' (perceiving the market environment correctly) and 'veridical interpretation' (ability to interpret the dynamics of the situation correctly and act accordingly). They argue that alert individuals possess mental models or schemas that guide information processing. Alert individuals have more complex schemas, enabling them to see emerging patterns. This, they suggested, could explain the differences between experts and novices (or between experienced individuals who have developed a depth of industry knowledge and nascent entrepreneurs who may lack such tacit understanding). Alert individuals apprehend the changing environment and realize they need to reassess the economic and/or market situation. If they decide not to ignore the situation, they would then consider its possible impacts and engage in counterfactual thinking and mental simulations (Gaglio and Katz, 2001). This would lead to realization that they should break with their current way of doing business. Reconfiguring perceived information would result in an insight and potential innovation. These researchers further suggested that such alert individuals would be more sensitive to market disequilibria and the potential for radical innovation. Alert individuals would also make fewer cognitive processing mistakes and their decisions would be timely. Moreover, they have greater domain-specific knowledge in respect of the market environment. Their integrative capability enables them to draw information together from different sources. Engagement in counterfactual thinking ('what-if') allows them to test out a new means–end framework. Hence frame-breaking is fundamental to entrepreneurial alertness (Kirzner, 1985) and a necessary step for genuine innovation. Essentially, alert individuals are sensitive to the economic potential of an opportunity; entrepreneurs and innovators aim to create value, which in economic terms means profit and wealth. Gaglio and Katz (2001) have argued that this theory accounts for non-alert behaviours and individuals of various types. They emphasized that this theory concerns the identification of market opportunities wherever they occur and is not about business creation or self employment. Shane (2003) discussed a variety of evidence supporting this view of the discovery of opportunities. One problem, however, is the assumption that a market exists and that the alert individual can spot the gap in the market. However, with some innovations there is no market and this presumably requires a different behaviour set.

Dutta and Crossan (2005) have argued that by exploring both ontological positions of opportunity discovery and emergence and enactment it would be possible to gain greater insights into the process from an organizational learning perspective. Their framework is resonant with Nonaka and Takeuchi's (1995) theory of tacit knowledge and includes the processes of intuition, interpretation, integration and institutionalization. It suggests that as a consequence of their prior knowledge and understanding, individuals recognize new patterns, which they attempt to make sense of; they explore and interpret an idea further and begin to share their understanding with others. Through this process of integration they develop coordinated action. If the coordinated action is recurrent and significant they will then begin to institutionalize knowledge, and routine sequences of activity will become embedded into the organizational repertoire (Dutta and Crossan, 2005). Evidence of intuition in entrepreneurs and senior executives does exist (Allinson et al., 2000; Sadler-Smith and Shefy, 2004). Witt (1998; 1999) has considered some of the behavioural implications for the entrepreneurial firm. He theorizes the importance of imagination and strong leadership. The envisioning process is important because the entrepreneur must develop a convincing business idea. But the idea potentially has rivals so the entrepreneur must have communication and social skills to mount convincing arguments in support of the idea in order to see off potential rivals, garner support and reduce the likelihood of opportunism. However, there is a need for detailed empirical research to test how opportunities are realized in the process of innovation.

The process of innovation or entrepreneurship goes beyond the so-called individual–opportunity nexus (Shane, 2003) to encompass the necessary steps for exploitation. These are generally thought to be the garnering of resources for opportunity development (Stevenson and Jarillo, 1990). However, from a human capital perspective what additional skills and competences might be helpful to this stage in the entrepreneurial endeavour? Two characteristics have been offered – entrepreneurial self-efficacy (ESE) and social competence.

Boyd and Vozikis proposed that ESE is 'an important explanatory variable in determining both the strength of entrepreneurial intentions and the likelihood that those intentions will result in entrepreneurial actions' (1994: p. 65). Self-efficacy beliefs have a social learning aspect to them and are thus strengthened through enactive mastery, observational learning, social persuasion and judgement of one's own physiological state such as anxiety or emotionality, which may make individuals vulnerable to reduced performance. Chen et al. (1998) suggested that ESE in the five key skill areas of marketing, innovation, management, risk-taking and financial control, differentiate between people actively interested in setting up a business and those who have already started. Studies continue to show, however, the strength of character and resolve that is needed to found a business. For example, Markman et al. (2005) have shown that because of the formidable and daunting task, entrepreneurs would require personal perseverance and self-efficacy. Baum and Locke (2004) examined the possible impact of ESE on venture growth. Forbes (2005) examined the way strategic decisions made in new ventures exert a significant influence on the ESE of entrepreneurs who manage them.

Social competence
A large proportion of nascent enterprises are founded by more than one individual. Furthermore, at the very early stage in getting established, the nascent entrepreneur(s) draw other people into the enterprise and therefore developing, managing and leading a team is an important social competence to have. Where nascent enterprises are developed within corporations this role is often taken by a person who champions opportunity development. But in both cases the need for the team to feel efficacious is important. Feeling motivated and rewarded, sharing thoughts, perceiving the path of opportunity development to be feasible, desirable and supported are important behaviours and attitudes (Shepherd and Krueger, 2002). The entrepreneur or champion uses persuasive language to ensure 'buy-in' by team members, especially where tangible support is given. They may do this by recognizing critical skills and knowledge needed to move forward. Furthermore, the social norms and attitudes toward the enterprise should value and reinforce entrepreneurial activity – this would not be expected to be an issue in a nascent independent enterprise.

Baron and Markman (2003) distinguish between social capital – the resources that individuals bring to their relationships with others – and social competence – effectiveness in interacting with others. To be effective, they have argued, requires various social skills. Social capital can enable an entrepreneur to 'get in the door' (Baron and Markman, 2003: p. 44), but social competence can influence the entrepreneur's success. Social competences include impression management, accurately perceiving others, persuasiveness and the ability to adapt to a range of others. The result might also be more communication with others, greater cooperation, more effective personal relationships and the ability to gain others' trust and confidence. In sum, these researchers identified five elements to social competence which they posited might affect the financial success of an enterprise: social perception; impression management; persuasiveness; social adaptability; and expressiveness. They tested this on two samples, the first were female sales contractors in the cosmetics industry and the second were predominantly male, top executives in high-tech entrepreneurial firms. They found social perception to be significant in both samples and social adaptability in the cosmetics industry sample, while expressiveness was found to be important in the high-tech group. Their conclusion was that social competence is important and likely to play a part in the success of entrepreneurially-led ventures.

Summary
Researchers have sought alternatives to trait approaches. Mischel and Shoda (1995) put forward their CAPS model, and whilst it has not been tested in entrepreneurial situations, it appears to have potential, not least because it encompasses social learning. Research on opportunity recognition is indicative of a prototypical cognitive pattern in entrepreneurs. Several theories have been put forward about how this process works. From an HRM perspective, it is important to understand how this might impact on others. Further work is needed to test the three positions: (1) opportunities are tangible and are discovered; (2) opportunities are intangible and created by individuals with unique insight; (3) opportunities are initially intangible, but as they are explored and interpreted, and the information is shared with others, they become more tangible. However, it would appear that where opportunities are frame-breaking, (2) and (3) are more likely to apply. Hence the research that supports the importance of ESE and social competence would appear to identify critical skills in these circumstances. It is perhaps not surprising therefore that some entrepreneurs are described as 'larger than life' or 'charismatic' as they are persuasive and influential and able to carry others along with them. Thus, entrepreneurs who are successful, have the ability to produce results and the social flair to convince others to back them are likely to be attractive to others. Clearly human capital and its development in entrepreneurial firms is crucial: resource rich enterprises attract more resources, whilst resource poor enterprises fail to do so and in this sense 'more begets more'. Further evidence to support this view is drawn upon in the next section.

The entrepreneurial process model 3: human and social capital
Criticism of the trait approach and recognition of entrepreneurship as a process have resulted in the development of process models (Chell, 1985; Low and Macmillan, 1988) positing the importance of human and social capital elements. Two, not necessarily mutually exclusive, approaches can be considered: (a) surveys of human capital that are hypothesized as impacting entrepreneurial outcomes; (b) resource-based theory (RBT) that assumes distinctive human and social capital elements are combined to produce competitive advantage in entrepreneurially-led situations.

Human capital

Surveys of human capital of nascent entrepreneurs have measured various demographics including education, age, gender and parental occupation. The Global Entrepreneurship Monitor (GEM) has surveyed nascent entrepreneurs in a range of countries over many years (Minniti et al., 2005; Reynolds et al., 2004). Whilst trends in country differences (especially between high income and middle income countries) in levels of entrepreneurial activity and the factors purported to determine such levels have been found, the observations were correlations and not theory-led. Items such as gender, marital status and education do not of themselves explain entrepreneurial activity, but contribute to countries' socio-cultural fabric. Whilst GEM includes measures of entrepreneurial opportunities and entrepreneurial capacity, such survey work cannot observe the nuances and subtleties of entrepreneurial behaviour and decision making as described above. It can inform policy at a macro level and, whilst it is at such a high order of generality, it is encouraging to see evidence-based policy.

Early studies included demographic characteristics and were largely unsuccessful in establishing an entrepreneurial profile (Shook et al., 2003). Later studies attempted to link various characteristics, such as skills and competences, with firm performance (Baum, 1994; Chandler and Hanks, 1994) or demographics, such as experience, personality, human capital and ethnic origin factors with employment growth (Storey, 1994). Delmar and Davidsson (2000) surveyed nascent entrepreneurs before they had taken the step of founding a business. Their results confirmed previous observations: nascent entrepreneurs were more likely to have self-employed parents; be more highly educated; have more management experience and were more likely to reside in large cities. Nascent entrepreneurs were also found to have higher incomes and personal wealth. In addition, they tended to be younger and male. However, when logistic regression analysis was used, the model's ability to classify female nascent entrepreneurs correctly was low. Clearly the variables identified had a low explanatory and predictive power where female nascent entrepreneurs were concerned.

A later study by Davidsson and Honig (2003) went beyond that of measuring human capital and also measured social capital factors in an attempt to examine the gap in understanding between these two sets of factors as they were posited to impact nascent entrepreneurship. This shift from demographic to human and social capital drew on the theory that education, knowledge and experience were more likely to affect the probability and successful exploitation of entrepreneurial opportunities. Social capital that included strong ties (bonding) and weak ties (bridging) was theorized as providing networks that facilitate the discovery of opportunities and the identification and allocation of scarce resources for successful exploitation.

The researchers found that those nascent entrepreneurs with greater levels of human capital were more likely to discover opportunities, and this included tacit knowledge, such as work and start-up experience. Human capital, however, did not reliably differentiate between successful and unsuccessful entrepreneurial processes. Explicit human capital such as formal education increased the pace of gestation, but was not found to affect critical outcomes. The implication was that different factors were at work in the discovery and exploitation stages. Social capital – in particular close ties – was strongly associated with discovery and was important in predicting successful exploitation. Weak ties, specifically being a member of a business network, were significant at both discovery and exploitation stages. Social capital therefore became increasingly important as the venture process progressed. These findings underlined entrepreneurship as a 'social game' and that when the objective is continued and successful exploitation, then more specialized knowledge, contacts and actions are required.

Baum and Locke (2004), building on an earlier study, developed and tested a revised conceptual model of the impact of human capital factors on venture growth. Specifically, they carried out a six-year follow-up study examining the impact of traits and skill (passion, tenacity and new resource skill) and situation-specific motivation (communicated vision, self-efficacy and goals) on venture growth. No direct effects of traits and skill on venture growth were found. Tenacity was related to new resource skill, while the motivational factors were significantly related to venture growth. Self-efficacy had the strongest impact on venture growth; vision and goals were also highly significant predictors of venture growth, and vision was significantly related to goals. The findings for communicated vision were thought to be particularly interesting and resonate with both the leadership and small business literature (Chell and Tracey, 2005; Filion, 1991). Further, they suggested that traits operated indirectly through mechanisms such as goals, efficacy and vision. New resource skill – the ability to acquire and organize the operating resources needed to start and grow a business venture – worked through motivational mechanisms. Thus, these authors suggested, the larger the organization the more the links require coordinating between the CEO/entrepreneur's vision, traits and goals and organizational performance (Baum and Locke, 2004: p. 596). As experience underpins skill development, new resource skills are important for explaining why habitual and serial entrepreneurs are more reliable founders of successful businesses. New resource skills were found to be a stronger predictor of venture growth than organizational skill because they were more closely related to vision, goals and self-efficacy. It was also found to be a significant ($p < .10$) predictor of venture growth.

Resource-based theory (RBT)

RBT has been applied to entrepreneurship in order to answer economic, psychological and social questions about the process of entrepreneurship (Alvarez and Busenitz, 2001). Resources are assumed to be heterogeneous and defined as 'socially complex assets'. The question is how do entrepreneurs organize such resources to gain competitive advantage? The answer partially depends on assuming that entrepreneurs have a unique mindset enabling them to make decisions using heuristic methods enabling them to take short cuts – imaginative leaps in logic and inspired guesses. Quicker decision-taking, faster learning and innovative interpretations of information result. Entrepreneurs are also able to frame situations opportunistically, discovering opportunities without search (Shane, 2003). The entrepreneur's capability is tacit generalized knowledge, which has been referred to as the ability to integrate synthetically knowledge and information from disparate sources (Chell, 2007) in contrast to domain-specific expert knowledge. It is how the entrepreneur organizes these resources – knowledge, technology, human resources, skills and other know-how – that creates differences which are difficult to imitate. Once this knowledge becomes explicit and common then the entrepreneurial firm loses its competitive advantage. A further dimension is the interaction between the entrepreneurial mindset and wider society, which raises the question of how we can explain the entrepreneurial hunch that an idea is an opportunity and should be exploited. This is particularly important when considering new technologies (like ring tones). It has been suggested that entrepreneurs expose themselves to a wider cross-section of society that 'gives them the opportunity to extrapolate and make extensions regarding new venture opportunities' (Alvarez and Busenitz, 2001: p. 768). In sum, entrepreneurship generally involves the entrepreneur's unique awareness of opportunities, the ability to acquire resources needed to exploit the opportunity and the organizational ability to combine homogeneous inputs to create heterogeneous outputs. Entrepreneurial resources in this process are alertness, insight, entrepreneurial knowledge and ability to coordinate resources in an inimitable way.

Rausch et al. (2005) have also contributed to RBT by examining the relationships between human capital, human resource development and utilization, and business performance, measured in terms of employment growth. Measures were taken at two points in time (with a four-year gap); thus at T1 the average age of the firms was 2.3 years and at T2 they were 6.3 years. The average number of employees grew from 6.28 (at T1) to 6.46 (at T2). Three models of the independent variables were tested on employment growth. They found the direct effects model had the strongest support showing that the human capital of business owners, but not their employees, significantly affected employment growth. Human resource development (HRD) and utilization also affected employment growth significantly. It was suggested that a finer grained assessment of employees' human capital might have shown positive results. Training and development of employees, decision-making involvement, goal communication and support for personal initiative were all HRD practices that affected employment growth. These represented investments and tended to have a delayed effect on employment growth. One hypothesis they were unable to test was the effect of HRD on human capital but they showed that the effect of HRD on employment growth was moderated by employees' human capital. Thus HRD and utilization was found to be more effective when there were high levels of employee human capital in the firm. Clearly this implies the importance of HRM issues in the establishment and growth of new and start-up enterprises.

Social capital

The process of nascent entrepreneurship goes beyond opportunity recognition to the ability to garner resources in its exploitation. This process involves the use of social capital principally through the development of social networks. Social networks include the entrepreneur's personal network of family and friends, which are known as strong ties, and contacts, which could be business acquaintances (Chell and Baines, 2000). In addition to these, entrepreneurs also develop weak ties which are more remote in their personal network structure but may be sources of diverse information (Aldrych, 1999; Granovetter, 1973). Two key structural elements potentially affect the nascent entrepreneur: diverse sources of information that facilitate opportunity recognition; and, the external network organizational structure of the competition. Where the latter is very tight it presents difficulties for the entrepreneur to access and leverage information or contacts, whereas the absence of network ties externally creates 'structural holes', which entrepreneurs may use to their advantage (Burt, 1992). Hence, nascent entrepreneurs with the capability to synthesize diverse information and who occupy advantageous positions may access emerging opportunities and critical resources. On the other hand, in impoverished locations entrepreneurs tend to fall back on their close ties or utilize the brokerage services such as a business support adviser or venture capitalist (Aldrych, 1999).

An implication of this process is 'vision communication'. The exploitation of opportunities that require imitation involves others in known routines and as such may not be challenged. However, in the case of a 'frame-breaking' innovation the entrepreneur has potentially more to do to convince others of the value of his/her vision (Witt, 1998). Vision communication, transformational leadership and the development of trusted relationships are critical (Bass, 1985; Chell and Tracey, 2005; Filion, 1991).

Discussion and implications for HRM

This chapter has focused on nascent entrepreneurs and the process of early stage entrepreneurship, where the exploitation of opportunity requires the garnering of resources, including those of human and social capital. The requirement for financial, legal, technical or other resources was not discussed. In narrowing the focus to human and social resources in the nascent enterprise, efforts were concentrated on the implications for HRM. Thinking about HRM has embraced the notion of strategic development and deployment of human capital to achieve organizational objectives. In so doing it has tended to assume large-scale, established organizations where HRM policies can be shaped to boardroom policy, rather than the nascent and rather fragile germinal enterprise. Does or should HRM have anything to contribute to the nascent enterprise? Should the nascent entrepreneur consider HRM issues as being critical to the development of the nascent enterprise?

In exploring the interface between entrepreneurship and HRM/D various models of entrepreneurship that included human and/or social capital elements were considered. Further work from an HRM perspective is needed in order to make progress, specifically:

- to understand the human capital element of the entrepreneurial process at its various discrete phases – recognition, formation and exploitation;
- to develop/adopt a contemporary model of entrepreneurship that is evidence-based;
- to be able to position the theory of the entrepreneur and entrepreneurial process in the social science literature;
- to deduce the probable attributes of entrepreneurial behaviour that result in effectiveness, for example, in respect of leadership and management; and
- to contribute to HRM policy in innovation and entrepreneurship at firm, regional and central government levels – including the ability of entrepreneurial firms gaining competitive advantage, making an impact on employment growth, contributing to productivity and a national competitiveness agenda.

From three contemporary models of entrepreneurship presented in this chapter the interface with HRM can be developed. With Model 1, the trait approach, there may be an argument for revisiting individual or constellations of traits conceptually in terms of them being socially learnt behaviours, contingent on socio-economic context and cultural factors. In terms of HRM/D the measurement of individual differences focuses on the individual but fails to explore the impact on other people. How do other people cope with a leader that is highly achievement oriented, controlling and appears to take bigger risks than they are comfortable with? The entrepreneur may be able to tolerate ambiguity, but colleagues may prefer to know more clearly (and unambiguously) what they are doing and why. Hence, there are clear implications for leadership and management of others in the nascent (as well as the established) enterprise.

Model 2 focuses on cognitive-based behaviour. Opportunity recognition research has the advantage of economic theoretical underpinnings and associated characteristics that include ESE and social competence. The HRM implications are primarily strategic and policy oriented at firm and government levels. For example, is there sufficient understanding of the process of opportunity recognition, formation and exploitation? Is the model robust? Is the socio-economic and cultural environment sufficiently supportive to enable entrepreneurs to be efficacious and thus to feel self-confident? Do entrepreneurs have the social and leadership skills to persuade others of the importance of the perceived (by the entrepreneur) opportunity? This is most fundamentally important if the entrepreneur is to garner resources, especially in this case, human resources, and see off potential rivals.

Model 3 focuses on human and social capital. Human capital factors taken alone were found to have weak predictive power, but when combined with social factors (such as strong and weak ties) have stronger explanatory value in the different phases of recognition and exploitation. Social awareness is needed to assess the value of opportunities. Entrepreneurs need leadership skills, while the training and development of them and their employees around effective participation in decision making, communication of vision and goals and support for personal initiative is critical. Nascent entrepreneurial firms with a relatively strong human capital base have greater potential to learn, contribute to HRD and its effective utilization. The development of social capital has strategic implications for the effectiveness of the nascent enterprise. It is important to train entrepreneurs to reach out to their extended network of remote contacts and communicate their vision effectively where appropriate by building trusted relationships and be an effective leader.

In this chapter human and social capital issues have been shown as being critical to the recognition and exploitation of opportunities for the creation of new enterprises. There is some evidence to support the influence of traits, but their influence is small and there is not yet the weight of evidence needed to be conclusive. However, the influence of personality cannot be dismissed and there remain questions to be answered. The idea that there is a single trait that typifies the entrepreneur can probably be rejected in favour of a constellation of person characteristics. This can be done because in engaging with a perceived opportunity the entrepreneur must: (a) synthesize tacit and explicit knowledge to recognize a potential opportunity; (b) formulate an idiosyncratic idea which will become their vision; (c) make a judgement to pursue the idea further; and (d) commence the process of garnering resources in order to exploit the idea. This complex process takes time and requires imagination, insight, creativity, sound judgement, confidence and leadership. The connection between experience, learning and entrepreneurial effectiveness has implications for the development of individuals and possibly teams of entrepreneurs.

Undoubtedly human and social capitals are the resources that the nascent entrepreneur and his/her associates bring to the enterprise. So what of traits? It is difficult to argue that each of the traits reviewed necessarily influences the entrepreneurial or innovative process in a significant way. However, small contributions, particularly where they occur on more than one occasion, could be significant in pertinent contexts. To explore these ideas sophisticated research designs are needed, which use samples of potential entrepreneurs, have a longitudinal design and measure effectiveness as well as enterprise performance.

Thus understanding the various human capital inputs and the social process gives a basis for HRM and HRD policies and practices that are relevant to the nascent enterprise (Chell, 2001). This would enable the enterprise team to be professional about the deployment of human capital at early and subsequent stages of the enterprise. Such an approach helps with the process of impression management when dealing with venture capitalists, bankers and investors. It gives a sense of understanding and valuing extant resources, and control in the direction and development of human capital requirements. That is, the enterprise team would not only understand what resources they already have, but what they do not have and why they might need them.

It is far easier to argue the necessity of a technical resource and overlook the fact that such a resource may not be sufficient to achieve success. Entrepreneurial alertness, social competence, efficacy (self and team) and various team building and leadership skills are arguably just as important. Nascent enterprises are by definition small and fragile: it is important that recruitment and selection strategies are right as new individuals can alter team dynamics. All need to contribute effectively to the overall endeavour as this type of enterprise cannot afford 'passengers' (Chell and Tracey, 2005). If individuals are to make a valuable contribution to the overall endeavour then efforts to retain them are also critical. Vision communication is crucial to convince and retain valued individuals (Witt, 1998) and from an HRM perspective, recognition and reward become critical.

Nascent enterprises are known to place heavy demands on the founding team in terms of flexibility, time and effort. Hence, the lead entrepreneur should know how to engage and communicate effectively and enthusiastically with the team, gaining commitment by rewarding performance. Some entrepreneurs operate with a right-hand person they have groomed and whose judgement they trust (Chell and Tracey, 2005). Within this dyad, there are important dimensions to effective interrelating: veridical perception and environmental comprehension; role complementarity; an appropriate management style; and effective vision communication. A soft HRM policy stressing the importance of skills, commitment and flexibility can be effective, and entrepreneurs should therefore build a flexible resource base, anticipate expansion and build up knowledge and resource skills. This underscores the importance of training and development and the expectation that learning heuristically will characterize the nascent enterprise for all parties.

Skill supply strategies are important as the nascent enterprise is orientated in its sector. Knowing how to recruit people with specialized skills, the sector-specific skills needed and ascertaining whether they are in plentiful supply or scarce (Hendry et al., 1995) are all important. Awareness that some skills are more difficult to identify, such as the non-routine ones based on experience, tacit and requiring sound judgement, is also needed. The entrepreneur should be able to work out what skills, competences and capabilities give the enterprise its particular competitive advantage and shape the HRM strategy around that knowledge. Without such critical understanding, the ability to develop and sustain the enterprise over the medium to long term would appear to be very precarious indeed.

References

Aldrich, H. (1999), *Organizations Evolving*, London and Thousand Oaks, CA: Sage.

Allinson, C.W., E. Chell and J. Hayes (2000), 'Intuition and entrepreneurial behaviour', *European Journal of Work and Organizational Psychology*, **9**, 31–43.

Alvarez, S.A. and L.W. Busenitz (2001), 'The entrepreneurship of resource-based theory', *Journal of Management*, **27**, 755–75.

Amit, R., L. Glosten and E. Muller (1993), 'Challenges to theory development in entrepreneurship research', *Journal of Management Studies*, **30**, 815–34.

Bandura, A. (1977), *Social Learning Theory*, Englewood Cliffs, NJ: Prentice Hall.

Baron, R.A. and G.D. Markman (2003), 'Beyond social capital: The role of entrepreneurs' social competence in their financial success', *Journal of Business Venturing*, **18**, 41–60.

Bass, B.M. (1985), *Leadership and Performance Beyond Expectations*, New York: The Free Press.

Bateman, T.S. and J.M. Crant (1993), 'The proactive component of organizational behavior: A measure and correlates', *Journal of Organizational Behavior*, **14**, 103–18.

Baum, J.R. (1994), 'The relation of traits, competences, motivation, strategy, and structure to venture growth', unpublished doctoral dissertation, The University of Maryland, US.

Baum, J.R. and E.A. Locke (2004), 'The relationship of entrepreneurial traits, skill, and motivation to subsequent venture growth', *Journal of Applied Psychology*, **89**, 587–98.

Becherer, R.C. and J.G. Maurer (1999), 'The proactive personality disposition and entrepreneurial behavior among small company presidents', *Journal of Small Business Management*, **37**, 28–36.
Begley, T.M. and D.P. Boyd (1986), 'Psychological characteristics associated with entrepreneurial performance', in R. Ronstadt, J.A. Hornaday, R. Peterson and K.H. Vesper (eds), *Frontiers of Entrepreneurship Research*, Wellesley, MA: Babson College, pp. 146–65.
Bonnett, C. and A. Furnham (1991), 'Who wants to be an entrepreneur: A study of adolescents interested in a young enterprise scheme', *Journal of Economic Psychology*, **12**, 465–78.
Bouchikhi, H. (1993), 'A constructivist framework for understanding entrepreneurship performance', *Organization Studies*, **14**, 549–70.
Boyd, N. and G. Vozikis (1994), 'The influence of self-efficacy on the development of entrepreneurial intentions and actions', *Entrepreneurship: Theory and Practice*, **18**(4), 63–77.
Brockhaus, R.H. (1980), 'Risk-taking propensity of entrepreneurs', *Academy of Management Journal*, **23**, 509–20.
Brockhaus, R.H. (1982), 'The psychology of the entrepreneur', in C.A. Kent, D.L. Sexton and K.H. Vesper (eds), *Encyclopaedia of Entrepreneurship*, Englewood Cliffs, NJ: Prentice Hall, pp. 39–56.
Burt, R.S. (1992), 'The social structure of competition', in N. Nohria and R.G. Eccles (eds), *Networks and Organizations: Structure, Form, and Action*, Cambridge, MA: Harvard University Press, pp. 57–91.
Buttner, E.H. (1992), 'Entrepreneurial stress: Is it hazardous to your health?' *Journal of Managerial Issues*, **4**, 223–40.
Caird, S. (1991), 'Testing enterprising tendency in occupational groups', *British Journal of Management*, **2**, 177–86.
Caird, S. (1992), 'Self assessments of participants on enterprise training courses', *British Journal of Education and Work*, **4**, 63–80.
Carland, J.W., J.C. Carland, F. Hoy and W.R. Boulton (1988), 'Distinctions between entrepreneurial and small business ventures', *International Journal of Management*, **5**, 98–103.
Carland, J.W., F. Hoy, W.R. Boulton and J.C. Carland (1984), 'Differentiating entrepreneurs from small business owners: A conceptualization', *Academy of Management Review*, **9**, 354–9.
Carsrud, A.L. and N.F. Krueger Jr (1995), 'Entrepreneurship and social psychology: Behavioural technology for the new venture initiation process', in J.A. Katz and R.H. Brockhaus Sr (eds), *Advances in Entrepreneurship, Firm Emergence and Growth*, Greenwich, CT: JAI Press, pp. 73–96.
Casson, M. (1982), *The Entrepreneur – An Economic Theory*, Oxford: Martin Robertson.
Casson, M. (2005), 'Entrepreneurship and the theory of the firm', *Journal of Economic Behavior and Organization*, **58**(2), 327–48.
Chandler, G.N. and S.H. Hanks (1994), 'Founder competence, the environment, and venture performance', *Entrepreneurship: Theory and Practice*, **18**(3), 77–89.
Chell, E. (1985), 'The entrepreneurial personality: A few ghosts laid to rest?', *International Small Business Journal*, **3**, 43–54.
Chell, E. (2000), 'Towards researching the "opportunistic entrepreneur": a social constructionist approach and research agenda', *European Journal of Work and Organizational Psychology*, **1**, 63–80.
Chell, E. (2001), *Entrepreneurship: Globalization, Innovation and Development*, London: Thomson Learning.
Chell, E. (2007), 'The training and development of managers and entrepreneurs: The role of integrative and innovative capability', in M. Ozbilgin and A. Malach-Pines (eds), *Career Choices in Entrepreneurship and Management*, Cheltenham, UK and Northampton, MA, USA: Edward Elgar.
Chell, E. (2008), *The Entrepreneurial Personality*, Oxford: The Psychology Press (forthcoming).
Chell, E. and S. Baines (2000), 'Networking, entrepreneurship and micro-business behaviour', *Entrepreneurship and Regional Development*, **12**, 195–215.

Chell, E. and R. Burrows (1991), 'The small business owner-manager', in J. Stanworth and C. Gray (eds), *Bolton 20 Years On: The Small Firm in the 1990s*, London: Paul Chapman, pp. 151–77.

Chell, E. and P. Tracey (2005), 'Relationship building in small firms: The development of a model', *Human Relations*, **58**, 577–616.

Chell, E., J.M. Haworth and S.M. Brearley (1991), *The Entrepreneurial Personality: Concepts, Cases and Categories*, London: Routledge.

Chen, C.C., P.G. Greene and A. Crick (1998), 'Does entrepreneurial self-efficacy distinguish entrepreneurs from managers?', *Journal of Business Venturing*, **13**, 295–316.

Ciavarella, M.A., A.K. Buchholtz, C.M. Riordan, R.D. Gatewood and G.S. Stokes (2004), 'The big five and venture survival: Is there a linkage?', *Journal of Business Venturing*, **19**, 465–83.

Collins, C.J., P.J. Hanges and E.A. Locke (2004), 'The relationship of achievement motivation to entrepreneurial behavior: A meta-analysis', *Human Performance*, **17**, 95–117.

Crant, J.M. (1996), 'The proactive personality scale as a predictor of entrepreneurial intentions', *Journal of Small Business Management*, **34**, 42–9.

Davidsson, P. and B. Honig (2003), 'The role of social and human capital among nascent entrepreneurs', *Journal of Business Venturing*, **18**, 301–31.

Delmar, F. and P. Davidsson (2000), 'Where do they come from? Prevalence and characteristics of nascent entrepreneurs', *Entrepreneurship and Regional Development*, **12**(1), 1–23.

Dutta, D.K. and M.M. Crossan (2005), 'The nature of entrepreneurial opportunities: Understanding the process using the 4I Organizational Learning Framework', *Entrepreneurship: Theory and Practice*, **29**, 425–49.

Engle, D.E., J.J. Mah and G. Sadri (1997), 'An empirical comparison of entrepreneurs and employees: Implications for innovation', *Creativity Research Journal*, **10**, 45–9.

Envick, B. and M. Langford (2000), 'The five factor model of personality: Assessing entrepreneurs and managers', *Academy of Entrepreneurship Journal*, **6**, 6–17.

Filion, L.J. (1991), 'Vision and relations: Elements for an entrepreneurial meta-model', *International Small Business Journal*, **9**, 16–40.

Fineman, S. (1977), 'The achievement motive construct and its measurement: Where are we now?', *British Journal of Psychology*, **68**, 1–22.

Forbes, D.P. (2005), 'The effects of strategic decision making on entrepreneurial self-efficacy', *Entrepreneurship: Theory and Practice*, **29**, 599–626.

Furnham, A. (2007), *Personality and Intelligence at Work: Exploring and Explaining Individual Differences in the Workplace*, London: The Psychology Press.

Gaglio, C.M. and J.A. Katz (2001), 'The psychological basis of opportunity identification: Entrepreneurial alertness', *Small Business Economics*, **16**, 95–111.

Gartner, W.B. (1988), ' "Who is an entrepreneur?" Is the wrong question', *American Journal of Small Business*, **12**, 11–31.

Gooding, R.Z. (1989), 'Decision-making and the structure of strategic problems', The Working Conference on Managerial Cognition, Washington, DC.

Granovetter, M. (1973), 'The strength of weak ties', *American Journal of Sociology*, **78**, 1360–80.

Hampson, S.E. (1982), *The Construction of Personality*, London: Routledge & Kegan Paul.

Hampson, S.E. (1988), *The Construction of Personality*, London: Routledge.

Hansemark, O.C. (2003), 'Need for achievement, locus of control and the prediction of business start-ups: A longitudinal study', *Journal of Economic Psychology*, **24**, 301–19.

Harris, J.A., R. Saltstone and M. Fraboni (1999), 'An evaluation of the job stress questionnaire with a sample of entrepreneurs', *Journal of Business and Psychology*, **13**, 447–55.

Hébert, R.F. and A.N. Link (1988), *The Entrepreneur – Mainstream Views and Radical Critiques*, New York: Praeger.

Hendry, C., M.B. Arthur and A.M. Jones (1995), *Strategy Through People: Adaptation and Learning in the Small-Medium Enterprise*, London and New York: Routledge.

Huefner, J.C., K.H. Hunt and P.B. Robinson (1996), 'A comparison of four scales predicting entrepreneurship', *Academy of Entrepreneurship Journal*, **1**, 56–80.

Johnson, B.R. (1990), 'Towards a multidimensional model of entrepreneurship: The case of achievement motivation and the entrepreneur', *Entrepreneurship: Theory and Practice*, **14**(3), 39–54.

Kaish, S. and B. Gilad (1991), 'Characteristics of opportunities search of entrepreneurs versus executives: Sources, interests, general alertness', *Journal of Business Venturing*, **6**, 45–61.

Kickul, J. and L.K. Gundry (2002), 'Prospecting for strategic advantage: The proactive entrepreneurial personality and small firm innovation', *Journal of Small Business Management*, **40**, 85–97.

Kirton, M.J. (1980), 'Adaptors and innovators in organizations', *Human Relations*, **3**, 213–24.

Kirzner, I.M. (1973), *Competition and Entrepreneurship*, Chicago: Chicago University Press.

Kirzner, I.M. (1979), *Perception, Opportunity and Profit*, Chicago: Chicago University Press.

Kirzner, I.M. (1985), *Discovery and the Capitalist Process*, Chicago: Chicago University Press.

Knight, F.H. (1921), *Risk, Uncertainty and Profit*, New York: Houghton Mifflin.

Korunka, C., H. Frank, M. Lueger and J. Mugler (2003), 'The entrepreneurial personality in the context of resources, environment, and the start-up process: A configurational approach', *Entrepreneurship: Theory and Practice*, **28**, 23–42.

Leavitt, H. (1988), *Managerial Psychology: Managing Behavior in Organizations*, Chicago: Dorsey Press.

Lee, D.Y. and E.W.K. Tsang (2001), 'The effects of entrepreneurial personality, background and network activities on venture growth', *Journal of Management Studies*, **38**, 583–602.

Low, M.B. and I.C. Macmillan (1988), 'Entrepreneurship: Past research and future challenges', *Journal of Management*, **14**, 139–61.

Markman, G.D., R.A. Baron and R.A. Balkin (2005), 'Are perseverance and self-efficacy costless? Assessing entrepreneurs' regretful thinking', *Journal of Organizational Behavior*, **26**, 1–19.

Matthews, G., I.J. Deary and M.C. Whiteman (2003), *Personality Traits*, 2nd edn, Cambridge: Cambridge University Press.

McClelland, D.C. (1961), *The Achieving Society*, Princeton, New Jersey: D. Van Nostrand Company Inc.

Meredith, G.G., R.E. Nelson and P.A. Neck (1982), *The Practice of Entrepreneurship*, Geneva: ILO.

Miller, D. and J.M. Toulouse (1986), 'Chief executive personality and corporate-strategy and structure in small firms', *Management Science*, **32**, 1389–409.

Miner, J.B. and N.S. Raju (2004), 'Risk propensity differences between managers and entrepreneurs and between low- and high-growth entrepreneurs: A reply in a more conservative vein', *Journal of Applied Psychology*, **89**, 3–13.

Minniti, M., W.D. Bygrave and E. Autio (2005), *Global Entrepreneurship Monitor*, Wellesley, MA: Babson College and London, UK: London Business School.

Mischel, W. (1973), 'Towards a cognitive social learning reconceptualisation of personality', *Psychological Review*, **80**, 252–83.

Mischel, W. and Y. Shoda (1995), 'A cognitive-affective system-theory of personality: Reconceptualizing situations, dispositions, dynamics, and invariance in personality structure', *Psychological Review*, **102**, 246–68.

Mitchell, J.R., P.N. Friga and R.K. Mitchell (2005), 'Untangling the intuition mess: Intuition as a construct in entrepreneurship research', *Entrepreneurship Theory and Practice*, **29**, 653–79.

Mueller, S.L. and A.S. Thomas (2000), 'Culture and entrepreneurial potential: A nine country study of locus of control and innovativeness', *Journal of Business Venturing*, **16**, 51–75.

Muller, G.F. and C. Gappisch (2005), 'Personality types of entrepreneurs', *Psychological Reports*, **96**, 737–46.

Nonaka, I. and H. Takeuchi (1995), 'Organizational knowledge creation', in I. Nonaka and H. Takeuchi (eds), *The Knowledge-Creating Company: How Companies Create the Dynamics of Innovation*, Oxford: Oxford University Press, Chapter 3.

Palich, L.E. and D.R. Bagby (1995), 'Using cognitive theory to explain entrepreneurial risk-taking: Challenging conventional wisdom', *Journal of Business Venturing*, **10**, 425–38.

Park, J.S. (2005), 'Opportunity recognition and product innovation in entrepreneurial hi-tech start-ups: A new perspective and supporting case study', *Technovation*, **25**, 739–52.

Rausch, A., M. Frese and A. Utsch (2005), 'Effects of human capital and long term human resource development and utilization on employment growth of small scale businesses: A causal analysis', *Entrepreneurship: Theory and Practice*, **29**, 681–98.

Reynierse, J.H. (1997), 'An MBTI model of entrepreneurism and bureaucracy: The psychological types of business entrepreneurs compared to business managers and executives', *Journal of Psychological Type*, **40**, 3–19.

Reynolds, P.D., N.M. Carter, W.B. Gartner and P.G. Greene (2004), 'The prevalence of nascent entrepreneurs in the United States: Evidence from the panel study of entrepreneurial dynamics', *Small Business Economics*, **23**, 263–84.

Robinson, P.B., J.C. Stimpson, J.C. Huefner and H.K. Hunt (1991), 'An attitude approach to the prediction of entrepreneurship', *Entrepreneurship: Theory and Practice*, **15**, 41–52.

Rotter, J.B. (1966), 'Generalized expectancies for internal versus external control of reinforcement', *Psychological Monographs*, **80**(1), 1–28.

Sadler-Smith, E. and E. Shefy (2004), 'The intuitive executive: Understanding and applying "gut feel" in decision-making', *Academy of Management Executive*, **18**, 76–91.

Sagie, A. and D. Elizur (1999), 'Achievement motive and entrepreneurial orientation: A structural analysis', *Journal of Organizational Behavior*, **20**, 375–87.

Sarasvathy, D.K., H.A. Simon and L. Lave (1998), 'Perceiving and managing business risks: Differences between entrepreneurs and bankers', *Journal of Economic Behavior and Organization*, **33**, 207–25.

Schere, J.L. (1987), 'Tolerance of ambiguity as a discriminating variable between entrepreneurs and managers', *Academy of Management Proceedings*, pp. 404–408.

Schumpeter, J.A. (1934), *The Theory of Economic Development*, Cambridge, MA: Harvard University Press.

Sexton, D.L. and N.B. Bowman (1984), 'Personality inventory for potential entrepreneurs: Evaluation of a modified JPI/PRF-E test instrument', in J.A. Hornaday, F. Tarpley, J.A. Timmons and K.H. Vesper (eds), *Frontiers of Entrepreneurship Research*, Wellesley, MA: Babson College, pp. 513–28.

Shackle, G.L.S. (1972), *Epistemics and Economics: A Critique of Economic Doctrines*, Cambridge: Cambridge University Press.

Shackle, G.L.S. (1979), *Imagination and the Nature of Choice*, Edinburgh: Edinburgh University Press.

Shane, S. (2000), 'Prior knowledge and the discovery of entrepreneurial opportunities', *Organization Science*, **11**, 448–69.

Shane, S. (2003), *A General Theory of Entrepreneurship*, Cheltenham, UK and Northampton, MA, USA: Edward Elgar.

Shepherd, D.A. and N.F. Krueger (2002), 'An intentions-based model of entrepreneurial teams' social cognition', *Entrepreneurship: Theory and Practice*, **27**, 167–86.

Shoda, Y., S. LeeTiernan and W. Mischel (2002), 'Personality as a dynamic system: Emergence of stability and constancy from intra- and inter-personal interactions', *Personality and Social Psychology Review*, **6**, 316–25.

Shook, C.L., R.L. Priem and J.E. McGee (2003), 'Venture creation and the enterprising individual: A review and synthesis', *Journal of Management*, **29**, 379–99.

Stevenson, H.H. and J.C. Jarillo (1990), 'A paradigm of entrepreneurship: Entrepreneurial management', *Strategic Management Journal*, **11**, 17–27.

Stewart, W.H. and P.L. Roth (2001), 'Risk propensity differences between entrepreneurs and managers: A meta-analytic review', *Journal of Applied Psychology*, **86**, 145–53.

Stewart, W.H., W.E. Watson, J.C. Carland and J.W. Carland (1999), 'A proclivity for entrepreneurship: A comparison of entrepreneurs, small business owners, and corporate managers', *Journal of Business Venturing*, **14**, 189–214.

Storey, D.J. (1994), *Understanding the Small Business Sector*, London and New York: Routledge.

Thornton, P.H. (1999), 'The sociology of entrepreneurship', *Annual Review of Sociology*, **25**, 19–46.

Timmons, J.A., L.E. Smollen and A.L.M. Dingee (1985), *New Venture Creation*, Homewood, Ill.: Irwin.

Utsch, A., A. Rauch, R. Rothfuss and M. Frese (1999), 'Who becomes a small scale entre-preneur in a post-socialist environment: On the differences between entrepreneurs and man-agers in East Germany', *Journal of Small Business Management*, **37**, 31–42.
Witt, U. (1998), 'Imagination and leadership: The neglected dimension of an evolutionary theory of the firm', *Journal of Economic Behavior and Organization*, **35**, 161–77.
Witt, U. (1999), 'Do entrepreneurs need firms? A contribution to a missing chapter in Austrian Economics', *Review of Austrian Economics*, **11**, 99–109.

3 Entrepreneurship capital: a regional, organizational, team and individual phenomenon
David Audretsch and Erik Monsen

Introduction
In the fields of economics and management five types of capital have been identified as drivers of economic growth: physical capital, human capital, knowledge capital, social capital, and most recently entrepreneurship capital. In this chapter we define entrepreneurship capital as a subset of social capital, which refers to those social and relational factors, forces and processes that promote or hinder the interaction of various economic agents and their ability to employ, integrate and exploit physical, human and knowledge capital for entrepreneurial ends.

In this chapter the concept of entrepreneurship capital is shown to be an important factor for regional economic performance. This concept is extended to explain the economic and entrepreneurial performance of organizations, teams and individuals or in other words the economic and entrepreneurial performance of a region's or firm's human resources.

At the regional and industry levels, we define entrepreneurship capital as those factors related to social capital influencing and shaping the capacity of a region or industry to generate entrepreneurial activity.

At the firm level we define entrepreneurship capital as those organizational factors related to social capital influencing and shaping an organization in such a way as to be more conducive to the creation of new entrepreneurial business units (such as external ventures, joint ventures or internal ventures).

At the team level we define entrepreneurship capital as those interpersonal factors related to social capital influencing and shaping a team in such a way as to be more conducive to the enactment of entrepreneurial behaviours by individual managers and employees.

At the individual level we define entrepreneurship capital as those personal factors related to social capital influencing and shaping cognitions and actions of entrepreneurs, managers and employees in such a way as to be more conducive to the discovery and creation of entrepreneurial opportunities and the active pursuit of entrepreneurial opportunities.

Drawing on existing entrepreneurship and social capital research at and across these four levels of analysis we demonstrate our proposition that researchers at various levels of analysis are in fact modelling the same underlying concept of entrepreneurship capital. In our review we identify the specific elements of entrepreneurship capital at each level and corresponding independent and dependent variables. Where there are gaps in the existing literature we suggest perspectives and approaches that researchers could use to fill those gaps.

Thus, in this chapter we suggest a new direction for research, public policy and management practice that focuses not only on enhancing the human capital of a region's or a company's labour force, but also those additional organizational, interpersonal and personal factors of entrepreneurship capital which promote entrepreneurial action at the firm, team and individual level. Given also that entrepreneurship is inherently a multi-level phenomenon we discuss why it is important for researchers to investigate entrepreneurship capital at multiple levels and why it is important for practitioners and policy makers to coordinate and align efforts to promote entrepreneurship capital at the individual, team, organizational and regional levels.

From entrepreneurship to economic and firm growth

Over the past two decades, a number of researchers have developed theory and produced evidence to link entrepreneurship (also known as innovation and technological change), to economic growth (Aghion and Howitt, 1992; Carree et al., 2002; Romer, 1986; Wennekers and Thurik, 1999). Improvements in the quality of the data for example through the Global Entrepreneurship Monitor study (see Minniti et al., 2005; Reynolds et al., 2005) and its analysis, have made it possible to draw more nuanced conclusions about this generally positive yet complex relationship (Acs and Varga, 2005). For example, it has been demonstrated that the internal motivation for entrepreneurship (necessity vs. opportunity driven; no-growth vs. high-growth firms) and the external business environment (less vs. more economically developed; geographic/cluster effects) play a substantial role in the relationship between entrepreneurship and economic growth (Minniti et al., 2005; Rocha and Sternberg, 2005; van Stel et al., 2005; Wennekers et al., 2005; Wong et al., 2005).

In this chapter, we begin by discussing those aspects of social capital at the economy level which influence and shape economic actors and create an environment that is more conducive to the creation of new firms, more specifically known as entrepreneurship capital (Audretsch and Keilbach, 2004a). Our definition of social capital is similar to that of Adler and Kwon's definition as it being 'the goodwill available to individuals or groups. Its source lies in the structure and content of the actor's social relations. Its effects flow from the information, influence, and solidarity it makes available to the actor' (2002, p. 23).

While our definition of social capital is certainly not the only one, it is consistent with that used in mainstream strategic management and entrepreneurship research. For example, Nahapiet and Ghoshal (1998) and Leana and Van Buren III (1999) state that social capital 'comprises both the network and the assets that may be mobilized through that network' (Nahapiet and Ghoshal, 1998: p. 243) and is 'a resource reflecting the character of social relations within the firm . . . which create value by facilitating successful collective action' (Leana and Van Buren III, 1999: p. 538). Further, our definition admits both the positive and negative aspects of social capital. On the one hand, social capital increases individual commitment and flexibility (Leana and Van Buren III, 1999); the efficiency of individual and collective action (Leana and Van Buren III, 1999; Nahapiet and Ghoshal, 1998); and contributes to adaptive efficiency, creativity and learning (Nahapiet and Ghoshal, 1998). On the other hand, there are aspects of social capital that can detract from entrepreneurial effectiveness and success (Coleman, 1990; Leana and Van Buren III, 1999; Nahapiet and Ghoshal, 1998).

Following this line of reasoning we incorporate related ideas and findings in the research literature to extend this concept down to the firm, and lastly, to the team and individual levels. Sternberg and Wennekers (2005) in their introduction to a special issue in *Small Business Economics*, suggest there is a precedent for research into the determinants and the effects of entrepreneurial activity at not only the macro/country level but also at the regional as well as micro/individual level. Davidsson and Wiklund (2001) provide a more fine-grained review of the literature, likewise reporting on research at the micro (individual, team and firm) and macro/aggregate (industry, region) levels of analysis. Thornton (1999) provides a related literature from the sociological viewpoint, highlighting supply and demand-side perspectives in entrepreneurship research. A more formal model of the conditions for, the crucial elements and impact of entrepreneurship was proposed several years earlier by Wennekers and Thurik (1999, see Figure 3.4, p. 51). What they propose as conditions for entrepreneurship for the individual, firm and macro levels, we see as important aspects of entrepreneurship capital. In this review we build on their basic typology and define entrepreneurship capital at the economic (region and industry), organizational and personal (team and individual) levels of analysis as follows.

Economic entrepreneurship capital
Economic entrepreneurship capital is defined as those social and relational factors related to social capital which promote entrepreneurship in an

economic region or industry, consisting of multiple firms, markets and other economic actors. Following Wennekers and Thurik (1999) these include cultural and institutional conditions as well as elements of variety, competition and selection. In the next two sections we review the relevant research at the level of analysis of the economic region and the industry.

Economic region
The formal concept of entrepreneurship capital was first introduced at the economic level of analysis (Audretsch and Keilbach, 2004a; 2004b; 2004c; 2005). In its original form, entrepreneurship capital is defined as a subset of social capital which promotes entrepreneurial activity and includes legal, institutional and social factors (Audretsch and Keilbach, 2004a). For an excellent review of social capital as it applies to entrepreneurship as well as a discussion of how social capital (for example social structures, networks and memberships) relates to human capital (for example tacit and explicit knowledge) we refer the reader to Davidsson and Honig (2003).

There are a number of indirect and direct as well as objective and perceptual ways, to measure entrepreneurship capital in an economic region (see Arenius and Minniti, 2005). An indirect but key indicator is the number of start-ups per capita (Audretsch and Keilbach, 2004a). Narrow definitions of type of start-up, for example high-technology manufacturing or hardware and software businesses in the information technology sector, may more accurately reflect the risky nature of entrepreneurial start-ups (Audretsch and Keilbach, 2004a). More direct measures characterize the institutions, policies, demographic characteristics as well as historical, social and cultural traditions (Audretsch and Keilbach, 2004a). Alternate measures of a pro-entrepreneurship social capital have been proposed and empirically tested with mixed success, include parental self-employment and entrepreneurship rates (Davidsson and Honig, 2003; Kim et al., 2006; Mueller, 2006a), the level of entrepreneurial activity of household members (Mueller, 2006a) and start-up rates among close friends and neighbours and membership in business networks (Davidsson and Honig, 2003).

Several economic models of increasing complexity have been developed and empirically tested to demonstrate: 1) entrepreneurship capital contributes to economic output over and above traditional forms of capital (such as physical, labour and knowledge) (Audretsch and Keilbach, 2004a); 2) the impact of entrepreneurship capital is three to four times that of knowledge capital (Audretsch and Keilbach, 2004a); 3) high-technology entrepreneurship capital impacts labour productivity growth (Audretsch and Keilbach, 2004a); and 4) R&D intensive entrepreneurship capital has a greater long-term impact on long-term regional productivity, especially in urban compared with rural regions (Audretsch and Keilbach, 2005). In terms of theory, three mechanisms have been proposed to explain the positive impact of entrepreneurship capital on economic growth: knowledge spillovers, increased competition among the increased number of enterprises, and increased diversity among firms (Audretsch and Keilbach, 2004c).

Another example of a specific important component of entrepreneurship/social capital in regions is social networks. Studies of particular note in this area include those published by Cantner and Graf (2006) for Jena, in Germany; Neck et al. (2004) for Boulder County, Colorado; Lawson and Lorenz (1999) and Keeble et al. (1999) for Cambridge, England; and Casper and Murray (2005) for both Cambridge, England and Munich, Germany.

Industry
The next logical extension of the concept of entrepreneurship capital would be to look at specific industries within specific economic regions or across multiple economic regions. While there are industry-level studies addressing this for social capital and networks in general (see Podolny et al., 1996; Stuart and Sorenson, 2003a; 2003b), we found only one conceptual paper explicitly and specifically addressing entrepreneurship capital at the industry level of analysis. Building on related industry-level entrepreneurship and institutional research (Aldrich and Fiol, 1994; Rao, 1994) Lounsbury and Glynn (2001) propose that stories can be used to promote legitimacy, create competitive advantage, and build industry-level institutional capital. In their model, entrepreneurial stories produce entrepreneurial identity and legitimacy, which leads to the acquisition of resource and institutional capital, enabling wealth creation and a new round of entrepreneurial stories (Lounsbury and Glynn, 2001).

The concept of industry stories parallels the concepts of historical, social and cultural traditions at the economic level of analysis and most likely presents similar data-collection difficulties (see Audretsch and Keilbach, 2004a). A proxy, such as the number of new venture start-ups within an industry, with a potential focus of high-technology start-ups within an industry (see Audretsch and Keilbach, 2004a) may be a more readily and publicly available measure. This should not, however, discourage researchers from a richer, more qualitative industry-level analysis of start-up activity (see Christensen, 2000; Klepper, 2001, 2002; Klepper and Sleeper, 2005; Rao, 2004). In particular, the importance of inter-firm networks should not be ignored (Johannisson, 1998, 2000; Johannisson et al., 2002).

Organizational entrepreneurship capital

We now proceed from considering a population of organizations in an economic region or industry to considering a population of individuals in an organizational context. At this new level we define organizational entrepreneurship capital as those social and relational factors related to social capital which promote entrepreneurial activity within a single firm or a single unit of the firm, consisting of multiple individuals, teams and other corporate actors. Following Wennekers and Thurik (1999), these include conditions regarding business culture and incentives and elements regarding start-ups, entry into new markets, and innovations. While we primarily address research on private and for-profit organizations we do briefly address an emerging literature on entrepreneurial public and not-for-profit organizations.

Firm level – commercial organizations

In this section we begin by reviewing the social capital aspects of the current literature on entrepreneurial strategy, culture and the resulting firm-level performance implications. Following this introduction to the firm level of analysis, we will broaden the scope of our review to other more general works on entrepreneurship and social capital at the firm level.

To categorize the current literature on entrepreneurial strategy and culture, we were inspired by a framework from Chung and Gibbons (1997) which builds on an earlier cultural framework from Fombrun (1986) to focus on two aspects of organizational culture: the superstructure and the socio-structure. Whereas the superstructure includes the core beliefs, values and dominant assumptions of the organization (its ideology), the socio-structure includes learning, information exchange, norms and sanctions (social capital). Chung and Gibbons (1997) propose that these two aspects, along with human capital, play an influential role in corporate entrepreneurship. Applying this framework to current measures of entrepreneurial strategy and culture, entrepreneurial orientation (EO), entrepreneurial management (EM), and the corporate entrepreneurship activity index (CEAI), we find ideology has been the central focus of research to date, rather than social capital.

The oldest and most widely adopted measure of entrepreneurial strategy and culture is entrepreneurial orientation (EO). Building on earlier work by Khandwalla (1977) and Kets de Vries (1977), Miller (1983) defined a firm as being entrepreneurial when it behaves in a risk-taking, innovative and proactive manner. The most widely used catalogue of questionnaire items used to measure EO empirically (Kreiser et al., 2002; Lyon et al., 2000) was published by Covin and Slevin (1989; 1991) and later expanded upon by Lumpkin and Dess (1996; 2001) (see also Lumpkin, 1998). Cross-cultural validity of the multi-factor EO scale was demonstrated by Knight (1997), Antoncic and Hisrich (2001), and Kreiser et al. (2002).

While it has been demonstrated across a number of studies that higher levels of EO generally result in higher levels of firm performance (Rauch et al., 2004), a number of internal and external contingency factors have been identified which can moderate the relationship between EO and different measures of firm performance (Antoncic and Hisrich, 2004; Covin et al., 2006; Dess et al., 1997; Lumpkin and Dess, 2001; Wiklund and Shepherd, 2005). In fact it has been proposed that EO moderates the relationship between knowledge resources and firm performance (Wiklund and Shepherd, 2003), suggesting that EO may in fact be more closely related to human capital than social capital.

Less widely used but nonetheless well-established measures of entrepreneurial strategy and culture are entrepreneurial management (EM) and the corporate entrepreneurship activity index (CEAI). EM, a newer concept proposed by Stevenson and Jarillo (1990) and later empirically measured by Brown et al. (2001), encompasses six factors: strategic orientation, resource orientation, management structure, reward philosophy, growth orientation, and entrepreneurial culture. The CEAI has been around for over 20 years (Hornsby et al., 1993; Kuratko et al., 1990) and in its current form addresses five organizational factors: management support, work discretion, rewards/reinforcement, time availability, and organizational boundaries (Hornsby et al., 1999; Hornsby et al., 2002).

Following Chung and Gibbons' (1997) framework, close examination of the questionnaire items used to measure EO, EM and CEAI reveals that while they measure many aspects of a firm's entrepreneurial ideology, as reflected in the conditions proposed by Wennekers and Thurik (1999) (that is, conditions regarding business culture and incentives and elements regarding start-ups, entry into new markets and innovations) they do not explicitly address issues of social capital. While later extensions of EO do introduce the concepts of autonomy (Lumpkin and Dess, 1996; Monsen and Boss, 2004) and teamwork (Monsen, 2005), which are related to social capital, other measures of entrepreneurial strategy and culture need to be examined to find more explicit references to social capital.

With this key finding in mind we pose the question, how can social capital be better integrated into empirical research into entrepreneurial strategy and culture? In the more general literature on organizations, Nahapiet and Ghoshal's (1998) framework is well established. They propose three basic dimensions of social capital: structural (network ties, network configuration and appropriable organization), cognitive (shared codes, language and narratives) and relational (trust, norms, obligations and identification). Further, they propose four mechanisms (access, anticipation, motivation and capability) that can lead to the creation of new intellectual capital (see Nahapiet and Ghoshal, 1998, Figure 1: p. 251). Confirmatory empirical evidence supporting this model is provided by Tsai and Ghoshal (1998). By extending their model and linking the dimensions and mechanisms to our conception of entrepreneurship capital we propose that this new intellectual capital can in turn be exploited for innovation and entrepreneurship.

We encourage fellow entrepreneurship researchers to pursue theoretical and empirical work in this area. A significant amount of foundational work has been conducted in the innovation and entrepreneurship literatures in the area of strategic alliances (Cooper, 2002; Dickson et al., 2006; Eisenhardt and Schoonhoven, 1996; Weaver and Dickson, 1998) and inter-firm social networks (Cooper, 2002; Greve and Salaff, 2001; Hagedoorn and Roijakkers, 2002; Johannisson, 2000; Johannisson et al., 2002; Lechner and Dowling, 2003; Lechner et al., 2006). There are a number of additional starting points from which inspiration can be drawn, including research on stories and narratives (Lounsbury and Glynn, 2001) as well as from the results of related exploratory empirical studies, highlighted in the review article by Davidsson and Honig (2003).

Firm level – public organizations (labs and universities)
It should be noted that while social capital is typically addressed in the context of private and for-profit organizations, there is an emerging literature focusing on technology transfer and commercialization out of public and not-for-profit universities and research institutions, in which social capital plays an important role. The study of academic entrepreneurship and its impact on firms, industries and economic regions has been the subject of many studies over the past decade (Mansfield, 1998; Mowery et al., 2004; O'Shea et al., 2004; Shane, 2004; Thursby and Thursby, 2002). Beyond more traditional measures of human capital (Audretsch et al., 2005; O'Shea et al., 2005) in this chapter we are interested in the human and social mechanisms which enable technology transfer and commercialization and promote firm and regional growth.

Increasing attention has focused on knowledge flows and spillovers, involving the direct transfer of knowledge and personnel from universities and research centres to firms (Audretsch and Keilbach, 2005; Audretsch and Lehmann, 2004, 2006; Autio et al., Hameri and Vuola, 2004; Mueller, 2006b; Rothaermel and Thursby, 2005). More concretely, it has been found that active inventor engagement in technology transfer projects can substantially increase chances of commercialization and follow-on royalties (Agrawal, 2006).

In summary, while one can read between the lines of these research results and see the potential role of social capital in the technology transfer and commercialization process, its explicit role has yet to appear in the publication. Thus we urge researchers to pursue this line of research more explicitly and help to empirically identify those aspects of organizational entrepreneurship capital that have the most positive impact for public organizations, which need not be the same as for commercial organizations.

Personal entrepreneurship capital
Finally, we define personal entrepreneurship capital as those social and relational factors related to social capital which promote entrepreneurial behaviour within a single individual, either firm founders, mid-level managers, or their employees. Given the fact that teams of entrepreneurs often found firms, we also include entrepreneurial teams under this label. Following Wennekers and Thurik (1999) these include conditions pertaining to psychological endowments and elements of individual attitudes, skills and actions. After discussing the literature on entrepreneurial teams and firm founders, we proceed to discuss research on managers and employees who actually do the work in entrepreneurial firms.

Team level
Given that many firms are founded by teams instead of individual entrepreneurs, it is important to understand the social interactions of the team members that can often determine the success or failure of the new venture (see Ensley et al., 1999; Lechler, 2001). This is an area of research that has great promise, as the number of studies in this area is relatively small when compared to economic/industry-level, firm-level, and individual-level studies (Davidsson and Wiklund, 2001). For a review of the foundational literature in this area we refer the reader to Birley and Stockley (2000). Research into the top management teams has identified team cohesion, team potency, task conflict and shared strategic consensus as playing a central role in new venture performance (Ensley and Hmieleski, 2005; Ensley et al., 2003; Ensley and Pearson, 2005). While these factors are implicitly related to strong internal social capital, the authors rely on top management team theory (Hambrick and Mason, 1984), leaving it up to future researchers to draw the explicit connections and examine the actual mechanisms that drive these relationships. The importance for making these connections explicit is highlighted in an exploratory study of eight real-world entrepreneurial teams, in which 'social networks were most often mentioned as sources of venture capital and/or business partners' (Ensley et al., 1999: p. 280).

Is there empirical evidence and corresponding theory to back this claim? In fact, it has been demonstrated in independent studies that a balance between individualistic/autonomous behaviour and collectivistic/team behaviour is necessary to maximize entrepreneurial performance (Monsen, 2005; Morris et al., 1993; Morris et al., 1994). Voluntary knowledge transfer amongst team members, in part driven by positive social identification and consequent organizational learning, has been proposed as the mechanism which makes this possible (Dutta and Crossan, 2005; Monsen, 2005). It could also be argued that such a balanced social context not only produces learning and innovations, but could also be a good climate for the emergence and growth of social capital within the work group as well as with other external groups and actors. It should be noted that Dickson and Weaver (1997) examined interaction of the individualism/collectivism dimension with uncertainty and entrepreneurial orientation; however, their outcome variable was alliance use/non-use and they did not report testing the U-shaped curve hypothesis for individualism/collectivism.

While the studies just mentioned do not explicitly draw on social capital theory, some recent research has done. For example, it has demonstrated that an entrepreneurial team's initial external social capital (external network density) and the growth of internal social capital over time (emotional closeness) can improve team performance (Weisz et al., 2004). In addition, reflecting the idea that not all forms of social capital can be classified as entrepreneurship capital, Hansen et al. (2001) demonstrated that social capital (non-redundant, strong external ties) accelerating product development teams engaged in exploration tasks was in fact a hindrance for teams pursuing exploitation tasks.

Research into team evolution and development suggests that time will be an important dimension to consider and we expect that different aspects of social capital will be more or less supportive of entrepreneurial activities, although this depends on the new venture team's stage of development (see Boeker and Wiltbank, 2005; Vanaelst et al., 2006). In addition, the entry and exit of team members (Ucbasaran et al., 2003), and in particular new member identification and selection processes (Forbes et al., 2006) can play a concrete role in the growth (or decline) of a new venture team's social networks and social capital.

Of course, there are measurement considerations which make this line of research a challenging task. One example of this is presented by Delmar and Shane (2006) in their study of founding teams and firm survival. In this study they examine the relationship between start-up experience, industry experience and new venture survival. In developing their hypotheses they argue that previous experience results in both corresponding knowledge (human capital) and networks (social capital) that can aid in firm survival (Delmar and Shane, 2006). Therefore, we caution researchers to be precise in their theoretical specifications and corresponding selection of indicator variables.

Founder and leader
While there is still substantial debate about what makes and motivates an entrepreneur (Baum and Locke, 2004; Blanchflower and Oswald, 1998; Shane et al., 2003), there is a significant body of literature about the individual founders and leaders of entrepreneurial ventures, what they have, and what they do to build, maintain and grow their personal entrepreneurship capital. For example, habitual entrepreneurs with an entrepreneurial mindset 'engage the energies of everyone', 'involve many people – both inside and outside the organization', 'create and sustain networks of relationships', and make 'the most of the intellectual and other resources people have to offer' while 'helping those people to achieve their goals as well' (McGrath and MacMillan, 2000: p. 3). Building on this conception entrepreneurial leadership has been quite relevantly defined as 'leadership that creates visionary scenarios that are used to assemble and mobilize a "supporting cast" of participants who become committed by the vision to the discovery and exploitation of strategic value creation' (Gupta et al., 2004: p. 242). The creation of visions and stories is just as important at the firm level as at the industry level to bring legitimacy to a new business (Lounsbury and Glynn, 2001).

If entrepreneurial leaders are able to follow through with these actions and engage (and grow) their social capital and professional network contacts in order to gather the information they need to do business in a competent manner, research suggests this will lead to greater performance for their firm (Baron and Markman, 2003; Bosma et al., 2004; Glaeser et al., 2000). Additional studies have found similar positive links between an entrepreneur's personal networks and new firm performance (Witt, 2004), while others have proposed a similarly positive relationship for informal networks and social capital in internal corporate ventures (Hayton, 2005). In addition, research has demonstrated how different types of networks are more appropriate for commercial and academic entrepreneurial contexts (Johannisson, 1998). For a more in-depth review of the relationship between entrepreneurial networks and performance, we recommend Cooper (2002). In the area of social capital and cognitive biases we recommend a conceptual paper by De Carolis and Saparito (2006). Additionally, for a review of the broader social network context we refer the reader to both Aldrich and Ruef (2006) and Borgatti and Foster (2003).

Middle-managers and employees
Gartner (2001) retells the classic tale of the six blind men and the elephant. We would like to add a new twist to the tale. In our version a traditional strategic management scholar studies the head of the elephant, measuring all possible dimensions and then times how fast the elephant can run. That

same scholar next examines a large sample of elephants, randomly selecting them from herds all across India. After many months s/he draws the conclusion that the larger the elephant's head, the faster it can run. This may be a statistically significant result but is it interesting? What would happen if the researcher instead measured the elephant's legs and correlated that with its running speed; might s/he not get even more accurate results? Along the lines of this thought experiment we now review the spartan literature of personal entrepreneurship capital regarding managers and employees.

At the level of the middle-manager Hornsby et al. (1999) and Hornsby et al. (2002) have applied their corporate entrepreneurship activity index (CEAI) to determine differences in the perceived entrepreneurial environment in a company across different managerial levels (lower middle, middle and upper middle management) (Hornsby et al., 2002) and countries (Hornsby et al., 1999). However, as mentioned earlier in this chapter, the questionnaire items of the CEAI do not explicitly address social capital factors.

Other researchers have begun to integrate the needs and motivations of middle-managers into a model of entrepreneurship. One of the first attempts was made by Miles and Covin (2002) who proposed a framework in which a manager's needs and biases (such as need for control, ability and willingness to commit resources, and entrepreneurial risk accepting propensity) interact with the company's corporate venturing objectives (for example, organizational development and cultural change, strategic benefits and real option development and quick financial returns) and in turn impact the optimal structuring of the new corporate venture. In Kuratko et al.'s (2005) more sophisticated, causal model of middle-level managers' entrepreneurial behaviour the establishment of new social networks is introduced as a possible model outcome.

Conceptual models including employees in the causal chain between entrepreneurial strategy/culture and performance are slowly emerging in the published literature (Antoncic, 2003; Hayton, 2005) but actual collection of data from both managers and employees is sparse. What is available provides interesting insights into the communication of entrepreneurial vision from supervisor to subordinate (Baum and Locke, 2004), the impact of supervisor entrepreneurial behaviours on subordinate satisfaction (Pearce II and Kramer, 1997) and the impact of entrepreneurial strategies on individual role attitudes, organizational identification and job performance (Monsen, 2005). While Monsen (2005) goes further than Baum and Locke (2004) by considering the social context (autonomy and teamwork) as moderating factors, he does not explicitly address social capital.

Filling this gap will better enable us to hire, reward, compensate and train workers and management using approaches that increase their individual and collective social capital (Leana and Van Buren III, 1999) and in turn their personal and organizational entrepreneurship capital. Human resource practices that leverage and promote entrepreneurship capital will increase the ability of workers and management to perform, promote and handle organizational change (see Cardon and Stevens, 2004; Hayton, 2003; Leung, 2003; Leung et al., 2006; Levesque, 2005). Likewise, research into the role of a worker's personal networks in the workplace will help us to train more socially mobile (see Podolny and Baron, 1997) and more entrepreneurially effective and successful workers.

Integrating the levels of analysis

Having reviewed the literature for each of the levels of analysis, we now proceed to discuss the current research literature that crosses levels of analysis as well as propose future multi-level streams of research. Following this, we will discuss additional new directions for research, public policy and management practice.

Multi-level approach

'Future entrepreneurship research should address the effects of individual-level traits, organizational and market-level variables, and population-level characteristics in models of the founding of new ventures' (Thornton, 1999: p. 35). At the start of this chapter we reported Davidsson and Wiklund's (2001) call for more multi-level research. We also looked at Wenneckers and Thurik's (1999) multi-level framework. Both not only propose conditions for entrepreneurship for the individual, firm and macro levels, but also propose that the entrepreneurship elements at one level can impact entrepreneurship elements at other levels. For example, Wennekers and Thurik (1999) contend that entrepreneurial attitudes, skills and actions can lead to start-ups, entry into new markets and innovations at the firm level. These can lead to variety, competition and selection at the economic level. Specific measures of these outcomes at each level would include personal wealth, firm performance and economic growth and competitiveness, respectively (Wennekers and Thurik, 1999).

Davidsson and Wiklund (2001) propose a more comprehensive typology based on outcomes being differentially positive or negative at the individual and societal levels of analysis, suggesting a broader spectrum of entrepreneurs and entrepreneurship than has previously been studied. Similarly, Ibarra et al. (2005) propose a related two-dimensional model where the differential (high or low) levels of social capital at the individual and communal levels result in very different entrepreneurial environments in a region. This has implications for researchers examining the effects of individual-level entrepreneurial activity and networks on markets and economic regions (see Bygrave and Minniti, 2000; Minniti, 2005). For a related organization-level discussion on the need to balance individual and organizational social capital see Leana and Van Buren III (1999). The next step would be to empirically test these multi-level propositions and their implications for entrepreneurial action and outcomes.

One such multi-level approach is suggested by a recent book by Miles et al. (2005) in which they describe a futuristic network-based organization, OpWin, which embodies continuous innovation and collaborative entrepreneurship. Information critical for innovation is not owned by any one organization, but is shared throughout the network through the efficient use of technology with a focus on group outcomes (Miles et al., 2005). This novel is based on Miles and Snow's (1995) human investment model, which espouses that investments in capabilities and trust should be made at the level of the individual, the team, the firm and the network. Multi-level models of entrepreneurship and fundamental processes such as organizational learning (Crossan et al, 1999; Dutta and Crossan, 2005) are needed to better understand how the different levels of analysis form and inform each other. Reviews of the more general literature on network-organizations are presented by Podolny and Page (1998) and by Contractor et al. (2006).

Alternative approaches can be drawn from recent overview articles on entrepreneurship in established firms, which is often labelled as strategic entrepreneurship and corporate entrepreneurship. When large and established firms act entrepreneurially it is called different things depending on the actor and the level of analysis: corporate venturing, intrapreneurship, strategic renewal and domain redefinition (see Sharma and Chrisman, 1999; Stopford and Baden-Fuller, 1994). Ireland et al. (2003) define strategic entrepreneurship as incorporating an entrepreneurial mindset, an entrepreneurial culture, entrepreneurial leadership, strategic management of resources and the application of creativity to develop innovations. Resources to be managed strategically include financial, human and social capital. Of particular interest to us in this chapter are social capital resources, which are defined as the set of relationships 'between individuals (internal social capital) and between individuals and organizations (external social capital) that facilitate action' (Ireland et al., 2003: p. 976). Whereas 'internal social capital is related to realized social capital . . . external social capital can serve as a source of new knowledge and as a result, is related to potential absorptive capacity' (Ireland et al., 2003: pp. 976–7). Empirical evidence of the moderating effect of absorptive capacity on the relationship between social capital and evidence is provided by Tsai (2001). We can see promise and potential for further research into the intersection of entrepreneurship capital and absorptive capacity at all four levels of analysis with a particular focus on influences across the levels of analysis.

Dess et al's (2003) review article of corporate entrepreneurship research likewise applies an organizational learning lens and calls for future research. Specifically they highlight the emerging and critical role of social exchange in the corporate entrepreneurship process. Further they call for a reassessment of the outcomes of corporate entrepreneurship research and in particular research into how social, human and intellectual capital can be used to create competitive advantage and wealth. One proposed measure of a firm's social capital is its network of relationships that can provide valuable tangible and intangible resources (Adler and Kwon, 2002). Additional measures can be borrowed from the more general literature on social capital in organizations, referred to earlier in this chapter (Leana and Van Buren III, 1999; Nahapiet and Ghoshal, 1998), as well as related multi-level literature on social networks (Brass et al., 2004). Following learning theory, outcomes might 'include rapid, deep, and broad learning of new technologies and skills' (Dess et al., 2003: p. 372).

New directions for research, public policy and management practice
One new direction is to go beyond this study and to address other agents and levels of analysis. For example in reviewing the literature on strategic leadership in entrepreneurial firms, Daily et al. (2002) identified not only CEOs/founders and top management teams, which we address in this chapter, but also boards of directors and venture capitalists, who we do not address. For example, Podolny (2001) demonstrated a link between social network characteristics (structural holes), two types of market uncertainty and the distribution of venture capital funding rounds. Sorenson and Stuart (2001) explore how information flows and inter-firm networks can impact the geographic and industry clustering of VC investments. De Clercq and Sapienza (2006) found that the amount of relational capital in the venture capitalist–portfolio company dyad and the venture capitalists' commitment to the portfolio company are both related to perceived performance. In fact they propose that learning enhanced by relational capital and commitment will increase perceived performance (De Clercq and Sapienza, 2006). Another potential interaction between social/entrepreneurship capital and learning can be seen as an explanatory mechanism.

Additional new directions can be found in the integration of ideas from the field of organizational development and change (ODC). Historically rooted in social psychology the ODC field is by definition multi-level, integrating human-processual aspects at the individual and team levels with techno-structural elements at the firm level to produce beneficial outcomes for actors at all levels within the organization (Friedlander and Brown,

1974). Depending on the entrepreneurial goal, different models of change (punctuated or continuous), may be more or less appropriate (Weick and Quinn, 1999). Also given the degree of change required and the potential degree of resistance in the organization, industry or economic region, the entrepreneurial effort, to learn new routines and adopt new values, will need to be carefully structured (see Argyris, 1976; Argyris, 2002; Austin, 1997). Naturally, one needs to consider relationships between agents at each level of analysis and across levels of analysis (see Hage, 1999).

Yet another rich potential research area is to integrate the different types of entrepreneurship capital across the various units of analysis in systematic studies. How is entrepreneurship capital at the individual and team level related to or influenced by entrepreneurship capital at, say, the regional and industry levels? Are they independent or are there some types of positive interactions resulting in a virtuous circle generating entrepreneurship capital and ultimately competitive advantage?

Of course, this chapter is not complete. There are other streams of research from all levels of analysis that we could examine. These include individual behaviours that contribute to building social networks (Obstfeld, 2005) and social capital (Bolino et al., 2002), opportunity recognition and exploitation (Arenius and De Clercq, 2005; De Carolis and Saparito, 2006), low vs. high-tech entrepreneurs (Liao and Welsch, 2003), family firms (Zahra et al., 2004), customer relations (Yli-Renko et al., 2001), R&D alliances (Dickson et al., 2006), open-source community-based innovation (Shah, 2006), internationalization (Coviello, 2006), and national culture (Hayton et al., 2002; Steensma et al., 2000). With these final suggestions we would like to again urge readers to pursue research in this area of entrepreneurship and human resources management, at all levels of analysis and to instil a more social and humanistic spirit in their entrepreneurship research.

References

Acs, Z.J. and A. Varga (2005), 'Entrepreneurship, agglomeration and technological change', *Small Business Economics*, **24**(3), 323–34.
Adler, P.S. and S.W. Kwon (2002), 'Social capital: Prospects for a new concept', *Academy of Management Review*, **27**(1), 17–40.
Aghion, P. and P. Howitt (1992), 'A model of growth through creative destruction', *Econometrica*, **60**(2), 323–51.
Agrawal, A. (2006), 'Engaging the inventor: Exploring licensing strategies for university inventions and the role of latent knowledge', *Strategic Management Journal*, **27**(1), 63–79.
Aldrich, H. and C.M. Fiol (1994), 'Fools rush in? The institutional context of industry creation', *Academy of Management Review*, **19**(4), 645–70.
Aldrich, H. and M. Ruef (2006), *Organizations Evolving* (2nd edn), Thousand Oaks: Sage Publications Inc.
Antoncic, B. (2003), 'Risk taking in intrapreneurship: Translating the individual level risk aversion into the organizational risk taking', *Journal of Enterprising Culture*, **11**(1), 1–23.

Antoncic, B. and R.D. Hisrich (2001), 'Intrapreneurship: Construct refinement and cross-cultural validation', *Journal of Business Venturing*, **16**(5), 495–527.

Antoncic, B. and R.D. Hisrich (2004), 'Corporate entrepreneurship contingencies and organizational wealth creation', *Journal of Management Development*, **23**(6), 518–50.

Arenius, P. and D. De Clercq (2005), 'A network-based approach on opportunity recognition', *Small Business Economics*, **24**(3), 249–65.

Arenius, P. and M. Minniti (2005), 'Perceptual variables and nascent entrepreneurship', *Small Business Economics*, **24**(3), 233–47.

Argyris, C. (1976), 'Single-loop and double-loop models in research on decision making', *Administrative Science Quarterly*, **21**(3), 363–75.

Argyris, C. (2002), 'Double-loop learning, teaching, and research', *Academy of Management Learning and Education*, **1**(2), 206–18.

Audretsch, D.B. and M. Keilbach (2004a), 'Does entrepreneurship capital matter?', *Entrepreneurship: Theory and Practice*, **28**(5), 419–29.

Audretsch, D.B. and M. Keilbach (2004b), 'Entrepreneurship and regional growth: An evolutionary interpretation', *Journal of Evolutionary Economics*, **14**(5), 605–16.

Audretsch, D.B. and M. Keilbach (2004c), 'Entrepreneurship capital and economic performance', *Regional Studies*, **38**(8), 949–59.

Audretsch, D.B. and M. Keilbach (2005), 'Entrepreneurship capital and regional growth', *Annals of Regional Science*, **39**(3), 457–69.

Audretsch, D.B. and E.E. Lehmann (2004), 'Mansfield's missing link: The impact of knowledge spillovers on firm growth', *The Journal of Technology Transfer*, **30**(1–2), 207–10.

Audretsch, D.B. and E.E. Lehmann (2006), 'Entrepreneurial access and absorption of knowledge spillovers: Strategic board and managerial composition for competitive advantage', *Journal of Small Business Management*, **44**(2), 155–66.

Audretsch, D.B., E.E. Lehmann and S. Warning (2005), 'University spillovers and new firm location', *Research Policy*, **34**(7), 1113–22.

Austin, J.R. (1997), 'A method for facilitating controversial social change in organizations: Branch Rickey and the Brooklyn Dodgers', *Journal of Applied Behavioral Science*, **33**(1), 101–18.

Autio, E., A.P. Hameri and O. Vuola (2004), 'A framework of industrial knowledge spillovers in big-science centers', *Research Policy*, **33**(1), 107–26.

Baron, R.A. and G.D. Markman (2003), 'Beyond social capital: The role of entrepreneurs' social competence in their financial success', *Journal of Business Venturing*, **18**(1), 41–60.

Baum, J.R. and E.A. Locke (2004), 'The relationship of entrepreneurial traits, skill, and motivation to subsequent venture growth', *Journal of Applied Psychology*, **89**(4), 587–98.

Birley, S. and S. Stockley (2000), 'Entrepreneurial teams and venture growth', in D.L. Sexton and H. Landström (eds), *Blackwell Handbook of Entrepreneurship*, Oxford: Blackwell Publishing Ltd, pp. 287–307.

Blanchflower, D.G. and A.J. Oswald (1998), 'What makes an entrepreneur?', *Journal of Labor Economics*, **16**(1), 26–60.

Boeker, W. and R. Wiltbank (2005), 'New venture evolution and managerial capabilities', *Organization Science*, **16**(2), 123–33.

Bolino, M.C., W.H. Turnley and J.M. Bloodgood (2002), 'Citizenship behavior and the creation of social capital in organizations', *Academy of Management Review*, **27**(4), 505–22.

Borgatti, S.P. and P.C. Foster (2003), 'The network paradigm in organizational research: A review and typology', *Journal of Management*, **29**(6), 991–1013.

Bosma, N., M. van Praag, R. Thurik and G. de Wit (2004), 'The value of human and social capital investments for the business performance of startups', *Small Business Economics*, **23**(3), 227–36.

Brass, D.J., J. Galaskiewicz, H.R. Greve and W. Tsai (2004), 'Taking stock of networks and organizations: A multilevel perspective', *Academy of Management Journal*, **47**(6), 795–817.

Brown, T.E., P. Davidsson and J. Wiklund (2001), 'An operationalization of Stevenson's conceptualization of entrepreneurship as opportunity-based firm behavior', *Strategic Management Journal*, **22**(10), 953–68.

Bygrave, W. and M. Minniti (2000), 'The social dynamics of entrepreneurship', *Entrepreneurship: Theory and Practice*, **24**(3), 25–36.

Cantner, U. and H. Graf (2006), 'The network of innovators in Jena: An application of social network analysis', *Research Policy*, **35**(4), 463–80.

Cardon, M.S. and C.E. Stevens (2004), 'Managing human resources in small organizations: What do we know?', *Human Resource Management Review*, **14**(3), 295–323.

Carree, M., A. Van Stel, R. Thurk and S. Wennekers (2002), 'Economic development and business ownership: An analysis using data of 23 OECD countries in the period of 1976–1996', *Small Business Economics*, **19**(3), 271–90.

Casper, S. and F. Murray (2005), 'Careers and clusters: Analyzing the career network dynamic of biotechnology clusters', *Journal of Engineering and Technology Management*, **22**(1/2), 51–74.

Christensen, C.M. (2000), *The Innovator's Dilemma*, New York: HarperBusiness.

Chung, L.H. and P.T. Gibbons (1997), 'Corporate entrepreneurship: The roles of ideology and social capital', *Group and Organization Management*, **22**(1), 10–30.

Coleman, J.S. (1990), *Foundations of Social Theory*, Cambridge, MA: Harvard University Press.

Contractor, N.S., S. Wasserman and K. Faust (2006), 'Testing multi-theoretical, multilevel hypotheses about organizational networks: An analytic framework and empirical example', *Academy of Management Review*, **31**(3), 681–703.

Cooper, A.C. (2002), 'Networks, alliances, and entrepreneurship', in M.A. Hitt, R.D. Ireland, S.M. Camp and D.L. Sexton (eds), *Strategic Entrepreneurship: Creating a New Integrated Mindset*, Malden, MA: Blackwell Publishing, pp. 203–22.

Coviello, N.E. (2006), 'The network dynamics of international new ventures', *Journal of International Business Studies*, **37**(5), 713–31.

Covin, J.G. and D.P. Slevin (1989), 'Strategic management of small firms in hostile and benign environments', *Strategic Management Journal*, **10**(1), 75–87.

Covin, J.G. and D.P. Slevin (1991), 'A conceptual model of entrepreneurship as firm behavior', *Entrepreneurship: Theory and Practice*, **16**(1), 7–25.

Covin, J.G., K.M. Green and D.P. Slevin (2006), 'Strategic process effects on the entrepreneurial orientation–sales growth rate relationship', *Entrepreneurship: Theory and Practice*, **30**(1), 57–81.

Crossan, M.M., H.W. Lane and R.E. White (1999), 'An organizational learning framework: From intuition to institution', *Academy of Management Review*, **24**(3), 522–38.

Daily, C.M., P.P. McDougall, J.G. Covin and D.R. Dalton (2002), 'Governance and strategic leadership in entrepreneurial firms', *Journal of Management*, **28**(3), 387–412.

Davidsson, P. and B. Honig (2003), 'The role of social and human capital among nascent entrepreneurs', *Journal of Business Venturing*, **18**(3), 301–31.

Davidsson, P. and J. Wiklund (2001), 'Levels of analysis in entrepreneurship research: Current research practice and suggestions for the future', *Entrepreneurship: Theory and Practice*, **25**(4), 81–99.

De Carolis, D.M. and P. Saparito (2006), 'Social capital, cognition, and entrepreneurial opportunities: A theoretical framework', *Entrepreneurship: Theory and Practice*, **30**(1), 41–56.

De Clercq, D. and H.J. Sapienza (2006), 'Effects of relational capital and commitment on venture capitalists' perception of portfolio company performance', *Journal of Business Venturing*, **21**(3), 326–47.

Delmar, F.D.R. and S. Shane (2006), 'Does experience matter? The effect of founding team experience on the survival and sales of newly founded ventures', *Strategic Organization*, **4**(3), 215–47.

Dess, G.G., G.T. Lumpkin and J.G. Covin (1997), 'Entrepreneurial strategy making and firm performance: Tests of contingency and configurational models', *Strategic Management Journal*, **18**(9), 677–95.

Dess, G.G., R.D. Ireland, S.A. Zahra, S.W. Floyd, J.J. Janney and P.J. Lane (2003), 'Emerging issues in corporate entrepreneurship', *Journal of Management*, **29**(3), 351–78.

Dickson, P.H. and K.M. Weaver (1997), 'Environmental determinants and individual-level moderators of alliance use', *Academy of Management Journal*, **40**(2), 404–25.

Dickson, P.H., K.M. Weaver and F. Hoy (2006), 'Opportunism in the R and D alliances of SMES: The roles of the institutional environment and SME size', *Journal of Business Venturing*, **21**(4), 487–513.

Dutta, D.K. and M.M. Crossan (2005), 'The nature of entrepreneurial opportunities: Understanding the process using the 4I organizational learning framework', *Entrepreneurship: Theory and Practice*, **29**(4), 425–49.

Eisenhardt, K.M. and C.B. Schoonhoven (1996), 'Resource-based view of strategic alliance formation: Strategic and social effects in entrepreneurial firms', *Organization Science*, **7**(2), 136–50.

Ensley, M.D. and K.M. Hmieleski (2005), 'A comparative study of new venture top management team composition, dynamics and performance between university-based and independent start-ups', *Research Policy*, **34**(7), 1091–105.

Ensley, M.D. and A.W. Pearson (2005), 'An exploratory comparison of the behavioral dynamics of top management teams in family and nonfamily new ventures: Cohesion, conflict, potency, and consensus', *Entrepreneurship: Theory and Practice*, **29**(3), 267–84.

Ensley, M.D., A. Pearson and C.L. Pearce (2003), 'Top management team process, shared leadership, and new venture performance: A theoretical model and research agenda', *Human Resource Management Review*, **13**(2), 329–46.

Ensley, M.D., J.C. Carland, J.W. Carland and M. Banks (1999), 'Exploring the existence of entrepreneurial teams', *International Journal of Management*, **16**(2), 276–86.

Fombrun, C.J. (1986), 'Structural dynamics within and between organizations', *Administrative Science Quarterly*, **31**(3), 403–21.

Forbes, D.P., P.S. Borchert, M.E. Zellmer-Bruhn and H.J. Sapienza (2006), 'Entrepreneurial team formation: An exploration of new member addition', *Entrepreneurship: Theory and Practice*, **30**(2), 225–48.

Friedlander, F. and L.D. Brown (1974), 'Organization development', *Annual Review of Psychology*, **25**, 313–41.

Gartner, W.B. (2001), 'Is there an elephant in entrepreneurship? Blind assumptions in theory development', *Entrepreneurship: Theory and Practice*, **25**(4), 27–39.

Glaeser, E.L., D. Laibson and B. Sacerdote (2000), 'The economic approach to social capital', *NBER Working Paper*, No. 7728.

Greve, A. and J.W. Salaff (2001), 'The development of corporate social capital in complex innovation processes', *Research in the Sociology of Organizations*, **18**, 107–34.

Gupta, V., I.C. MacMillan and G. Surie (2004), 'Entrepreneurial leadership: developing and measuring a cross-cultural construct', *Journal of Business Venturing*, **19**(2), 241–60.

Hage, J.T. (1999), 'Organizational innovation and organizational change', *Annual Review of Sociology*, **25**(1), 597–622.

Hagedoorn, J. and N. Roijakkers (2002), 'Small entrepreneurial firms and large companies in inter-firm R and D networks: The international biotechnology industry', in M.A. Hitt, R.D. Ireland, S.M. Camp and D.L. Sexton (eds), *Strategic Entrepreneurship: Creating a New Integrated Mindset*, Malden, MA: Blackwell Publishing, pp. 223–52.

Hambrick, D.C. and P.A. Mason (1984), 'Upper echelons: The organization as a reflection of its top managers', *Academy of Management Review*, **9**(2), 193–206.

Hansen, M.T., J.M. Podolny and J. Pfeffer (2001), 'So many ties, so little time: A task contingency perspective on corporate social capital in organizations', *Research in the Sociology of Organizations*, **18**, 21–57.

Hayton, J.C. (2003), 'Strategic human capital management in SMEs: An empirical study of entrepreneurial performance', *Human Resource Management*, **42**(4), 375–91.

Hayton, J.C. (2005), 'Promoting corporate entrepreneurship through human resource management practices: A review of empirical research', *Human Resource Management Review*, **15**(1), 21–41.

Hayton, J.C., G. George and S.A. Zahra (2002), 'National culture and entrepreneurship: A review of behavioral research', *Entrepreneurship: Theory and Practice*, **26**(4), 33–52.

Hitt, M.A., L. Ho-Uk and E. Yucel (2002), 'The importance of social capital to the management of multinational enterprises: Relational networks among Asian and Western firms', *Asia Pacific Journal of Management*, **19**(2/3), 353–72.

Hornsby, J.S., D.F. Kuratko and R.V. Montagno (1999), 'Perception of internal factors for corporate entrepreneurship: A comparison of Canadian and US managers', *Entrepreneurship: Theory and Practice*, **24**(2), 9–24.

Hornsby, J.S., D.F. Kuratko and S.A. Zahra (2002), 'Middle managers' perception of the internal environment for corporate entrepreneurship: Assessing a measurement scale', *Journal of Business Venturing*, **17**(3), 253–73.

Hornsby, J.S., D.W. Naffziger, D.F. Kuratko and R.V. Montagno (1993), 'An interactive model of the corporate entrepreneurship process', *Entrepreneurship: Theory and Practice*, **17**(2), 29–37.

Ibarra, H., M. Kilduff and W. Tsai (2005), 'Zooming in and out: Connecting individuals and collectivities at the frontiers of organizational network research', *Organization Science*, **16**(4), 359–71.

Ireland, R.D., M.A. Hitt and D.G. Sirmon (2003), 'A model of strategic entrepreneurship: The construct and its dimensions', *Journal of Management*, **29**(6), 963–89.

Johannisson, B. (1998), 'Personal networks in emerging knowledge-based firms: Spatial and functional patterns', *Entrepreneurship and Regional Development*, **10**(4), 297–312.

Johannisson, B. (2000), 'Networking and entrepreneurial growth', in D.L. Sexton and H. Landström (eds), *Blackwell Handbook of Entrepreneurship*, Oxford: Blackwell Publishing, 368–86.

Johannisson, B., M. Ramírez-Pasillas and G. Karlsson (2002), 'The institutional embeddedness of local inter-firm networks: A leverage for business creation', *Entrepreneurship and Regional Development*, **14**(4), 297–315.

Keeble, D., C. Lawson, B. Moore and F. Wilkinson (1999), 'Collective learning processes, networking and "institutional thickness" in the Cambridge region', *Regional Studies*, **33**(4), 319–32.

Kets de Vries, M.F.R. (1977), 'The entrepreneurial personality: A person at the crossroads', *Journal of Management Studies*, **14**(1), 34–57.

Khandwalla, P.N. (1977), *The Design of Organizations* (1st edn), New York: Harcourt Brace Jovanovich.

Kim, P., H. Aldrich and L. Keister (2006), 'Access (not) denied: The impact of financial, human, and cultural capital on entrepreneurial entry in the United States', *Small Business Economics*, **27**(1), 5–22.

Klepper, S. (2001), 'Employee startup in high-tech industries', *Industrial and Corporate Change*, **10**(3), 639–74.

Klepper, S. (2002), 'The capabilities of new firms and the evolution of the US automobile industry', *Industrial and Corporate Change*, **11**(4), 645–66.

Klepper, S. and S. Sleeper (2005), 'Entry by spinoffs', *Management Science*, **51**(8), 1291–306.

Knight, G.A. (1997), 'Cross-cultural reliability and validity of a scale to measure firm entrepreneurial orientation', *Journal of Business Venturing*, **12**(3), 213–25.

Kreiser, P.M., L.D. Marino and K.M. Weaver (2002), 'Assessing the psychometric properties of the entrepreneurial orientation scale: A multi-country analysis', *Entrepreneurship: Theory and Practice*, **26**(4), 71–94.

Kuratko, D.F., R.V. Montagno and J.S. Hornsby (1990), 'Developing an intrapreneurial assessment instrument for an effective corporate entrepreneurship environment', *Strategic Management Journal*, **11**(4), 49–58.

Kuratko, D.F., R.D. Ireland, J.G. Covin and J.S. Hornsby (2005), 'A model of middle-level managers' entrepreneurial behavior', *Entrepreneurship: Theory and Practice*, **29**(5), 699–716.

Lawson, C. and E. Lorenz (1999), 'Collective learning, tacit knowledge and regional innovative capacity', *Regional Studies*, **33**(4), 305–17.

Leana, C.R. and H.J. Van Buren III (1999), 'Organizational social capital and employment practices', *Academy of Management Review*, **24**(3), 538–55.

Lechler, T. (2001), 'Social interaction: A determinant of entrepreneurial team venture success', *Small Business Economics*, **16**(4), 263–78.

Lechner, C. and M. Dowling (2003), 'Firm networks: External relationships as sources for the growth and competitiveness of entrepreneurial firms', *Entrepreneurship and Regional Development*, **15**(1), 1–26.

Lechner, C., M. Dowling and I. Welpe (2006), 'Firm networks and firm development: The role of the relational mix', *Journal of Business Venturing*, **21**(4), 514–40.

Leung, A. (2003), 'Different ties for different needs: Recruitment practices of entrepreneurial firms at different developmental phases', *Human Resource Management*, **42**(4), 303–20.

Leung, A., J. Zhang, P.K. Wong and M.D. Foo (2006), 'The use of networks in human resource acquisition for entrepreneurial firms: Multiple "fit" considerations', *Journal of Business Venturing*, **21**(5), 664–86.

Levesque, L.L. (2005), 'Opportunistic hiring and employee fit', *Human Resource Management*, **44**(3), 301–17.

Liao, J. and H. Welsch (2003), 'Social capital and entrepreneurial growth aspiration: A comparison of technology- and non-technology-based nascent entrepreneurs', *Journal of High Technology Management Research*, **14**(1), 149–70.

Lounsbury, M. and M.A. Glynn (2001), 'Cultural entrepreneurship: Stories, legitimacy, and the acquisition of resources', *Strategic Management Journal*, **22**(6/7), 545–64.

Lumpkin, G.T. (1998), 'Do new entrant firms have an entrepreneurial orientation?', Paper presented at the Academy of Management annual meeting, San Diego, California.

Lumpkin, G.T. and G.G. Dess (1996), 'Clarifying the entrepreneurial orientation construct and linking it to performance', *Academy of Management Review*, **21**(1), 135–72.

Lumpkin, G.T. and G.G. Dess (2001), 'Linking two dimensions of entrepreneurial orientation to firm performance: The moderating role of environment and industry life cycle', *Journal of Business Venturing*, **16**(5), 429–51.

Lyon, D.W., G.T. Lumpkin and G.G. Dess (2000), 'Enhancing entrepreneurial orientation research: Operationalizing and measuring a key strategic decision making process', *Journal of Management*, **26**(5), 1055–85.

Mansfield, E. (1998), 'Academic research and industrial innovation: An update of empirical findings', *Research Policy*, **26**(7/8), 773–6.

McGrath, R.G. and I. MacMillan (2000), *The Entrepreneurial Mindset: Strategies for Continuously Creating Opportunity in an Age of Uncertainty*, Boston: Harvard Business School Press.

Miles, M.P. and J.G. Covin (2002), 'Exploring the practice of corporate venturing: Some common forms and their organizational implications', *Entrepreneurship: Theory and Practice*, **26**(3), 21–40.

Miles, R.E. and C.C. Snow (1995), 'The new network firm: A spherical structure built on a human investment philosophy', *Organizational Dynamics*, **23**(4), 5–18.

Miles, R.E., G. Miles and C.C. Snow (2005), *Collaborative Entrepreneurship: How Communities of Networked Firms use Continuous Innovation to Create Economic Wealth*, Stanford, CA: Stanford University Press.

Miller, D. (1983), 'The correlates of entrepreneurship in three types of firms', *Management Science*, **29**(7), 770–91.

Minniti, M. (2005), 'Entrepreneurship and network externalities', *Journal of Economic Behavior and Organization*, **57**(1), 1–27.

Minniti, M., W.D. Bygrave and E. Autio (2005), 'Global Entrepreneurship Monitor 2005 Executive Report', Babson College and London Business School.

Monsen, E. (2005), 'Employees do matter: Autonomy, teamwork and corporate entrepreneurial culture', unpublished dissertation, University of Colorado, Boulder, CO.

Monsen, E. and R.W. Boss (2004), 'Mapping the differential impact of entrepreneurial orientation on performance in a healthcare organization', Paper presented at the Babson-Kauffman Entrepreneurship Research Conference, University of Strathclyde, Glasgow, Scotland.

Morris, M.H., R.A. Avila and J. Allen (1993), 'Individualism and the modern corporation: Implications for innovation and entrepreneurship', *Journal of Management*, **19**(3), 595–612.

Morris, M.H., D.L. Davis and J.W. Allen (1994), 'Fostering corporate entrepreneurship: Cross-cultural comparisons of the importance of individualism versus collectivism', *Journal of International Business Studies*, **25**(1), 65–89.

Mowery, D.C., R.R. Nelson, B.N. Sampat and A.A. Ziedonis (2004), *Ivory Tower and Industrial Innovation: University–Industry Technology Transfer before and after the Bayh-Dole Act in the United States*, Stanford, CA: Stanford University Press.

Mueller, P. (2006a), 'Entrepreneurship in the region: Breeding ground for nascent entrepreneurs?', *Small Business Economics*, **27**(1), 41–58.

Mueller, P. (2006b), 'Exploring the knowledge filter: How entrepreneurship and university–industry relationships drive economic growth', *Research Policy*, forthcoming.

Nahapiet, J. and S. Ghoshal (1998), 'Social capital, intellectual capital, and the organizational advantage', *Academy of Management Review*, **23**(2), 242–66.

Neck, H.M., G.D. Meyer, B. Cohen and A.C. Corbett (2004), 'An entrepreneurial system view of new venture creation', *Journal of Small Business Management*, **42**(2), 190–208.

Obstfeld, D. (2005), 'Social networks, the Tertius Iungens orientation, and involvement in innovation', *Administrative Science Quarterly*, **50**(1), 100–130.

O'Shea, R.P., T.J. Allen, A. Chevalier and F. Roche (2005), 'Entrepreneurial orientation, technology transfer and spinoff performance of US universities', *Research Policy*, **34**(7), 994–1009.

O'Shea, R.P., T.J. Allen, C. O'Gorman and F. Roche (2004), 'Universities and technology transfer: A review of academic entrepreneurship literature', *Irish Journal of Management*, **25**(2), 11–29.

Pearce II, J.A. and T.R. Kramer (1997), 'Effects of managers' entrepreneurial behavior on subordinates', *Journal of Business Venturing*, **12**(2), 147–60.

Podolny, J.M. (2001), 'Networks as the pipes and prisms of the market', *American Journal of Sociology*, **107**(1), 33–60.

Podolny, J.M. and J.N. Baron (1997), 'Resources and relationships: Social networks and mobility in the workplace', *American Sociological Review*, **62**(5), 673–93.

Podolny, J.M. and K.L. Page (1998), 'Network forms of organizations', *Annual Review of Sociology*, **24**(1), 57–76.

Podolny, J.M., T.E. Stuart and M.T. Hannan (1996), 'Networks, knowledge, and niches: Competition in the worldwide semiconductor industry, 1984–1991', *American Journal of Sociology*, **102**(3), 659–89.

Rao, H. (1994), 'The social construction of reputation: Certification contests, legitimation, and the survival of organizations in the American automobile industry: 1895–1912', *Strategic Management Journal*, **15**(8), 29–44.

Rao, H. (2004), 'Institutional activism in the early American automobile industry', *Journal of Business Venturing*, **19**(3), 359–424.

Rauch, A., J. Wiklund, M. Frese and G.T. Lumpkin (2004), 'Entrepreneurial orientation and business performance: Cumulative empirical evidence', Paper presented at the Babson-Kauffman Entrepreneurship Research Conference, University of Strathclyde, Glasgow, Scotland.

Reynolds, P., N. Bosma, E. Autio, S. Hunt, N. De Bono, I. Servais, P. Lopez-Garcia and N. Chin (2005), 'Global entrepreneurship monitor: Data collection design and implementation 1998–2003', *Small Business Economics*, **24**(3), 205–31.

Rocha, H.O. and R. Sternberg (2005), 'Entrepreneurship: The role of clusters. Theoretical perspectives and empirical evidence from Germany', *Small Business Economics*, **24**(3), 267–92.

Romer, P.M. (1986), 'Increasing returns and long-run growth', *Journal of Political Economy*, **94**(5), 1002–37.

Rothaermel, F.T. and M. Thursby (2005), 'University–incubator firm knowledge flows: Assessing their impact on incubator firm performance', *Research Policy*, **34**(3), 305–20.

Shah, S.K. (2006), 'Motivation, governance, and the viability of hybrid forms in open source software development', *Management Science*, **52**(7), 1000–14.

Shane, S. (2004), *Academic Entrepreneurship: University Spinoffs and Wealth Creation*, Cheltenham, UK and Northampton, MA, USA: Edward Elgar.

Shane, S., E.A., Locke and C.J., Collins (2003), 'Entrepreneurial motivation', *Human Resource Management Review*, **13**, 257–79.

Sharma, P. and J.J. Chrisman (1999), 'Toward a reconciliation of the definitional issues in the field of corporate entrepreneurship', *Entrepreneurship Theory and Practice*, **23**(3), 11–27.

Sorenson, O. and T.E. Stuart (2001), 'Syndication networks and the spatial distribution of venture capital investments', *American Journal of Sociology*, **106**(6), 1546–88.

Steensma, H.K., L. Marino, K.M. Weaver and P.H. Dickson (2000), 'The influence of national culture on the formation of technology alliances by entrepreneurial firms', *Academy of Management Journal*, **43**(5), 951–73.

Sternberg, R. and S. Wennekers (2005), 'Determinants and effects of new business creation using global entrepreneurship monitor data', *Small Business Economics*, **24**(3), 193–203.

Stevenson, H.H. and J.C. Jarillo (1990), 'A paradigm of entrepreneurship: Entrepreneurial management', *Strategic Management Journal*, **11**(4), 17–27.

Stopford, J.M. and C.W.F. Baden-Fuller (1994), 'Creating corporate entrepreneurship', *Strategic Management Journal*, **15**(7), 521–36.

Stuart, T.E. and O. Sorenson (2003a), 'The geography of opportunity: Spatial heterogeneity in founding rates and the performance of biotechnology firms', *Research Policy*, **32**(2), 229–53.

Stuart, T.E. and O. Sorenson (2003b), 'Liquidity events and the geographic distribution of entrepreneurial activity', *Administrative Science Quarterly*, **48**(2), 175–201.

Thornton, P.H. (1999), 'The sociology of entrepreneurship', *Annual Review of Sociology*, **25**, 19–46.

Thursby, J.G. and M.C. Thursby (2002), 'Who is selling the ivory tower? Sources of growth in university licensing', *Management Science*, **48**(1), 90–104.

Tsai, W. (2001), 'Knowledge transfer in intraorganizational networks: Effects of network position and absorptive capacity on business unit innovation and performance', *Academy of Management Journal*, **44**(5), 996–1004.

Tsai, W. and S. Ghoshal (1998), 'Social capital and value creation: The role of intrafirm networks', *Academy of Management Journal*, **41**(4), 464–76.

Ucbasaran, D., A. Lockett, M. Wright and P. Westhead (2003), 'Entrepreneurial founder teams: Factors associated with member entry and exit', *Entrepreneurship: Theory and Practice*, **28**(2), 107–27.

van Stel, A., M. Carree and R. Thurik (2005), 'The effect of entrepreneurial activity on national economic growth', *Small Business Economics*, **24**(3), 311–21.

Vanaelst, I., B. Clarysse, M. Wright, A. Lockett, N. Moray and R. S'Jegers (2006), Entrepreneurial team development in academic spinouts: An examination of team heterogeneity', *Entrepreneurship: Theory and Practice*, **30**(2), 249–71.

Weaver, K.M. and P.H. Dickson (1998), 'Outcome quality of small- to medium-sized enterprise-based alliances: The role of perceived partner behaviors', *Journal of Business Venturing*, **13**(6), 505–22.

Weick, K.E. and R.E. Quinn (1999), 'Organizational change and development', *Annual Review of Psychology*, **50**, 361–86.

Weisz, N., R.S. Vassolo and A.C. Cooper (2004), 'A theoretical and empirical assessment of the social capital of nascent entrepreneurial teams', paper presented at the Academy of Management Annual Meeting.

Wennekers, S. and R. Thurik (1999), 'Linking entrepreneurship and economic growth', *Small Business Economics*, **13**(1), 27–55.

Wennekers, S., A. van Wennekers, R. Thurik and P. Reynolds (2005), 'Nascent entrepreneurship and the level of economic development', *Small Business Economics*, **24**(3), 293–309.

Wiklund, J. and D. Shepherd (2003), 'Knowledge-based resources, entrepreneurial orientation, and the performance of small and medium-sized businesses', *Strategic Management Journal*, **24**(13), 1307–14.

Wiklund, J. and D. Shepherd (2005), Entrepreneurial orientation and small business performance: A configurational approach', *Journal of Business Venturing*, **20**(1), 71–91.

Witt, P. (2004), 'Entrepreneurs' networks and the success of start-ups', *Entrepreneurship and Regional Development*, **16**(5), 391–412.

Wong, P.K., Y.P. Ho and E. Autio (2005), 'Entrepreneurship, innovation and economic growth: Evidence from GEM data', *Small Business Economics*, **24**(3), 335–50.

Yli-Renko, H., E. Autio and H.J. Sapienza (2001), 'Social capital, knowledge acquisition, and knowledge exploitation in young technology-based firms', *Strategic Management Journal*, **22**(6/7), 587–613.
Zahra, S.A., J.C. Hayton and C. Salvato (2004), 'Entrepreneurship in family vs. non-family firms: A resource-based analysis of the effect of organizational culture', *Entrepreneurship: Theory and Practice*, **28**(4), 363–81.

4 Interpretivist approaches to entrepreneurship
Catherine Cassell and Sara Nadin

Introduction

Entrepreneurship as one of the newest fields of management (Wortman, 1987) is interdisciplinary and has become the object of a large variety of research work (Cunningham and Lischeron, 1991). Research has been conducted at a variety of levels with a considerable diversity of foci. At a macro level research has focused on areas of financing entrepreneurial activities and characteristics of the economic environment (Kuratko and Hodgetts, 1998). At the micro level research has covered individual traits of the entrepreneur (for example, Allinson et al., 2000; Cromie, 2000), entrepreneurial behaviour in relation to creating new ventures (Stevenson and Jarillo, 1990) and the processes of strategy formulation and strategic direction. More recently there has been an increased interest in the links between entrepreneurship and HRM as this present collection testifies.

This growing field is characterized by diversity in a number of ways. Apart from being diverse in content and scope, entrepreneurship has been informed by a number of insights from other social science approaches such as anthropology, economics and history. Indeed as Grant and Perren suggest, 'much of the development of the field has been achieved by drawing on theoretical frameworks from outside' (2002: p. 185). Despite this diversity the methodological underpinnings of the field have remained fairly uniform, with the majority of published research being located within a functionalist paradigm informed by a positivist epistemology. A number of authors have drawn attention to this situation. For example Grant and Perren (2002) conducted a meta-analytic review of articles published in the year 2000 by leading authors in the small business and entrepreneurship journals. They concluded that most research could be classified as being located within a functionalist paradigm and issued a 'call for paradigmatic experimentation, engagement and debate' (Grant and Perren, 2002: p. 202). Other writers have also drawn attention to this condition (for example, Blackburn and Stokes, 2005; Gartner and Birley, 2002; Hill and McGowan, 1999; Jennings et al., 2005) with Perren and Jennings bemoaning the fact that 'Much of the research in the area is so dominated by the discourse of functionalism that most researchers do not even bother to state their philosophical position and certainly do not appear to consider that they may be living in the hegemony of a functionalist discourse' (2002: p. 360).

The reasons for this state of affairs are explored by Coviello and Jones (2004) who consider the methodological basis of 55 studies in the new and emerging field of international entrepreneurship. Their conclusion is also that the bulk of research they review is located within a logical positivist tradition where the emphasis is upon the quantification and analysis of statistical data. They speculate as to why this may be the case and suggest that the methodological focus in this area 'perhaps reflects a perceived need to provide "significant" empirical evidence in order to justify research in a new field' (Coviello and Jones, 2004: p. 499). Arguably, when developing a research domain, the security and credibility that comes with the use of more traditional approaches seems preferable to the uncertainty that may be associated with more interpretivist paradigmatic stances.

A similar picture emerges in the HRM field. Publications in refereed journals are predominantly positivist in orientation, often seeking to establish cause and effect relationships using statistical techniques (Hoobler and Johnson, 2004). Again such methods serve a legitimating function in terms of endowing HRM with the credentials of 'science'. The limitations of an almost exclusive use of positivist methods are recognized by both exponents and critics of HRM. Wall and Wood (2005) challenge the purported causal links between HRM and performance, highlighting the fragmented nature of research to date and calling for more large-scale and long-term research achieved through partnerships between research, practitioner and government communities. Fleetwood and Hesketh (2006) suggest that the dominance of the 'scientific approach' and the largely unchallenged pursuit of simplistic causal relationships in HRM have resulted in under-theorization, which seriously limits and threatens the explanatory power of HRM.

Although interpretivist approaches are becoming more widely used in the fields of entrepreneurship and HRM, an examination of the content of the so-called 'top' journals in the field shows papers informed by alternative approaches to positivism to be in the minority. In this chapter we argue that alternative approaches to positivism provide many opportunities for researchers working in the field of entrepreneurship. Specifically we argue that the adoption of interpretivist approaches to entrepreneurship has much to offer in terms of the theoretical and methodological development of the discipline and the integration of ideas from the field of HRM. We begin by outlining what is meant by interpretivist approaches and what they have to offer. This is examined firstly in the context of theory development in the field, and then in relation to methodology. We then explore some of the barriers to the increased use of interpretivist approaches and conclude by assessing the challenges facing those seeking to apply interpretivist approaches to the entrepreneurship field.

Defining interpretivist approaches

A wide range of different philosophical approaches are located under the umbrella label of interpretivism. Examples are phenomenological approaches, constructivism and hermeneutics. Seale (1999) suggests that interpretivist positions, which informed early practitioners of qualitative research, challenge the notion of methodological monism as a basis for studying the social world. It is argued that the phenomena we study in the social sciences are very different from the subject matter of the natural sciences. Humans are sentient beings whose behaviour is influenced by motivation, mood and a whole range of other issues. As Seale suggests, 'the objects of social science are different from those of natural science, in that they are capable of independent volition' (1999: p. 21). Consequently the methods used in the natural sciences cannot always be usefully appropriated for studying the social sciences world.

The emphasis of interpretivist approaches is on understanding the complex nature of human experience from the point of view of those who live it. Interpretivist researchers and thinkers are keen to access the 'sense making' processes of individuals (Weick, 2001) and understand how they come to interpret what occurs in the world around them. Schwandt (2003) suggests that the goal of an interpretivist researcher is that of 'verstehen' or understanding meaning and grasping an actor's definition of a situation. In order to understand the actor's world one must interpret it, and hence the label interpretivism. As Grant and Perren suggest, 'Interpretivists are portrayed as taking a subjective view of reality, being concerned with explaining individuals' perceptions of their organizations and society' (2002: p. 188).

In methodological terms interpretivists focus on accessing subjective realities through the use of qualitative methods. In relation to the world of work, Alvesson and Deetz suggest,

> The express goals of interpretive studies is to show how particular realities are socially produced and maintained through norms, rites, rituals and daily activities. In many of the writings a clear preservationist, communitarian, or naturalist tone exists. It moves to save or record a life form – with its complexity and creativity – that may be lost to modern, instrumental life or overlooked in it (2000: p. 34).

From this tradition entrepreneurship can be constructed in a different way. For understanding the intersection between entrepreneurship and HRM it suggests a need to access the reality of practice on a day-to-day basis from the perspective of the entrepreneur and others in the entrepreneurial venture. The opportunities this different construction provides are investigated in more detail in the next section.

The opportunities provided by interpretivist research

Hill and McGowan (1999) argue that individual and unique characteristics of entrepreneurial small firms need to be taken into account if their dynamics are to be understood. However, doing so requires in-depth research programmes to be applied, utilizing qualitative techniques located within an interpretivist approach. They suggest that ontologically the researcher investigating the small firm needs to embrace the notion of multiple realities. Epistemologically too, the researcher who seeks to understand the individual entrepreneur needs to minimize the distance between the subject and themselves, hence the appropriateness of an interpretivist approach. They argue that prior research into small firms rooted in positivist thinking has failed to yield a rich understanding of the key issues impacting on the potential for enterprise development. This point is taken further by Gartner and Birley who argue that 'many of the important questions in entrepreneurship can only be asked through qualitative methods and approaches' (2002: p. 387). These arguments are further reinforced if we look at the patterns of HRM practices used by entrepreneurs and small business owners. The adoption of HRM practices is rarely strategic and they are often informal, bearing little resemblance to the ideas about best practice characterizing the HRM literature (Cardon and Stevens, 2004; Reid et al., 2002). This renders traditional positivist approaches to the study of HRM of limited value unless they are also complemented by in-depth contextualized accounts enabling us to understand the highly nuanced approach to HRM of entrepreneurs and small business owners.

Heneman et al. (2000) suggest that the small samples that reside in smaller firms, often the location of entrepreneurship research, may preclude the use of quantitative data analysis. This is a theme taken up by other authors who have used in-depth case studies as a way of gaining information about what happens in smaller firms. Cassell et al. (2002) argue that use of quantitative data is of relatively little value given the diverse nature of smaller firms. Holliday (1995) also questions whether survey or questionnaire-based research is entirely relevant to the study of a deeply heterogeneous small firm sector, while Blackburn and Stokes (2005) argue that focus groups have much to offer. They argue that quantitative techniques tend to only provide a 'snapshot' of what goes on within smaller firms while qualitative and longitudinal research can provide rich, detailed accounts.

Another comment on this issue comes from Mitchell (1997) who argues that past research on entrepreneurs and entrepreneurship has failed to sufficiently 'de-mystify' the profession. Through an in-depth analysis of the life histories and stories told by entrepreneurs he presents data suggesting that entrepreneurial success is not as mystical as large-scale quantitative studies with their differing conclusions present. The last few years have seen increased use and interest in this kind of in-depth analysis. Narrative analysis (for example, Hamilton, 2006; Johansson, 2004; Rae, 2000) has been increasingly applied and identifies three particular areas where it has the potential to make a contribution to our understanding of entrepreneurship. First it enables the exploration of how the entrepreneurial identity is constructed through life story accounts (see Mallon and Cohen, 2001). Another potential contribution is the analysis of stories and how they serve to articulate entrepreneurial learning. Third, the use of narrative helps to 'conceptualize and re-conceptualize enterprise' (Johansson, 2004: p. 285), enabling entrepreneurship and entrepreneurs to be explored and understood from various angles. Rae (2000) argues the advantage of narrative approaches is in the richness and authenticity they provide to the 'real lived experience' of entrepreneurs. Such understanding is a crucial element of exploring the entrepreneurship phenomenon.

The content and focus of the entrepreneurial field coupled with piecemeal and informal HRM practices operating in smaller firms appear to lend support for use of interpretivist approaches and qualitative techniques. Theory development in the field of entrepreneurship could also benefit as a result. The dominance of functionalist approaches has led to the production of masculinized normative models presenting entrepreneurship as something which is neutral and fixed (Bruni et al., 2004; Mirchandani, 1999; Ogbor, 2000). Theoretically this fails to capture and explain alternative forms of entrepreneurship practised by women and men. Interpretivist approaches, however, enable alternative forms of entrepreneurship to be explored. This would challenge normative assumptions and help to ensure the continued relevance and utility of academic theorizing in this field.

To understand the potential theoretical contribution interpretivist approaches could make it is worth considering how theory can be conceived. Alvesson and Deetz neatly summarize the conception of theory within interpretivist approaches in the following way, 'Theory is given a different conception and a different role here. While theory may provide important sensitizing conceptions, it is not a device of classification nor tested in any simple or direct manner. The key conceptions and understandings must be worked out with the subjects under study' (2000: p. 33).

They continue by suggesting that there are three basic functions of theory: directing attention; organizing experiences; and enabling useful responses. It is worth considering each of these in terms of what interpretivist approaches can contribute to theoretical developments in entrepreneurship. In doing this we highlight some examples from our own research.

In terms of directing attention, interpretivist approaches provide us with a range of issues to consider and research questions to ask. Our study (Cassell et al., 2002) of change management in an SME environment can be used as an example. Managing Directors were asked about the nature of recent changes in their firms and their experiences of introducing those changes. Initially the interview data was analysed using a standard template analysis approach (King, 2004). The initial template was devised from the interview schedule and proceeded through a number of iterations. From the final template an interpretation of the data was produced addressing the specific research questions about the kinds of changes introduced and the experience of introducing those changes. A report was written and this satisfied the funding body. However whilst conducting the interviews and analysing the data, the way in which the interviewees talked about their role in the change process and their role in the organization generally, emerged as an issue to pursue. The discourses they drew upon to describe and account for their roles as change agents were interesting. A different epistemological perspective had to be adopted to explore how individuals were creating their own understandings of the change process through the interview situation and the impact this had on how they accounted for their role in that process. An interpretivist approach drawing on the principles of social constructivism was appropriate therefore to examine how an individual constructs meaning through the process of talk. Interview transcripts were examined in detail for the interpretive repertoires (Potter and Wetherall, 1987) interviewees had used to account for their change experiences.

The point being made is that the use of an interpretivist approach led to paying attention to different types of research questions. Their analysis of the transcripts highlighted four repertoires interviewees used to account for their role in the change process. The notion of resource poverty in SMEs was drawn upon and interviewees talked a lot about the lack of resources available to them. This ranged from a lack of expertise in the human resources area, to the skill shortages in the manufacturing industry. Resource poverty was used as a way of organizing and making sense of their experience in seeking to change their companies. A second key repertoire drawn upon was that of the organizational culture being 'stuck' and therefore being unable to change things in the organization. The barriers interviewees faced were often attributed to culture and its pervasiveness and inertia. The third repertoire was whether small was good or bad. This informed the discussion about how change was managed. Smallness was linked to issues of control and being at the mercy of outside agents, for example, the difficulties that emerge from being an SME in a market where the big boys 'call the shots'. This was constructed as small is good and big is bad, although some pointed to the advantages of being small. The final repertoire permeating the accounts was that of the interviewee as change agent. The interviewees talked of themselves as being responsible for engineering change in their organizations, almost in the role of heroes, taking the moral responsibility for the development of the firm.

By taking an interpretivist approach, this study provided insights into the experience of those driving and managing change in an SME environment. Rather than focusing on the types of changes and how those changes had occurred as the original analysis had done, the adoption of an interpretivist approach allowed the focus on a different type of issue: how the individual made sense of their organizational world. Therefore attention was directed to a different set of theoretical issues.

The second role of theory (Alvesson and Deetz, 2000) is that of organizing experience. Theories enable us to organize the wide range of information we have about entrepreneurship in different ways. In this context, an interpretivist approach provides a relatively flexible way of organizing knowledge about entrepreneurs and entrepreneurship. Through the use of sensitizing concepts, or providing directions in which to look (Blumer, 1954), the overall organizing aim is that of 'verstehen' – understanding the meaning that an actor has of a given situation.

How this operates can be illustrated through another piece of our research (Nadin and Cassell, 2007). We sought to understand the dynamics of the psychological contract located specifically within small firms from the perspective of the owner–manager. By adopting an interpretive approach we collected in-depth accounts about the psychological contracts and related issues through semi-structured interviews. Whilst existing theoretical ideas about the psychological contract were used to inform the interview schedule, the open-ended nature of the questions meant participants were encouraged to explore their own ideas about psychological contracts in as much detail as possible. Template analysis (King, 2004) was then used and it resulted in the identification of a range of important themes in the data, some of which were commensurate with existing theoretical ideas about the psychological contract, others which were new or which challenged extant theory. By using the psychological contract as a basic organizing theoretical framework and by adopting interpretive techniques which lent to this flexibility, a contribution was made to understanding the psychological contract within the specific domain of the small firm, an understanding which was grounded in the experiences and interpretations of the participants.

The third role for theory is in enabling useful responses. This is a pragmatic view, but one that is useful to those of us working in the field of management research and consultancy, where there is an increasing concern with producing knowledge of use to the practising manager (Aram and Salipante, 2003; Huff, 2000; Maclean and Mackintosh, 2002; Tranfield and Starkey, 1998; van Aken, 2004). Such concerns are also central to the domain of HRM which is reflected in the plethora of research on HRM and performance, coupled with the recognition that what is good for the large firm is not necessarily good for the small firm (Hendry et al., 1995; Marlow and Patton, 1993).

Interpretivist approaches enable a useful contribution to be made here, they enable different realities and interpretations to be recognized, as an account of those different interpretations can be made. Any intervention on the basis of research findings needs to take into account the multiple realities experienced in a given situation by a range of individuals or groups. Therefore instead of giving clear prescriptions for good practice, recommendations for interventions are contextually located. Legge (2005) voices similar concerns in relation to HRM, suggesting the need for alternatives to positivism and the adoption of methods to give voice to 'the submerged voice of those who experience HRM initiatives'. She calls for accounts that are culturally and historically located. Blackburn and Stokes (2005) provide an example of this in relation to the use of focus groups to research SMEs. They argue that the worlds of the academic researcher and the SME owner are culturally different, therefore focus groups are a way of breaking down barriers. The in-depth understanding of the issues entrepreneurs face which is generated from such an approach can lead to higher quality policy initiatives.

So far we have argued that interpretivist approaches fit with the subject matter of entrepreneurship and the integration of ideas from HRM, enabling practical and theoretical developments in the field. A third reason for extending interpretivist approaches draws on the diversity of methodological tools available to interpretivist researchers to access the subtle meanings individuals ascribe to entrepreneurship. Critical incident technique (Chell, 2004), repertory grid technique (Cassell et al., 2000), oral history (Mitchell, 1997), critical discourse analysis (Perren and Jennings, 2002; 2005), open-ended interviews (Jack and Anderson, 2002), archival studies (Kisfalvi, 2002), metaphorical analysis (Dodd, 2002; Goss, 2005; Nicolson and Anderson, 2005), narrative analysis (Johansson, 2004; Hamilton, 2006; Rae, 2000) and matrices analysis (Nadin and Cassell, 2004) have all been used in the entrepreneurship and small business fields. The diversity of techniques means traditional questions can be explored in different ways. It also offsets the criticism that entrepreneurship research is mono-method.

In summary, arguments to extend interpretivist approaches focus on the nature of the subject matter, the opportunity for theory development, and the added richness that results from using a diverse range of qualitative methods. But given the potential contribution, why have interpretivist approaches not been used more within the field of entrepreneurship? In the next section we identify a series of challenges for researchers using these approaches.

Challenges for interpretivist researchers in the entrepreneurship area
Earlier we highlighted Coviello and Jones' (2004) suggestion that the need to justify empirical work on international entrepreneurship accounts for the dominance of studies drawing on a positivist paradigm and emphasizing statistical techniques. In other areas of management research such as HRM, the lack of published research drawing upon qualitative research methods (for example, Cassell et al., 2006; Kiessling and Harvey, 2005; Legge, 2005) gives rise to the argument that a heavy reliance on the positivist paradigm prevents innovation in the discipline. Symon and Cassell (1999) identify seven barriers to innovation in research practice which they see as interrelated and emanating from a variety of social-psychological and political processes. The use of alternative approaches to positivism may be seen as a threat to the 'scientific' status of a discipline and therefore actively discouraged. Symon and Cassell (1999: p. 394) also identify the role and significance of 'epistemological gatekeepers' such as journal editors, reviewers, conference organizers and professional associations who can shape perceptions of accepted practice in a discipline for academic and practitioner audiences. Research drawing on an interpretivist approach may be difficult to get published. Gartner and Birley (2002) also draw attention to some of these issues in their editorial for a special issue of *Journal of Business Venturing* on qualitative methods in entrepreneurship. They contrast the content of their special issue with an *Academy of Management Journal* special issue on international entrepreneurship (McDougall and Oviatt, 2000) in which all articles drew on quantitative techniques. The contributions in the *Journal of Business Venturing* special issue were non-United States-based scholars, whereas of those contributing to the *Academy of Management Journal* special issue, only two of the 17 authors were based outside the US. They contend that other than there perhaps being a European tradition of qualitative research, issues of timescale may also be important, 'Qualitative data (particularly ethnographic longitudinal studies) take much longer to collect and analyze, which often means that this time scale does not always fit doctoral program, tenure decision, and promotion track in United States-based Universities' (Gartner and Birley, 2002: pp. 392–3). Similar trends have been noted in HRM research, with US research serving a legitimating function in terms of attempting to establish causal links between HRM and performance. The nature of

academic training in the US means quantitative methods are understood and frequently used by researchers and they also offer a quick route to publication (Hoobler and Johnson, 2004). This may deter researchers from engaging with alternative qualitative techniques. Given the international movement to measure academic research using metrics they suggest, 'There does seem to be a trend in more European Universities to promote more research productivity, particularly as measured by publications in United States-based journals. Does this trend bode well for qualitative research?' (Gartner and Birley, 2002: p. 393). These issues have been raised elsewhere in relation to management research (see Symon et al., 2008) and clearly this is something that needs to be monitored as the field develops.

A further issue to examine in order to address the question of what prevents researchers from dabbling with interpretivist approaches is critiques of the approach more generally. Schwandt (2003) argues that there are a number of challenges that critics of interpretivist approaches often present, including the lack of critical purchase, the problem of inquirer authority and privilege and the problem of criteria for evaluation. The first problem of too much description (Schwandt, 2003) and sometimes the reporting of interpretivist research may be critiqued somewhat unfairly from this perspective. Mitchell (1997), referring to the use of oral histories, suggests that outsiders who have not been involved in a piece of in-depth research may perceive its value only on the basis of 'surface features', rather than understanding the detail and richness of the profession of entrepreneurship. It is precisely these rich insights that emerge from immersion in the accounts of entrepreneurs that interpretivist researchers seek to provide. However, presenting those accounts in a format where their critical and rich nature is exposed is a craft that develops over time and with practice.

The second challenge that Schwandt (2003) outlines is the problem of inquirer authority and privilege. The argument is that interpretivist researchers do not appropriately appraise the accounts they produce, rather they present them regardless of any overarching critique. This privileges the accounts of those being researched. This criticism is clearly located within a particular epistemological stance. This is only a problem if the researcher does not recognize that there are multiple realities, and that any account presented needs to be viewed within its socio-historical context rather than accepted as a given truth. This can also be addressed through reflexive processes where the researchers address issues such as the impact of their philosophical approach on how knowledge is produced to the impact of the research methods used on the interpretations given (for example, Alvesson and Skoldberg, 2002; Cunliffe, 2003; Johnson and Duberley, 2003; Nadin and Cassell, 2006; Weick, 2002).

The third challenge highlighted by Schwandt (2003) deals with the appropriateness of criteria for the assessment of quality in interpretivist entrepreneurial research (see Symon et al., 2000). Although there may be considerable consensus amongst management researchers about appropriate criteria for positivist informed research, such as reliability, replicability, validity and generalizability, a different set of criteria is needed to evaluate research in an interpretivist perspective as it is underpinned by a different set of philosophical assumptions. This has led to some interpretivist researchers generating alternative sets of criteria to apply when evaluating the quality of qualitative research (for example Lincoln and Guba, 2003; Morse, 1994). Whether this is useful or indeed desirable is a controversial issue, with some writers arguing that the use of checklists would encourage uniformity and detract from the diversity and richness associated with interpretivist perspectives. Despite these concerns there are regular requests for a universal set of assessment criteria for this type of research (see Sandberg, 2005).

However, interpretivist approaches are characterized by a diversity of methods while researchers hold different philosophies and assumptions. There has been a call for greater philosophical transparency in this area (Cope, 2005) and one way of addressing the issue of criteria would be to consider the appropriateness of different sets of criteria within different philosophical approaches. Johnson et al. (2006) propose the notion of a 'contingent criteriology' where research using qualitative techniques is evaluated through a different set of criteria depending upon the tradition within which it is located. To this extent, we can assess a piece of interpretivist research alongside the quality criteria that match that tradition. This may be a way forward in seeking appropriate criteria with which to evaluate work within an interpretivist tradition.

Interpretivist researchers face a number of challenges in this field and these stem from confronting the status quo. Our suggestion is that regardless of epistemological position, methodological rigour is the cornerstone of valuable research, something which is itself contingent upon transparency in the research process. By making explicit the philosophical assumptions underlying any piece of research – including positivist research – it can be evaluated according to the merits of the appropriate paradigm. Whilst the barriers associated with epistemological gatekeeping are more problematic, the more these concerns are voiced and the more interpretivist research is conducted, the less it can be ignored.

Conclusions
In this chapter we have argued that the use of interpretivist approaches presents a number of new opportunities for those researching at the intersection

of entrepreneurship and HRM. By asking different types of research questions and applying different methodological techniques new theoretical developments can be made. We have identified a series of challenges for interpretivist researchers in this field and argued that these are informed by critiques of interpretivism located in other epistemological traditions. Frese et al. (2000) argue that entrepreneurship is one of the most important areas to research in the current millennium. Employing the range of different methodological approaches available to social scientists can only enhance our understanding of the processes of entrepreneurship and the role of HRM through the sense-making processes of the entrepreneur.

References

Allinson, C.W., E. Chell and J. Hayes (2000), 'Intuition and entrepreneurial behaviour', *European Journal of Work and Organizational Psychology*, **9**(1), 31–44.

Altheide, D.L. and J.M. Johnson (1994), 'Criteria for assessing interpretive validity in qualitative research', in N.K. Denzin and Y.S. Lincoln (eds), *Handbook of Qualitative Research*, Thousand Oaks, CA: Sage Publications, pp. 485–99.

Alvesson, M. and S. Deetz (2000), *Doing Critical Management Research*, London: Sage Publications.

Alvesson, M. and K. Skoldberg (2002), *Reflexive Methodology: New Vistas for Qualitative Research*, London: Sage Publications.

Aram, J.D. and P. Salipante (2003), 'Bridging scholarship in management: Epistemological reflections', *British Journal of Management*, **14**, 189–205.

Blackburn, R. and D. Stokes (2005), 'Breaking down the barriers: Using focus groups to research small and medium-sized enterprises', *International Small Business Journal*, **19**(1), 44–67.

Blumer, H. (1954), 'What's wrong with social theory', *American Sociological Review*, **19**(1), 3–10.

Bruni, A., S. Gherardi and B. Poggio (2004), 'Entrepreneur-mentality, gender and the study of women entrepreneurs', *Journal of Organizational Change Management*, **17**(3), 256–68.

Cardon, M. and C. Stevens (2004), 'Managing human resources in small organizations: What do we know?', *Human Resource Management Review*, **14**, 295–323.

Cassell, C.M., A. Buehring, G. Symon and P. Johnson (2006), 'Qualitative methods in management research: An introduction to the themed issue', *Management Decision*, **44**(2), 161–6.

Cassell, C.M., P. Close, J.P. Duberley and P. Johnson (2000), 'Surfacing embedded assumptions: Using repertory grid methodology to facilitate organizational change', *European Journal of Work and Organizational Psychology*, **9**(4), 561–74.

Cassell, C.M., S.J. Nadin, M. Gray and C.M. Clegg (2002), 'The use of HRM practices in small and medium-sized enterprises', *Personnel Review*, **31**(6), 671–92.

Chell, E. (2004), 'Critical incident technique', in C.M. Cassell and G. Symon (eds), *Essential Guide to Qualitative Methods in Organizational Research: A Practical Guide*, London: Sage Publications, pp. 45–60.

Comte, A. (1853), *The Positive Philosophy of Auguste Comte*, London: Chapman.

Cope, J. (2005), 'Researching entrepreneurship through phenomenological inquiry: Philosophical and methodological issues', *International Small Business Journal*, **23**(2), 163–89.

Coviello, N.E. and M.V. Jones (2004), 'Methodological issues in international entrepreneurship research', *Journal of Business Venturing*, **19**, 485–508.

Cromie, S. (2000), 'Assessing entrepreneurial inclinations: Some approaches and empirical evidence', *European Journal of Work and Organizational Psychology*, **9**(1), 7–30.

Cunliffe, A. (2003), 'Reflexive inquiry in organizational research: Questions and possibilities', *Human Relations*, **58**(8), 983–1003.

Cunningham, J.B. and J. Lischeron (1991), 'Defining entrepreneurship', *Journal of Small Business Management*, **29**(1), 45–61.

Delantey, G. (1997), *Social Science: Beyond Constructivism and Relativism*, Buckingham: Open University Press.

Dodd, D. (2002), 'Metaphors and meaning: A grounded cultural model of US entrepreneurship', *Journal of Business Venturing*, **17**(5), 519–35.

Fleetwood, S. and A. Hesketh (2006), 'HRM-performance research: Under theorized and lacking explanatory power', *International Journal of Human Resource Management*, **17**(12), 1977–93.

Frese, M., E. Chell and H. Klandt (2000), 'Introduction', *European Journal of Work and Organizational Psychology*, **9**(1), 3–6.

Gartner, W.B. and S. Birley (2002), 'Introduction to the special issue on qualitative methods in entrepreneurship research', *Journal of Business Venturing*, **17**(5), 387–95.

Goss, D. (2005), 'Schumpeter's legacy? Interaction and emotions in the sociology of entrepreneurship', *Entrepreneurship: Theory and Practice*, **29**(2), 205–18.

Grant, P. and L.J. Perren (2002), 'Small business and entrepreneurial research: Meta-theories, paradigms and prejudices', *International Small Business Journal*, **2**(2), 185–211.

Guba, E. and Y. Lincoln (1989), *Fourth Generation Evaluation*, Newbury Park, CA: Sage Publications.

Hamilton, E. (2006), 'Narratives of enterprise as epic tragedy', *Management Decision*, **44**(4), 536–50.

Hendry, C., M.B. Arthur and A.M. Jones (1995), *Strategy Through People: Adaptation and Learning in the Small-Medium Enterprise*, London: Routledge.

Heneman, R.L., J.W. Tansky and S.M. Camp (2000), 'Human resource management practices in small and medium-sized enterprises: Unanswered questions and future research perspectives', *Entrepreneurship: Theory and Practice*, Fall, pp. 11–26.

Hill, J. and P. McGowan (1999), 'Small business and enterprise development: Questions about research methodology', *International Journal of Entrepreneurial Behaviour and Research*, **5**(1), 5–18.

Holliday, R. (1995), *Investigating Small Firms: Nice Work?*, London: Routledge.

Hoobler, J.M. and N.B. Johnson (2004), 'An analysis of current human resource management publications', *Personnel Review*, **33**(6), 665–76.

Huff, A.S. (2000), 'Changes in organizational knowledge production: 1999 Presidential Address', *Academy of Management Review*, **25**(2), 288–93.

Jack, S.L. and A.R. Anderson (2002), 'The effects of embeddedness on the entrepreneurial process', *Journal of Business Venturing*, **17**, 467–87.

Jennings, P.L., L. Perren and S. Carter (2005), 'Guest editors' introduction: Alternative perspectives on entrepreneurship research', *Entrepreneurship: Theory and Practice*, **29**, 145–52.

Johansson, A.W. (2004), 'Narrating the entrepreneur', *International Small Business Journal*, **22**(3), 273–93.

Johnson, P. and J. Duberley (2003), 'Reflexivity in management research', *Journal of Management Studies*, **40**(5), 1279–303.

Johnson, P., A. Buehring, G. Symon and C.M. Cassell (2006), 'Evaluating qualitative management research: Towards a contingent criteriology', *International Journal of Management Reviews*, **8**(3), 131–56.

Kiessling, T. and M. Harvey (2005), 'Strategic global human resource management research in the 21st century: An endorsement of the mixed-method research methodology', *International Journal of Human Resource Management*, **16**(1), 22–45.

King, N. (2004), 'Template analysis', in C.M. Cassell and G. Symon (eds), *Essential Guide to Qualitative Methods in Organizational Research: A Practical Guide*, London: Sage Publications, pp. 11–22.

Kisfalvi, V. (2002), 'The entrepreneur's character, life issues, and strategy making: A field study', *Journal of Business Venturing*, **17**, 489–518.

Kurakto, D.F. and R.M. Hodgetts (1998), *Entrepreneurship: A Contemporary Approach*, 4th edn, Orlando: The Dryden Press.

Leahey, T. (1991), *A History of Modern Psychology*, Englewood Cliffs, NJ: Prentice Hall.
Legge, K. (2005), *Human Resource Management: Rhetorics and Realities*, Anniversary Edition, Basingstoke: Palgrave Macmillan.
Lincoln, Y.S. and E.G. Guba (1985), *Naturalistic Inquiry*, Beverly Hills: Sage.
Lincoln, Y.S. and E. Guba (2003), 'Paradigmatic controversies, contradictions, and emerging confluences', in N.K. Denzin and Y.S. Lincoln (eds), *The Landscape of Qualitative Research: Theories and Issues*, Thousand Oaks, CA: Sage, pp. 252–91.
Maclean, D. and R. Mackintosh (2002), 'On the challenges of management research', *European Management Journal*, **20**(4), 383–92.
Mallon, M. and L. Cohen (2001), 'Time for a change? Women's accounts of the move from organizational careers to self-employment', *British Journal of Management*, **12**(3), 217–30.
Marlow, S. and D. Patton (1993), 'Managing the employment relationship in the smaller firm: Possibilities for human resource management', *International Small Business Journal*, **11**(4), 57–64.
McDougall, P.P. and B.M. Oviatt (2000), 'International entrepreneurship: The intersection of two research paths', *Academy of Management Journal*, **43**(5), 902–9.
Mirchandani, K. (1999), 'Feminist insight on gendered work: New directions in research on women and entrepreneurship', *Gender, Work and Organization*, **6**(4), 224–35.
Mitchell, R.K. (1997), 'Oral history and expert scripts: Demystifying the entrepreneurial experience', *International Journal of Entrepreneurial Behaviour and Research*, **3**(2), 122–39.
Morse, J.M. (1994), 'Emerging from the data: The cognitive process of analysis in qualitative enquiry', in J.M. Morse (ed.), *Critical Issues in Qualitative Research Methods*, London: Sage, pp. 23–43.
Nadin, S. and C.M. Cassell (2004), 'Matrices analysis', in C.M. Cassell and G. Symon (eds), *Essential Guide to Qualitative Methods in Organizational Research: A Practical Guide*, London: Sage, pp. 271–87.
Nadin, S. and C.M. Cassell (2006), 'Increasing reflexivity through the use of research diaries', *Qualitative Research in Accounting and Management*, **3**(3), 208–17.
Nadin, S. and C.M. Cassell (2007), 'New deal for old? Exploring the psychological contract in a small firm environment', *International Small Business Journal*, **25**(4), 417–43.
Nicholson, L. and A.R. Anderson (2005), 'News and nuances of the entrepreneurial myth and metaphor: Linguistic games and entrepreneurial sense making and sense giving', *Entrepreneurship: Theory and Practice*, **29**(2), 153–72.
Ogbor, J.O. (2000), 'Mythicizing and reification in entrepreneurial discourse: Ideology-critique of entrepreneurial studies', *Journal of Management Studies*, **37**(5), 605–35.
Perren, L. and P. Jennings (2002), 'Discourses of domination at the edge of entrepreneurial life-worlds', *Proceedings of the 2002 Small Business and Entrepreneurship Development Conference*, Bradford: European Research Press.
Perren, L. and P. Jennings (2005), 'Government discourses on entrepreneurship: Issues of legitimization, subjugation and power', *Entrepreneurship: Theory and Practice*, **9**(2), 173–84.
Potter, J. and M. Wetherall (1987), *Discourse and Social Psychology: Beyond Attitudes and Behaviour*, London: Sage.
Rae, D. (2000), 'Understanding entrepreneurial learning: A question of how?', *International Journal of Entrepreneurial Behaviour and Research*, **6**(3), 145–55.
Reid, R., T. Morrow, B. Kelly and P. McCartan (2002), 'People management in SME's: An analysis of human resource strategies in family and non-family businesses', *Journal of Small Business and Enterprise Development*, **9**(2), 245–59.
Sandberg, J. (2005), 'How do we justify knowledge produced within interpretive approaches?', *Organization Research Methods*, **8**(1), 41–69.
Schwandt, T.A. (2003), 'Three epistemological stances for qualitative enquiry: Interpretivism, hermeneutics and social constructivism', in N.K. Denzin and Y.S. Lincoln (eds), *The Landscape of Qualitative Research: Theories and Issues*, 2nd edn, Thousand Oaks, CA: Sage, pp. 252–91.
Seale, C. (1999), *The Quality of Qualitative Research*, London: Sage Publications.
Stevenson, H.H. and J.C. Jarillo (1990), 'A paradigm of entrepreneurship: Entrepreneurial management', *Strategic Management Journal*, **11**, 17–27.

Symon, G. and C.M. Cassell (1999), 'Barriers to innovation in research practice', in M. Pinha, E. Cunha and C. Alves Marques (eds), *Readings in Organizational Science*, Lisbon: ISDPA, pp. 387–98.

Symon, G., C. Cassell and R. Dickson (2000), 'Expanding our research and practice through innovative research methods', *European Journal of Work and Organizational Psychology*, **9**(4), 1–6.

Symon, G., A. Buehring, P. Johnson and C. Cassell (2008), 'Positioning qualitative research as resistance to institutionalization in the academic labour process', *Organization Studies* (forthcoming).

Tranfield, D. and K. Starkey (1998), 'The nature, social organization and promotion of management research: Towards policy', *British Journal of Management*, **9**, 341–53.

van Aken, J. (2004), 'Management research based on the paradigm of the design sciences: The quest for field tested and grounded technological rules', *Journal of Management Studies*, **41**(2), 219–46.

Wall, T.D. and S.J. Wood (2005), 'The romance of human resource management and business performance, and the case for big science', *Human Relations*, **58**(4), 429–62.

Weick, K.E. (2001), *Making Sense of the Organization*, Oxford: Blackwell.

Weick, K.E. (2002), 'Real-time reflexivity: Prods to reflection', *Organization Studies*, **23**(6), 892–8.

Wortman Jnr., M.S. (1987), 'Entrepreneurship: An integrating typology and evaluation of the empirical research in the field', *Journal of Management*, **13**(2), 259–79.

PART II

THE NATURE OF HRM IN SMALLER AND ENTREPRENEURIAL FIRMS

5 Human resource management as an entrepreneurial tool?
Cinzia Dal Zotto and Veronica Gustafsson

Introduction

A firm's primary goal is to be profitable. To reach this goal a firm can grow and improve its market competitiveness. Growth can enhance economic efficiency, increase market share or lead to the creation of new markets. For this purpose innovation is key, and the process of introducing innovative products or services to the market is known as entrepreneurship (Schumpeter, 1934; Shane and Venkataraman, 2000). This is underpinned by creativity which can see the initial inspiration leading to the creation of new products or services. Talent, education and cognitive skills can drive inspiration. However, for this to become a daily driving force and lead to continuous innovation, high levels of creativity are required and attained only through intrinsic motivation (Amabile, 1996; Oldham and Cummings, 1996). Within such an unpredictable context, when competence and motivation are necessary for innovation, human resource management (HRM) becomes a crucial factor. It is therefore important and theoretically interesting to explore the contribution of HRM to the entrepreneurial growth of new and established firms.

As our chapter is exploratory by nature, it aims, first, to review the relationship between entrepreneurship and HRM. Second, we wish to point out the differences and similarities which characterize HRM in entrepreneurial and established firms, and therefore highlight the potential function of HRM in both sustaining growth and fostering intrapreneurship. We explore these insights through the analysis of two case studies of firm-level HRM in the media industry.

Entrepreneurship may lead to the creation of new organizations (Gartner, 1988) or may be pursued within already existing firms (intrapreneurship). Entrepreneurs who choose to start a new firm are usually categorized as being novices (founders of their first independent business) or habitual entrepreneurs (founders of several companies consecutively). We assume that, due to the liability of newness (Stinchcombe, 1965) novice entrepreneurs lack HRM competences. As the firm grows, the size of the entrepreneurial team and the dynamic of its composition increase (Chandler et al., 2005). This makes the need for HRM competence all the more pronounced. Personnel are considered a crucial resource for the successful performance of a firm which, if it aims at rapid growth, should manage its employees accordingly (Barringer et al., 2005).

There are several ways to generate HRM competence and lower the probability of mistakes. External consultants can be asked for help, entrepreneurs can attend courses and/or seminars (Klaas et al., 2005), or the HRM function can be outsourced (Cardon and Stevens, 2004; Cooke et al., 2005). Our argument is that HRM tasks can be shared amongst all members of an entrepreneurial start-up venture and the tasks are taken on as a part-time job. The result is a kind of networked learning process for which the ability of the members involved to learn and work in a team becomes crucial. This can also lead to the development of managerial resources in the start-up as those involved in networked HRM acquire competences they can use as future managers or executives.

In the case of habitual entrepreneurs, it is plausible to assume HRM competences are already present but intrinsic, and to see habitual entrepreneurs as experienced in acquiring and motivating personnel. As it is difficult to transfer tacit knowledge (Polanyi, 1967) they take the HRM functions upon themselves to decrease the probability of mistakes such as hiring the wrong people. However, the risk is that if the habitual entrepreneur decides to leave the firm the HRM competences also leave with him/her.

Entrepreneurs are motivated by uncertainty, which they recognize as an opportunity. In order to pursue this opportunity they are ready to start up a new firm and take on the related risk. However, to turn an opportunity into a viable business, having the right team is critical. Only an appropriately composed team can turn inventions into concrete and marketable innovations (Chandler et al., 2005). The same holds true when opportunities are recognized within an established firm. Entrepreneurship can therefore be understood as the management process by which a group of individuals, starting up a new firm or launching a new product or market, accept risk and pursue an opportunity (Schumpeter, 1934; Timmons, 1999). Clearly those involved have to be selected, empowered, developed, motivated and supported. HRM can be seen as the tool to retrieve, revive and reinforce entrepreneurial spirit and innovative capabilities of the new and emerging organization as well as established firms. It is within this context that HRM becomes important to new and growing ventures, and we will investigate how this occurs in two case studies.

In the next section of the chapter we point out the specificities of HRM in new and young firms, as well as its potential links with intrapreneurship. This is followed by a brief overview of the research method and context. We then introduce and analyse two case studies: the first is a start-up e-book firm in Finland, while the second, a free newspaper based in

Sweden, deals with the attitudes both of a start-up and an established firm. The cases were selected from firms operating in the Scandinavian media industry. The environmental dynamics of this industry are such that firms constantly change, innovate, and are characterized by an entrepreneurial spirit.

HRM in emerging and rapidly-growing firms
For firms, the investment in human resources can improve the fulfilment of personnel's labour contracts. A lack of investment in human resources or inappropriate leadership can decrease performance and lead to the loss of valuable competence as employees quit. This holds true for firms whether they are new and growing or established. Empirical studies have demonstrated that new firm survival as well as growth strongly depend on the firm's endowments with qualified and experienced personnel (Brüderl et al., 1998; Ziegler, 2000). HRM is a critical function even at the very early stage of the firm's founding.

According to a growing body of research, HRM in small, rapidly-growing firms is different from both their slowly-growing counterparts and large companies (see Barringer et al., 2005; Heneman and Tansky, 2002; Katz et al., 2000). Compared to large established companies, small firms may be subjected to liabilities of smallness and newness, which often demonstrate themselves through the scarcity of resources including employer's legitimacy (see Cardon and Stevens, 2004; Stinchcombe, 1965; Williamson et al., 2002 as well as chapters by Cardon and Tarique (Chapter 17), and Williamson and Robinson (Chapter 18) in this handbook). Even rapidly-growing companies can suffer from a lack of HRM experience; as a result, it is quite possible to expect small companies to abstain from elaborate and expensive HRM practices (such as formal training programmes; see Cardon and Stevens, 2004). However, while their HRM systems may be less formal they are more likely to be innovation-oriented compared to those in established firms.

A necessary part of all firms' HRM system is wages and salaries, together with payment of associated taxes and charges such as pensions and insurance. However, entrepreneurs also have other HRM functions such as planning, acquiring and especially selecting the personnel to employ. A unified HRM system will also address issues such as leadership, personnel motivation and development, compensation as well as performance management. This needs to be aligned or harmonized with all other firm strategies especially those concerning product portfolios, marketing and financing. The importance of this alignment increases with the size of the firm. As resources are limited and novice entrepreneurs may not have HRM competences they may concentrate on two of the most critical functions: acquisition of personnel and leadership. However, if emerging firms are to grow rapidly and be successful, then other HRM issues must be considered and dealt with (Drumm, 2003; Cardon and Stevens, 2004).

We argue that HRM practices can be considered one of the core competences of rapidly-growing firms. To this end we will consider the evidence on recruitment, compensation, leadership, development and performance management in entrepreneurial ventures. We will also discuss some other factors critical for emerging firms, such as the outsourcing of HRM and the use of contingent labour.

Recruitment

According to the HRM literature, all companies, however small, practise HRM even though this function can be implicit (Aldrich and Von Glinow, 1991). Recruitment seems to be one of the most challenging HRM tasks for smaller firms due to their lack of financial and material resources (Hannan and Freeman, 1984). In emerging firms the problem is a lack of experience. Given that HRM often becomes the responsibility of the general manager rather than a trained HRM professional (Longenecker et al., 1994), then attracting and selecting competent personnel can become problematic for emerging firms (Arthur, 1995).

Barney (1991) posits that many companies, instead of suffering the liability of newness, turn their condition of emergence into a competitive advantage. Their hiring practices depart from industry norms and this might be seen in the absence of job descriptions (or having only vague ones) or the absence of stock-based compensation (Alexander, 1999). Rapidly-growing firms are often founded with the idea of being 'anti-bureaucratic' and their approach to hiring is characterized by providing realistic job descriptions, communicating both positive and negative aspects of a job (Deshpande and Golhar, 1994). Such firms also exhibit strong tendencies to use the informal approach to work and to empower their employees (Cardon and Tolchinsky, 2006).

Extant literature indicates that core employees of entrepreneurial firms are often acquired through networks. Leung et al. (2006) provide an important insight into the hiring practices of entrepreneurial firms by highlighting how firms shift their network pools during different stages of emergence and growth. During the start-up phase the core team members are recruited from both social and business networks, whereas in the growth phase, recruitment is carried out almost solely from business networks. In other words, through the start-up and growth phases key personnel are recruited using strong ties (Granovetter, 1973). Moreover, in new ventures, those employed to initiate the business are not necessarily the same type of people who are needed to sustain the firm. At the beginning, founders usually hire generalists who are willing to put a lot of effort into and feel very passionate about the new venture. Later, when the firm starts to grow, more seasoned professionals are employed, who through their knowledge and experience can accelerate the business and foster growth (Swiercz and Lydon, 2002). The inability to foresee how and if a given individual will fit at the next level of firm growth can be a major problem for the founders as far as recruitment is concerned. It can also be compounded by recruiting core employees through social networks during the start-up phase.

Compensation
Alongside recruitment, compensation is a crucial area for small firms' survival and growth. Appropriate compensation is extremely important for emerging firms in acquiring core talents (Cardon and Stevens, 2004). Rewarding creativity, innovation, willingness to take risks, cooperation, interactive behaviour and tolerance for ambiguity and uncertainty is necessary in entrepreneurial firms (Balkin and Logan, 1988). Rewards systems are usually based on bonuses which may include both profit- and stock-sharing (Cardon and Stevens, 2004). By creating a sense of ownership, such systems allow emerging firms to retain core talents (Barringer et al., 2005; Cardon and Stevens, 2004). Financial incentives and stock options are a distinctive feature of fast-growing (gazelle) firms compared to their slowly-growing counterparts (Barringer et al., 2005). Barringer et al. (2005) argue that by providing personnel with modest salaries and generous bonuses if the firm performs well, rapidly-growing firms are able to shift a portion of the business risk to their employees.

Entrepreneurial firms tend to have flat organizational structures, and employees may be treated in an egalitarian fashion as far as compensation is concerned (Graham et al., 2002). In such firms financial rewards are not indicative of an employee's status, as traditional hierarchical distinctions are kept to a minimum (Balkin and Logan, 1988). Instead, entrepreneurial firms provide a multi-dimensional reward based on the payoff of acting in uncertain environments, which includes gambling on innovations. The satisfaction and responsibility of having a stake in the business adds up to the perceived feeling of reward (Graham et al., 2002). Rapidly-growing firms often operate without a formal compensation policy and instead it is negotiated on an individual basis depending on the needs and resource constraints of the firm and, on the other hand, on the skills and experience of the employees (Balkin and Swift, 2006). However, care must be taken that this does not compromise the qualities of such entrepreneurial ventures.

Leadership, training and development
Through direct involvement, entrepreneurs usually lead a process that creates value for stakeholders by bringing together a package of resources

in order to exploit a recognized opportunity. In fulfilling this process, entrepreneurs innovate, take risks and act proactively (Morris et al., 2004). By innovating they search for creative solutions to operational problems or needs. According to Schumpeter (1934) a successful innovation requires an act of will and not of intellect. Therefore innovation, which should not be confused with an invention, especially depends on leadership and not only on intelligence (Hébert and Link, 1988).

The concept of entrepreneurial leadership is important for founder-driven organizations but can also be used to foster entrepreneurial orientation within larger firms (Darling et al., 2007). The entrepreneur typically identifies an opportunity, and then surrounds herself/himself with individuals to help pursue it, while providing the necessary leadership to develop and motivate these individuals (Martins and Terblanche, 2003). This happens in new firms as well as in established ones when, for example, a new organizational unit is set up to develop a new product or service. Entrepreneurial leadership is all about breaking new ground and going beyond the known. It is about helping people to engage in new opportunities (McLagan and Nel, 1995). Therefore, the entrepreneur's ability to deal with opportunities effectively through the dynamics or an organizational setting can determine the success of a firm. Failures sometimes refer back to organizations being over-managed and under-led. This happens when entrepreneurs or managers excel in their ability to handle the daily routine, yet never question whether the routine should be done at all (Darling et al., 2007).

Through appropriate means and with sufficient competence, an entrepreneurial leader inspires a group or individuals to become willing participants in the fulfilment of innovative goals. For this purpose entrepreneurial leaders must have an exciting and contagious vision to encourage others to commit to organizational achievement. But they must also communicate this vision. Openness and dynamic contacts between individuals, teams and departments within an organization facilitate the acceptance of new perspectives and represent relevant traits of organizational cultures able to stimulate creativity and innovation (Martins and Terblanche, 2003; Mumford et al., 2002). Open communication is fostered by teamwork which provides the conditions for a dynamic mixture of ideas and competencies (Fong, 2003). Furthermore, by delegating some decisions, entrepreneurs can give responsibility to employees, and by assigning stimulating tasks create the preconditions for the development of their internalized motivation (Drumm, 2003).

Acting in this way entrepreneurs reflect the characteristics of both transformational and charismatic leadership (George and Jones, 2005). Transformational leaders pay attention to the developmental needs of followers by helping them look at problems in new ways. The result is that followers tend to increase their level of trust in the entrepreneur and be motivated to put extra effort to achieve group goals (Cacioppe, 1997; Darling et al., 2007). Charismatic leaders have a vision of how things could be, clearly communicate it to their followers and, through their excitement, motivate them to support this vision (Darling et al., 2007). Both leadership styles contribute to the building up of an organizational culture based on learning, tolerance and trust (Cardon and Stevens, 2004: p. 310). However, entrepreneurs tend to be authoritarian and to take all decisions themselves. This behaviour discourages highly skilled employees in particular (Drumm, 2003).

Personnel development is an important issue in the context of entrepreneurial leadership and therefore requires close research attention. Employees' skills and knowledge are valuable assets. Yet smaller companies are known for abstaining from formalized training programmes, mostly due to their financial cost and the loss of employees' immediate working time (Banks et al., 1987). Training and learning exist in small firms, but are at times unstructured and supplemented (if not even substituted) by organizational socialization (Chao, 1997). Barringer et al. (2005) argue that fast-growing firms, compared to their slow-growing counterparts, put stronger emphasis on the training and development of employees, as multi-tasking and role transitions are important factors (May, 1997).

The concept of networked leadership can be applied as a personnel development measure in smaller firms (Dal Zotto, 2001). Here the leader's authority is granted by her/his expertise and ability to provide professional and psychological support to the entrepreneurial team. Serving as mentor and coach to employees helps to develop them as leaders and is considered to be one of the competencies of entrepreneurial leadership (Comelli and von Rosenstiel, 1995; Swiercz and Lydon, 2002).

Performance management

Although performance appraisal is of crucial importance in fostering entrepreneurship (Morris and Jones, 1993), very little research has been undertaken on this issue (Cardon and Stevens, 2004). A possible explanation, indirectly supported by Barringer et al.'s (2005) findings, is that in rapidly-growing entrepreneurial firms, employee performance is evaluated and apprised through financial incentives and stock options, rather than through other established HRM procedures.

Another explanation is provided by Heneman and Tansky (2002). According to their study, a high turnover of employees can be expected in the companies oriented towards innovation and flexibility. This steady in-flow of new knowledge and skills brought by new employees can be desirable. Nevertheless, intensive employee turnover can be detrimental for companies aiming at fast growth (Baron and Hannan, 2002) especially in knowledge-intensive industries, as organizational knowledge can be lost without appropriate practices in place for its capture and retention.

Outsourcing HRM practices
A number of studies show that outsourcing HRM and increasing reliance on contingent labour are becoming more common among small firms (Cardon, 2003; Cardon and Tolchinsky, 2006; Klaas, 2003). Advantages would be: reduced costs and administrative burden; diverse skills and talents accessed through a contingent labour force; and superior HRM skills gained by using a professional employer organization (PEO). All these factors combined can, in turn, lead to increased competitive advantage.

However, the outcomes of outsourcing HRM could be different depending on the small firm's prime goal (Klaas, 2003). If the desire is to reduce costs and administration, then hiring a PEO might quickly lead to competitive advantage. On the other hand, if the desire is to improve HRM practices, then a successful collaboration with a PEO requires time in order to establish trust and gain firm-specific knowledge (Klaas, 2003).

Hiring temporary staff from employment agencies can avoid the risk related to the fixed cost of employment. When specific qualifications are required and the need for personnel increases in terms of time, then the firm is bound to hire employees on a permanent basis. Executives for new or young firms can be sourced – for a limited period of time – through older, experienced managers who previously served in older or larger companies and who are approaching retirement (Niedhof, 1999). This could present an attractive challenge for these executives, while allowing young firms to bridge a phase in which their development is still uncertain and future executives still need to be developed or hired. Furthermore, the presence of experienced managers for a period of time can trigger learning processes among all the staff within the firm. This interim management acquisition strategy can be carried out with the help of specialized consultants. Assistance with selection can be important to overcome biased decision making; candidates can play-act and know by heart the guides to job applications (Beitz and Loch, 1996), while decisions could also be made on the basis of the favourable appearance of candidates.

HRM and intrapreneurship
Corporate entrepreneurship, which is also known as intrapreneurship (Pinchot, 1985), is a prominent feature in large organizations concerned with increased profitability through creativity and innovation (Zahra, 1996). Intrapreneurship facilitates individual risk acceptance and promotes

entrepreneurial contribution (Hayton, 2005). However, it implies organizational learning. HRM practices could therefore play a prominent role in fostering intrapreneurship. Indeed, the existing small (albeit growing) body of literature demonstrates consensus on this issue, although, according to Hayton (2005) the empirical evidence is somewhat inconclusive and the theoretical clarity is lacking. This state of things can be partially explained by the fact that intrapreneurship is a complex phenomenon which includes innovation, venturing and strategic renewal (Guth and Ginsberg, 1990). Sharma and Chrisman define this phenomenon as 'the process whereby an individual or a group of individuals, in association with an existing organization, create a new organization, or investigate renewal or innovation within that organization' (1999: p. 18). Innovation implies a process of turning inventions into marketable products or services, venturing means that a new business is created either through establishing a new business unit, acquisition of a new business or partnership with another company (Hayton, 2005). Strategic renewal is a process of organizational transformation through renewal of the organization's key ideas (Guth and Ginsberg, 1990). This process is infrequent and rarely observed empirically (Covin and Miles, 1999). As a result, the interplay of HRM and intrapreneurship is most commonly studied within the process either of innovation or venturing (Hayton, 2005).

According to established opinion, intrapreneurship requires decentralization of authority, participation in decision-making, cooperation, decrease of bureaucracy and encouragement of risk-taking and creativity (Luchsinger and Bagby, 1987). In large organizations a crucial role in fostering intrapreneurship belongs to the middle management (Kuratko et al., 2005). Even if precise HRM practices to support such behaviour are difficult to find and may be contradictory, Hayton's recent study (Hayton, 2005) identified that:

- HRM should encourage internal and external knowledge acquisition and integration, which facilitates the ability of management to 'endorse, refine, and shepherd entrepreneurial opportunities and identify, acquire and deploy resources needed to pursue these opportunities' (Kuratko et al., 2005: p. 705).
- HRM should encourage the formation of cooperative and trusting relationships which enable sharing of tangible and intangible resources (including knowledge).
- HRM practices should focus on encouraging behaviour which accepts risk-taking and tolerates failure. This is crucial, as risk and uncertainty are inherent features within a context of entrepreneurship or innovation.

Moreover, studies have pointed to HRM practices focusing on innovative input rather than on rewarding the outcomes (Balkin et al., 2000).

A general framework for analysis

From the analysis of the extant literature it appears that for emerging firms HRM practices are more important than entrepreneurs would expect. In particular, the fact that HRM competence is not typically available within the founding team, means that the application of different HRM practices is important to overcome this deficiency. As general managers rather than trained professionals are usually responsible for HRM, in order to recruit core talent, emerging firms need to combine sourcing from social and business networks with attractive compensation measures. Such measures also foster feelings of ownership among newly acquired employees, the existence of which is important when firms grow and entrepreneurs need to delegate responsibility.

Further, as emerging firms exist under conditions of uncertainty, entrepreneurial leaders need to inspire as well as motivate employees by openly communicating an exciting vision and by helping them to develop professional skills. By applying a combination of transformational and charismatic leadership approaches, entrepreneurs can overcome the typical problem of being too authoritarian and therefore discouraging skilled employees. While a certain amount of turnover cannot be avoided in emerging firms, in order for turnover not to be detrimental, rapidly-growing and knowledge-intensive firms need to invest in knowledge management systems from an early stage. Last but not least, as the risk of hiring the wrong people is very high among inexperienced entrepreneurs, outsourcing HRM practices to professional organizations or using a contingent labour force when no specific qualifications are required, can be a way of minimizing the chances of making mistakes.

We can therefore argue that the implementation of a unified HRM system – not simply fragmented practices such as recruiting and leadership – would be important to the success of emerging firms. Such a system can help maintain and further develop entrepreneurial orientation and thus foster innovation within new but also established firms operating in highly dynamic environments.

The media industry provides a fertile ground for entrepreneurial and intrapreneurial processes due to the development and adoption of technological innovation by media companies. In two case studies of small and rapidly-growing media companies we explore whether the HRM practices they use enable growth and encourage entrepreneurial behaviour. How we go about doing this is outlined below.

Method

The application of HRM measures both to foster growth in emerging firms and to enhance entrepreneurial behaviour in established firms is under-researched (Leung et al., 2006). Our purpose is to fill in this gap, thus this study is exploratory by nature. HRM is regarded here as a pool of management techniques – such as empowerment, personnel acquisition, motivation, development – which aim to strategically integrate labour management into the future plans of the organization, individualizing the effort assessment with differentiated rewards in terms of pay and conditions, as well as enhancing not only the commitment to managerial decisions (Marlow, 1997) but also the willingness to engage in entrepreneurial behaviour and act proactively (Brown, 1996; Wiklund, 1998). Because of the complexity and the dynamic setting of the phenomenon under study (Eisenhardt, 1989), the case study method is suitable. Unlike quantitative methodology that seeks to predict behaviour, qualitative research methods are suited for understanding meanings, context and processes in their natural settings (Maxwell, 1998). They give insight through rich details and are typically conducted using different methods for gathering empirical material (Pettigrew, 1997; Stake, 1995).

As the access to data is determinant for the case studies to fulfil their purpose, two cases from the media industry were selected. One of the authors works at a research institute for media management and therefore it was convenient to access data from companies which were already within the institute's network of contacts. Furthermore, the media industry is populated by well established and emerging firms that operate within a very dynamic environment and they are therefore bound to have quick reactions and to be proactive. This context is well suited for testing the application of HRM practices as entrepreneurial tools. While conducting the case studies we found it useful to think of the chosen firm as the case and of the HRM practices as the unit of analysis. This means that we did not focus on analysing the firms themselves but rather on capturing the influence of HRM on entrepreneurial behaviour by investigating which HRM practices were applied by the firms for which purpose. The first case of Ellibs was chosen as an example of a typical start-up, while the second, Metro, was both a start-up and a spin-off from a well-established media firm, thus presenting a case in intrapreneurship. With this choice we could also explore the influence of experience in the application of HRM measures for entrepreneurial purposes.

To collect the empirical material, a multi-method approach (Denzin and Lincoln, 1994) was followed. Semi-structured interviews were conducted with the CEOs of both firms while we also spoke to other managers at Metro, including the Vice President for Human Resources and Head of

Research at Metro's headquarters in London. Secondary data were sought from the firms' websites, press releases and firms' reports. Documents enable researchers to investigate and reconstruct ongoing processes that are not available for direct observation (Lindlof, 1995). This method is ideal to complement primary data when analysing young firms within a dynamic context such as the media industry.

Case 1: Ellibs.com

The company
Ellibs.com was founded by Kristian Laiho. Being the manager of an events portal for three cities in Finland – Turku, Tampere and Oulu – Kristian realized that users did not seem to be interested in the content being produced and made available on the Internet. In 2001 Kristian recognized that there was a need for quality and qualified knowledge on the Internet, for which surfers would be willing to pay.

To carry out his idea of selling quality information, Kristian had to find a viable business model. He decided to commission some market research which identified an interest in buying electronic books. Thirty-five per cent of people interviewed said they would buy e-books, and 17 per cent said they would prefer e-books to paper books. In 2001 the non-fiction book market in Finland was worth 180 million euros so Kristian recognized that e-books were an opportunity. He talked about his idea with Idea Development, which agreed to help him create a suitable website: Eweline.com.

After checking publishers' interest in the idea he contacted all major telecommunication companies. He made an agreement with Elisa Innovation, a mobile phone provider in Finland, who agreed to sell Eweline.com a Digital Right Management System allowing the handling of pdf files. The first step was to put out a press release about the cooperation between the two partners for a big project on e-books and in this way hold back competitors and inform the public about Eweline.com. Kristian's second step was to contact small publishers that were trying to become more visible, as well as publishers that were already dealing with e-books. A small publisher in the US, Dorrance Publishing, agreed on a contract for 30 books to be published online. This allowed Kristian to start his adventure.

Kristian received the first 35 000 euros of seed financing in the form of a loan from the Government Bank. During 2002 the money was mainly spent on book fairs and on getting the web system operational. In November Eweline.com was launched and online surfers could start buying e-books. Word of mouth saw the first Finnish quality publisher and the biggest IT book publisher in the Nordic countries – Docendo – contact Eweline.com and agree on a contract. Through an agreement with the University Library in Helsinki, Kristian succeeded in becoming a mediator between publishers and libraries, which is the way that bookstores operate.

In order to contact libraries and look for subscriptions Kristian hired a call centre offering them a revenue-sharing agreement: the call centre would retain 30 per cent of the fee. This agreement lasted until the 16th sale, when Kristian decided to hire Marlene, who had been in charge of the task at the call centre. As the company was growing, Kristian realized he needed real office space so he entered into a cooperation with the Turku Science Park Incubator, which offered facilities supporting 45 per cent of all the company's costs, including the salaries. This support started at the beginning of 2004 and lasted for one year. Kristian was now ready to hire the staff he needed which included: a technical support person; a content manager to put the books online; and Marlene, who was in charge of selling books to libraries. After a first venture capital round in spring 2004 and further support from the Government Bank, Eweline.com was ready to enter the UK market. To facilitate this process the company name was changed to Ellibs as it was easier to pronounce in English.

Human resource management practices
When the research was undertaken Ellibs had one part-time and seven full-time employees. Several students were working as content managers. There were also two key account managers, a manager of publishing operations, a content manager, two technical developers, a technical support person and the CEO. The new employees were hired along the way, and responsibility was delegated following an 'empowerment' pattern. The leadership style could be considered both task- and people-oriented with a charismatic touch. An incentive system existed and was based on bonuses, which were paid when performance targets on sales and development were achieved. Flexible working time was allowed as the company was managed by objectives.

A human resource development programme had also been introduced. It was partly outsourced, as the former managing director of the World Trade Centre in Turku had been hired as an HRM consultant. She came in one afternoon every second month and with Kristian led a seminar on a topic they had previously agreed. Basically the programme aimed to sum up the actual situation of the company and inform employees about the next goals and steps, as well as to suggest to them possible pathways for reaching those goals. Employees were then to find the best way they could to reach the set objectives. In enabling them to make their own decisions about their own projects, the programme tried to make employees feel like intrapreneurs or self-employed. For example the sales people could decide which clients they preferred to deal with, while developers could choose to work on the projects they were most interested in. Every Monday the Ellibs team met in a briefing to discuss what had happened in the previous week. In this way employees felt they belonged to a team and participated in the day-by-day development of the company.

According to the CEO, when starting his company, the first problem he encountered was the acquisition of personnel, that is, finding skilled employees. Kristian Laiho thought that the solution to this problem could be found in personnel marketing, which for start-ups is problematic because of their lack of image or their newness (Stinchcombe, 1965). The first employee at Ellibs was a friend of an employee at Idea Development, the company where Kristian was previously working. She was tertiary qualified and looking for a job. Kristian hired her when Eweline.com got the contract with Docendo. The first developer was a friend of a friend and was recommended as 'being good'. The first sales person was Marlene, who had been working for the telemarketing company which was hired to find the agreements with the libraries. The situation here supports Leung et al.'s findings (2006) of the importance of networks for the recruitment of personnel to entrepreneurial firms.

The second technical developer joined the firm when the first one, Miska, had to join the army. When Miska returned, the second developer decided to stay with the company. When Ellibs got new office space at the Turku Science Park and the first venture capital investment came in, the situation was good enough for the company to be promoted as the biggest e-book seller in Europe and to gain a positive image. Hiring people became easier, and more qualified people (such as those who knew the publishers' business) could be hired. When Marlene left because she felt she was not skilled enough for the job, an advertisement was posted on Ellibs' own News Bulletin on their website. An employee of WSOY, one of the most famous publishers in Finland, read the advertisement and was recruited to Ellibs as the public relations manager.

Managing employees is not easy. For Kristian, developing experience has been the critical factor in learning to manage people. Experience has been key to evaluating people's potential and learning not to overestimate their capabilities.

Case 2: Metro

The company
The world's largest chain of free newspapers is run under the brand name Metro. Metro was started as a subsidiary of the Modern Times Group (MTG), which in turn was part of the Kinnevik Investment Group in Sweden. During the late 1980s and early 1990s Kinnevik acted almost like

an incubator launching several companies, which now represent market-leading international brands within the fixed phone line and mobile telecommunications, free-to-air, pay-TV broadcasting, publishing as well as financial services industries. As a subsidiary of MTG, Metro became profitable after only one year in operation. In order to secure its expansion, Metro International SA was first incorporated in Luxemburg as a holding company for all Metro operations. In 2000 the company was listed on both the Stockholm and New York stock exchanges, while it is still controlled by the Kinnevik Group.

The first edition of Metro was published in Stockholm and distributed in the Stockholm underground. The concept of the free commuter paper was developed in Sweden in 1992. However, it took three years to convince investors and the Stockholm public transport system to support the new paper. Today the newspaper is still primarily distributed through public transport systems while the newspaper's name may vary due to trademark issues. For instance the Chilean and Mexican editions are called Publimetro and the Danish Metro is named MetroXpress.

All Metro editions carry headline local, national and international news in a standardized and accessible format and design, which enables commuters to read the newspaper during a typical journey time of less than 20 minutes. Metro's editorial content aims at being independent and focuses on giving readers the news they need at the time they read, rather than comment or views. Following this strategy Metro has become the largest and fastest-growing international newspaper in the world. Seventy daily Metro editions are published in more than 100 major cities in 21 countries in 19 languages across Europe, North and South America and Asia. Metro has a unique global reach and attracts a young, active, well-educated audience of more than 20 million daily readers and over 42 million weekly readers. Metro has an equal number of male and female readers, of which 70 per cent are under 45 years of age. This demographic group does not typically read a daily newspaper but is most attractive for advertisers. By targeting a new generation of newspaper readers Metro's advertising sales have grown at a compound annual growth rate of 41 per cent since the first edition was launched in 1995.

However, not every Metro launch has been a success. Operations in Switzerland, Argentina and the UK were terminated after some time, while a free afternoon paper (almost every free newspaper is a morning paper) in Stockholm was closed within a few months of its launch. Furthermore, while profitability goals have been reached by almost every edition within three years, overall profits have not been realized by the company so far. The high launching costs and the interest on loans used for these launches have contributed to this.

Human resource management practices

When the research was conducted, Metro employed around 1500 people, of which 500 were part of the editorial staff (journalists, photographers and editors) and 750 were salespeople. There were also employees in the distribution area. Although the company grew rather rapidly the working style has remained very informal. Efforts have been made to maintain the entrepreneurial spirit of the start-up. In order to foster the entrepreneurial orientation, managing directors delegated responsibility for the projects to their employees. Because of their small size, empowerment measures were also facilitated at Metro headquarters. Further, as MTG supported its staff when they came up with the idea of a free newspaper, Metro has also supported a research project called Metro Life Panel. With this employees have created a panel of online readers which has been expanded to seven countries and includes 20 000 readers. Readers give their opinion on advertisements in the newspaper and these are used to improve both the newspaper, which can be more customer-oriented, and the advertising performance. Readership statistics can also be obtained through readers' online registrations, and this data is then sold as research services. This activity has the potential for spin-off should it become profitable.

New staff were acquired according to their fit with the entrepreneurial and informal organizational culture of Metro. Usually managing staff were recruited from the radio, Internet or magazine industry. There Metro could source professionals who were fresh to, and therefore challenged by, the newspaper business. The sales employees were acquired from any part of the media industry. The criteria for their recruitment was youth and an aggressive attitude. In the editorial department positions of editors-in-chief were mostly filled with experienced journalists who were bored with traditional ways of working in other newspaper companies. The Metro editor-in-chief in Denmark was editor of a traditional Danish newspaper company. After four years as editor-in-chief and managing director at Metro he became global editor-in-chief and then left for a position as CEO at the Danish TV2.

With regard to personnel development Metro holds two formally organized conferences each year: one for the sales staff and managing directors and the other for the editorial and distribution staff. During these conferences, which usually run for three days, staff are informed about company results and any new goals. In addition award ceremonies for outstanding achievements take place. Metro promoted a management programme, which was open to all the staff, allowing skilled and dedicated employees to speed up their career by following a fast-track training as assistants to the CEO. Through this programme one trainee became an Executive Vice

President after four years. In the sales department staff were offered the opportunity to attend the sales training academy.

Compensation at Metro was based on sales volume for the sales staff, while for managers and marketing people the company offered bonuses related to the overall company performance as well as personal performance. For the editorial staff Metro did not provide specific compensation measures as it was apparent to the staff that working for Metro was already a great experience. Moreover it was thought that compensation incentives could affect the overall content quality.

In order for the HRM function to be successfully implemented at Metro, a Vice President for HRM was appointed at the headquarters and in each country location.

Discussion and conclusions

Both the Ellibs and the Metro case studies show the importance of HRM practices, if in different ways. Still being in an early stage of its development, Ellibs relies on a very informal HRM. However, its application is very clear. The founder tries to minimize the risk of hiring the wrong people by looking for skilled employees within his network of social and business relations. This method appears to have been successful so far as only one person left the company, and therefore turnover is low. In order to keep fixed costs under control the company's compensation system is based on low salaries complemented by performance-related bonuses. Empowerment is encouraged through the delegation of responsibility and giving employees choice over the type of project they wish to work on. Flexible working time is also used to motivate employees. The employee development programme stimulates knowledge transfer and learning processes.

At Metro the HRM system looks more established, and some of its features already have a formal character. This stresses the importance the company puts on HRM and their goal-oriented management. Despite the fact that it is already 11 years old, the working style remains very informal and is based on empowering employees. Staff are acquired according to their fit with the entrepreneurial orientation of the company. Metro counts on its image as being an unconventional and fast-growing company, which seems to appeal to young and ambitious potential employees. For managerial and sales staff, compensation is based on a fixed salary and complemented by bonuses. Training and development is considered critical. In fact, formal measures such as informational conferences, the management executive programme and the sales training academy are part of the firm's culture. Multi-tasking and role transition practices take place regularly as staff are promoted to different departments and sometimes to different countries. Furthermore, a multi-skill strategy is supported by the acquisition of staff coming from different parts of the media industries, not only newspapers. This also permits the firm to pursue multi-media development, which is necessary for the future of newspapers. The leadership style at Metro encourages innovative ideas, and is proving to be successful both for keeping an entrepreneurial spirit within the company and for enhancing innovation and firm growth.

A limitation of this study can be in the selection of cases which may suffer from a cultural bias: one firm is Swedish and the other is Finnish. They are therefore influenced by the Scandinavian social culture. As all organizations exist within a framework of national cultures, different historical traditions and political systems influence the way organizations come into existence and operate. Every effort to introduce standardized modern instruments of HRM will therefore be impacted by national factors.

As stated earlier, the aim of this chapter was to understand if and how HRM practices can foster growth in new and young firms as well as stimulate entrepreneurial spirit within more established firms. The exploration of HRM in the two case study firms and the review of the existing literature concerning HRM practices in rapidly-growing firms, points out that with their financial resources constrained, new and young firms would benefit from a thoughtful application of HRM measures. Recruiting personnel from pre-existing social and business networks is not expensive and allows firms to avoid the risk of hiring the wrong employees. The development of a compensation structure based on a modest salary plus profit as well as stock-sharing oriented bonuses represents both a motivational factor for employees and a way for emerging firms to share the risk with their staff. Furthermore, stock options give the employees a highly motivating feeling of being themselves entrepreneurs. By offering employees stimulating assignments and delegating responsibilities while assuring a coaching presence allows the entrepreneur to be a charismatic but motivational leader. Finally, emphasizing the development of multi-tasking skills and role transitions makes employees feel they are considered important. At the same time this prevents young firms from relying only on highly competent and experienced employees, whose departure would mean a loss of key competences and replacement problems for the company.

HRM practices appear to be highly important for established firms, too. Their main concern is not the lack of resources. On the contrary, the abundance of resources may cause a lack of entrepreneurial creativity as no urgency for innovation is felt. HRM measures might therefore help incumbents to re-introduce or keep alive some entrepreneurial spirit and act proactively.

References

Aldrich, H.E. and M.A. Von Glinow (1991), 'Business start-ups: The HRM imperative', in S. Subramony (ed.), *International Perspectives on Entrepreneurship Research, Vol. 18*, New York: Elsevier Science Publishers, pp. 233–53.

Alexander, S. (1999), 'Recruiting big as a small shop', *Computer World*, **33**, 55.

Amabile, T.M. (1996), *Creativity in Context*, Boulder, CO: Westview Press.

Arthur, D. (1995) *Managing Human Resources in Small and Mid-sized Companies*, New York: American Management Association.

Balkin, D.B. and J.W. Logan (1988) 'Reward policies that support entrepreneurship', *Compensation and Benefit Review*, **20**(1), 18–25.

Balkin, D.B. and M. Swift (2006), 'Top management team compensation in high-growth technology ventures', *Human Resource Management Review*, **16**, 1–11.

Balkin, D.B., G.D. Markman and L.R. Gomez-Mejia (2000), 'Is CEO pay in high technology firms related to innovation?', *Academy of Management Journal*, **43**, 1118–29.

Banks, M.C., A.L. Bures and D.L. Champion (1987), 'Decision making factors in small business: Training and development', *Journal of Small Business Management*, **25**, 19–25.

Barney, J. (1991), 'Firm resources and sustained competitive advantage', *Journal of Management*, **17**, 99–120.

Baron, J.N. and M.T. Hannan (2002), 'Organizational blueprints for success in high-tech start-ups: Lessons from the Stanford project on emerging companies', *California Management Review*, **13**, 253-6.

Barringer, B.R., F.F. Jones and D.O. Neubaum (2005), 'A quantitative content analysis of the characteristics of rapid-growth firms and their founders', *Journal of Business Venturing*, **20**, 663–87.

Beitz, H. and A. Loch (1996), 'Assessment Center, Erfolgstips und übungen für Bewerberinnen und Bewerber', 3rd edn, Niedernhausen: Falken Verlag GmbH.

Brown, T.E. (1996), 'Resource orientation, entrepreneurial orientation and growth: How the perception of resource availability affects small firm growth', Unpublished Dissertation, Rutgers University, Newark, NJ.

Brüderl, J., P. Preisendörfer and R. Ziegler (1998), 'Der Erfolg neu gegründeter Betriebe: Eine empirische Studie zu den Chancen und Risiken von Unternehmensgründungen', 2nd edn, Berlin: Duncker & Humblot.

Cacioppe, R. (1997), 'Leadership moment by moment!', *Leadership and Organization Development Journal*, **18**(7), 335–45.

Cardon, M.S. (2003), 'Contingent labor as an enabler of entrepreneurial growth', *Human Resource Management Journal*, **42**(4), 357–73.

Cardon, M.S. and C.E. Stevens (2004), 'Managing human resources in small organizations: What do we know?' *Human Resource Management Review*, **14**, 295–323.

Cardon, M.S. and P. Tolchinsky (2006), 'To hire or not to hire? Implications of alternative staffing models for emerging organizations', in J.W. Tansky and R.L. Heneman (eds), *Human Resource Strategies for the High Growth Entrepreneurial Firm*, Greenwich, CT: Information Age Publishing, pp. 69–98.

Chandler, G., B. Honig and J. Wiklund (2005), 'Antecedents, moderators and performance consequences of membership change in new venture teams', *Journal of Business Venturing*, **20**, 705–25.

Chao, G.T. (1997), 'Unstructured training and development: The role of organizational socialization', in J.K. Ford (ed.), *Improving Training Effectiveness in Work Organizations*, Mahwah, NJ: Erlbaum.

Comelli, G. and von Rosenstiel, L. (1995), *Führung durch Motivation*, Munich: Vahlen.

Cooke, F., J. Shen and McBride, A. (2005), 'Outsourcing HR as a competitive strategy? A literature review and an assessment of implications', *Human Resource Management*, **44**(4), 413–32.

Covin, J.G. and M.P. Miles (1999), 'Corporate entrepreneurship and the pursuit of competitive advantage', *Entrepreneurship Theory and Practice*, **23**(3), 47–63.

Dal Zotto, C. (2001), *Die Simultaneität und Permanenz von Personal- und Organisationsentwicklung*, Frankfurt/Main: Peter Lang.

Darling, J., M. Gabrielsson and H. Seristö (2007), 'Enhancing contemporary entrepreneurship: A focus on management leaders', *European Business Review*, **19**, 4–22.

Denzin, N.K. and Y.S. Lincoln (1994), 'Introduction: Entering the field of qualitative research', in N.K. Denzin and Y.S. Lincoln (eds), *Handbook of Qualitative Research*, Newbury Park, CA: Sage Publications.

Deshpande, S.P. and D.Y. Golhar (1994), 'HRM practices in large and small manufacturing firms: A comparative study', *Journal of Small Business Management*, **32**(2), 49–56.

Drumm, H.J. (2003), 'Personalwirtschaft für Gründer', in M. Dowling and H.J. Drumm (eds), *Gründungsmanagement*, 2nd edn, Berlin: Springer Verlag.

Eisenhardt, K.M. (1989), 'Building theories from case study research', *Academy of Management Review*, **14**, 532–50.

Fong, P. (2003), 'Knowledge creation in multidisciplinary project teams: An empirical study of the processes and their dynamic interrelationships', *International Journal of Project Management*, **21**, 479–86.

Gartner, W.B. (1988), ' "Who is an entrepreneur?" Is the wrong question', *American Journal of Small Business*, **12**, 11–31.

George, J. and G. Jones (2005), *Understanding and Managing Organizational Behavior*, 4th edn, Upper Saddle River, NJ.: Pearson Prentice Hall.

Graham, M.E., B. Murray and L. Amuso (2002), 'Stock-related rewards, social identity, and attraction and retention of employees in entrepreneurial SMEs', in J.A. Katz and T.M. Welbourne (eds), *Managing People in Entrepreneurial Organizations, Volume 5*, Amsterdam: JAI Press, pp. 107–45.

Granovetter, M. (1973), 'The strength of weak ties', *American Journal of Sociology*, **78**, 1360–80.

Guth, W.D. and A. Ginsberg (1990), 'Guest editors' introduction: Corporate entrepreneurship', *Strategic Management Journal*, **11**, 5–15.

Hannan, M.T. and J. Freeman (1984), 'The population ecology of organizations', *American Sociological Review*, **49**, 149–64.

Hayton, J.C. (2005), 'Promoting corporate entrepreneurship through human resource management practices: A review of empirical research', *Human Resource Management Review*, **15**, 21–41.

Hébert, R.F. and A.N Link (1988), *The Entrepreneur – Mainstream Views and Radical Critiques*, New York: Praeger.

Heneman, R.L. and J.W. Tansky (2002), 'Human resource management models for entrepreneurial opportunity', in J.A. Katz and T.M. Welbourne (eds), *Managing People in Entrepreneurial Organization: Learning from the Merger of Entrepreneurship and Human Resource Management*, Boston: JAI Press, pp. 54–81.

Katz, J.A., H.E. Aldrich, T.M. Welbourne and P. Williams (2000), 'Guest editors' comments. Special issue on human resource management and the SME: Towards a new synthesis', *Entrepreneurship: Theory and Practice*, **25**, 7–10.

Klaas, B. (2003), 'Professional employer organizations and their role in small and medium enterprises: The impact of HR outsourcing', *Entrepreneurship: Theory and Practice*, **28**, 43–61.

Klaas, B.S., J.A. McClendon and T. Gainey (2000), 'Managing HR in the small and medium enterprise: The impact of professional employer organizations', *Entrepreneurship: Theory and Practice*, **25**(1), 107–23.

Klaas, B.S., H. Yang, T. Gainey and J.A. McClendon (2005), 'HR in the small business enterprise: Assessing the impact of PEO utilization', *Human Resource Management*, **44**(4), 433–48.

Kuratko, D.F., R.D. Ireland, J.G. Covin and J.S. Hornsby (2005), 'A model of middle-managers' entrepreneurial behaviour', *Entrepreneurship: Theory and Practice*, **29**, 699–716.

Leung, A., J. Zhang, P.K. Wong and M.D. Foo (2006), 'The use of networks in human resource acquisition for entrepreneurial firms: Multiple "fit" considerations', *Journal of Business Venturing*, **21**, 664–86.

Lindlof, T.R. (1995), *Qualitative Communication Research Methods*, 3rd edn, Thousand Oaks: Sage Publications.

Longenecker, J.G., C.W. Moore and J.W. Petty (1994), *Small Business Management: An Entrepreneurial Emphasis*, Cincinnati: South Western.
Luchsinger, V. and D.R. Bagby (1987), 'Entrepreneurship and intrapreneurship: Behaviors, comparisons and contrasts', *SAM Advanced Management Journal*, **52**(3), 10–13.
Marlow, S. (1997), 'The employment environment and smaller firms', *International Journal of Entrepreneurial Behaviour and Research*, **3**(4), 143–8.
Martins, E.C. and F. Terblanche (2003), 'Building organizational culture that stimulates creativity and innovation', *European Journal of Innovation Management*, **6**, 64–74.
Maxwell, J.A. (1998), 'Designing a qualitative study', in L. Bickman and D.J. Rog (eds), *Handbook of Applied Social Research Methods*, Thousand Oaks: Sage Publications, pp. 69–100.
May, K. (1997), 'Work in the 21st century: Understanding the needs of small businesses', *Industrial and Organizational Psychologist*, **35**(1), 94–7.
McLagan, P. and C. Nel (1995), *The Age of Participation*, San Francisco, CA.: Berrett-Koehler.
Morris, M., M. Schindehutte and R. LaForge (2004), 'The emergence of entrepreneurial marketing: Nature and meaning', in H. Welsch (ed.), *Entrepreneurship: The Way Ahead*, New York: Routledge, pp. 91–104.
Morris, M.H. and F.F. Jones (1993), 'Human resource management practices and corporate entrepreneurship: An empirical assessment from the USA', *International Journal of Human Resource Management*, **4**, 873–96.
Mumford, M., G. Scott, B. Gaddis and J. Strange (2002), 'Leading creative people: Orchestrating expertise and relationships', *The Leadership Quarterly*, **13**, 705–50.
Niedhof, S.D. (1999), 'Start-ups brauchen Führungskompetenz', *Personalwirtschaft*, no. 11, 70–72.
Oldham, G.R. and A. Cummings (1996), 'Employee creativity: Personal and contextual factors', *Academy of Management Journal*, **39**, 607–34.
Pettigrew, A. (1997), 'What is a processual analysis?', *Scandinavian Journal of Management*, **13**, 337–48.
Pinchot, G. III (1985), *Intrapreneuring: Why You Don't Have to Leave the Corporation to Become an Entrepreneur*, New York: HarperCollins.
Polanyi, M. (1967), *The Tacit Dimension*, New York: Anchor Books.
Schumpeter, J. (1934), *The History of Economic Development*, Cambridge, MA: Harvard University Press.
Shane, S. and S. Venkataraman (2000), 'The promise of entrepreneurship as a field of research', *Academy of Management Review*, **25**, 217–26.
Sharma, P. and J.J. Chrisman (1999), 'Toward a reconciliation of the definitional issues in the field of corporate entrepreneurship', *Entrepreneurship: Theory and Practice*, **23**, 11–27.
Stake, R.E. (1995), *The Art of Case Study Research*, London: Sage Publications.
Stevenson, H.H. and W.A. Sahlman (1989), *Small Business and Entrepreneurship*, New York: MacMillan Education Ltd.
Stinchcombe, A.L. (1965), 'Social structure and organizations', in J.D. March (ed.), *Handbook of Organizations*, Chicago, IL: Rand McNally, pp. 153–93.
Swiercz, P.M. and S.R. Lydon (2002), 'Entrepreneurial leadership in high-tech firms: A field study', *Leadership and Organizational Development Journal*, **23**(7), 380–89.
Timmons, J. (1999), *New Venture Creation: Entrepreneurship for the 21st Century*, Homewood, IL: Irwin-McGraw Hill.
Wiklund, J. (1998), 'Small firm growth and performance: Entrepreneurship and beyond', Doctoral Dissertation, Jönköping International Business School, Jönköping.
Williamson, I.O., D.M. Cable and H.E. Aldrich (2002), 'Smaller but not necessarily weaker: How small businesses can overcome barriers to recruitment', in J.A. Katz and T.M. Welbourne (eds), *Advances in Entrepreneurship, Firm Emergence and Firm Growth*, Greenwich, CT: JAI Press, pp. 83–10.
Woodman, R.W. (1995), 'Managing creativity', in D.A. Gioia, C.M. Ford, D. Bjorkegren, K.E. Sveiby and H. Nystrom (eds), *Creative Action in Organizations: Ivory Tower Visions and Real World Voices*, Thousand Oaks, CA: Sage Publications, pp. 60–64.

Zahra, S.A. (1996), 'Governance, ownership and corporate entrepreneurship: The moderating impact of industry technological opportunities', *Academy of Management Journal*, **39**, 1713–35.
Ziegler, R. (2000), 'Überlebens- und Erfolgschancen neu gegründete Betriebe in den alten und den neuen Bundesländern', in G. Büttler, H Herrman, W. Scheffler and K.-I. Voigt (eds), *Existenzgründung, Rahmenbedingungen und Strategien*, Heidelberg: Physica Verlag, pp. 33–48.

6 The formality and informality of HRM practices in small firms
Rowena Barrett and Susan Mayson

Introduction

The nature of human resource management in small firms is understood to be characterized by ad hoc and idiosyncratic practices. The liability of smallness (Heneman and Berkley, 1999) and resource poverty (Welsh and White, 1981) presents unique challenges to managing human resources in small firms. The inability to achieve economies of scale can mean that implementing formalized HRM practices is costly in terms of time and money for small firms (Sels et al., 2006a; 2006b). These, combined with small firm owner–managers' lack of strategic capabilities and awareness (Hannon and Atherton, 1998) and a lack of managerial resources and expertise in HRM (Cardon and Stevens, 2004) can lead to informal and ad hoc HRM practices. For some this state of affairs is interpreted as problematic as the normative and formalized HRM practices in the areas of recruitment, selection, appraisal, training and rewards are not present (see Marlow, 2006 and Taylor, 2006 for a critique). However, a more nuanced analysis of the small firm and its practices in their context can tell a different story (Barrett and Rainnie, 2002; Harney and Dundon, 2006).

In this chapter we contribute to our understanding of small firm management practices by investigating a series of questions in relation to HRM in small firms. The purpose is to understand what HRM practices are used in small firms and how they are applied. In light of the debates about the applicability of more formalized large-firm models of HRM in small firms, we particularly focus on the notion of formality and consider how this might emerge in small-firm HRM practice. We do this through interviews with owner–managers of 11 small firms in Victoria, Australia. Our concern is not simply whether or not practices are formalized, but with the logic of formalization or its purpose and look to older ideas about bureaucracy to pursue this.

In the next sections we outline our methodology and the context within which the study took place. Understanding the context is important as Australia has quite a particular system of industrial relations which affects the way firms frame terms and conditions of employment. We will outline some of the more pertinent changes occurring in the IR system at the time

111

we undertook the study. We follow this with a discussion of our findings and in the final section we explore the logic of formalization and suggest avenues for future research.

The study
Similar to other developed Western economies, Australian small firms are important contributors to the economy and they dominate all private sector industries as well as playing a significant role in rural and regional economies and communities. However, because Australian small firms are defined as firms that employ less than 20 employees, the small business population is large and heterogeneous. In number, they make up 97 per cent or 1.23 million firms in the Australian private sector (ABS, 2005) and they make a large contribution as a source of employment. Underlining the importance of understanding small firm management practices, particularly their HRM practices, it is important to note that nearly 3.6 million people work in private sector non-agricultural small firms, with 30 per cent as owner–managers or self-employed and 70 per cent as employees (ABS, 2005).

In this chapter we report on an analysis of qualitative interview data collected from a small sample of 11 firms. These firms were drawn from a group who volunteered to be involved out of a larger group of 410 small firms in Victoria (SE Australia) which participated in our survey of small business HRM practices in late 2004 (see Barrett and Mayson, 2005; Barrett, Mayson and Warriner, Chapter 9, this handbook). The sample was restricted to Victoria as a single industrial relations system operates in this state which is in contrast to the situation in other Australian states where dual Federal/State systems operate.

The questionnaire results for the 11 firms are used in this chapter as a basis to move beyond 'what' small firms' owner–managers say they do, to a more interpretivist analysis of 'how' and 'why' they do the things they do. Such an approach enabled us to address Curran and Blackburn's (2001) comment that very few studies of small business go beyond the question of 'what' (for example, 'what HRM practices are used' or 'what aspects of HRM are perceived as a "problem"'). We explore the how and why through the analysis of in-depth semi-structured interviews conducted with owners or owner–managers who volunteered to be interviewed for the study. Interviews were conducted between November 2005 and March 2006, while questions covered organizational and owner demographics, issues employers encountered when managing staff, existence of and responsibility for HRM policies, how they were used, and the relationship between HRM and business goals. This allowed us to explore not only what employers did to recruit, select, motivate and retain their employees but how this worked in practice. Importantly, exploring survey results through qualitative interviews permits an interpretivist approach that has much to offer theory development (see Cassell and Nadin, Chapter 4, this handbook) because the approach generates a richness of understanding (Weick, 2007) of the practical realities of small-firm management.

All interviews were tape recorded and transcribed. The data was analysed manually using a coding sheet derived from the interview schedule and key themes identified from the literature review. After initial coding, the data was categorized into key themes using a simple count (number of respondents). The coding was cross-checked by the authors to ensure that identified themes accurately reflected the patterns found in the data. Given the small sample size, a manual process, rather than a more automated system, was deemed appropriate. Such an approach enabled analysis of themes within and across interviews (Miles and Huberman, 1994).

The context
To contextualize the study it is important to understand the industrial relations (IR) environment at the time when the interviews were being conducted as this affects the regulatory environment in which human resources are managed. We will only focus on two aspects, while more comprehensive accounts of the IR system and changes to it can be found in Sappey et al. (2006) and Hall (2006 and 2007).

In 1996 the Victorian state government referred the majority of its IR powers to the Commonwealth government. But despite Victorian firms falling within the jurisdiction of the *Workplace Relations Act* 1996 (Commonwealth) many, and mainly small firms, would have had their employees' terms and conditions of employment covered by the five minimum conditions set out in Schedule 1A of that Act. To improve the conditions of the 350 000 or so Schedule 1A employees in Victoria, legislation was passed to enable the spread of federal awards (which specify minimum terms and conditions of employment for industries or occupations) through the implementation of common rule awards. During 2005 common rule awards commenced operation in Victoria. This meant that on 1 January 2005 in firms where employees were not already covered by a federal award or agreement, an existing federal award was declared to operate as common rule. This applied to all employers and employees in a particular industry or occupation who were performing the type of work outlined in the classifications of the award. The majority of firms affected would have been small firms as they are least likely to have already been covered by a federal award. The effect of common rule awards would be to force many small-firm owners to have a look at the terms and conditions of employment they offered against those specified in common rule awards.

Additionally during the period leading up to and during the interviews there was extensive national debate around the federal government's ongoing neo-liberal IR reforms and the proposed WorkChoices legislation. This came into effect on 27 March 2006 and had a number of implications for incorporated firms (see Hall, 2006 and 2007). In particular the effect for small firms, or those employing less than 100 employees, was an exemption from the unfair dismissal provisions in the legislation. Also under this new legislation the number of allowable matters that could be retained in awards was reduced and this meant more employment matters were to be subject to negotiation and bargaining at the workplace. Furthermore, minimum wage rates were to be excluded from awards and instead would be set and adjusted by the new Australian Fair Pay Commission (see https://www.workchoices.gov.au/ourplan/). The effect of these changes was to put pressure on all firms, but especially small firms which have traditionally relied on the award system, to begin to take greater responsibility for their own employment relations. This is the context in which this study was conducted.

Demographics of the small firms
Table 6.1 summarizes key demographic information about each of the firms drawn from the questionnaire data. The table shows that six firms, MaterialCo, WoodCo, RoadCo, AirCo, PrintCo and GardenCo operated in the manufacturing sector. The nature of the work within them ranged from unskilled work such as packing work in a warehouse (for example, GardenCo and TileCo) to highly technical work such as developing infrared business and safety applications at TechCo and aircraft engineering at AirCo. As indicated earlier, the legal form of the business has implications for whether firms would be affected by the WorkChoices legislation. Incorporated businesses such as MaterialCo, WoodCo, TechCo, MoneyCo, TileCo, ExecCo, AirCo, PrintCo and GardenCo potentially faced substantial changes to their employment practices whereas RoadCo and LandCo, being family businesses and operating as trusts, would not be affected.

In Australia, small firms are defined as firms that employ less than 20 employees. As Table 6.1 shows, the number of people employed in these firms ranged from seven in MaterialCo to 18 in AirCo, GardenCo and PrintCo. The average number of people employed was 14.7. The majority of the businesses were founded by their current owner. The oldest business, MaterialCo, was established in 1937 and the youngest, WoodCo, was established in 1996. The average age of the firms was 21.7 years.

In terms of these firms' size and age compared to the general population of small firms in Australia, they are older and larger than the average Australian small business. For example, some 56.3 per cent of Australian

Table 6.1 Sample firm demographics*

	Business activity	Year business established	Legal form	2004 total number employed	2003–2004 change in employment	Owner's entry to business	2004 sales revenue	2003–2004 sales revenue	Interviewee Nov 2005– March 2006
MaterialCo	Textile distribution	1937	Private company	7	Same	Bought business in 1999	A$1–2 million	Increased 1–5%	Owner–manager
WoodCo	Manufacture wood panels	1996	Private company	11	Decrease	Owner founded	A$1–2 million	No change	Owner–manager
LandCo	Landscape design	1991	Trust	14	Same	Owner founded	A$1–2 million	Increased 6–10%	Director
TechCo	Infra-red technology applications	1988	Private company	14	Same	Bought business in 2001	A$1–2 million	Increased 10%+	Owner–manager
MoneyCo	Finance brokerage	1984	Private company	14	Increase	Owner founded	A$0.5–1 million	Increased 10%+	Owner
TileCo	Import and wholesale tiles	1993	Private company	15	Increase	Owner founded	A$5 million +	Increased 10%+	Internal HRM 'expert'
RoadCo	Civil construction	1992	Trust	15	Increase	Owner founded	A$5 million +	Increased 1–5%	Internal HRM 'expert'
ExecCo	Executive search and recruitment	1992	Private company	18	Increase	Owner founded	A$1–2 million	Increased 10%+	Manager

Table 6.1 (continued)

	Business activity	Year business established	Legal form	2004 total number employed	2003–2004 change in employment	Owner's entry to business	2004 sales revenue	2003–2004 sales revenue	Interviewee Nov 2005–March 2006
AirCo	Aircraft electronics service and repair	1988	Private company	18	Decrease	Owner founded	A$5 million +	Decreased 5%+	Manager
PrintCo	Commercial printing	1988	Private company	18	Same	Bought business in 1999	A$2–5 million	Increased 10%+	Owner–manager
GardenCo	Wholesale horticultural supplies and gardenware	1978	Private company	18	Increase	Bought business in 1980	A$5 million +	Increased 10%+	Owner–manager

Note: * Columns 1–8 based on responses to questionnaire in August 2004 (see Barrett, Mayson and Warriner, Chapter 9 in this handbook for full details of the survey and findings).

small firms employ no one and only 10.9 per cent employ between five to 19 employees (ABS, 2005). In terms of age, in June 2004 some 33.5 per cent of all Australian small businesses were less than five years old, although they do get larger as they get older (ABS, 2005). Research tells us that firms of increased size and age have an increased chance of survival as the liabilities of newness and smallness have been overcome, accommodated or neutralized (Aldrich, 1999). Arguably firms of increased size are also more likely to have formalized HRM practices in place as a response to the increased complexity that comes from greater numbers of employees.

We have argued elsewhere (Barrett and Mayson, 2005; 2007 and Barrett, Mayson and Warriner, Chapter 9, this handbook) that growth is a salient factor in the formalization of HRM practices in small firms. In the survey, we asked questions about firm growth. The responses to these questions were captured in the two measures reported in Table 6.1: change in employment numbers and change in sales revenue. Gathering data on multiple growth indicators, particularly those related to sales and employment, provides richer information (Birley and Westhead, 1990; Davidsson and Wiklund, 2000; Weinzimmer et al., 1998) than relying on a single measure. It also recognizes that employment and revenue growth measures do not necessarily correlate. As research has indicated, increased employment, for example, can have a negative impact on profitability but positive impact on sales performance (Smallbone and Wyer, 2000). Furthermore, as firms do not all grow in the same way, data on a variety of growth measures can help us better understand the growth process (Delmar et al., 2003).

An examination of Table 6.1 shows that in 2003–4 there were five firms – MoneyCo, TileCo, RoadCo, ExecCo and GardenCo – growing in terms of both employment and sales revenue. While interview questions did not address sales revenue, given the sensitive nature of financial information in small firms, we did find that between the time of the questionnaire responses and the interview TileCo, RoadCo, ExecCo and AirCo had each increased their staffing by two or three employees.

Of the two firms reporting a decrease in employment and decrease and/or no change in sales revenue on the questionnaire – AirCo and WoodCo – only WoodCo had decreased employee numbers (by three). In contrast, at AirCo the situation had changed since the questionnaire and they were slowly growing their employment because of increased sales. The manager explained, 'Oh well it has been a rather gradual thing, up until probably about 18 months ago, where we've tried to increase staff due to the workload. We'd still like to have probably another 5 to 7 people' (Interview, AirCo).

We would expect that different HRM issues would arise in firms based on whether they were growing or not (Huang and Brown, 1999). And while the literature commonly refers to HRM problems related to attracting and retaining skilled staff (see Deshpande and Golhar, 1994), at WoodCo the downturn in business brought on by cheap Chinese imports meant staff needed to be 'put off'. This was being carefully managed by the firm so that their reputation as an 'employer of choice' in the regional town in which they operated was not affected. As the owner–manager said, 'everyone knows everyone so employment issues become public knowledge very quickly' (Interview, WoodCo).

Business practices

Planning in small firms is generally ad hoc, and planning documents are often produced for one-off finance purposes rather than as strategic documents used to guide business decisions (Gibb and Scott, 1985; Hannon and Atherton, 1998). Our survey asked questions about firms' use of business and staffing plans, and Table 6.2 lists whether in the firms we studied there

Table 6.2   Planning and HRM*

	Does the business have or use a formal business plan?	Does the business have or use a staffing plan with dedicated budget?	Who primarily provides HRM advice to this business?
MaterialCo	Yes	No	Independent business consultant or lawyer
WoodCo	Yes	Yes	Internal HRM 'expert'
LandCo	Yes	No	Accountant
TechCo	Yes	No	Independent business consultant or lawyer
MoneyCo	Yes	No	Independent business consultant or lawyer
TileCo	No	No	Internal HRM 'expert'
RoadCo	Yes	No	Internal HRM 'expert'
ExecCo	Yes	Yes	Accountant
AirCo	No	No	Industry or employer association
PrintCo	No	No	Industry or employer association
GardenCo	Yes	No	Industry or employer association

Note: * Based on responses to survey and interview questions. See Barrett, Mayson and Warriner (Chapter 9 in this handbook) for full details of the survey and findings.

was a formal business plan and/or staffing plan with dedicated budget, and who provided them with HRM advice. A formal business plan was defined as a document which sets out business goals and means of achieving them. Table 6.2 shows that in eight of the 11 firms such a plan existed. In the interview at PrintCo – one of the firms without a business plan – the owner reported that he was under pressure from one of his new managers who 'wants to formalize the business plan as we have been operating for 16 and a half years without one, but that isn't advisable because it's in here [pointing to his head]' (Interview, PrintCo). In the interviews at AirCo and TileCo, the other two businesses which reported on the questionnaire not to have a business plan, this was no longer the case. In both firms the owners were responsible for the business plan and the managers we spoke to had no formal role or input in the development of those plans. As one manager explained, 'it is not something that I would have any influence over' (Interview, TileCo).

The informal and ad hoc nature of planning in small firms may contribute to firms' inability to grow (see Barrett and Mayson, 2005; 2007; Barrett et al., Chapter 9, this handbook). Table 6.2 also shows that in only two firms was a staffing plan with a dedicated budget said to exist. Consistent with the literature, the rationale for such a plan at ExecCo was explained by the manager as necessary to support the firm's growth strategy (Interview, ExecCo). In contrast, as indicated above, at WoodCo the plan was used by the internal HRM expert to preserve the firm's reputation and to manage the negative impact on staffing costs that the competitive pressure from cheap Chinese imports was exerting on the firm (Interview, WoodCo).

The interviews did, however, reveal additional information around firms' planning and staffing activities and while few firms had a staffing plan with a dedicated budget, it became apparent in the interviews that considerable costing around various human resource issues and activities was undertaken. At MoneyCo, for example, while there was said to be neither a formal business plan nor a staffing plan, the owner did update cash flow projections every three months which included updating the staffing budget and costs (Interview, MoneyCo).

Small firms rarely have managerial resources and expertise in HRM or employment matters (Chandler and McEvoy, 2000; Hornsby and Kuratko, 1990; Klaas et al., 2000; Kotey and Sheridan, 2001; McEvoy, 1984; McLarty, 1999). In only three firms was someone dedicated to the function. At RoadCo, part of the responsibility of the HR expert, who was the owner's son and a recent HRM graduate, was to create an HR manual, which he had done (Interview, RoadCo). He had also implemented a training plan which was fully costed.

At TileCo there was an internal HRM expert who had been appointed three years previously to replace the owner's wife after she had convinced her husband that the job was too big for her (Interview, TileCo). The complexity of the job was demonstrated by a story the HR manager told about his first day at TileCo, when he was called upon to break up a fight between one of their sales representatives and a storeman. After looking in the firm's HR manual to see how to deal with the fight he found 'it was completely silent about things like respect, honesty and behavioural stuff . . . nothing in your duty statement says you are entitled to snot someone' (Interview, TileCo). This was his cue for revising the whole manual. Interestingly, because he only worked part-time, he was not responsible for a range of key HRM activities. For example, he relied on supervisors to tell him when more staff were needed and then left the recruitment process to management. He adapted to this situation by focusing on the administration and orientation needs of new hires, as he explained, 'at the point they [management] hire, I do the documentation and start them [new employees] up' (Interview, TileCo).

HRM practices
We argue in this chapter that in light of the literature, while we might know something of the number or lack of HRM activities found in small firms we know very little about the reasons why such practices may or may not exist, and if they do exist, why and how they operate in the small-firm context. The interviews reported on in this chapter explicitly focus on how and why these practices were used. Table 6.3 shows the HRM practices as reported in the questionnaire and interviews for each of the firms interviewed.

Recruitment activities in small firms are typically unplanned, informal and as McEvoy (1984) argues, 'unimaginative'. It generally follows that owners or managers of small firms like to maintain direct control of recruitment and they employ practices that are convenient and inexpensive (Heneman and Berkley, 1999). In our survey we asked questions about recruitment practices and methods and these questions were followed up in the interviews. The responses are summarized in Table 6.3.

Table 6.3 shows that a common practice was to use a list of skills or qualifications in the hiring process. For example in RoadCo formal recruitment and selection practices were needed to ensure road crew employees had the necessary and current licences to operate heavy machinery on the job. For some jobs at RoadCo, GardenCo and AirCo, information about the completion of an apprenticeship had to be verified before successful applicants could begin work. In some firms, recruits with higher level qualifications needed to be attracted for some positions. For example at MoneyCo employees needed not only to have specialized knowledge of banking and finances, but also to have completed statutory compliance training. At TechCo the

Table 6.3   *HRM practices**

	Use list of skills/quals when recruiting?	Main recruitment method used?	Main selection method used?	How wages and conditions specified?	Rate for employees' wages?	How are valued employees rewarded?	Performance appraised on regular basis?	Type of training mainly offered?	Other written policies**
MaterialCo	Yes	Referrals	Interviews	Award	Industry rate	Increased pay	Yes	Formal delivered in-house	OHS Internet usage AA Harassment/ Bullying Discipline Grievance Drug & Alcohol use
WoodCo	Yes	Agency	Interviews	Award	Award rate	Promotion	No	Job rotation	OHS Overtime Internet usage Discipline
LandCo	Yes	Agency	Interviews	Individual written contracts	Industry rate	Increased pay	Yes	On-the-job	Overtime
TechCo	Yes	On-line ads	Interviews	Individual written contracts	Industry rate	Equity or profit sharing	Yes	Formal delivered externally	None
MoneyCo	Yes	Referrals	Interviews	Individual written contracts	Industry rate	Increased pay	No	Formal delivered in-house	None

Table 6.3 (continued)

	Use list of skills/quals when recruiting?	Main recruitment method used?	Main selection method used?	How wages and conditions specified?	Rate for employees' wages?	How are valued employees rewarded?	Performance appraised on regular basis?	Type of training mainly offered?	Other written policies**
TileCo	Yes	On-line ads	Interviews	Award	Industry rate	Employee share plan	Yes	Formal delivered in-house	OHS EEO PML Internet usage Harassment Discipline Grievance Drug & Alcohol use
RoadCo	Yes	Agency	Trial period	Award	Award rate	Non-financial rewards	Yes	Formal delivered externally	OHS Overtime Harassment/ Bullying Grievance Drug & Alcohol use
ExecCo	Yes	Referrals	Interviews	Individual written contracts	Industry rate	Equity or profit sharing	Yes	On-the-job	OHS EEO Internet usage AA Harassment/ Bullying

AirCo	Yes	Referrals	Interviews	Individual verbal agreement	Industry rate	Increased pay	Yes	Job rotation	OHS Overtime Drug & Alcohol use
PrintCo	Yes	Agency	Interviews	Award	Industry rate	Non-financial rewards	Yes	On-the-job	OHS EEO PML Flexible work hours Overtime Harassment/Bullying Discipline Drug & Alcohol use
GardenCo	Yes	Newspaper ads	Interviews	Award	Award rate	Increased pay	Yes	On-the-job	OHS PML Overtime Harassment/Bullying Discipline Grievance Drug & Alcohol use

Notes:
* Based on responses to survey and interview questions. See Barrett, Mayson and Warriner (Chapter 9 in this handbook) for full details of the survey and findings.
** OHS = Occupational Health and Safety; EEO = Equal Employment Opportunity, AA = Affirmative Action; PML = Paid Maternity Leave.

technicians needed to have IT training, while landscape architecture qualifications were needed by employees who worked at LandCo. At ExecCo, recruitment and selection was less straightforward and while some of the consultants had legal training this was not requisite. What was required, however, was specialized knowledge of the particular sector they supplied executives for as was previous experience as a business consultant.

In a number of the firms specialist salespeople were employed and therefore sales experience was requisite for those employees. Recruiting and selecting staff with practical professional experience but without recognized qualifications can be more challenging than simply finding staff with formal qualifications and licences. This was confirmed by the difficulty many of the firms shared in finding good salespeople. For example, the manager at PrintCo described the problems of accessing appropriately skilled staff, saying 'It's very hard to get a good salesperson, not that we are after a real gung ho salesperson, we only want them to service our accounts properly . . . just someone who is solid and reliable' (Interview, PrintCo).

It is frequently reported that in small firms, staff are recruited according to informal 'fit' criteria in contrast to best practice HRM advice that 'fit' can be facilitated by having formal person or job specifications and formal training. However, as one of our interviewees demonstrated, formalizing the recruitment process by using a recruitment agency and having a list of skills and qualifications was not a guarantee of the 'right' person being employed. The owner–manager at TechCo told the story of recruiting a new salesperson which he described as 'a particularly bad experience' (Interview, TechCo). He said,

> I went though two [recruitment] companies with the full on 'here's the brief, go away and come back with your shortlist, I'll then cut that down to a shorter list and I'll interview them'. I went through their lists and shaved them down then went up to Sydney and interviewed five people in a day. It was hard work and I was exhausted. The person I chose, whose references checked fantastically, I recommended. I had him on for six months and I think he sold about $5000 worth of equipment . . . he was not right at all (Interview, TechCo).

Most interviewees highlighted the importance of 'fit' for new employees, and agencies were not seen as being particularly helpful in this regard. This was illustrated at MaterialCo where the owner–manager explained what happened when they used an agency to try to recruit a new accountant.

> I had to find someone to fill a role which was quite focused but there wasn't anybody. So I went out and I started employing these employment agencies that have experience in the area. One was $5000 for a placement and they sent me bimbos. All they were interested in was getting their money (Interview, MaterialCo).

Despite this experience the manager at MaterialCo persevered and an accountant was sourced through an agency and she did work out very well for the firm.

The problem with agencies highlights the (incorrect) assumption that small firms will have well developed orientation and training processes in place to facilitate the 'fit' of the new employee and the firm. This was well put by the Director at LandCo,

> They [agencies] don't understand the business. They just hope that because we are looking for someone we will make them fit, which can sometimes work because you can teach people skills. But it's the person that's important and we really try to be specific about the person that we are wanting (Interview LandCo).

At WoodCo and RoadCo recruitment agencies were only used when the firm was seeking casual labourers.

It is well recognized in the literature that informal recruitment practices such as 'walk-in' and referrals from trusted 'others' – employees, former colleagues or others in the industry – are a means used by small firms to try to ensure new recruits fit. Interestingly, the referral method has become increasingly popular in larger firms with the 'war for talent' forcing firms to employ 'off-market' recruitment practices (see Fernandez et al., 2000). The interviews showed that this was the case with some of the firms. TileCo had 'picked up some people through friends and acquaintances of employees' (Interview, TileCo), while the early employees at MoneyCo were former colleagues in the banking industry where the owner had previously worked. All other staff at MoneyCo were recruited through personal contacts or through personal referrals.

At AirCo the small size of the specialized industry meant referrals and personal contacts were used for recruitment. The manager explained,

> Between the three of us here we would know virtually all of the suitable people in Australia. . . . we might know of somebody but we don't know what their work standard is like and that has happened. We rang up the guy up there and said 'hey [Name] what is he like?' He said, 'oh he is good, no problems'. And we go 'okay' and, you know, you go okay (Interview, AirCo).

At MaterialCo the position of Invoice Clerk was filled on the recommendation of the Chinese Accountant, '[Accountant's name] said, "Oh [Owner–manager's name], I have a friend". So I said, "well bring her in". So we brought [Friend's name] in and they know each other and speak their own language. As I say, I have no problems' (Interview, MaterialCo).

While referrals were used because they were underpinned by trust, there could also be problems with this form of recruitment as the story told by the Manager at ExecCo suggested.

> One problem we had recently was a business developer we employed. Well I hadn't recruited him, the Managing Director met him in Europe and there was this personal relationship when he was employed. He was based in Sydney and he was misusing our internet and our emails. He was using it for pornographic material and also dating services. He was emailing, you know, all sorts of things back and forth. So, you know, I had to go to Sydney and deal with him. It was obviously a summary dismissal and . . . he was actually sponsored out of England . . . so he had five weeks basically to get out of the country. We thought that was punishment enough. It also affected, obviously, his personal life here because he had a relationship with a woman, so that had to end (ExecCo).

While most of the firms used interviews as a key method of selecting new employees, another practice some of them used to see whether the new recruit 'fitted' was probation or an initial period of employment on a casual (hourly) employment contract. At WoodCo and RoadCo all new employees were first employed as casuals, enabling the employer 'to check their attitude and if we like them, we put them on contract' (Interview RoadCo). Similarly at MaterialCo the rationale for a three-month trial period was 'to see if you like us and we like you'. At TileCo a three-month probation period was used in the warehouse although 'some of them don't even last that period of time, we have had them for two or three days out in the warehouse and it's not their cup of tea' (Interview, TileCo). The work in the warehouse involved manual lifting of heavy and awkward tiles and the HR manager acknowledged that it was not a very pleasant job. In other cases at TileCo administrative staff had been dismissed after their period of probation. As the HR manager explained, 'It's really about fit . . . and despite, you know, regular performance reviews and keeping an eye on people during probation, on D day I would say, "Right. Life skills". Bang, people would go' (Interview TileCo).

As suggested in the earlier discussion about the IR context of this study, terms and conditions of employment would be established through an award. Alternatively employers could have taken the option to pursue a collective agreement with their staff (with or without union representation) or formalized individual terms and conditions of employment in what is known as an Australian Workplace Agreement (AWA) (see Sappey et al., 2006). As Table 6.3 shows, in manufacturing sector firms, an award was used to underpin employees' terms and conditions of employment, while in services sector firms, individual contracts were utilized. Essentially an award was used to specify the minimum (but not maximum) wage rate and other general terms and conditions around annual and sick leave. At PrintCo the minimum rate of pay in the award was used as guidance while there was also an accepted 'industry rate' for some employees. As the owner–manager said, 'In our industry it is very, very competitive, and at the moment we have an award rate and most printers pay within that award rate. But to get the right people you would generally pay quite well above it. There is an industry standard if you like' (Interview, PrintCo).

A similar situation operated at AirCo as the following exchange between the manager and interviewer showed.

> Manager: 'We follow the guidelines in the award, apart from the wages'.
> Interviewer: 'Okay. Do you pay clearly above award wages?'
> Manager: 'Oh mate!'
> Interviewer: 'Way above?'
> Manager: 'Yes, way above.'
> Interviewer: 'Highly competitive is it?'
> Manager: 'Extraordinarily.'
> Interviewer: 'Understood!'
> Manager: 'We would be paying, I suggest, very close to double what the award asks for.'
> Interviewer: 'Really?'
> Manager: 'We have to do that to keep staff.'
> (Interview, AirCo).

The owner–manager of GardenCo explained how they relied on an award:

> I don't really want to get tied down to individual contracts. I personally prefer working within an award as we currently do. . . . Basically, what we do is say, 'This is the award we use, we'll give you all the entitlements. . . .' We give them holiday loading, we give them more although they're not entitled to it, because they don't work shifts. But we continue those things on because we won't get staff otherwise. That is the issue. The retention of staff is a huge issue and we have had to play it by the award to maintain staff (Interview, GardenCo).

However, they had recently converted the warehouse and despatch managers from wages to salary, 'because they were getting good money but racking up lots of hours. So there was a quality of life issue' (Interview, Garden Co). Despite taking a pay cut, there had not been any problems and in fact for the warehouse manager the owner–manager explained,

> It means that he isn't here at 2 o'clock in the morning and that sort of thing. But also over the course of bringing the job up, it forced him to give some of the workload away and they [warehouse and despatch managers] actually work as a team a lot better (Interview, GardenCo).

The changing IR context has also influenced management's (uncertain) perceptions of the employment options available to them, the risks and benefits of available options and how to manage them. At TileCo the HR manager told us how he had suggested to the owner that moving from an award to a non-union collective agreement might be beneficial. The suggestion was driven by the implementation of common rule awards in Victoria as well as the firm's relocation from an inner city location to an outer suburban industrial estate where he thought a union was more likely to be active in recruiting members. As he said,

> I thought the minute we lob here the union is going to come in and try and see what's going on and do a bit of recruitment. But they haven't been here so far, so that didn't happen. But I said to him [the owner], 'Given that what is going to happen with the common rule awards and the fact that you might have unions kicking your door in when we move, then from a risk management point of view, you might want to look at doing a collective agreement, rather than AWAs [individual agreements], which would be the policy manual and maybe fiddle around with that a bit. But just basically register it and it's your agreement. That locks your unions out and locks your conditions in. It gives you that certainty into the future but you've got the freedom to adjust wages if you want to, same as you've got now, but it gives you some legal protection' (Interview, TileCo).

However, the owner did not want to go down that path, and as the HR manager explained, 'I think he had a bit of a problem getting his head around why I would be saying that and whether or not I had his interests at heart' (Interview, TileCo).

A previous Australian study of HRM in small firms indicated that reward management practices predominantly relied on salary increases with some firms offering equity sharing or non-financial rewards (Barrett and Mayson, 2005). This study had largely consistent findings. Increased wages or some form of profit sharing was the predominant way in which staff, particularly valuable employees, were rewarded or retained in nine of the firms. Other methods were also used, for example at LandCo the Director was very aware of the desires of their 'rising stars', as she called them. One wanted to travel for three months while another wanted a promotion – and the Director was very keen to try to accommodate them as much as possible. With the one who wanted to travel, the Director's approach was to say that the firm would hold the job over but she wanted to 'get [the employee] actively involved and see if she can help find a contractor to replace her, so put a bit of responsibility back on her too' (Interview, LandCo).

Performance appraisal practices in small firms have been found to be informal and continuous and often used for monitoring rather than developmental purposes (Barrett and Mayson, 2005; Gilbert and Jones, 2000). In our study formal performance appraisal was one way employers determined employees' value, and in nine of the firms this was said to occur on a regular basis. At TechCo this was more about monitoring than simply speaking to employees. As the owner–manager said, 'when we designed the layout here, it was done so that this office can overlook the line, and so I can see all the way down to the back' (Interview, TechCo). In ExecCo, the firm's value statement was an important document and the appraisal of performance was underpinned by these values. The manager explained,

> Earlier this year we went through an activity of clarifying our values and our behaviours and everyone has agreed to those. If ever we have an issue we always refer back to our values and behaviours. In reception you'll see our values framed – they are not large enough to read and you have to get very close to them – but everyone has agreed to them and anyone who comes to work for us is made aware of what we expect (Interview, TechCo).

Changes to the IR system in Australia have placed more emphasis on internal HRM systems and practices to manage wages and conditions. This was evident in the study, where having a record of performance was said to be necessary in order to protect employers from accusations of unfair dismissal if any employee had their employment terminated. While the new WorkChoices legislation exempts incorporated small firms from unfair dismissal provisions, employers still must ensure their dismissals are not unlawful. However as the HR manager from TileCo said, 'The thing about unfair dismissal – I don't think it ever caused me any difficulty – what it did do, I think, was cause people grief because they didn't have their HR systems covered off or well applied' (Interview, TileCo). The importance of formalized systems in relation to performance matters is similarly underlined by the owner–manager at GardenCo when he told the following story.

> We had a bullying incident 12 months ago and it ended up being frivolous. But it came down to us. It came down to incorrectly changing a person for a role. I didn't do the interview, my partner did the interview . . . and it was the wrong person to do the task. We ended up with someone who was, um, tardy, and slow and not very . . . not suited to the role and she got hassled by one of the other employees. So you can imagine what happened. Needless to say she left and put in a stress claim and a bullying claim. Of course we had Workcover here, but they threw it out. I summarily dismissed the other guy but I went through a process of finding out what went on underneath, and such like. He had been given a couple of warnings about his temper and other things, so it just, it worked out for the best, but it was a very awkward situation (Interview, GardenCo.).

In small firms, training has been found to be reactive while the cost of formal training programmes can make them prohibitive (Barrett and Mayson, 2005; Storey and Westhead, 1997). Our study showed training to be delivered in different ways throughout the firms with a mix of formal and informal approaches. Table 6.3 shows that in four firms on-the-job training was predominantly used and in another two job rotation was used. In three firms formal training delivered in-house, while in another two formal training was delivered externally for staff. The nature of the training provided depended on the nature of work being undertaken. For example, occupational health and safety (OHS) training was very important in the manufacturing sector firms. At RoadCo they had previously dismissed an employee because of 'a bad work attitude' and the belief that if he had stayed he would have risked other workers' safety on site (Interview, RoadCo). OHS training was very important for employees working in the warehouse at TileCo. As the HR manager explained,

> Well in the warehouse it's a different environment. It's a lot of heavy manual han-dling of tiles, and boxes of tiles are awkward and heavy. It's literally back break-ing work. It's the worst. We have been doing a lot to try to avoid back injuries but also, you know, cuts and abrasions (Interview, TileCo).

'Literally back breaking' was true.

> We had a major back injury going back over a year. A guy came in who was a very big guy, you know, thickset, muscular, 26 years old, and he went out there, lifted up a couple of boxes and broke his back. Severe back injury. Now there were instructions in place – inadequate as it turned out – that said don't lift those, cut the straps, undo the boxes and so on . . . So now it's really about educating people to make sure they know what the risks are and how to lift properly and how not to lift (Interview, TileCo).

Similarly, induction training has been found to be ad hoc and informally implemented in small firms (Gilbert and Jones, 2000; Kotey and Sheridan, 2001). At GardenCo OHS was said to be 'an induction thing' (Interview, GardenCo.), while at TechCo the owner–manager made safety the first item on the agenda of the weekly staff meetings. LandCo employees who had to go out to other sites where they were undertaking landscaping work all held industry OHS red cards. More generally the LandCo Director was keen to develop staff more generally. As she explained,

> Well one, two things that we are doing at the moment with staff who are oh, one who just sort of, 'I want to do this and I want to do that', and the next day 'I'm bored'. I say, 'so why is that you want to do that?' 'Oh, I just thought that would be good' and I say, 'well why don't you set out a bit of your own job description and the areas that you want to work in and then we can look at what the best development course would be. Is it, you know, oh, I'd like to do public speaking and is that because you want to do more projects where you go out and talk to the community about community projects, or do you want to be an expert witness at the planning tribunal?' You know, I think it's just sort of you've got to grab that with staff (Interview, LandCo).

At PrintCo they were moving from on-the-job training to more formal training but delivered internally. Their approach to increasing levels of staff competency was a simplified form of skills gap analysis where they planned to use 'a simple chart of the people that we have here and the skills that we want to acquire' (Interview, PrintCo) and use the training to address those skills gaps.

The informal nature of HRM in small firms has been by a lack of written-down and regularly referred to policies to guide HRM practice. In the final column of Table 6.3 the range of other written HRM policies that were reported on the questionnaire to exist in these firms are indicated. Interestingly many of these matters are not mandated, for example, paid maternity leave (PML) or equal employment opportunity (EEO). Interviews revealed that in many of the firms these policies were usually part of an HR manual and employees were made aware of their existence either by incorporating them in their contract or going through them at induction. For example at TileCo the HR manager explained,

> I run through it [HR manual] in induction with them [new hires] pointing out significant stuff as well as the interest stuff, like where they can find their leave conditions if they want to. Health and safety, our code of conduct, grievance procedures – how we do it here – it's right in front of them (Interview, TileCo).

At TechCo new employees went through induction, the purpose of which was,

> . . . to make sure that you know who you talk to to get all the payroll sorted out and understand all that side of the system, timesheets and all that sort of stuff. We give a direct report about where they are, what they are going to do and their responsibilities. When we talk to the workshop guys we make sure they understand what they can and can't do down in the workshop . . . it involves pointing out the obvious things about safety in terms of what we do to get out of the place and occupational health and safety more generally (Interview, TechCo).

While the existence of a manual indicated that some thought had gone into the type of behaviour that the firm required and/or expected from employees, it did not necessarily mean that the way in which these expectations or behaviours were to be achieved had been budgeted for or was seen as a priority.

Locating the findings and implications
Informality is said to be a defining characteristic of small firm HRM (see for example Cardon and Stevens, 2004); however, our concern has been in exploring how the HRM practices that operate in small firms apply and to some extent trying to determine why. Can we say that the HRM practices in these 11 firms are characterized by informality? For example, recruitment and selection in small firms has received much attention from researchers, and practices have been labelled 'unimaginative'. However, our

interviews show that the lack of imagination in recruitment procedures, particularly the use of referrals, is exceeded only by the desire of the owner–manager to make sure they get people who 'fit'. Similar notions of fit underpin selection procedures, such as the use of probation and trial periods of casual employment prior to permanent employment being offered.

What these interviews suggest is that it is not a conscious or programmatic choice that small-business owner–managers make between two alternatives. Instead formal and informal HRM practices can co-exist within the one firm. Informal recruitment processes may be used as the desire is for new employees to 'fit'. But formal performance management processes can also be used as the firm needs to be protected against any future claims of discrimination or dismissal from 'unhappy' former employees.

To explain why formal and informal HRM practices co-exist we can consider the Janus faces of bureaucracy and look to Gouldner's (1954) study of 'rules' in a gypsum factory. He argued that bureaucratic measures are a result of tension and a breakdown in social relationships. They are not necessarily a function of firm size or anything else in particular although increasing employee numbers or the need to manage across more than one location, for example, may lead to tension. Increased firm size is one of the problems for which bureaucracy is a solution; however, it is not inevitable. Similarly it is not inevitable that once initiated it will persist – bureaucracy is not immortal. The issue is really one of logic – what is the logic of the rules or what tension does a rule seek to resolve?

We would argue that the logic of formalization is where attention should be focused. So for example, a range of issues thrown up in the interviews go to the debate around the informality of HRM in small firms and whether this is a 'good' or 'bad' thing. Clearly the writing of HR manuals or specific policies around safety behaviour suggest that some rules were perceived as 'good' as they served the interests of both employer and employee (Gouldner, 1954). Largely however these manuals represented what Adler and Borys (1996) term 'enabling formalization', in that they contained procedures that captured organizational memory and lessons learned from experience. Enabling formalization is represented in those rules that do not try to foolproof the system but instead capture organizational learning and experience. These rules codify best practice routines (to date) and stabilize and diffuse organizational capabilities. These are 'good' procedures and like those representative bureaucratic rules (Gouldner, 1954), which serve the interests of managers and workers, they are set and followed because they do not violate either party's values. These rules are likely to elicit cooperation and consent from employees as they can both legitimate management control as well as give workers some control over their work.

This is apparent from the interviews where the enabling logic (Adler and Borys, 1996) seemed to prevail in the management of people more generally – at least from the employers' perspective. At MoneyCo it was described as 'give and take on both sides', while at MaterialCo it was said to be 'a two way thing'. At PrintCo it was put more fully by the owner–manager as follows.

> I'm a realist and know that they are going to have a sick day. I know that their kids are going to be sick and I know that with the stringent requirements placed on kindergartens these days that if your kid is sick you can't take them to kinder. All of this sort of thing. I make allowances and I tell my people, I say, 'Look, I know that you are going to have to go to the dentist. I know that you have got to go to the doctor. I know this. Just go early in the morning or go late at night, but I also know that when you have got to go, you have got to go.' But they look to make up time when they go. They feel guilty when they take time off, and so they come to work every day (Interview, PrintCo).

Perhaps the prevailing enabling logic was a result of the relative lack of experience with HRM across these firms. While there were more rules at TileCo where there was an experienced HR Manager and at RoadCo to a slightly lesser extent, where there was a newly graduated HR Manager, these procedures were still reported to be enabling. At TileCo this may have been a result of the owners' desire to 'look after their people' (as reported by the HR Manager) and their continued control over the business, which tempered the extent to which the HR Manager could implement policies.

The alternative logic of formalization is coercive. Rules such as those in punishment-centred bureaucracies (Gouldner, 1954) substitute rather than complement employee commitment. These rules serve as a means of legitimating one party's right to sanction the other in areas of conflict and when a discipline pattern is applied by management the rules enforce reluctant compliance and extract recalcitrant effort as any deviance from them is deemed to be 'bad'.

It could be a shortcoming of the research method and a lack of desire on the interviewees' part to tell the interviewer how the rules were applied coercively – as Adler and Borys (1996) write, 'the coercion logic tends to be pursued behind the scenes' (p. 82). But there is some indication of these operating, in for example the monitoring and surveillance of employees undertaken at TechCo. We can also see it in the interview with the owner–manager of PrintCo who explained how he had addressed a situation where another manager had been unable to manage the amount of Monday and Friday sick days that one of his staff members was taking. As he said, 'it's about continuously addressing those issues, where we have to implement them for the whole staff. So if you are sick on Friday you have to come in with a doctor's certificate on Monday. . . .' (Interview, PrintCo).

Similarly it can also be seen in the interview with the owner–manager of GardenCo when he said,

> I think it's about trust, communication, and people comfortable enough to say, 'Look I need to go to a doctor's appointment. Can I leave half an hour earlier?' And me saying, 'Yeah, that's fine.' You don't dock them as you know they'll make it up. But, look, not everyone is going to do that. That's the problem you know (Interview GardenCo).

Gouldner (1954) did identify a third type of bureaucracy as a 'mock bureaucracy'. This occurs when rules exist but are ignored by all parties because enforcing them would be inconsistent with the values of either party. These 'dead letter rules' were imposed by outsiders and in the gypsum factory he studies, the 'no smoking' rule was the classic example, being imposed by insurance requirements and only enforced when there was an insurance inspector around. It was a 'dead letter rule' as everyone (workers and management) smoked despite the rule existing. Written policies which are then not enacted would be dead letter rules. In this study a number of firms reported the existence of a range of written polices (see final column, Table 6.3) covering matters such as EEO, affirmative action (AA), PML, Internet usage and drug and alcohol usage. These policies were infrequently applied and therefore they were not strictly examples of mock bureaucracy. In fact it was interesting some of these matters were addressed at all as there is no legislated regime of PML in Australia while the Equal Opportunity for Women in the Workplace Act 1999 does not require firms with less than 100 employees to establish a workplace programme to remove the barriers to women entering and advancing in these organizations.

The implication of this discussion is that the question for small-firm HRM researchers should not just be whether rules do or do not exist or the degree to which rules exist. Instead their concern should be with the type of rules that exist, their logic and the outcomes in terms of attitudes and behaviours. In this study, by talking only to management we could only go part of the way down this path. A key limitation of our study is the lack of employee perspective. Without this it is difficult, if not impossible, to know the effect of the way HRM is managed on the firm and on individuals. Do employees find the way HRM practices are enacted to be enabling or coercive? What are their levels of satisfaction and commitment and do these differ depending on the nature of the work being undertaken? Do employees suffer from role stress or role conflict and would they prefer more or less formalized procedures? While it would be important to know what current employees thought it would also be fruitful to explore why others had left and how they perceived the situation. This of course exposes the limitation of studies that rely on a snapshot of what happens in small firms, and suggests that further in-depth ethnographic work is required.

References

Adler, P. and B. Borys (1996), 'Two types of bureaucracy: Enabling and coercive', *Administrative Science Quarterly*, **41**, 61–89.

Aldrich, H.E. (1999), *Organizations Evolving*, Thousand Oaks, CA: Sage Publications.

Australian Bureau of Statistics (ABS) (2005), *Characteristics of Small Business (Main Features Reissued)*, Cat. No. 8127.0, Canberra: ABS.

Barrett, R. and S. Mayson (2005), *Getting and Keeping Good Staff: An Analysis of Human Resource Management 'Problems' In Small Firms*, report to CPA Australia <http://www.cpaaustralia.org.au>.

Barrett, R. and S. Mayson (2007), 'Human resource management in growing small firms', *Journal of Small Business and Enterprise Development*, **14**, 307–20.

Barrett, R. and A. Rainnie (2002), 'What's so special about small firms? Developing an integrated approach to analysing small firm industrial relations', *Work Employment and Society*, **16**, 415–32.

Birley, S. and P. Westhead (1990), 'Growth and performance contrasts between "types" of small firms', *Strategic Management Journal*, **11**, 535–57.

Cardon, M. and C. Stevens (2004), 'Managing human resources in small organizations: What do we know?', *Human Resource Management Review*, **14**, 295–323.

Chandler, G. and G. McEvoy (2000), 'Human resource management, TQM, and firm performance in small and medium-sized enterprises', *Entrepreneurship: Theory and Practice*, **25**, 43–58.

Curran, J. and R. Blackburn (2001), *Researching the Small Enterprise*, London: Sage.

Davidsson, P. and J. Wiklund (2000), 'Conceptual and empirical challenges in the study of firm growth', in D.L. Sexton and H. Landstrom (eds), *The Blackwell Handbook of Entrepreneurship*, Oxford: Blackwell, pp. 26–44.

Delmar, F., P. Davidsson and W.B. Gartner (2003), 'Arriving at the high-growth firm', *Journal of Business Venturing*, **18**, 189–216.

Deshpande, S. and D. Golhar (1994), 'HRM practices in large and small manufacturing firms: A comparative study', *Journal of Small Business Management*, **32**(2), 49–56.

Fernandez, R.M., E.J. Castilla and P. Moore (2000), 'Social capital at work: Networks and employment at a phone centre', *American Journal of Sociology*, **105**, 1288–356.

Gibb, A. and M. Scott (1985), 'Strategic awareness, personal commitment and the process of planning in small business', *Journal of Management Studies*, **22**, 597–631.

Gilbert, J. and G. Jones (2000), 'Managing human resources in New Zealand small business', *Asia Pacific Journal of Human Resources*, **38**, 55–68.

Gouldner, A.W. (1954), *Patterns of Industrial Bureaucracy*, New York: The Free Press.

Hall, R. (2006), 'Australian industrial relations in 2005: The WorkChoices revolution', *Journal of Industrial Relations*, **48**, 291–303.

Hall, R. (2007), 'The first year of WorkChoices: Industrial relations in Australia in 2006', *Journal of Industrial Relations*, **49**, 207–309.

Hannon, P. and A. Atherton (1998), 'Small firm success and the art of orienteering: The value of plans, planning and strategic awareness in the competitive small firm', *Journal of Small Business and Enterprise Development*, **5**, 102–19.

Harney, B. and T. Dundon (2006), 'Capturing complexity: Developing an integrated approach to analysing HRM in SMEs', *Human Resource Management Journal*, **16**, 48–73.

Heneman, H. and R. Berkley (1999), 'Applicant attraction practices and outcomes among small businesses', *Journal of Small Business Management*, **37**, 53–74.

Hornsby, J. and D. Kuratko (1990), 'Human resource management in small business: Critical issues for the 1990s', *Journal of Small Business Management*, **28**(3), 9–18.

Huang, X. and A. Brown (1999), 'An analysis and classification of problems in small business', *International Small Business Journal*, **18**, 73–84.

Klaas, B., J. McClendon and T. Gainey (2000), 'Managing HR in the small and medium enterprise: The impact of professional employer organizations', *Entrepreneurship: Theory and Practice*, **25**(1), 107–23.

Kotey, B. and A. Sheridan (2001), 'Gender and the practice of HRM in small business', *Asia Pacific Journal of Human Resources*, **39**(3), 23–40.

Marlow, S. (2006), 'Human resource management in smaller firms: A contradiction in terms?', *Human Resource Management Review*, **16**, 467–77.

McEvoy, G. (1984), 'Small business personnel practices', *Journal of Small Business Management*, **22**(4), 1–8.

McLarty, R. (1999), 'The skills development needs of SMEs and focus on graduate skills application', *Journal of Applied Management Studies*, **8**, 103–12.

Miles, M. and A. Huberman (1994), *Qualitative Data Analysis: An Expanded Sourcebook*, 2nd edn, Thousand Oaks: Sage Publications.

Sappey, R., J. Burgess, M. Lyons and J. Buultjens (2006), *Industrial Relations in Australia: Work and Workplaces*, Sydney, Australia: Pearson Education.

Sels, L., S. De Winne, J. Maes, J. Delmotte, D. Faems and A. Forrier (2006a), 'Unravelling the HRM–performance link: Value-creating and cost-increasing effects of small business HRM', *Journal of Management Studies*, **13**, 319–42.

Sels, L., S. De Winne, J. Maes, J. Delmotte, D. Faems and A. Forrier (2006b), 'Linking HRM and small business performance: An examination of the impact of HRM intensity on the productivity and financial performance of small businesses', *Small Business Economics*, **26**, 83–101.

Smallbone, D. and P. Wyer (2000), 'Growth and development in the small firm', in S. Carter and D. Jones-Evans (eds), *Enterprise and Small Business*, Harlow: Financial Times/Prentice-Hall, pp. 409–433.

Storey, D. and P. Westhead (1997), 'Management training in small firms: A case of market failure?', *Human Resource Management Journal*, **7**(2), 61–71.

Taylor, S. (2006), 'Acquaintance, meritocracy and critical realism: Researching recruitment and selection processes in smaller and growth organizations', *Human Resource Management Review*, **16**, 478–89.

Weick, K.E. (2007), 'The generative properties of richness', *The Academy of Management Journal*, **50**, 14–19.

Weinzimmer, L.G., P.C. Nystrom and S.J. Freeman (1998), 'Methods for measuring organizational growth: Issues, consequences, and contingencies', *Journal of Management*, **24**, 235–62.

Welsh, J. and J. White (1981), 'A small business is not a little big business', *Harvard Business Review*, **59**, 18–32.

7 Human resource management and corporate performance: evidence from UK and US small firms
Jonathan Michie and Maura Sheehan

Introduction

In a special issue of *Human Resource Management* in small and medium sized enterprises (SMEs) the editor observed that, 'the science and practice of entrepreneurship has advanced dramatically in recent years' and that 'the general business press, too frequently highlights the importance of SMEs for job creation and economic growth' (Huselid, 2003: p. 297). He went on to ask, 'How has the field of human resource management made a contribution to the emergent field?' concluding 'perhaps surprisingly our contribution has been very limited', calling for more research and a greater dialogue on HR in SMEs (Huselid, 2003: p. 297). This chapter is a response to that call. It builds upon our previous work on the links between human resource management (HRM) and corporate performance in large UK companies by examining these relationships in small firms (employing between ten and 100 employees) and places the analysis in an international context by comparing results between UK and US small firms in matched industries.

The key purpose of this chapter is to examine what contribution HRM practices make to the competitive success of small firms. Competitive success is proxied here by three variables: whether the firm has introduced a product and/or process innovation in the past three years; labour productivity; and financial performance, and so subjective and objective measures of performance are examined. In doing this we take forward the literature examining the HRM–performance linkage (for example, Becker and Gerhard, 1996; Dyer and Reeves, 1995; Guest and Hoque, 1994; Huselid, 1995; Osterman, 1994; Pfeffer, 1994, 1998) and contribute additional insight from original material and analysis to the small firm HRM literature (of, for example, Cassell et al., 2002; Chandler and McEvoy, 2000; Ciavarella, 2003; Deshpande and Golhar, 1994; Drummond and Stone, 2006; Duberley and Walley, 1995; Hayton, 2003; Nguyen and Bryant, 2004; Sels et al., 2006a, 2006b; Way, 2002).

In the next section we briefly review the HRM–performance linkage before examining the types of HRM practices and policies used, how these practices vary between firms, and the relationship between these practices and firm performance, using original data collected from a sample of small firms in matched manufacturing and service sectors in the UK and US.

Review of the literature on human resources and organizational performance

Numerous studies have analysed the relationship between the use of HRM practices on the one hand, and corporate performance on the other (see, for example, Appelbaum et al., 2000; Becker and Gerhart, 1996; Becker and Huselid, 1998; Guest et al., 2000, 2003; Hoque, 1999; Huselid, 1995; Ichniowski et al., 1994, 1997; MacDuffie, 1995; Michie and Sheehan, 2001, 2003, 2005; Osterman, 1994, 1999; Richardson and Thompson, 1999; Wood, 1999; Wood and de Menezes, 1998). In this literature, which is largely US-based but which increasingly includes several studies analysing UK data, is the finding of a degree of positive association between the use of HRM practices – such as the bundles of practices generally termed 'High Commitment Work Systems' or 'High Performance Work Systems' and organizational outcomes and corporate performance. However, the strength and significance of the associations found varies across studies. Some researchers have found such associations vary according to specified characteristics such as the corporate strategies being pursued by the firms under study (see Michie and Sheehan, 2005).

Not only does the strength and significance of the HRM–performance association vary across studies but issues of causality also bedevil the interpretation of these observed relationships (see Wall and Wood, 2005). Moreover, few studies focus exclusively on small firms, which is problematic as it is assumed that the case for HRM–performance association will hold for both large and small firms. Although this assumption has not previously been tested explicitly it is based on two linked arguments; that the effective HRM offers a basis for competitive advantage (Barney, 1995); that effective use of HRM depends on the application of a distinctive combination of practices, often described as 'bundles' of practices (MacDuffie, 1995) or HRM 'systems' (Becker and Huselid, 1998). Some researchers have attempted to categorize HRM practices in terms of 'high performance work systems' (Appelbaum et al., 2000), while others have described a system of 'high-commitment management' (Arthur, 1994; Pfeffer, 1994, 1998; Wood and de Menezes, 1998) or 'high-involvement management' (Guthrie, 2001). Despite the terminology, the point is that once the case for HRM has been made, attempts to establish what form of HRM is likely to be most effective have been undertaken.

In the HRM–performance literature the concept of performance has been addressed in a variety of ways. For financial performance, measures of return on investment and Tobin's Q (firm market value/book value; see Huselid, 1995) would be the most obvious. However, it can be argued that financial performance lies at the end of the causal chain and that outcome measures more closely linked to HRM might be more appropriate. Moreover, small firms are unlikely to be publicly traded and therefore Tobin's Q is not a practical measure of performance. Other measures of performance could be used including profitability, productivity, turnover and innovation rates (see Kleinknecht, 1998; Kleinknecht et al., 1997; Michie and Sheehan, 2003 for analyses of the relationship between HRM and innovative activities in firms).

Subjective measures of company performance are widely used in research and typically interpreted as being equivalent to objective measures. Yet the assumption of equivalence is open to challenge. In previous work (Wall et al., 2004), we tested this assumption in three separate samples. We found first that subjective and objective measures of company performance were positively associated (convergent validity); second that those relationships were stronger than those between measures of differing aspects of performance using the same method (discriminant validity); and third that the relationships of subjective and objective company performance measures with a range of independent variables were equivalent (construct validity). In this chapter, we test for convergent validity for two performance measures – financial performance and labour productivity – and estimate the relationship between HRM and performance using both subjective and objective measures.

Hypotheses tested
The purpose of this study is to explore the HRM–performance relationship using a range of performance measures in a sample of small UK and US firms, where both subjective and objective indicators of performance are used. Specifically our hypotheses are as follows:

Hypothesis 1a: There will be an association between greater use of HRM practices and higher labour productivity.

Hypothesis 1b: There will be an association between greater use of HRM practices and higher profitability.

Hypothesis 1c: There will be an association between greater use of HRM practices and a greater probability of innovating.

Hypothesis 2: Any HRM–performance relationship will be equally significant whether objective or subjective measures of performance are used.

The research framework

The research method and sample
The data used in the analysis were derived from a stratified sample of firms from the Dun and Bradstreet databases in the UK and US respectively. Two dimensions were used to stratify the sample: organizational size and the primary sector of business activity. In relation to size, the selection criterion was that the firms employed between ten and 100 employees. Nine sectors were identified – five in manufacturing and four in services – using the 1992 UK and US Standard Industrial Classification (SIC) codes. The matched SIC codes are as follows:

Manufacturing – medical:
2833 – Medicinal Chemicals and Botanical Products
2834 – Pharmaceutical Preparations
3827 – Optimal Instruments and Lenses
3841 – Surgical and Medical Instruments and Apparatus
3844 – Radiology/Electrical Medical Equipment

Services – health:
8071 – Medical and Scientific Laboratories
8072 – Dental Laboratories
8051 – Skilled Nursing Facilities

Services – other:
5411 – Grocery Stores/Supermarkets

Dun and Bradstreet supplied a total of 1281 firms with the above characteristics in the UK and 1470 in the US (see Table 7.1 for sample details). The medical manufacturing and health-service SIC codes were selected because these represent industries of significant growth – both current and expected – in the UK and US, and are generally associated with high skill and training levels. The grocery store industry was selected to serve as a comparative industry. This is a large industry with a high expected rate of growth, although not known for high skill or training levels.

By focusing on specific industries, we aimed to reduce the problem of firm heterogeneity that bedevils small firm research. We also sought to examine how the specific industrial characteristics in these sectors moderate both the use and effectiveness of particular HRM practices and bundles of practices. We did this in response to Datta, Guthrie and Wright's (2005) detailed examination of how industrial characteristics moderate the effectiveness of high-performance work systems.

Table 7.1   Sample details

	Number of UK companies (per cent)	Number of US companies (per cent)	Total sample (per cent)
Establishment size			
10–25	35 (38.5)	37 (37.8)	72 (38.1)
26–50	32 (35.2)	30 (30.6)	62 (32.8)
51–75	10 (10.9)	12 (12.2)	22 (11.6)
76–100	14 (15.4)	19 (19.4)	33 (17.5)
Total	91 (100.0)	98 (100.0)	189 (100.0)
Age			
Mean	25.1 years	20.3 years	23.2
Range	491–1.5 years	114–1.1 years	491–1.1 years
Industry: Manufacturing			
2833 – Medicinal chemicals and botanical products	6	7	13
2834 – Pharmaceutical preparations	7	9	16
3827 – Optimal instruments and lenses	4	5	9
3841 – Surgical and medical instruments and apparatus	9	11	20
3844 – Radiology/electrical medical equipment	4	5	9
Total	30 (33.0)	37 (40.7)	67 (35.4)
Industry: Services			
8071 – Medical and scientific laboratories	9	10	19
8072 – Dental laboratories	8	7	15
8051 – Skilled nursing facilities	25	23	48
5411 – Grocery stores	19	21	40
Total	61 (67.0)	61 (62.2)	122 (64.6)
Large firm affiliation	31 (34.0)	40 (40.8)	71 (37.6)
Trade union members	17 (18.5)	14 (14.3)	31 (16.4)
ISO recognition and/or industry specific quality recognition	32 (35.2)	54 (55.1)	86 (45.5)
External assistance	35 (38.5)	19 (19.4)	54 (28.6)

As the firms employed less than 100 people we thought they would be unlikely to have an HR Department or HR Director/Specialist (see Klaas et al., 2000). Letters were therefore sent to the company's CEO/Owner/ Director or the most senior person that could be identified from the Dun and Bradstreet database. Given low responses to postal surveys, in particular from SMEs (Dennis, 2003), a telephone survey of the selected companies was conducted. The following protocol was followed.

1. The contact person was sent a briefing on the objectives of the survey and the expected length of the interview. Confidentiality was emphasized.
2. The person was then contacted to see if they would agree to the telephone interview and if agreeable, a date and time was set. They were then faxed a 'glossary' of HRM terminology and definitions of the financial variables that they would be asked about. It was found, however, that this fax had a negative effect on people completing the telephone survey. This was a particular problem in the US. It was likely that small business owners did not wish to reveal financial information, despite our assurances of confidentiality. Once this problem was identified, the financial variable information was dropped.

Interviews were conducted by telephone with the company's CEO/Owner/ Director in 87 per cent of cases in the UK and 83 per cent of cases in the US. The remaining interviews were carried out with the Director of Human Resources/Personnel/Employee Relations. Targeting the CEO/Owner/ Director of the company contrasts with most HRM studies where the HRM manager is the respondent. However Sels et al. (2006a, 2006b) use a similar approach and argue, 'The simple management structure of a small business implies that the business manager often has a clearer view on the various management practices in the organization' (2006a: p. 328).

Many of the interviewees appeared extremely interested in the research. Thus, in around half of the interviews, quite lengthy discussions took place. Summaries of these discussions, comments and feedback were entered into the final databases, which were used in the analysis and helped to provide us with an understanding of the processes behind the quantitative data. Some clear themes emerged from the analysis of these quantitative data. We found that in companies where more HRM practices were used, these managers had previously worked for a large organization and thus had been exposed to, and were familiar with, the use of HRM practices. These same managers also indicated that having formal HRM practices in place was crucial to employee morale, reducing labour turnover, increasing returns on investing in their employees (in part through reducing voluntary turnover) and running an organized company. Furthermore these managers were more likely than the survey population to have a university degree. Finally these managers often did note that HRM had to be 'adapted' to meet the needs of small firms.

On this last point, several of these managers – namely those who had previously worked for a large organization where they had been exposed to, and hence were familiar with, the use of HRM practices – emphasized the need for 'balance'. They suggested that too much formalization of HRM practices was inappropriate, unnecessary and costly in small firms, while too little would result in a workforce that was 'unaccountable'.

In total 1173 companies were asked to participate in the survey in the UK (holding companies and companies where it was clear that they had been categorized in the wrong SIC were excluded). Of these, 1051 declined, 31 agreed but subsequently failed to complete the interview and 91 interviews were completed successfully (a response rate of 8 per cent). In the US, 1221 companies were asked to participate, 1066 declined, 56 agreed but subsequently failed to complete the interview and 98 interviews were completed successfully (again, a response rate of 8 per cent). Based on response rates to the pilot telephone interviews, our sampling aim was to obtain a total quota of 5 per cent of our population and to achieve representation within the stratified sample cells. Where possible, potential interviewees were asked why they declined to participate: the main reason was 'time constraints'. Many of the business owners commented that they worked long hours, often seven-day weeks, and even though many stated that the study seemed interesting and that they did need to learn more about 'personnel management' and 'how to manage their employees more effectively', they simply could not 'spare the time'. The other main reason for not participating in the study was 'confidentiality concerns', particularly in the US firms.

To check for response bias, we undertook t-test comparisons of the size bands and the SIC category of the responding firms with the same data for the non-responding firms (that is, the full sample supplied by Dun and Bradstreet for both the UK and US. No significant differences (p <. 001) between these two subgroups were found for size. Firms in the manufacturing industries were significantly (p<.001) more likely to respond than firms in the service industries in both the UK and US. Firms in the grocery store industry were the least likely to participate in the study in both samples.

Measures of HRM practices
There is considerable debate in the HRM–performance literature on which variables to include as measures of HRM: whether selected practices should be given equal weights in estimations; whether a single HRM index is an appropriate measure; whether the use of more HRM practices means more effective HRM or more importantly whether observed links between HRM practices and organizational performance are causal or merely

reflect pre-existing differences between firms. Godard (2004) provides a comprehensive critique of the HRM–performance paradigm.

In time series studies by Cappelli and Neumark (2001), Wright et al. (2005), Sels et al. (2006a, 2006b), which were conducted on a sample of small firms employing ten to 100 people, it was found that there were serious cost implications of implementing HRM practices and that perhaps these were more significant for small firms compared to large firms. These costs significantly weakened or came close to eliminating altogether the correlation of HRM practices and firm performance in these studies.

Since our data are cross-sectional, they cannot reveal much about causality and the cost implications of the introduction of HRM practices. In terms of the selection of HRM practices we follow previous studies of HRM in small and large organizations. Since knowledge is still limited about which practices 'matter' for small firms, we chose not to weight any of the measures.

The selection of the core HRM measures used in this study was influenced by the Harvard HRM model developed by Beer et al. (1984). This informed the initial identification of relevant HRM categories. In addition though we examine the potential relevance of strategic human resource management in the context of small firms (see, for example, the classic work of Delery and Doty, 1996) and therefore a 'strategy' domain is included in our index.

HRM practices were measured through 21 items in the interview schedule, as outlined in Table 7.2. These 21 items were drawn from the existing literature on HRM in large and small firms. From the large-firm literature we relied on Becker and Gerhard (1996), Bowen and Ostroff (2004), Delery and Shaw (2001), Dyer and Reeves (1995), Guest and Hoque (1994), Huselid (1995), Ichniowski et al. (1997), and Pfeffer (1994, 1998). Studies of small-firm HRM by Cassell et al. (2002), Chandler and McEvoy (2000), Ciavarella (2003), de Kok and Uhlaner (2001), Deshpande and Golhar (1994), Duberley and Walley (1995), Guthrie (2001), Hayton (2003), Nguyen and Bryant (2004), Sels et al. (2006a, 2006b) and Way (2002) also informed our research.

Based on this previous empirical work and much influenced by Beer et al.'s (1984) seminal study, we initially piloted eight main areas of HRM. These included the amount of effort and resources used to recruit the right people, employment security and the use of internal career ladders, formal training systems, formal results-orientated appraisals, performance-based compensation, employee voice and consultation, broadly defined jobs and decentralization, and strategic HRM.

However, to ensure these fitted with what HRM looks like in small firms, we conducted several pilots of the survey. The pilot stage commenced with a focus group of half a dozen small business CEOs in the US. The survey was modified after the focus group and then further pre-survey/pilot interviews with eight companies in the UK and US were conducted to

Table 7.2   HRM practices used in UK and US small firms

HRM practices	Mean UK N=91	Mean US N=98	Mean All N=189
Recruitment and selection			
Use of at least one of the following selection methods: formal application form; formal interview; work sample; test of job skills; assessment of job skills	0.889	0.913	0.91
Performance appraisal			
Formal appraisal of majority (>50 per cent) of managerial and non-managerial employees on a regular basis or at least annually	0.605	0.721	0.665
Performance-based compensation			
Individually-based performance pay	0.521	0.650	0.563
Profit sharing (or some other type of company-based reward system)	0.100	0.152	0.126
Employee stock options	0.022	0.053	0.037
Team-based performance	0.208	0.285	0.249
Training–education achievement-linked bonus	0.199	0.152	0.175
Training and development			
Formal induction programme for new employees	0.912	0.936	0.926
The majority (>50 per cent) of managerial and non-managerial employees received formal (NVQ and/or off-the-job) training in past 12 months	0.612	0.489	0.550
The majority (>50 per cent) of managerial and non-managerial employees received informal (on-the-job) training in past 12 months	0.802	0.785	0.794
Employee voice and participation			
Employee representation at board/senior management meetings	0.462	0.412	0.434
Joint consultative committees (JCCs)	0.203	0.221	0.211

Table 7.2   (continued)

HRM practices	Mean UK N=91	Mean US N=98	Mean All N=189
Employee voice and participation			
Employees surveyed on regular basis, at least annually	0.788	0.792	0.794
Employees consulted about new hires	0.332	0.255	0.291
Where financial targets are set (59 per cent of UK firms; 68 per cent of US firms), employees are informed about the status of these targets (i.e. whether exceeded, met or not met)	0.205	0.153	0.180
Formal employment documentation			
Written employment contract	0.934	0.615	0.768
Written job description	0.553	0.592	0.572
HRM strategy			
HR department or specialist	0.033	0.073	0.059
Analysis of recruitment methods at least annually	0.333	0.388	0.360
Recruitment plan for next year	0.312	0.436	0.374
Training and development plan for next year	0.533	0.484	0.510

check what types of HRM practices were likely to be found in the small firms in our selected industries and what terminology small-firm owners were familiar with in relation to HRM practices in the above areas.

We also considered the types of HRM practices used for different employee groups within the firm (Osterman, 1994) at the pre-survey stage. Where interviewees indicated that a practice was used, we investigated how widely dispersed this was across the firm. In particular, we examined whether certain categories of employees, such as non-managerial ones, were not affected by a particular HRM practice.

The majority of CEOs interviewed in the pilot stage emphasized that given the risk and uncertainty inherent in owning and working in a small company, employment security was not a realistic objective. One interviewee stated, 'To be a successful entrepreneur you must have the mentality that in any given month you will need to shut your doors, lay off all of your employees (including family members) and file for bankruptcy – there is no security in running your own business'. The interviewees emphasized that the companies were all quite horizontal, so prospects for promotion (internal career ladders) were limited, and that all employees were expected to be functionally flexible and thus jobs were broadly defined. In addition, it was emphasized that where an HRM practice was used (such as performance appraisals, performance-related pay or employee surveys) it almost always applied to all groups of employees – managerial and non-managerial – due to the horizontal structure of the firms. Thus the method often used in studies of HRM in large firms of asking interviewees about the 'proportion of the workforce that experienced a particular practice' was also modified, as in the focus groups and during the pilot interviews, this question was challenged as being 'not applicable' to small firms.

In terms of decentralization, again for various reasons interviewees did not feel this was applicable to small firms. Some interviewees said that employees were consulted frequently, especially about any major changes or initiatives, and this was viewed as 'decentralized' decision-making. In other cases it was felt that management needed to 'get on and make the key decisions' and thus decentralization of decision-making was simply not appropriate.

Thus, perhaps not surprisingly given the nature of small firms, it was found that two categories of HRM practices used widely in HRM–performance studies for large firms – 'employment security and the internal labour market' and 'broadly defined jobs and decentralization' – were not applicable and were excluded from the survey.

Unlike the situation in large firms, not all small firms are likely to issue written employment contracts (required by law in the UK but not in the US) or written job descriptions. The pre-survey interviews found these two factors seemed important for small firms and their presence was correlated to a general awareness and use of HRM practices. They are therefore included in a category called 'written employment documentation'.

Seven aggregate HRM practices are used in the analysis. These categories are broadly consistent with those used in other HRM–performance studies (Hoque, 1999; Ichniowski et al., 1997). As in these other studies, there was a slight imbalance in the number of practices included in each category, driven basically by the number of practices that were relevant within each of the seven broad categories. These are shown in Table 7.2.

While experience of certain work practices (performance appraisals, performance-related pay and training) did vary slightly between managerial and non-managerial employees, in general if a practice was used, all employees in the category (managerial or non-managerial) were either exposed to it or had the opportunity to avail themselves of the practice. In small firms there was little management will or indeed opportunity to exclude employees from HRM practices. Therefore when constructing the HRM index an

HRM practice was counted if it applied to 'the majority (> 50 per cent) of both managerial and non-managerial employees'.

Factor analysis of the seven aggregate HRM practices revealed no coherent factors or what might be described as 'bundles' of practices. We therefore measured the overall human resource system, based on the score on an HRM index, which encompasses the seven HRM categories. This is similar to the approach used by other researchers including those examining the links between HRM–performance in small firms (see Nguyen and Bryant, 2004; Sels et al., 2006a, 2006b; Way, 2002). Like our research, these studies were influenced by Becker and Huselid's (1998) conclusion of a preference in this research 'for a unitary index that contains a set (though not always the same set) of theoretically appropriate HRM practices derived from prior work' (p. 63).

The mean number of practices used in the UK sample was 12.1 and 14.7 for the US sample. Thus, our measure of HRM used to test the hypotheses is cumulative, with each firm being ranked according to the extent to which they adopted the 21 HRM practices. All practices are coded as 1 if they are used and meet the criteria described in Table 7.2, and 0 otherwise. The Cronbach alpha score for the HR index is 0.71, indicating that the multidimensional concept of HRM practices can be approximated by our one-dimensional index.

Performance variables
Estimates of labour productivity and financial performance were obtained from respondents being asked to rate each on a scale of one (much worse) to five (much better):

1. How well does labour productivity at your company compare with other companies in the same industry?
2. How does financial performance – profitability – at your company compare with other companies in the same industry over the past financial year?
3. During the past three years, has the company introduced any product or process innovations? (Companies introducing at least one innovation are classified as 'innovators').

Interviewees seemed acutely aware of where their company ranked compared to others in the same industry. Indeed, 63 per cent and 74 per cent of the UK and US companies respectively had benchmarked (examined the way things are done at other workplaces and compared them with their own company) in the past two years.

For the majority of sample companies (60 per cent in both the UK and US), we were able to obtain independent financial data from Dun and

Bradstreet. Objective financial performance was measured using financial data supplied by Dun and Bradstreet as part of the original sample framework (the 'population') and then supplemented with additional data from its Comprehensive Financial Reports for the sample companies where data was not supplied with the original sample. Financial data were obtained for a sub-sample of 55 of the 91 sample firms in the UK and 59 of the 98 sample firms in the US.

Objective measures were constructed from these data. Productivity was calculated as gross sales per employee. Profit was calculated as the pre-tax financial value of sales divided by the number of employees (that is, profit per employee) because 'cost per employee' data were not available. The profit variable was deflated by the producer price index in which the company belonged. To deal with the non-normal deviations of the data we used the logarithm of the raw scores. The means and standard deviations for UK companies were: M=4.89, SD=3.01 and M=6.85, SD=2.25 for profitability and productivity respectively; and for US companies M=5.14, SD=3.41 and M=7.77, SD=3.16 for profitability and productivity respectively.

These data allow us to address the issue of convergent validity between the subjective and objective measures of performance (see the Appendix for how we tested these relationships) and also to test Hypothesis 2, that any HRM–performance relationship will be equally significant whether objective or subjective measures of performance are used. The findings on convergent validity for the subjective and objective measures of company performance demonstrated a relatively high degree of consistency between subjective performance measures and their objective counterparts.

Control variables
We used a number of control variables that have previously been used in research into HRM and performance in SMEs (Aragon-Sanchez and Sanchez-Marin, 2005; Bacon et al., 1996; Duberley and Walley, 1995). Descriptive statistics on these variables are given in the Appendix. The control variables, with the name used to identify them in the results tables given in parentheses, are as follows.

1. Number of employees (Size).
2. Age of the company (Age) where age was 2005 (the year of the study) minus the founding year.
3. Sector dummies for 'Industry (Manufacturing)' comprising companies in the 2833, 2834, 3827, 3841, 3844 SIC codes; companies in the 8051, 8071 and 8072 SIC codes were placed in the 'Industry (Services)'

category; and companies in the 5411 SIC code in the 'Industry (Other)' category. The omitted category is 'Industry (Other)'.

4.   Whether the company has a large firm affiliation (34 per cent and 41 per cent for UK and US companies respectively) (Large Firm Affiliation) (yes=1, no=0). This variable investigates whether the firm has access to a larger company supplier or customer closely associated with the small company (the small company, however, is not a subsidiary of the larger company). This variable is used as de Kok and Uhlaner (2001) found that this type of relationship between a small firm and a large firm influenced the degree of formalization of HRM practices, while we also found in our pilot interviews that it affected the use and formalization of HRM practices.

5.   Market environment (1 = declining; 2 = turbulent; 3 = stable; 4 = growing; and 5 = growing rapidly) (Market Conditions).

6.   Trade union presence (18.5 per cent and 14 per cent for UK and US companies respectively) (Trade Union Presence) (yes = 1, no = 0).

7.   ISO 9000 series recognition (41.1 per cent and 49.5 per cent for UK and US companies respectively) (ISO Recognition) (yes = 1, no = 0). Surveys of ISO 9000 recognition in small firms indicate that installing such a system is a major exercise, is costly, especially in the short run, must be well planned and usually requires an internal champion, particularly the CEO (McAdam and McKeown, 1999; McTeer and Dale, 1996; Porter and Rayner, 1991; and Taylor, 1995). Thus, similar to investment in HRM practices, ISO recognition in small firms requires significant investment and is a recognition by management that this type of investment will improve the company's performance, at least in the medium to long term. There is also overlap between requirements for ISO recognition and formalization of HRM practices, especially in relation to training and education of the workforce. Indeed, the pilot interviews found that firms with ISO recognition were more likely to have more formalized HRM systems in place, which is why we use recognition as a control variable.

8.   Whether the company received external assistance from organizations. In the UK this could be from Business Links or the Small Business Advisory Service, the Small Firms Loan Guarantee scheme or the EU (38 per cent). In the US this could include assistance from the Small Business Administration, Chambers of Commerce, or Business Administration Centers (19 per cent). (External Assistance) (yes = 1, no = 0); and

9.   A country dummy variable is added to the full sample regressions (Country) (UK = 0 and US = 1).

The results

Descriptive results
The correlations among the items, the means and standard deviations for the full sample are shown in Table 7.3.

Almost all the variables displayed the signs consistent with other HRM–performance studies and descriptive results reported in other studies of HRM practices in small firms (Aragon-Sanchez and Sanchez-Marin, 2005; Cassell et al., 2002; Chandler and McEvoy, 2000; Ciavarella, 2003; Duberley and Walley, 1995). In particular we find significantly positive correlations between firm size, age, having a large firm affiliation, operating in a growing market, having ISO certification and having received external assistance, on the one hand, and the use of most of the HRM practices and having an HRM strategy in place, on the other hand. Firm size and age are marginally negatively correlated with the use of employee voice and participation methods.

In relation to the receipt of external assistance, significantly negative correlations are found in relation to company size and age which is what is to be expected – small, young start-up companies are more likely to seek external assistance than larger, more established companies.

Significant positive correlations between the HRM practices themselves are found, suggesting the practices are not independent of one another. The positive relationship between having an HRM strategy in place is particularly highly correlated with firm size, age, having written employment documentation and formal training.

UK–US differences were positive and significant for the use of performance appraisals, performance-related pay, strategic HRM, subjective and objective labour productivity and innovation. Having written employment documentation was significantly negatively correlated with being a US firm, reflecting regulatory differences.

In terms of the subjective and objective performance variables, these are significantly positively correlated with one another and between the variables themselves, suggesting validity of these measures.

The association between HRM and subjective indicators of performance
Hierarchical regression analysis was used to test the hypotheses for productivity and financial performance. Standardized beta coefficients are reported for these variables. Since innovation is a bivariate variable, it is estimated by using a logit model. The regression coefficients and standard errors are therefore reported for the innovation variable. For firm age the natural log is used to account for a somewhat skewed distribution within these data.

Table 7.3　Means, standard deviations and correlations among main study variables: all firms[a]

Variable	Mean	SD	1	2	3	4	5	6	7	8
1. Size	35.01	18.93								
2. Age	23.20	35.45	0.49							
3. Industry (Manuf.)	0.35	0.46	0.50	0.21						
4. Industry (Services)	0.43	0.52	0.09	0.10	0.01					
5. Large firm affil.	37.60	0.33	0.44	0.35	0.25	0.11				
6. Market condit.	3.88	1.62	0.47	0.18	0.09	0.11	0.22			
7. TU presence	16.40	0.51	0.55	0.45	0.15	0.13	0.09	0.08		
8. ISO recog.	45.50	0.22	0.60	0.49	0.30	0.10	0.52	0.20	0.07	
9. Ext. assist.	28.62	0.55	−0.61	−0.51	−0.09	0.27	0.55	0.19	0.09	0.19
10. Country	0.52	0.54	0.22	0.07	0.06	0.08	0.08	0.10	−0.11	0.33
11. Recruit. & selection	90.01	10.01	0.21	0.27	0.21	0.25	0.41	0.20	0.13	0.25
12. Perf. App.	66.50	9.82	0.25	0.20	0.19	0.30	0.41	0.19	0.08	0.09
13. Perf. rel pay	52.43	11.92	0.26	0.22	0.27	0.44	0.23	0.49	0.05	0.42
14. Formal train.	69.34	12.22	0.22	0.06	0.20	0.33	0.60	0.50	0.15	0.48
15. Employee voice & partic.	55.31	12.50	−0.16	−0.15	0.09	0.17	0.14	0.21	0.18	0.20
16. Written empl. docum.	66.53	19.22	0.62	0.60	0.11	0.35	0.58	0.35	0.32	0.41
17. Strategic HR	25.70	13.53	0.68	0.59	0.17	0.33	0.37	0.32	0.14	0.35
18. Lab. prod.	3.96	0.61	0.15	0.10	−0.02	0.15	0.42	0.46	0.06	0.41
19. Fin. perf.	3.40	0.70	0.17	0.11	−0.05	0.22	0.44	0.50	0.10	0.39
20. Innovated	0.77	0.43	0.10	0.09	0.23	0.32	0.21	0.44	0.07	0.43
21. Sales/ employee	38492.12	21866.23	0.15	0.13	0.05	0.11	0.35	0.48	0.03	0.45
22. Profit/ employee	1615.23	31276.45	0.19	0.15	0.08	0.19	0.39	0.45	0.06	0.53

Notes:
[a]　All reports by interviewees with the exception of sales per employee and profit per employee.
For correlations > 0.11, $p < 0.05$; correlations > 0.15, $p < 0.01$; and correlations > 0.19, $p < 0.001$.

9	10	11	12	13	14	15	16	17	18	19	20	21
0.10												
0.12	0.10											
0.15	0.25	0.44										
0.19	0.39	0.46	0.82									
0.41	0.10	0.52	0.51	0.67								
0.09	0.08	0.17	0.28	0.25	0.35							
0.67	−0.32	0.66	0.53	0.48	0.70	0.68						
0.55	0.54	0.58	0.58	0.42	0.73	0.61	0.79					
0.08	0.39	0.11	0.22	0.22	0.41	0.26	0.19	0.44				
0.20	0.10	0.14	0.23	0.17	0.32	0.28	0.17	0.32	0.41			
0.10	0.29	0.15	0.21	0.20	0.53	0.44	0.25	0.45	0.53	0.44		
0.10	0.33	0.17	0.19	0.19	0.38	0.28	0.23	0.40	0.45	0.35	0.53	
0.19	0.09	0.20	0.31	0.22	0.35	0.19	0.15	0.38	0.35	0.48	0.38	0.41

Hypothesis 1 proposes a positive correlation between greater use of HR and higher labour productivity, better financial performance, and an increased probability of innovating. Results for the test of the link between these variables are shown in Table 7.4. It should be noted that all of these variables pertain to reports from the interviewees.

We found firm size significantly positively correlated with all of the performance variables. The age of the company was also positively and

Table 7.4 Results for Hypothesis 1[a]

	Labor productivity			Financial performance			Innovation		
	Full	UK	US	Full	UK	US	Full	UK	US
Size	0.21***	0.19***	0.22***	0.21***	0.22***	0.20***	0.305 (0.119)**	0.298 (0.117)**	0.413 (0.115)***
Age	0.12*	0.13*	0.12*	0.20***	0.19**	0.21***	0.218 (0.164)	–0.213 (0.101)*	0.102 (0.070)
Industry (Manufacturing)	0.12*	0.14*	0.13*	0.18**	0.21***	0.19*	0.173 (0.073)**	0.162 (0.065)**	0.159 (0.082)*
Industry (Services)	0.09	0.07	0.10	0.20***	0.11	0.25***	0.225 (0.087)**	0.218 (0.110)*	0.284 (0.088)***
Large Firm Association	0.15**	0.16**	0.16**	0.21***	0.22***	0.20***	0.387 (0.115)**	0.260 (0.138)*	0.207 (0.058)***
Market Conditions	0.16**	0.14*	0.17**	0.24***	0.22***	0.24***	0.406 (0.150)**	0.397 (0.178)**	0.352 (0.177)*
Trade Union Presence	0.08	0.12*	0.06	0.02	0.03	0.01	0.103 (0.066)	0.202 (0.126)	0.087 (0.083)
ISO Recognition	0.19**	0.24***	0.18**	0.16*	0.25***	0.12*	0.267 (0.107)**	0.112 (0.049)**	0.318 (0.092)***
External Assistance	0.18**	0.23***	0.16*	0.18**	0.20***	0.15*	0.172 (0.079)*	0.263 (0.105)**	0.162 (0.084)*
Country	0.17**	–	–	0.08	–	–	0.176 (0.088)*	–	–
HR Index:	0.24***	0.23***	0.27***	0.17**	0.12*	0.18**	0.452 (0.125)***	0.338 (0.141)**	0.588 (0.129)***
Adjusted R-squared	0.14	0.17	0.13	0.08	0.05	0.07	–	–	–

F	3.213***	2.521**	2.814***	2.552**	2.192*	2.104*	–	–		
Pseudo R^2	–	–	–	–	–	0.093	0.082	0.091	0.091	
N	186	90	96	181	88	93	187	90	97	97

Notes:

[a] This and the following table show beta weights for labour productivity and financial performance derived from the regressions in which all of the items in each column are entered simultaneously. For innovation, logit analysis is used and the coefficients given (standard errors in brackets).

*** significant at 1 per cent;

** significant at 5 per cent; and

* significant at 10 per cent in all models.

significantly correlated with labour productivity and financial performance. In terms of innovation, age is positive but not significant for the full and US samples but negatively and significantly correlated with age for the UK sample. Thus, older firms in the UK were less likely to innovate. Having an affiliation with a large firm and ISO recognition were both significantly positively correlated with all the performance measures, and especially so for UK companies. The same was found in relation to having received external assistance, where the coefficient was positive and significant, again especially for UK companies.

Trade union presence was positive but not significant for all of the performance variables. Note that only a small number of companies in the sample had trade union members. In terms of market conditions, operating in a growing market is significantly positively correlated with all of the performance variables.

In relation to the HRM practices and performance (Hypothesis 1), significantly positive correlations are found for all the performance variables. The HR index is significantly positively related to the likelihood of innovating, especially for US firms, but also for UK firms and for the combined sample. The HR index is significantly positively related to labour productivity for US and UK firms. Given that these HR practices are costly in terms of time and money to introduce and implement, it might be expected that investing in such practices would be more likely to enhance productivity and innovation than profitability. This indeed is what our results show. However, although the positive link between the HR index and profitability is statistically weaker than the link with either innovation or productivity, it does not disappear entirely.

HRM practices and objective estimates of firm performance
The productivity and profitability data are based on Dun and Bradstreet data and are presented for a subset of sample firms as described above to test Hypothesis 2. Table 7.5 shows there are no consistent differences between the results based on subjective and objective measures of performance. The betas on the objective measures and the significance levels are higher than for the subjective measures, but since the samples are not identical, no inferences can be drawn from this. We thus cannot reject Hypothesis 2, which suggests that there would be similar sets of results using subjective and objective performance measures.

For both sets of results, the correlations between the HR index and financial performance is weaker compared to the other performance variables. This presumably reflects the costs of investing in such HRM practices, so that even where they have a positive effect on performance measures such as productivity or innovation, the financial cost of investing in the practices will detract

Table 7.5   Results for Hypothesis 2

Variable	Labor productivity			Financial performance		
	Full	UK	US	Full	UK	US
Size	0.19**	0.20***	0.19***	0.17**	0.16*	0.22***
Age	0.15**	0.16*	0.13*	0.18**	0.15*	0.11*
Industry (Manufacturing)	0.11*	0.11*	0.09	0.16**	0.11*	0.18**
Industry (Services)	0.07	0.10	0.12*	0.12*	0.07	0.18**
Large Firm Association	0.16**	0.15*	0.17**	0.19**	0.17*	0.15*
Market Conditions	0.20***	0.16**	0.19**	0.26***	0.25***	0.28***
Trade Union Presence	0.02	0.03	0.00	0.03	0.05	0.01
ISO Recognition	0.15*	0.16**	0.15*	0.14*	0.13*	0.12*
External Assistance	0.16**	0.18**	0.14*	0.13*	0.15*	0.08
Country	0.25***	–	–	0.10	–	–
HR Index:	0.35***	0.28***	0.36***	0.20***	0.15**	0.19***
Adjusted R^2	0.18	0.15	0.13	0.07	0.03	0.05
F	3.554***	2.321***	2.514***	2.219**	1.913*	1.887*
N	114	55	59	114	55	59

Notes:
*** significant at 1 per cent;
** significant at 5 per cent;
* significant at 10 per cent.

from their profitability. However, there is still a statistically positive correlation between our HR index and profitability from both sets of results, namely those using subjective measures and those using objective measures.

Conclusion
It might well be thought by managers of small firms that the HRM–performance link applies particularly to large firms able to invest in an HRM Department and in the range of practices that the literature suggests need to be pursued in combination. The introduction of such practices for a small firm might either not bring about the improved productivity which studies relying on datasets of mainly large firms have found, or any productivity gain that is achieved might boost the firm's finances by less than the overall cost of introducing such practices, leaving the firm worse off financially. We

therefore tested three performance measures – innovation, labour productivity and financial performance – against the use of HRM practices.

Our results demonstrated significantly positive correlations between HRM practices on the one hand, and corporate performance on the other. Thus, the generally positive HRM–performance results emerging from the literature for innovation and productivity are also found for our sample of small firms. But with cash flow at such a premium for small firms, can they afford to invest in and maintain the types of HRM practices examined in this study, however desirable the performance outcomes such as improved productivity might be? Is the financial payback from higher productivity and enhanced innovation greater or less than the financial outlay required to deliver these outcomes?

To answer these questions, we tested for the financial outcome as a third performance measure. As expected, given the cost of these HRM practices, the correlation between the presence of the HRM practices and financial performance was weaker than the correlation between the presence of these HRM practices and the other performance measures of innovation and productivity. Although the correlation with financial performance was weaker it was nevertheless still positive and statistically significant. For these small firms, our results suggest that the HRM practices do appear to pay.

These findings should be interpreted bearing in mind the following caveats. First, the sample size is relatively limited even for small business research where survey response rates are always a problem. This is especially so in relation to financial performance. Second, the data are cross-sectional and so can only be used to test for correlations rather than causality. Third, the data were collected from one individual in each firm, and so there may be common method variance. Finally, we did not investigate whether the impact of HRM practices on outcomes were mediated through employee attitudes (on which see Godard, 2001; Ramsay et al., 2000).

Such issues are being addressed theoretically, methodologically and empirically in the continuing HRM–performance literature and research agenda, although generally with a view to the corporate sector as a whole rather than small firms. Similar work focused on the small firm sector might help illuminate the HRM–performance processes in general, as well as contribute to our understanding of the dynamics of small firms and performance management within them.

References

Appelbaum, E., T. Bailey, P. Berg and A.L. Kalleberg (2000), *Manufacturing Advantage: Why High-Performance Work Systems Pay Off*, Ithaca, NY: Cornell University Press.
Aragon-Sanchez, A. and G. Sanchez-Marin (2005), 'Strategic orientation, management characteristics and performance: A study of Spanish SMEs', *Journal of Small Business Management*, **43**(3), 287–309.

Arthur, J.B. (1994), 'Effects of human resource systems on manufacturing performance and turnover', *Academy of Management Journal*, **31**, 670–87.

Bacon, N., P. Ackers, D. Storey and D. Coates (1996), 'It's a small world: Managing human resource management in small businesses', *International Journal of Human Resource Management*, **1**(1), 82–98.

Barney, J. (1995), 'Looking inside for competitive advantage', *Academy of Management Executive*, **9**, 49–61.

Becker, B. and B. Gerhard (1996), 'The impact of human resource management on organizational performance: Progress and prospects', *Academy of Management Journal*, **39**, 779–801.

Becker, B.E. and M.A. Huselid (1998), 'High performance work systems and firm performance: A synthesis of research and managerial implications', in G.R. Feffis (ed.), *Research in Personnel and Human Resources*, Vol. 16, Stanford, CT: JAI Press, pp. 53–101.

Beer, M., P. Spector and E. Walton (1984), *Managing Human Assets*, New York: Free Press.

Bowen, D. and C. Ostroff (2004), 'Understanding HRM–firm performance linkages: The role of the "strength" of the HRM system', *Academy of Management Review*, **29**, 203–21.

Capelli, P. and D. Neumark (2001), 'Do "high performance" work practices improve establishment-level outcomes?', *Industrial and Labor Relations Review*, **54**, 737–75.

Cassell, C., S. Nadin, M. Gray and C. Clegg (2002), 'Exploring human resource management practices in small and medium sized enterprises', *Personnel Review*, **31**(5/6), 671–92.

Chandler, G. and G. McEvoy (2000), 'Human resource management, TQM and firm performance in small and medium-size enterprises', *Entrepreneurship: Theory and Practice*, Fall, pp. 43–57.

Ciavarella, M. (2003), 'The adoption of high-involvement work practices and processes in emergent and developing firms: A descriptive and prescriptive approach', *Human Resource Management*, **42**(4), 337–56.

Datta, D., J. Guthrie and P.M. Wright (2005), 'Human resource management and labor productivity: Does industry matter?', *The Academy of Management Journal*, **48**(1), 135–45.

de Kok, J. and L. Uhlaner (2001), 'Organizational context and human resource management in small firms', *Small Business Economics*, **17**(4), 273–91.

de Kok, J., M. Uhlaner and R. Thurik (2002), *Human Resource Management within Small and Medium-Sized Firms: Facts and Explanations*, Zoetermeer: EIM/Erasmus University Rotterdam.

Delery, J. and D.H. Doty (1996), 'Models of theorizing in strategic human resource management: Tests of universalistic, contingency, and configurational performance predictions', *Academy of Management Journal*, **39**(4), 802–35.

Delery, J. and D. Shaw (2001), 'The strategic management of people in work organizations: Review, synthesis and extension', *Research in Personnel and Human Resource Management*, **20**, 165–97.

Dennis, W.J. (2003), 'Raising response rates in mail surveys of small business owners: Results of an experiment', *Journal of Small Business Management*, **41**, 278–95.

Deshpande, S. and D. Golhar (1994), 'HRM practices in large and small manufacturing firms: A comparative study', *Journal of Small Business Management*, **32**(2), 49–56.

Drummond, I. and I. Stone (2006), 'Exploring the potential of high performance work systems in SMEs', *Employee Relations*, **29**(2), 192–207.

Duberley, J.P. and P. Walley (1995), 'Assessing the adoption of HRM by small and medium-sized manufacturing organizations', *International Journal of Human Resource Management*, **4**(4), 891–909.

Dyer, L. and L. Reeves (1995), 'Human resource strategies and firm performance: What do we know and where do we need to go?', paper presented to the 10th IIRA World Congress, Washington, 31 May–4 June.

Godard, J. (2001), 'High performance and the transformation of work? The implications of alternative work practices for the experience and outcomes of work', *Industrial and Labor Relations Review*, **54**, 776–805.

Godard, J. (2004), 'A critical assessment of the high-performance paradigm', *British Journal of Industrial Relations*, **42**(2), 349–78.

Guest, D. and K. Hoque (1994), 'The good, the bad and the ugly: Employment relations in new non-union workplaces', *Human Resource Management*, **5**, 1–14.
Guest, D., J. Michie, M. Sheehan and N. Conway (2000), *Employee Relations, HRM and Business Performance: An Analysis of the 1998 Workplace Employee Relations Survey*, London: Chartered Institute of Personnel and Development.
Guest, D., J. Michie, N. Conway and M. Sheehan (2003), 'A study of human resource management and corporate performance in the UK', *British Journal of Industrial Relations*, **41**(2), 291–314.
Guthrie, J.P. (2001), 'High-involvement work practices, turnover, and productivity: Evidence from New Zealand', *Academy of Management Journal*, **44**, 180–90.
Hayton, J. (2003), 'Strategic human capital management in SMEs: An empirical study of entrepreneurial performance', *Human Resource Management*, **42**(2), 375–91.
Hoque, K. (1999), 'Human resource management and performance in the UK hotel industry', *British Journal of Industrial Relations*, **37**(3), 419–43.
Huselid, M. (1995), 'The impact of human resource management on turnover, productivity and corporate financial performance', *Academy of Management Journal*, **38**(3), 635–72.
Huselid, M. (2003), 'Editor's Note: Special issue on small and medium-sized enterprises: A call for more research', *Human Resource Management*, **42**(4), 297.
Ichniowski, C., K. Shaw and G. Prennushi (1994), *The Effects of Human Resource Management Practices on Productivity*, New York: Columbia University Press.
Ichniowski, C., K. Shaw and G. Prennushi (1997), 'The effects of human resource management on productivity: A study of steel finishing lines', *American Economic Review*, **87**(3), 291–313.
Klaas, B., J. McClendon and T. Gainey (2000), 'Managing HR in the small and medium enterprise: the impact of professional employer organizations', *Entrepreneurship: Theory and Practice*, **25**(1), 107–23.
Kleinknecht, A. (1998), 'Is labour market flexibility harmful to innovation?', *Cambridge Journal of Economics*, **22**(3), 387–96.
Kleinknecht, A., R. Oostendorp and M. Pradhan (1997), *Flexible Labour, Firm Growth and Employment: An exploration of Micro Data in the Netherlands*, mimeo, 2 December 1997.
MacDuffie, J. (1995), 'Human resource bundles and manufacturing performance: Organizational logic and flexible production systems in the world auto industry', *Industrial and Labour Relations Review*, **48**(2), 197–221.
McAdam, R. and M. McKeown (1999), 'Life after ISO 9000: An analysis of the impact of ISO 9000 and total quality management on small businesses in Northern Ireland', *Total Quality Management*, **10**(2), 229–41.
McTeer, M.M. and B.G. Dale (1996), 'The process of ISO 9000 series recognition: An examination in small companies', *International Journal of Production Research*, **34**(9), 2379–92.
Michie, J. and M. Sheehan (2001), 'Labour market flexibility, human resource management and corporate performance', *British Journal of Management*, **12**(4), 287–306.
Michie, J. and M. Sheehan (2003), 'Labour market deregulation, flexibility and innovation', *Cambridge Journal of Economics*, **27**(1), 123–43.
Michie, J. and M. Sheehan (2005), 'Business strategy, human resources, labour market flexibility and competitive advantage', *International Journal of Human Resource Management*, **15**(3), 445–64.
Nguyen, T. and S. Bryant (2004), 'A study of the formality of HRM practices in small and medium sized firms in Vietnam', *International Small Business Journal*, **22**, 595–618.
Osterman, P. (1994), 'How common is workplace transformation and who adopts it?', *Industrial and Labor Relations Review*, **47**(2), 173–88.
Osterman, P. (1999), *Securing Prosperity*, Princeton: Princeton University Press.
Pfeffer, J. (1994), *Competitive Advantage Through People*, Boston: HNS Press.
Pfeffer, J. (1998), *The Human Equation*, Boston: HBS Press.
Porter, L. and P. Rayner (1991), 'BS 5750/ISO 9000: The experience of small and medium sized businesses', *International Journal of Quality and Reliability*, **18**(6), 16–29.
Ramsay, H., D. Scholarios and B. Harley (2000), 'Employees and high-performance work systems: Testing inside the black box', *British Journal of Industrial Relations*, **38**, 501–31.

Richardson, R. and M. Thompson (1999), *The Impact of People Management Practices on Business Performance: A Literature Review*, London: Institute of Personnel and Development.

Sels, L., S. De Winne, J. Maes, J. Delmotte, D. Faems and A. Forrier (2006a), 'Unravelling the HRM–performance link: Value-creating and cost-increasing effects of small business HRM', *Journal of Management Studies*, **43**(2), 319–42.

Sels, L., S. De Winne, J. Delmotte, J. Maes, D. Faems and A. Forrier (2006b), 'Linking HRM and small business performance: An examination of the impact of HRM intensity on the productivity and financial performance of small businesses', *Small Business Economics*, **26**, 83–101.

Taylor, W. (1995), 'Organisational differences in ISO 9000 implementation practices', *International Journal of Quality and Reliability*, **12**(7), 10–38.

Wall, T.D. and S.J. Wood (2005), 'The romance of HRM and business performance, and the case for big science', *Human Relations*, **58**(2), 429–62.

Wall, T., J. Michie, M. Patterson, C. Clegg and M. Sheehan (2004), 'On the validity of subjective measures of company performance', *Personnel Psychology*, **57**(1), 95–118.

Way, S. (2002), 'High performance work systems and intermediate indicators of firm performance within the US small business sector', *Journal of Management*, **28**, 765–85.

Wood, S. (1999), 'Getting the measure of the transformed high-performance organization', *British Journal of Industrial Relations*, **37**(3), 4391–417.

Wood, S. and L. de Menezes (1998), 'High commitment management in the UK: Evidence from the Workplace Industrial Relations Survey, and Employers' Manpower and Skills Practices Survey', *Human Relations*, **51**, 485–515.

Wright, P.M., T. Gardner, L. Moynihan and M. Allen (2005), 'The relationship between HR practices and firm performance: examining causal order', *Personnel Psychology*, **58**(2), 409–46.

Appendix: Spearman rank-order correlations between subjective and objective performance measures

Method

Subjective performance was measured as: 'How does financial performance, that is profitability, at your company compare with other companies in the same industry over the past financial year?' and 'How does your labour productivity compare with that in other companies in the same industry?' Responses were obtained on a five-point response scale running from 'much worse' to 'much better'. The mean and standard deviation for these variables for UK companies were: M=3.33, SD=.65; and M=3.96, SD=.58 for profitability and productivity respectively; and for US companies were: M=3.51, SD=.79; and M=4.02, SD=.68 for profitability and productivity respectively.

Objective financial performance was measured using financial data supplied by Dun and Bradstreet as part of the original sample framework (the 'population') and then supplemented with additional data from its Comprehensive Financial Reports for the sample companies where data were not supplied with the original sample. Financial data were obtained for a sub-sample of 55 of the 91 sample firms in the UK and 59 of the 98 sample firms in the US (for both samples, the least amount of financial data were available for skilled nursing home facilities and grocery stores).

Objective measures were constructed from these data. Productivity was calculated as gross sales per employee. Profit was calculated as the pre-tax financial value of sales divided by number of employees (that is, profit per employee) because cost per employee data were not available. To control for price movements, the profit variable was deflated by the producer price index in which the company belonged. To deal with the non-normal deviations of the data, we used the logarithm of the raw scores. The means and standard deviations for UK companies were: M=4.89, SD=3.01 and M=6.85, SD=2.25 for profitability and productivity respectively; and for US companies M=5.14, SD=3.41 and M=7.77, SD=3.16 for profitability and productivity respectively.

Results

Even after logarithmic transformations the data were not normally distributed, so the appropriate non-parametric, Spearman rank-order correlation was used. We conducted the analysis for each sample as a whole and by sector – manufacturing, health care, and grocery stores – and did find differences in the patterns of results; thus we present these results by sector.

While objective financial data were available for the majority of firms in the sample, the overall subset becomes 55 companies in the UK and 59 in the US, so when broken down by sector, the cell sizes become small. In addition, all of the analysis presented here is cross-sectional so only convergent validity can be tested and not discriminant analysis. Having said this, the results are remarkably consistent for both the US and UK subset of firms and the overall results are broadly consistent with our previous work in this area for large firms that utilized larger samples.

The findings in Tables 7.A1 and 7.A2 show that the relationships between the directly corresponding subjective and objective performance measures (see on-diagonal in bold) are the strongest in both the UK and US samples. The relationships are strongest in the manufacturing sector, then services, and weakest (although all of the direct measures are significant) for the services 'other' sector (grocery stores). These patterns are not surprising, especially since it is well recognized that productivity is generally easier to measure in the manufacturing sector compared to the service sector.

An additional financial performance variable 'current ratio' – indicating a firm's liquidity, measured by its liquid assets (current assets) relative to its

Table 7.A1   *Spearman rank-order correlations between subjective*
                performance and objective financial performance, UK firms

Objective performance	Manufacturing (N=26)		Services (N=20)		Services (other) (N=9)	
	Profit	Productivity	Profit	Productivity	Profit	Productivity
Profit	.61**	.39**	.42**	.29**	.25**	.19
Productivity	.37**	.51**	.25**	.39**	.18	.26**

Note: *p<.01; **p<.001.

Table 7.A2   *Spearman rank-order correlations between subjective*
                performance and objective financial performance, US firms

Objective performance	Manufacturing (N=28)		Services (N=21)		Services (other) (N=10)	
	Profit	Productivity	Profit	Productivity	Profit	Productivity
Profit	.63**	.43**	.47**	.22**	.30**	.21
Productivity	.40**	.58**	.20**	.41**	.16	.27**

Note: *p<.01; **p<.001.

liquid debt (short-term or current liabilities) – was available for this same sub-sample of companies. The correlation between profitability and the current ratio was 0.82** for UK companies and 0.73** for US companies. These high correlations imply that the current ratio, an asset-based measure, is also a good proxy for a firm's financial performance. We next tested the correlations between subjective financial performance and the objective current ratio. For UK firms, this correlation was 0.58**, and for US firms it was 0.63**.

8 Human resource strategies of high-growth entrepreneurial firms
Robert L. Heneman, Judith W. Tansky and S. Michael Camp

Introduction

High growth is often a strategic objective of entrepreneurial firms. It has been related to a variety of measures of business success including survival, market share, profit and net worth. For example in Cox and Camp's (1999) survey of 672 firms considered as leaders in entrepreneurial achievement, the following were reported:

- averaging 10 per cent growth per year doubles the chance of firm survival;
- high-growth firms have relative gains in market share five times greater than low-growth firms;
- the level of profitability for high-growth firms is 25 per cent more than for low-growth firms; and
- net worth for high-growth companies grows three times faster than that for low-growth firms.

Given these impressive figures, it is not surprising that many studies have been conducted on factors related to the growth of entrepreneurial firms (Whyte, 1998). In addition, many models of various growth stages have been developed (Hanks et al., 1993). What is surprising, however, is the lack of study regarding the management of human resources (HR) in high-growth entrepreneurial firms (Heneman and Tansky, 2003). Many years ago Penrose (1959) stated that, 'All the evidence indicates that the growth of a firm is connected with attempts of a particular group of human beings to do something; nothing is gained and much is lost if this fact is not explicitly recognized' (p. 2). With high growth comes the need for additional employees and as additional employees are added, the complexity of managing increases rapidly. Most important of all, however, is that if managed properly, HR can be a source of sustained competitive advantage to the organization (Barney and Wright, 1998). According to the resource-based view (RBV) of the firm, sustained competitive advantage is derived from the control of scarce, valuable and inimitable assets (see Barney, 1991;

Penrose, 1959). Hayton (2006) argues that the RBV represents a configurational perspective on the relationship between human resource management (HRM) and firm performance (Heneman and Tansky, 2002) in that a firm's HRM practices must be both internally consistent and fit externally with the business strategy (Huselid, 1995; Wright and Snell, 1998). In fact, Alvarez and Molloy (2006) argue that the objective of HRM is to maximize firm performance (Noe et al., 2006).

The purpose of this chapter is to build on our knowledge of the HR strategies associated with high growth in entrepreneurial firms. To do so, we provide a brief review of the strategy literature that focuses on HR as a source of potential sustained competitive advantage for firms. Next we present the results of a survey, an archival dataset and focus groups that compare HR strategies in high versus low-growth firms. Finally, we present a case study of a Toyota dealership in the USA to illustrate high-growth HR strategies in action.

Human resource strategies and firm performance
Recently a considerable amount of theory, research and practice has been devoted to assessing the value of HR strategies to organizations (see for example Goswami et al., 2006; Wright et al., 1999). Several conclusions stand out from this body of literature, which in turn have important implications for high-growth entrepreneurial firms.

First, it has been shown that HR strategies are related to measures of financial performance of the firm (Huselid, 1995; Huselid et al., 1997). In particular, HR strategies are related to intermediate human outcomes such as productivity and turnover, and in turn, are related to more distant outcomes such as financial performance of the firm. Hence wealth creation in organizations is a function of not only capital and technology, but is also of HR as assets. Notable examples here include: a review of studies that showed that the implementation of a Management by Objectives (MBO) system is associated with an average productivity increase of 45 per cent (Rodgers and Hunter, 1991); another study that reported an increase in shareholder wealth of US$41 000 per employee based on the implementation of high performance work systems (Huselid as reported in LeBlanc, 1999); and a study that concluded that HR practices like skilled temporary employees, positive employee relations, and an emphasis on training employees resulted in higher rates of innovation in IPO software firms, the higher levels of innovation leading to improved financial performance in the form of higher stock prices (Vogus and Welbourne, 2003).

Second, some HR strategies are universally likely to have an impact on organizational effectiveness. The sharing of wealth with employees is one such example. Weitzman and Kruse (1990) reported in a review of research that the average productivity increase associated with profit-sharing is 12 per cent. The implication here is that when managing the HR asset in organizations, best practices need to be considered. The use of best practice HR strategies is especially critical for organizations that need to move from below to average levels for firms in their industry (Barney, 1997).

Third, some HR strategies are more likely to impact business performance than are other strategies. In particular, HR strategies that other organizations have a difficult time copying are most likely to be successful and to help the organization attain above-average business performance for their industry (Barney, 1997). Barney and Wright (1998) review notable companies that have achieved above-average returns in their industry through HR strategies. This implies that organizations must carefully craft HR strategies that are tailor-made to their business environment and are thus unlikely to be as useful to their competitors.

Fourth, HR strategies are more likely to be effective when they are tailored to the type of organization and the business conditions faced by the firm. For example, several studies (Cleveland et al., 1989; Jackson et al., 1989; Saari et al., 1988) have found that HR strategies vary as a function of industry, business strategy, technology and organizational structure. These findings suggest that HR strategies need to be tailored to the strategy, structure, process and people in the organization (Lawler III, 1996).

Fifth, theoretical developments in HR strategy suggest that combinations of HR strategies or 'bundles' are more likely to be associated with organizational effectiveness because synergy exists between various strategies. For example, a pay-for-performance system is more effective when accompanied by a well-developed performance measure. In the absence of a well-developed performance measure, employees are unlikely to perceive a relationship between their performance and pay, and therefore have little motivation to perform (Heneman, 1992). Although in theory the need for synergistic HR systems seems important, the empirical research has not provided a great deal of support to date. This lack of empirical support may be due to either poor theory development regarding important combinations of activities or to poor research methods (Wright et al., 1999). Thus, the theory of synergy between HR strategies should be considered as a potential means to improve organizational effectiveness.

Taken together, these five major sets of findings indicate that HR strategies are indeed related to firm performance. Interestingly however, few of these studies explicitly look at firm growth as an important measure of organizational effectiveness. In this chapter we explicitly consider growth as a measure of organizational effectiveness. Because growth is correlated with other measures of organizational effectiveness including shareholder value as previously discussed, we expect that HR strategies will also be related to firm growth. In order to demonstrate the importance of HR strategies to firm growth we gathered data to investigate whether HR strategies differentiated between high- and low-growth firms.

Data sources
Participants in the study were 37 CEOs of entrepreneurial firms, of whom 16 were from high-growth firms (growth rate of 50 per cent or more) while 21 were from low-growth firms (growth rate of less than 50 per cent). Characteristics of the studied sample are shown in Table 8.1.

Data was collected by the Kauffman Foundation for Entrepreneurial Leadership using both a survey instrument and focus groups. The survey was based on questions developed by Delery and Doty (1996) as a result of 'best practice' HR strategies they identified in the literature. Focus group data was collected using procedures set forth by Krueger (1988). Trained moderators conducted the focus groups around a series of prepared questions designed to prompt the entrepreneurs to recall specific lessons learned and critical issues raised, regarding HR during the growth of their firm.

Table 8.1   Sample characteristics

		High growth (%) (N=16)	Low growth (%) (N=21)
Years in business	1 year	18.8	0.0
	1 to 5 years	25.0	20.0
	5 to 10 years	37.5	30.0
	More than 10 years	18.7	50.0
Number of employees	Less than 5 employees	0.0	5.3
	6 to 10 employees	0.0	0.0
	11 to 25 employees	43.8	42.1
	26 to 50 employees	18.8	26.3
	51 to 100 employees	25.0	21.1
	101 to 200 employees	6.2	0.0
	More than 200 employees	6.2	5.2
Revenue per year	Less than US$500 000	6.2	0.0
	US$500 000 to less than 1M	0.0	10.0
	US$1M to less than 5M	62.5	60.0
	US$5M to less than 10M	6.2	15.0
	US$10M to less than 25M	18.9	10.0
	US$25M to less than 50M	6.2	5.0
Founded company		93.8	85.0

The focus groups were recorded and content analysis was performed on the computerized transcripts using the procedures specified by Abrahamson and Park (1994).

Because of the small sample size of the survey and focus groups, an archival database with a larger sample size was also secured. The archival data is based on the *1998 Survey of Innovative Practices* mailed in Fall 1998 to 6000 Entrepreneur of the Year® Institute (EOYI) members. The EOYI membership is comprised of regional finalists from the Ernst & Young Entrepreneur of the Year® Awards Program. EOYI members are CEOs (primarily founders) from arguably the most innovative and admired firms in the world. They represent the 'best of the best' in terms of their contribution to growth, profitability, job creation and economic impact. The survey was commissioned to explore key non-financial items that were believed to impact a firm's ability to achieve and sustain a high rate of growth. The significance of the relationships between annual sales growth and growth strategy, employee compensation structure, equity compensation and other HR functions was explored.

Six hundred and seventy-two usable responses were received. Although 20 per cent of the firms had less than US$5 million dollars in annual sales in 1997, the firms averaged US$89 million in sales. The 672 firms averaged 5.9 per cent net profit, 18 years in business, and employed an average of 269 employees in 1995. Although retail trade was somewhat under-represented and manufacturing was over-represented, the distribution across industrial sectors was fairly representative.

Results

Focus group
Representative comments from the focus group are shown in Table 8.2. Taken together the comments appear to address the philosophies regarding HR of high versus low-growth firms.

High-growth firms appear to have a 'visionary' philosophy regarding HR. That is, a vision for the organization is to be set that is reflected in the culture of the organization and specific HR strategies for the firm. In turn employees are matched to that culture in careful ways in order to build a sense of commitment or psychological ownership to the firm. This can be contracted with low-growth firms that appear to have more of a 'reactive' philosophy towards HR. The focus is on solving immediate HR problems confronting the firm. In today's US economy with very low unemployment, the immediate problem predictably is hiring people. Concern is expressed about an immediate fit to the job rather than long-term growth with the firm. Decision-making regarding HR is left to others whenever possible in

Table 8.2   Representative comments from high- and low-growth firm
          participants

High-growth firms	Low-growth firms
• Developing the management talent (personally and team) to support rapid growth. I continue to believe that the primary limiting factors to _____'s growth are my own management skills and my ability to build a strong management team. I need to rapidly learn how to manage a much larger organization. I also need to find, recruit, and retain a strong team to help me achieve our goals.	• Motivating and retaining quality employees. In the technology industry you must work hard. The life cycle for technology is six months, which requires constant learning. It has been a challenge to find people who want to work as hard as you must to be successful.
• Keeping the values that brought us to this point alive for staff as we grow beyond 20 people. As we grow, I can see it happening before my eyes – what seems obvious to me, is murky to everyone else. How do I get the most junior staff, who I now rarely interact with, to 'get it'? To share my vision, value the same principles, dedicate the same level effort and commitment that I did when working alone or when the team was four people? How do I keep everyone excited, motivated and moving forward?	• How do I attract high caliber employees willing to work on a commission or revenue-generated basis?
• Lead by example, but always LISTEN to your people and give mission type orders (what to accomplish not how to do it).	• How to find and attract top talent in my industry.
• Defining new positions to address our changing needs.	• Attracting qualified employees: I will keep positions open rather than hire an unqualified person.
• Develop a flexible profit sharing plan.	• Attracting and retaining excellent people.
• Maintaining quality of service. As the workload has expanded beyond what the core employees can handle, it is difficult to find individuals who are as zealous in their work. As a result, the ability of the company to continue its rapid growth rate has been compromised.	• Finding talented employees.
	• Attract capable people.
	• Staffing.
	• Shortage of qualified employees to sustain growth.
	• Use outsourcing whenever you can.
	• Employees: Find great contract labor as a starting position. Use the information that the people bring with them to your enterprise. Hire your weaknesses immediately. Use only those that are refereed generously and check the references.
	• Make it very difficult for your top producers to leave the company. Don't be stupidly greedy. Start with a good 'golden handcuffs' program and add to it over time.

Table 8.2   (continued)

High-growth firms	Low-growth firms
• Creating a corporate identity and culture. The need to create a framework and culture is critical to developing new employees. The larger the organization becomes, the less amount of daily contact there is between individual employees and the founding 'spirits' of the company. • Additional strategies for identifying, recruiting, hiring, training and retaining key management staff. We are exploring various employee recruiting and retention strategies that include the ESOP and non–qualified SOP. • Finding key employees that buy into the long-term vision of the company and then putting in place systems to keep that vision alive for them so that they become anchors in the company. • Create a good culture and work hard to maintain it. • Hire quality/experienced staff. We are very particular when hiring new staff. Minimum requirements have been established to secure that each new employee can integrate their expertise and experience with the existing 'team'. We never hesitate to terminate staff when we feel the work or integration with the team is not working out. • Corporate culture building. We attribute much of our success to the corporate culture we have created and sustained through culture reinforcing management practices. The culture itself has helped speed up learning by new staff by allowing all employees to reinforce values and methods in our corporate way. Annually we have corporate retreats and senior	Be honest: People don't have to agree with you; but they must believe that what you tell them is the truth and that your actions will be consistent with your words. • Red flags during the hiring process and initial employment period are important and should be acted upon sooner rather than later. Things tend to get worse not better. • Hire well. Believe. Encourage. And, get out of the way. I am closely involved with the day-to-day operations of my company, but it's our great people who make us what we are, and I have faith in their abilities. When I begin to tamper, that's when we begin to have problems. • It's all about people – employees. The majority of your time will be spent on employees. When I made my plan, I glossed over employees – it was obvious to me that we would attract the best people out there . . . that they would be lined up wanting to work for us. Now, most of our time is spent on people issues – our own people! • Giving people a chance to prove themselves and listening to your gut. Building strong and confident team players and getting out of their way.

Table 8.2   (continued)

High-growth firms	Low-growth firms
management retreats that have been essential in reinforcing the core values of the firm and developing teaming relationships within our firm. • Believe in people, you will suffer some disappointment but that will be offset by the incredible satisfaction of helping others to succeed. • Never assume your past experience will give you the correct perspective in the current situation, challenge every assumption.	

Table 8.3   HR philosophies

Visionary philosophy for high growth	Reactive philosophy for low growth
• Clearly define HR strategies • Build and maintain a corporate culture • Match people to the organization rather than to the job • Create a sense of psychological ownership	• Focus on immediate HR problems (e.g., attraction, retention, motivation) • Match people to the job rather than to the organization • Outsource as much as possible • Use 'gut' feelings to manage people

the form of outsourcing, and when decisions are made, they are made 'on the spot'. Consideration of the longer-term strategic implications of outsourcing such as reduced skill levels (Lei et al., 1996) do not appear to be considered. The two philosophies are summarized in Table 8.3.

As Table 8.3 indicates, high-growth firms seem to have more of a strategic focus than low-growth firms. Consistent with current theory on HR strategy there is a concern about vertical alignment and horizontal integration (Wright et al., 1999) by high-growth firms. Vertical integration takes place when HR activities are aligned with the goals of the organization. In the present case one such goal is the building of a corporate culture with HR. Horizontal integration refers to the integration of HR strategies with corporate goals. Matching people to the job in order to create a psychological sense of ownership results from a synergistic set of HR strategies.

In interpreting the results of the focus group data, a note of caution should be interjected. The comments from CEOs of high-growth firms appear to be more in-depth than the comments from the CEOs of low-growth firms. These differences in comments may be a reflection of more thoughtful and effective leadership in high-growth than in low-growth firms. Our methodology does not allow for us to control for this leadership variable. As a result of this weakness to our focus group data, we gathered survey data, examined archival data and conducted a case study as well.

Survey
The survey results are shown in Table 8.4. Comparing the pattern of results for high-growth firm respondents versus low-growth respondents reveals a pattern of HR strategies being used consistently with either a visionary or reactive philosophy to HR. A summary of the contrasting set of HR strategies is shown in Table 8.5.

High-growth firms appear to follow more sophisticated HR strategies that have been shown in the research literature to be associated with organizational effectiveness. For example the positive impact of employee participation in decision-making (or their involvement) on organizational effectiveness has been clearly established (Lawler III et al., 1998). Moreover, high-growth firms appear to be more willing to take risks on newer HR strategies where it has not yet been clearly established that a link exists between the HR strategy and organizational effectiveness. Competencies and team rewards are examples here because while the preliminary evidence is favorable (Heneman et al., 2000), not a great amount of research has been conducted. Lastly, it is interesting to note that much of the visionary HR strategy revolves around reward systems in the broadest sense (for example, career advancement, feedback, pay and ownership). Rewards clearly seem to be viewed as a critical HR strategy. Also these somewhat more risky reward approaches are very consistent with the changing nature of work in high-growth companies (Heneman et al., 2000).

By contrast low-growth firms seem to follow more traditional HR strategies as would be predicted by their reactive HR philosophy. When the concern is about immediate HR problems such as attraction and retention as is the case in today's low unemployment economy, then traditional HR strategies shown in Table 8.5 are relevant. For example it is much less time-consuming and requires fewer applicants to fit the person to the job rather than to the organization. In terms of retention, traditional rewards such as job security, formal training and individual rewards are likely to be valued by employees and can be more easily implemented and administered strategies than are the more risky HR strategies used by high-growth firms.

Table 8.4   Survey results

	High growth		Low growth	
	M	SD	M	SD
Staffing				
1. Most employees were hired from outside the organization.	5.69	1.35	6.60	.68
2. Employees have clear career paths within the organization.	4.47	1.30	4.15	1.14
3. Employees have very little future within this organization.	1.63	1.26	2.15	1.46
4. Employees' career aspirations within the company are known by their immediate supervisors.	4.06	1.18	4.65	1.46
5. Employees who desire promotion have more than one potential position they could be promoted to.	4.81	1.47	4.55	1.79
Training				
1. Extensive training programs are provided for employees.	4.06	1.69	4.30	1.34
2. Other employees usually go out of their way to help new employees learn their job.	4.69	1.25	4.90	1.68
3. Employees will normally go through training programs every few years.	3.88	1.71	4.65	2.08
4. There are formal training programs to teach new hires the skills they need to perform their jobs.	4.38	2.22	4.45	2.04
5. Formal training programs are offered to employees in order to increase their promotability in this organization.	3.56	2.03	4.45	1.70
Performance appraisal				
1. Performance appraisals usually focus on the bottom line.	3.69	2.06	3.35	1.69
2. Performance appraisal feedback is usually evaluative rather than developmental.	4.25	1.29	3.7	1.59
3. Performance is more often measured with objective quantifiable results.	4.31	1.58	3.95	1.47
4. The focus of the performance appraisal is the behavior of the employee.	4.38	1.45	4.55	1.57
5. The focus of the performance appraisal is on how (in what manner) the job is performed rather than on how well (results).	2.81	1.47	2.95	1.57

Table 8.4 (continued)

	High growth		Low growth	
	M	SD	M	SD
6. The primary objective of appraisals is to improve performance.	5.13	1.78	4.6	1.90
7. Performance appraisals are based on objective, quantifiable results.	4.31	1.58	4.25	1.48
8. Performance appraisals are very informal. There is little written documentation.	3.50	2.48	3.75	2.29

Compensation

	High growth		Low growth	
1. Compensation is solely in the form of base pay.	2.31	1.58	2.10	1.62
2. Employees receive bonuses based on the profit of the organization.	5.25	1.84	5.00	2.15
3. All employees are paid approximately the same amount.	1.81	1.11	2.90	1.86
4. Employees receive pay rises only on the basis of seniority.	1.50	.82	1.80	1.67
5. Bonuses are paid based on a gain-sharing plan.	3.67	1.68	3.40	2.14
6. Employees are given stock (or stock options) in the organization as an incentive.	4.06	2.67	2.85	2.30
7. Pay rates are determined primarily by market rates for similar jobs.	4.19	1.76	4.60	1.82
8. Pay rates are determined primarily by comparison to other jobs within the organization.	3.44	1.55	3.40	1.50
9. The amount earned during each pay period is determined primarily by an incentive plan rather than by a guaranteed-income plan.	3.00	1.55	3.75	2.07
10. Pay rates are determined currently above the rates of our major competitors.	4.69	2.02	4.30	1.17
11. Employees receive pay rises on the basis of individual performance.	5.25	1.61	5.55	1.10
12. Employees receive pay rises on the basis of group performance.	4.00	1.41	3.45	1.54
13. Employees receive a considerable amount of time off with pay.	4.44	1.71	4.20	1.80

Table 8.4   (continued)

	High growth		Low growth	
	M	SD	M	SD
Job security				
1. Employees can expect to stay in the organization for as long as they wish.	4.13	1.86	4.50	2.06
2. It is very difficult to dismiss an employee.	3.06	1.95	3.30	1.34
3. There are formal policies that protect employees from being fired.	2.19	1.91	2.60	1.19
4. An employee's superior must get approval before he/she can fire that employee.	3.25	1.91	4.42	1.89
5. Job security is almost guaranteed to employees.	2.00	1.41	2.26	1.24
6. If the company were facing economic problems, employees would be the last to get cut.	4.19	1.87	4.20	1.54
7. When employees are laid off, they are given comprehensive severance packages.	2.93	1.67	4.89	2.02
Employee voice				
1. There are formal grievance systems for employees.	3.13	2.25	3.30	1.75
2. Employees are allowed to make many decisions.	5.88	.96	5.55	1.19
3. Employees are often asked by their superior to participate in decisions.	6.06	.93	5.55	1.47
4. Employees are provided the opportunity to suggest improvements in the way things are done.	6.06	.99	6.20	1.01
5. Superiors keep open communication with employees.	5.81	1.05	6.20	.83
Job descriptions				
1. The duties of most employees are clearly defined.	4.50	1.51	5.25	1.74
2. Employees are often asked to do things that are not in their job description.	5.56	1.32	5.35	1.50
3. Most jobs have an up-to-date job description.	3.75	1.61	3.85	1.79
4. The job description contains all of the duties performed by individual employees.	2.94	1.61	3.42	1.77
5. Most jobs are narrowly defined.	3.00	2.39	2.47	1.17
6. The actual job duties are shaped more by the employee than by a specific job description.	4.63	1.36	4.05	1.73

Table 8.5   HR strategies

High growth	Low growth
• Promote from within • Provide on-the-job training • Use evaluative and results-oriented performance appraisals • Provide equity ownership • Provide team rewards • Focus on employee participation in decision making	• Bring senior talent in from outside the organization • Provide extensive formal training opportunities • Use performance appraisals for developmental reasons with focus on behavior rather than results • Pay for individual rather than team results • Pay for the value of the job rather than the person • Provide job security • Focus on vertical communications • Define jobs in terms of duties to be performed

Caution must be exercised in interpreting the results of the survey, as there are several limitations to the methodology employed. We did not conduct tests of statistical significance on mean differences. We did not do so because of the small sample size and the risk of capitalizing on Type I error by conducting multiple tests of statistical differences. Our samples of high and low-growth firms are not directly comparable in all instances, as shown in Table 8.1. In particular, high-growth firms are somewhat younger than low-growth firms. Firms that may have been in operation longer may have established more HR practices (for example, training). Also, again because of the small sample size, we were not able to control for industry differences between the samples. Because of these limitations to the survey, we have supplemented the survey with focus group data, archival survey data and a case study.

Archival data
We examined an area of the questionnaire that asked: 'On a scale from one to five with "one" being "no impact" and "five" being "big impact", please indicate how your firm's ability to manage each of the following HR functions impacts the growth of your firm.' Table 8.6 lists the ten individual HR functions and shows the results of a principal components factor analysis with varimax rotation. Two factors with Eigenvalues of over 1 were found. Factor 1 represents 26.9 per cent of the variance and Factor 2 represents 23.9 per cent. Appraising employee performance and maintaining employee

Table 8.6   Factor analysis of human resource functions and their impact on growth

	Factor 1 Visionary human resources	Factor 2 Reactive human resources
Training and development	**.561**	.125
Complying with employment regulations	.111	**.796**
Appraising employee performance	**.632**	**.345**
Maintaining employment records	.268	**.757**
Setting competitive compensation levels	**.631**	.205
Maintaining employee health/wellness	**.547**	**.438**
Managing workers' compensation	.165	**.707**
Maintaining productivity	**.721**	−.000
Maintaining morale	**.800**	−.000
Dealing with labor/union issues	−.000	**.549**

Note: Bold indicates variables contributing to Factor 1 and Factor 2 respectively.

health/wellness were dropped as they loaded on both factors. Appraising employee performance is done either formally or informally in almost all organizations as a means of either proactively rewarding performers or reactively deciding who has problems that must be corrected to prevent the person from being terminated. Because of the way 'appraising employee performance' was worded, loading on both factors makes sense. The same is true for maintaining employee health/wellness. It can be proactive if the organization has club facilities or programs to help or support employee health problems. On the other hand, responding to safety measures required by OSHA (Occupational Safety and Health Act) and other government agencies is reactionary.

Factor 1, labeled 'visionary management of HR for growth', includes several proactive methods of managing HR. The second factor is called 'reactive management of HR for growth'. This factor focuses on the activities that are required in an organization to avoid legal issues and to react to government regulations. It includes complying with employment regulations, managing employment records, managing workers' compensation and dealing with labor/union issues.

Although all the firms in this sample had been recognized as leaders in entrepreneurial firms, they would not all be considered high-growth. The sample was divided at the 30th, 60th and 90th percentiles following the format used by Cox and Camp (1999). Four groups emerged (low, medium, high and hyper) with average annual sales growth, from 1995 to 1997 of

5 per cent, 21 per cent, 60 per cent and 110 per cent. We correlated proactive management of HR with low, medium, high and hyper growth with the following results. Proactive management of HR was negatively and significantly correlated with low growth ($r = -.12, p < .01$), negatively correlated with medium growth but not significant, positively correlated with high growth but not significant, and positively and significantly correlated with hyper growth ($r = .10, p<.05$). The higher the growth in average annual sales from 1995 to 1997, the more likely the company was to take a proactive approach to HR, which included training and development, competitive compensation and an emphasis on productivity and morale.

Case study of a high-growth Toyota dealership
In order to solidify the HR strategies associated with a high-growth firm, a case study of a high-growth firm was conducted. The firm studied was a Toyota dealership in the US Midwest known to all three authors. The points made in Tables 8.3 and 8.5 will be apparent in this case.

Toyota is presently the number three auto maker in the world, but strives to become number one by the year 2010. A key component of Toyota's growth is Toyota Motor Sales, USA Inc. (TMS), which has grown beyond sales to incorporate manufacturing and a credit corporation. The Toyota dealer group in the US comprises of some 1200 Toyota dealers franchised by TMS. The first franchises were offered in the mid-1960s to American auto dealers. TMS faced challenges convincing the Japanese corporation that it needed to build different types of cars, especially different colors. Fighting tariffs and overcoming the American opinion of Japanese merchandise was aided by the oil crisis of the early 1970s. Suddenly a small car that could get 30 to 40 miles per gallon was in great demand.

One visionary dealer in the Midwest who had three small town Chrysler dealerships was the butt of many jokes by his peers when he signed on with Toyota for four franchises: one in each of his small town locations and one in the state capital. Upon returning from World War II, he had started on the path to becoming an auto dealer because of his belief that one of the fastest growing industries in the US would be cars. In fact, he was convinced that the first thing every returning soldier would want was a car.

Housed first with a parts store owned by the dealer, the metropolitan Toyota dealership opened in its own location in 1967. In 1970 the son of the original dealer took over the metropolitan dealership. Continuous growth led TMS to push the dealer into moving to a new and larger location. In 1985, the dealership moved to a location on the northwest side of the county, which was later to become the busiest intersection in town. Leaving the body shop at its original location, the dealer struggled to staff and operate two locations at the same time.

In December 1992 the dealership had 60 employees and sales of US$17.8 million (1103 cars were sold). In December 2006, the dealership included the facility that opened in 1985 and a body shop and used car-reconditioning department housed in a facility that is the largest body shop in the state. As of December 2006 the dealership had 108 employees and sales of US$67.24 million (3119 cars were sold). In an industry where an outstanding net profit is 1.5 to 2 per cent of gross sales and the average is below 1 per cent, it is not easy to survive. This dealership, however, has not only survived for over 35 years but has been very successful the last eight years. In fact, the regional office of TMS has indicated that they view it as having the best growth potential of any Toyota dealership in their four-state region.

When the dealer (the son who took over in 1970) was asked why he thought the dealership had been successful, he was the first to argue that it was all due to people, to his employees. In fact, when he started working after graduating from college, his father, knowing that family relationships often suffered as a result of a family business, sent his best manager from his small town dealerships to train his son (clear HR strategy, on-the-job training).

The dealer had a strategy of promoting from within (promote from within). He has always hired young people who work hard and has developed their technical skills. His parts manager and one of his certified mechanics started as lot techs (washing cars and running errands) and were trained on-the-job for the positions they now hold (match people to organization, on-the-job training). One mechanic who came as a refugee from Thailand during the Vietnam War has been with the organization since 1973. Not only does this benefit the employee but it has also helped to establish a culture of training: opportunities are available for employees who work hard (build and maintain corporate culture). This has also helped to create a sense of psychological ownership (psychological ownership). Employees can see their contribution to the firm's success and they take pride in their achievements as well as the success of the dealership.

The dealership has grown its own mechanics, body repairers and detailers by providing on-the-job training and paying for employees to participate in Toyota training such as Mechanic Certification Training (clear HR strategy, on-the-job training, external training, promote from within). The office staff are also trained in-house. In fact the firm has not outsourced any of its functions or used temporaries or employment agencies. The philosophy has for the most part focused on hiring the 'right' people who fit the culture, developing them, encouraging them to offer their opinions and insights and then rewarding them based on outcomes (corporate culture, match people to organization, promote from within, on-the-job training, evaluative and results-oriented performance appraisals).

The dealer was willing to discuss what he called lessons he learned the hard way. Pressured by TMS to hire a general manager because they believed the organization had reached the point where the dealer could no longer handle all the daily activities, a manager with experience was sought. This contrasted with his normal approach of hiring from within but he knew he had nobody internally to handle the job. It became obvious within several months that the manager did not share the owner's value system. The culture the new manager tried to create in the sales department was only successful because he hired several assistant managers with his same belief system. The whole situation developed into a crisis when several tenured sales people left, customer complaints started to increase and Toyota sales satisfaction scores started to decrease. The dealer and manager had to 'part company' while the assistant managers who had been hired by the manager also left. The dealer found it necessary to start hiring sales staff so he could 're-create the culture' in the sales department and once again have a unified dealership. There was no doubt that this situation stunted the organization's growth and probably cost the organization some good employees (did not follow philosophy of maintaining corporate culture, matching people to the organization, promoting from within and focusing on employee participation in decision making).

Another difficult lesson focused around recognizing that all good employees do not make good managers and good managers can become outdated or outgrown. A former lot tech who had become a mechanic was put in charge of the body shop when he hurt his hand in an accident. He did a good job as long as the body shop had four employees and a small work area. When the body shop moved into its new facility and tripled in size he did not have the competencies to manage the people or the systems necessary for success. The job and the required competencies had outgrown him. The body shop struggled for a year before he and the owner reached a mutual agreement that he should leave. Moving a master mechanic from his technical position to shop manager at the satellite location resulted in the same problem. The mechanic was excellent at training apprentices but lacked the necessary competencies to schedule work, interact with customers and manage expenses.

Both examples were expensive lessons in learning to define, as clearly as possible, the competencies needed for a position. The dealer commented that internal movement is not always the best decision if you cannot develop the skills needed for the person to be successful in the new position. These two lessons helped the dealer to define HR strategies more clearly, as well as helping him to learn how to make use of evaluative performance results which would have indicated more quickly that these two people were not right for the growing needs of the organization. This is a hard lesson for entrepreneurs to learn as this case study and the focus group indicated. This was also the point at which the owner learned to get employee participation in decision making, as employees often have more information about other employees.

Although a formal performance appraisal system had never been implemented, almost all personnel had their pay based on performance or the outcomes they achieved. The departmental managers were paid on the net profit of their departments. They had accountability for expenses and participated in decisions that affected their departmental sales or expenses. Sales people and finance managers were paid on a percentage of the profit they generated on a sale and their customer satisfaction scores. Mechanics and body repairers were paid an hourly rate based on the flat rate hours they turned (the flat rate hours for each job was determined by TMS). Parts and service managers were paid on the sales they generated and handled. Only office workers and lot techs were paid an hourly rate or salary, but the owner also had a longstanding policy of giving monthly bonuses to high performers in these two areas. This compensation was a clear HR strategy that not only created psychological ownership but also was a form of equity ownership.

The dealer emphasized that the key to his success in a highly competitive industry with a low profit margin was his people. He has to be able to anticipate the market, make changes as quickly as possible and communicate his vision. However, he also chose people that shared his values and helped them to develop the necessary competencies – this is what has grown his business. His 'visionary' philosophy with clearly defined HR strategies has helped him to build and maintain a corporate culture in which people are matched to the organization and a sense of psychological ownership is created. These HR strategies (some of which have evolved after what he called a time of crisis) included promoting from within when possible because the person has the ability to learn the right skills, providing on-the-job training, using evaluative and results oriented performance information, providing a form of profit sharing and focusing on employee participation in decision making.

Conclusion

Little information exists regarding appropriate HR strategies for high-growth firms. We have begun to fill this void by offering focus group comments, survey results, archival data and a case study to show some of the HR strategies that help to differentiate between high and low-growth firms. The results show a consistent pattern of findings across the comments, survey results, archival data and case study. High-growth firms follow a visionary HR philosophy. In turn they are likely to use contemporary HR strategies, some of which may be considered somewhat risky. Emphasis is placed on total rewards programs in high-growth firms. HR strategies are aligned with the business and integrated with one another. As indicated in the introduction, high growth is associated with several measures of organizational effectiveness. In order to achieve high growth it appears that the human asset must be managed as carefully as capital, physical and technological assets in the organization.

Future research needs to be conducted with a larger sample and controlling for industry, company age and leadership qualities of the CEO. We hope that our preliminary results presented here guide future research with more comprehensive sets of variables in this direction. The data that we present does provide some preliminary findings showing systematic differences in HR strategies between high- and low-growth firms.

Also, to control for the possibility that the results presented are based on the measures used, future research should use other measures of HR strategies. Additional construct validity procedures (for example, convergent or discriminant validity) can be followed to assess the dimensionality of differences in HR strategies by growth of the firm. It should be noted, however, that the current measure used was reported to have adequate construct validity properties (Delery and Doty, 1996). Hence, we have some confidence in the measure used in the survey portion of our study.

Lastly, in terms of future research, more attention needs to be given to issues of theory than to practice. In our study and most other studies with an HR strategy perspective, the focus is often more on benchmark practices to follow than theory to guide practice. Future research in this area should be guided by more deductive, theoretical perspectives – social capital theory (Leana and Van Buren III, 1999) for example – to guide the more inductive, practice-driven data that we have presented in this study. Both deductive and inductive processes are likely to be needed to generate new knowledge about using HR to drive business growth.

Alvarez and Molloy (2006) posit that we must identify why differences exist between HRM in established firms and in entrepreneurial firms and use this information to aid both theoretical and descriptive research. We challenge you to begin to build this theory that will help us explain people/ employees in small and entrepreneurial firms as well as the processes that develop as a result of growth.

Acknowledgement
An earlier version of this chapter was presented at the 2000 Babson/ Kauffman Entrepreneurship Research Conference. We wish to express our appreciation to the Kauffman Center for Entrepreneurial Leadership for funding this project.

References

Abrahamson, E. and C. Park (1994), 'Concealment of negative organizational outcomes: An agency theory perspective', *Academy of Management Journal*, **37**, 1302–34.

Alvarez, S.A. and J.C. Molloy (2006), 'Why human resource management differs in entrepreneurial and established firms: Theoretical foundations', in J.W. Tansky and R.L. Heneman (eds), *Human Resource Strategies for the High Growth Entrepreneurial Firm*, Greenwich, CT: Information Age Publishing, pp. 1–12.

Barney, J.B. (1991), 'Firm resources and sustained competitive advantage', *Journal of Management*, **17**(1), 99–120.

Barney, J.B. (1997), *Gaining and Sustaining Competitive Advantage*, Reading, MA: Addison-Wesley.

Barney, J.B. and P.M. Wright (1998), 'On becoming a strategic partner: The role of human resources in gaining competitive advantage', *Human Resource Management*, **37**, 31–46.

Cleveland, J.N., K.R. Murphy and R.E. Williams (1989), 'Multiple uses of performance appraisal: Prevalence and correlates', *Journal of Applied Psychology*, **74**, 130–35.

Cox, L.W. and S.M. Camp (1999), *A Survey of Innovative Practices*, Kansas City, MO: Kauffman Center for Entrepreneurial Leadership.

Delery, J.E. and J.H. Doty (1996), 'Modes of theorizing in strategic human resource management: Tests of universalistic, contingency, and configurational performance predictions', *Academy of Management Journal*, **39**, 802–35.

Goswami, R.M., G.C. McMahan and P.M. Wright (2006), 'Understanding strategic human resource management', in J.W. Tansky and R.L. Heneman (eds), *Human Resource Strategies for the High Growth Entrepreneurial Firm*, Greenwich, CT: Information Age Publishing, pp. 13–50.

Hanks, S.H., C.J. Watson, E. Jansen and G.N. Chandler (1993), 'Tightening the life cycle construct: A taxonomic study of growth stage configurations in high technology organizations', *Entrepreneurship: Theory and Practice*, **18**, 5–29.

Hayton, J.C. (2006), 'Human capital management practices', in J.W. Tansky and R.L. Heneman (eds), *Human Resource Strategies for the High Growth Entrepreneurial Firm*, Greenwich, CT: Information Age Publishing, pp. 51–68.

Heneman, R.L. (1992), *Merit Pay: Linking Pay Increases to Performance Ratings*, Reading, MA: Addison-Wesley.

Heneman, R.L. and J.W. Tansky (2002), 'Human resource management models for entrepreneurial opportunity', in J.A. Katz and T.M. Welbourne (eds), *Managing People in Entrepreneurial Organization: Learning from the Merger of Entrepreneurship and Human Resource Management*, Boston: JAI Press, pp. 54–81.

Heneman, R.L. and J.W. Tansky (2003), 'Introduction to the special issue on human resource management in SMEs: A call for more research', *Human Resource Management*, **42**(4), 299–302.

Heneman, R.L., G.E. Ledford and M. Gresham (2000), 'The changing nature of work and its effects on compensation design and delivery', in S. Rynes and B. Gerhart (eds), *Compensation in Organizations: Current Research and Practice*, Society for Industrial and Organizational Psychology Frontiers of Industrial and Organizational Psychology Series, San Francisco: Jossey-Bass, pp. 195–240.

Huselid, M.A. (1995), 'The impact of human resource management practices on turnover, productivity, and corporate financial performance', *Academy of Management Journal*, **38**, 635–72.

Huselid, M.A., S.E. Jackson and R.S. Schuler (1997), 'Technical and strategic human resource management effectiveness as determinants of firm performance', *Academy of Management Journal*, **40**, 171–88.

Jackson, S.E., R.S. Schuler and J.C. Rivero (1989), 'Organizational characteristics as predictors of personnel practices', *Personnel Psychology*, **42**, 727–86.

Krueger, R.A. (1988), *Focus Groups: A Practical Guide for Applied Research*, Newbury Park, CA: Sage.

Lawler III, E.E. (1996), *From the Ground Up: Six Principles for Building the New Logic Corporation*, San Francisco: Jossey-Bass.

Lawler III, E.E., S.A. Mohrman and G.E. Ledford Jnr (1998), *Strategies for High Performance Organizations: Employee Involvement, TQM, and Reengineering in Fortune 1000 Companies*, San Francisco: Jossey-Bass.
Leana, C.R. and H.J. Van Buren III (1999), 'Organizational social capital and employment practices', *Academy of Management Review*, **24**, 538–55.
LeBlanc, P.V. (1999), 'Valuing human capital', *Perspectives*, **9**(1), 2–9.
Lei, D., M.A. Hitt and R. Bettis (1996), 'Dynamic core competences through meta-learning and strategic context', *Journal of Management*, **22**, 549–69.
Noe, R., J. Hollenbeck, B. Gerhart and P. Wright (2006), *Human Resource Management: Gaining a Competitive Advantage*, 5th edn, New York: McGraw Hill Irwin.
Penrose, E.T. (1959), *The Theory of the Growth of the Firm*, Oxford: Basil Blackwell.
Rodgers, R. and J.E. Hunter (1991), 'Impact of management by objectives on organizational productivity', *Journal of Applied Psychology*, **76**, 322–36.
Saari, L.M., T.R. Johnson, S.D. McLaughlin and D.M. Zimmerle (1988), 'A survey of management training and education practices in US companies', *Personnel Psychology*, **41**, 731–45.
Vogus, T.J. and T.M. Welbourne (2003), 'Structuring for high reliability: HR practices and mindful processes in reliability seeking organizations', *Journal of Organizational Behavior*, **24**, 877–903.
Weitzman, M.L. and D.L. Kruse (1990), 'Profit sharing and productivity', in A.S. Blinder (ed.), *Paying for Productivity: A Look at the Evidence*, Washington, DC: The Brookings Institute, pp. 95–142.
Whyte, W. (1998), *Bibliography*, The Institute for Entrepreneurship, Innovation, and Growth, Richard Ivey School of Business.
Wright, P.M. and S.A. Snell (1998), 'Toward a unifying framework for exploring fit and flexibility in strategic human resource management', *Academy of Management Review*, **23**(4), 756–72.
Wright, P.M., L.D. Dyer, J.W. Boudreau and G.T. Milkovich (1999), *Research in Personnel and Human Resources Management Supplement 4: Strategic Human Resources Management in the Twenty-First Century*, Stamford, CT: JAI Press.

9 The relationship between small firm growth and HRM practices

Rowena Barrett, Susan Mayson and Niel Warriner

Introduction

In this chapter we explore the relationship between small firms' growth orientation, their business planning efforts and the role the owner plays and whether or not formal HRM practices are used. Formal HRM practices are assessed in terms of whether they are written down, regularly applied or assured to take place. We take on board Heneman et al.'s (2000) suggestion that 'surveys of employer practices across SMEs [would] be [a] valuable addition to the strategic human resource management literature' (p. 23) and report the results of an online and paper survey of a sample of 1753 small firms (defined as those employing less than 20 people) in the state of Victoria (SE Australia). Our particular interest in this chapter, which is based on an analysis of 410 responses to the survey, is whether growth-oriented small firms adopt formal HRM practices. This research contributes to understanding whether more formal organizational systems and routines are more likely to be used (or not) to nurture human capital in growth-oriented small firms. Moreover by focusing on firm growth, this chapter, consistent with recent calls in the literature (see Baron, 2003; Barrett and Mayson, 2006; Katz et al., 2000; Tansky and Heneman, 2003), contributes to a better understanding of issues at the intersection of entrepreneurship and HRM research.

In the next section we address the literature on small firms, growth and HRM in order to develop propositions for exploration in our survey research. We then outline the research approach and analysis techniques and report the results of the data. In the final section we discuss the results and draw some conclusions about our results and their implications for what we know at the intersection of HRM and entrepreneurship.

Small firms, growth and HRM

There are a range of studies indicating that small firms are characterized by informal HRM practices (see Cardon and Stevens, 2004 for an overview). In terms of recruitment, 'unimaginative' (McEvoy, 1984), convenient and inexpensive practices that are directly controllable by the firm

(Heneman and Berkley, 1999) are used, while selection procedures (such as face-to-face interviews, reference checks, job try outs and application blanks) are also chosen for ease of use and convenience (Deshpande and Golhar, 1994; Gilbert and Jones, 2000; Kotey and Sheridan, 2001; McEvoy, 1984). Formal training is problematic and either not undertaken through 'ignorance' or because the cost is too high (Storey and Westhead, 1997). Studies have found induction training to occur but on an informal basis while internal and external training was not linked to employee performance appraisals (Gilbert and Jones, 2000; Kotey and Sheridan, 2001). Performance appraisal practices in small firms tend to be informal and continuous and often used for monitoring and control rather than development purposes (Gilbert and Jones, 2000). Some suggest that there is a greater sophistication in HRM practices in small firms than would be expected (Duberley and Walley, 1995), while others argue that informal practices are effective means of ensuring new recruits 'fit in' (Marlow, 2000).

However, the increased complexity that comes with growth and particularly with the increase in employee numbers associated with growth, as the literature on the attributes of growing firms implies, demands that there should be different HRM practices in place than those in non-growth oriented small firms (Arthur, 1995; Mazzarol, 2003). For example, in a study of 2903 US family firms with fewer than 500 employees, Rutherford et al. (2003) identify four growth stages – no growth, low growth, moderate growth, high growth – and show that 'as firms achieve increasing levels of growth, HR issues seem to shift' (p. 332).

As small firms grow, the formalization of HRM activity also changes. For example, Barrett and Mayson (2007) show that growing small firms were more likely than non-growing small firms to have formal HRM practices where that meant practices were either written down, regularly applied or assured to take place (de Kok and Uhlaner, 2001). Similarly Kotey and Slade (2005) found increasing standardization and documentation of HRM practices as the firm grew. This was more likely to begin early in the growth process rather than later as size increased. Nguyen and Bryant (2004) attribute this to the founder's blueprint for HR formality during the founding of the firm as this has a significant impact on the firm's current levels of HR formality. In doing so they draw on Baron et al.'s (1996) work which shows that the owner's blueprint for HRM at the founding of the firm exerts a significant effect over the type, nature and speed of HRM practices adopted over the evolution of the firm.

In essence the general argument in the literature and the findings of recent studies of HRM in small firms suggest that as small firms grow they are likely to exhibit greater formality in their HRM practices. As a result we propose (P1) there is a positive relationship between small firm growth and the use of formal HRM practices.

Small firms, strategic planning and HRM

An understanding of the role of HRM in growth-oriented small firms can be drawn from the literature on strategic HRM. This is a theoretical base for understanding how firms develop their human capital to enhance their competitive advantage through aligning HRM policies and practices with business growth strategies (see, for example, Delery, 1998; Wright et al., 2001). It has been found that growth in entrepreneurial firms is related to the implementation of both proactive and reactive strategies (Gray, 2002). Evidence suggests that in small firms the strategic awareness of managers predicts some level of formal business planning (Gibb and Scott, 1985; Hannon and Atherton, 1998). Yet a barrier to realizing the value of their strategic planning is the owner not 'letting go' and delegating responsibility for HRM (Heneman et al., 2000). This will depend on the owner's management style and personality (Mazzarol, 2003) and as Scase (1995) argues, those small business owners who are unable to change their style act as a barrier to firm growth. More recently, Drummond and Stone (2007) point to the critical role of the small business owner in the establishment, operation and coherence of high performance work systems.

The ability to overcome the 'managerial capacity problem' (Barringer et al., 1998) depends in part on the owner recognizing the importance of HRM to the small firm's performance, but as Ardichvili et al. (1998) showed, the delegation of HRM issues lags well behind the delegation of accounting, production and information systems in small firms. This is problematic given Hornsby and Kuratko's (2003) argument that managerial incompetence in handling HRM issues is a major source of firm failure.

So while the formalization of HRM policies becomes desirable as firms grow, the ability for this to occur in small firms depends on the recognition of the owner of the strategic need for delegation and then the possibility of delegating that task. This suggests two further propositions: (P2) There is a positive relationship between strategic planning and the use of formal HRM practices; and (P3) there is a positive relationship between having an owner–manager who delegates some or all of their activities and the use of formal HRM practices.

Method

In Australia small firms are defined by the Australian Bureau of Statistics as those employing fewer than 20 people (ABS, 2002). A database of 2500 small firms purchased from Dunn and Bradstreet included the business name, address, name of the CEO and contact details. The database was

confined to the state of Victoria (SE Australia) in order to minimize juris-
dictional issues pertaining to employment and workplace relations (see also
Barrett and Mayson, Chapter 6 this handbook). Twenty-four per cent of
all small firms are located in the state of Victoria, which is the second
highest state-based population of small firms in Australia (ABS, 2002). By
selecting a general sample of small firms we minimized the likelihood of
gaining a non-representative sample of small firms (see, for example,
Bandilla et al., 2003).

The survey was administered in two rounds. Round one utilized an online
survey tool developed at Monash University and housed on a university
website. Survey methodologists have considered some of the potential
problems of using the Internet and we incorporated their suggestions into
the questionnaire design and the survey process (Bandilla et al., 2003). For
example, an explanatory letter was sent to the CEO in early August 2004
inviting their participation in the survey and providing them with a unique
username and password that would enable them to access the online survey.
The letter advised them about how long the survey would remain open and
how they could review their responses and check their performance against
the rest of the respondents after the survey closed. Technical issues such as
the amount of time the questionnaire would take to complete, the browser
settings required and where assistance could be found should any technical
difficulties be encountered were also addressed in the letter.

While in Australia there is a very high penetration of the Internet into
businesses and home – for example, the Australian Bureau of Statistics
(2003) reports that 65 per cent of micro firms (0–4 employees) and 80 per
cent of small firms (5–19 employees) have Internet access – the letter also
stated that respondents could request a paper copy of the questionnaire if
they were unable to complete it online. This was in line with Saxon et al.'s
(2003) suggestion that this should address non-response rates and sampling
bias. To increase the response rate a reminder letter was sent two weeks
after the original letter to all who had not yet participated in the survey.

In the first round of the survey there were a total of 193 responses. In
addition there were 147 return to sender (RTS) letters or refusals to participate in the research for a variety of reasons including that they employed
more than 20 employees or that the business was no longer operating. As a
result of this low response rate a paper version of the questionnaire with a
covering letter was sent early in November 2004 to 1600 of the small firms
remaining on the database (those participating in the first round, RTS and
refusals were excluded, as were another 557 businesses that, when their
details were checked, were found not to be private-sector small businesses).
In this second round of the survey there were 217 completed returns as well
as 42 RTS or refusals to participate in the research for a variety of reasons

including that they employed more than 20 employees or that the business was no longer operating.

Statistical checks show no difference between responses by questionnaire type and therefore the sample consists of 410 useable questionnaires, with 53 per cent completing the paper-based survey and 47 per cent completing the survey online. From an effective sample size of 1753, the 410 returns represent a response rate of 23 per cent.

Dependent variable
Formal HRM practices: while there is some debate in the literature about the practices that make up an HRM system (Way, 2002), we included those dealing with recruitment, selection, training, appraisal and rewards. This is consistent with Delery (1998), Nguyen and Bryant (2004), Pils and McDuffie (1996) and Way (2002). We assessed the level of formality of these practices in terms of whether the practice was either written down, regularly applied or assured to take place (Barrett and Mayson, 2007; de Kok and Uhlaner, 2001; Mayson and Barrett, 2006). A further element in the formality of the firm's HRM practices would be indicated if the firm used a written staffing plan with a dedicated budget. The practices are defined in Table 9.1, and were coded 0 if the answer was in the negative and 1 if there was an affirmative response.

Independent variables
Growth: there are multiple ways business growth may be measured, for example in terms of relative or absolute increases in (new) employment, productivity, sales, turnover, profitability or assets as well as greater market

Table 9.1   Definition of formal HRM practices

Practice	Definition
Recruitment criteria	When recruiting new staff is there a written list of skills and qualifications sought?
Selection criteria	Is there a written job description for all staff?
Formal training	Does the business offer formal training delivered internally or externally to staff?
Formal performance appraisal	Does the firm have a written policy on performance appraisal?
Formal rewards	To keep a valued staff member would you use an employee share plan, equity in the business or promotion?
Staffing plan	Does this firm have a written staffing plan with dedicated budget?

share or expansion and/or diversification. Applying multiple growth indicators, particularly those related to sales and employment, is supported by various researchers because they are able to provide richer information (see for example Davidsson and Wiklund, 2000). Such an approach recognizes that measures do not necessarily correlate (Smallbone and Wyer, 2000) and that not all firms grow in the same way. For this study three measures of growth were used dealing with the firm's past and future growth orientations: employment growth over the past 12 months, sales growth over the past 12 months and intention to increase employment in the next 12 months. These were all coded 0 = No and 1 = Yes.

Planning: the existence of a business plan is evidence of some form of strategic thinking which is more planned than emergent (Marlow, 2000). On the questionnaire a formal business plan was defined as a plan setting out business goals and means of achieving them. Respondents were also asked whether they had a written business plan and indicated that this would usually be used for gaining finance. Both these were coded 0 if the business did not have or use such plans or 1 if they did.

Owner's role: the definition of the role the owner plays in the business was drawn from Scase and Goffee (1982) and Scase (1995) who differentiate between self-employed, small employers, owner–controllers and owner–director. The latter two roles see owners delegate some or all management responsibilities to managers. While determining different owner roles based upon the mix of capital and labour does not necessarily imply there are unvarying forms of practice (Edwards, 1995) within each of these types, they do suggest that the more the owner delegates, the more likely they are to utilize formal HRM practices and therefore exert more formal than informal control over employees. Responses were coded 0 if they described their role as small employer (owner works alongside employees as well as undertakes administrative and managerial tasks associated with running the business) and 1 if the owner described their role as owner–controller (owner does not work alongside employees as they are solely and singularly responsible for administration and management) or owner–director (owns and controls the business which has a management hierarchy). Those describing their role as 'self-employed' were excluded from the analysis.

Results

Descriptive statistics
All firms in our sample employed fewer than 20 people. The average size of responding firms was 12.5 employees (SD = 3.9, N=408) with a range of two to 19 people employed. These firms were older, with an average age of 26.5 years (SD = 20.7, N = 338) with a range of two to 151 years. The

sample was fairly evenly split between firms operating in the manufacturing sector (43.9 per cent, N = 178) and those operating in services (55.9 per cent, N = 229).

Nearly half (48 per cent, N = 363) of the firms had or used a formal business plan in which their goals and means of achieving them were outlined. However, only 27.3 per cent of firms (N = 365) had or used a written business plan which was defined as a plan which is used for gaining external funding for the business. In 43.9 per cent of firms (N = 398) the owner delegated some or all of their responsibilities for management. In terms of growth orientation some 62.2 per cent (N=393) had increased sales growth over the past 12 months; some 32.4 per cent (N = 371) had increased the number of employees in the past 12 months; and some 53.2 per cent (N = 371) indicated they intended to employ more staff in the next 12 months. Table 9.2 indicates the proportion of firms using the six formal HRM practices.

Exploratory data analysis
In order to test each of the three propositions Pearson's correlations were undertaken to determine the level of association between the variables. For Proposition 1 each of the three indicators of growth (past employment growth, past sales growth and future employment growth) were correlated with each of the six HRM practices (recruitment criteria, formal training, formal performance appraisals, selection criteria, formal rewards and plan). Growth did not indicate a strong association with any of the HR practices. But Table 9.3 indicates there were weak and positive correlations between future growth and having a formal performance appraisal practice (r = .161, N = 361, p = .002, two-tailed). Offering formal training and using selection criteria demonstrated a weak and positive association with each of the three indicators of growth.

As Table 9.3 also shows, formal training was correlated more strongly with future employment growth (r = .144, N = 361, p = .006, two-tailed) and past

Table 9.2   Proportions of firms using formal HRM practices

	Per cent	N
Recruitment criteria	64.6	369
Selection criteria	47.6	372
Formal performance appraisal	32.2	361
Formal training	28.5	361
Formal rewards	17.1	360
Staffing plan	19.3	362

Table 9.3   Correlations between growth and formal HRM practices

		1	2	3	4	5	6	7	8
1. Have sales grown in last 12 months	Pearson Correlation	1.00							
	N	393							
2. Has employment grown over last 12 months	Pearson Correlation	.333							
	Sig. (2-tailed)	.000							
	N	366	371						
3. New staff in next 12 months	Pearson Correlation	.153	.224						
	Sig. (2-tailed)	.003	.000						
	N	367	370	371					
4. Written list skills/quals when recruiting	Pearson Correlation	.084	.039	.122					
	Sig. (2-tailed)	.110	.452	.020					
	N	363	367	367	369				
5. Written job desc. all staff	Pearson Correlation	.124	.111	.112	.374				
	Sig. (2-tailed)	.017	.033	.031	.000				
	N	366	370	370	369	372			
6. What training mainly offered	Pearson Correlation	.123	.138	.144	.071	.190			
	Sig. (2-tailed)	.020	.009	.006	.180	.000			
	N	357	360	361	358	361	361		
7. Written policy on performance appraisal	Pearson Correlation	.063	.109	.161	.259	.359	.253		
	Sig. (2-tailed)	.237	.039	.002	.000	.000	.000		
	N	357	360	361	358	361	355	361	

Table 9.3 (continued)

		1	2	3	4	5	6	7	8
8. What offered to keep valued staff	Pearson Correlation	.016	.058	.054	.033	.030	-.081	-.009	
	Sig. (2-tailed)	.756	.266	.297	.531	.558	.122	.862	
	N	393	371	371	369	372	361	361	410
9. Have or use a staffing plan with dedicated budget	Pearson Correlation	.051	.110	.061	.122	.219	.168	.282	-.067
	Sig. (2-tailed)	.339	.037	.244	.021	.000	.001	.000	.202
	N	358	362	362	359	362	355	359	362

employment growth (r = .138, N = 360, p = .009, two-tailed), than with past sales, whilst having selection criteria showed the highest correlation with past sales growth (r = .124, N = 366, p = .017, one-tailed) rather than with employment growth. Using recruitment criteria (that is having a formal written list of skills when recruiting new staff) was only weakly associated with future employment growth (r = 0.122, N = 367, p = .020, one-tailed).

Proposition 2 suggested that there would be a relationship between using a formal or written business plan with each of the six measures of formal HRM practices. As Table 9.4 indicates, planning (having or using a written business plan and having or using a formal business plan) demonstrated weak to moderate correlations with most of the HRM practices. Table 9.4 shows that both aspects of planning correlated the strongest with the HRM practice of having a staffing plan. Having or using a formal business plan demonstrated stronger correlations with the practice of formal performance appraisals (r = .245, N = 357, p = .0005, two-tailed) and with using selection criteria (r = .213, N = 363, p = .0005, two-tailed), but also demonstrated positive and weaker correlations with using recruitment criteria (r = .144, N = 362, p = .031, one-tailed) and formal training (r = .127, N = 356, p = .016, one-tailed). The use of a written business plan was also weakly correlated with formal performance appraisals (r = .166, N = 360, p = .002, two-tailed), and with using selection criteria (r = .127, N = 365, p = .015, one-tailed). The HRM practice of using formal rewards was not significantly correlated with either of the measures of planning.

The third proposition investigated the owner's role and its relationship to each of the six formal HRM practices. Table 9.5 indicates that when the owner delegates some of their responsibility for management then there is a significant correlation (although weak), with the HRM practices of using selection criteria (r = .135, N = 368, p = .010, two-tailed), formal performance appraisals (r = .122, N = 357, p = .021, one-tailed) and a staffing plan (r = .123, N = 358, p = .020, one tailed). The owner's role was not correlated significantly with formal training, using recruitment criteria, or formal rewards.

Discussion
We argued in this chapter that we would see growing small firms use formal HRM practices strategically to gain or maintain a competitive advantage. The literature suggested there was a need for growth-oriented small firms to more carefully recruit, select, manage and reward employees if firm growth was to be sustained. We identified six indicators of formal HRM practices. Firms were more likely to use criteria when recruiting (that is have a list of skills and qualifications when recruiting new staff) and least likely to use formalized rewards to keep valued staff. This finding is consistent

Table 9.4 *Correlations between planning and formal HRM practices*

		1	2	3	4	5	6	7
1. Written list skills/quals when recruiting	Pearson Correlation N	1.00 369						
2. Written job desc. all staff	Pearson Correlation Sig. (2-tailed) N	.374 .000 369	372					
3. What training mainly offered	Pearson Correlation Sig. (2-tailed) N	.071 .180 358	.190 .000 361	361				
4. Written policy on performance appraisal	Pearson Correlation Sig. (2-tailed) N	.259 .000 358	.359 .000 361	.253 .000 355	361			
5. What offered to keep valued staff	Pearson Correlation Sig. (2-tailed) N	.033 .531 369	.030 .558 372	-.081 .122 361	-.009 .862 361	410		
6. Have or use a staffing plan with dedicated budget	Pearson Correlation Sig. (2-tailed) N	.122 .021 359	.219 .000 362	.168 .001 355	.282 .000 359	-.067 .202 362	362	

7. Have or use a written business plan	Pearson Correlation Sig. (2-tailed) N	.051 .329 362	.127 .015 365	.050 .350 357	.166 .002 360	-.028 .591 365	.217 .000 361	 365
8. Have or use a formal business plan (goals & means to achieve)	Pearson Correlation Sig. (2-tailed) N	.114 .031 362	.213 .000 363	.127 .016 356	.245 .000 357	-.036 .491 363	.257 .000 358	.466 .000 360

Table 9.5 Correlations between owner's role and formal HRM practices

		1	2	3	4	5	6
1. Written list skills/quals when recruiting	Pearson Correlation N	1.000 369					
2. Written job desc. all staff	Pearson Correlation Sig. (2-tailed) N	.374 .000 369	372				
3. What training mainly offered	Pearson Correlation Sig. (2-tailed) N	.071 .180 358	.190 .000 361	361			
4. Written policy on performance appraisal	Pearson Correlation Sig. (2-tailed) N	.259 .000 358	.359 .000 361	.253 .000 355	361		
5. What offered to keep valued staff	Pearson Correlation Sig. (2-tailed) N	.033 .531 369	.030 .558 372	-.081 .122 361	-.099 .862 361	410	

6. Have or use a staffing with dedicated plan budget	Pearson Correlation		-.067	.282	.168	.219	.122
	Sig. (2-tailed)		.202	.000	.001	.000	.021
	N		362	359	355	362	359
7. Best description of owner's role	Pearson Correlation	.123	.028	.122	.102	.135	.057
	Sig. (2-tailed)	.020	.575	.021	.053	.010	.275
	N	358	398	357	357	368	365

with the viewpoint that the most commonly found HRM practices tend to reflect operational needs and pragmatic concerns which include record keeping, staffing activities and recruitment and selection of staff, and to a lesser extent reward practices. The data indicates that a firm's growth orientation is a consideration in determining the extent of formal HRM practices. HRM practices can be a source of competitive advantage and therefore contribute to firm performance, and as such, our results indicate that past sales tend to correlate with having a formal list of written skills for recruiting staff. The adoption of performance appraisal correlated with future employment growth which supports the notion that in order to gain competitive advantage the adoption of such practices would be required.

Additionally, in this study we explored the relationship between formal HRM practices, the owner's role and planning. We argued that growing small firms, small firms where there was evidence of planning, and small firms where the owner delegated some or all of their responsibility for management would use formal HRM practices. Having a written business plan or using a formal business plan correlated with using selection criteria, using a formal performance appraisal practice and having a staffing plan. Having a formal business plan also correlated with using criteria when recruiting and offering formal training. The existence of planning documentation should correlate with all aspects of formal HRM practices given that it is taken as some form of evidence of strategic thinking. As our results indicate, the planning aspects correlated with most of the formal HRM practices, which suggests that attempts to set out business goals and a means for achieving them would require more formalized HRM practices.

Finally, the owner's role correlated with using selection criteria, a formal performance appraisal practice and having a staffing plan. These correlations tend to suggest that our findings are consistent with the proposition that the more the owners delegate management responsibilities, the more likely they are to use formal HRM practices. The lack of significant correlations with training, recruitment and rewards could suggest that the HRM practices best used are the ones that contribute to firm performance as indicated by the resource-based view.

The only HRM practice that did not correlate with growth, planning or owner's role was formal rewards. This may have been because of the way this was defined – offering a salary increase was defined as an informal rather than formal practice and many of our respondents said that this was primarily what they would do to retain a valued staff member.

Conclusion
A strategic approach to managing employees is vital for the success of all firms (Dyer, 1993; Pfeffer, 1994; 1998). In growth-oriented small firms the

existence of formal HRM practices is desirable to help cope with the increase in complexity resulting from greater numbers of employees if growth is to be sustained (Arthur, 1995). However, research indicates that small firms are characterized by informal and ad hoc planning in general and this can cause difficulty in taking a strategic approach to HRM (Gibb and Scott, 1985; Hannon and Atherton, 1998). Unless owners recognize the need to plan, which will also most likely entail delegating some responsibilities for direct supervision to other managers, then they are unlikely to succeed in using formal HRM practices. Our results support these arguments.

There are some limitations with the data we use. First, the questions used to define the formal HRM practices were not all asked in the same manner – some offered respondents a choice while others required a yes or no response. Second, the sample was truncated at firms that employed 20 people or less, and therefore to explore the relationship between size and formality more meaningfully we would need to have small, medium and large firms in our sample. The average size of the responding firms was 12.5 employees (SD = 3.9) and this is larger than the average Australian small business, of which some 56.3 per cent employed no one and only 10.9 per cent employed between five and 19 employees (ABS, 2005). In addition the average age of the 410 firms in our sample was 26.5 years, which makes our sample older than the average Australian small firm: for example, some 33.5 per cent of all Australian small businesses were less than five years old in June 2004, although they do get older as they get larger (ABS, 2005). Firms of increased size and age are more likely to increase their chances of survival as the liabilities of newness and smallness are able to be overcome or neutralized (Aldrich, 1999).

Furthermore, we do not have any specific performance measures in the data. We did measure total sales over the last 12 months and this measure is positively associated with growth. For example, 34.9 per cent of firms that had past employment growth and 25.4 per cent of firms with a future employment growth orientation had total sales over A$5 million. While we might like to attribute higher total sales in growing firms to a more careful approach to managing HRM, we would prefer to explore this issue through further qualitative analysis of small firms.

Entrepreneurship generates economic growth (Schumpeter, 1934) and this occurs by combining resources in new ways to create and exploit new opportunities (Shane and Venkataraman, 2000; Stevenson and Jarillo, 1990). While much of the literature focuses on new and emergent firms or start-ups as the place in which entrepreneurship occurs, the above definition does not limit entrepreneurial activity in such a manner. This research contributes to an understanding of the nature of HRM in growth-oriented small firms in Australia, where small firms are considerably smaller than their European and US counterparts. This research helps to understand whether more formal organizational systems and routines are more likely to be used (or not) to nurture human capital in growing small firms. In so doing, this research, consistent with recent calls in the literature (Baron, 2003; Barrett and Mayson, 2006; Katz et al., 2000; Tansky and Heneman, 2003), contributes to a better understanding of issues at the intersection of entrepreneurship and HRM research.

Acknowledgements

The authors would like to acknowledge the funding support from CPA Australia in carrying out this project.

References

Aldrich, H.E. (1999), *Organizations Evolving*, Thousand Oaks, CA: Sage Publications.
Ardichvili, A., B. Harmon, R. Cardozo, P. Reynolds and M. Williams (1998), 'The new venture growth: Functional differentiation and the need for human resource development interventions', *Human Resource Development Quarterly*, **9**, 55–70.
Arthur, D. (1995), *Managing Human Resources in Small and Mid-Sized Companies*, New York: American Association of Management.
Australian Bureau of Statistics (ABS) (2002), *Small Business in Australia 2001*, Cat. No. 1321.0, Canberra: ABS.
Australian Bureau of Statistics (ABS) (2003), *Business Use of Information Technology, 2001–2*, Cat. No. 8129.0, Canberra: ABS.
Australian Bureau of Statistics (ABS) (2005), *Characteristics of Small Business (Main Features Reissued)*, Cat. No. 8127.0, Canberra: ABS.
Bandilla, W., M. Bosnjak and P. Altdorfer (2003), 'Survey administration effects? A comparison of web-based and traditional self-administered surveys using the ISSP environment module', *Social Science Computer Review*, **21**, 235–43.
Baron, J.N., M.D. Burton and M.T. Hannan (1996), 'The road taken: Origins and early evolution of employment systems in emerging companies', *Industrial and Corporate Change*, **5**(2), 239–73.
Baron, R. (2003), 'Editorial: Human resource management and entrepreneurship: Some reciprocal benefits of closer links', *Human Resource Management Review*, **13**, 253–6.
Barrett, R. and S. Mayson (2006), 'Exploring the intersection of HRM and entrepreneurship. Guest editors' introduction to the special edition on HRM and entrepreneurship', *Human Resource Management Review*, **16**, 443–4.
Barrett, R. and S. Mayson (2007), 'Human resource management in growing small firms', *Journal of Small Business and Enterprise Development*, **14**(2), 307–20.
Barringer, B., F. Jones and P. Lewis (1998), 'A qualitative study of the management practices of rapid-growth firms and how rapid-growth firms mitigate the managerial capacity problem', *Journal of Developmental Entrepreneurship*, **3**, 97–122.
Cardon, M. and C. Steven (2004), 'Managing human resources in small organizations: What do we know?', *Human Resource Management Review*, **14**, 295–323.
Davidsson, P. and J. Wiklund (2000), 'Conceptual and empirical challenges in the study of firm growth', D.L. Sexton and H. Landstrom (eds), *The Blackwell Handbook of Entrepreneurship*, Oxford: Blackwell, pp. 26–44.
de Kok, J. and L. Uhlaner (2001), 'Organization context and human resource management in the small firm', *Small Business Economics*, **17**, 273–91.
Delery, J. (1998), 'Issues of fit in strategic human resource management: Implications for research', *Human Resource Management Review*, **8**, 289–309.

Deshpande, S. and D. Golhar (1994), 'HRM practices in large and small manufacturing firms: A comparative study', *Journal of Small Business Management*, **32**, 49–56.

Drummond, I. and I. Stone (2007), 'Exploring the potential of high performance work systems in SMEs', *Employee Relations*, **29**(2), 192–207.

Duberley, J. and P. Walley (1995), 'Assessing the adoption of HRM by small and medium sized manufacturing organizations', *International Journal of Human Resource Management*, **6**, 891–909.

Dyer, L. (1993), *Human Resources as a Source of Competitive Advantage*, Ontario: IRC Press.

Edwards, P. (1995), 'The employment relationship', in P. Edwards (ed.), *Industrial Relations: Theory and Practice in Britain*, Oxford: Blackwell, pp. 3–26.

Gibb, A. and M. Scott (1985), 'Strategic awareness, personal commitment and the process of planning in small business', *Journal of Management Studies*, **22**, 597–631.

Gilbert, J. and G. Jones (2000), 'Managing human resources in New Zealand small business', *Asia Pacific Journal of Human Resources*, **38**, 55–68.

Gray, C. (2002), 'Entrepreneurship, resistance to change and growth in small firms', *Journal of Small Business and Enterprise Development*, **9**, 61–72.

Hannon, P. and A. Atherton (1998), 'Small firm success and the art of orienteering: The value of plans, planning and strategic awareness in the competitive small firm', *Journal of Small Business and Enterprise Development*, **5**, 102–19.

Heneman, H. and R. Berkley (1999), 'Applicant attraction practices and outcomes among small businesses', *Journal of Small Business Management*, **37**, 53–74.

Heneman, R.L., J.W. Tansky and S.M. Camp (2000), 'Human resource management practices in small and medium-sized enterprises: Unanswered questions and future research perspectives', *Entrepreneurship: Theory and Practice*, **25**, 11–26.

Hornsby, J. and D. Kuratko (2003), 'Human resource management in US small business: A replication and extension', *Journal of Developmental Entrepreneurship*, **8**, 73–92.

Katz, J.A., H.E. Aldrich, T.M. Welbourne and P. Williams (2000), 'Guest Editors' comments. Special issue on human resource management and the SME: Towards a new synthesis', *Entrepreneurship: Theory and Practice*, **25**, 7–10.

Kotey, B. and A. Sheridan (2001), 'Gender and the practice of HRM in small business', *Asia Pacific Journal of Human Resources*, **39**, 23–40.

Kotey, B. and P. Slade (2005), 'Formal human resource management practices in small growing firms', *Journal of Small Business Management*, **43**, 16–40.

Marlow, S. (2000), 'Investigating the use of emergent strategic human resource management activity in the small firm', *Journal of Small Business and Enterprise Development*, **7**, 135–48.

Mayson, S. and R. Barrett (2006), 'Human resource management in small firms: Evidence from growing small firms in Australia', in R. Heneman and J. Tansky (eds), *Human Resource Strategies for the High Growth Entrepreneurial Firm*, Greenwich, CT: Information Age Publishing, 223–44.

Mazzarol, T. (2003), 'A model of small business HR growth management', *International Journal of Entrepreneurial Behaviour and Research*, **9**, 27–49.

McEvoy, G. (1984), 'Small business personnel practices', *Journal of Small Business Management*, **22**, 1–8.

Nguyen, T. and S. Bryant (2004), 'A study of the formality of HRM practices in small and medium sized firms in Vietnam', *International Small Business Journal*, **22**, 595–618.

Pfeffer, J. (1994), *Competitive Advantage through People*, Boston: Harvard University Press.

Pfeffer, J. (1998), *The Human Equation*, Boston: Harvard University Press.

Pils, F. and J. McDuffie (1996), 'The adoption of high-involvement work practices', *Industrial Relations*, **35**, 423–56.

Rutherford, M., P. Buller and P. McMullan (2003), 'Human resource management problems over the life cycle of small to medium-sized firms', *Human Resource Management*, **42**, 321–35.

Saxon, D., D. Garratt, P. Gilroy and C. Cairns (2003), 'Collecting data in the Information Age: Exploring web-based survey methods in educational research', *Research in Education*, **69**, 51–66.

Scase, R. (1995), 'Employment relations in small firms', in P. Edwards (ed.), *Industrial Relations: Theory and Practice in Britain*, Oxford: Blackwell, pp. 569–95.

Scase, R. and R. Goffee (1982), *The Entrepreneurial Middle Class*, London: Croom Helm.
Schumpeter, J. (1934), *The Theory of Economic Development*, Cambridge, MA.: Harvard University Press.
Shane, S. and S. Venkataraman (2000), 'The promise of entrepreneurship as a field of research', *Academy of Management Review*, **25**, 217–26.
Smallbone, D. and P. Wyer (2000), 'Growth and development in the small firm', in S. Carter and D. Jones-Evans (eds), *Enterprise and Small Business*, Harlow: Financial Times/Prentice-Hall, pp. 409–33.
Stevenson, H. and J. Jarillo (1990), 'A paradigm of entrepreneurship: Entrepreneurial management', *Strategic Management Journal*, **11**, 17–27.
Storey, D. and P. Westhead (1997), 'Management training in small firms: A case of market failure?', *Human Resource Management Journal*, **7**, 61–71.
Tansky, J. and R. Heneman (2003), 'Guest Editors' note: Introduction to the special issue on human resource management in SMEs: A call for more research', *Human Resource Management*, **42**, 299–302.
Way, S. (2002), 'High performance work systems and intermediate indicators of firm performance within the US small business sector', *Journal of Management*, **28**, 765–85.
Wright, P., B. Dunford and S. Snell (2001), 'Human resources and the resource based view of the firm', *Journal of Management*, **27**, 701–21.

10 Formalizing relationships? Time, change and the psychological contract in team entrepreneurial companies

Lynn M. Martin, Shaheena Janjuha-Jivraj, Charlotte Carey and Srikanth Sursani Reddy

Introduction

In this chapter the main focus is the 'formalization' of human resource management (HRM) practices and processes in the growing small firm. More formal HRM practices, such as regular performance appraisal and employer-based training programmes, are usually associated with larger organizations (De Kok and Uhlaner, 2001).

Larger firms are generally more formal and bureaucratic in their practices than smaller firms, and this can be seen in their approaches to recruitment (Barber et al., 1999) and training (Storey, 2004). Smaller firms, on the other hand, are characterized as operating in informal ways and adopting more formal modes only when forced to do so by breakdowns in communication and other pressures (Vinten, 1999).

Despite the growing importance of strategic HRM, the available knowledge about HRM in small firms is highly descriptive and fragmented (Brand and Bax, 2002). Nankervis et al. (1996) found little empirical evidence on HRM strategies and practices in small and medium enterprises (SME) while Marlow (2000) suggests that there is little information on how or if SME owners make strategic use not only of their own skills but also of their management team to achieve business aims and growth.

There are, however, studies showing that more formalized HRM may be connected to improved performance in small firms. Carlson et al. (2006) show HRM practices such as training and development, recruitment packages, use of performance appraisals, and competitive compensation are important for high sales growth firms. Beaver and Hutchings (2005) also suggest that SMEs with a strategic approach to training and human resource development will profit not only from a competitive position in their marketplace but also will be well placed to adjust to changing and often uncertain externalities in their business environment. In such cases HRM may therefore be described as contributing to the competitive advantage of these companies (Ferligoj et al., 1997).

The focus of this chapter is small entrepreneurial companies, which are often started by loosely grouped teams, and which operate informally with little regard for formal workplace practices. Our concern is with their development into more formally constituted workplaces. To contextualize the data we first explore the literature on team entrepreneurship and examine how this maps onto the psychological contracts literature as a way to focus on formalization of relationships in these firms. While the HRM literature mainly pertains to employees, the body of work on the psychological contract deals with the contract between employees and employer.

Here the context is the evolution of the psychological contract during the development of small firms with HRM seen by participants in their words as part of the formalization or 'professionalization' of the firm. Formalization is explored in this chapter in the context of a longitudinal study funded by the European Union and carried out in the United Kingdom. Thirty companies were tracked from start-up through to established business (or business exit) over a six-year period from 1999 to 2005.

Employers and employees saw formalization in terms of the introduction of written procedures to carry out functions such as recruitment, the development of documentation and processes to replace what had been seen as ad hoc and informal practices. We show that both the pattern and nature of the relationships between company members changed to fit the requirements of the business during different stages of development. These were team-based firms. Founding business relationships were mainly based on friendship and shared vision supported by synergy and chance, plus family-based relationships in some cases. The founding teams all reflected the social network of the founder(s) (Huse, 2004). As the firms developed, grew, faced crises and sometimes disappeared, these relationships needed to be re-negotiated in order for more formal workplace relationships to evolve. How psychological contract was originally perceived and how those perceptions changed demonstrate the transition to formality, as well as the potential difficulties in this transition. The impacts on trust and power in workplaces and the additional problems in workplaces with family members where emotion is also evident are explored in this chapter. However, in the next section we explore the literature on team entrepreneurship to provide a context for the firms in this study before elaborating on the study design and research methods.

Entrepreneurial team start-ups and change

There is an established body of research exploring the nature of team-based entrepreneurship (Birley and Stockley, 2000; Byers et al., 1998; Schoonhoven and Romanelli, 2001; Stam and Schutjens, 2006). Definitions of team entrepreneurship focus not only on the team directly involved in forming the company but also on the wider team providing informal support to the firm at start-up and through growth (Donckels and Lambrecht, 1995). In partnerships or team start-ups, the collective resources are important since individual entrepreneurs may lack critical resources to grow their businesses (Birley and Stockley, 2000; Kamm et al., 1990).

Although ventures founded by teams appear to achieve better performance than those founded by individuals (Chandler et al., 2005; Weinzimmer, 1997), studies into team entrepreneurship appear to be limited (Ucbasaran et al., 2001), especially in terms of examining the dynamics of team entrepreneurship (Birley and Stockley, 2000). Where research has been conducted on such firms, work relationships have not been the focus. For example, studies have explored the comparative performance of individually-based entrepreneurship and have looked at relative growth and loss or entry of team members, but few have explored the psychological contract perspective, either at the outset or through the lifetime of the firm. In exploring team membership Chandler et al. (2005) suggest that the greater the number of members in emerging ventures the more likely they are to add members, as size has no effect on team departures. The human dynamics underlying these actions is under-reported, contributing to a lack of research into the nature of entrepreneurial founder team turnover (Ucbasaran et al., 2003).

The life cycle of a firm can help us understand this issue. The life cycle stages have been described as typically consisting of an entrepreneurial stage, a collectivity stage, a 'formalization and control' stage and an 'elaboration of structure' stage (Huse, 1998, 2004). Reflecting these stages, the rationale and operation of boards also varies according to the company's point in this life cycle (Huse, 1998; Lynall et al., 2003). Where crises occur, directorial roles may vary in order to respond to critical situations (Huse et al., 1989), but different crises affect these roles in different ways. The power and activities of the individual director may increase or decrease with ensuing pressures across team relationships (Huse, 2004). It has been suggested that the composition of the board of directors also changes according to the stage in the company's life cycle (Lynall et al., 2003). Hence during venture creation – the entrepreneurial stage described above – boards reflect the social network of the founders. During the collectivity stage or the formalization and control stage, boards may reflect the company's resource needs, unless the power lies externally with a financial body, when it will reflect the requirements of the institutional environment. However there has been little research considering how work relationships change as firms move through their life cycle. Similarly the effects on trust and power or the psychological contract have not been explored. In terms of changed relationships with the firm there is an assumption that SMEs resist formalization. This is based on the view that smaller firms tend to have organic structures, an informal organizational form, little standardization or documentation and instead loose and informal working relationships. The perceived resistance to formality has been attributed to a lack of resources, for example, to accomplish corporate governance developments (Huse, 2004; Markman et al., 2001). This state has also been linked to the owner–manager wishing to retain power and resist the delegation of duties and responsibilities that are implied by formalization (Ghobadian and Gallear, 1997; see also Marlow and Thompson, Chapter 11 this handbook).

The owner–manager's attitude is reflected in the organizational culture, given the pivotal role of the owner–managers in small firms. If the organizational culture is informal, based on intuition and easily able to respond to market needs, this may also mean that it is resistant to written procedures, fixed roles and hierarchical structures. Where smaller firms implement quality systems, for instance, these are hindered by the perceived formality implied in these quality standards and mechanisms such as IS0900 (Van der Wiele and Brown, 1998). Similarly, Vyakarnam, Jacobs and Handelberg (1999) have described the need to slim down a five-page policy document seen by directors as 'bureaucratic' to reflect the culture of the business. Part of the problem may be that in smaller firms, organizational leaders are often responsible for the HR function, an area where they typically have limited training and experience (Klaas et al., 2005).

Time, formalization and the psychological contract
Formalization has been a focus in the small firm literature, especially in the areas of training, innovation processes, regulatory impacts and in studying the effects of cooperation with other organizations. The views are mixed. While innovation is thought to occur in more informal workplaces, cooperation, training and regulation evident in better-performing small firms encourages the formalization process. A common thread in the literature is the effect of time on formalization. Less established owner–managers dominate 'informal structures' in their firms, while more established firms are more likely to be at an early formalization stage, and are more 'functionally organized' with perhaps a 'bureaucratic' structure (Mukhtar, 2002). Roles in established businesses may be based on function, and decision-making requires delegation and the decentralization of authority. This implies that owner–managers of established firms would be more sophisticated in their managerial structure. They might be 'less autocratic, more formal, practice greater delegation of authority, have a more formal approach towards strategic and operational planning, and practice decision making that is dictated by business objectives' (Mukhtar, 2002: p. 298).

Formalization can therefore be affected by the life cycle stage a firm is in over time as different skills are called for and different tasks are required of owners, managers and employees with the company's development. Those setting up the business may know how to enter a new niche market, but may not be equipped to tackle the problems of growth within a company (Ray and Hutchinson, 1983). Over time there may be greater understanding of the specialist skills required in the business and increased recognition of the need for specialized roles (Storey, 2004). There is also a possibility that over time the team's portfolio of managerial skills could lose their relevance and old skills may need updating or specialized personnel may need to be hired.

When the company develops, the entrepreneurial perspective needs to encompass managerial roles together with the legal and formal requirements of being a director. As team members emerge from the founding team as managers and directors, inevitably fellow workers may be perceived as resources to be managed, led or directed. This may represent a significant change in the mindset of the entrepreneur and other team members or employees, where these categories are differentiated within the firm.

Differences and difficulties may emerge from how members of the firm viewed their psychological contract. Psychological contracts are defined as the beliefs employees hold about the terms and conditions of the exchange agreement between themselves and their organizations (Rousseau, 1989). Work relationships are seen as having both social and economic aspects built on formal and informal processes and structures (Cullinane and Dundon, 2006). While legal contracts can cover some of the economic aspects, other factors loosely grouped under the heading 'social' (such as, motivation, trust, commitment and loyalty), are outside the scope of the legal contract and all part of the 'psychological contract'. While the original psychological contract may be based on shared responsibilities, values and ideas, this may not be the case as the company grows. To support company development, attitudes change and the team approach may suffer.

Previous studies of the psychological contract have placed emphasis on employee rather than employer perceptions (Turnley et al., 2003). Here the psychological contract is described as the mental model formed by the individual of his or her relationship with the organization – based not only on promises made but also on implied promises. However, the mutuality of employer–employee views and a shared understanding of commitments in the workplace form the basis for the psychological contract (Rousseau, 2000). Where the employer and employee have different perceptions about what the contract actually involves, one or other may feel that promises have been broken or that there has been a violation of the psychological contract (Robinson, 1996; Robinson and Rousseau, 1994). Perceptions of a psychological contract breach cause significant changes in employee attitudes, demonstrated in negative behaviour such as lower commitment, diminished organizational citizenship behaviour and eventually higher turnover of staff (Lester et al., 2002). Breaches of the psychological contract can lead to loss of commitment to the organization and job (Schein, 1965).

Similar outcomes can result when the psychological contract has to be repositioned in the context of employment legislation, rather than solely on the background relationship with the owner–managers of the firm or being part of the group that started the company, via loose and informal relationships. Extra difficulties emerge in family workplaces. Here the original drive to support other family members to be part of the enterprise may continue as the firm grows. There is potential for issues to arise that may damage family relationships. If original roles are not recognized, then conflicts may arise. Boundaries may need to be redrawn and new external employees brought in to extend the firm's capacity or sometimes to replace family members. Again, the growing firm may not address these issues, leading not only to personal difficulties for that family member but also to the potential problems for the family and the firm. Formalization of workplace relations may address these aspects or it may not, while the way in which a firm undertakes the transition to formally constructed rules may have negative consequences for the firm and family.

The study
In order to consider the way in which the psychological contract evolved in the particular human dynamics of team start-ups, an exploratory study of 30 team start-ups was undertaken over a six-year period from 1999 to 2005. The human dynamics surrounding team operations were a key focus and especially how changes within the firms affected the psychological contracts of team founders and of other employees. Most importantly how these affected the formalization of relationships in the firm, including its impact on HRM and other functions in the firms was examined.

The 30 companies were located in the Midlands region of the UK and we followed them from initial start-up and through the next stages of their business development over the six-year period. The companies were all set up by teams with between two to five people officially involved and on average another three unofficially involved. The official team members went on to become directors, managers or key technicians within the firms while the unofficial members remained as advisors, or provided financial or other practical support. The 30 firms were drawn from two sectors where project-based work was the norm in sometimes short-lived, loosely-based teams. These were creative sector and high-technology firms.

In selecting a research method, it was apparent that most work on the psychological contract encompassed larger samples and quantitative methods; this included the development of the psychological contract inventory (Rousseau, 2000). Usually a survey was used to ask direct questions exploring perceptions and attitudes. A five-point scale indicating the extent to which respondents believed the organization was obligated to provide items (from a list derived from other survey work) is commonly used (Coyle-Shapiro and Conway, 2005; Ho et al., 2006; Robinson and Rousseau, 1994). We took a different approach and participants were encouraged to use narrative as a way to explain their views. Questions were used as cues and these formed the basis for semi-structured interviews. Ho (2006) has identified that although the way in which workers experience the organization via signals sent by formal practices is important, equally so are workers' experiences in the informal organization (Ho et al., 2006; Ho and Levesque, 2005). We wished to explore the informal organization and its reflection in the formal organization to see how this shaped the psychological contract. Richer insights were needed and what was said and how it was said was to be important. Taking a qualitative and narrative approach and using language as a key means to explore attitudes of company members to others and the company meant a different perspective of the psychological contract could be obtained, as could an understanding of how time affected this when companies faced critical incidents, grew or ceased operating.

Data was collected through interviews, focus groups, participant observations and from a review of relevant documents. The different datasets were evaluated and analysed using appropriate software such as N'Vivo and SPSS to explore emerging themes, and to test ideas about relevance and interrelationships. The relationship between employer and employee was explored using qualitative means via narrative and semi-structured interview techniques.

How the firms progressed over the six-year period is shown in Table 10.1. We can see that the original 30 firms reduced to 21 at the end of six years.

Table 10.1 Company progress over the six-year period

	Year 1	Year 2	Year 3	Year 4	Year 5	Year 6
At the start of the year	N=30	N=29	N=28	N=24	N=24	N=22
Company growth	22	18	11	10	11	8
Company static	6	9	7	11	9	11
Company decline	1	1	6	1	2	2
End of company	1	1	4	0	2	1

During the period only eight firms grew in terms of turnover and the numbers of employees. One in three of the original firms had two or more family members as part of the founding team. These firms proved to be more resilient than the other non-family firms, with only one closing during the six-year period. Moreover in the sixth year of our study four of the eight firms that enjoyed growth in terms of increased sales and turnover were family firms.

In those firms that grew in terms of employment, the new employees were a source of new skills and expertise but they also meant firms had to comply with health and safety and other employment regulations and to train and try to embed these new people into small, close-knit teams. For these firms increased numbers of staff also meant investing in premises for the first time. The regulatory burden of staffing plus the extra financial requirements of supporting both new employees and premises caused difficulties. Owner–managers were drawn away from their core role to deal with governmental legislation and to undertake different types of reporting. The financial impact of having new employees meant that profits were reduced and that a larger income was needed on a regular basis to meet salary commitments. The original team members also had to see themselves as employers for the first time, rather than as 'partners in crime', as one company director described it. For example the director of one firm commented on growth issues in the following way. 'Up until then it had been happening very quickly and really we were almost playing at it. Once employees come on board it's like you have to grow up and deal with real issues; other people depend on you' (Director, Computer firm, three-member original team).

Business advisors tried to assist by suggesting some firms moved to incubator units and pointed managers to schemes, providing incentives to employ staff. Owner–managers felt pressured to change advisors, as one said, 'For a time things got out of control, other people expected us to have proper premises, whereas we had managed very well up to then without them' (Computer firm, four original partners).

Despite support from external advisors and through incentive schemes, the extra work for managers in supervising and training staff and new premises and staff saw managers distracted from core business and this was described as problematic by team members. There were issues around who supervised new staff, with employees complaining of lack of a coherent management style across team members. In some teams different directors competed to 'build empires' as the company grew and this caused friction and damaged relationships. As the managing director of one firm said:

> With proper premises come employees you hadn't really considered before, cleaners, admin . . . Things changed in the team too as we couldn't just be a loose

team . . . of equals. When you have employees someone has to manage them, someone else has to ensure the sales cover their salaries . . . (Creative sector firm, original team of three).

Growth and development would be perceived as problematic by team members and as requiring a renegotiation of roles and behaviours. 'Once you have employees you have to act as a manager' was the rather wistful comment from one of three directors at a high-growth creative sector firm. He perceived the success of the firm as what had changed it from a very creative and unconventional environment into being 'more professional'. By this he meant the firm was more conventional and more focused on business functions with a recognized hierarchy. Previously he felt he was 'acting as a creative focus' whereas now he needed to change and learn to administrate and supervise more effectively. In this firm this trend across the three directors was a source of internal differences and bickering as no one wanted to take responsibility for this side of things although they all commented that they 'felt they had to'.

Table 10.2 indicates some of the changes that occurred in the firms over the six-year period. Growth in sales, turnover and numbers of employees all caused difficulties especially in terms of maintaining consistent products or services and guaranteeing quality when customer or supplier arrangements changed unexpectedly. These also sometimes triggered the employment of new staff, not always with satisfactory results since expectations were not

Table 10.2   Firm changes over the six-year period

	Year 1	Year 2	Year 3	Year 4	Year 5	Year 6
Extra employees	0	6	4	3	3	2
Team members leave	2	4	5	5	2	1
Customer issues	8	9	9	5	6	5
Supplier issues	3	5	5	3	2	4
Capacity issues	8	11	13	15	15	8
Changes in organizational structure	7	3	6	5	2	1
Formalization of recruitment and induction	1	8	6	6	0	0
Changes due to						
Regulatory needs	3	3	2	0	1	0
Interpersonal difficulties	4	3	6	4	2	1
Customer needs	1	0	0	1	0	0
	N=30	N=29	N=28	N=24	N=24	N=22

explored thoroughly during recruitment and both sides held unrealistic perceptions of the new recruit's role and the rewards being offered. To some extent this might have been anticipated given that most teams had little experience of recruitment processed and there were no formal HR departments. To counter this, some firms used outsourcing agencies with mixed success, as agencies had not understood what the firms were about. This led to candidates expecting unrealistic working conditions and returns (in the eyes of their employers) and to a pattern of non-delivery and high staff turnover. Unfortunately this would lead to the process beginning again in some firms.

Most did learn, however. Comments from three managing team members (A, B and C) at a software firm show the difficulties of translating their tacit knowledge of each other and the meaning attached to their actions and words to new employees. Their comments show their realization that they entered the employer–employee relationship unprepared to deal with this.

> A: Because we all knew each other so well, it was hard for us to know what to tell people so that they would become one of the team.
> B: So that they would just know what we meant without us having to explain.
> C: We expected them to be able to interpret signals we're used to giving to each other. It took a while for us to realize that what is in our heads is not so obvious but based on who we are and how long we've known each other . . .
> B: But it was very tedious having to spell everything out and I resented the time spent doing that . . . I never felt that that employee pulled their weight, maybe as a result of that.

After the employee left they worked through a set of instructions for new employees and agreed a process for recruiting and managing before they employed someone else.

> C: This was our first attempt at capturing our company and how it did things on paper, it showed us lots of things we were doing badly so helped with processes but it also meant that the next person started on a better footing with us.
> A: They started on a much clearer basis, knowing what we were expecting of them.
> B: . . . although you can't write everything down, new people have to be . . .
> A: . . . intuitive . . .
> C: . . . show initiative . . .
> B: . . . to understand how things work around here.

This exchange was typical where team members had remained together in the firm, with sentences being shared or completed by others. This was not recognized by participants but was an outcome of a long-term, trusting relationship and their experience of working as a team. The same dynamics were not observed in firms where teams had changed. Table 10.2 also shows that 22 of the firms changed their organizational structure during the six-year period, while two changed their form more than once. This often accompanied the departure of key members of the original team or it preceded the inclusion of new members at director level. The addition of new board members or employees was often accompanied by more formalized approaches to selecting and orienting them to the company.

Formal processes

By year six a third of the firms had implemented formal processes. This might mean a process such as 'induction' was defined in writing. In some firms there were pre-joining agreements for new employees and in three cases these existed for new directors and were termed 'prenuptial agreements'. Their purpose was to avoid some of the difficulties encountered with previous team members, who had not fulfilled the tasks or responsibilities expected by others in the team. The managing director of a computer firm that started out a team of three described why they used agreements for members after two original members left: 'We had known each other such a long time that you wouldn't expect to have to spell it out but we have learned the hard way' (Computer firm MD; original team of three, now five). Roles were defined in writing with minimum requirements identified for responsibilities such as reporting to the board, or attending board meetings.

In exploring organizational change, interpersonal difficulties were reported and observed in 16 firms (two had more than one change, and both changes were attributed to interpersonal difficulties as well as regulatory or customer needs). In these firms employees and employers defined formalization as the implementation of 'written' and 'procedural' steps to 'professionalize' their firms. This included:

- Using written agreements, such as pre-joining agreements for new directors, which had not occurred with the original team members;
- Having written procedures for induction measured and checked as having occurred;
- Having formal annual appraisals;
- Introducing disciplinary procedures;
- Taking steps to meet diversity and disability targets and keeping records of these steps; and
- Recruiting staff via formal and repeated processes of advertisement, application, interview and monitoring and so on rather than as an ad hoc recognition of someone's potential and immediate agreement (although this still did happen on occasion).

Employers described this as 'adding transparency', 'being more professional' and 'being more grown up about what we are doing'. Employees saw the benefit of being 'more organized' but expressed regrets about the distance it put between employer and employee. One said, 'We were very close at first – it was very friendly, very informal and we just worked across roles and got on with things; its very different now, we are definitely not part of the team but employees; we work here but we don't belong here.'

Psychological contract – changes and perceptions

Over the period of the study the psychological contract was renegotiated not only between team members and employees but also between team members. This affected the way the relationship was perceived by parties and could be seen in the language used to describe the relationship. The way the relationship not only impacted on but also was affected by the formalization process to deliver different types of behaviour was also affected.

The language and the way it was used signals how participants perceived the changes in the psychological contract as change occurred – whether the source was good or bad. The first stages of business start-up were described by all members of staff with enthusiasm, expressions of enthusiasm, warmth and belief in the future of the firm and their own role in it. This was expressed through words such as 'hope' and 'belief', as shown in Table 10.3. Team members spoke well of each other and of the joint venture. In family firms the family members also included other family and community members in their views of who constituted the team, even when they were not on the payroll, confident they could call on them for finance, advice and providing extra time (for low/no pay) if it could help to develop the firm.

The psychological contract was originally seen as being based on trust, a belief in the promise of firm growth and that inclusion in the process would be kept in both surviving and exiting firms. This changed in both surviving and exiting companies as critical incidents occurred and changes resulted to the way things were organized and managed. The original conception of the team changed. Many of the employees who worked in these firms soon after start-up (and who had accepted poor conditions because of their belief in the opportunities that would come from being part of the growing firm) went from being 'in' to 'out' in their own eyes and in the comments of their managers. The transition from 'inclusive part of the firm' to 'employee' was signalled by the directors' changing attitudes towards them. This was also reflected in new entrants to the management team treating them as employees and by being affected by processes being formalized. What had once been an informal working relationship, characterized by a shared but often unstated understanding had become documented. As a

Table 10.3 Language used to describe relationships at different stages of the firm's development

For firms ending during the research period (N=9)

	Start-up	Mid-course	End
Team	Faith, hope, belief, respect, affection, knowledge (of other person), trust, innovative	Trust, competitive, accountable, innovative 'the honeymoon's over'	Lack of trust, incompatibility, lack of cooperation
	High trust	Reduced trust	No trust
Employee	Trust, faith, hope, belief, creative	Lack of trust, responsibility, accountability (as in he or she should take responsibility)	Lack of management skills, lack of understanding of employee
	High trust	Reduced trust	needs/feelings No trust

For firms surviving during the research period (N=21)

	Start-up	Mid-course	End
Team	Faith, hope, belief, respect, affection, knowledge (of other person) trust, innovative	Trust, competitive, accountable, innovative 'the honeymoon's over'	Experience, better knowledge of partners, reliable,
	High trust	Reduced trust	Trust
Others – Employee	Trust, faith, hope, belief, creative	Anxiety about change, lack of trust, responsibility (as in he or she should take responsibility), perceptions of	Perceptions of breach but acceptance of the process, less commitment to the firm more interest outside,
	High trust	breach of contract as formalization occurs, no longer part of the team but employees Reduced trust	Reduced trust

result relationships became more explicit and different from the way they had been before. Employees described a loss of personal relationships at work as a result of increasing formalization of processes. Typical comments made in many firms are seen in what employees at a computer company which had experienced rapid growth over a short time had to say:

> D: The best thing about it at first was the way you all worked together . . . it was like a family . . . [Now however] it's just like anywhere else, just us and them . . . you might work here but you don't matter in the same way you did.

> E: I really felt very close to [two of the original team members] I mean I thought of them as friends, as people I could rely on and look up to. I thought they felt the same way but it turns out that was just in my head; they are directors and I am a technician and the friendship evaporated as the company grew.

As we can see in Table 10.4, directors talked about employees as having a lack of realism about their role in the firm. They frequently forgot the start-up process and the loyalty and efforts employees had made. When they were reminded by reviewing interview transcripts from those early periods they put their views down to naivety and inexperience. 'Friendship doesn't have a place at work; being professional and pleasant. . .really it's not about feelings' (MD at the computer company). They also saw their earlier views (about all being part of one team and sharing rewards) as evidence that they had not been 'professional' when they had started the company. Here employees attributed breach to the organization's intentional disregard for earlier implied commitments while directors explained this as being beyond the organization's direct control and unrealistic on the employee's part (reflecting work by Lester et al., 2002).

There was also a lack of common understanding of terms. For example employers described the 'rewards' of firm growth for the employer to be rising wages and improving conditions. Employees, however, saw part of their reward as being included in the process, and having their efforts seen as valuable and recognized as such. This was also the case with some team members being 'edged out' as their skills and experience meant they either could not contribute effectively to company development or they were felt to be incompatible with the team. Again their perceived loss of potential financial rewards was also compounded by feelings of rejection by the team and a lack of recognition of their earlier value and contributions.

These changes were viewed emotionally by team members and their feelings were signalled by the language they used. Parallels between home and work were apparent and changes were described in terms of divorce. In a creative sector firm one of the four original directors explained: 'The four of us were very close at the start but we drifted apart, maybe we didn't talk enough . . . after the break up [i.e., with two team members leaving] we

*Table 10.4   How employers described the role of employees at different
stages of firm development*

	Start-up	Mid-course	End
Of the firm at different stages	We're all in this together	We need to develop properly as a firm	We need to evaluate how to use our resources
Of themselves at different stages	We're equals/partners/ family; we know each other really well	We're partners despite ups and downs	We've had to grow up and see ourselves differently as managers, for instance; some of the team weren't happy to do that
Of employees	Few had employees at start-up As the firm grows so the team will grow	The employees/staff/ the rest of the firm	The employees/staff/ the rest of the firm

made sure we had a process before anyone else joined; a kind of prenuptial agreement . . .'

In a software firm going through rapid growth, a departing director commented: 'I gave the firm everything, gave up things for the firm, supported them through really difficult times during the time we were starting up but they have replaced me with someone new now. I couldn't believe it when things went wrong, that they wanted me to leave.'

Perceptions of breaches of the psychological contract are most likely to differ on the extent to which the organization violated its obligations to provide fair pay, advancement opportunities, and a good employment relationship (Lester et al., 2002). Here the breach resulted from more fuzzy expectations not being met, from the organization devaluing the individual and his or her contribution and not living up to its earlier promise of nurturing employees.

As the literature on psychological contracts indicates, when there is a breach, team members become alienated. For example an employee who had been in at the company's founding ceased to work effectively with the rest of the team either as director or an employee and this further exacerbated the situation. While others become accustomed to them working communally, they did not include them in discussion and the person felt more isolated. Despite the literature identifying that deviant behaviours might be displayed as a result (see Conway and Briner, 2002; Kickul, 2001; Kickul et al., 2001; Lester et al., 2002; Robinson and Rousseau, 1994; Robinson, 1996; Robinson and Morrison, 2000; Turnley et al., 2003) this was not evident in the companies in the study.

In common with Lester et al. (2002), employees' perceptions of psychological contract breach were linked with lower commitment to the organization and decreased job performance (as rated by their supervisor). Employees who remained with their firm came to terms with the situation, although as some commented, 'their heart was not in it'.

> I feel quite sad sometimes coming to work but I have got past it, I just come in, do the stuff asked of me in the time required and go home; no extras, no ideas. It pays the rent but I can't say it feels like it did at first. I am looking for another job but I wouldn't go into the same type of company again – you put your heart into it and it's not appreciated (Designer, creative sector firm).

Conclusion

These 30 firms provide insights into the human dynamics accompanying business development in companies started by teams. O'Gorman and Doran (1999) suggest that as small businesses grow their managers become increasingly distant from employees and their strong entrepreneurial vision may no longer be shared by new staff or new investors. In these firms the team entrepreneurs also became more distant from each other, with interpersonal difficulties arising as different problems emerge. In this study we focused on growing firms, and the problems we observed were caused by issues around growth in terms of numbers of employers and consistently meeting quality targets. Emotions were high and negative and positive feelings were expressed during the course of the business developing or exit. The language used to describe work relationships reflected that used in personal spheres of home and family.

The study shows how formalization in the firms can emerge and the potentially negative impacts of the transition on company members if it is not carried out in an inclusive way. This can be seen in the transition of original team members who thought they were 'part of a team', to become employees. The psychological contract between the team of founding directors was also shown to change in this process, as loyalties changed and people seen as valuable at start-up became less so during company development. The impact of formalized processes on HRM on these relationships is indicated but warrants further research to fully understand how these shifts in the psychological contract occur over time. From the directors' viewpoint, formalizing processes and structures made the firms and themselves more 'professional'. This could be an area for further research given the image of the owner–manager that directors felt they should embody in running their companies.

Harney and Dundon (2006) used findings from a multiple case study to show that a complex interplay of external structural factors and internal dynamics shaped HRM. Hence HRM was not the coherent set of practices typically identified in the literature but rather was often informal and emergent. Our study supports their view and suggests that more research needs to be done in the small-firm area, to explore further how psychological contracts are formed and how they develop in smaller workplaces where often more is implied than written. Also the context of the family firm provides a new dimension to the study of the psychological contract. There is little research to show how the psychological contract differs in family and nonfamily firms, how it is differentiated between home-based relationships, and whether one impacts upon or reflects the other.

References

Barber, A.E., M.J. Wesson, Q.M. Roberson and S. Taylor (1999), 'A tale of two job markets: Organizational size and its effects on hiring practices and job search behavior', *Personnel Psychology*, **52**(4), 841–67.

Beaver, G. and K. Hutchings (2005), 'Training and developing an age diverse workforce in SMEs: The need for a strategic approach', *Education + Training*, **47**(8/9), 592–604.

Birley, S. and S. Stockley (2000), 'Entrepreneurial teams and venture growth', in D.L. Sexton and H. Landstrom (eds), *The Blackwell Book of Entrepreneurship*, Oxford, UK: Blackwell Publishers, pp. 287–307.

Brand, M.J. and E.H. Bax (2002), 'Strategic HRM for SMEs: Implications for firms and policy', *Education + Training*, **44**(8/9), 451–63.

Byers, T., H. Kist and R.I. Sutton (1998), 'Characteristics of the entrepreneur: Social creatures, not solo heroes', in R.C. Dorf (ed.), *The Technology Management Handbook*, Boca Raton, FL: CRC Press LLC, pp. 1-1–1-6. (Also available at http://www.stanford.edu/class/e145/materials/Characteristics.html).

Carlson, D.S., N. Upton and S. Seaman (2006), 'The impact of human resource practices and compensation design on performance: An analysis of family-owned SMEs', *Journal of Small Business Management*, **44**(4), 531–43.

Chandler, G.N., B. Honig and J. Wiklund (2005), 'Antecedents, moderators, and performance consequences of membership change in new venture teams', *Journal of Business Venturing*, **20**, 705–25.

Conway, N. and R. Briner (2002), 'A daily diary study of affective responses to psychological contract breach and exceeded promises', *Journal of Organizational Behavior*, **23**, 287–302.

Coyle-Shapiro, J.A.-M. and N. Conway (2005), 'Exchange relationships: An examination of psychological contracts and perceived organizational support', *Journal of Applied Psychology*, **90**(4), 774–81.

Cullinane, N. and T. Dundon (2006), 'The psychological contract: A critical review', *International Journal of Management Reviews*, **8**(2), 113–29.

DeKok, J. and L.M. Uhlaner (2001), 'Organization context and human resource management in the small firm', *Small Business Economics*, **17**, 273–91.

Donckels, R. and J. Lambrecht (1995), 'Networks and small business growth: An explanatory model', *Small Business Economics*, **7**, 273–89.

Ferligoj, A., J. Prasnikar and V. Jordan (1997), 'Competitive advantage and human resource management in SMEs in a transitional economy', *Small Business Economics*, **9**(6), 503–14.

Ghobadian, A. and D. Gallear (1997), 'TQM and organization size', *International Journal of Operations and Production Management*, **17**(2), 121–63.

Harney, B. and T. Dundon (2006), 'Capturing complexity: Developing an integrated approach to analysing HRM in SMEs', *Human Resource Management Journal*, **16**(1), 48–73.

Ho, V.T. (2006), 'Social influence on evaluations of psychological contract fulfillment', *Academy of Management Review*, **30**, 113–28.

Ho, V.T. and L.L. Levesque (2005), 'With a little help from my friends (and substitutes): Social referents and influence in psychological contract fulfillment', *Organization Science*, **16**, 275–89.

Ho, V.T., D.M. Rousseau and L.L. Levesque (2006), 'Social networks and the psychological contract: Structural holes, cohesive ties, and beliefs regarding employer obligations', *Human Relations*, **59**(4), 459–81.

Huse, M. (1998), 'Researching board–stakeholder relations', *Long Range Planning*, **31**, 218–26.

Huse, M. (2004), 'Corporate governance in advanced market economies: Understanding important contingencies', *Committee For Trade, Industry And Enterprise Development*, Economic Commission For Europe Paper No. 17, available online at http://www.unece.org/indust/sme/morten.doc.

Huse, M., J.W. Lorsch and E. MacIver (1989), *Pawns and Potentates: The Reality of America's Corporate Boards*, Boston: Harvard Business School Press.

Kamm, J.B., J.C. Shuman, J.A. Seeger and A.J. Nurick (1990), 'Entrepreneurial teams in new venture creation: A research agenda', *Entrepreneurship: Theory and Practice*, **14**(4), 7–17.

Kickul, J. (2001), 'When organizations break their promises: Employee reactions to unfair processes and treatment', *Journal of Business Ethics*, **29**(4), 289–307.

Kickul, J.R., G. Neuman, C. Parker and J. Finkl (2001), 'Settling the score: The role of organizational justice in the relationship between psychological contract breach and anticitizenship behavior', *Employee Responsibilities and Rights Journal*, **13**(2), 77–93.

Klaas, B.S., T. Gainey and J.A. McClendon (2005), 'HR in the small business enterprise: Assessing the impact of PEO utilization', *International Journal of Human Resource Management*, **16**(3), 383–404.

Lester, S.W., W.H. Turnley, J.M. Bloodgood and M.C. Bolino (2002), 'Not seeing eye to eye: Differences in supervisor and subordinate perceptions of and attributions for psychological contract breach', *Journal of Organizational Behavior*, **23**(1), 39–56.

Lynall, M.D., B.R. Golden and A.J. Hillman (2003), 'Board composition from adolescence to maturity: A multi-theoretical view', *Academy of Management Review*, **28**, 416–31.

Markman, G., D. Balkin and L. Schjoedt (2001), 'Governing the innovation process in entrepreneurial firms', *Journal of High Technology Management Research*, **12**, 273–93.

Marlow, S. (2000), 'Investigating the use of emergent strategic human resource management activity in the small firm', *Journal of Small Business and Enterprise Development*, **7**(2), 135–48.

Mukhtar, S.M. (2002), 'Differences in male and female management characteristics: A study of owner–manager businesses', *Small Business Economics*, **18**, 289–311.

Nankervis, A., R. Compton, L. Savery and T. McCarthy (1996), *Strategic Human Resource Management*, Melbourne: Nelson Thomson.

O'Gorman, C. and D. Doran (1999), 'Mission statements in small and medium-sized businesses', *Journal of Small Business Management*, **37**(4), 59–66.

Ray, G.H. and P.J. Hutchinson (1983), *The Financing and Financial Control of Small Enterprise Development*, Aldershot: Gower.

Robinson, S.L. (1996), 'Trust and breach of the psychological contract', *Administrative Science Quarterly*, **41**, 574–600.

Robinson, S.L. and E.W. Morrison (2000), 'The development of psychological contract breach and violation: A longitudinal study', *Journal of Organizational Behavior*, **21**, 525–46.

Robinson, S.L. and D.M. Rousseau (1994), 'Violating the psychological contract: Not the exception but the norm', *Journal of Organizational Behavior*, **15**, 245–59.

Rousseau, D.M. (1989), 'Psychological and implied contracts in organizations', *Employee Responsibilities and Rights Journal*, **2**, 121–39.

Rousseau, D.M. (2000), 'Psychological contract inventory', *Technical Report. No. 2000–02*,

The Heinz School of Public Policy and Management, Carnegie Mellon University, Pittsburgh, PA.

Schein, E.H. (1965), *Organizational Psychology*, Englewood Cliffs, NJ: Prentice Hall.

Schoonhoven, C.B. and E. Romanelli (2001), *The Entrepreneurship Dynamic: The Origins of Entrepreneurship and the Evolution of Industries*, Stanford: Stanford University Press.

Stam, E. and V. Schutjens (2006), 'The fragile success of team start-ups', in R. Oakey, W. During and S. Kauser (eds), *New Technology-based Firms in the New Millennium*, Volume V, Oxford: Elsevier Science.

Storey, D.J. (2004), 'Exploring the link between management training and firm performance among small firms: A comparison between the UK and other OECD countries', *International Journal of Human Resource Management*, **15**(1), 112–30.

Turnley, W.H., M.C. Bolino, S.W. Lester and J.M. Bloodgood (2003), 'The impact of psychological contract fulfilment on the performance of in-role and organizational citizenship behaviors', *Journal of Management*, **29**(2), 187–206.

Ucbasaran, D., P. Westhead and M. Wright (2001), 'The focus of entrepreneurial research: Contextual and process issues', *Entrepreneurship: Theory and Practice*, **24**(4), 57–81.

Ucbasaran, D., A. Lockett, M. Wright and P. Westhead (2003), 'Entrepreneurial founder teams: Factors associated with member entry and exit', *Entrepreneurship: Theory and Practice*, **28**, 107–27.

Van der Wiele, T. and A. Brown (1998), 'Venturing down the TQM path for SMEs', *International Small Business Journal*, **16**(2), 50–69.

Vinten, G. (1999), 'Corporate communications in small- and medium-sized enterprises', *Industrial and Commercial Training*, **31**(3), 112–19.

Vyakarnam S., R. Jacobs and J. Handelberg (1999), 'Exploring the formation of entrepreneurial teams: The key to rapid growth business?', *Journal of Small Business and Enterprise Development*, **6**(2), 153–65.

Weinzimmer, L.G. (1997), 'Top management team correlates of organizational growth in a small business context: A comparative study', *Journal of Small Business Management*, **35**(3), 1–9.

11 Growing pains: managing the employment relationship in medium-sized enterprises
Susan Marlow and Amanda Thompson

Introduction
There is a growing body of literature on the management of labour in small and medium-sized enterprises (SMEs), usually defined as those with fewer than 250 employees (DTI, 2004). However, the bulk of this literature focuses on small firms, which are those with fewer than 50 employees. This literature is said to represent, 'a key exemplar of analytical advance [where] research has made empirical and analytical progress' (Ram and Edwards, 2003: p. 719). Whilst mindful of heterogeneity within the sector, the evidence suggests informal management of the effort-wage bargain (Holliday, 1995; Marlow, 2003; Marlow et al., 2004; Moule, 1998; Ram and Edwards, 2003; Ram et al., 2001). Arguably this informality arises and persists from the spatial and social proximity between employers and employees. Additionally owner–managers have limited awareness or regard for formal policy and practice, which in turn leads to a devaluing of HRM and a consequent reluctance to delegate labour management to professionals (Marlow, 2002; Marlow et al., 2004; Mazzarol, 2003; Ram et al., 2001).

Since 1998 the UK Workplace Employment Relations Survey (WERS) has paid attention to SMEs including firms with as few as 10 employees in 1998 and five employees in 2004. The findings from these surveys indicate that while the extent of formalization varies within and across smaller firms, in general, formality increases with organizational size, (indicated by employee numbers and financial performance) (Cully et al., 1999; Kersley et al., 2006). Informality arising from social and spatial proximity dissipates with growth so, whilst still able to embrace degrees of informality, larger organizations tend towards more bureaucratic, formal ordering of the employment relationship in order to operate effectively, efficiently and lawfully.

When reviewing contemporary analyses of the employment relationship, it is apparent that research on managing labour in large firms is well established and there is a growing seam of literature focused upon small firms, but little attention has been afforded to independently-owned and managed medium-sized enterprises. Those firms that have more than 50 but fewer than 250 employees are not well understood despite employing approximately 12 per cent of the labour force (DTI, 2004). It might be expected that these organizations will have grown too large to depend upon informal management approaches but are unlikely to have fully adopted sophisticated, formal bureaucratic systems. They are likely to differ from both their smaller and larger counterparts in having a distinct approach to labour management, which may still demonstrate degrees of informality whilst having to become more cognizant with a professional approach to labour management. It has been noted (Mazzarol, 2003; Wilkinson, 1999; Wynarcyzk et al., 1993) that as a firm grows the processes required to effectively manage labour become more sophisticated. Indeed a common reason owners give for avoiding growth is their reluctance to either delegate labour management or to deal with the ensuing complexity themselves. Twenty employees would therefore be considered a critical threshold in the life of the organization, as beyond this number of employees it becomes difficult to maintain and support informal social relations (Wilkinson, 1999).

Nevertheless, many independently-managed firms do grow beyond the 20 employee threshold and face the problems of managing increasing complexity in the employment relationship. Complexity is not only related to regulatory compliance issues but also the challenge of managing a growing and increasingly diverse group of both managers and employees in an efficient and effective manner. A professional HR manager is not a priority appointment in many SMEs, as owners are reluctant to delegate labour management (Marlow and Patton, 2002; Taylor, 2006; Wynarczk et al., 1993) and afford HRM low status and value. Arguably then, managing labour in medium-sized firms, whether undertaken by owners, general managers or HR professionals, has particular challenges quite different from those identified in the small firm where informality in a context of proximity is feasible and indeed, considered rational (Taylor, 2006). Moreover, the formal bureaucratic systems evident in many large organizations are unlikely to be found in firms where owners, uninformed and/or unskilled in labour management maintain prerogative over the employment relationship. How then do owners and managers address the increasing complexity of dealing with an expanding workforce and manage the process of implementing more formal and professional policies and practices?

The chapter is organized as follows to explore this question. First a conceptual framework using the notions of informality and formality in the employment relationship will be explored and established; the relationship between these concepts and firm size will be considered, particularly how firm growth influences the dynamic of informality. Second, these arguments will be investigated empirically using the findings from a qualitative study of six medium-sized firms where owners, managers and employees were interviewed at length to ascertain their views and opinions about the process of growth and change. Finally, the implications of these findings are discussed in broader terms.

Conceptual framework: informality and formality in the management of labour

Considerable attention has been focused on the informal nature of labour management in small firms since the 1990s. Ram et al. define informality as 'a process of workforce engagement, collective and/or individual, based mainly on unwritten customs and the tacit understandings that arise out of the interaction of the parties at work' (2001: p. 846). Marlow et al. suggest that an informal approach is 'largely emergent, flexible and loosely structured' (2004: p. 5). In small firms, informality becomes the norm when the owner or a general manager manages the employment relationship and so there is a lack of professional personnel input and formalized systems. Instead practices are idiosyncratic and apply on the owner–manager's terms. This approach to ordering the employment relationship can be compared to a formal stance where the terms and conditions of employment are laid down within written policies and articulated by professional practitioners.

This is not to suggest simplistic dichotomies between informality and formality where these notions can be uncritically associated with small and large firms respectively. As Ram et al. argue, informality and formality are dynamic constructs which co-exist in differentiated forms in time and space such that 'informality in small firms is a matter of degree and not kind' (2001: p. 846). So for example Cully et al. (1999) and Kersley et al. (2006) find that small firms do adopt formal procedures and this is particularly evident in the case of discipline and grievance policies, where even many of the smallest firms claim to have written policies. On balance though smaller organizations are likely to have fewer policies and practices in place than their larger counterparts but it is the exception where there is a complete absence. Qualitative studies of labour management in smaller firms (Bacon et al., 1996; Gilman et al., 2002; Marlow, 2002) have found a degree of 'over claiming' and 'mock formality' in the use of formal policy and practice and this must be kept in mind when dealing with surveys of the presence of formal practices. Bacon et al. (1996) for example, found that some 30 per cent of respondents claimed they had adopted HRM practices, which they hadn't, while Marlow (2002) found respondents did indeed have formal, written policies in their filing cabinets, but that was usually where they remained even when problems arose. Her study found owners preferred to maintain their own idiosyncratic approaches to managing the employment relationship and rarely consulted or used formal procedures.

Other research considers a range of influences on the propensity of firms to formalize, and size, whilst important, is only one of several. So for example, in their work upon the adoption of the National Minimum Wage, Arrowsmith et al. (2003) identified how sector influenced formality. Bacon and Hoque (2004) drew attention to the impact of the internal context such as the demand for skills, and influences from the external context such as key customers upon promoting formality, and Kinnie et al. (1999) have emphasized supply chain influences on managerial practice.

This also suggests that it is also too simplistic to assume that large organizations operate in a purely formal, bureaucratic manner. It is evident that whilst the employment relationship is defined through formal policy and bureaucratic systems, custom and practice also abounds (Elger and Smith, 1998; Webb and Palmer, 1998). This is usefully illustrated in Taylor's (2006) critical analysis of recruitment and selection practices where attention is drawn to the fact that even though the selection process in large firms is highly regulated, given the need to amalgamate the requirements of the organization with government-imposed ethical standards, informality still exists. During selection in particular, 'managerial agency allows for interpretation and contestation of norms; in other words, tools such as interview and psychometric testing are filtered through managerial politics, individual preferences and prejudices, organizational or local cultures and instrumental demands' (Taylor, 2006: p. 480). As such, managers in large organizations navigate between rationality, formality, personal preference and idiosyncrasy.

In assessing informality and formality in relation to firm size, Marlow (2002) suggests that key differences lie in the legitimacy of informality to order the employment relationship. As such, in large organizations, custom and practice may be tolerated and indeed its efficacy in smoothing the path of production fully appreciated. However, the effort-wage bargain will be formally defined and bounded because it has to be. Where managerial authority is delegated down through hierarchies, systems must be in place to make a coordinated and planned production process possible. Within this process, though, employees and managers will make 'room to manoeuvre' and this has been recognized and analysed through notions such as 'manufacturing consent' and the well-established concept of sharing control in order to gain employee consent to be managed (Buroway, 1979; Flanders, 1968). But when questions, challenges, tensions and/or disputes arise, the line manager does not possess the ultimate authority of the employer and the employee is not embedded within a paternalistic relationship with the owner (and may also have representation through a trade union), so recourse to formality is essential for both parties. Moreover, areas and issues of tension and dispute can also be delegated to or overseen by HR managers who can assist in dissipating personal animosity between groups. Thus, as Marlow et al. (2004: p. 7) note, 'informality in large firms, although an enduring feature of the employment relationship, is a more subversive activity . . . it is only ever discretionary'.

In contrast, informality in small firms strengthens social ties and supports an environment of social obligation. As Taylor (2006) argues, blurring the divisions between employers and employees supports cultural continuity in the organization and facilitates the persistence of a family analogy suggesting that all are working towards similar and shared goals. As Ram et al. (2001) note, informality also works to disguise highly exploitative employment relationships and should not be taken to be synonymous with harmony. Informality is, however, seen to be more legitimate because of flatter structures, social and spatial proximity and a presumption of shared ambition.

There will be a range of variables that combine to influence the manner and pace of firms adopting more formal procedures to cope with complexity. Formality and informality are dynamic and are shaped by context, and as Ram et al. argue, 'all firms combine formality and informality just as they combine control and consent. The balance differs as conditions vary', (2001: p. 859). The purpose of this chapter is to explore how the balance of formality and informality shifts as firms grow. Given that the SME sector is heterogeneous there will be differences in the degree and extent of formality. But as firms grow and become more complex the social relations of production will become stretched by hierarchical and spatial distance, and organizations will be obliged to adopt and utilize greater formality. This will challenge prevailing norms and relationships and it is this process and related tensions that are of interest.

We do not assume that formality has an overwhelmingly detrimental impact on an organization. As firms grow and become more hierarchical and bureaucratic, greater formality can ensure that managerial systems and processes are utilized appropriately and efficiently. In the case of the employment relationship, as employee numbers grow formal systems are required to enable the delegation of labour supervision and management. Employment numbers trigger many aspects of the regulation shaping the employment relationship; in the UK this includes the Employment Relations Act (1998) and the Information and Consultation of Employees Regulation (2004). To ensure employers and employees comply with such regulation, a professional approach to policy and practice is essential. So, the elasticity of informality is useful for smaller firms but can act as an impediment to growth if personalized and idiosyncratic managerial approaches are not underpinned by formal policy and process.

In comparison to the literature on labour management in small firms, there is relatively little attention afforded to medium-sized organizations. There is a tendency to talk about SMEs which groups all firms with ten to 249 employees. The purpose of this chapter is to explore the process whereby growing firms adopt greater formality within the employment relationship and in so doing, considers what motivates the adoption of formality; the challenges and tensions associated with such changes and how these are perceived and understood within the organization.

As Ram et al. argue, limited attention has been afforded to how informality evolves over time, 'the tendency has been to treat it as an essentially unchanging way of oiling the wheels, but we also need to consider in what direction the wheels are heading' (2001: p. 846). To explore this process of change, findings from in-depth interviews with owners, Chief Executive Officers (CEO), HR managers and employees in six independently owned and/or managed medium-sized firms are reported.

Methodology

In previous studies (Bacon and Hoque, 2004; Cully et al., 1999; Heneman et al., 2000; Kersley et al., 2006; Kinnie et al., 1999) formality has been measured by the number of formal policies and practices an organization has in place to manage the employment relationship. We earlier indicated that in survey work there can be over-reporting of the extent and complexity of policy. Moreover, there has been some tendency to conflate formality and HRM practices; however, the former might be indicated by the use of written policy whilst the latter may be used to presume a level of strategic engagement and complexity in the approach to labour management. The problem of searching for, and finding, HRM in smaller firms has been critically explored by Taylor (2004) and Marlow (2006) who argue that an HRM approach is not synonymous with employment relations and the term should be used with care, particularly in respect to smaller firms. In our study formality refers to the presence and consistent use of written policy and procedure within key areas of the employment relationship. Our concern is not with how many of these policies and procedures are in place, rather, our aim is to explore if, when, why and how formal policy has been introduced and to what degree it has become embedded within the management of employment relationship.

A qualitative approach is adopted to explore these issues. The difficulty of relying on qualitative data has been noted and as Blackburn argues, they 'are methodologically inadequate to unearth the real nature and processes of employment relations in the workplace and offer an overly simplistic picture of the complexities of employment relations in the workplace' (2004: p. 58). Others have also suggested that qualitative case study research is needed if 'the actual as opposed to the espoused' (Dickens and Hall, 2005: p. 34) is to be uncovered when considering employment relations practices at the workplace.

The characteristics of the firms participating in this study are described in Table 11.1, and those of the respondents in Table 11.2. The respondent firms were at the smaller end of the medium category (between 50 and 100 employees) but we thought that in this size band changes to the employment relationship would be more evident, as although the 20 employee threshold had been exceeded the firms were not yet so large that the process of developing formal policy would be forgotten or dismissed. Moreover, the firms had experienced employee-related growth during the last two years, hence the dynamics and challenges associated with change could be readily recalled.

Table 11.1   Firm characteristics

Firm	Sector	Age (yrs)	2004 Employment size: full time (part-time)	2006 Employment size: full time (part-time)	2004 Turnover (£ millions)	2006 Turnover (£ millions)
BoxCo	Manufacturing	12	38 (3)	72 (6)	4.1	5+*
HaulCo	Road haulage	13	45 (4)	75 (4)	3.8	5+*
IntelCo	Training	9	48 (12)	68 (10)	3.1	5+*
WomCo	Support	9	36 (10)	58 (25)	2.7	3.3
PropCo	Property development	16	50 (6)	84 (8)	12	15
ChefCo	Manufacturing	12	47 (5)	64 (4)	5+*	5+*

Note: *Turnover not specified but given as 5+.

Table 11.2   Respondents

	Management	Employees
BoxCo	Owner	Production employee (1)
HaulCo	Owner	Owner's PA; other administrative staff (2)
IntelCo	CEO	–
WomCo	CEO	Administrative staff (2)
PropCo	Owner	Administrative staff (2)
ChefCo	Owner, HR manager	–

Getting into smaller firms as a researcher is then difficult given the resistance of owners to external scrutiny and the more mundane issue of time pressures (Curran and Blackburn, 2001; Scase, 1995). To overcome this problem, key employees were identified who then established the researcher's credentials. These employees were identified through a snowball approach starting with a self-employed book-keeper known to the researchers who specialized in completing VAT and tax returns for SMEs in the region. Trust and access was then gained through the credibility of the key contact who was able to vouch for the researcher.

While our findings cannot be generalized to a whole population, this is not the aim. Instead the purpose is to add to the understanding of the dynamics of formality and informality in the employment relationship, and particularly to explore the fluidity between these concepts during a time of firm growth. We take a similar stance to Ram et al. and argue, 'we are not seeking to generalize to a population but to examine "soft" processes and dynamics . . . we generalize to the level of theory rather than any notion of representativeness' (2001: p. 849).

To explore the process of change in the employment relationship, respondents were asked to describe contemporary policy in a range of practices from recruitment to dismissal. To assess change over time, a critical incident approach was adopted (Cope and Watts, 2000). This approach was useful as the incident was a point for discussion particularly in terms of how it prompted change. Our concern was with an incident that the respondents felt had affected the approach to labour management and specifically had caused the owner or management team to adopt greater formality. Respondents were asked to discuss what they thought were the causes and consequences of these incidents, and from the six firms, interviews with 15 respondents ensured a wealth of data focused around the critical elements of the employment relationship.

Findings
Interviewees were asked to describe the extent (if any) to which formality had been adopted over time as the firm had grown. In the only organization (ChefCo) with a professional HR manager, formality was associated with changes in performance and labour management issues, 'the firm is much more efficient, people feel more secure as we have better communication and systems'. Yet, when the owner of the firm was asked the same question, he associated formality with change in the social relations of production,

> it has become much more formalized. It has become much more difficult to treat people as individuals, they are much more legal entities, you have to be very

careful what you say and do and I think that you have to create a formal structure, it has dehumanized a lot of work relationships which is a shame.

Indeed, this was a common sentiment from owners and managers that formality was strongly associated with an erosion of social relations; for example the owner of PropCo said, 'at one time, I knew all of my staff members personally and now I couldn't tell you 50 per cent of their names on sight, it means I have to delegate control and you lose the personal touch, it does upset me'. There was some agreement that in general, formality meant doing things 'properly' with due recognition of rules and regulations rather than depending upon intuition and idiosyncrasy. It was interesting to contrast these views with those of the employees as some differences did emerge. For instance, when asked to comment on changes in the organization as it had grown, an employee at PropCo claimed, 'Well, I think they have carried on trying to do things the same way but just making adjustments here and there to try and make it carry on working but it does fall apart'. Despite her employer stating that formality was established within the organization, an accounts clerk at HaulCo felt things were quite chaotic and ended her interview with the comment, 'they are trying to get things better, getting rid of the relatives but it is still bad; I really hope it gets better, I really do'.

The interviewees were asked about policy and practice in key areas such as recruitment and selection, training and development, appraisal, reward, employee voice, employment regulation, discipline and grievance as well as any critical incidents they felt had changed the employment relationship in a significant way. Some general observations can be drawn out about their relationship with the management of these processes, how they had changed over time and to firm growth. In the ChefCo organization, which employed a Chartered Institute of Personnel and Development (CIPD) qualified HR manager, there was a broad range of policies in place and they were used as the norm. This was apparent when the HR manager described how specific elements of the employment relationship were managed and gave clear examples and instances of formal management practices. In a subsequent interview, ChefCo's owner said he no longer interfered in labour management issues and these were delegated to the HR manager. However, he emphasized his regret about encroaching formality as he felt this had changed the culture of the business.

Embedded formality was not so evident in the other firms. None of these had a professional HR manager but in each instance the owner or CEO and a staff member, usually the CEO's personal assistant, took joint responsibility for the employment relationship. In these firms it was claimed that formality had encroached on the management of employees but closer examination revealed a fluid notion of formality. So, when discussing broad policy issues related to HR practice and policy, the intersection of formality and informality was apparent. Recruitment and selection is a useful example where all firms used formal recruitment methods such as advertisements, the job centre or agency referrals. None mentioned the grapevine or relying on family members as applicants, which is a common practice in small and micro firms. Selection was less rigorous, and in the case of WomCo, while much was invested in formal advertising, when it came to interviewing it was agreed that the approach was poor as no one really had the necessary expertise. In fact, there was a high dependency on an agency employee who, because she was assertive and seemed informed, had been leading on selection interviews for permanent members of staff. When asked about this practice, the agency employee commented, 'well, they are all a bit hopeless, it's not rocket science, ask appropriate questions, assess if they can do the job and if they are not obviously bonkers they will probably be alright'. IntelCo's CEO had previously been a professional HR Director, but found that in one of the branches the person responsible for recruitment selection 'placed proper adverts but it is amazing how people end up there, he words it in such a way that he gets the people he wants'. There was a general lack of awareness and expertise regarding selection. In all firms an equal opportunities policy covering recruitment and selection practices was said to exist. Its application, however, might be problematic as we can see when the owner of PropCo remarked, 'we do believe we offer equal opportunities, yes I think I treat every one equally as long as they do their job'.

Similar instances of the sliding interface between formal policy and idiosyncratic practices were evident in most firms. One particular area where this might be problematic is grievance and discipline. The literature notes that in small and micro firms such issues can be managed through close proximity of the employer and employee, in that employers can exploit the more intimate social relationship to address any problems or simply ignore them in the absence of formal voice mechanisms (Marlow, 2002; Ram, 1994). However, as the firm grows, this approach is no longer so effective and indeed it has been of some concern to the UK government that so many Employment Tribunal cases for unfair dismissal arise from smaller firms. In an attempt to address this problem the UK Employment Act (2002) laid down the requirement for firms to have formal discipline and grievance procedures. The degree to which firms complied with the regulation was explored in some depth and we found all had formal, written grievance and discipline policies in place but used them in rather different ways. Not unsurprisingly, the HR manager at ChefCo managed all such issues and encouraged the line managers to bring all issues, however minor, to her attention. This can be contrasted with the situation at WomCo where polices were in place, but 'they are not really used, the line managers generally sort it out there and then'. A similar situation existed at PropCo and HaulCo. Only at BoxCo was more consideration given, with the owner reflecting that:

> One day I came across a section manager having a row with one of the blokes, he can be a bit bolshie and the manager was on for it. I did calm it down and actually, the bloke had a fair point so I organized a meeting and impressed the need to use the policies. In the past a bit of chat and banter might sort it out but not now, we're too big and it's too risky.

The employee from BoxCo could not recall any grievance issues but did comment with discipline or dismissal, 'if someone is in trouble, they are less likely to sort it out there and then now, in fact it usually gets taken upstairs and sorted properly, we don't get to see it'. The situation was a little different in IntelCo as the CEO had struggled with various members of management to introduce change and had himself been subject to the grievance procedure. This was somewhat ironic as prior to this the CEO claimed that such policies had never been used, noting that 'prior to that, we just got rid of people, I don't know how we did it'.

Finally, the respondents were asked to describe a critical event which had changed the manner in which the firm was managed and which had also impacted upon the management of employment relationships. In each case this was possible, so for instance, the reason why ChefCo embraced formality and sought to embed policy and practice as the norm stemmed from the recognition that previous poor management practice and in-fighting were constraining performance. A management consultant was employed to analyse the cause of the problems; his key recommendations were the appointment of a dedicated HR manager and the need for greater delegation of responsibilities down through the managerial hierarchy. The current HR manager was previously the owner's PA but grasped the opportunity to study for a professional qualification in HRM and formalized their approach to labour management. Creating the role of HR Manager at ChefCo diluted and deflected the idiosyncratic and autocratic influence of the owner and enabled a more professional approach to emerge and be embedded as the norm. The HR manager suggested that initially her appointment caused some problems as some senior managers were reluctant to 'let go' but she noted,

> I've done this for a few years now, the new people coming in only know me as the HR manager, so they come to me first; it is very formal now, the CEO (owner) and managers were quite bullying and we had tribunal cases we were lucky to

win and we weren't doing well. Now though, it's different, the CEO has backed off and we are doing well.

During the period of change there was some battling for position as the newly appointed HR manager tried to establish her authority over the management of the employment relationship. It was clear she was determined to attain ownership of the HR manager's role. Not only were the owner and other senior managers reluctant to step back from managing employees, some employees had established relationships with certain managers and preferred to use these channels to address employment relations issues. The HR manager felt she only established her role by constantly referring to the consultants' report, linking her job to firm performance and by seeking and achieving the support of the owner to introduce formal policy. Once this was achieved, her specific role as HR manager became easier to protect and defend as the complexity of the systems introduced made it more difficult for other managers to either interfere or act independently in labour management decisions.

At IntelCo, it was partially the attempt by the CEO to introduce formality which created a crisis. Other members of the management team had established niches for themselves in different branches of the organization when financial incompetence came to light as procedures were tightened. However, the prevailing management structure and culture came under scrutiny. Resentment ensued and the grievance case against the CEO (mentioned above) was taken with 'interference' and 'manner' as the focus. The grievance was unsuccessful but during this period of unrest other areas of the business were neglected and consequently their Investors in People (IiP) accreditation was lost. The CEO described this chapter in the organization's history as 'character forming'. Subsequently management redundancies were made and the business re-structured. Early indications suggested the business was slowly turning around, although there was recognition that managing culture change had been very difficult, as had introducing greater formality into the management of the employment relationship. As the CEO reflected, 'I had to break down barriers, take the staff with me, we went through two years to sort it out but unless you put it in [formality] and bed it down and enforce it, it slips back to the old ways.' The CEO now employs the services of a professional HR consultant who visits the firm on a regular basis to update policy and practice and to deal with any specific HR issues. IiP accreditation had not been regained at the time of the research. In this case the rationale for greater formality did not appear to be understood and similarly the social dynamic shaping the employment relationship. Here, the introduction of formality had a detrimental impact upon the performance of the organization.

Changes had been prompted at two firms, WomCo and PropCo, when they were threatened with employment tribunal applications from disgruntled employees. When asked to discuss these events, the CEO of WomCo said, 'how long have you got?' To summarize a long story, a director was found to be systematically bullying staff and causing stress to all concerned but no one knew how to deal with the situation; there were not policies in place and no one felt they had the authority to challenge the director. Eventually a formal complaint was made and the director resigned but she then threatened to go to tribunal that resulted in her being paid compensation. She was not replaced and all senior staff were 'acting up' to another post. Consequently, the organization had become dependent on agency staff to fill gaps at lower levels but this led to high labour turnover and associated costs. Whilst it was too early to evaluate the implications of this event, the organization is now planning to appoint an HR manager to 'turn it all around, to make sure this never happens again; we have all talked about the necessity of changing things but it is just finding the time'.

At PropCo the owner had been accused of sexual harassment and was threatened with a tribunal application.

> I suppose this made us realize we needed proper procedures to deal with these events when we can't settle informally. Until then I really would have said it was like a family here, I thought everyone got on and if there were any problems, they would be talked through. This hit like a bolt from the blue; it was resolved with apologies and the person left with a deal, but to be honest, I was very upset – it made me realize that you can't have a bit of fun. We went for IiP to tighten up our procedures. I'd like to think that wouldn't happen again.

What is interesting here is that the owner frequently referred to the IiP accreditation as proof of formality and doing things properly, yet from interviews with employees a different picture emerged. It was claimed that bullying was still a feature of the organization and a recent case was cited where the owner's PA had tried to encourage adherence to formal policy but this had caused friction with another director. An employee said,

> She went away on holiday, came back for her appraisal and was told she was leaving. A [the director] had gone to C [the owner] and just complained all the time so, she was told to tell us she was being made redundant but that's a lie. She was really upset and I know they have had to pay her off.

The loss of a major customer was a critical incident for HaulCo and BoxCo. For BoxCo this created problems, as they had to make people redundant but were unsure of the process. The Arbitration, Conciliation and Advisory Service (ACAS) advised and the situation was resolved; it exposed weaknesses in customer dependence and labour management practices. As the owner remarked, 'we are moving away from everyone knowing each other to recognizing the importance of doing things properly. People still just do their own thing without thinking of the consequences. I try and explain you just can't, but it is a hard slog.' The response at HaulCo was more ad hoc. Redundancies were made but were relatively unproblematic. Their annual labour turnover of about 50 per cent made it easier to let people go. The real impact was felt on the financial side and there was some uncertainty whether the firm would survive. Investment of personal funds by the owners prevented failure. Whilst the main focus was on the financial implications of this crisis, the subsequent growth saw attention given to labour management and costs. The PA responsible for the employment relationship quite candidly stated that the biggest problem was the owner. She said,

> Stopping the MD from still doing everything and undermining other managers, it's difficult as he owns the place! Also, we need to get a professional tier of managers in, which we have started to do, and get rid of the family; we need the right people in the right jobs.

To continue growth and professionalize the business two new managers were employed at considerably higher salaries than existing staff. However, it was recognized that they would also have to be professionally managed if they were to be retained. The employees were not so positive about the extent of change, as the accounts clerk revealed:

> Everyone here is on weekly pay because they can't afford a monthly pay roll; the new managers earn loads more than the others, there will be hell to pay if they find out and I feel sorry for G [the PA], she is really trying but the old guard here, they don't like it, they make her job so hard.

Discussion and conclusions
Since the early 1990s a robust body of evidence has grown on the management of the employment relationship in small and micro firms (those with fewer than 50 employees), however there is little written about labour management in medium-sized firms, and in particular how it differs from that within small and large organizations. Research on small firms has established that although there is heterogeneity in the sector with respect to approaches to managing labour, there is a trend towards informality but as firms grow increasing complexity challenges this tendency (Cully et al., 1999; Kersley et al., 2006). In this chapter the focus was on independently managed medium-sized firms to consider if, when and why they adopt more formal employment policies to manage labour.

The evidence suggests that these owners found themselves 'pushed' towards formality by increasing size and then regretted the distance that grew between them and their employees. There was a considerable reluctance to delegate the management of labour to others and rely on policy rather than instinct. Consequently, there is some evidence for what Marlow (2002) has referred to as 'mock bureaucracy' as owners and managers frequently referred to and described policy that they did not actively use at appropriate times.

Employee views of the employment relationship reveal how good managerial intentions became lost in the daily need to manage and produce. All of these firms had a formal policy framework in place for key employment issues but there were clear differences apparent in the manner and extent to which these policies were embedded into practice. The presence of an HR manager who was determined to take ownership of the personnel function and was supported by a professional management consultant's report, enabled the successful incorporation and acceptance of formality at ChefCo. This could be compared to HaulCo where the PA tried to introduce and adhere to formal policies but was being undermined by the firm owner and also other family members of management. By focusing on critical incidents we could see crisis forced change as well as realization of the need for change. At BoxCo the firm was on the path to formality as the owner recognized that the employment relationship was too complex to be effectively managed by non-professionals.

While critical events in these firms indicated a need to adopt formal policies, the task of instituting changes to labour management processes in growing firms was not easy. For example, the CEO of IntelCo faced trouble from his management team when he tried to instigate a more formal approach. Although this problem had been addressed by the time our research was conducted and many of the old management team had since left, the CEO still sensed that he needed to constantly be 'on patrol' to keep order and prevent slippage back to old, informal ways of managing labour. The PA at PropCo, who the employee saw as a key instigator of change, had in fact lost her job altogether due to resentment from other members of senior staff. Consequently the effect of formalizing in growing firms is not unproblematic.

Formality was defined as having policy in place and using it as a matter of practice. The results show that most of the firms here did not willingly or consistently take a formal approach to labour management. It might have been imagined that formality might be more apparent if these firms had over 65 employees and were ambitious to grow further. Clearly it is important to recognize the difference between the presence of formal policies and their acceptance as the norm and this is a critical difference that is not always acknowledged in the literature. The key elements to facilitate transition to embedded formality would seem to be a critical incident related to labour management, the willingness of the owner to delegate responsibility but also, support from other managers and employees in observing and engaging with the formal policies. What is of particular interest here is the dynamic nature of the adoption of formality. It is clearly not just a case of employing HR staff and developing policies that comply with regulation and reflect good practice. Quite clearly, owner, managers and employees themselves have to accept and embrace these formal policies. Whilst the literature does acknowledge the reluctance of owners to adopt and support greater formality, employee compliance is also essential if policies are to become embedded as custom and practice. It is notable that the evidence of such embeddedness was drawn from the one organization with a HR manager; however, achieving this had not been easy and persistent reference to performance issues was essential for acceptance.

In this chapter informality and formality of labour management has been analysed drawing on evidence from medium-sized firms, a group of firms that have hitherto commanded little attention. What is shown is that although the need for formality is recognized and appreciated when firms grow in size, making the transition towards it is challenging. Informality can be stretched and moulded to fit the needs of middle-sized firms through a combination of ignorance and idiosyncrasy but its dynamics are hidden by the presence, if not the use of, formal policies. In-depth qualitative information on the management of a wide spectrum of HR processes in medium-sized organizations was generated and this enabled broad discussion of the nuances of formality and informality in the conduct of employment relations. There are a number of ways in which this research could be developed further, including replicating the research exercise with a sample of slightly larger medium-sized firms, for example those organizations employing between 100 and 150 people, to see if a size threshold begins to emerge at which those in firms tend to recognize the need for formality and take action to embed it. Moreover the role of employees themselves in facilitating or resisting formal policy and its embedding in practice would be interesting to explore as it may challenge established social networks. Consequently, there is much scope for further research in this area.

References

Arrowsmith, J., M. Gilman, P. Edwards and M. Ram (2003), 'The impact of the National Minimum Wage in small firms', *British Journal of Industrial Relations*, **41**(3), 435–56.

Bacon, N. and K. Hoque (2004), 'HRM in the SME sector: Valuable employees and coercive networks', *International Journal of Human Resource Management*, **16**, 1976–99.

Bacon, N., P. Ackers, J. Storey and D. Coates (1996), 'It's a small world: Managing human resources in small businesses', *The International Journal of Human Resource Management*, **7**, 82–100.

Blackburn, R. (2004), 'Researching the employment relationship in small firms: What are the contradictions from the employment relations and small firms literature', in

S. Marlow, D. Patton and M. Ram (eds), *Managing Labour in Small Firms*, London: Routledge.

Buroway, M. (1979), *Manufacturing Consent: Changes in the Labour Process under Monopoly Capitalism*, Chicago: University of Chicago Press.

Cope, J. and G. Watts (2000), 'Learning by doing: An exploration of experience, critical incidents and reflections in entrepreneurial learning', *International Journal of Entrepreneurial Behavior and Research*, **6**(3), 104–24.

Cully, M., A. O'Reilly, N. Millward, J. Forth, S. Woodland, G. Dix and A. Bryson (1999), *The 1998 Workplace Employee Relations Survey*, London: Routledge.

Curran, J. and R.A. Blackburn (2001), *Researching the Small Enterprise*, London: Sage.

Department of Trade and Industry (DTI) (2004), *SME Statistics of the UK 2003*, available online at www.sbs.gov.uk/content/statistics/stats 2002.xls.

Dickens, L. and M. Hall (2005), *Review of Research into the Impact of Employment Relations Legislation*, Employment Relations Research Series No. 45, London: Department of Trade and Industry. Available online at www.dti.gov.uk/er/inform.htm.

Elger, T. and C. Smith (1998), 'Exit, voice and mandate: Management strategies and labour practices of Japanese firms in Britain', *British Journal of Industrial Relations*, **36**(2), 185–208.

Flanders, A. (1968), 'Collective bargaining: a theoretical analysis', in A. Flanders (1975), *Management and Unions*, London: Faber and Faber, pp. 213–40.

Gilman, M., P. Edwards, M. Ram and J. Arrowsmith (2002), 'Pay determination in small firms in the UK: The case of the response to the National Minimum Wage', *Industrial Relations Journal*, **33**, 52–68.

Heneman, R., J. Tansky and M. Camp (2000), 'HRM practices in small and medium sized enterprises: Unanswered questions and future research perspectives', *Entrepreneurship: Theory and Practice*, Fall, pp. 11–26.

Holliday, R. (1995), *Investigating Small Firms, Nice Work?*, London: Routledge.

Kersley, B., C. Alpin, J. Forth, A. Bryson, H. Bewley, G. Dix and S. Oxenbridge (2006), *Inside the Workplace: First Findings from the Workplace Employment Relations Survey 2004*, London: Department of Trade and Industry.

Kinnie, N., J. Purcell, Terry M. Hutchinson, M. Collinson and H. Scarborough (1999), 'Employment relations in SMEs: Market driven or customer shaped?', *Employee Relations*, **21**(3), 218–35.

Marlow, S. (2002), 'Regulating labour management in small firms', *Human Resource Management Journal*, **12**(3), 285–95.

Marlow, S. (2003), 'Formality and informality in employment relations', *Environmental Planning C: Government and Policy*, **21**, 531–47.

Marlow, S. (2006), 'Human resource management in smaller firms: A contradiction in terms?', *Human Resource Management Review*, **16**, 467–77.

Marlow, S. and D. Patton (2002), 'Minding the gap between employers and employees: The challenge for smaller manufacturing firm owners', *Employee Relations*, **24**, 523–39.

Marlow, S., D. Patton and M. Ram (2004), *Managing Labour in Small Firms*, London: Routledge.

Mazzarol, T. (2003), 'A model of small business HR growth management', *International Journal of Entrepreneurial Behaviour and Research*, **9**(1), 27–49.

Moule, M. (1998), 'Regulation of work in small firms: A view from the inside', *Work, Employment and Society*, **12**, 635–53.

Ram, M. (1994), *Managing to Survive: Working Lives in Small Firms*, Oxford: Blackwell.

Ram, M. and P. Edwards (2003), 'Praising Ceasar not burying him: What we know about employment relations in small firms', *Work, Employment and Society*, **17**, 719–30.

Ram, M., P. Edwards, M. Gilman and J. Arrowsmith (2001), 'The dynamics of informality: Employment regulations in small firms and the effects of regulatory change', *Work, Employment and Society*, **15**, 845–61.

Scase, R. (1995), 'Employment relations in small firms', in P. Edwards (ed.), *Industrial Relations, Theory and Practice*, London: Blackwell, pp. 569–95.

Taylor, S. (2004), 'HRM in small firms: Hunting the Snark?', in S. Marlow, D. Patton and M. Ram (eds), *Managing Labour in Small Firms*, London: Routledge, pp. 18–42.

Taylor, S. (2006), 'Acquaintance, meritocracy and critical realism: Researching recruitment and selection processes in smaller and growth organisations', *Human Resource Management Review*, **16**, 478–89.

Webb, M. and G. Palmer (1998), 'Evading surveillance, making time: An ethnographic view of the Japanese factory floor in Britain', *British Journal of Industrial Relations*, **36**(4), 611–28.

Wilkinson, A. (1999), 'Employment relations in small firms', *Employee Relations*, **21**, 206–17.

Wynarczyk, P., D. Storey, H. Short and K. Keasey (1993), *Managerial Labour Markets in Small and Medium Sized Enterprises*, London: Routledge.

12 Paternalism and people management in a low-tech manufacturing company
Jeff Hyman, Fraser Osborne and Sarah Jack

Introduction

Paternalism, an approach to management that extends back to the early days of industrialization, has rarely received good press. Reasons for this include the fact that little control is extended to employees over their working lives and indeed, in more extreme manifestations, employees may be expected to put their employer's interests firmly in advance of their own. Benevolent paternalism, whilst offering a softer, more Dickensian model of behaviour, may be seen as manipulative and condescending to employees. Nevertheless many small business employers often act in paternalistic ways and the outcomes are not necessarily negative. In this chapter a case study of benevolent paternalism as it operates in a small company is presented and the positive behaviour reciprocated by employees suggests that under some conditions, benevolent paternalism may indeed offer some insights into effective management.

This chapter therefore contributes to an understanding of the human resource (HR) aspect for building successful organizations. This is important as despite the volume of work that attempts to understand entrepreneurial behaviour, HR in small entrepreneurial ventures is frequently overlooked. Indeed, we know remarkably little about the dynamics of management and employee behaviour within small and growing entrepreneurial ventures. Reviewing North American literature, Ram and Edwards report that a search over the past ten years 'produced no significant examples of research papers on behaviour in small firms' (2003: p. 719). We do know that HRM practices have been found to become more formalized with the growth of the organization, a process that accelerates with size. We also know that formal HRM policies lag behind operational-level practices in smaller firms (Kotey and Slade, 2005). The small business owner–manager may lack understanding about what HRM actually means. Heneman et al. (2000) found interpretation of the term to be wide, ranging from employee management in its entirety to specific concerns about issues over recruitment or compensation. Nevertheless, Heneman et al. (2000) conclude that scholars are commenting on the dearth of available information about managing HR in small entrepreneurial ventures.

In small firms two dominant cultural paradigms prevail – the 'happy family' led by an authoritarian but essentially well-disposed father (or mother) figure as opposed to 'bleak house' where apparent harmony is a façade disguising conflictual (but not necessarily overtly expressed) antagonisms predicated on owner hegemony (Barrett and Rainnie, 2002; Ram and Edwards, 2003). The 'happy family' syndrome is closely associated with paternalism which early research helped to identify as a dominant feature of small-firm employee relations (Wray, 1994). Dyer (1986) offered a more developed cultural paradigm that suggested that family business consists of three inter-related cultures of firm, family and board, and each of these 'sub-cultures' can vary along different dimensions (Stavrou et al., 2005). Schematically these different dimensions are demonstrated in Table 12.1 below.

One problem of such a model of course is that these various configurations co-exist and compete on a dynamic behavioural rather than static structural basis (Kotey and Slade, 2005). Also the dependency links between the variables can be hard to discern, although studies do suggest that in smaller firms cultures can be traced to the influence of key individuals and to a lesser extent family members (Feltham et al., 2005). Organizational culture studies generically have of course been criticized for presenting culture largely from the perspective of senior organizational members as a source of organizational change to meet new demands (see for example, Burawoy, 1979; Rosen, 1985; van Maanen, 1991). Many of the above studies are based on surveys of key personnel within the firms from which highly useful models relating to managerial and ownership views can be discerned. Their weakness is that the attitudinal and behavioural orientations of employees, which contribute to organizational culture, risk being overlooked. The present study therefore adds to these perspectives by providing a voice for employees through a single company studied longitudinally for over a year.

In the next section we briefly consider the organizational culture of smaller firms and the ways in which the domination by owner–managers manifests itself in the management of people. As such the focus is on

Table 12.1   Small-firm culture

Firm culture	Family culture	Board culture
Paternalistic	Patriarchal	Paper
Laissez-faire	Collaborative	Rubber stamp
Professional	Conflicted	Advisory overseer

Source: Derived from Dyer (1986) and Stavrou et al. (2005).

factors that influence HRM within small entrepreneurial organizations and a more extended review can be found in Jack et al. (2006). In the following section we present our methodological approach and then our findings from the study. Finally some conclusions and directions for future research are presented.

The organizational culture of smaller ventures
At its heart, the complexity of culture can be distilled down to 'the way we do things round here' (Schein, 1992) and for the purposes of this discussion this straightforward definition provides an appropriate foundation. With smaller ventures, the feature common to any examination of culture is provided by personal and direct management, interest and stewardship of owners. Organizations may respond differently to different product and labour market signals (Blackburn and Hart, 2002), but it is through the owners that these signals and responses are largely channelled and mediated. Therefore, leadership and management style become crucial aspects for the small entrepreneurial venture and are also likely to be a significant shaping influence on organizational culture. This links directly to people management in the enterprise as the probability of commercial success may be enhanced if HR is developed and utilized effectively (Rauch et al., 2005). Further evidence suggests that reasons for small venture success and/or failure are often attributed to personnel-related issues (McEvoy, 1984). This leads to (unresolved) questions about whether there is an effective leadership style for growth or indeed, survival (Thakur, 1998). The ability to find competent workers but also to motivate and effectively manage them is recognized as important for small-venture viability (McEvoy, 1984). Within smaller entrepreneurial ventures recruitment practices are typically informal with managers and staff often recruited by word of mouth.

Hence the motives and ideologies which inform owner–manager behaviour as well as their material circumstances and wide range of individual responsibilities they assume (Arrowsmith et al., 2003), are critical factors in helping us to understand processes of HRM in small entrepreneurial ventures. Scase and Goffee (1980) identified both desired independence of action alongside high levels of personal control as principal aspirations for small business owners. We can see this when an owner–manager in a case study ascribed his ownership motivation as driven principally by: 'having control over my own destiny' (Hyman et al., 2004: p. 58). An orientation toward relational informality is a contiguous principal identified characteristic of small business owners (Ram, 1991; 1994), as is 'preference for informality and an antipathy towards external regulation' (Vickers et al., 2005: p. 149). In consequence it is argued that smaller firms rarely have formal HR policies or specialized HR staff (Cardon and Stevens, 2004).

Arguably, these values can be linked back to the primacy of an individualist ideology among small business owners, which is especially prevalent among active owner–managers (Cully et al., 1999).

Individualism and its link to unitarism and contingent behaviours serves as an important or even defining influence in small business management and employee relationships, as can be seen in stances toward trade unions. For example, in the 'small is beautiful' or 'happy family' scenario (Rainnie, 1989), the relations between owner–managers and employees are relatively informal with direct communication, task flexibility and easy access to paternalistic senior management or owners basically negating the need for more formal and structured employee relations involving external bodies and influences. However, the darker 'bleak house' (Wilkinson, 1999) interpretation of small business unitarism, for which there is substantial evidence, is that union representation is anathema to small business owners whose allegiance to individualistic direct relations with employees is more founded on their preference for independence from external influences or regulation and opposition to any manifestations of collective representation.

Firm size of course plays its part also, but employment relations in smaller firms are not simply determined by size alone (Barrett and Rainnie, 2002). As these and other authors (see for example, Wilkinson, 1999) point out, it is size coupled with other contextual factors, or the 'totality of the firm's economic relations' (Barrett and Rainnie, 2002: p. 427), which serve to determine the structures and fuel the dynamics within which employment relationships are conducted. There are also internal factors specific to small entrepreneurial ventures that can clearly influence, along with other criteria, the management approach and potential effects on employment relations.

Effects can be in terms of work–life balance, and the take-up of performance management, training, reward, involvement and worker welfare practices. Proponents for informality assert that more casual, unstructured direct relations with owner–managers typical to smaller firms provide the means to secure employee commitment and preclude the need for more formalized participative procedures. As Walton (1985) argued, it is through employee commitment that organizational change can be manipulated most beneficially. However, the 'control' model of small business management might cast doubts on the extent to which owners or their managers actually behave in this enlightened way. Indeed involvement in organizational decision-making more generally may well conflict with individualistic values held by small business owner–managers and help explain low rates of financial participation. In particular, involvement through financial participation is a management decision (Baddon et al., 1989), which suggests very strongly that, notwithstanding structural constraints, the absence of such arrangements is a consequence of owner–manager preferences or awareness and these preferences are sustained despite the potentially positive performance effects which might accrue.

While there are important structural differences between smaller and larger organizations in terms of management approaches and potential effects on employment relations, there are also observable differences amongst smaller firms that need to be explained. The processes through which relationships between managers and employees are mediated have received less attention and provide a main empirical focus for this study. In the next section we outline our methodology and then focus on findings of our longitudinal case study of the dynamics of employee relations in a low-tech small firm.

Methodology and research context
The research reported here addresses the related issues of cultural processes and their relationships to the dynamics of people management in a relatively low-tech, low-skill environment. The objectives of this research relate to understanding the meanings that lie behind actions (Hammersley, 1992; Oinas, 1999) and the influences these can have on a small venture. To investigate and explore these complex issues a longitudinal single qualitative case study approach was used.

The chosen venture was a small manufacturing business concerned with the design, manufacture, supply and installation of signs based around an oil-dominant city in the North East of Scotland. The company (which we call SignCo) was established in 1951 and had expanded from the original branch to two sites. The current owner, Paul, took over in 1997 and subsequently rescued one branch from liquidation. Since his arrival at SignCo the workforce has steadily increased from 25 to 37 members of staff over two sites, with a sizeable proportion of staff having over ten years' experience, and turnover has steadily increased to £1.6m. It has a number of established major competitors plus an ever-increasing number of new companies entering the market due to the low barriers to entry. SignCo has grown with technology and produces a number of diverse products such as neon signage, engraving, vinyl wraps, digital printing and fascia signs for a variety of clients, including large oil operations, retail outlets, hospitals and medical facilities plus many smaller customers. Although the company may not be particularly fast-growing or entrepreneurial it does face considerable challenges in an extremely competitive environment. Nevertheless, it has been very successful in not only meeting these challenges but also overcoming them. The company is currently amongst the top five in Scotland for sign making and offers a complete integrated range of services to its customers. Concern about its long-term future in an increasingly competitive environment has led to the need to look at how SignCo can adapt in order to grow and survive. To achieve this it is looking to change the culture throughout the organization and improve business performance and profitability as a basis for further revenue growth. To deal with this concern the managing director recently initiated performance-related changes within the company.

The longitudinal nature of the research provided an opportunity to monitor and assess the impact of change over time and the processes and mechanisms through which change was brought about (Bryman and Bell, 2003). One of the researchers was located full-time in the venture between 2004 and 2006. Throughout this time he interacted with employees and managers both formally and informally, which provided the opportunity to understand the way people behaved (Easterby-Smith et al., 1991), how they interacted and collaborated (Gill and Johnson, 1997), to learn about the culture and the perspectives of the group being studied (Curran and Blackburn, 2001; Gill and Johnson, 1997; Gummesson, 2000). The remaining two researchers were involved in setting the research agenda, in regular meetings and discussions with the company and the participating researcher.

In addition to formal and informal interactions, interviews were carried out with the business owner and a selection of employees during April 2005. A semi-structured interview schedule was used containing specific areas on which respondents were questioned at length. This schedule was organized around the research questions and themes of the study: culture, communication and owner–employee relations. The sampling technique used to identify appropriate respondents was purposive (Punch, 2005; Silverman, 2000). This method was used because the researchers wanted to understand the situations of individuals at various levels within the organization, who were involved in different types of activities and varied in length of service. Of the 37 employees, 15 were interviewed and are used for this study. Table 12.2 illustrates the role of each respondent, their background prior to joining the business, the number of years they have been with SignCo and whether they saw long-term prospects with the company.

A framework for data collection and analysis was developed from the literature reviewed. This not only provided theoretical understanding and background for the research but also illustrated that culture, communication and owner–employee relations were appropriate themes for analysis. Investigating these themes provided a way to focus data collection. Questions were derived from an understanding generated by the literature. Initially, we aimed to explore how and why issues related to respondents' views, feelings and perceptions of the culture of the organization. This was achieved by exploring issues related to what culture actually represented

Table 12.2   Details about interviewees at SignCo

Name	Role	Role prior to joining	Years employed	Perception of long-term prospects
Barry	Manager	School leaver	20	Probably
Emma	Admin	Admin	8	None
Frank	Manager	School leaver	25	Yes
James	Sales	Agency	2	Unsure
Jason	Fitter	Joiner	2	No
John	Printing/ Design	Admin and art	23	Probably
Kate	Admin	Admin	1	No
Kevin	Manager	Mechanic	18	Yes
Mary	Admin	Employed with another company	4	Yes
Michael	Printing/ Design	Art	23	Probably
Paul	Managing Director and owner	Sales	10	Yes, until retirement
Richard	Machine operator		15	Likes to think so
Russell	Engraver	School leaver	22	Definitely
Steven	Vinyl	Sign business	5	Yes
Stuart	Engraver	Unemployed	2	Unsure

and meant for each respondent and how they felt about this particular aspect of the organization. Second, we wanted to identify internal organizational communications. To do so we asked a range of questions relating specifically to how people actually communicated with each other, whether communication was effective and how respondents perceived it. Our third key area of interest related to the owner–employee relationship, how respondents perceived it and if so, how and why this worked for the organization. In-depth, confidential, semi-structured individual interviews were carried out with the 15 respondents. Interviews were taped and transcribed. The data was then analysed using the constant comparative method (Alvesson and Sköldberg, 2000; Silverman, 2000) and analytic induction (Glaser and Strauss, 1967). Responses were analysed and compared to determine categories and general patterns of activities. Each incident was continually compared with others within the emergent categories to refine both description and explanation. Throughout the process of data collection, interview probes were used to ensure response consistency (see Easterby-Smith et al., 1991). The findings from the interviews used here are supplemented with observations of the researchers during the two-year period in which the study took place.

Findings

Culture
All organizations have a culture, and understanding an organization means understanding its culture (Clegg et al., 2005). The culture of an organization consists of many small acts of obedience and transgression that informally define the rules that constitute behaviour (Clegg et al., 2005). When asked to actually define or describe the culture of SignCo the owner Paul commented:

> Culture is a difficult one. I see the culture as the unwritten rules, you know the things you take for granted. Everybody must respect everybody else's opinions. I think that's quite important. We listen to people, people come to us, they've got domestic problems, you know we'll try to sort that out, if somebody needs a lawyer, we'll give them a lawyer . . . It's got a family feel to it, of course it has. And paternalistic companies, that's not the style of management nowadays, it's got to be ruthless, it's got to be figures, figures, figures now but we're not like that, we can still achieve the figures.

The cultural orientation was openly paternalistic and Paul believed that the employees and their welfare were important to him. At the same time, Paul's perception was that he tried to encourage people and involve them in decision-making; he tries to stimulate relationships, built on high levels of mutual trust. However, this was undertaken within the unstated parameters of his control. Paul chooses with whom he will discuss issues and at what depth, leading to inner and outer circles of influence in the 'family', as the following quotes indicate.

> Some people have been here at the company for a long time so have more say than people who don't. That's the main kind of problem here (Stuart).

> If things are good then everybody's happy but a lot of them are disgruntled not knowing what's going to happen . . . (Emma).

Nevertheless, for most, there was an overall sense of belonging and feeling of loyalty to the firm. In reviewing the culture, employees commented on the atmosphere, the people, loyalty and its family feel as being contributory factors.

> I think the atmosphere is quite good . . . I think they probably have their underlying sort of loyalty. . . . the majority of people in here have the attitude that we are here to help and if we can get something done then we'll do it (Barry).

> It's a happy atmosphere . . . like a big family really. It's a family type. People do interact pretty well (John).

> It can be really like a family when everyone pulls together . . . there is no major conflict between departments. There is a blame culture which pisses me off but usually it's good that we can pull together and if there's a crisis everyone has to work (James).

Evidently employees saw culture in terms of the family atmosphere of the organization and overall this seemed to be a positive factor. People seemed to enjoy working for the organization and were happy at work. The impression was that people were optimistic despite the ever-present threat of change:

> It's a family-run business and with that they don't like change. Change is happening all around but we don't want it in here but unfortunately that's overtaken and they have to compromise. We have to have these changes (Emma).

In SignCo the overall view was that it ran as a close-knit business and that it had a family feeling to it. Among employees, there was certainly this notion of the company as a family and a feeling of social community was frequently expressed.

Employee reasons for remaining with SignCo

SignCo had a history of people joining the company and staying long term. We felt this was a key feature to understanding its culture and looked to identify why people remained with the business. There were key patterns in the data, which reflected their reasons for remaining with the company. These could be grouped into three broad but clear categories: the people, the work and the variety in their work. More specifically, staff continually mentioned the extent to which they enjoyed their work and the people they worked with as the following quotes indicate.

> I enjoy the work. The people I work with are good (Steven).

> I like a lot of the people that's here mainly (Richard).

> It's the actual guys I work alongside, the actual workforce. They're a really great bunch of guys. You get a good laugh and most folk are willing to help each other out . . . there seems to be a team effort. It's a good laugh and you get on with pretty much everybody and vice versa. It's a bit disheartening sometimes but there's never a day I've come in and just thought 'I could walk out'. It's not that bad. I'm happy to come in every day as opposed to some jobs I've been at (Jason).

> I enjoy the job . . . there's always the odd day, everyone's the same I think, you feel like jacking the whole lot in but the majority of the time I enjoy it . . . I enjoy the guys I work with as well. I get on pretty well with the majority (Frank).

Most of the people are nice. It's a small company, friendly people. I like the actual work I do, it's something I'm very familiar with (Mary).

It's a good working environment, everyone's friendly and the main thing is it's easy. You get stuck in a routine would be the best way of describing it (Stuart).

A continuing strand in organizational behaviour prescription concerns the problems of gaining employee commitment to the services of the organization. In the present case, there was an important social element to working within the company. In many ways this reflected the sense of belonging and community bonding with which classical notions of culture are strongly engaged (Roethlisberger and Dickson, 1939). Employees tended to be local and to have strong links with the local community. They were often used to source new employees. SignCo was very much a local business, primarily serving the local market and had been built, developed and grown around local industries. Interestingly, there were very few negative comments relating to the company. Empowerment and team-working were frequently cited as participative variables linked to stimulating positive employee responses. Yet formal structures for the provision of these activities are generally lacking in smaller firms, but informal and undefined participative processes clearly offer opportunities for employee expression, even within a paternalistic cultural context. At SignCo there was an unspoken/unwritten understanding that employees were empowered to get on with the job they were employed to do. Employees were trusted to work on their own initiative and they saw this as a positive feature.

I'm pretty much sort of left to be my own boss quite a lot of the time so I do quite like that as well (Mary).

You get the chance of doing different jobs and there are different things come in all the time so it's good. I seem to get a challenge . . . (Russell).

I've got quite a lot of freedom. I mean you're not constantly having someone over your shoulder making sure you're doing everything right. You know you're allowed to use your initiative on quite a lot of things. The management are quite good as well (Stuart).

I'm always getting trained up on different things, so I haven't seen any need to go and do anything else (Steven).

Probably because in a short period of time I became quite good at the job. I think I was recognized within the first year. I was given more responsibility quite quickly . . . and the money for some of the time I was in here has been quite good. For the last four or five years I've been moving up the ladder (Barry).

> I like seeing a job go right and when it finishes and you see it up on the wall and it's a nice job and the customer's happy. . . . yes satisfaction (Kevin).

> They leave me to get on with it. They know what my role is and nobody's breathing down my neck, 'do this, do that', reaching targets and that. So, I work on my own initiative and I enjoy that . . . nobody gets on at me. . . . I'm allowed to speak my mind and nobody takes that to heart and you can be yourself in that respect (Emma).

These freedoms were linked to employee commitment, an outcome which many empowerment commentators seek but rarely find in the more structured empowerment initiatives of some larger companies (see, for example, Cunningham et al., 1996). In turn the ability of employees to develop and get on with the job led to them representing a key and tapped human capital resource. Although limitations could be identified, these related to individual situations and circumstances and shortcomings in communication practice. By comparison the benefits of working for SignCo not only outweighed the limitations, but consistent patterns emerged, for example, good colleagues; positive work atmosphere; interesting nature of the job; and people encouraged to work on their own initiative.

Communication
Communicating with employees, team working, team briefing, employee input and channels of and for communication have been identified as key cultural factors which can also promote the development of trust (see, for example, Heller et al., 1998). There was a visible management structure in place and this was recognized throughout the company. Furthermore, all levels within this structure were viewed as being approachable, prepared and willing to discuss things and respondents felt that they could go directly to their managers. Although, as we have seen, some employees felt they may not always be listened to – their views 'fall on deaf ears' – and would like their ideas taken on board, the overall perception was that they knew how to make their views known. Effective channels for communication were available and people appeared to have a clear idea of lines of responsibility. By comparison, the actual communication itself appears to represent an issue, a point succinctly noted by Paul, the owner, as well as by employees.

> Any time we have anybody in to write about it, the communication is shite. We don't communicate with anybody, nobody knows anything that's happening, you know, and of course the issues are always the same (Paul).

> Communication between us all, between ourselves. It's getting better but there's still a lot of work to be done (Michael).

> Communication problems, definitely (Kate).

Although decision-making was clearly hierarchical, informal processes and consensual value systems identified in the study were associated with and encouraged by Paul, as he said,

> I listen to what's going on, speak to people and say 'do you think it's a good idea?' and try and get them, if you like, to come round to my way of thinking but the change is not dramatic, there isn't a need for change dramatically. I'm concerned about tomorrow. That's my main job is looking where we are going and to be doing tomorrow and everything that that embraces. Have we got enough money, have we got the right people in the right place, are we selling the right products? What, how are we going to react to what happens tomorrow and I try to keep my nose out of the day-to-day tactical things. I try and stand back from that but of course you can't do that because, for example, this week the sales manager's father-in-law has popped his clogs.

Discussion and analysis
What the data clearly illustrates is that under favourable conditions, small and informal can indeed be (relatively) beautiful. In this instance, positive conditions were linked with the benevolent paternalistic approach adopted by the owner–manager. This finding emerges strongly, clearly reflected in the enjoyment individuals take from working at the company. People were committed and a strong sense of loyalty existed not only to the organization but also to each other. In many ways this is based on social bonds, social ties and embeddedness within the organization. Although respondents perceive and describe SignCo as having a family firm culture the firm was not a typical family type as described in the literature and displayed few features normally associated with these types of firms (see Thompson and McHugh, 2002). The culture was paternalistic in that although Paul had delegated some authority, in terms of decision-making he had the final say and retains all key information about operations and future developments. That is not to say that he saw his employees as untrustworthy but instead saw himself as a father figure accepting his obligations and taking them seriously. Significantly, when asked to explain his role within the business, Paul commented,

> I am the Managing Director. I'm the manager of a train set, I'm the owner. I own all the shares. I think we've created a platform, we've created a culture and I would hope that I'm actually quite good.

The paternalistic culture that grew with the company appears to work. It is a very open culture. People felt a sense of belonging and understood how they contribute to the organization. There was also a sense of mutual respect within SignCo. Paul respected his staff and on the whole they seem to respect him, based on reciprocal behaviours as the following quote shows.

Paul now, you help him out. You come in, you work, you work overtime if asked, and he pays you for it. If you ask a favour of him, if he can help you, he will (Russell).

Paul particularly trusted those who had been in place for a long time and long before he took over the company. Despite several changes in ownership, what was interesting was that the workforce (particularly the core) had remained. As one long-term employee explained,

I've been here for 25 years so SignCo has played a very big part of my life and hopefully will do in the future so I want to see SignCo up there. We can rely on the expertise, the workforce who can do it. We've got the quality so we make a push. And that's what we've got to strive towards and keep it going basically (Frank).

Nevertheless, seniority within the company seemed to be related with length of service rather than job specificity or performance and for the 'outsiders', the pace of change and opportunity for individual advancement appeared to be restricted. As one employee said,

I'm just clinging to the hope that maybe somebody would see some of the potential and I could go somewhere in the company (James).

Most employees seemed ambitious for the company to succeed and, using Paul's terminology, to be part of its arrival at the next station. Indeed, employees could be seen to be pushing the train along. As well as being the driver, Paul was also the train's owner, who oversaw but also facilitated change. He not only held the purse strings but also managed them, retaining the final say. In many ways he not only represented the father figure but also played out the role of the father who allowed the children to play. It would seem that this was a deliberate strategy on Paul's part and certainly the company was successful under his control. But with growth, the grounds on which the 'children' played show signs of fragmentation and lack integration. An issue that some employees reported was a division between sales, administration and manufacturing and that individuals needed to be better informed about the roles, activities and requirements of the different departments.

It's office staff or a salesman, they are so fascinated by getting them replaced as opposed to dealing with the workforce and to be honest, if you don't have a workforce, you don't have a company. You'll always have a problem between sales and production because sales want to sell but it puts the likes of us under pressure (Jason).

The company is too sales driven for my liking and four of the five people have never made things, which is fair enough for Paul and Kevin but if the other sales guys got the actual knowledge and experience of how things are made and fitted it would benefit the company big time (Barry).

Therefore, the paternalistic nature of the organization could be dysfunctional or divisive despite employees being important to Paul. This was evident when he said,

I take time with people even though I'm always rushed but I still take time to speak to people . . . that's what the business is all about. It's all about people.

As the company expands it is moving towards more bureaucratic procedures, for instance performance appraisals and monitoring systems. It will be interesting to monitor the extent to which the current paternalistic and somewhat laissez-faire approach can be compatible with a more structured and formalized HR managerial approach.

Conclusions and future directions
Paternalism can be seen as an expression of a strong and potentially integrative culture, traditionally associated with smaller firms (Cully et al., 1999). This unitarist culture is often reinforced through the active workplace intervention of owner–managers. Paternalism is usually projected in somewhat pejorative terms as a result of its association with employer dominance and employee dependence, and many organizations of paternalistic origins have shifted to more structured personnel policies with distancing of owner–managers from day-to-day management and increasing organizational size (Cully et al., 1999). SignCo was also taking tentative steps to move toward a more formalized relationship with its employees. Performance appraisals had been introduced and the company's plan to develop a more formalized communications and training approach was signalled by its intention to apply for Investors in People (IiP) accreditation.

A potential tension is that the present system, although firmly founded in paternalism, appears to work successfully within its size limits. Almost by stealth, an empowered culture emerged from within a paternalistic framework, and this culture is both appreciated by employees and appears to contribute to their motivation and commitment and satisfaction with the company. Whether this approach can be sustained under a shift to a more formal management regime, driven by a perceived need to accommodate change, is an open question. Nevertheless, any shift toward formalization in smaller firms, a trend noted in other studies (Kotey and Slade, 2005), has clear implications for owner–managers in terms of the practical aspects of managing people, particularly for those who are more attuned to more direct and informal styles of employee relations.

Whilst the paternalistic culture which is evident in our case may be typical of smaller firms and a dominant feature of small-firm employee relations, this study demonstrates how in many ways it has been successfully managed and allowed to develop, either intentionally or accidentally. For SignCo it clearly works and has been a vital factor in allowing the company to survive in a very competitive industry. There is a 'firm but fair' leadership style. Employees have a clear understanding of the role they play within the organization.

While behaviour in smaller firms has been relatively under-researched, considerable inroads into our understanding are gradually being made. Owner–managers have a clear preference for informal direct relationships, including negotiation of statutory requirements (Edwards et al., 2003). Abstinence from formal HR policies is another manifestation of this inclination for informality, as is the declining presence of trade unions in the small firm sector. This is not to suggest that all small firms share identical behaviours. Studies indicate that other factors can influence the employment relationship and patterns of HRM. These factors include size, sector, market competition, and are derived from product market, labour market structures and dynamics. Nevertheless, there are common cultural strands of strategic deficiency, individualism and informality and increasingly these are being confronted by the spread of regulation to small ventures, especially in the form of legislation. Recent developments in the UK include the introduction of the statutory national minimum wage, universal health and safety regulations and requirements to consult and communicate with employees (Dix and Oxenbridge, 2003). These encroaching pressures sit uneasily with small company traditions of economic informality and a policy preference for limiting administrative demands on small businesses (Hampton, 2004). Owner–managers need to be better informed about legislation, the implications for how people are managed means they must establish systems needed in order to comply with growing regulation. Increasing formality is going to confront current (and long-standing) traditions of informality, raising vital questions of the potential impact on small venture creation, growth and behaviour, and by extension, on their performance.

Our discussion clearly demonstrates the importance of HRM for entrepreneurship, not only in helping to shape strategies but also for the growth and healthy development of effective organizations (Thakur, 1998). However, managing people is a functional role (McEvoy, 1984) requiring skills and energy that entrepreneurs would often prefer to channel into dealing with other aspects of entrepreneurial activity. In SignCo this was not the case, and the outcomes appear to be rewarding to both company and to employees. Entrepreneurship researchers have tended to focus on trying to understand the founding process, traits of the individual entrepreneur and characteristics of high-growth firms (Katz et al., 2000). However, the challenge for the future seems to be to widen our understanding of HRM practices within the smaller entrepreneurial venture and to consider more specifically the ways these practices can evolve into strategies which contribute to success or indeed failure. Empirical research in small firm HRM is relatively sparse, despite the human element receiving increasing attention. There is clearly an issue in that although the importance of HRM is recognized, many studies are descriptive rather than analytical (Heneman et al., 2000; Hornsby and Kuratko, 1990; Rauch et al., 2005) and static rather than dynamic. More intensive case study and longitudinal research work may offer ways to expand our knowledge and understanding about HRM and the smaller entrepreneurial venture.

This study has important implications for both researchers and practitioners. It highlights the need for a greater appreciation of the importance and relevance of culture and how it can influence and impact on the viability of the smaller business. It also suggests that many smaller firms have taken larger organization policies and procedures as their reference points for effective organizational performance (although not necessarily following them). However, the success of the informal and open approaches adopted by SignCo could offer equally important lessons not only to other smaller firms but also to those larger firms, whose regimented management styles and accompanying structured participative and empowerment initiatives have failed to provide the organizational cohesion and effective performance evidenced by the present study.

References

Alvesson, M. and K. Sköldberg (2000), *Relexive Methodology: New Vistas for Qualitative Research*, London: Sage Publications.

Arrowsmith, J., W. Gilman, P. Edwards and M. Ram (2003), 'The impact of the national minimum wage in small firms', *British Journal of Industrial Relations*, **41**, 435–56.

Baddon, L., L. Hunter, J. Hyman, J. Leopold and H. Ramsay (1989), *People's Capitalism? A Critical Analysis of Profit-Sharing and Employee Share Ownership*, London: Routledge.

Barrett, R. and A. Rainnie (2002), 'What's so special about small firms?', *Work, Employment and Society*, **16**(3), 415–31.

Blackburn, R. and M. Hart (2002), 'Small firms' awareness and knowledge of individual employment rights', *Employment Relations Research Series, No. 14*, London: Department of Trade and Industry.

Bryman, A. and E. Bell (2003), *Business Research Methods*, Oxford: Oxford University Press.

Burawoy, M. (1979), *Manufacturing Consent: Changes in the Labour Process Under Monopoly Capitalism*, Chicago: Chicago University Press.

Cardon, M.S. and C.E. Stevens (2004), 'Managing human resources in small organizations: What do we know?', *Human Resource Management Review*, **14**, 295–323.

Clegg, S., M. Kornberger and T. Pitsis (2005), *Managing and Organizations*, London: Sage Publications.

Cully, M., S. Woodland, A. O'Reilly and G. Dix (1999), *Britain at Work*, London: Routledge.

Cunningham, I., J. Hyman and C. Baldry (1996), 'Empowerment: The power to do what?', *Industrial Relations Journal*, **27**(2), 143–55.

Curran, J. and R. Blackburn (2001), *Researching the Small Enterprise*, London: Sage Publications.

Dix, G. and S. Oxenbridge (2003), 'Information and consultation at work: From challenges to good practice', *Research Paper 03/03*, London: ACAS.

Dyer, G. (1986), *Cultural Change in Family Firms*, San Francisco: Jossey-Bass.

Easterby-Smith, M., R. Thorpe and A. Lowe (1991), *Management Research: An Introduction*, London: Sage Publications.

Edwards, P., M. Ram and J. Black (2003), 'The impact of employment legislation on small firms: A case study analysis', *Employment Research Series No 20*, London: Department of Trade and Industry.

Feltham, T., G. Feltham and J. Barnett (2005), 'The dependence of family businesses on a single decision-maker', *Journal of Small Business Management*, **43**(1), 1–15.

Gill, J. and P. Johnson (1997), *Research Methods for Managers*, 2nd edn, London: Paul Chapman Publishing Limited.

Glaser, B.G. and A.L. Strauss (1967), *The Discovery of Grounded Theory: Strategies for Qualitative Research*, New York: Aldine.

Gummesson, E. (2000), *Qualitative Methods in Management Research*, Thousand Oaks: Sage Publications.

Hammersley, M. (1992), *What's Wrong with Ethnography? Methodological Explorations*, London: Longmans.

Hampton, P. (2004), *Reducing Administrative Burdens: Effective Inspection and Enforcement*, London: HM Treasury.

Heller, F., E. Pusic, G. Strauss and B. Wilpert (1998), *Organizational Participation: Myth and Reality*, Oxford: Oxford University Press.

Heneman, R.L., J.W. Tansky and S.M. Camp (2000), 'Human resource management practices in small and medium-sized enterprises: Unanswered questions and future research perspectives', *Entrepreneurship: Theory and Practice*, **25**, 11–21.

Hornsby, J.S. and D.F. Kuratko (1990), 'Human resource management in small business: Critical issues for the 1990s', *Journal of Small Business Management*, **28**, 9–18.

Hyman, J., C. Lockyer, A. Marks and D. Scholarios (2004), 'Needing a new program? Why is union membership so low among software workers', in G. Healy, E. Heery, P. Taylor and W. Brown (eds), *The Future of Worker Representation*, Basingstoke: Palgrave, pp. 37–61.

Jack, S., J. Hyman and F. Osborne (2006) 'Small entrepreneurial ventures culture, change and the impact on HRM: A critical review', *Human Resource Management Review*, **16**(4), 456–66.

Katz, J.A., H.E. Aldrich, T.M. Welbourne and P.M. Williams (2000), 'Guest editors' comments: Special issue on human resource management and the SME: Toward a new synthesis', *Entrepreneurship: Theory and Practice*, **25**, 7–10.

Kotey, B. and P. Slade (2005), 'Formal human resource management practices in small growing firms', *Journal of Small Business Management*, **43**(1), 16–40.

McEvoy, G.M. (1984), 'Small business personnel practices', *Journal of Small Business Management*, **22**, 1–8.

Oinas, P. (1999), 'Voices and silences: The problem of access to embeddedness', *Geoforum*, **30**, 351–61.

Punch, K. (2005), *Introduction to Social Research: Quantitative and Qualitative Approaches*, London: Sage Publications.

Rainnie, A. (1989), *Industrial Relations in Small Firms*, London: Routledge.

Ram, M. (1991), 'The dynamics of workplace relations', *International Journal of Small Business*, **10**, 44–53.

Ram, M. (1994), *Managing to Survive: Working Lives in Small Firms*, Oxford: Blackwell.

Ram, M. and P. Edwards (2003), 'Praising Caesar, not burying him: What we know about employment relations in small firms', *Work, Employment and Society*, **17**(4), 719–30.

Rauch, A., M. Freese and A. Utsch (2005), 'Effects of human capital and long-term human resources development and utilization on employment growth of small-scale businesses: A causal analysis', *Entrepreneurship: Theory and Practice*, **29**, 681–98.

Roethlisberger, F.J. and W.J. Dickson (1939), *Management and the Worker*, Cambridge, MA: Harvard University Press.

Rosen, M. (1985), 'Breakfast at Spiro's: Dramaturgy and dominance', *Journal of Management Studies*, **11**, 31–48.

Scase, R. and R. Goffee (1980), *The Real World of the Small Business Owner*, London: Croom Helm.

Schein, E. (1992), *Organizational Culture and Leadership*, San Francisco: Jossey-Bass.

Silverman, D. (2000), *Doing Qualitative Research: A Practical Handbook*, London: Sage Publications.

Stavrou, E., T. Kleanthous and T. Anastasiou (2005), 'Leadership personality and firm culture during hereditary transitions in family firms: Model development and empirical investigation', *Journal of Small Business Management*, **43**(2), 187–206.

Thakur, S.P. (1998), 'Size of investment, opportunity choice and human resources in new ventures: Some typologies', *Entrepreneurship: Theory and Practice*, **14**, 293–309.

Thompson, P. and P. McHugh (2002), *Work Organisations*, 3rd edn, Basingstoke: Palgrave.

Van Maanen, J. (1991), 'The smile factory: Working at Disneyland', in P. Frost, L. Moore, M. Louis, C. Lundberg and J. Martin (eds), *Reframing Organizational Culture*, Newbury Park, CA: Sage, pp. 58–76.

Vickers, I., P. James, D. Smallbone and R. Baldock (2005), 'Understanding small firm responses to regulation: The case of workplace health and safety', *Policy Studies*, **26**, 149–69.

Walton, R. (1985), 'From control to commitment in the workplace', *Harvard Business Review*, March–April, pp. 77–84.

Wilkinson, A. (1999), 'Employment relations in SMEs', *Employee Relations*, **21**, 206–17.

Wray, D. (1994), 'Paternalism and its discontents: A case study', Paper presented to 12th International Labour Process Conference, Aston.

13 Barriers to growth in family-owned smaller businesses
Richard Harris and Renee Reid

Introduction

The literature on family-owned businesses (FoBs) has struggled to define what distinguishes such firms from others. Early researchers concentrated on the coincidence of shareholder (ownership), governance and management roles and particularly the problems surrounding intergenerational succession, while there has long been recognition of the intrinsic fragility of FoBs arising from the potential conflict between family and business goals. For many the focus is on trans-generational value creation which, as Chrisman et al. point out 'captures multiple goals and a purpose that transcends profitability, better than wealth creation that really represents the means rather than the ends of family enterprise' (2003: p. 468). Definitions of FoBs have focused on their 'intention' (Litz, 1995), 'vision' (Shanker and Astrachan, 1996) or 'behaviour' (Chua et al., 1999). Chrisman et al. (2003) argue that FoBs consist of: (i) the intention to maintain family control; (ii) family involvement that leads to a unique, inseparable and synergistic set of resources and capabilities; and (iii) the planning and execution of family succession issues. Unfortunately researchers often do not have access to the requisite information to make such distinctions and thus tend to operate using a more pragmatic approach (Daily and Dollinger, 1993). In this study we are constrained by the question asked in the 2004 Workplace Employment Relations Survey (WERS) about ownership and FoBs are defined as those firms where 50 per cent or more of the business is owned by one person or a family (Kersley et al., 2006).

Arguments as to why FoBs should act differently generally appeal to agency theory and the associated costs that arise when owners (who are also engaged in the management of the company) face the moral hazard problem of how to engender a higher level of worker output (Chami, 2001). According to agency theory, owner-management should minimize agency costs, as ownership aligns managers' attitudes towards growth opportunities and risk and there is much less need to reach, monitor and enforce agreements between owners and managers (Jensen, 1998). However, the extant FoBs literature tends to reach the opposite conclusion by providing evidence that the use of governance procedures and adoption of practices in such firms would seem to act as barriers to growth. This has led to the extension of agency theory to incorporate altruism when looking at FoBs. The problems associated with altruism arise when the owner–manager (typically the founder) attempts to help family members (such as children) who free-ride and shirk (Schulze et al., 2003). Thus Greenwood (2003), when commenting on Schulze et al. (2003), states several reasons why we might expect agency costs to be higher in FoBs including: family members are often not the best qualified for positions to which they have the inside track; they may shirk or free-ride in their work roles; owners may be unwilling to relinquish control even though they are no longer capable of effective management; and the possibility of owners interfering with family members charged with managing the firm.

Altruism (towards members of the family) is also likely to lead to a more general paternalistic approach to the workforce. There is the likelihood that in FoBs paternalistic behaviour reinforces and is reinforced by a high degree of altruism on the part of family members. The firm does not necessarily seek to just increase efficiency but is also concerned with equity issues (for example employees are 'looked-after' and treated fairly in return for their loyalty and effort). As shown in Chami (2001) when trust between owner, non-family managers and the workforce is low and/or altruism is asymmetric then the agency problem in the FoBs is exacerbated and can impact on the survival of the business.

Thus FoBs are likely to take a different approach to employee involvement (EI) practices such as consultation and communication and indeed other HRM strategies. How this links into economic performance at the establishment level is clearly an important area for research, with academic, public policy and business-related outcomes. In this chapter we use a nationally representative UK dataset that contains information on EI practices and economic performance to explore the relationship to family ownership. The general failure in the mainstream literature to recognize, embrace and deliberately incorporate FoBs is our rationale for doing so. This exclusion of the 'family' variable may mean that management theories do not apply to the vast majority of organizations in the UK and elsewhere. As Leach (1994) and Cromie et al. (1995) point out, FoBs comprise the great majority of enterprises in the UK. Indeed as Barclays Bank (2002) showed, three out of every five businesses in the UK with an annual turnover of less than £5 million are owned and managed by family members.

Much of the theory relating to FoBs emphasizes their operation under a different set of constraints and often with different objectives compared to non-FoBs (Chrisman et al., 2003; Lansberg, 1983; Mitchell et al., 2003). In the FoB a single family (usually) exercises significant managerial and financial authority (Goffee, 1996; Kirchoff and Kirchoff, 1987; Ward and Aronoff, 1991). Families seldom relinquish control to non-family managers (Francis, 1980) and consequently there is often a tension between rational profit-seeking activities and the non-commercial objectives of the family business. It has been argued that FoBs may adopt strategies that allow them to accomplish family goals such as maintaining family control and avoiding debt (Berembeim, 1990; Harris et al., 1994; Mishra and McConaughy, 1999). Non-family managers are kept on a tight rein (Goffee and Scase, 1985) and ownership allows the family to pursue such non-commercial objectives as ensuring intergenerational employment for family members and a paternalistic approach to running the company with a particular culture that is strong on trust, loyalty and inclusion (Dyer, 1986).

In addition to the pursuit of non-commercial objectives FoBs are often managed differently (Leach, 1990, 1994; Reid et al., 1999; Ward, 1997). Carlock and Ward (2004) suggest that a general lack of strategic planning contributes to their high failure rate as they attempt to survive from one generation to the next. It is well documented that only a small proportion of FoBs survive to the second or third generation (Kets de Vries, 1993; Lansberg, 1988; Santarelli and Lotti, 2005). Resistance to the process of succession by individuals and groups is characterized by 'fear of losing status' in the family and the firm (Sonnenfeld and Spence, 1989), rivalry between the different generations (Davis and Tagiuri, 1989; Levinson, 1971), the strong psychological link between founder and firm (Levinson, 1971) and difficulties in accepting mortality (Lansberg, 1988).

Despite the numbers of FoBs and their 'difference' from other firms there is little research examining barriers to their growth. The purpose of this chapter is to look at UK data to examine the extent to which FoBs do indeed differ across a wide range of attributes that are linked to economic growth. Our approach here is mainly descriptive, leaving more detailed and sophisticated statistical analysis to follow as part of a wider research programme in which we are engaged.

Importance of family ownership in the UK
In this chapter we use the 2004 WERS data which was gathered from a survey of a nationally weighted sample of some 2500 plants (not businesses) employing five or more employees. Our analysis is limited to the private sector.

Our analysis finds that family-owned plants (36 per cent of all plants) employed some 24 per cent of the workforce (in plants employing five or more employees) (see Figure 13.1). Restricting the comparison to those plants with fewer than 250 employees and to ownership groups that by definition include family ownership (for example, PLCs, private limited

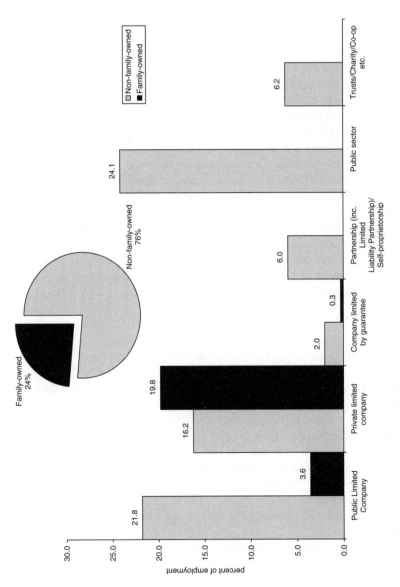

Figure 13.1 Employment share by ownership status

263

companies and companies limited by guarantee) then we see family-ownership of 77.3 per cent of all plants accounting for 70.2 per cent of total employment. This confirms earlier work that such firms do indeed comprise the great majority of (smaller) business enterprises in Britain.

Family-owned plants are concentrated in the smallest employment size-band comprising 50 or fewer employees (67.1 per cent of plants belonging to family-owned firms are in this group) whereas 71.9 per cent of plants belonging to non family-owned firms are part of enterprises that employ 250 plus workers in the UK. This difference in the size distribution is likely to have a major impact on any analysis and consequently we restrict our analysis to the sample of plants employing fewer than 250 people (those we term small and medium enterprises – SMEs).

Our analysis also suggests that plants with family ownership are more likely to be found in certain industries, namely wholesale and retail, manufacturing, other business services and construction.

In looking at the difference between various characteristics of family and non-family-owned plants we conduct t-tests to test for significant differences between groups. However these do not take into account any differences in the size or industrial distribution of the plants which we found to be important. Therefore in Table 13.1 we also report the results based on a second t-test.

$$y_i = \alpha_i + \alpha_2(FO)_i + \sum_j \beta_j SIZE_{ij} + \sum_k \delta_k INDUSTRY_{ik} + \varepsilon_i \quad (13.1)$$

We estimate the above model where y refers to one of the variables listed in Appendix 13.A1, *FO* is a dummy variable that refers to whether plant is family-owned (or not), *SIZE* is the employment size-band to which the plant belongs, with j bands being used (covering less than 50; 50–99; 100–149; and 150–249 people employed) and *INDUSTRY* refers to the industrial classification of the plant (12 groups were used). We test the null hypothesis $H_0: \alpha_2 = 0$ having controlled for the influence of size and industry and report the t-statistic obtained. When the dependent variable is continuous (for example the number of employees in the establishment) we use OLS regression to test whether $\alpha_2 = 0$. If y is a dichotomous dummy variable (for example foreign-owned or not) we use a logit model to test the null hypothesis.

The characteristics of family-owned and non-family-owned plants across a wide range of variables are contained in Table 13.1. Definitions of variables can be found in Appendix 13.A1. Table 13.1 shows that family-owned plants belonging to an SME are on average smaller. Their significantly lower employment is based on them being concentrated in the 'less than 50' size-band, rather than them necessarily being smaller across

Table 13.1 Weighted means of characteristics of SME plants, by family ownership

	Non-family-owned	Family-owned	T-test (1)	T-test (2)
No. employed	30	18	−3.48	−0.93
No. plants	4	2	−3.02	−0.07
Age (years)	27	22.6	−1.52	−0.79
Foreign-owned	15.1	5.3	−3.75	−3.74
US-owned	5.1	0.4	−3.88	−2.90
UK MNE	3.5	1.1	−1.83	−1.14
HQ plant	81.8	84.6	0.74	1.14
Union density	7.4	2.2	−3.92	−4.23
Part-time	18.3	21.2	1.17	0.47
Female workers	36.7	40.9	1.48	3.80
Manual workers	42.8	59.9	5.48	4.03
Temporary workers	9.1	7.0	−0.83	−0.71
Ethnic workers	6.5	4.9	−1.07	−0.32

Notes:
Sample based on PLCs, private limited companies and companies limited by guarantee that employ 5–249 workers.
(1) Test of the null that mean values are different.
(2) Test of the null that family-owned dummy is significant in regression (see equation 13.1).

all size-bands. Controlling for size removes any statistically significant relationship between family ownership and the number of people employed in the plant. Non-family-owned firms operate more plants than family-owned ones (although the overwhelming majority of all firms in the sample are single-plant enterprises) and the difference is statistically significant using a standard univariate t-test. However, after controlling for size and industry effects this difference becomes insignificant.

Table 13.1 shows that family-owned plants belonging to an SME are on average younger (under 23 years compared to 27 years) although the statistical significance attached to this difference is weak. Figure 13.2 provides a better indication of any difference and by calculating a two-sided Kolmogorov–Smirnov (KS) statistic it is possible to test whether the age distribution of one group of plants lies to the right of another. We can see that the age distribution of non-family-owned plants (when ranked from lowest to highest) mostly lies to the right of the distribution for family-owned plants. By showing a first-order stochastic dominance between such (random) variables we have conducted a stricter test than simply comparing the mean age levels across the two groups. By using the KS to test the null hypothesis that the difference between the two distributions is favourable to

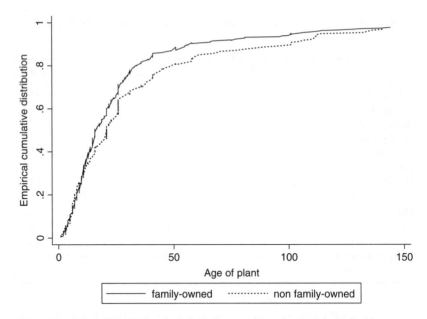

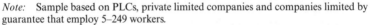

Note: Sample based on PLCs, private limited companies and companies limited by guarantee that employ 5–249 workers.

Figure 13.2   Age differences between family-owned and non-family-owned plants

non-family-owned over family-owned plants, we were able to accept this null hypothesis.

Only for the youngest plants (up to around ten years) is there some evidence of any difference between the ages of the two groups. This either suggests family-owned plants were relatively more likely to be started in more recent years (hence a lower average age) and/or they have experienced higher closure rates (that is on average plants do not survive as long and thus have a lower mean age). Both explanations could be true but only with time-series panel data could we say more on the dynamics of plant opening and closure across sub-groups. Both explanations would be consistent with the hypothesis that family-owned plants have a lower overall probability of survival.

Table 13.1 also shows family-owned plants belonging to SMEs are much less likely to be foreign-owned. This result is statistically significant on the basis of both t-tests. Moreover, they are also less likely to be UK multinational companies. Statistically this difference is only significant using the standard t-test.

In terms of workforce issues family-owned plants are much less likely to be unionized and overall they tend to employ more part-time workers (although the difference is not statistically significant). A higher proportion of female workers are employed in family-owned plants while they employ relatively more manual workers. There is little statistical significance in the proportion of temporary or ethnic workers employed in family-owned plants.

Overall Table 13.1 shows family-owned plants tend to be smaller, younger, UK-owned, with relatively fewer unionized members but with more female, manual and part-time workers. The t-tests confirm that after controlling for size these differences remain. In short this data tells us that family-owned plants are different from other private sector SME plants. While these differences are important our real interest is in whether there is also a different approach to HRM (and thus EI practices) in these firms and then whether this impacts on their relative economic performance vis-à-vis non-family-owned plants.

Family-owned plants, HRM and employee involvement
Mizrahi reports 'a remarkable consensus . . . regarding the fundamental principles needed to achieve competitiveness in individual enterprises . . . (such as) high standards of employee selection, broad task design and teamwork, employee involvement in problem-solving, and a climate of co-operation and trust' (2002: p. 690). In this section we concentrate on whether family-owned plants take a different approach with respect to EI and other HRM strategies designed to elicit worker effort. The primary focus is on communication and consultation aspects of EI as they relate to activities at the workplace. These could be the extent of self-managed work teams, worker involvement in the design of EI programme, the extent of Total Quality Management (TQM), committees on productivity, worker involvement in work processes, formal suggestion or complaint systems, formal information-sharing with employees and surveys of workers regarding their satisfaction (Freeman et al., 2000).

Such a focus is important as it has been argued (see for example Addison et al., 2000) that greater involvement increases employee loyalty, responsibility and effort and thus increases efficiency. Consultation and cooperation can lead to creative outcomes and shared goals (especially in 'tough times') as set out in the Freeman and Lazear (1995) works council/ employee involvement model. We do, however, recognize the debate about the extent to which EI achieves these outcomes or whether these measures actually lead to work intensification (see Marchington and Grugulis, 2000). The fundamental issue is whether EI leads to greater employee empowerment (Wilkinson, 1998) or whether it is a mechanism for the appropriation of employee knowledge, and while giving workers greater specific control over their day-to-day tasks nevertheless allows management greater general control over the work system as a whole. This is an important debate, but if the outcome is still greater productivity of the workforce (through empowerment or greater control), then it might be argued that EI initiatives still can achieve their goals.

A consideration of communication and consultation practices is also particularly relevant when considering cultural differences between FoBs and non-FoBs. For example, Dyer (1986) points out that the most common type of culture in FoBs can be described as paternalistic (see also Hyman, Osborne and Jack, Chapter 12, this handbook). In such an environment family members make the significant decisions and closely supervise employees in a 'what is good for business is good for employees' mentality (Ram and Holliday, 1993; Scott et al., 1989). Dyer (1986) also identifies other less common cultural forms of family-owned firms, including laissez-faire (which is similar to paternalistic but employees are trusted and given greater scope to accomplish the strategy determined by management) and participative (which he argues is rare in FoBs as it involves team-working, downplays the family's power and has a more fully-developed HRM strategy).

Wray (1996) points out that FoBs often start out with a traditional paternalistic approach that relies on face-to-face deference between workers and owner–managers. Owner–managers deal personally with their workers and not through sophisticated management techniques or formal procedures while the employment relationship is regulated for the employees and not by them. However, growth of the FoBs makes this difficult to sustain and owner–managers resort to a more sophisticated paternalistic approach with devolved managerial systems, above-average remuneration, training and EI mechanisms – all of which is in the image of 'best practice HRM' (Dundon et al., 1999). However, Wray (1996) points out that this type of paternalism should not be confused with EI initiatives as associated with HRM:

> both incorporate employees through mechanisms of consultation and involvement . . . the defining difference is to be found in the underpinning rationale for each style of management. Sophisticated paternalism remains loyal to the familial culture of traditional paternalism, becoming 'sophisticated' only in attempts to maintain that culture in the face of the contingencies of modern industrial society (1996: p. 703).

In summary, if FoBs engage in EI initiatives, they are likely to take a different approach. But with any EI initiatives there is a risk that workers will want to increase their share of the firm's profits, and with greater EI they will have the information and ability to pursue this. So while EI increases productive efficiency, inefficiency can set in if greater rent-seeking is encouraged. For management the optimal level of EI is usually (considerably) below the maximal level possible and this suggests that the profit–EI trade-off curve is an inverted U shape. Thus, in both FoBs and non-FoBs there are limits to EI, although the limit in the FoBs will set in at a (much) lower level. This is also likely to be reinforced by a culture that means EI is seen as less necessary because workers are 'looked after'. EI could be seen as a threat to the FoBs culture if it engenders rent-seeking and challenges to the way the business is run by family members.

Given the above, we turn to the WERS data to see whether family-owned plants are less likely to engage in EI and other HRM strategies as well as whether they are less likely to communicate directly and consult with their workforce, compared to non-family-owned plants. As earlier, we control for firm size given the general acceptance in the literature of informal approaches to employment relations, and indeed that formal 'communication strategies are often non-existent' (Wilkinson, 1999: p. 209). Even where practices are adopted, for example because they become embedded in supply-chain relationships, the form of EI is often more informal than formal (Bacon, Ackers, Storey and Coates 1996). Although most FoBs are also likely to be SMEs, it is important to separate them out. For example, Goffee (1996) argues that,

> Even when it is acknowledged that ownership . . . remains largely concentrated within a single private family, such information is rarely applied to explanations of managerial or organizational behavior. By thus divorcing the issue of ownership from that of managerial control it is possible to construct organizational models which depict small- and medium-sized (family) business as 'simple' . . . while larger (publicly owned) enterprises are regarded as 'complex'. Such analyses miss the point that most family businesses . . . involve highly complex interrelationships between . . . the family and the business (p. 36).

Table 13.2 presents the (weighted) mean values for EI and other HRM practices. 'Internal fit' summarizes the extent to which the plant adopts a wide range of practices and it relates to the 'synergistic benefits resulting from the introduction of HRM as an institutionally supported package of practices that cohere with and mutually reinforce each other' (Hoque, 1999: p. 422). It draws on the contingency approach to HRM. Internal fit is measured by counting the number of appropriate HRM practices (as listed in Table 13.2) that are used, with the list of such practices based on Hoque (1999, Table 2) and defined in Appendix 13.A1.

Arguably 'external fit' is also an important intervening variable in terms of how EI practices affect performance. Only if the firm's HRM strategy is meshed with a business strategy that emphasizes quality enhancement or innovation (Schuler, 1989; Schuler and Jackson, 1987) will EI prove to be effective. External fit is measured by whether or not workplaces set targets for the quality of the product or service (in a similar way to targeting sales and/or costs and/or profits for example).

Overall, Table 13.2 shows that on average family-owned plants use significantly fewer numbers of HRM practices, although this disappears

Table 13.2   Weighted means of HRM and EI practices of SME plants, by family ownership

	Non-family-owned	Family-owned	T-test (1)	T-test (2)
Grievances policy	80.6	66.0	−3.19	−1.25
EO/managing diversity policy	57.3	37.6	−4.04	−1.49
Job security	7.2	9.7	0.86	0.69
Induction programmes	70.8	61.2	−1.99	0.19
Personality tests	8.6	10.6	0.66	1.77
Performance tests	42.3	34.7	−1.57	−0.21
Worker appraisal	65.2	41.4	−4.87	−2.53
Investor-in-People	22.6	11.8	−3.11	−1.52
Multi-tasked	28.3	29.1	0.18	0.75
Discretion over work	25.2	42.4	3.55	3.27
Designated teams	59.3	46.3	−2.62	−0.55
Quality circles	12.1	14.0	0.53	2.12
Performance pay	29.4	26.5	−0.65	−0.27
Profit pay	10.4	14.8	1.28	1.53
Internal fit	5.2	4.5	−2.97	−0.84
External fit	45.8	27.9	−3.86	−2.54

Notes:
Sample based on PLCs, private limited companies and companies limited by guarantee that employ 5–249 workers.
(1) Test of the null that mean values are different.
(2) Test of the null that family-owned dummy is significant in regression (see equation 13.1).

when controlling for size and industry. These plants are also significantly less likely to target product quality (overall some 28 per cent adopt such targets compared to nearly 46 per cent of non-family-owned SMEs). However, underlying internal fit is an array of practices and Table 13.2 shows that family-owned plants are less likely to: use grievance procedures; have policies dealing with equal opportunity issues; have an induction programme; undertake appraisal of non-managerial workers; be accredited to the Investors-in-People (IiP) programme; and use designated teams. However, they do allow more discretion over how people work and use quality circles, while there is some indication that they are more likely to link pay to profits.

Do these results help us to discern any patterns that might suggest that family-owned plants have a culture of (sophisticated) paternalism or are they just as engaged in pursuing best practice HRM policies as non-family-owned plants? Arguably the results suggest that employees are 'looked after' by there being informal work procedures with less managerial control (evidenced by more discretion over work and the greater use of quality

Table 13.3   Weighted means of consultation and communication practices of SME plants, by family ownership

	Non-family-owned	Family-owned	T-test (1)	T-test (2)
Brief workforce	59.8	51.5	−1.65	−0.01
Used JCCs	11.3	3.1	−3.78	−2.17
Surveys	19.8	16.6	−0.84	−0.82
Information about investment plans	40.5	31.7	−1.85	−1.89
Information about financial position	47.3	33.4	−2.89	−2.31
Meetings	70.0	67.2	−0.59	−1.12
Management chain	55.2	33.8	−4.46	−2.74
Suggestion schemes	14.2	13.2	−0.29	−0.64
Newsletters	30.5	14.0	−4.38	−2.93
Email	39.4	21.3	−4.20	−1.65
No consultation	6.5	15.4	3.18	2.65

Notes:
Sample based on PLCs, private limited companies and companies limited by guarantee that employ 5–249 workers.
(1) Test of the null that mean values are different.
(2) Test of the null that family-owned dummy is significant in regression (see equation 13.1).

circles) and therefore family-owned plants do seem to have a different (more paternalistic) culture. There is also some evidence to suggest that family-owned plants are relatively less likely to use bundles of HR practices. This evidence does therefore seem to support other research highlighting differences in the way FoBs are managed and operated.

If paternalism is the more prevalent culture, then turning to a more specific consideration of the extent of differences in consultation and communication practices means we would expect FoBs to share relatively less information with their employees. Table 13.3 presents the results across a wide range of practices. The overall picture is that in family-owned plants managers are significantly less likely to: consult with employees through the use of joint consultation committees; provide information about investment plans or the financial position of the plant/company; communicate down through the management chain; and use newsletters and emails. Evidence suggests that there is a greater tendency for managers not to communicate directly with employees if the plant is family-owned.

We recognize there can be quite important differences between information sharing, communication and consultation practices as they relate to empowering employees. However, as Wilkinson (1998) argues, management

Table 13.4   Summary of type of communication/consultation practised in SME plants, by family ownership

Type	Non-family-owned (%)	Family-owned (%)	Total (%)
Direct communication only	86.4	86.8	86.7
Direct communication only + use of JCC	11.4	3.1	5.1
No direct communication/consultation	2.3	10.1	8.2

Notes:
Sample based on PLCs, private limited companies and companies limited by guarantee that employ 5–249 workers.
χ^2-tests reject the null of no association for each two-way cross-tabulation, at the 1 per cent significance level.

increases downward communication typically via newsletters, the management chain or team briefings, which should result in greater employee commitment. Upward problem solving (through say the use of quality circles or suggestion schemes) should also have similar impacts. What is important to distinguish is whether such practices are either absent or are direct or mediated by employee representation (such as through joint consultative committees (JCCs)). As a result we regroup the practices in Table 13.3, presenting them in Table 13.4 to show plants involved in direct communication only, those involved in direct communication but also negotiating with JCCs, and those plants with no direct communication/consultation procedures. The data in Table 13.4 confirms that overall family-owned plants were nearly four times less likely to use JCCs and were more than four times more likely to have no direct communication and/or consultation. These results are consistent with the hypothesis that FoBs are more likely to have a culture of (sophisticated) paternalism, rather than to pursue best practice HRM policies because they can improve worker performance. It is to the economic performance of these plants which we now turn.

Economic performance
Economic performance (in terms of financial performance, labour productivity, and the quality of the product or service) was measured in WERS by asking management to provide a ranking relative to others operating in the industry to which they belong. While such perceptual data can be biased, Wood et al. (2002) argue that as long as it is uniform then it will not invalidate the measures used.

Table 13.5 reveals little difference in the perceived financial performance of family-owned and non-family-owned plants. Family-owned plants

Table 13.5 Workplace performance[a] of SME plants, by family ownership

	Non-family-owned	Family-owned	T-test (1)	T-test (2)
Financial performance	0.46	0.46	−0.03	−0.47
Labour productivity	0.87	0.58	−3.65	−2.75
Quality of product/service	1.02	1.18	2.21	2.74
'Best' plants[b]	33.6	25.5	−2.80	−2.54

Notes:
Sample based on PLCs, private limited companies and companies limited by guarantee that employ 5–249 workers.
(1) Test of the null that mean values are different.
(2) Test of the null that family-owned dummy is significant in regression (see equation 13.1).
[a] Mean values reported based on 'lot better than average'=2; 'better than average'=1; 'average' = 0; 'below average' = −1; 'lot below average' = −2.
[b] 'Best' plants scored '2' on all 3 indicators of performance.

reported lower sales per worker compared to industry rivals but on average produce a better quality product or service than non-family-owned plants. Given such differing results we classified plants into two groups with the 'best plants' defined as those rated 'a lot better than average' on all three indicators of performance. Using this definition we show in Table 13.5 that family-owned plants belonging to SMEs were significantly less likely to belong to the best group (only some 25 per cent compared to nearly 34 per cent of the non-family-owned plants).

The question then becomes whether the form that consultation and communication (linked to family ownership) takes is important in explaining workplace performance. Before we use the 2004 WERS data to explore the factors determining whether a plant belongs to the 'best' category or not we revisit previous work involving the estimation of a (weighted ordered probit) model using the 1998 WERS data (see Harris et al., 2003). That relied on much the same variables as we use here (see Appendix 13.A1) to obtain the results which are set out in Table 13.6.

The first row in Table 13.6 shows that in 1998 (having controlled for other impacts) family-owned plants were some 17.5 per cent less likely to report a level of performance that was 'a lot better than average', while family-owned plants were 30 per cent more likely to believe their financial performance was average or below average. However, of particular interest are those variables relating to direct communication/consultation and no communication with the workforce. Table 13.6 shows that plants having EI schemes involving direct communication with the workforce are more likely to report better than average performances compared to plants that negotiate with JCCs. For example, the probability of being a lot better than

Table 13.6   *Marginal effects of workplace financial performance*[a]
(WERS, 1998)

Variables	$\partial(y=0)/\partial x$	$\partial(y=1)/\partial x$	$\partial(y=2)/\partial x$	$\partial(y=3)/\partial x$
Family-owned	0.098	0.202	−0.126	−0.175
Internal fit	−0.007	−0.015	0.010	0.013
Direct communication with workforce	−0.068	−0.140	0.087	0.121
Direct communication × family-owned	0.060	0.123	−0.077	−0.106
No communication with workforce	−0.148	−0.305	0.190	0.263
No communication × family-owned	0.160	0.330	−0.205	−0.284
No communication × family-owned × external fit	−0.178	−0.368	0.229	0.317
ln age of plant	−0.015	−0.031	0.019	0.027
ln employment size × family-owned	−0.033	−0.068	0.042	0.059
Single establishment enterprise	−0.032	−0.067	0.041	0.057
TU density 10–49 per cent	0.026	0.055	−0.034	−0.047
TU density 50+ per cent	−0.038	−0.078	0.048	0.067
Little workplace change last 5 years	0.033	0.068	−0.042	−0.058
No workplace change last 5 years	0.063	0.129	−0.080	−0.112
Per cent part-time	0.001	0.002	−0.001	−0.002
Per cent female	−0.001	−0.001	0.001	0.001
Employees receive profit-related pay × family-owned	0.054	0.111	−0.069	−0.095
Gini coefficient relating to FT male earnings	−0.076	−0.158	0.098	0.136
Outsourcing in last 5 years	0.028	0.057	−0.036	−0.050
Temporary/fixed term workers	0.039	0.082	−0.051	−0.070
Supply national/ international markets	0.038	0.080	−0.049	−0.069

Notes:
Only significant effects included based on Table A2 in Harris et al. (2003).
[a]   Financial performance coded 0 = below average to 3 = a lot better than average.

average is 12.1 per cent higher if there is direct communication. However, if the plant is family-owned then these benefits largely disappear. This is seen by adding together the two rows of data for the direct communication variables, to obtain the probability of being in any financial performance sub-group when the plant is family-owned. In other words the probability of being 'a lot better than average' is only 1.5 per cent (12.1–10.6) higher if there is direct communication in a family-owned plant.

Where there is no direct communication/consultation with the workforce, workplaces also benefit in terms of their financial performance when compared to the benchmark group comprising plants that have JCCs (indeed the relationship is even stronger). Here the probability of being a lot better than average is 26.3 per cent higher with no communication, for a non-family-owned plant. Again, if the plant is family-owned, these benefits generally disappear (as can be seen by adding together the two relevant rows in Table 13.6). The exception is those family-owned plants with no direct communication but who target the quality of the product or service produced (external fit). For this relatively small group (2.6 per cent of family-owned workplaces) the probability of being a lot better than average is 29.6 per cent higher (obtained from summing 0.317, −0.284 and 0.263).

Using the 1998 WERS data, Harris et al. (2003) therefore found that while direct communication/consultation improves the financial performance of non-family-owned plants, these effects are largely absent in family-owned establishments, implying that not only do such establishments have lower levels of this aspect of EI, when EI is present this does not translate into greater economic benefits.

If we now analyse the 2004 WERS data, the results in Table 13.7 are from estimating a (weighted) logit model with best plant (coded 1 if true) as the dependent variable and a selection of the variables listed in Appendix 13.A1 as the right-hand-side determinants. In this analysis we omit the number of people employed in the plant and instead use UK enterprise employment grouped into size-bands. We also only include 'internal' and 'external' fit from the HRM practices and procedures list, and only 'no consultation' is used from the consultation and communication list. Given collinearity problems with entering too many variables from the list of HRM practices and consultation and communication we used factor analysis to see if we could obtain principal components spanning these different lists. We found that the major principal component for HRM practices was strongly linked to the 'internal fit' measure (with a correlation of over 90 per cent) and 'no consultation' was strongly linked to the main principal component spanning the consultation and communication list. Consequently, neither principal component survived when using a stepwise regression approach to estimation.

Table 13.7   Marginal effects of workplace performance[a] in SME plants, by family ownership (WERS, 2004)

Variables	$\partial \hat{p}/\partial x$	z-value	$\bar{x}$
Family-owned*	−0.167	−1.87	0.760
Age	−0.002	−2.37	23.675
HQ plant*	0.089	1.85	0.839
Foreign-owned*	0.169	2.10	0.076
Foreign-owned × family-owned	−0.173	−1.91	0.040
Per cent ethnic	−0.007	−2.04	5.312
Per cent ethnic × family-owned	0.008	2.21	3.756
Strategic plan* × family-owned	0.170	2.45	0.284
Exports*	−0.233	−3.40	0.131
Exports × family-owned	0.310	1.58	0.080
Product innovation*	0.229	2.14	0.288
Product innovation × family-owned	−0.141	−1.87	0.185
Process innovation*	−0.092	−1.87	0.419
Quality standards*	−0.106	−2.00	0.216
Hotels & Restaurants sector	0.150	2.30	0.066
50–99 employees in UK enterprise*	0.114	2.19	0.079
150–249 employees in UK enterprise *	0.333	3.70	0.046
Pseudo R^2	0.10		
N	544		
Log pseudo-likelihood	−288.3		
Link test[b]: H0: $\beta_2 = 0$	0.86		

Notes:
Sample based on PLCs, private limited companies and companies limited by guarantee that employ 5–249 workers.
[a] 'Best' plants coded 1.
[b] Tests of model misspecification are based on 'best' = $\beta_1(x\hat{\beta}_x) + \beta_2(x\hat{\beta}_x)^2$. Under the correct specification, $\beta_1 = 1$ and $\beta_2 = 0$; thus we test $\beta_2 = 0$.
The significance level for rejecting the null is reported here.
* Dichotomous variable coded 1 if true.

In conducting our logit analysis we allowed all the right-hand-side regressors to be entered a second time after they were multiplied by the family-owned dummy variable. This allowed family ownership effects to work through the other covariates rather than just through the impact of the (0, 1) dummy variable. A stepwise procedure was applied, and marginal effects, $\partial \hat{p}/\partial x$, rather than parameter estimates, $\hat{\beta}$, are reported as these indicate the change in the probability of belonging to the 'best plant' sub-group given a change in each determinant, having controlled for other impacts.

The single most important result is that family-owned plants are nearly 17 per cent less likely to belong to the best group having controlled for the impact of all other factors. Older plants are also less likely to belong to that group while HQ (rather than branch) plants are nearly 9 per cent more likely to belong. Foreign ownership increases the probability of the plant being classified as best (by 17 per cent) except if the foreign-owned plant is also family-owned (then the overall probability of being the best is largely unaffected by foreign ownership). Having more ethnic workers as a proportion of the workforce lowers the probability of being one of the best although not in family-owned plants. Family-owned plants with formal strategic plans setting out objectives and how they will be achieved are 17 per cent more likely to be in the best group having controlled for other covariates. While only a small proportion of family-owned plants have these plans (37.4 per cent compared to 60.9 per cent of non-family-owned plants), our results show they are associated with significantly better levels of performance.

Surprisingly we found plants selling into international markets do not rate themselves as the best, which may say something about the level of competition (and the quality of the competitors) they face when exporting. Family-owned exporters, however, are 7.7 per cent more likely to belong to the best group.

Product innovators have a 22.9 per cent higher probability of being in the best group except if the plant is family-owned (then the impact falls to only an 8.8 per cent higher likelihood). Interestingly, process innovators (which presumably compete more on cost than quality when compared to product innovators) and plants that have attained quality standards are less likely to be in the best group. This may indicate that quality Kitemarks are used as a substitute for achieving better performance but this is just a tentative conclusion without further research. Lastly, plants with 50–99 (150–249) employees in the UK enterprise are 11.4 per cent (33.3 per cent) more likely to belong to the best group (compared to plants in other size-bands), as are plants in the hotels and restaurants sector which are 15 per cent more likely.

In summary, by using the 2004 WERS data we can show that after controlling for a range of other factors that impact on whether a plant is amongst the best, those that are family-owned do significantly worse. Family ownership meant they were 17 per cent less likely to belong to the best group while also mitigating against the positive impacts of being foreign-owned and introducing product innovations. However, we found no separate role for HRM and EI factors in determining best economic performance, rather factors associated with the technological side of production dominated our results. That is not to say that HRM and EI and the impact that family ownership can have through these variables are not important. However, the model needs to be further developed so we can adequately map out the (structural) influences of all the likely factors (including extending the role of HRM and consultation/communication factors) which determine performance, and this is work in progress.

Summary and conclusions

We began this chapter by reviewing the literature to assert that FoBs would take a different approach to EI practices and indeed to other HRM practices designed to elicit worker effort. By drawing on WERS 2004, which is a representative plant-level database for the UK, we were able to examine the relative importance of family ownership and confirmed earlier work that FoBs comprise the great majority of (smaller) business enterprises in the UK. These family-owned plants tended to be smaller, younger, UK-owned (and less likely to be multinational), with relatively fewer unionized members, but more female, manual and part-time workers.

We then turned to consider HRM and EI practices in these plants. We found that on average family-owned workplaces used (significantly) fewer HRM practices. In terms of specific HRM practices, these plants were less likely to use a grievance procedure; have a policy dealing with equal opportunity issues; appraise non-managerial workers; have gained IiP accreditation; and make use of designated teams. On the other hand they were more likely to offer discretion over how people work; use quality circles; and link pay to profits (although the last difference was statistically insignificant).

Given these differences we then considered whether family-owned plants had a culture of (sophisticated) paternalism or whether they were equally as likely as non-family-owned plants to pursue best practice HRM policies. We found that family-owned plants seemed to operate with a different (more paternalistic) culture and when we added the evidence that these plants were also relatively less likely to use a bundle of HR practices, our overall conclusion was of important differences in the management and operation of family-owned plants.

What of the consultation and communication practices? We thought that if family-owned plants were less engaged in such activities then this would provide further evidence of paternalistic cultures. We found that family-owned plants were significantly less likely to: consult with their employees through the use of JCCs; communicate through providing information about investment plans or the financial position of the plant/company; communicate down through the management chain; use newsletters and emails; and use any of the standard methods of direct communication with employees. Overall, we found that family-owned establishments were nearly four times less likely to use JCCs and were more than four times more likely to have no direct communication and/or consultation with employees. As such our findings were consistent with the argument that in FoBs a culture of (sophisticated) paternalism operates. Culture rather than improving workforce performance would explain the use of best practice HRM practices.

When we turned to plant performance there was no evidence that family-owned plants did better or worse than others in terms of perceived financial performance. Differences in terms of labour productivity and quality of goods and services did emerge. Overall, however, the results on the economic performance of family-owned plants (relative to non-family-owned plants) were mixed. Could this be a result of differences in the communication and consultation practices of family-owned plants? The evidence presented (using 1998 data) showed that while direct communication/consultation improved the financial performance of non-family-owned plants, these effects were largely absent in family-owned establishments. This implied that not only did such plants have lower levels of EI but also when EI was present this did not translate into greater economic benefits. When we drew on the WERS 2004 data we did not find a direct role for HRM and/or communication and consultation practices (the model estimated was only an initial step in considering the determinants of economic performance), but we did find evidence that plants that are family-owned performed less well than non-family-owned plants.

Research on the FoBs is relatively underdeveloped, especially from an HRM perspective. The availability of representative datasets such as WERS enables a range of studies to be undertaken. We would argue this is necessary given the evidence that family ownership makes a difference especially with regard to the type of HRM policies and business growth strategies pursued by these firms.

References

Addison, J.T., W.S. Siebert, J. Wagner and X. Wei (2000), 'Worker participation and firm performance: Evidence from Germany and Britain', *British Journal of Industrial Relations*, **38**, 7–48.

Bacon, N., P. Ackers, J. Storey and D. Coates (1996), 'It's a small world: Managing human resources in small businesses', *International Journal of Human Resource Management*, **7**, 83–100.

Barclays Bank (2002), *A Family Affair, Today's Family Businesses*, London: Barclays Bank.

Berembeim, R.E. (1990), 'How business families manage the transition from owner to professional management', *Family Business Review*, **3**, 69–100.

Carlock, R.S. and J.L. Ward (2004), *Strategic Planning for the Family Business: Parallel Planning to Unify the Family and Business*, New York: Palgrave.

Chami, R. (2001), 'What is different about family businesses?', *IMF Working Paper*, WP/01/70.

Chrisman, J.J., J.H. Chua and R. Litz (2003), 'A unified systems perspective of family firm performance: An extension and integration', *Journal of Business Venturing*, **18**, 467–72.

Chua, J.H., J.J. Chrisman and P. Sharma (1999), 'Defining the family business by behavior', *Entrepreneurship: Theory and Practice*, **23**, 19–39.

Cromie, S., B. Stephenson and D. Monteith (1995), 'The management of family firms: An empirical investigation', *International Small Business Journal*, **13**, 11–34.

Daily, C.M. and M.J. Dollinger (1993), 'Alternative methodologies for identifying family-versus nonfamily-managed businesses', *Journal of Small Business Management*, **31**, 79–90.

Davis, J.A. and R. Tagiuri (1989), 'The influence of life stage on father–son work relationships in family companies', *Family Business Review*, **2**(1), 47–74.

Dundon, T., I. Grugulis and A. Wilkinson (1999), 'Looking out of the black-hole: Non-union relations in an SME', *Employee Relations*, **21**, 251–66.

Dyer, Jr. W.G. (1986), *Cultural Change in Family Firms: Anticipating and Managing Business and Family Transactions*, San Francisco: Jossey-Bass.

Francis, A. (1980), 'Families, firms and finance capital: The development of UK industrial firms with particular reference to their ownership and control', *Sociology*, **14**, 1–27.

Freeman, R.B. and E.P. Lazear (1995), 'An economic analysis of works councils', in J. Rogers and W. Streek (eds), *Works Councils: Consultation, Representation and Cooperation in Industrial Relations*, Chicago: University of Chicago Press, pp. 27–52.

Freeman, R.B., M.M. Kleiner and C. Ostroff (2000), 'The anatomy of employee involvement and its effect on firms and workers', *NBER Working Paper 8050*.

Goffee, R. (1996), 'Understanding family business: Issues for further research', *International Journal of Entrepreneurial Behaviour & Research*, **2**, 36–48.

Goffee, R. and R. Scase (1985), 'Proprietorial control in family firms', *Journal of Management Studies*, **22**, 53–68.

Greenwood, R. (2003), 'Commentary on: "Toward a Theory of Agency and Altruism in Family Firms" ', *Journal of Business Venturing*, **18**, 491–4.

Harris, G., J.I. Martinez and J.L. Ward (1994), 'Is strategy different for the family-owned business?', *Family Business Review*, **7**, 159–74.

Harris, R., R. Reid and R. McAdam (2003), 'Consultation and communication in family businesses', *International Journal of HRM*, **15**(8), 1426–46.

Hoque, K. (1999), 'Human resource management and performance in the UK hotel industry', *British Journal of Industrial Relations*, **37**, 419–43.

Jensen, M.C. (1998), *Foundations of Organizational Strategy*, Cambridge: Harvard University Press.

Kersley, B., C. Alpin, J. Forth, A. Bryson, H. Bewley, G. Dix and S. Oxenbridge (2006), *Inside the Workplace: Findings from the 2004 Workplace Employment Relations Survey*, London: Routledge.

Kets de Vries, M.F.R. (1993), 'The dynamics of family controlled firms: The good and the bad news', *Organisational Dynamics*, **21**, Winter, 59–71.

Kirchoff, B.A. and J.J. Kirchoff (1987), 'Family contributions to productivity and profitability in small business', *Journal of Small Business Management*, **25**, 25–31.

Lansberg, I. (1983), 'Managing human resources in family firms: The problem of institutional overlap', *Organisation Dynamics*, **12**(1), 29–38.

Lansberg, I. (1988), 'The succession conspiracy', *Family Business Review*, **1**(2), 119–43.

Leach, P. (1990), *Managing the Family Business in the UK*, London: Stoy Hayward.

Leach, P. (1994), *The Stoy Hayward Guide to Family Business*, London: Kogan Page.

Levinson, H. (1971), 'Conflicts that plague family businesses', *Harvard Business Review*, Mar–Apr, pp. 90–98.

Litz, R. (1995), 'The family business: Toward definitional clarity', *Family Business Review*, **8**, 71–81.

Marchington, M. and I. Grugulis (2000), 'Best practice human resource management: Perfect opportunity or dangerous illusion?, *International Journal of Human Resource Management*, **11**(6), 1104–24.

Mishra, C.S. and D.L. McConaughy (1999), 'Founding family control and capital structure: The risk of loss of control and the aversion to debt', *Entrepreneurship: Theory and Practice*, **23**, 53–64.

Mitchell, R.K., E.A. Morse and P. Sharma (2003), 'The transacting cognitions of nonfamily employees in the family business setting', *Journal of Business Venturing*, **18**, 533–51.

Mizrahi, S. (2002), 'Workers' participation in decision-making processes and firm stability', *British Journal of Industrial Relations*, **40**, 689–707.

Ram, M. and R. Holliday (1993), 'Relative merits: Family culture and kinship in small firms', *Sociology*, **27**, 629–48.

Reid, R., B. Dunn, S. Cromie and J. Adams, (1999), 'Family orientation in family firms: A model and some empirical evidence', *Journal of Small Business & Enterprise Development*, **6**(1), 55–65.

Santarelli, E. and F. Lotti, (2005), 'The survival of family firms: The importance of control and family ties', *International Journal of Economics and Business*, **12**, 183–92.

Schuler, R. (1989), 'Strategic human resource management and industrial relations', *Human Relations*, **42**, 157–84.

Schuler, R. and S. Jackson (1987), 'Linking competitive strategies with human resource management practices', *Academy of Management Executive*, **1**, 207–19.

Schulze, W.S., M.H. Lubatkin and R.N. Dino (2003), 'Towards a theory of agency and altruism in family firms', *Journal of Business Venturing*, **18**, 472–90.

Scott, M., I. Roberts, G. Holroyd and D. Sawbridge (1989), 'Management and industrial relations in small firms', *Department of Employment Research Paper*, London.

Shanker, M.C. and J.H. Astrachan (1996), 'Myths and realities: Family businesses' contributions to the US economy', *Family Business Review*, **9**, 107–23.

Sonnenfeld, J.A. and P. Spence, (1989), 'The parting patriarch of a family firm', *Family Business Review*, **2**(4), 355–75.

Ward, J. (1987), *Keeping the Family Business Healthy*, San Francisco: Jossey-Bass.

Ward, J.L. (1997), 'Growing the family business: Special challenges and best practices', *Family Business Review*, **10**, 323–37.

Ward, J.L. and C.E. Aronoff (1991), 'To sell or not to sell', *Nation's Business*, **78**, 63–64.

Wilkinson, A. (1998), 'Empowerment: Theory and practice', *Personnel Review*, **27**(1), 40–56.

Wilkinson, A. (1999), 'Employment relations in SMEs', *Employee Relations*, **21**, 206–17.

Wood, S.J., L.M. de Menezes and A. Lasaosa (2002), 'High involvement management and performance', mimeo.

Wray, D. (1996), 'Paternalism and its discontents: A case study', *Work, Employment & Society*, **10**, 701–15.

Appendix

Table 13.A1   Definitions

Variables	Definition
Family-owned*	A plant is classified as family-owned if a single individual or family own at least 50 per cent of the enterprise
Basic characteristics	
No. employed	Number of employees employed in plant (not UK enterprise)
No. employees in UK enterprise	This variable is used to define an SME and to obtain size-bands (<50; 50–99; 100–149; 150–249)
No. of plants in UK enterprise	Number of plants operated by the UK enterprise (single plant enterprise$=1$)
Age	How many years plant has been in operation (all addresses)
Foreign-owned*	Establishment is (>51 per cent) foreign-owned
US-owned*	Whether HQ is in the USA
Single plant*	Whether a single-plant enterprise
HQ plant*	Whether plant is the HQ plant of the enterprise
UK MNE*	Whether enterprise is UK-owned and operates plants in other countries
Union density	Per cent of employees who are members of a trade union (or staff association) whether recognized or not
Part-time	Per cent of workforce who are part-time
Female	Per cent of workforce who are female
Manual	Per cent of workforce who are manual workers
Temporary	Per cent of workforce who are temporary/fixed-term workers
Ethnic	Per cent of workforce who are from ethnic minorities
HRM practices and procedures	
Grievances policy*	Formal procedure for dealing with individual grievances at plant
EO/managing diversity policy*	Formal written policy on EO/managing diversity
Job security*	Guaranteed job security/no compulsory redundancies for any group

Table 13.A1 (continued)

Variables	Definition
Induction programmes*	Standard induction for new employees in largest occupation group
Personality tests*	Conduct personality or attitude tests when filling vacancies
Performance tests*	Conduct performance or competency tests when filling vacancies
Worker appraisal*	>50 per cent non-managerial workers have performance formally appraised
Investor-in-People*	Workplace accredited as Investor-in-People (IiP)
Multi-tasked*	>50 per cent non-managerial workers are multi-tasked
Discretion over work*	Largest occupation group has a lot of discretion over how they work
Designated teams*	>50 per cent of largest occupation group in formally designated teams
Quality circles*	Groups to solve specific problems or aspects of performance/quality
Performance pay*	>50 per cent non-managerial workers receive performance-related pay
Profit pay*	>50 per cent non-managerial workers receive profit-related pay
Internal fit	Number of HRM practices used from the above list of 14
External fit*	Workplace targets quality of product or service

Consultation and Communication	
Used JCCs*	Any committees of managers/employees primarily concerned with consultation rather than negotiation
Brief workforce*	Any system of briefings for any section of workforce
Surveys*	Whether formal survey of employees' views in last 5 years
Information about investment plans*	Regularly supply employees with information on internal investment plans
Information about financial position*	Regularly supply employees with information on financial position of establishment
Meetings*	Regular meetings of entire workforce present
Management chain*	Systematic use of management chain/cascading of information

Table 13.A1   (continued)

Variables	Definition
Suggestion schemes*	Use suggestion schemes
Newsletters*	Regular newsletters distributed to all employees
Emails*	Use emails
No consultation*	None of last 9 schemes used

Innovation and Workplace Change

Strategic plan*	Workplace is covered by a formal strategic plan which sets out objectives and how they will be achieved
Exports*	Market for main product/service is national or international
Product innovation*	Introduction of technologically new or significantly improved product or service in last 2 years
Process innovation*	Introduction or upgrading of other types of new technology in last 2 years
Quality standards*	Workplace has attained either of the quality standards BS5750 or ISO9000
No change last 2 years*	None of 8 following have been introduced/changed in last 2 years: performance pay; computers (or upgrades); other new technology; working time arrangements; organization of work; work techniques; involvement of employees; new products or services

Economic performances

Financial performance and Labour productivity and Quality of product/service	Compared to other establishments in the industry, did management rate the plant: 'a lot better than average' (coded 2); 'better than average' (coded 1); 'average' (coded 0); 'below average' (coded -1); 'a lot below average' (coded -2)

Note: * Dichotomous variable coded 1 if true.

14 Human resource management in small and medium-sized enterprises in Jiangsu, China

Li Xue Cunningham and Chris Rowley

Introduction

The purpose of this chapter is to explore the extent to which human resource management (HRM) practices are applied in small and medium-sized enterprises (SMEs) in China. There are several reasons for doing this beyond the importance of SMEs in the Chinese economy. SMEs have become vital as a source of employment and as contributors to the economy and structural reform. In 2002 for instance the number of registered SMEs in China was over 10 million (99 per cent of total enterprises) with their gross industrial output value, sales income, taxes and profits, and gross export volume representing around 60 per cent, 57 per cent, 40 per cent and 60 per cent respectively of the national totals (*People's Daily*, 30 July 2002). SMEs also provided around 75 per cent of job opportunities for cities and towns, thus absorbing job seekers (*People's Daily*, 30 July 2002). While helping to expand the scale of the market economy SMEs also contributed to the creation of a socialist market economic system as a whole. Most management systems in China, as an example, first began in SMEs and then became widespread (Fan, 2003).

While the numbers of SMEs have increased, this has been in spite of a range of obstacles. Following China's World Trade Organization (WTO) accession SMEs have faced intense market competition and in China's South Eastern and coastal provinces, where many multinational companies (MNCs) are located, the pressures are considerably higher (Luo, 1999). SME survival is a key issue, and theoretical and empirical studies conclude that HRM can have an impact (Boxall and Purcell, 2003; Wright and Barney, 1998).

Although evidence showing a correlation between HRM and performance is promising (for example, Boxall and Purcell, 2003; Guest, 1987; Storey, 2004), the transferability of HRM has been questioned by many HRM scholars and researchers. For example Guest (1990) claims that the values underlying HRM represent the 'American dream', while Brewster (1993) has argued that the concept of HRM defined by some American commentators is inadequate in the European situation. Rowley and Benson (2004) have also questioned the extent to which HRM applies in Asian firms.

The degree of adoption of HRM is also a matter of some debate. On the one hand many international researchers are only now beginning to appreciate that the Asian bloc is far from homogeneous. They argue that differences in HRM systems reflect different national histories and cultures (Rowley, 1997; Rowley and Bae, 2002; Zhu and Warner, 2003). On the other hand Western management theories do have an effect in China (Rowley and Lewis, 1996). The high level of foreign direct investment (FDI) and the Chinese modernization programme show the possibility that employment systems may become more 'Westernized' (Cooke, 2005).

While many pertinent issues relating to the transfer and adoption of HRM in China have been considered by international scholars, SMEs have not yet been the focus of attention. For example in discussions on the differences between traditional Chinese personnel management (PM) systems (see 'Three Old Irons' in Ding and Warner, 2001) and Western HRM (see Child, 1994; Ding et al., 2000; 2002; Warner, 1997; Zhao, 1994; Zhu and Warner, 2003) the focus has primarily been on large-sized enterprises (1000 plus employees) and particularly joint ventures (JV) and state-owned enterprises (SOE).

With few studies of SMEs in China (see Cooke, 2002; 2005; Zheng, 1999) the nature of HRM in them needs further investigation. In this chapter the following questions are explored. To what extent do SMEs in China use people management practices? Can this be seen as 'traditional' PM or 'newer' HRM? What is the role of HR/personnel managers in the strategy-making process? What methods are adopted by SMEs in relation to four major HRM practices, namely recruitment, training, rewards and employee involvement? What are the key characteristics of labour-management relations? To what extent do external bodies such as the trade unions have influence over the employment issues?

Research methodology

A survey approach combined with in-depth, semi-structured interviews is used to explore these questions. Underpinning this approach is an attempt to gather as much information as possible so that a realistic and holistic perspective on HRM development in SMEs in China can be developed.

As there is no generally agreed definition of what constitutes an SME, an upper limit of 500 employees is applied in the study. This accords with other definitions of SMEs and a number of HRM studies (for example, Deshpande and Golhar, 1994; 1997; Hayton, 2003; Kinnie et al., 1999; Storey, 2004). While many researchers argue that size may be a key factor explaining HRM practices in SMEs, by itself it is not sufficient to make generalizations for the sector as a whole, since other factors influence practices, including product market, industry, technology, labour markets, sector, family culture, and ownership (for example Ram, 1991; Wilkinson, 1999).

In this chapter we focus on urban SMEs of four major ownership types: private enterprises (PEs), collective-owned enterprises (COEs), SOEs, and foreign-invested enterprises (FIEs). These firms operate in a variety of industries.

The research was conducted in Jiangsu, a province located in the middle of China's East coast and on the lower reaches of the Yangtze River. With a total area of 102 600 square kilometres (1.07 per cent of China), and a population of 74.75 million in 2005 (5.75 per cent of China), Jiangsu plays an important role in the nation's economy. In 2005, for instance, its GDP ranked third in the country (producing 10 per cent of the nation's total) after Guangdong and Shandong; it was also the third largest consumer market in the country as its retail sales of consumer goods reached RMB570 billion (US$69.5 billion at an exchange rate of 8.2), accounting for 8.5 per cent of China's total; it also ranked top in attracting FDI (utilized amount) among all the provinces and municipalities (21.9 per cent of China's total). Furthermore the share of industrial output of the seven pillar industries, which are electronics, telecommunications, chemicals, textiles, machinery, equipment and metallurgy in the province was 60.9 per cent of the nation's total in 2005 (*Jiangsu Statistical Yearbook*, 2006; *China Statistical Yearbook*, 2006).

Jiangsu was chosen due to its significant role in China's economy and because the highly competitive market puts considerable pressures on SMEs to become sustainable. Jiangsu's industries have become externally oriented and exports increased by 40.6 per cent to US$123 billion while imports grew by 25.9 per cent to US$105 billion in 2005 (*Jiangsu Statistical Yearbook*, 2006). Wholly foreign-owned companies have overtaken joint ventures as the dominant mode of FDI in Jiangsu in 2005 (79 per cent compared to 19 per cent). Foreign investments are mainly engaged in the manufacturing sector, as utilized foreign investment in this sector amounted to US$10.9 billion, accounting for 82.9 per cent of the provincial total in 2005 (*Jiangsu Statistical Yearbook*, 2006). Jiangsu's services sector has become another site for foreign investment after China's WTO accession and market liberalization. In 2005 FDI in the service sector amounted to nearly US$1.9 billion, accounted for 14.1 per cent of the total, growing from 6.5 per cent in 2001 (*Jiangsu Statistical Yearbook*, 2006). The statistical evidence clearly shows that Jiangsu's business environment is heavily influenced by FDI and foreign-owned companies. This can lead to the introduction of Western management concepts and practices as well as increased competition at a local level. In order to compete successfully local firms tend to learn and/or copy 'best practices' (Cooke, 2005) and as Ding and Warner (2001) conclude, people-management systems in firms located in the key urban areas may be said to 'converge' with international HRM practices. In this study we assume that the influence of the market would increase the likelihood of firms adopting HRM practices.

Most importantly, the reason for choosing Jiangsu was that it is known for the number of SMEs (see Byrd and Zhu, 1989) and its strong private sector. Production by the private sector accounted for around 93.5 per cent of the province's total industrial output in 2005 (*Jiangsu Statistical Yearbook*, 2006). Further, the famous economic development model – the Southern Jiangsu model (SU-NAN Model), which included the rules, regulations and policies pertaining to SMEs in Jiangsu – has been widely applied in other Southern provinces in China.

Jiangsu province is therefore quite an appropriate location for assessing the transfer and adoption of HRM in SMEs in China.

To undertake the study a questionnaire with open- and close-ended questions was used to assess the extent to which HRM was applied in the organization. The questionnaire was translated into Chinese and then translated back into English to ensure the accuracy of the original translation (Brislin and Sinaiko, 1973). Previous organizational studies in cross-national settings, including China, have demonstrated the validity of this procedure (see Tan and Litschert, 1994; Zhu and Dowling, 2002; Zhu et al., 2005). The questionnaire and administrative procedures were also pilot-tested with an effective sample size of $N = 10$ (interviewees) with four SMEs in July 2004, and as a result some translations were adjusted.

It is widely acknowledged that personal contact is very important for doing research in China (Glover and Siu, 2000; Schlevogt, 2001; Wright et al., 2002; Zheng, 1999). Often owner–managers are reluctant to participate, seeing their participation as time consuming, politically unwise, or the study being of no interest to them. Hence, the questionnaire was distributed via personal networks to personnel or HR managers or officers. These were then collected in person to seek higher response rates and to ensure that complete information was provided.

Some 168 questionnaires were sent out between February and May 2005 and 142 were returned by June 2005 (83 per cent response rate). Returns with incomplete information were omitted, leaving a sample of 114. Thirteen companies granted us further access, and in early 2006 some 43 semi-structured in-depth interviews were conducted across these firms with owners, senior managers, line managers, HR managers, trade union representatives and employees in order to help verify the survey findings and explore HRM issues in more detail. In Table 14.1 the details of the 13 companies which participated in the qualitative component of this study are outlined.

Four major categories of HRM practices are often examined as giving a good coverage of the main areas of HRM, namely employee resourcing,

Table 14.1   Interview sample details

Firm	Ownership	No. employees	Industry	Interviewees
C1	PE	<500	Construction	VP, HR Director, Dep. Head (Law Dept.) Employee
C2	PE	<300	Manufacturing	GM (Owner), HR manager, Line manager, Employee
C3	PE	<200	Manufacturing	GM (Owner), HR manager, Line manager, Employee
C4	PE	<200	Services	GM (Owner), HR manager, Dept. manager, Employee
C5	SOE	<500	Services	GM, HR manager, Assistant manager, Employee
C6	PE	<300	Manufacturing	GM (Owner), HR manager, Shop manager, Employee
C7	SOE (77%)	181	Services	CEO, HR manager, Director, Employee
C8	SOE (60%)	202	Manufacturing	Acting Deputy Plant Manager
C9	JVE (HK 75%)	200	Manufacturing	HR manager, Finance manager, Employee
C10	COE	300	Manufacturing	GM (relocated), HR manager, Employee
C11	SOE (55%)	60	Manufacturing	Finance manager
C12	FIE (US 17.8%)	300	Financial	GM, HR manager, Line manager, Employee
C13	JVE (HK)	128	Utilities	GM, HR manager, Line manager

development, rewards and relations (Rowley, 2003). For example in a review of 104 empirical research articles published in pre-eminent international refereed journals between 1994 and 2003, Boselie et al. (2005) found that training and development, contingent pay and reward schemes, performance management (including appraisal), and careful recruitment and selection were top HRM practices which might 'reflect the main objectives of most conceptualizations of a strategic HRM program' (Boselie et al., 2005: p. 73). However, in the SME context communication, direct participation, decision-making, and labour–management relations can have a direct impact on the adoption of HRM practices (Wilkinson, 1999). In this chapter we focus on these data and not those relating to contextual factors, such as enterprise characteristics, institutional impacts, and cultural influences.

Findings

Sample characteristics
All firms employed less than 500 people while nearly 30 per cent had less than 300 employees, 15.8 per cent between 50–100 employees, 15.8 per cent between 100–150 employees, 21.9 per cent between 150–300 employees and 16.7 per cent between 300–500 employees.

Most companies were set up after 1992 (mean firm age = 13.35 years). On average, firms with 151–300 employees were the oldest, with the majority being more than 18 years old. In addition, services firms dominated the sample (55 per cent) regardless of firm size. In contrast to a small portion of SOEs (14 per cent, 16 companies), other companies were PEs (39.5 per cent, 45 companies), FIEs (25.4 per cent, 29 companies), and Employee Shareholding Cooperatives (ESHs) (17.5 per cent, 20 companies). Only 2.6 per cent (three companies) remained in collective ownership. The statistics also show that the average age of employees was about 31 years old. More than 70 per cent of the employees had long-term labour contracts (over one year) with their company.

In Table 14.2 demographic information about the 43 interviewees in the 13 companies who granted further access is provided. In order to give a balanced point of view on HRM in SMEs, it shows that information was drawn from different levels of the organization, which included senior managers, other department/line managers, HR managers/officers, and employees. The informants ranged in age from 23 to 56 years and had served an average of 7.29 years with their firm.

The role of the HRM function
Rowley (2003) argues that the major difference between HRM and traditional personnel management (PM) seems to be about integration, strategy and implementation. A distinction between traditional PM and HRM is that HRM is a key part of senior management decision-making. In

Table 14.2   Interviewee demographics

Job title	No. interviews	Female	Male	Ave. age	Age range
General manager	7	1	6	49	38–65
Owner–manager	4	1	3	43	38–53
HR Manager/Officer	11	6	5	36	25–51
Dept./Line Manager	11	6	5	42	31–56
Employee	10	8	2	32	23–45
Total	43	22	21	40	

looking at strategic qualities and managerial roles of HRM, we found that the personnel/HR department role was more operational than strategic. For example, although 61.4 per cent of firms had a personnel or HR department, their top three major functions were recruitment (78.9 per cent), training and development (65.8 per cent) and labour relations (64 per cent). Collective bargaining, career planning and top management involvement were the least common functions (10.5 per cent, 22.8 per cent and 27.2 per cent respectively).

In the interviews we found a similar situation. Most companies did not have a separate HR department. Responsibility for HRM was normally found in financial, administrative or logistical departments, perhaps because the personnel tasks were simple and basic. For example, personnel managers mostly dealt with payroll, filing documents, recording clock-ins and paying social benefits. The major responsibilities of personnel managers were to support other business departments by managing organizational issues and soothing relations among employers, managers and employees. Further, 'personnel' ('renshi guanli') was still used as a word to describe how people were managed, yet the slang of HRM ('renli ziyuan guanli') was often mentioned during the interviews. This suggests that traditional Chinese PM seems to prevail in these firms.

While traditional Chinese PM (more details see Warner, 1995) seems persistent, interview evidence suggested the importance of HR had been acknowledged. For example, in C1, C2 and C9 a new HR department had been established, and in C3, C4 and C12 qualified HR staff had been hired. Top managers were more sensitive to the importance of HR issues than in the past. A majority of owners and managers recognized HR might help to improve commitment, business performance and competitive advantage in the long term, particularly those in C2, C3 and C6.

Nevertheless, conflicts and problems emerged in practice. For example, one HR manager from C3 complained that: 'The knowledge that I learned from the book is so different from the real world. I have received a number of negative feedbacks from employees because of rules and regulations I am trying to apply within the company.' There were not only difficulties in practising effective HRM but also inconsistency with respect to understanding the role of HRM among top management, HRM itself, line managers and employees. For instance, while the CEO and the personnel manager in C7 considered HRM as a strategic player in their firm, conversely a female company worker stated that:

> There is no HRM in our company at all. The personnel person is only taking care of social welfare, such as paying for our insurance. Even the payroll, which is a common role for traditional PM in China, is handled by the finance department. The personnel person only fills in the Excel form for database purposes.

Current HRM practices

In terms of employee resourcing the survey found that inheritance of jobs ('dingti') applied in just 2.6 per cent of firms, and government allocation had almost ceased, with it applying to just 7.9 per cent of firms. This is due to the PM reforms, especially the 'san gaige' reforms in 1992 (see Warner, 1995). Internal job bidding (50.9 per cent) and referral (50 per cent) were the most popular recruitment methods. Employee recommendations, advertising and agencies were also frequently used. Only 25.4 per cent of firms adopted promotion as a recruitment strategy. Educational institutions were used as a channel for looking for the right candidates, but this was not crucial.

While the findings showed a more diverse labour resource provided by the market in contrast to the one in the pre-reform period (see Warner, 1995), the interviews revealed that key employees such as senior managers and skilled workers were recruited through personal recommendations or internal promotion. Most senior managers admitted that applicants who were introduced through personal connections were more reliable and trustworthy, better quality and had stronger loyalty to the firm. Personal relations seem to be essential in employee resourcing in SMEs, especially in helping to build trust in business relations. In addition, the difficulty in finding highly qualified employees in the labour market was highlighted during the interviews. It is interesting to note that the labour market was mainly used when hiring manual workers or cheaper labour (especially in C2, C6, C9), whereas in seven companies (C1, C4, C6, C10, C11, C12, C13) advertising was said to be the most useful method for general recruitment.

During the selection process the survey found interviews to be the most popular method to select candidates, whereas graphology, psychometric testing and assessment centres were the least used methods. Similarly, the interviewees reported that application forms and probationary periods were often used before making the final decision.

Employee development

The survey showed that most firms made efforts to improve training. For example 83.3 per cent offered training programmes, although the interviews revealed that training was still at its initial stage and the extent limited and piecemeal. For instance, few interviewees claimed that the company had a training plan, budget or performance-related assessment. Training needs were evaluated informally, mainly based on personal perceptions and expectations. Training was short and often 'on-the-job'. Training content was commonly firm-specific, covering company policies and procedures, legal regulations, new product introductions and some basic techniques in the workplace. Most interviewees claimed that assessment would be conducted after training but there was no following check-up and the assessment was not linked to employee performance. Furthermore, a number of barriers to informal, on-the-job training were reported during the interviews, such as time constraints and lack of internal trainers. The HR manager at C13 said:

> I feel drained by the training, since the programmes (from HQ) are always rigid and mandatory without reference to the production plan. Therefore, it is difficult for employees and managers to focus on training while they are busy with production at the same time. Consequently, the training is ineffective even if we have spent lots of time attending all different types.

Bjorkman and Lu (1999) argue that attitudes towards technical training were gradually changing in Chinese JVs. Although only two participating companies were Joint-Venture Enterprises (JVEs), our survey findings verify such arguments by showing that the main purpose of training was to improve employees' technical job ability (82.5 per cent of the companies). At the same time, however, the interviewees disclosed that the approach to staff morale education was weakened. Moreover, employees' learning attitudes were undermined, especially in some traditional, less competitive, SOEs (such as C5).

Employee rewards
In terms of pay rewards the survey found merit pay was the most common method (78.1 per cent), whereas stock options were least used and rare, operating in just 3.5 per cent of firms. Payment by results, annual bonuses and commissions were used at various levels based on different circumstances. Interviews found all companies were practising merit pay to some extent, and this was directly linked with various economic objectives, such as profits, sales, number of new clients, number of complaints or the completion of projects. As such the findings indicate widespread use of performance-related pay schemes.

In interviews we found that, when deciding the initial pay levels among employees, ten firms (C1, C3, C5, C7, C8, C9, C10, C11, C12 and C13) gave weight to the type of job held (positional wage) and in four (C1, C7, C11 and C12) to the length of time worked (seniority wage). All 13 companies emphasized responsibilities and performance at individual and/or group level in the design of pay systems. Workplace attitudes and behaviour, such as respect for rules and discipline, orientation of quality and competence and loyalty to the firm, were also underlined as part of reward criteria in seven companies (C3, C4, C5, C6, C9, C12 and C13). Economic stimulation (such as monetary rewards), employee future development (promotion), and 'spirit inspiration' or honour were the major incentive

Table 14.3   Reward strategies

Firm	Pay and benefits
C1	Pay rise, Travel, Housing allowance, Training
C2	Pay rise
C3	Pay rise, Travel
C4	Pay rise, Bonus, Share of stock
C5	Money award
C6	Pay rise, Money award
C7	Profit sharing, Travel, Car allowance, Holiday
C8	Pay rise
C9	Pay rise
C10	Share of stock
C11	Bonus
C12	Money award
C13	Money award

mechanisms deployed in the reward system by the interviewed companies. Indeed, monetary rewards (such as pay rise, bonus and monetary award) were amongst the most important retention devices in use (see Table 14.3).

While a performance-oriented reward system has gradually emerged, employee benefits are minimal. For example, although the survey showed that social insurance (80.7 per cent) and medical insurance (79.8 per cent) were major components among 14 benefits applied, the interviews confirmed that none actually provided a full range of social welfare (including health, pension, unemployment and minimum living standard insurance) for employees except in state-involved companies (such as state-holding, SOE). A manager from a legal department in C1 said: 'There is no need for the company to pay the pensions of employees as long as nobody makes complaints.' The interviews illustrated that the companies tried to reduce the costs of employee benefits to the bare minimum by only meeting basic legislative requirements.

Besides overlooking legislative requirements even when they were applicable, the survey found that few companies offered free schooling or nursery provisions (19 per cent and 26 per cent respectively). There was very little sponsorship of sporting activities (21 per cent), libraries (7 per cent) or medical clinics (7.9 per cent). Interviewees reported that companies offering canteens and transport to the workplace did so largely because they were located away from the city centre where public transport did not operate. Evidence therefore shows that employers provide few benefits that could be expected to operate in Chinese firms.

In several firms problems had arisen in the implementation of the reward system. Some companies found the reward system did not motivate employees and conversely led to resistance or resentment, high key employee turnover and anxieties between the individual/team and employer. Some also questioned the reliability of reward criteria, especially ones relating to non-quantified measures. In one firm (C1) a deputy manager from the legal department revealed the conflicts between pay confidentiality and the regulations based on the 1995 Labor Law, saying:

> According to the labor law, the employment contract should include the length of the contract, work content, health and safety protection and working conditions, remuneration, discipline, conditions for termination of contract, and liability for violating the employment contract. However, the boss insists on vagueness with regard to the pay package. Therefore, the contract is left as incomplete. This incompleteness creates a number of problems at a later stage, especially in employee dismissal. Additionally, the effect of the reward system becomes minor since neither managers nor employees know the exact criteria for the reward.

Employee relations
In the case of involvement and participation, the survey showed 7 per cent of respondents felt their company had problems with sharing information among departments. In addition 78.9 per cent rated the exchange of information between supervisors and subordinates as 3 (to some extent) or above. However, employee involvement in the decision-making process within the company was only rated 5 (to a great extent) in 5.3 per cent. Less than 17 per cent rated the extent to which employees were informed of important business and operational issues at 5 (to a great extent). Therefore, the survey findings seem to imply that communication was well conceived at operational levels, such as among departments, employees and managers, but that participation of employees was limited or confined to the strategic level.

While validating the lack of involvement at strategic level, the interviewees provide a more complex and pessimistic picture of employee engagement at the operational level (see Table 14.4). For example, ten of the 13 senior managers acknowledged that there was little interaction either among different departments or between employees and managers, although information was exchanged regularly and freely among senior managerial levels. Moreover, the information passed to middle managers and employees was selective and mostly based on business needs (C6 and C7). For instance, the owner manager of C6 admitted that middle managers only obtained information related to their departmental operations while employees were only informed when the contents were performance-related

Table 14.4   Employee involvement

Company code	Organization structure	Employee involvement		
		Dept vs. dept	Dept vs. individuals	Channels
C1	Top-down	✘	−	Meetings
C2	Top-down	✘	−	Face-to-face interview, Individual summary
C3	Top-down	✓	+	Team briefings and meetings, Individual summary
C4	Top-down	✓	+	Text message, Team briefings and meetings
C5	Top-down	✘	−	Suggestion box, Meetings
C6	Top-down	✘	+	Weekly meetings, Regular team briefings
C7	Top-down	✘	+	Team briefings and meetings, Suggestion box, Newspaper, Intranet, Weekly report, Summaries
C8	Top-down	✓	−	Meeting
C9	Top-down	✘	−	Technical discussion
C10	Top-down	✘	−	Report
C11	Top-down	✓	+	Team briefings and meetings, Feedback, Notice board
C12	Top-down	✘	−	Weekly meetings, Team briefings, Intranet, Company magazine
C13	Top-down	✘	−	Meeting, Intranet

Notes: Dept vs. Dept: ✘ = not applicable; ✓ = applicable: Dept vs. Individual: − = one-way communication; + = two-way communication.

and/or motivation-oriented. Furthermore, one-way, downward communication was the most common form of direct communication in most companies, with channels limited to regular meetings, summaries and performance reports. Intranet and suggestion schemes were used by some companies but the effects were reported to be insignificant.

In spite of a lower level of employee involvement and a hierarchical organizational structure among the companies, most interviewees (32) expressed satisfaction with the management–employee relationship. Employee relations in most companies were claimed to be good, harmonious and cooperative. The working environment was pleasant and friendly. The growth of direct communication with the workforce, such as team briefings and meetings between senior managers and the workforce, was the clearest trend (see Table 14.4). Companies could be seen as 'carers' who were looking after employees not only at work but also outside. For example, some employees described their relationship with their owner–managers as a 'brotherhood' or 'friendship'. A line manager from C3 illustrated this, saying: 'Our boss knows every employee's family background and personal interests. He also remembers every new employee's name. It is not a big deal but workers are touched.'

Although 'harmonious' was not an uncommon way employee relations were described by interviewees, the evidence suggests that power in the workplace was unbalanced and tilted towards employers. To prevent problems during dismissals, for instance, some companies took action well beforehand while others used economic punishment to force workers to leave by themselves without further complaints or negotiation. Overall, as an HR manager from C3 concluded:

> The employees are still in a weak position in the labor–management relations. To employees, this is a catch 22 situation. None of the companies would like to keep a 'trouble' employee. In the end, it is the employee who will lose the job no matter whether he/she wins the case or not.

The picture of trade union (TU) representation was not promising. Firms favoured direct communication methods without union recognition and in four small PEs (C2, C3, C4 and C6) there was not a TU. It seems that ownership and company size were two determinants of TU representation while some interviewees said that there was no legal obligation on owner–managers to have a union in the company.

Where unions existed (nine of the 13 companies, C1, C5, C7, C8, C9, C10, C11, C12 and C13) their influence was said to be trivial, with them existing in name only. TUs played a traditional role organizing entertainment or social activities, taking care of workers' welfare and coordinating relations between management and workers. Most interviewees claimed that the role of the TU was a 'carer' for employees or to be a 'conveyor belt' between the company and workers. Furthermore, most of the leaders of a TU were delegated by the company. It is interesting that interviewees noted that most TU chairs were older, had worked with the company for a long time and had obtained a positive reputation among workers. Nevertheless, the chair had no negotiating power and an interviewee at C12 indicated the dilemma their TU chair faced:

On one hand, he is the 'tongue' of workers. His main task is to represent the workers' interest. On the other hand, he is an employee, who is the same as the rest of us. He needs to sign a labor contract with the company as well. Therefore, the chair is always under pressure that his contract may be terminated if he doesn't act on the owner's behalf.

Even where Workers' Congresses remained (C5, C7, C10 and C11), TU influence had declined. There were few issues that could be solved or implemented after the annual meeting, as one manager put it:

As the master of the enterprise, workers' representatives are able to raise issues of concern freely in the annual meeting. However, these concerns, if they are still mentioned after the meeting, will be treated as harmful rumors which obstruct effective production and cause disorder within the company. Therefore, in fact, major issues are still in the control of top management hands.

Discussion

In this chapter we have looked at HRM in SMEs at two levels. The managerial role of HRM in the organization was analysed while four key HRM practices were also discussed and examined. Several key themes relating to HRM development in SMEs were highlighted. Little evidence was found of a key role played by the personnel manager or HR department in senior management decision-making.

In terms of the four HRM practices we found the following. For employee resourcing, the selection of key employees still largely remained internal. For employee development, opportunities for training were very limited. Training programmes tended to be narrow, generally task-related and seen as a necessary choice rather than the key to competitive success. Employee reward systems were becoming more sophisticated, yet they had little impact in motivating the workforce and attracting key employees. Employee relations were seemingly harmonious but there was no real involvement or participation in managerial decision-making processes.

Despite these results the importance of HRM was recognized by top management. Most companies provide training to their employees and there was an emphasis on technical training. Also, there was an attempt to implement a performance-related reward strategy in order to attract and motivate highly qualified employees. The extent to which HRM practices were adopted was complicated and fragmented rather than simple and straightforward.

The findings of the study contribute to understanding not only the development of SMEs but also the debates of possible convergence or continuation of divergence of HRM and the relationship between human capital and organizational performance. The study sheds some light on the applicability and transferability of Western management concepts and techniques to China, and suggests that PM practices which are embedded with traditional Chinese characteristics (such as respect for seniority, harmony, emphasis on personal relations), may need to be kept alongside elements of Western management practices.

Most early studies of SMEs were focused on advanced market economies and those in other economies remain by and large an unexplored and important research agenda (Cooke, 2005). However, some limitations of this study do need to be noted; in particular the focus was only on urban SMEs with less than 500 employees in Jiangsu province, Eastern China. No inference can necessarily be made to SMEs from rural and/or other regions in China. While we employed a multi-method approach, the survey findings were limited by future expectations, as the actual level of rating was difficult to interpret. For instance, one respondent argued that it was difficult to evaluate the effectiveness of training since the standards of the companies were different. Therefore a low rating to a particular item might reflect the fact that the firm did not pursue the issue or it might reflect the fact that the firm was already very good in the area under question and so no longer thought the issue critical. In addition, during analysis of interviews data bias could be introduced. Thus a more comprehensive analysis of HRM in SMEs in China would require involvement of enterprises from different regions and perspectives while a systematic comparative study across regions, sectors and countries could provide interesting information about convergence of HRM practices in SMEs.

Conclusion
SMEs are recognized as important to economic development in many economies, and China is no exception. Central Chinese government officials claim that SMEs are in a better position to adapt to the WTO environment since they lack the social, managerial and financial 'baggage' of most large SOEs. Officials have also said that SMEs can further integrate themselves into MNC supply chains so they can one day become 'big giants' in their own right (see www.usembassy-china.org.cn/econ/smes 2002).

As competition in the market environment increases, our research demonstrates that a change of people management is taking place in SMEs in China. Conversion from a traditional Chinese PM towards Western HRM practices is in process but the progress is slow. The transition appears at different levels within the organization (such as managerial and employee) and the degrees are various among different practices (for example employee resourcing, development, rewards and relations). In the meantime, the evidence illustrates that the old mindset and behaviour still has a strong impact on people's behaviour and, therefore, influences the extent of the adoption of HR practices in companies. Those cultural factors may hinder the movement towards 'Westernized' HRM practices. In other words, HRM will play an important role in helping SMEs to become more efficient. However, there are strong cultural factors which limit the adoption of many features of HRM in SMEs in China. Therefore, the research findings suggest that a convergence with Western HRM practices, along with 'Chinese characters', will be a trend in the development of HRM in SMEs in China.

References

Bjorkman, I. and Y. Lu (1999), 'The management of human resources in Chinese–Western joint ventures', *Journal of World Business*, **34**(4), 306–24.

Boselie, P., G. Dietz and C. Boon (2005), 'Commonalities and contradictions in HRM and performance research', *Human Resource Management Journal*, **15**(3), 67–94.

Boxall, P. and J. Purcell (2003), *Strategy and Human Resource Management*, Basingstoke, UK: Palgrave Macmillan.

Brewster, C. (1993), 'European human resource management: Reflection of, or challenge to the American concept?' in P. Kirkbride (ed.), *Human Resource Management in the New Europe of the 1990s*, London: Routledge, pp. 56–89.

Brislin, R.W. and H.W. Sinaiko (1973), 'Evaluating language translations: Experiments on three assessment methods', *Journal of Applied Psychology*, **57**(3), 328–34.

Byrd, W.A. and N. Zhu (1989), 'Market interactions and industrial structure', in W.A. Byrd and Q. Lin (eds), *China's Rural Industry: Structure, Development, and Reform*, New York: Oxford University Press, pp. 85–111.

Child, J. (1994), *Chinese Management during the Age of Reform*, Cambridge: Cambridge University Press.

China Statistical Yearbook (various), Beijing: China Statistic Press, National Bureau of Statistics, available from http://www.stats.gov.cn.

Cooke, F.L. (2002), 'Ownership change and reshaping of employee relations in China: A study of two manufacturing companies', *Journal of Industrial Relations*, **44**(1), 19–40.

Cooke, F.L. (2005), *HRM, Work and Employment in China*, London and New York: Routledge.

Deshpande, S.P. and D.Y. Golhar (1994), 'HRM practices in large and small manufacturing firms: A comparative study', *Journal of Small Business Management*, **32**(2), 49–56.

Deshpande, S.P. and D.Y. Golhar (1997), 'HRM practices of large and small Canadian manufacturing firms', *Journal of Small Business Management*, **35**(3), 30–38.

Ding, Z.D. and M. Warner (2001), 'China's labour-management system reforms: Breaking the "Three Old Irons" (1978–1999)', *Asia Pacific Journal of Management*, **18**, 315–34.

Ding, D.Z., K. Goodall and M. Warner (2000), 'The end of the iron rice bowl: Whither Chinese HRM?', *International Journal of Human Resource Management*, **11**(2), 217–36.

Ding, D.Z., K. Goodall and M. Warner (2002), 'The impact of economic reform on the role of trade unions in Chinese enterprises', *International Journal of Human Resource Management*, **13**(3), 431–49.

Fan, C. (2003), 'Government support for small and medium-sized enterprises in China', *Problems of Economic Transition*, **45**(11), 51–8.

Glover, L. and N. Siu (2000), 'The human resource barriers to managing quality in China', *International Journal of Human Resource Management*, **11**(5), 867–82.

Guest, D. (1987), 'Human resource management and industrial relations', *Journals of Management Studies*, **24**(5), 503–21.

Guest, D.E. (1990), 'Human resource management and the American dream', *Journal of Management Studies*, **27**(4), 378–97.

Hayton, J.C. (2003), 'Strategic human capital management in SMEs: An empirical study of entrepreneurial performance', *Human Resource Management*, **42**(4), 375–91.

Jiangsu Statistical Yearbook (various), Beijing: China Statistic Press, National Bureau of Statistics.

Kinnie, N., J. Purcell, S. Hutchinson, M. Terry, M. Collinson and H. Scarbrough (1999), 'Employment relations in SMEs – market-driven or customer-shaped', *Employee Relations*, **21**(3), 218–35.

Luo, Y. (1999), 'Environment–strategy–performance relations in small businesses in China: A case of township and village enterprises in southern China', *Journal of Small Business Management*, **37**(1), 37–50.

People's Daily (30 July 2002), 'Legally promote sound development of small and mid-sized enterprises', Available http://www.peopledaily.com.cn.

Ram, M. (1991), 'Control and autonomy in SFs: The case of the West Midlands clothing industry', *Work, Employment and Society*, **14**, 610–19.

Rowley, C. (1997), 'Reassessing HRM's convergence', *Asia Pacific Business Review*, **3**(4), 197–210.

Rowley, C. (2003), *The Management of People: HRM in Context*, Spiro Press: USA.

Rowley, C. and J. Bae (2002), 'Globalisation and transformation of human resource management in South Korea', *International Journal of Human Resource Management*, **13**(3), 522–49.

Rowley, C. and J. Benson (2004), *The Management of Human Resources in the Asia Pacific Region: Convergence Reconsidered*, London: Cass.

Rowley, C. and M. Lewis (1996), *Greater China – Political Economy, Inward Investment and Business Culture*, London: Frank Cass and Co.

Schlevogt, K. (2001), 'The distinctive structure of Chinese private enterprises: State versus private sector', *Asia Pacific Business Review*, **7**(3), 1–33.

Storey, D.J. (2004), 'Exploring the link, among small firms, between management training and firm performance: A comparison between the UK and other OECD countries', *International Journal of Human Resource Management*, **15**(1), 112–30.

Tan, J.J. and R.J. Litschert (1994), 'Environment-strategy relationship and its performance implications: An empirical study of the Chinese electronics industry', *Strategy Management Journal*, **15**(1), 1–20.

Warner, M. (1995), *The Management of Human Resources in Chinese Industry*, London: Macmillan.

Warner, M. (1997), 'Management–labour relations in the new Chinese economy', *Human Resource Management Journal*, **37**(4), 30–43.

Wilkinson, A. (1999), 'Employment relations in SMEs', *Employee Relations*, **12**(3), 205–17.

Wright, P. and J. Barney (1998), 'On becoming a strategic partner: The role of human resources in gaining competitive advantage', *Human Resource Management*, **37**(1), 31–46.

Wright, P., W.F. Szeto and L.T.W. Cheng (2002), 'Guanxi and professional conduct in China: A management development perspective', *International Journal of Human Resource Management*, **13**(1), 157–82.

Zhao, S. (1994), 'Human resource management in China', *Asia Pacific Journal of Human Resources*, **32**(2), 3–12.

Zheng, C. (1999), 'The relationship between HRM and Chinese SME performance', *International Journal of Organisational Behaviour*, **4**(4), 125–37.

Zhu, C.J.H. and P.J. Dowling (2002), 'Staffing practices in transition: Some empirical evidence from China', *International Journal of Human Resource Management*, **13**(4), 569–97.

Zhu, C.J.H., B. Cooper, H.D. Cieri and P.J. Dowling (2005), 'A problematic transition to a strategic role: Human resource management in industrial enterprises in China', *International Journal of Human Resource Management*, **16**(4), 513–31.

Zhu, Y. and M. Warner (2003), 'Human resource management "with Chinese characteristics": A comparative study of the People's Republic of China and Taiwan', *Asia Pacific Business Review*, **9**(2), 21–42.

PART III

FUNCTIONAL ASPECTS
OF HRM

15 Small firms' strategic stickiness and the impact of state interventions
Robert Blackburn and David Smallbone

Introduction

In this chapter we will explore how the motivations and 'world perspectives' of small firm owner–managers, combined with their various market positions, affect the ways in which they respond to externally-imposed state interventions. Our argument is that external interventions are more often met with resistance rather than acceptance although there is some variation. The factors underlying their responses are many, including sector, resource availability and business objectives, but in the main they are inextricably linked with the motivation of the small firm owner–manager. A number of key studies have helped unpack the so-called 'real world' of business owners, drawing on psychological and sociological literature. These analyses often present them as having a strong 'internal locus of control' with risk-taking propensities and a strong need for independence (Chell, 1991). These factors combine to create what we call 'strategic stickiness' – that is a drive for stability rather than change and a reluctance of owner–managers to readily embrace externally-imposed changes. Such a strategic orientation tends to engender 'steady state' conditions in small firms, and resistance rather than radical or even step changes in the firm's mission or ways of working. This perspective provides the context for considering a variety of state interventions for small firms, but is particularly applicable in the case of state regulations. For many small firm owner–managers, state regulations represent a veil of interference and a distraction from achieving their business objectives. Thus while 'strategic stickiness' applies generally, in this chapter we investigate it in relation to health and safety regulation and employment legislation.

Conceptually we draw on the social science literature which emphasizes the importance of the small firm owner–manager and associated notions of independence, autonomy and informality. We summarize two examples of intervention to illustrate owner–manager responses and the effects on the business together with the factors behind these responses. In this context, notions of dynamism and entrepreneurship, often associated with smaller firms, disappear into thin air as they are shown to clash rather than to be commensurate with externally-imposed changes. Instead, owner–managers prefer to stick to what they know best. As a result, changes in strategy resulting from external initiatives or forces vary over time and are less so as a deliberate strategy. Whilst the general notion of 'strategic stickiness' holds, the results show some diversity across small firms. We draw the main themes together to help us understand the challenges of changing strategy and practice in smaller firms. In doing so we contribute to the growing literature emphasizing diversity of labour management, learning and training in smaller firms, while we also point to issues around methods of researching smaller firms.

Strategy in small firms and state interventions
As a backcloth to analysing the strategic behaviour of owner–managers in relation to regulatory compliance it is important to understand their motivations, world views, business objectives and *modus operandi*. This provides the lens through which external interventions are interpreted and responses made. However, it is fair to say that there is no general theory of owner–managers' responses to interventions and the relationship with strategy. Instead a variety of underlying concepts can help us to develop an understanding of observed responses.

A distinguishing feature of small firms is the use of emergent rather than planned strategy (Beaver and Prince, 2004; Mintzberg, 1995; Whittington, 1993). This may be key to understanding owner–managers' responses to regulation. Incrementalism, informality and intuition typify management in smaller firms where emergent strategy operates. This suggests responses to environmental change are likely to be based on rules of thumb and prior experiences rather than detailed, codified information and scientific management practices. Of course, decisions about 'what business are we in?' and 'how do we compete in this business?' are also driven by personal objectives, resource constraints and opportunities. As Curran highlights, the difference between strategy in small versus large organizations is that in smaller firms 'strategy is much less of a conscious process based on detailed prescriptive models or sophisticated techniques, and more of an instinctive, flexible approach to survival consistent with the owner's broad personal and business goals' (1996: p. 4513). Having to redeploy business resources in order to understand, implement and monitor regulations will distract if not irritate many owner–managers from 'doing the business' and may negatively affect the business.

In assessing the effects of regulation on strategy in small firms it is also important to appreciate the value system and world views of owner–managers. Gibb (2000) highlighted the 'culture clash' between corporate business values, beliefs and ways of seeing and doing things compared with those in smaller firms. These are shown in Table 15.1 where there essentially appears to be a disjuncture with the state and small business practices.

Table 15.1   *The business approach to entrepreneurship in the small business: the potential culture clash*

Government/Corporate (looking for)	Small business (as being)
Order	Untidy
Formal	Informal
Accountability	Trusting
Information	Personal observation
Clear demarcation	Overlapping
Planning	Intuitive
Corporate strategy	'Tactically strategic'
Control measures	'I do it my way'
Formal standards	Personally monitoring
Transparency	Ambiguous
Functional expertise	Holistic
Systems	Freely
Positional authority	Owner-managed
Formal performance appraisal	Customer/network exposed

Source: Figure 2 (p. 17) in Gibb (2000).

This also helps us to understand the likely responses of owner–managers to regulations. Interactions from seemingly external agents are unlikely to be met with enthusiasm irrespective of the 'objective' benefits or otherwise to the firm. Attitudes to government intervention tend to be particularly adversarial because they often interfere with the status quo of the running of the business.

Given the direct and personal ways of managing staff, product and service delivery, then owner–managers may perceive regulation as disturbing their ability to control what goes on and to undermine one of the key reasons why many operate smaller firms: that is, independence. This suggests that many owner–managers have a 'fortress' mentality about external interventions (Curran and Blackburn, 1994) and any fundamental shifts are undertaken only under extreme pressure.

Caution against generalization
Whilst we emphasize the notion of 'strategic stickiness' in this chapter, we also accept that generalization about strategy in small firms is problematic as there is a growing body of literature which emphasizes diversity rather than cohesion. Scase (2004) for example classifies smaller firms in relation to managerial strategies based on their skill requirements, product and market bases. He argues that managerial strategies in low-skill, manual or

craft businesses 'will be organized according to different principles compared to those prevailing in the professional services, high technology and science sectors of the economy' (Scase, 2004: p. 66).

When the above arguments of culture clash with the state and diversity within the small business population are combined, then in Table 15.2 is some typical survey evidence of the most important problems small firm

Table 15.2   Most important problem, by number of employees, excluding proprietor/partner

	0 employees (%)	1–2 employees (%)	3–4 employees (%)	5–9 employees (%)	10–19 employees (%)	20+ employees (%)
Govt. regulations and paperwork	14	18	17	18	32	25
General economic climate	17	11	9	12	10	7
Lack of skilled employees/High pay	2	5	11	8	9	18
Sector-specific demand/problems	8	7	8	10	8	7
Cashflow/Payments/ Debtors	13	8	7	7	5	8
Lack of time/ capacity	10	11	11	9	7	1
Total tax burden	5	5	12	5	7	7
Competition	6	8	8	12	3	9
No problems	9.	3	3	1	3	0
Marketing problems	9	5	3	3	1	2
Inflation/Cost of materials, supplies	0	1	1	3	3	4
Other costs (for example, premises or transport)	1	1	0	1	3	2
Exchange rates	0	1	3	2	2	3
Interest rates/Access to finance	1	1	1	1	1	1
Other (please specify)	2	14	7	7	5	6
No response	1	2	0	0	0	0
N	86	168	101	153	88	108

Source: Based on SERT/Natwest 2004 Q4.

owner–managers claim they face. Clearly government regulations and paperwork rank high. Interventions are therefore likely to be set within a context of owner–manager negativity.

Regulation appears to be an obstacle for firms of increasing size and this is confirmed elsewhere (Atkinson and Hurstfield, 2004). While the reasons are not clear they may be associated with lower levels of awareness or a lower likelihood of regulation being applicable (including possible exemptions) to the smallest firms. If there is a case for examining the effects of interventions on small firm strategy, then we do need to look at the effects of regulation. However, we also need to move beyond evidence based on perception to actually show how 'problems' affect smaller firms and their strategy.

Regulation as a stimulant for strategic change, innovation and learning?

There is a growing amount of literature on learning within smaller firms (Spicer and Sadler-Smith, 2006) although little evidence has been presented on the extent to which external interventions can stimulate change and learning. Historically, self-generated motivations to change have been difficult to detect. As Marlow (2004) has stated,

> One facet of effective strategic development is to enhance opportunities for individual and organisational learning and training. However, drawing on the extant literature, it would appear that smaller firm owners, in general, invest few resources in formally developing either themselves, their managers or employees (p. 11).

However, in assessing the effects of regulation on small firms, arguably they may act as a stimulant for change and management learning. The application of management learning and organizational learning theories to small firms is relatively new, but what evidence we do have suggests that changes in the firm's environment and the search for information to help adjust to these changing conditions can lead to process and product changes within the firm (Cope, 2003; Zhang et al., 2006). The literature shows that learning and subsequent changes in activities and performance can begin with events or 'jolts' from environmental changes, for example in terms of competition. In the management learning literature there is little explicit connection made between regulation, organizational response and management learning. However, a new regulation may be regarded as a 'shock' and as such may lead to a change in business behaviour or perhaps a search for information outside the business.

In the small business and entrepreneurship fields 'shocks' have not been studied extensively and much remains to be done. *A priori* an external 'shock' may lead to new information being sought from networks which may then lead to questioning about products and processes and subsequently the implementation of strategic changes. Certainly networking can lead to innovations, but much depends on the rationale for networking and the underlying motivations of owner–manager to network. Networking and the exchange of tacit information can lead to changes in organizational culture. For example, Pittaway et al. (2004) have shown how networking can lead to improved competitiveness, although this is contingent on a range of factors.

What does this strategic context mean for state–small business relations and the effects on the employment relationship? Evidence suggests that small firms have been reluctant participants in state-led interventions even when these have been designed to improve their performance. Patton's (2004) review of the body of evidence related to the take-up of government-led training highlights the significance of informal training in small firms and the mis-match between what is on offer, the methods of delivery and business needs. Holliday's (1995) examination of the introduction of the quality system (BS5750, now ISO9001) in a small firm found evidence of mock bureaucracies with both managers and workers 'colluding to fool inspectors as they visited factories to check that systems were thoroughly implemented. When they left, practices returned to normal' (p. 174). The significance of this study was the emphasis on the owner–managers' multiple rationales for achieving their objectives rather than succumbing to any externally-imposed system based on an alternative all-embracing rationale such as the profit motive. Holliday (1995) argued, 'The emphasis on multiple rationales at work in small firms militates against all positivistic reasoning of much production research, which places all its emphasis on an unproblematic rationality' (p. 174). Thus, providing an overall view of the responses to interventions may be intrinsically unrealistic.

Research by Edwards, Ram and Black (2003) using a qualitative interview approach examined the effects of employment regulations on small firm practices. The case study approach focused on the effects of the UK national minimum wage (NMW), the formalization of disciplinary practices after an Employment Tribunal case and other legal developments applying to smaller firms. They found the effects of regulation were mediated by the overall attitudes of owner–managers, the nature of individual laws, the market context in which the firm operated and the internal dynamics of each firm. In a few instances, they were able to identify positive effects including the 'modernization' of employment relations procedures and a 'moving up market'. Interestingly, though, respondents found it hard to produce concrete estimates of the cost of regulation.

Evidence on the relationship between regulation and external searches for information and learning is scarce. In an investigation of the NMW on an Asian clothing firm, Ram et al. (2003) found that although legislation was commonly reported to be burdensome, it also acted as a 'positive shock' in terms of stimulating more efficient practices and a move into niche markets.

Arrowsmith and Gilman (2004) also analysed the effects of the NMW on small firms in the hotel and catering and clothing sectors. Although the majority responded by implementing the NMW, they did find a minority of employers who 'used the occasion of the NMW to revise existing arrangements' (p. 165). Again they emphasized the interplay of numerous factors: 'This dual context of difficult business conditions and the almost defining feature of informal employment relations mediated the procedural and substantive regulatory "shock" of the NMW' (p. 171). The outcomes of the NMW across the sectors were classified as either achieving fairness/efficiency, little change, 'low road' or illegality. The biggest single effect appeared to be little change. In terms of pay determination, stickiness of existing pay and working time was as much a result of owner–managers' conceptions of fairness as external factors. Clearly, whilst diversity does exist, the ability to instil change in small firms from 'top down' or external interventions is open to question.

The above discussion helps to set out a framework for understanding small firm owner–managers' 'stickiness' in terms of management strategies. Synthesizing the key points suggests that there are different types of business owner–managers, who are motivated to operate a business for a variety of reasons and are situated within different socio-economic contexts. Gray provides a useful summary:

> Studies of small business owner-managers . . . have found consistently that their reasons for starting their businesses are more likely to be a desire for independence, autonomy, self-awareness, self-actualization and a sense of achievement rather than any of the more traditional economic motivations . . . Furthermore, it is equally clear that the traditional ideas of business motivation – such as growth, wealth, accumulation of capital or the maximisation of profits – have very little influence, even in a peripheral sense, on many small businesses (especially the self-employed) (1998: p. 133).

Whilst economic motivations are important, they are not the only reason for a small business owner running a business. The implication is that financial considerations such as incentives or penalties may not be sufficient to change the behaviour and practice of smaller business owner–managers, although there will be some diversity in responses.

However, there are many forms of regulation, and the SME population is highly heterogeneous. The above tells us little about responses to regulations and resultant change. What types of effects do specific regulatory interventions have on smaller firms? How do small firm owner–managers deal with these interventions? To what extent do interventions act as a catalyst for broader changes within the smaller firm? The purpose of this chapter is to present two examples to help show the variations in the effects of regulation and responses by small firm owner–managers. Broadly these cases illustrate the general case of 'strategic stickiness' in smaller firms.

Propositions
A body of literature indicates that effects of regulation will be mediated by a series of processes which are shaped by external and internal firm factors. Our aim is to contribute to this literature by investigating the extent to which small firms resist change in the face of external interventions. In other words, to what extent is strategy in smaller firms difficult to change? The following three propositions will be investigated:

1. The effects of regulations on small firms' strategies will vary between firms according to a variety of internal and external factors.
2. In searching for solutions to meet regulations, owner–managers are likely to engage with outside agencies and activate networks.
3. Engagement with agencies may lead to positive effects, including changes in practices, innovation and possibly learning.

Two projects with which both authors were involved are used to investigate these propositions. The first project was an investigation of the influences on attitudes and behaviour with respect to UK health and safety regulation in small firms (Vickers et al., 2003; Vickers et al., 2005). The second project was an examination of the effects of individual employment rights (IERs) on smaller firms in the UK (Blackburn and Hart, 2002). The advantages of drawing upon different empirical sources include the ability to explore the effects of different types of regulation, the opportunity to explore any common themes in relation to business responses and the ability to identify the relative merits of different methodologies in examining the effects on owner–manager strategies.

Case study one: the effects of health and safety legislation
Health and safety regulations often appear as one of the most common areas of intervention in business operations. This study (Vickers et al., 2003; 2005) aimed to identify the cultural influences that make employers and workers receptive and/or unreceptive to health and safety messages, recognize authoritative and credible channels of communication by which health and safety messages can be more widely disseminated and consider the impact of cultural influences on employer/employee expectations of the

UK Health and Safety Executive (HSE). Culture was defined as 'the shared practices, mental habits and norms which shape people's identities and influence their attitudes and behaviours' (Vickers et al., 2003: p. 3).

The data for this project was gathered using a mixed method approach and included a telephone survey of more than 1000 small firms (those with fewer than 50 employees), 73 face-to-face interviews with owner–managers and 21 employees, and interviews with key informants in selected intermediary organizations, health and safety inspectors and trade union representatives.

In relation to the first proposition this study found diversity in the effects of regulation and a threefold classification of firms according to their response was created:

(i)   avoiders/outsiders;
(ii)   reactors of which there were 'minimalist' and 'positive'; and
(iii)   proactive learners.

The majority of firms fell into the avoiders/outsiders and minimalist reactor categories. Their reasons for a lack of preparedness to change and low level of engagement included the firm's poor market position, a fear of officialdom and drive to minimize costs. These poor resource conditions were reinforced by management whose world view was of regulation as an unnecessary burden, common sense and the responsibility of individual employees (Vickers et al., 2003: p. 110). Thus the response of the majority was minimal and change would occur only when there was compulsion.

On the other hand the minority group of proactive learners showed a more positive response to interventions and a willingness to engage with inspectors. External influences included: characteristics of the market, particularly the degree and forms of competition, and sectoral context of the business; regulatory pressures, particularly the nature of enforcement; supply chain influences, particularly the requirements of large customers/contractors; and other government policies, including other regulatory and enterprise support policy.

'Internal' influences on management attitudes and behaviour resulted from their interrelationship with external influences, as well as with each other. Three main groups of internal influences included those relating to the nature of the technology, processes and premises utilized and associated hazards. These were often strongly sector-related, but were also size-related because of scale economies and/or cost factors.

Organizational characteristics also played a role including the degree of formality in the approach to management, separation of roles, degree of consultation and workforce representation and business performance/growth orientation. This group of influences was strongly size-related. Cultural characteristics were also important and these related to the nature of employer–employee relations, such as the propensity and ability of employees to demand improvements (in the absence of more formal representation), and the individual values and behavioural traits of managers and employees (as shaped by factors such as prior experience, education, training, gender characteristics, ethnic background) particularly as they impact on perceptions of risk. Together with organizational characteristics these influenced the receptiveness of the owner–manager towards, and ability to take advantage of, external advice and support.

The major influences on the firm therefore appeared to be the firm's culture, its resource constraints and competitive pressures. At the same time, how this influence was manifested varied between different firm types. The health and safety study showed that on many of the indicators adoption of health and safety management and improvement measures was strongly size-related, with larger firms (within the 1–50 employee sizeband) tending to perform better. Evidence from this study therefore confirms our first proposition.

In relation to our second proposition about regulation being a stimulant for engagement with outside agencies, the health and safety study found that less than a third of owner–managers had sought external information and advice in the past five years. Unsurprisingly this varied by size and sector as is shown in Table 15.3. This provides partial support for our second proposition.

Table 15.3   Use of external sources of information and advice on health and safety issues 1997–2002 (by sector and employment size)

	Count	%	N
Manufacturing	43	24	179
Construction	41	36	114
Health	56	29	192
Retail	61	24	250
Hospitality	113	32	352
Total	314	29	1087
1–9 employees	219	26	833
10–19 employees	59	39	152
20+ employees	32	38	85

Note: 17 missing cases by employment size.

Source: Vickers et al. (2003: p. 33).

However, counts of owner–managers seeking external advice tell us little of the content of the interaction or the effects on firm strategy. In this regard the role of the health and safety inspectors was of central importance. In the health and safety field, inspection duties are shared between the HSE and local authorities. The HSE are responsible for inspecting higher risk activities, such as construction and manufacturing, and local authority inspectors are responsible for less risky activities (for example, retail and hospitality). A complicating factor is that some activities (such as restaurants) are also subject to the food hygiene regulations, which are the responsibility of local authority Environmental Health Officers. While some local authorities have separate inspection teams for food hygiene and for health and safety, others tend to combine the two functions. In terms of frequency of inspection, this can range from once every five to seven years for businesses rated as low risk to annual inspections for high risk and food hygiene categories.

Nearly three-quarters of surveyed businesses had been visited by an inspector at some time and particularly larger firms (or those employing five or more staff). There were also variations in the frequency of inspection between sectors with firms in the hospitality (mainly catering) sector exhibiting by far the highest proportion of respondents recalling inspection visits (93 per cent). In terms of outcomes less than one third of inspected firms were required to take actions as a result of visits by inspectors, and the vast majority of those reported being able to undertake the required actions easily. Perhaps surprisingly was the generally positive experience surveyed firms reported in regard to inspectors' visits. Health and safety inspectors appeared to adopt a predominantly persuasive and educative role and only used enforcement action (such as prosecution) as a last resort. This is important and is a message that needs to be disseminated throughout the small business community, particularly to the more difficult-to-reach micro-enterprises. Inspectors themselves identified external pressures as the key influence on awareness and compliance with health and safety regulations in small firms.

Whilst the majority of firms either sought to avoid compliance with regulation and/or viewed it as an unnecessary burden, the minority in the proactive learner group often accepted the business case for regulation and viewed it as a possible means of gaining competitive advantage. Typically these were well managed, profitable and growing firms which were often operating in niche markets where product/service quality, innovation and responsiveness to customer needs were keys to business success. This contrasted with the avoiders and minimalist reactors whose competitiveness appeared to depend more on price. The positive responders and learners were also more likely to be higher visibility enterprises and involved in higher risk activities, thus they tended to attract more regulatory attention.

That those firms responding positively to regulation were likely to be proactively managed and profitable is supported by findings from other studies. For example, in a study of the implications of the completion of the EU Internal Market on SMEs in the food processing sector, Smallbone et al. (1996) identified a small number of firms that viewed changes in the regulatory regime as an opportunity to get 'one step ahead of the pack' by making necessary investments to comply with regulations that were to be introduced two or three years later, rather than waiting until the last minute. For one firm this meant an investment of more than half a million pounds sterling which the manager justified in terms of moving more quickly than their main competitors.

However, overall the results of the health and safety study suggest that influences on workplace health and safety practices were a result of a complex bundle of external and internal factors, not merely legislation. External factors such as the nature of the sector, market and competitive pressures on the firm were just as important. In some cases, engagement with large customers or contractors influenced the level of awareness and compliance. Internally, the nature of the technology, industry sub-culture, the degree of management formality and owner–managers' behavioural characteristics were also found to be very influential. These results are consistent with the literature which emphasizes the dominance of the owner–manager on the firm's management practices. But the study also showed diversity across the small firm population and that there was, under certain conditions, an ability and willingness to embrace change such that regulations could engender strategic developments over and above minimalist conformity with legislation.

Case study 2: employment regulations and small firms

Employment legislation is considered to be amongst the most influential regulatory areas faced by small firms. There has indeed been a raft of enhancements in individual employment rights (IERs) in the UK ranging from the NMW to working time regulations and rights to time off for family-friendly reasons. The data we draw on here was derived from a UK Department of Trade and Industry (DTI) study of IERs with a sample of 1071 owner–managers plus face-to-face interviews (Blackburn and Hart, 2002). It was subsequently built upon by Edwards et al. (2003) with further interviews and case studies. This study illustrates the advantages of large-scale surveys but also highlights the limitations of quantitative studies in investigating the broader effects of regulations on smaller firms.

The study found a strong positive relationship between business size and the presence of a personnel specialist: in firms employing fewer than 10 people 22.5 per cent stated that personnel matters were a significant part of their job compared with 42.9 per cent of those employing 20–49 people (Blackburn and Hart, 2002). As a result respondents in larger firms were more aware and confident in their knowledge about IERs than those in smaller firms. As Table 15.4 shows, just over a third of the 1071 respondents reported that IERs had had a significant effect on their business operations. In other words, two-thirds reported no influence of IERs on their business. Of those reporting an effect, the biggest single effect IERs had was on 'administrative workload' followed by the 'amount of legal advice'. Adjustments in the numbers employed or recruited in the past two years, the ways in which employees were managed and changes in employment contracts were also affected by IERs.

The effect of IERs on the administrative workload and legal advice sought was also found to be larger in the larger firms. This size effect may have been

Table 15.4   Influence of IERs legislation on business operations by size of enterprise

	1–9 employees (%)	10–19 employees (%)	20–49 employees (%)	All (%)
Administration workload	52.1	70.6	76.5	56.5
Amount of legal advice	37.4	50.0	64.7	41.2
Numbers employed over last 2 years	40.6	24.2	31.3	37.7
Overall business performance	34.2	38.3	41.2	35.3
Way employees are managed	33.2	35.3	41.2	34.0
Changes in employment contracts	27.3	38.2	43.8	30.0
Changes in employees' attitudes or performance	20.4	24.2	31.3	21.7
Balance between full and part-time	20.9	14.7	12.5	19.4
Use of agency or self-employed workers	15.6	14.7	17.6	15.6
Balance between males and females	8.6	0.0	5.9	7.1
N (Unweighted N)	187 (83)	33 (133)	17 (163)	237 (379)

Note: Only includes those respondents who stated that employee rights have had a significant impact on their business.

Source: Blackburn and Hart (2002).

a result of these firms employing significant numbers of staff and thus their owner–managers were more likely to have to come to terms with effects of IERs. There was also some indication that firms in the smaller size band were more likely to state that employment rights had affected their recruitment over the past two years although this relationship was not linear. However, the results also showed that these responses did not follow a simple pattern, and notions of a 'size threshold' as a means of understanding business responses to government regulations should be treated with caution. In short these results render support to the proposition that variations exist in the responses by firms to employment rights legislation depending on firm size.

An examination of the types of IERs affecting firms shows that the greatest reported effect was from the NMW, followed by basic terms and conditions and then maternity rights (Table 15.5). The bulk of employers tended to have negative views about the effects across the range of IERs although a minority perceived that they had positive effects (Table 15.5). The IER having the highest perceived positive effect on business performance was 'basic terms and conditions of employment' (3 per cent of the sample) and this was followed by 'maternity rights' and the NMW (1.7 per cent). It is important to note that although a high proportion of owner–managers had complained about the impact of IERs they were unable to provide responses in relation to specific IERs. Hence the numbers in Table 15.5 are low and this suggests that any 'shock' to strategy is likely to be limited to specific types of businesses.

Table 15.5   Negative and positive impact of IERs on business performance (n=1071)

	Negative effect	Positive effect	N
NMW	6.4	1.4	87
Basic terms and conditions	4.4	3.0	79
Maternity rights	4.7	1.7	68
Unfair dismissal	4.1	0.2	45
Extension of rights to part-timers	2.6	0.6	34
Limits on working week	1.8	0.2	22
Regular time off	1.3	0.5	19
Parental leave	1.1	0.5	18
Minimum work breaks	0.2	0.6	10
Disability rights	0.3	0	4
Anti-discrimination	0.1	0	2

Source: Blackburn and Hart (2002).

Further analysis (Hart and Blackburn, 2004) found these results to vary according to the composition of the labour force and the sector in which the business operated, thus lending further support to proposition 1. For example, an examination of the perceptions of the effects on the workforce showed that particular IERs had different effects according to the percentage of females in the labour force. Employers with at least 75 per cent females were most likely to perceive maternity rights and the extension of rights to part-timers as having a negative effect on business performance. Those employers with no female workers were more likely to perceive negative effects resulting from the NMW, basic terms and conditions, limits on the working week and rights to regular time off work – that is IERs with no specific gender target. There were also some expected but significant differences according to whether an employer had been taken to an employment tribunal and perceived effects on their business performance. The latter were much more likely to be negative about the impact of maternity rights and basic terms and conditions. Clearly notions of size need to be considered in light of other factors such as workforce composition.

The data also confirmed that expectations of an uneven effect as shown by the number of negative responses by employers were classified by business sector (see Hart and Blackburn, 2004). Employers in the distribution sector were especially negative about the effects of IERs. Those in the hotels and catering sector were the most negative about the extension of rights to part-timers, most probably reflecting their high use of a part-time labour force, and minimum work breaks. Business and professional services employers recorded the highest number of employers being negative about maternity rights. Although why these patterns emerge can only be investigated through further qualitative research, they do show that making blanket statements about the effects of IERs on small firms is problematic. In relation to our propositions, the findings support the first one, that is that the effects of regulations on strategy in small firms will vary between firms according to a variety of internal and external factors.

What of the use of external advice and support agencies? The survey revealed that the bulk of owner–managers were prepared to go outside for advice on IERs. As Table 15.6 shows, the most popular source of advice and information were accountants, followed by solicitors, government departments and then other owner–managers. Whilst the pattern of advice-seeking follows those of other studies, the fact that these responses were related to employment issues does bring to the fore other less common sources. Use of government departments and the Advisory, Conciliation and Arbitration Service (ACAS) was relatively high. Thus we can deduce that employment rights' legislation was stimulating external searches by owner–managers, which lends support to our second proposition.

Table 15.6   Single main source of advice on IERs

	1–9 employees (%)	10–19 employees (%)	20–49 employees (%)	All (%)
Accountant	21.4	14.9	5.7	20.4
Solicitor	11.8	8.0	14.3	11.6
Government department	8.7	8.0	11.4	8.8
Trade association	6.4	11.5	14.3	7.1
ACAS	5.6	10.3	11.4	6.2
Federation of Small Businesses	4.7	5.7	2.9	4.8
Friends/relatives generally	3.9	3.4	0	3.7
Another business owner	2.7	2.3	0	2.6
Business Link	2.7	2.3	0	2.6
Employee/Manager in the business	1.9	4.6	5.7	2.2
Citizens Advice Bureau	1.7	0	0	1.5
Forum of Private Business	1.5	1.1	0	1.4
Training and Enterprise Council	1.2	0	0	1.0
Employers' Federation	0.6	1.1	2.9	0.7
Chamber of Commerce	0.3	1.1	2.9	0.5
Employee/Manager other business	0.2	1.1	2.9	0.4
Bank manager	0	1.1	0	0.1
Other	6.1	12.6	20.0	7.1
No main source	18.4	10.3	5.7	17.4
Total	100	100	100	100
N (Unweighted N)	949 (349)	87 (363)	35 (359)	1071 (1071)

Source: Blackburn and Hart (2002).

Table 15.6 also shows the single most important source of advice about IERs by firm size. Smaller firm owner–managers were more dependent on accountants while those in larger firms were more likely to use trade bodies and ACAS. This was probably due to larger firms being more likely to have their own personnel expertise in-house. In contrast, owner–managers of smaller firms would be reliant on already established and trusted professional contacts even though this contact was initially in relation to financial and accountancy matters. These results confirm those of Harris (2000) but also provide partial support for proposition 2, that IERs stimulate external networking in order to help owner–managers deal with these rights.

Whether or not IERs had stimulated strategic changes, innovation or learning in the businesses was difficult to detect with any detail. Earlier, Table 15.4 showed us that IERs had some impact on firms in relation to the ways in which employees were managed (34 per cent), employment contracts (30 per cent) and the use of agency workers (15.6 per cent). However, these proportions were based on a subset of the overall sample and did not provide evidence of the details of these changes. All owner–managers were asked about the benefits of IERs for their business. Almost two-thirds answered 'none'; one in five said legislation provided them with guidelines and clarification in setting the conditions for their workers; and almost 10 per cent stated that IERs raised staff morale and engendered a feeling of security.

One possible interpretation is that IERs stimulated very little over and above achieving compliance, formalizing the employment relationship and buying in personnel-related advice. Follow-up questions provided little more evidence of the impact on learning beyond 'what IERs are' or 'what we have to do to comply'. Thus we must be mindful of the limitation of this data. First, owner–managers that reported a significant effect were included in the sample (indeed 754 did not report a significant effect). Second, the results do not tell us what these effects mean in terms of scale, how fundamental they were for the business or changes over time. Third, the data was based on owner–managers' perceptions. There are limitations to quantitative data and the results have a bounded validity. But it does pave the way for more in-depth research that could unpack the reasons for the reported effects.

Edwards et al. (2003) undertook this task and complemented the above study with 18 case studies and 101 face-to-face interviews. They found the impact of IERs on small firms to be contingent on the market context and the individual situation of the firm. The competitive situation of the firm was highlighted as particularly significant in how employment legislation affected the business. In relation to our third proposition they found some evidence of legislation contributing to modernization and formalization of business practices. However, these changes were at a cost to the firms while any benefits were more likely to be realized in the longer term and thus lead to negative rather than positive responses (Edwards et al., 2003). As such, their findings provide weak and partial support to our third proposition that regulation may lead to positive effects, including changes in practices, innovation and possibly learning.

Discussion and conclusion

A number of key themes emerge from this chapter which help our understanding of the effects of government interventions on the 'strategic stickiness' of small firms and owner–managers' responses to regulations. If we could generalize, then the most common theme to emerge relates to the impact on owner–managers regarding searching for solutions to comply with legislation. However, the depth of impact in terms of its effect on stimulating broader strategic changes within firms was minor. Hence, it appeared that the strength of numerous mediating factors led to a dissipation of any broader effects of legislative shocks on the firm. There was some diversity in responses, particularly in the Health and Safety study, where some deeper effects of interventions on the strategy of the business were reported. It was also clear that the desire to change and ability to change was contingent on the owner–manager and competitive context of the business.

In Table 15.7 the results of our three propositions are set out against the findings from the two studies. We show that effects of regulations varied between firms depending on a variety of characteristics over and above the

Table 15.7   Summary of analysis

Proposition	Case 1: Health and safety regulations	Case 2: Employment legislation
(1) The effects of regulations on small firms' strategies will vary between firms according to a variety of internal and external factors	– *Supported* – Contingent on culture of firm, nature of technology used and organizational characteristic	– *Supported* – Contingent on interaction of external and internal factors (e.g. business sector composition of labour force)
(2) In searching for solutions to meet regulations, owner–managers are likely to engage with outside agencies and activate networks	– *Supported* – Health and safety regulations led to external engagement with inspectorate	– *Supported* – Employment regulations stimulated search and engagement with outside agencies
(3) Engagement with agencies may lead to positive effects, including changes in practices, innovation and possibly learning	– *Supported* – Evidence showed that interactions with inspectors led to positive outcomes; minority of firms classified as 'learners'	– *Partial weak support* – This is a snapshot survey and owner–managers were neutral or negative about the effects. Subsequent follow-up study showed some effects.

size of the firm. Regulations stimulated a search for information and this went beyond tried and trusted networks. Small firms tended to operate with a culture of informality and independence and owner–managers gleaned information and made decisions on a 'need-to-know' basis. Hence these studies suggested that the effects of these external searches were limited to satisfying requirements of the particular piece of legislation rather than having broader effects. Again some variations existed but the overall result is that emergent strategies operated in smaller firms: owner–managers sought solutions to specific problems and then moved on to the next challenge. Legislation tended not to trigger responses other than the necessity of compliance.

Other research has shown how legislation may shock smaller firms and stimulate changes (Ram et al., 2003). Our results are consistent with these but also highlight the way in which penetrating the predominant customs and practices of small firms is difficult. Perhaps the absence of any widespread evidence of management learning and innovation is a result of the nature of the regulations we examined which tended to generate negative responses from owner–managers.

The evidence suggests that disturbing small firms' 'strategic stickiness' may require a variety of policy levers including, where necessary, legislation combined with readily available information through key agencies including accountants. Regulation alone is unlikely to be a catalyst for fundamental change. To be positive, regulations may need to be accompanied by other methods such as we saw with the role of the health and safety inspector in the first case, as the way a regulation is delivered can affect the outcome. This resonates with the recommendations in the Hampton Review (2004) for multiple approaches to be used to reach small firms with information if change is to be realized.

We have also shown that the generation of knowledge can be strongly influenced by the methodological approach adopted. Whilst quantitative-based evidence can map out the general effects of regulation, these approaches are inadequate for understanding these effects, particularly when they take time to permeate the business. Hence, this supports the view 'that business behaviour vis-à-vis regulatory law and enforcement is complex and multi-faceted, and not adequately captured by traditional economic models which assume that firms respond only to short-term economic incentives, including predicted costs of detection and punishment' (Gunningham and Kagan, 2005: p. 217).

Our chapter has implications for further research. Although it illustrates a variation in the ability to test a series of propositions according to the research method used, a more systematic attempt to compare different methodological approaches on the same topic would provide an important scientific way forward in understanding the effects of regulation. A key deficiency of our chapter is in relation to understanding the effects of regulation over time. But we suggest other analytical approaches that may be able to model the impact of government regulation on small firm owner–manager behaviour and assess the variety of responses this may stimulate. Whilst case studies have moved in this direction (Edwards et al., 2003) these may not be sufficient to unpack the effects of legislation as it is implemented. A longitudinal, qualitative methodology could yield fruitful results and help us to understand and model these processes and effects. An ethnographic element could also be built into this approach in order to tease out the day-to-day effects of regulation and what it means within the firm. Also the focus could be not only on owner–managers, their strategies, responses and learning but also on their employees who are significant agents in changing work practices and products. Thus, from the evidence presented, the 'strategic stickiness' thesis holds but with some qualifications in terms of outcomes and research methods.

References

Arrowsmith, J. and M. Gilman (2004), 'Small firms and the National Minimum Wage', in S. Marlow, D. Patton and M. Ram (eds), *Managing Labour in Smaller Firms*, London: Routledge, pp. 159–77.

Atkinson, J. and J. Hurstfield (2004), *Small Business Service Annual Survey of Small Businesses: UK 2003*, London: DTI Small Business Service.

Beaver, G. and C. Prince (2004), 'Management, strategy and policy in the UK small business sector: A critical review', *Journal of Small Business and Enterprise Development*, **11**, 24–49.

Blackburn, R. and M. Hart (2002), *Small Firms' Awareness and Knowledge of Individual Employment Rights*, DTI Employment Relations Research Series No. 14, Available at <http://www.berr.gov.uk/files/file11561.pdf>.

Chell, E. (1991), *The Entrepreneurial Personality*, London: Routledge.

Cope, J. (2003), 'Entrepreneurial learning and critical reflection: Discontinuous events as triggers for high level learning', *Management Learning*, **34**, 429–50.

Curran, J. (1996), 'Small business strategy', in M. Warner (ed.), *International Encyclopedia of Business and Management*, London and New York: Thomson Business Press, pp. 4510–20.

Curran, J. and R.A. Blackburn (1994), *Small Firms and Local Economic Networks: The Death of the Local Economy?*, London: Paul Chapman/ Sage Publications.

Edwards, P., M. Ram and J. Black (2003), *The Impact of Employment Legislation on Small Firms: A Case Study Analysis*, DTI Employment Relations Research Series No. 20, London. Available at <http://www.berr.gov.uk/files/file11518.pdf>.

Gibb, A. (2000), 'SME policy, academic research and the growth of ignorance: Mythical concepts, myths, assumptions, rituals and confusions', *International Small Business Journal*, **18**(2), 13–35.

Gray, C. (1998), *Enterprise and Culture*, London and New York: Routledge.

Gunningham, N. and R.A. Kagan (2005), 'Regulation and business behavior', *Law and Policy*, **27**, 213–18.

Hampton, P. (2004), *Reducing Administrative Burdens: Effective Inspection and Enforcement*, available at <http://www.hm-treasury.gov.uk/pre_budget_report/prebud_pbr04/assoc_docs/prebud_pbr04_hampton.cfm>.

Harris, L. (2000), 'Employment regulation and owner-managers in small firms: Seeking Support and guidance', *Journal of Small Business and Enterprise Development*, **7**(4), 352–62.

Hart, M. and R. Blackburn (2004), 'Labour regulation in SMEs: A challenge to competitiveness and employability?' in S. Marlow, D. Patton and M. Ram (eds), *Managing Labour in Smaller Firms*, London: Routledge, pp. 133–58.

Holliday, R. (1995), *Nice Work*, London: Routledge.

Marlow, S. (2004), 'Introduction', in S. Marlow, D. Patton and M. Ram (eds), *Managing Labour in Smaller Firms*, London: Routledge, pp. 1–17.

Mintzberg, H. (1995), 'Strategic thinking as seeing', in B. Garratt (ed.), *Developing Strategic Thought*, London: McGraw Hill, pp. 79–84.

Patton, D. (2004), 'Training in small firms', in S. Marlow, D. Patton and M. Ram (eds), *Managing Labour in Smaller Firms*, London: Routledge, pp. 83–108.

Pittaway, L., M. Robertson, K. Muir, D. Denyer and A. Neely (2004), 'Networking and innovation: A systematic review of the evidence', *International Journal of Management Reviews*, **5/6**(2&4), 137–68.

Ram, M., M. Gilman, J. Arrowsmith and P. Edwards (2003), 'Once more into the sunset? Asian clothing firms after the national minimum wage', *Environment and Planning C: Government and Policy*, **21**, 71–88.

Scase, R. (2004), 'Managerial strategies in small firms', in S. Marlow, D. Patton and M. Ram (eds), *Managing Labour in Smaller Firms*, London: Routledge, pp. 66–82.

Smallbone, D., A. Cumbers and R. Leigh (1996), 'The single European market and SMEs in the UK food processing sector', *International Small Business Journal*, **14**(4), 55–71.

Spicer, D. and E. Sadler-Smith (2006), 'Organizational learning in smaller manufacturing firms', *International Small Business Journal*, **24**(2), 133–58.

Vickers, I., P. James, D. Smallbone and R. Baldock (2005), 'Understanding small firm responses to regulation: The case of workplace health and safety', *Policy Studies*, **26**(2), 149–69.

Vickers, I., R. Baldock, D. Smallbone, P. James, I. Ekanem and M. Bertotti (2003), *Cultural Influences on Health and Safety Attitudes and Behaviour in Small Firms*, Health and Safety Executive Research Report 150, Sudbury: HSE Books.

Whittington, R. (1993), *What is Strategy and Does it Matter?*, London: Routledge.

Zhang, M., A. Macpherson and O. Jones (2006), 'Conceptualizing the learning process in SMEs: Improving innovation through external orientation', *International Small Business Journal*, **23**(3), 299–323.

16 Becoming an employer
Hefin David and Gerald Watts

Introduction

For most small firm owners the employment of others is an essential condition for firm growth, as it can overcome constraints on human capital and enable scale increases. It is a significant step for the owner, marking a shift to a new role with new responsibilities and perhaps changes to their self-concept. It can also signal change in the way the owner relates to the firm and thinks about its future.

The employment decision is also important for other stakeholders in the small firm. Most notably it is important for the new employee, who will become a significant member of the growing business and play an important role in its development. Governments (local, regional and national) also see the transition from non-employer to employer as being important in terms of the impact on employment, economic growth and social capital.

Literature examining the concept of human resource management (HRM) in small firms has grown significantly in recent years (see for example Barrett and Mayson, 2006; Marlow, 2006; Ram, 1994; 1999; Ram and Edwards, 2003; Taylor, 2006). Yet there is little research about the first employment decision, despite the criticality of this to the firm's growth and the owner's personal development. The purpose of this chapter, therefore, is to report on the initial findings of case studies of five small business owners, where their personal approach to the first employment decision is explored. In these cases, employment is conceptualized as a learning experience for the owner.

The chapter begins with a brief examination of the literature on employment and employment relationships in small firms as well as the process of reflection as an aide to learning from experience. This latter aspect is particularly important when learning to employ. The research methodology and context are briefly elaborated before the cases of the five small firm owners are reported. The discussion of pertinent issues emerging from the cases is undertaken and this is followed by a cross-case analysis in which similarities and differences in the experiences and philosophies of the owners are explored. As this research is still in the exploratory stages, issues for future research are highlighted in the conclusion.

Employment and small business

Small firms play an important role in developed and developing countries as a source of employment. In the UK for example, over two-thirds of the private sector workforce is employed by small firms (Curran and Blackburn, 2001). Yet, despite this significance, only 30 per cent of UK small firms have any employees and of these, three-quarters employ only between one and nine employees (DTI, 2006).

Studies of HRM in small firms have increased in number but there are few dealing with the first employment decision. Given many small firms' owners do not become employers, why they do not is an important question. While an array of resources offer advice to owners considering taking on their first employee (see on-line resources such as www.inc.com, www.firewheeldesign.com, and www.cbsc.org) and policy-orientated reports attempt to identify barriers to recruitment (see for example, the European Commission's (2005) report 'Obstacles to growth – recruiting the first employee'), there is little providing insight into what the individual is thinking when they are deciding whether or not to become an employer.

The European Commission report for example only considers the burden of legislation, regulations, administration and non-wage costs associated with recruitment as barriers to recruitment. The Canadian Government also examines the legal and financial responsibilities that must be considered when employing for the first time, and provides a source of advice for firm owners (www.cbsc.org). This, however, neglects a deeper understanding of the life-world of individual small firm owners and the fact that the first employment decision cannot be separated from their experiential history. While legislation and regulations may be barriers, the reluctance to employ also has a more complex psychological origin.

This view is supported by the work of Rae and Carswell (2001) who have noted that entrepreneurship is learned primarily by experience and discovery. They argue that 'the entrepreneur's own story is rarely heard' (p. 151) and produce a conceptual understanding of entrepreneurial learning that emphasizes the importance of early life experience. They argue that a number of experiential factors are essential for the development of confidence and self belief in the learning stage, namely relationships, known capabilities, and active learning.

They also argue that the entrepreneur develops personal theories about the way things should be done, and these allow the formation of individual mission statements or heuristics. The result of the learning process is a self-belief and confidence that releases the ability to determine personal values and to set and achieve ambitious goals, of which overcoming the reluctance to employ may be one.

Perceived self-efficacy refers to 'a judgement of one's ability to organize and execute given types of performances' (Bandura, 1997: p. 21) and is recognized by Chen et al. (1998) as having useful application to the field of entrepreneurship research. Their concept of Entrepreneurial Self-Efficacy (ESE) is used to find that individuals more likely to establish and grow ventures and become serial entrepreneurs had a higher ESE.

The ability to reflect upon and thus learn from experiences is a significant factor in developing ESE. Stuart and Binstead (1981) identify that this learning process is at least partially reliant upon reference to past and present work experiences. Heron (1998) further explores the 'digging-up' of life experiences through reflection and refers to exploratory reflection and 'hermeneutic' thinking as a mechanism for the cognition of life experiences as motivators of future actions. These ideas will be further explored later in this chapter around the development of a framework to help conceptualize employment as a learning experience.

The first employment decision is therefore likely to be influenced by a complex range of factors that are deeply personal to the small firm owner. In this sense, it is unlikely that widely applicable rules of behaviour can be established. Indeed, the term 'informal' is repeatedly used in literature referring to employment practices and relationships within small firms (see Barrett and Mayson, Chapter 6, this handbook; Kotey and Sheridan, 2004; Marlow and Patton, 2001; Ram, 1999 for example). This informality may manifest itself in the form of emergent rather than deterministic employment practices.

In a quantitative study Kotey and Sheridan (2004) demonstrate how informal HRM practices become formalized as the firm grows. This suggests that, at the time of the first employment decision, the recruitment process is at its most informal. Indeed Taylor recognizes that 'practices in smaller organizations tend to be seen as deviant according to the prescriptive norms of "good HRM"' (2006: pp. 480–81). While informality is not held as an exemplar in the development of HRM policy, its continued existence and its role in the social and economic development of the firm makes it an area worthy of detailed study.

Taylor and Thorpe (2004) would concur, arguing that informal networks are vital to the experiential learning process that guides individuals in the establishment and development of the business. By exploring relationships in and outside the firm, the social, historical and cultural contexts of learning can be taken into account and every individual that the owner has contact with may influence his or her decision making and behaviour. Larson and Starr (1993) identify three stages in the development of the owner's network culminating in a 'critical mass of dyads that establish the organization as a new entity' (p. 10).

Other factors will also play a role. For example, the industry will influence the type of employee to be recruited and the subsequent experience of employment. We can see this when Ram (1999) explored recruitment practices in small, high-technology professional service firms and found that, while recruitment was more informal and less systemic than in large firms, serious consideration was given to the type of employee required. Skills and experience were considered to be important but these were assessed through previous contacts that the employees had with the firm either as freelancers or as people known to the employers in a social capacity.

Recruitment practice may also be guided by earlier experiences. Many small firm owners may have taken part in recruitment and employment activity, particularly if they have worked as managers in other firms. Yet they may still encounter difficulties such as contending with legal responsibilities and the pool of labour available to them being different from that available to older or larger firms. In their chapters of this handbook, Williamson and Robinson (Chapter 18) and Cardon and Tarique (Chapter 17) address some of these legitimacy issues when small firms recruit.

A range of themes emerge from this discussion and these will be used to organize the analysis of the first employment decision and subsequent experiences of five small employers in the next section of this chapter. The learning process that the owner embarks on and the effect of this on attitudes to the initial and subsequent employment decisions will be explored. The degree of consideration given to the recruitment process and the extent to which an 'informal' process exists will also be assessed.

Case studies

This chapter is based on the lead author's doctoral research which aims to provide a deeper understanding of the first employment decision and subsequent experiences. It draws on semi-structured interviews with a purposive sample of five small firm owners in South Wales and the West of England. Brief demographic details of the owners are listed in Table 16.1

How the owner became an employer, their early experience as an employer, their personal views on employment and the way their experience informed their subsequent practice was the focus of the interviews. Respondents were also asked to reflect more broadly on their personal views on employment issues and the ways in which their experiences had informed their emergent employment strategy. In order to preserve anonymity, all of the names used in the case studies are fictitious. The scarcity of published research and limited conceptual development in the area of the first employment decision practices require that this research is exploratory in nature.

Table 16.1 Demographics of the sample

	Age	Nature of business (location)	Number of current employees	Previous work experience
Cathy Cole	50s	Business support events (Cardiff)	1	Similar full-time role in a university
Peter Martin	Early 40s	Insurance agent (South Wales)	12	Insurance agent for large firm
Mike Hart	Early 40s	Two retail clothing stores (Cardiff and Newport)	20–30	Worked in and bought business from previous owner
John Stuart	Late 30s	Graphic design (Cardiff)	5	Graphic design consultancy; Start-up; University teaching
Neil Jones	Late 30s	Events management (Bristol)	20	Army; Manager in large US firm

Case 1: Cathy Cole

Cathy established her business in July 2006. She previously had a career in academia, latterly as head of a university research centre, a position she had held from January 2000 until June 2006. Cathy established her current business in order to continue the work that she had been doing in the research centre, which involved obtaining European grants for short-term practical research projects. Her desire to set up on her own stemmed from a need to be able to take on riskier projects which the university would not sanction. Cathy employed one person in her business.

As head of the research centre she had employed a total of 26 staff during the time it existed. This had been her first experience of being responsible for the generation of income to pay staff salaries, albeit in the secure environment of a large organization.

Reflecting on her experiences as an employer in the research centre, Cathy said,

> When you employ staff, it's like buying a house. You spend half an hour looking through it. You don't know all the creaks and bangs and whether the central heating is going to break down . . . It's the same with staff . . . People can put on an act, they might be very good at interviews, they might be terrible at interviews and might make the best employee. So I think the actual recruitment process is very difficult.

Cathy said, 'it is different employing people in your own business', because she can develop opportunities without justifying it to a superior. Her employee, Jean, was funded by a public sector research project. Cathy employed Jean because Jean herself identified the project and the available funding, something that would not have happened in the university.

Cathy wanted her organization to develop a distinctive approach to employment. Rather than recruit staff, she wanted to work with self-employed associates on short-term contracts. She used the name 'Associates' in the business name and quoted Welsh Development Agency (WDA, 2006) research to support this approach. The need for this approach was also linked to the company relying on partnerships with public sector organizations to secure funding. Cathy said she often acted as a project manager with the project workers employed by the lead public sector body. Her objective was to grow the business and 'have associates linked to the business'.

Cathy suggested that having associates would reduce the need for significant layers of 'employer responsibility or employer legislation' and was 'the way in which people are going to work in the future'. Cathy may be described as a reluctant employer, stating that 'probably I would prefer not to take on employees'. Cathy initially seemed uncertain whether her type of research consultancy business would require employees and would depend on future developments. However, when asked directly whether she would need any employees in future, she recognized that relying solely on self-employed associates might prevent her objective of growing the business and, given the constraints on her own time, she would reluctantly have to take on more employees.

Case 2: Peter Martin

Peter Martin took the decision to start his own business after he had accumulated numerous clients whilst working for a large insurance agency. These clients were gained through his own contacts and he recognized that they were likely to stay with him rather than with his employer if he established his own firm. Following a successful period of working alone in his business, Peter realized that he was spending time on administrative work rather than business generation and that, in order to grow the business, some administrative help was required.

Peter recalled taking on his first employee as a result of necessity due to the increasing workload. He said, 'the first girl, Elsa, she was employed on a government scheme and I took her on after that. But it was very difficult because I had to find a wage for her and it was five or six thousand pounds, good God.'

Although he said little more about the first employment decision, as he built up his business he began to employ others, initially on a part-time and later on a full-time basis. These employees had remarkably similar profiles: female, aged below 40. When questioned on this approach, Peter said,

> Put it this way. I recently advertised in the local paper for an insurance advisor to work here. I interviewed twenty people this week. Out of those, I would say that there weren't three applicants who were male. I did interview one male for a job who wasn't suitable.

He did employ one male, Matt, who had previously owned a similar business which Peter had bought upon Matt's decision to retire at the age of 60. Matt clearly had a different role in the business from that of the female staff. Matt appeared to be an advisor and confidant whereas the female staff had more formal responsibilities such as office management, business quotes and renewals.

It was noted that Peter's employees were working in a small office on one site. Peter had opened another business on another site two years previously but quickly decided not to continue this venture.

> I couldn't keep my finger on the pulse. One of the girls over there was pinching money and it was because there were only two girls working there. When you are here everyone is checking each other and . . . it's impossible to fiddle in here. The only way a person could fiddle in here is if they were writing cheques and the only person who writes cheques is myself and Tanya [female office manager].

Peter stated that he wanted to make more use of the space in the existing premises but currently had no plans to move to new premises. He was 'a firm believer in doing things slowly' and his actions did typify this cautious, gradualist approach. He emphasized this by recalling that 'the people I know that have rushed into it all are not there now'.

Case 3: Mike Hart

Mike Hart started work as a school-leaver for the clothing retailer that he now owns. His employer was 'a real inspiration'. Mike gradually got promoted and increased his influence over 20 years until he became the general manager 'running the business day to day'. In this sense, he became a first line manager in the business. In the meantime, with the support of his employer Mike had also opened his own business elsewhere with his (now) ex-wife, which over a period of seven years expanded to three shops.

Mike was 'very conscientious as an employee' but found that as an employer 'you suddenly have the responsibility of not only making a living for yourself but your employees as well'. His general philosophy was to 'give so much but don't give everything because people will just take from you'. He learned this approach from his employer.

Mike started his own business because he 'wanted to succeed and prove to myself I could do it and not on the back of somebody else's success'. He felt that he was able to achieve this goal in his day-to-day work in the established company, again with the support of his employer. Mike recognized the closeness of the small clothing retail industry in South Wales and the fact that many owners establish their own businesses in the same way he had. He suggested his employment experience acted as an apprenticeship for his own business and this pattern was repeated with one of the other employees starting their own similar business.

Mike became an employer for the first time when his then wife became pregnant. He recruited by advertising in the local paper and recognized that he has learnt more about the selection process in the meantime. He found the first interview 'tough' and 'went for a good personality and gut feel' about the employee. In that instance, the employment was successful and repaid Mike's trust.

Mike spent 12 years not taking on new employees. He eventually saw a need to employ younger people in order to develop a unique company culture and began employing again. Employing young people had 'given the business a new lease of life'. Employees were encouraged to wear the company's products on the shop floor and were offered staff discounts. He also gained knowledge about current youth fashions from these employees. As Mike got older, young employees were important to help maintain the business in the market and the firm's youth culture.

Reflecting on his experiences of employment, Mike said that there were two kinds of employee. 'The first tends to rise to a certain level and is then happy to stay there. The others gain more and more experience and eventually leave for bigger and better things.' He classed himself and two previous employees, both now departed, in the latter category.

Case 4: John Stuart

John Stuart worked on his own for about nine months in the early 1990s building his business before he employed someone full-time. If he had any large jobs he would take on freelancers but his first employee was 'on the administrative side of things', doing the jobs that he didn't enjoy. He recruited this person through a newspaper advertisement and after interviewing six people, chose a graduate in business administration. He 'felt fine' about employing this person as he had been in charge of people before, while in employment.

John built up a strong working relationship with this person and she only left because she got married and moved away. John then took on a new employee, again a female graduate straight from university. Over the last eight years the business has grown, eventually employing five people. He didn't think that his approach to employment had changed in that time and he thought he had a very good team. He said, 'we are very careful' with the recruitment process. In fact the recruitment process for the last new employee was very gradual and took seven months. Among the reasons for this is that everyone in the company had joined straight from university 'so that I've been able to mould them . . . and they've all remained with me for [between] eight and five years'. Also, it was because in a small business,

> new people can have a huge effect on the dynamic of the business from a cultural point of view as well as from a normal business point of view. So finding the right person who not only has the requisite skills to do the job but also that one believes will fit in as a team member and not upset the balance. There is a fine balance . . .

John described the company culture as relaxed with very little hierarchy. He said that he was therefore relying on people. He used the word 'dangerous' to describe this approach and that 'people understand the different roles that they do and which is why the appointment process is crucial'. John felt a strong need to maintain his relaxed and trusting culture and felt that expansion could damage that. He therefore had no desire to grow the business beyond the current number of full-time employees. When going on holiday he felt he could leave staff in charge and did not want to lose that confidence. He hoped his staff would never leave and would eventually take over the running of the business as shareholders.

Case 5: Neil Jones

Neil Jones left school at 16 to join the Army and was one of the few state school leavers at the highly prestigious Royal Military Academy, Sandhurst. He was eventually encouraged to leave Sandhurst as his superiors felt he had the attitude of 'a great wartime officer but in peacetime I'd be a liability' and it was clear that 'his face didn't fit'. He felt his social and educational background had an effect on this. He was 'the only Valleys boy' and was 'a bit bolshy'. He recalled being a confident person and 'a bit cocky' beforehand but remembers Sandhurst as 'a big culture shock . . .. three doors down from me was a boy who is now King Hussein of Jordan'. He only joined the Army because he didn't want to tell his mother that he'd failed his A-levels and had no plans for his life. He said that his family was confident and 'everyone was expected to have an opinion around the dinner table'. Neil described himself as 'on the pacifist side of the line and also "a socialist" so was "a complete misfit" ' at Sandhurst.

His first experience of work after the Army was as a salesperson, dealing 'with quite senior people'. He recalled his grandfather saying to him 'in a strong Welsh accent: "remember that you are as good as anyone and better than bloody most"'. He said that in his first job, he learned a lot about 'dealing with different types of people' and that 'a lot of what you learn at Sandhurst is about leadership'. This became an important part of his later beliefs. He said that then going on to employ people 'wasn't so scary really'.

Neil's first experience as an employer came at the age of 23 when he ran an exhibition contracting business, similar to one that his father had developed. Prior to setting up his current business he worked in the US for a multinational as a 'Vice President for the East Coast'. He was responsible for multiple sites and 50 people, closing down offices and making people redundant. Despite what seems to have been an excellent apprenticeship, when asked if he wanted to be an employer Neil replied, 'God no – I don't think anyone wants to be an employer. I think that's an ego thing so it's always out of necessity.'

Neil reflected that in order to increase the number of people employed,

> you have to make sure that the groups have captains and that other people have leadership roles. We have tried to ensure that the best people don't become sales managers by being sales managers that are still selling and are leading by example, rather than being sales managers that are just leading a team. I do most of the training, interviewing and recruiting and I want them to take some responsibility but we are a long way from being perfect on that.

Analysis and discussion
We now turn to focus on the first employment decision, its motivation and the recruitment process. We will explore the early experience of being an employer and the consequences of this experience on the owner's later outlook.

The first employment decision
Peter's first employee was sought because of a strongly-felt need to change the balance of his work by employing someone to help with clerical work.

> Looking back, it was the best move I ever made because I had somebody in the office who was doing all the rubbish . . . so I thought . . . if I can do three or four new cases a day it will pay for my wage and it would pay for her wage.

Throughout the discussion, however, he seemed reluctant to dwell upon the experience. He talked at length about the operational and financial difficulties he faced in the first four years of his business, which perhaps reflects the marginal role he was willing to give the new employee. Despite this, the first employee was reliable and productive and remained with him for a number of years and did enable him to spend more time attracting new customers.

John also had difficulties recalling his first employment decision in any detail. The first employee worked for John for a number of years and it 'worked out really well'. Again, as in the case of Peter, the first decision was not considered to be significant, yet did lead to a good and productive working relationship that ended only when the employee moved away.

For Peter and John, the first employment decision was not something to which they gave much initial thought. They had a general idea of the kind of person they wanted to employ, but did not want to give that person a senior role in the business or direct contact with customers. This reluctance to see their role being taken on by others may be indicative of their lack of confidence as employers. Arguably the seniority of the first employee and the manner of their recruitment is related to the perceived self-efficacy of the owner as an employer.

Cathy found the first (and in her case only) employment decision a relatively easy one; the first employee effectively generated her own salary and had previously been employed by Cathy in a larger organization. In this case, Cathy had a strong confidence in her own ability to manage this employee, based on pervious experiences. The perceived future risk involved in the employment was minimal and consonant with the findings of Taylor and Thorpe (2004), the employee emerged from a pre-existent and supportive personal network. As with the other respondents, Cathy exhibited a clear reluctance to employ anyone else. The risks associated with an unknown figure were perceived to be higher and the language she used to describe the consequences of recruitment was negative, saying 'you employ someone for two years and you are stuck with them for two years'. Cathy did see the legislative and regulatory burdens involved with being an employer as being a deterrent and wanted to use 'associates' in order to avoid this problem.

Mike, who did recruit his first employee to a senior role, also exhibited a degree of reluctance. While he had some experience as a first line manager, he found employment a highly daunting task and approached it tentatively. For Mike, the first employment decision was a highly significant event. He describes the process as 'terrifying' and interviewing people was 'very, very tough and a very hard experience'. He had made the decision on a basis of 'gut feel' and recognized he had been apprehensive about placing a great deal of trust in one individual. Nonetheless, their relationship worked well and the employee remained with him for a number of years. Mike said that over time he gained experience as an employer and found he had an 'affinity with it'. His later experiences clearly increased his self-belief.

Neil took the view that the first employment decision was one of the most important decisions he could make. He reflected that 'each time then, when you employ somebody, you end up being less deliberative'. He attributed this to the first person and early employees 'shap[ing] the culture' of the business but later employees joining with that culture already established. Neil's first employment decision was clearly based on a great deal of thought about the kind of person he wanted to attract. He perceived that it would be significant in the development of the company and believed that he could find the right person.

His previous experiences as a senior manager in a large company, his training at Sandhurst and his self-declared confidence were obviously important. Having had positive experiences of leading and managing people, then for him becoming an employer was not such a significant step. Expressed differently, it is reasonable to argue that he had a strongly developed perceived self-efficacy when considering becoming an employer. Neil also differed from the others in his vision of his business as a developing organization. From the outset, he was concerned about the culture that would emerge and was conscious of the disproportionate role of the first employees in shaping it.

For all the respondents, the first employment decisions were positive and allowed them to learn from and build upon these experiences. In each case, despite a degree of reluctance or even trepidation when first approaching the decision to employ, there was evidence of increasing confidence and self-belief as their business grew and they took on more employees.

Experience, learning and evolving beliefs
How had respondents' experiences changed their views of employment over time and to what extent has this encouraged their personal confidence in their abilities as employers?

By the time of the interview Peter had appointed both a trusted general manager and a senior advisor who had previously run a similar business. John now employed four members of staff to work on product design. For Peter and John, their gradual increase in confidence as employers was reflected in the ways in which, as they became more experienced as employers, they gave more responsibility to their new employees.

As suggested by Rae and Carswell (2001), as they gained experience, all four of the owners had developed a personal philosophy about appropriate behaviour as an employer and the rules of employment. Their philosophy was clearly based on their experience as employers. For example, Mike felt employers should 'give so much but don't give everything because people will just take from you'. Neil believed 'you have to make sure that the groups have captains'. Peter stated 'I am a firm believer in doing things slowly. The people I know that have rushed into it all are not there now.' John recognized introducing a new employee would have a 'huge effect on the dynamic of the business from a cultural point of view'. Cathy's use of the house analogy suggested a general belief about recruitment that had its roots in her previous experiences as a manager in the public sector and one which, unlike the other respondents, would constrain the business growth.

While the link between beliefs and employer behaviours will be the focus of further research, there was evidence to suggest that these beliefs guide practice. John, for example, has a protracted process of recruitment to select a new employee. Mike, despite his declared relaxed approach to management, asked his first line manager and other senior managers to make new and younger staff aware of the importance of keeping to the leave rota and not taking inconvenient sick days. Cathy's apprehension about her ability to judge a member of staff at the recruitment stage explains why she chose to employ someone she knew well and had worked with before.

There was further evidence of these evolving beliefs in the patterns of employment. Peter employed mostly young and middle-aged females and John employed young graduates. Both denied explicitly choosing these as employment strategies, although John did joke that 'you can mould them in your image'. This pattern was represented slightly differently in Mike's and Neil's larger businesses. Mike had consciously changed his employment strategy. He recognized his target market was 25-year-olds and under, and so decided to employ young school-leavers of both sexes on the shop floor, instead of the lower-middle-aged males he had previously employed. This change was necessary if staff were to model his clothing range in the store. Neil recognized the impact of industry remuneration practice on his employment practice. Because the norm was to offer a basic salary with a high proportion of commission, his employees needed to be strongly financially motivated. He was only half-joking when he said that his ideal employee would be a 'young greedy guy with a fast car and . . . a gambling habit'. Neil lamented the fact that such people were hard to find outside of London.

In both these latter cases, accumulated experience and an increasing perceived self-efficacy as the firm grew led to more sophisticated decisions being made about the most appropriate type of employee who would fit. This may indicate that in the early days of the business, the recruitment process was based on, to quote Mike Hart, 'gut feel' whereas later experiences allow more informed, rational choices.

The issue of trust
The issue of trust was a theme that emerged during the later stages of the interviews. Each of the owners reflected on the extent to which they could trust their employees and we explore this further in this section.

Goel and Ranjan (2006) suggest that entrepreneurs with high perceived self-efficacy are likely to over-trust their staff. Trust was certainly an issue that emerged in some form in all five interviews, either explicitly identified or implied in their behaviour toward staff. Neil, the most experienced of the employers and arguably the one with the highest perceived self-efficacy as an employer, believed most strongly that he could trust his employees. He was surprised by minor pilfering from the office fridge but also cited examples of stressful occasions in which he placed his trust in staff and they reacted well. Cathy, who was certainly the most reluctant employer of the group, was also the least likely to place trust in her employees, preferring associates on short-term, arm's length contracts.

Peter did not place a great deal of trust in his staff. He had a cautious attitude to the growth of the business and following the aborted expansion to another site he became a more cautious employer. This was also exhibited in the fact that next to his desk was a large window that looked out directly onto the open plan office in which all his staff worked. It seemed that, until he decided that he would trust his employees without his supervision, the physical size of the premises would limit the growth of the business.

John trusted his employees to the point where he could leave them in charge when he was holidaying. This did not extend to new employees who were still outsiders to be carefully judged. He used a lengthy selection process as a result. In addition, he frequently expressed the fear that if expansion was not carefully managed then it could irrevocably alter and destroy the company culture.

Mike reflected on the difficulty of making judgements about trustworthiness, 'The way someone comes across doesn't mean much when it comes to honesty', perhaps bearing out his idea of not 'giving too much'. He told a story of an early employment experience in which he indulged his shop manager with a high level of autonomy but later found that this employee had been stealing money.

Each of the respondents expressed strong views about employee responsibility. Reflecting on his employees, Mike emphasized his feeling that younger members of staff 'almost expect to have sick leave' – which was very different to his view of work. He claimed to be 'quite hurt by that', feeling that those employees were letting him and their colleagues down. He felt they should feel a responsibility for the business. Neil shared this stance, saying that in his absence productivity fell and he had tried to explain to his staff they were effectively stealing from him if they relaxed their efforts when he was away.

Neil and Mike had formed similarly relaxed and realistic views of the extent to which they could trust employees. Peter's approach was loaded with reservation and caution. John felt able to trust, but only when he had a strong and close relationship with his employees. Clearly Peter's and John's issues with trust were factors in the slower growth of their businesses.

Cathy was very reluctant to employ others and her negative experiences as a manager, in one case invoking disciplinary action against an employee, had left her strongly wary of future employment. The future growth of her business would most likely be affected by this.

Conclusions

Contrary to the initial expectations of the authors, the first employment decision was not always recalled to have been of high salience. The reality was much more complex, bound up within patterns of motivations, expectations, employment practice and business goals. Two of the respondents made reluctant initial decisions to employ, both borne of necessity, and did not see this decision as a major step in the development of their businesses. By contrast, another two (Neil and Mike) did see the initial employment decision as very important but for different reasons. For Mike, it was an important plank in his growth strategy – he needed employees to scale up the business. Neil's early motivations to employ were also driven by growth aspirations but were also informed by a vision of his business as a developing organization. This active stance towards employment can be compared with Peter's and Stuart's passive one.

Cathy espoused a desire for business growth but this was severely constrained by her view of the inherent uncertainty and difficulty of being an employer. It may be said that Mike, Peter, Neil and John had all, to some extent, gained sufficient experience to increase their perceived self-efficacy such that they no longer feared being employers. Some form of negative experience was common to all and had, perhaps but for the case of Neil, formed a restraining influence on the pace of growth of the firm.

None of the respondents appeared to bear out the small firm stereotype of informality that was discussed earlier. All used a degree of formality in their initial recruitments, in that they all gave prior thought to the role and the sort of person who would be appropriate, advertised the position and selected from a number of candidates. However, rather than informality being a characteristic of the recruitment process, it could be argued that four of the five respondents displayed informality in their employment strategies, recruiting on an ad hoc basis rather than within a strategic vision of the business as a human organization.

Nevertheless, across the sample there was clear evidence of the emergence of a strategic view of employment, in the sense that it was seen to be of high criticality to performance and of long-term significance for the development of the business. Although only Neil had taken such a view of his business at the start, John, Mark and Peter had all learned to think strategically about the human capital in their business. Even Cathy, who had little experience of being an employer, recognized after reflection that the growth of the business would be constrained by her reluctance to employ in a conventional sense. She perceived that she would soon have to make a decision as to whether her reluctance as an employer would override her desire for business growth. This particular case is therefore worth revisiting in the development of this research.

Peter and John explicitly discussed culture, recognizing its criticality to performance, while the others referred to cultural issues in other terms. This considered and strategic view was not necessarily related to growth objectives. In particular, John restricted the size of his organization for fear of loss of direct control but was also very conscious of the evolving organizational culture.

As predicted by Rae and Carswell (2001) each of the owners interviewed was guided, driven and constrained by a set of heuristics: about themselves as an employer; about the most appropriate profile for their employees; about how to manage people; and about appropriate behaviour. Each espoused an employment philosophy derived from their accumulated experience as an employer and informed by earlier work experiences. The clearest case of this was Neil, who had substantial experience as a manager and this served him well as preparation for his role as employer. Trust clearly plays an important role and each of the respondents was able to recount critical incidents which made them reflect in depth on issues of trust.

Reflection, evaluation and implications

It is important to note that much emphasis has been placed upon the early experiences and learning processes of the five owners. Personality factors cannot be discounted: for example, the generally cautious approach demonstrated by two of the owners, which was probably evidence of more deeply-rooted personality traits. The exploration of such issues is, however, beyond the scope of this research.

Given the sample size, the fact that this was exploratory research and the complexity and diversity that was revealed, we are reluctant to make any generalizations or policy recommendations. However, significant themes emerged that will form focuses for further research, some of which have potential policy relevance.

The first of these is the learning process: the unique and highly complex set of experiences that contribute to an individual's personal development as an employer. Each of these owners made a unique and complex journey towards becoming an employer, which prepared them in different ways for the experience and impacted on the way they recruited and behaved in an employing role. Their subsequent experience clearly had a powerful formative role in developing both their practice as employers and the system of beliefs which underpinned it.

Figure 16.1 is our first attempt to integrate our findings into a conceptual framework and illustrate some key aspects of the decision to become an employer (to the left of the vertical line) and the learning process following this decision (to the right of the line). We draw on the earlier cited work of Stuart and Binstead (1981), Bandura (1997) and Chen et al. (1998). The key inputs to the decision are motivation, in the sense of felt need to become an employer, and beliefs about the reality of this role, ability to carry it out effectively and the impact that having employees has on work and life, comparable to the concept of Entrepreneurial Self-Efficacy (ESE). Each of these inputs is therefore moderated by prior experience. For example, Neil's experience as a manager contributed to his acceptance of the need to become an employer and his self-belief about carrying out this role. By contrast, Cathy's more difficult experience as a manager had made her a very reluctant employer.

In each case, the respondents' subsequent experiences as an employer led to reflection, introspection and a degree of re-evaluation of their beliefs and practices. Each of the respondents was able to articulate their employment philosophy and could attribute this to their accumulated experience. In this respect, there was a clear difference between the experienced employers and Cathy, who was new to the role and was reconsidering the possible impact of her employment philosophy on the growth of her business.

At this stage it is only possible to make some tentative observations about implications for policy and practice and these are at the conceptual level only. An interesting finding not highlighted in the discussion above was that only one of the respondents discussed regulations or 'red tape'. Although they all talked at length and in depth about the complex inter-personal issues surrounding being an employer, only Cathy Cole mentioned the impact of statutory requirements and legislative burdens of becoming an employer.

This is not to suggest that such factors are unimportant or unworthy of consideration. Indeed, the earlier cited work of Taylor and Thorpe (2004) and Larson and Starr (1993) would suggest that such issues are of major significance as aspects of the owner's external network and should have an influence on their behaviour. Thus, the model described in Figure 16.1 should not be seen as a closed system but an early conceptualization of a previously unconsidered component of a wider open system. Further research focusing on external influences in relation to the first employment decision is required in order to identify how this may interact with the wider system.

Far more significant for all of the respondents in this study was the extent to which they could trust their employees and encourage them to care about the business as much as they did. It was a factor which caused at least two

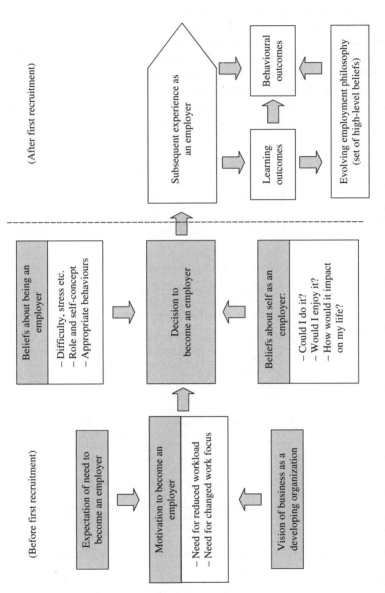

(Before first recruitment)

(After first recruitment)

Figure 16.1   Employment as a learning experience – a first step in conceptualization

of the owners to exhibit a strong reluctance to employ and this could limit their firm's growth. Yet the owner who had overcome this reluctance, Neil, saw that in trusting his employees he was repaid and this was a highly rewarding experience from which he drew a great deal of confidence.

For each of the owners employment was a complex and highly personal experience, involving deep-rooted beliefs about themselves and others. This is in stark contrast with much of the available support for small firm employers, which tends to focus on legal, administrative and procedural issues. It raises the question as to how, if at all, the respondents might have been helped along the tortuous path towards becoming a proficient employer.

References

Bandura, A. (1997), *Self-Efficacy: The Exercise of Control*, New York: Freeman.
Barrett, R. and S. Mayson (2006), 'Exploring the intersection of HRM and entrepreneurship: Guest editors' introduction', *Human Resource Management Review*, **16**, 443–6.
Chen, C.C., P.G. Greene and A. Crick (1998), 'Does entrepreneurial self-efficacy distinguish entrepreneurs from managers', *Journal of Business Venturing*, **13**(4), 295–316.
Curran, J. and R. Blackburn (2001), *Researching the Small Enterprise*, London: Sage Publications.
Department of Trade and Industry (DTI) (2006), 'Annual Small Business Survey 2005: Executive summary', Available online at http://www.dti.gov.uk/files/file38237.pdf, accessed 13 June 2007.
European Commission (2005), 'Obstacles to growth – recruiting the first employee', Available online at www.europa.eu.int (accessed 2 January 2007).
Goel, S. and K. Ranjan (2006), 'Entrepreneurs, effectual logic and over-trust', *Entrepreneurship: Theory and Practice*, **30**, 477–94.
Heron, J. (1998), *Co-operative Inquiry – Research into the Human Condition*, London: Sage.
Kotey, B. and A. Sheridan (2004), 'Changing HRM practices with firm growth', *Journal of Small Business and Enterprise Development*, **11**, 474–85.
Larson, A.L. and J.A. Starr (1993), 'A network model of organization formation', *Entrepreneurship: Theory and Practice*, **17**(2), 5–15.
Marlow, S. (2006), 'Human resource management in smaller firms: A contradiction in terms?', *Human Resource Management Review*, **16**, 467–77.
Marlow, S. and D. Patton (2001), 'Minding the gap between employers and employees: The challenge for owner-managers of smaller manufacturing firms', *Employee Relations*, **24**, 523–39.
Rae, D. and M. Carswell (2001), 'Towards a conceptual understanding of entrepreneurial learning', *Journal of Small Business and Enterprise Development*, **8**, 150–58.
Ram, M. (1994), *Managing to Survive*, London: Routledge.
Ram, M. (1999), 'Managing autonomy: Employment relations in small professional service firms', *International Small Business Journal*, **17**(2), 2–17.
Ram, M. and P. Edwards (2003), 'Praising Ceasar not burying him: What we know about employment relations in small firms', *Work, Employment and Society*, **17**, 719–30.
Stuart, R. and D. Binstead (1981), *New Approaches to Management Development*, Aldershot: Gower.
Taylor, D. and R. Thorpe (2004), 'Entrepreneurial learning: A process of co-participation', *Journal of Small Business and Enterprise Development*, **11**, 203–11.
Taylor, S. (2006), 'Acquaintance, meritocracy and critical realism: Researching recruitment and selection processes in smaller and growth organizations', *Human Resource Management Review*, **16**(4), 478–89.
Welsh Development Agency (2006), *Cyfenter Research Report: Post Business Start Up*, Cardiff: WDA.

17 Organizational attractiveness of small businesses

Melissa S. Cardon and Ibraiz Tarique

Introduction

The last two decades have seen a significant increase in research at the nexus of human resource management and entrepreneurship. Several reviews of this literature have been done (for example, Cardon and Stevens, 2004; Heneman and Tansky, 2002; Heneman et al., 2000) and special issues of journals such as *Human Resource Management, Human Resource Management Review* and *Entrepreneurship: Theory and Practice* have been devoted to relevant manuscripts. Yet despite the increase in research at this nexus, there is still much we do not know about even basic functions within small and/or emerging ventures. Cardon and Stevens (2004) provide a comprehensive review of this literature while in Tansky and Heneman's (2006) edited book several new promising lines of research in this area are detailed.

The majority of research at the intersection of entrepreneurship and human resources is in the area of recruitment and selection. For example, Cardon and Stevens (2004) found 15 of the 37 articles reviewed included these topics. What we know about selection in small firms is that it is important (Hornsby and Kuratko, 1990), but difficult (Gupta and Tannenbaum, 1989), because these firms often lack resources and stability (Bruderl and Schussler, 1990; Ranger-Moore, 1997) and may be seen as illegitimate employers to potential applicants (Williamson, 2000; Williamson et al., 2002). Learning how to attract the best applicants has become critical but small firms have a problem with their 'organizational attractiveness'. In addition, much of our knowledge of hiring practices in small firms is from the organizational perspective, examining issues such as the type of hiring practices used (for example, Baker and Aldrich, 1994), whether recruiting or other HR functions should be outsourced (for example, Klaas et al., 2000) or non-permanent labor recruited (Cardon, 2003; Cardon, and Tolchinsky, 2006) and comparisons of small and large firms regarding their methods of recruitment and selection (Deshpande and Golhar, 1994; Heneman and Berkley, 1999).

Interestingly, despite the recognition that recruitment and selection is difficult, there is very little empirical data concerning the applicant perspective or what draws people (or does not) to entrepreneurial firms instead of larger or more established firms. One notable exception is work by Alison Barber and colleagues (Barber et al., 1999; Barber, 2006), who empirically examine the impact of firm size on recruitment practices utilized, as well as job seeker preferences for work in large versus small firms and the impact on their job search behaviors. This early work (Barber et al., 1999) raises the question of whether the organizational attractiveness problem of small firms is based on organizational attributes, such as size, age, resources or their perceived instability, or individual attributes of their applicant pool, such as self-efficacy, risk-taking propensity or aspects of personality such as extraversion. Which of these is most relevant is an important question because it could profoundly affect approaches to recruiting, whether organization image or legitimacy (for example, Williamson, 2000; Williamson et al., 2002) with their existing applicant pool is the focus or whether recruitment activities are targeted to people who are likely to be most attracted to specific organizations, such as those with greater self-efficacy or higher risk-taking propensity. In this chapter we discuss an initial empirical study of this question where we examine potential applicant perceptions of organizational attractiveness and how these are influenced by the size and age of the firm, as well as by the extraversion and risk-taking propensity of the applicant. While preliminary, the results are quite interesting and suggest the need for more work in this area.

The recruiting problem in small firms – organizational attractiveness

Recruitment and selection is an important challenge for small and new firms (Mehta, 1996), because these firms and their entrepreneurial owner-managers often lack resources (Hannan and Freeman, 1984) and legitimacy (Williamson, 2000) and trained members who know how to perform the necessary tasks involved (Longenecker et al., 1994). Of particular difficulty is effectively attracting candidates to the firm (Arthur, 1995; Cardon and Stevens, 2004). Some scholars recommend specific strategies to help address this problem, such as imitating standard methods of job advertising or other recruiting practices that reflect industry norms (Williamson et al., 2002) in order to gain legitimacy, or attending job fairs to gain access to a larger pool of potential applicants (Buss, 1996). However, other scholars (for example, Barber et al., 1999) have noted that labor markets for small firms and large firms are inherently different and that merely adopting the practices of larger firms may not be an effective way to address the recruiting challenge.

We concur with this latter approach but go a step further to suggest that even within the broad category of 'small firms' there may be different mini-labor markets, in terms of different preferences among potential applicants for what size organization they are interested in or willing to work for. More specifically, while firms in the USA are generally considered small when they have fewer than 250 employees (for example, Taylor and Banks, 1992), we suggest that there may be significant differences in recruiting for firms that are very small, such as those with ten employees, moderately small, with say 50 employees, and those closer to the limits of the small category, with 200–250 employees.

In addition, Cardon and Stevens (2004) point out that liabilities of small-ness (for example, Bruderl and Schussler, 1990), such as resource constraints are different from liabilities of newness (Stinchcombe, 1965), such as lack of legitimacy or the firm being unknown within their industry or job market. This suggests that the relative newness or age of a firm may also impact their ability to effectively attract and recruit new employees. Again we suggest that simply being 'young' versus 'old' as a firm may not tell the entire story, and that we need to examine more closely the relative age of firms within the category of 'young' (generally organizations in existence less than eight years), differentiating between brand new firms (perhaps less than one year old), new firms (one to three years old) and young firms (three to eight years old). Taken together we suggest that instead of a 'tale of two labor markets' (Barber et al., 1999) we may have a 'coat of many colors'.

We rely on the established literature focused on applicant attraction to organizations to shed light on this problematic area for entrepreneurial firms. The study of organizational attractiveness is one of the most often researched topics in recruitment literature (Chapman et al., 2005) and has received considerable theoretical and empirical attention during the last few years. Some studies have examined the effects of organizational attri-butes on potential applicants' attraction to a firm (for example, Turban and Greening, 1996), while others have analyzed the influence of individual characteristics on attraction to firms (for example, Rentsch and McEwen, 2002). In addition, several studies have utilized the interactionist perspec-tive, focusing on how individual characteristics moderate the influence of organizational characteristics on attraction to firms (for example, Turban et al., 2001). Overall this stream of research has contributed to a better understanding of relevant predictor and outcome variables related to appli-cant attraction and job choice processes.

In a recent meta-analysis Chapman et al. (2005) describe a classifica-tion of recruiting outcomes in four categories: job pursuit intentions; job–organization attraction; acceptance intentions and job choice. Job pursuit intentions refer to a job seeker's desire to submit an application, attend a site visit or second interview, or otherwise indicate a willingness to enter or stay in the applicant pool without committing to a job choice. Job–organization attraction captures the applicant's overall evaluation of the attractiveness of the job and/or organization. Acceptance intentions assess the likelihood that an applicant would accept a job offer if one were forthcoming. Finally, job choice is defined as choosing whether to accept a real job offer involving an actual job. In this study we focus on job pursuit intentions that help explain job seekers' thoughts (compare with Highhouse et al., 2003) about small businesses during the early stages of the job search process. Our primary purpose in doing so is to provide a better understanding of potential job seekers' desires or intentions to enter or stay in an applicant pool for these entrepreneurial firms. More specifically we take an interactionist perspective (Turban and Keon, 1993) to examine the interactive effects of two individual characteristics (extroversion and risk-taking propensity) and organizational attributes (size and age) on job pursuit intentions.

Although there are surely many organizational and individual attributes, prior research (Lievens et al., 2001; Turban and Keon, 1993) has provided guidelines for identifying and selecting organizational and individual attributes that influence the initial assessment of organizational attractiveness. Organizational attributes should be salient and visible during the early stages of the job search process, reflect organizational values and cultures of the potential employer and vary across organizations (Lievens et al., 2001). Similarly individual attributes should influence individuals' reactions to environmental cues, both as applicants in the job search process and as employees; and be related to employees' work behaviors and attitudes (Turban and Keon, 1993). We believe that age and size (organizational attributes) and extroversion and risk-taking propensity (individual attributes) meet these criteria.

As one of the first studies examining organizational attractiveness of entrepreneurial firms, it is difficult to draw from enough relevant literature to develop detailed hypotheses. However, we expect some general trends in the data that reflect what we do know about small and new firms and those that work in them. First, we expect that potential job seekers will be more attracted to firms that are moderate in both size and age, within the confines of our focus on businesses with fewer than 250 employees in existence for less than eight years. We base this expectation on the work of Barber and others, who discuss the difficulties of recruitment for such firms (Barber et al., 1999; Barber, 2006; Williamson, 2000). Secondly, we expect that extroversion and risk-taking propensity will moderate the influence of these organizational characteristics on job pursuit intentions. We base this expectation on the work of Turban and colleagues (Turban and Greening, 1996; Turban and Keon, 1993; Turban et al., 2001), who find strong support for the perspective that both organizational and individual elements will interact in their influence on organizational attractiveness, including job pursuit intentions. Our conceptual model is depicted in Figure 17.1.

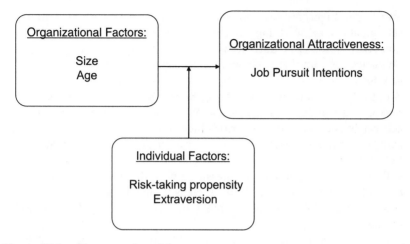

Figure 17.1   Conceptual model

Methods

Our experimental design is a three by three between-subjects factorial design. The design includes three levels of SME size (less than ten employees – Size10; about 50 employees – Size50; and about 200 employees – Size200), and three levels of SME age (less than one year old – Age1; three to eight years old – Age3; and more than eight years old – Age8), resulting in nine separate organizational descriptions that were randomly distributed to participants. Data were collected at two points in time. At time 1, 122 participants completed the first questionnaire developed to measure demographics, control variables and the independent variables. At time 2 (four weeks later), 109 participants completed the second questionnaire designed to assess the dependent variables concerning organizational attractiveness of entrepreneurial firms. For this assessment, participants were asked to read a hypothetical description of an organization and indicate their attraction to the small business enterprise as a possible future employer.

Ninety-six participants completed both questionnaires. Participants were undergraduate students enrolled in introductory organizational behavior and management courses. They completed both questionnaires during class time for course credit. The majority of students were juniors (39 per cent) and seniors (38 per cent), and 20 per cent of the sample were sophomores.

Measures

Job pursuit intentions were measured with four items adapted from Schwoerer and Rosen (1989) and Turban et al. (2001). Each item used a seven-point Likert response scale, (ranging from 1 = very little extent to 7 = very great extent), with higher scores indicating greater job pursuit intentions. Sample items include, 'To what extent would you pursue employment opportunities with this organization?' Reliability for job pursuit intentions was .86.

Extroversion was measured using Saucier's (1994) mini-markers. The scale consists of eight adjectives that reflect the trait. Participants rate how accurately each adjective describes them on a nine-point scale (ranging from 1 = extremely inaccurate to 9 = extremely accurate). Reliability for this scale was .81.

Risk-taking propensity was measured with the ten-item Zhao, Siebert and Hills (2005) scale, using items such as 'I am willing to take significant risk if the possible rewards are high enough'. Reliability for risk-taking propensity was .71.

Interaction terms were created to test the moderation hypotheses by first standardizing extraversion and risk-taking propensity, and then calculating their interaction with the manipulated size and age variables.

Results

Manipulation checks
Before testing the hypotheses, we examined whether our intended manipulations in fact worked as intended. The manipulated experimental conditions were dummy coded to reflect three levels of firm age (dummy coded into two age variables – Age3 and Age8, both as compared to Age1) and three levels of firm size (dummy coded into two size variables – Size50, Size200, both as compared to Size10). The age variables were then regressed onto two separate measures of firm age embedded elsewhere within the questionnaire at time 2, and the size variables regressed onto two separate measures of firm size. The age dummies did significantly predict both age measures ($p < .001$ for all coefficients) and the size dummies did significantly predict both size measures ($p < .001$ for the first size measure and $p < .01$ for the second size measure). Thus we are confident that our manipulations of organizational age and size were effective.

Tests of hypotheses
Descriptive statistics and correlations among measures are reported in Table 17.1. Moderated regression analysis was used to test our hypotheses, using a hierarchical regression model, where independent variables were entered in four steps (see Table 17.2). In step 1, organizational variables of age and size were entered. In step 2, independent variables of extraversion and risk-taking propensity were entered. In step 3, interaction terms with

Table 17.1   Correlation matrix and descriptive statistics for study variables

	Mean	SD	1	2	3	4	5
1. Job pursuit intentions	5.42	1.14	(.86)				
2. Extraversion	4.35	0.86	.226*	(.81)			
3. Risk-taking propensity	4.20	0.73	−.139	.257**	(.71)		
4. Size (0=10 employees; 1 = 50; 2 = 200)	1.04	0.82	.158	−.086	−.017	–	
5. Age (0 = 1 year; 1=3 years; 2 = 8 years)	0.94	0.81	.216*	−.080	−.004	−.010	–

Notes: * p <. 05; ** p <. 01.
Numbers in parentheses represent scale reliabilities.

Table 17.2   Regression analysis exploring interaction effects on job pursuit intentions

Step and source	Step 1	Step 2	Step 3	Step 4
1. Organizational characteristics				
Firm Size, 50 employees (compared to 10)	.041	.030	.022	−.009
Firm Size, 200 employees (compared to 10)	.188	.220*	.225*	.179+
Firm Age, 3 years (compared to 1)	.205+	.227*	.217*	.208*
Firm Age, 8 years (compared to 1)	.280**	.311**	.217*	.299**
2. Personal characteristics				
Extraversion		.321**	.389*	.350***
Risk-taking propensity		−.222*	−.218*	−.549**
3. Extraversion interactions				
Extravers × Size-M (50 compared to 10)			−.139	
Extravers × Size-L (200 compared to 10)			−.010	
Extravers × Age-M (3 years compared to 1)			.008	
Extravers × Age-L (8 years compared to 1)			.006	
4. Risk-taking propensity interactions				
Risk-taking × Size-M (50 compared to 10)				.020
Risk-taking × Size-L (200 compared to 10)				.224+
Risk-taking × Age-M (3 years compared to 1)				.142
Risk-taking × Age-L (8 years compared to 1)				.214
R^2	0.095	0.213	0.226	0.278
Change in R^2	0.095**	0.117**	0.013	0.066
Adjusted R^2	0.055	0.159	0.133	0.192

Notes:
*** p <. 001; ** p <. 01; * p <. 05; + p <. 10.
Extraversion and risk-taking propensity were standardized before calculating interaction terms.
Standardized beta coefficients reported.

extraversion were entered, and in step 4 the interaction terms with risk-taking propensity were entered.

The results for step 1 show that organizational age does significantly influence job pursuit intentions such that, in general, subjects were more likely to pursue a job at older organizations than younger ones (p <. 01 for Age 8 vs. Age1; p <. 10 for Age3 vs. Age1). Size of the firm did not have a main effect, however, contrary to our expectations.

In step 2 we added two individual characteristics, extraversion and risk-taking propensity, which resulted in a significant change in R^2 for the model (change in R^2 = .117, p <. 01). Both individual characteristics contributed to this significant change, as both had significant effects on job pursuit intentions, although in opposite directions. Greater extraversion was associated with higher job pursuit intentions (B = .321, p <. 01) while greater risk-taking propensity was associated with lower job pursuit intentions (B = −.222, p <. 05).

In step 3, we explored the interactions between size, age and extraversion. The addition of the extraversion interaction terms did not result in a significant change in R^2, indicating that this did not improve the model. In addition, none of the interaction effects were significant.

In step 4, we explored the interactions between size, age and risk-taking propensity. Again, the addition of the interaction terms did not improve the model, and only one of the interaction terms approached significance, the interaction of risk-taking propensity and large firm size (p <. 10).

Post hoc analyses

Given the non-significant results for our moderation hypotheses, we sought to better understand the relationships among firm size and age and job pursuit intentions, and used exploratory graphing techniques and t-tests for mean differences between slopes in these graphs to do so. We plotted the two individual characteristics for the two organizational characteristics, after first splitting the individual characteristics into categorical variables of high and low based on the variable mean.

In Figure 17.2, we plotted the extraversion interactions, first for firm age (a) and then for firm size (b). The main effect of firm age found in step 1 of our regression model was clear in graph (a), as the line indicating the relationship between extraversion and job pursuit intentions was highest for Age8 and lowest for firms Age1. The main effect of extraversion, given the slope of the lines between extraversion and job pursuit intentions, was positive. In general, greater extraversion leads to greater job pursuit intentions. However, for Age1 firms (the bottom line), the slope is fairly flat. A t-test indicated that for those with high extraversion, job pursuit intention was significantly lower for Age1 firms (compared with either Age3 or Age8;

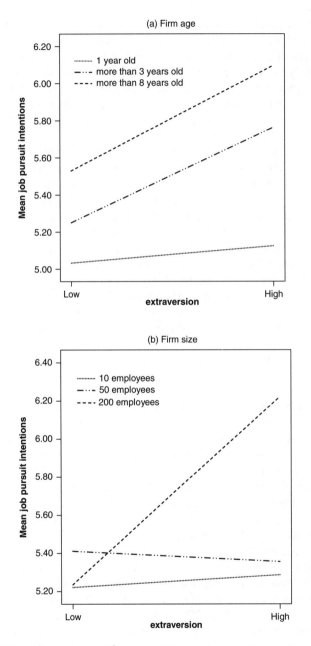

Figure 17.2   Interactions with extraversion

p <. 05). In graph (b) of Figure 17.2, there was a significant interaction between extraversion and firm size, such that for those high in extraversion, reading about a firm of 200 employees (vs. ten or 50 employees) led to significantly higher job pursuit intentions (p<.01). This indicated that individuals high in extraversion had the highest job pursuit intentions for firms that were older (at least three years old) and larger (200 employees or more). For those low in extraversion, job pursuit intentions were also higher for older firms, but size had little impact.

Figure 17.3 shows a similar pattern emerged for the interactions between organizational characteristics and risk-taking propensity. In graph (a) (see Figure 17.3) the slope of the risk-taking propensity to job pursuit intentions line was slightly positive for Age8 firms, slightly negative for Age3 firms and very negative for Age1 firms. T-tests indicated that when risk-taking propensity was high, job pursuit intentions for Age1 firms were significantly lower than Age8 firms (p <. 05), but not significantly different from Age3 firms. In graph (b) the interaction between risk-taking propensity and firm size shows that for those high in risk-taking propensity job pursuit intentions were highest when for Size200 firms compared to Size10 or Size50 (p <. 01). These results suggest that individuals high in risk-taking propensity had the lowest job pursuit intentions for firms that were extremely young (Age1) or very small (Size10). For individuals low in risk-taking propensity, older firms led to greater job pursuit intentions, and size had very little impact on this aspect of organizational attractiveness.

Discussion of contributions and limitations
The objective of this exploratory study was to examine if potential job seekers would be more attracted to firms moderate in both size and age, within the confines of small businesses, and whether extroversion and risk-taking propensity moderated the influence of these organizational characteristics on job pursuit intentions. The results provided support for the argument that the specific age and size of the firm matter, rather than just broad categories of 'small firm' or 'young firm'. More specifically, our results show that concerning size, Size10 and Size50 firms did not appear to be any different for potential organizational applicants, but Size200 firms did result in a higher intention to pursue jobs, both as a main effect, and when either risk-taking propensity or extraversion was high. This is in contrast to many studies, and in fact the US Small Business Administration, where firms with fewer than 250 employees are often lumped together into the category of 'small firm'. This is also in contrast with other research on organizational attractiveness, where the category of small firms refers to organizations with 'only several hundred employees' (Turban and Keon, 1993) in contrast with firms of 5000–6000 employees, termed medium

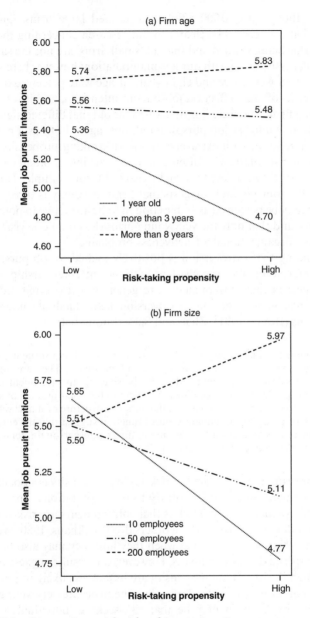

Figure 17.3   Interactions with risk-taking propensity

firms, or those with 50 000 employees, termed large firms. Our results suggest that we need to be clearer in our research concerning the specific size of firms being studied and that all 'small firms' are not the same.

A similar issue arose with our age manipulation; however here we found that firms that were three and eight years of age were perceived quite similarly in terms of their effect on job-pursuit intentions, and it was only the very young firms that were less than one year old that differed significantly, leading to much lower job pursuit intentions, again both as a main effect and in moderation with extraversion and risk-taking propensity. In contrast to other scholars, who often combine firms into a broad category of 'young' when they are less than eight years old (for example, Turban and Keon, 1993), our research suggests that firms as young as three years old might already be perceived as stable enough to be attractive to potential job applicants, and that only the very young firms (less than one year old) will suffer from organizational attractiveness problems.

The finding that extroversion is positively related to job pursuit intentions is interesting. This is consistent with the entrepreneurship literature, which suggests that entrepreneurs are generally extroverted individuals. Another reason may be that extroversion helps facilitate interpersonal interactions (Butler, 1991). Zhao and Seibert note that:

> Entrepreneurs must interact with a diverse range of constituents, including venture capitalists, partners, employees, and customers. They are often in the role of a salesperson, whether they are persuading an investment banker or venture capitalist to back their idea or a client to buy their product or service. In addition to these external relations, the minimal structure of a new venture and the lack of a developed human resource function suggest that the entrepreneur can expect to spend considerable time in direct interpersonal interaction with their partners and employees (2006: p. 26).

A surprise finding is that greater risk-taking propensity is associated with lower job pursuit intentions, contrary to our expectations. The presumption in entrepreneurship research is that entrepreneurs are risk-takers and in fact do not perceive risks where others do (Brockhaus, 1980; Weber and Milliman, 1997), suggesting that when they hire they may also be looking for other risk-takers as employees. However, our results suggest that individuals high in risk-taking propensity are in fact less likely to pursue jobs in these organizations, particularly when the firms are very young or very small. One explanation may be that risk-seeking individuals require a minimum level of job security – firms as young as three years might offer more job security than very young firms (less than one year old). Another explanation may be that risk-seeking individuals are more attracted to variable pay (Cable and Judge, 1994) and very young firms may not have the capabilities to institute different types of variable pay systems required to address the needs of individuals high in risk-taking propensity. Other explanations may be equally as plausible and additional research is needed to determine which explanation is accurate.

It must be acknowledged, as with all exploratory research, that this study has a number of limitations. First, the organizational scenarios we used provided limited information about the organization and the job. These hypothetical scenarios may not have evoked 'real' responses in our students. Yet this approach is used often in organizational attractiveness research (for example, Turban et al., 2001). Future research should examine how the results might differ if more information is provided or real companies with the necessary characteristics are used instead of hypothetical ones. Second, the small sample size is also a concern since with small samples weak effects may have failed to show significance even though they exert some influence. Third, the sample in this study is predominantly students and this raises the concern about generalizability of our results. Student samples can be a cause for concern given that many of the students are not actively looking for full-time jobs at the time of the study. However, student samples are commonly used in organizational attractiveness research, and are also the pool of potential job seekers for these firms. In particular, students are often more willing to work for less money or less stability than labor force 'veterans'. Many of the students in our sample were actively seeking internship jobs at the time of the study, making them an appropriate sample of potential job applicants for the small businesses in question. A fourth potential limitation is that we examine only two organizational and two individual characteristics, despite acknowledgement in the organizational attractiveness literature that other potential aspects might be considered. In order to build a more robust model of the organizational attractiveness of entrepreneurial firms, other variables could be measured, including individual characteristics such as self-efficacy (Zhao et al., 2005), need for achievement (McClelland, 1965) or locus of control (Sexton and Bowman, 1986) and organizational characteristics such as founder tenure or size of the founding team (for example, Aldrich, 1999). Other sub-dimensions of organizational attractiveness could also be explored, such as attraction to the job or intent to accept a job offer. Finally, common method bias is a potential concern when both the criteria and predictors are self-reported, as they are in this study. We attempted to reduce this bias by following the procedural remedies suggested by Podsakoff et al. (2003) such as creating a temporal separation by introducing a time lag between the measurement of the predictor and criterion variables.

Despite these limitations, as one of the first exploratory studies to show how organizational and personality characteristics make a difference in who is attracted to entrepreneurial firms, we have provided a foundation for future research and note some important academic and practical implications. For practitioners the findings can be used as a basis for attracting applicants who have a strong inclination toward the individual characteristics we examined, such as extraversion. The above findings provide preliminary support for the argument that particular age and size matter, not just broad categories of 'small firm' or 'young firm'. However, this study represents only an exploratory investigation of an otherwise complex causal relationship. As such, it provides some preliminary evidence upon which subsequent work can be developed.

References
Aldrich, H.E. (1999), *Organizations Evolving*, London: Sage.
Arthur, D. (1995), *Managing Human Resources in Small and Mid-Sized Companies*, New York: American Management Association.
Baker, T. and H.E Aldrich (1994), 'Friends and strangers: Early hiring practices and idiosyncratic jobs', in W.D. Bygrave, S. Birley, N.C. Churchill, E. Gatewood, F. Hoy, R.H. Keeley and W.E. Wetzel (eds), *Frontiers of Entrepreneurship Research*, Wellesley, MA: Babson College, pp. 75–87.
Barber, A.E. (2006), 'The hiring challenge: Recruitment in small firms', in J.W. Tansky and R.L. Heneman (eds), *Human Resource Strategies for the High Growth Entrepreneurial Firm*, Greenwich, CT: Information Age Publishing, pp. 99–113.
Barber, A.E., M.J. Wesson, Q.M., Roberson and M.S. Taylor (1999), 'A tale of two job markets: Organizational size and its effects on hiring practices and job search behavior', *Personnel Psychology*, **52**, 841–67.
Brockhaus, R.H. (1980), 'Risk taking propensity of entrepreneurs', *Academy of Management Journal*, **23**, 509–20.
Bruderl, J. and R. Schussler (1990), 'Organizational mortality: The liabilities of newness and adolescence', *Administrative Science Quarterly*, **35**, 530–47.
Buss, D.D. (1996), 'Help wanted desperately', *Nation's Business*, **84**(4), 16.
Butler, J. (1991), 'Toward understanding and measuring conditions of trust: Evolution of a conditions of trust inventory', *Journal of Management*, **17**(3), 643–63.
Cable, D.M. and T.A. Judge (1994), 'Pay preferences and job search decisions: A person–organization fit perspective', *Personnel Psychology*, **47**, 317–48.
Cardon, M.S. (2003), 'Contingent labor as an enabler of entrepreneurial growth', *Human Resource Management Journal*, **42**(4), 357–73.
Cardon, M.S. and C. Stevens (2004), 'Managing human resources in small organizations: What do we know?', *Human Resource Management Review*, **14**(3), 295–323.
Cardon, M.S. and P. Tolchinsky (2006) 'To hire or not to hire? Implications of alternative staffing models for emerging organizations', in J.W. Tansky and R.L. Heneman (eds), *Human Resource Strategies for the High Growth Entrepreneurial Firm*, Greenwich, CT: Information Age Publishing, pp. 69–98.
Chapman, D., K. Uggerslev, S. Carroll, K. Piasentin and D. Jonese (2005), 'Applicant attraction to organizations and job choice: A meta-analytic review of the correlates of recruiting outcomes', *Journal of Applied Psychology*, **90**, 928–44.
Deshpande, S.P. and D.Y. Golhar (1994), 'HRM practices in large and small manufacturing firms: A comparative study', *Journal of Small Business Management*, **32**(2), 49–56.
Gupta, U. and J.A. Tannenbaum (1989), 'Enterprise: Labor shortages force changes at small firms', *Wall Street Journal*, 27 June, pp. B-2.
Hannan, M.T. and J. Freeman (1984), 'The population ecology of organizations', *American Sociological Review*, **49**, 149–64.
Heneman, H.G. and R.A. Berkley (1999), 'Applicant attraction practices and outcomes among small businesses', *Journal of Small Business Management*, **37**, 53–74.

Heneman, R.L. and J.W. Tansky (2002), 'Human resource management models for entrepreneurial opportunity: Existing knowledge and new directions', in J.A. Katz and T.M. Welbourne (eds), *Managing People in Entrepreneurial Organizations, Vol. 5*, Amsterdam: JAI Press, pp. 55–82.

Heneman, R.L., J.W. Tansky and S.M. Camp (2000), 'Human resource management practices in small and medium-sized enterprises: Unanswered questions and future research perspectives', *Entrepreneurship: Theory and Practice*, **25**, 11–26.

Highhouse, S., F. Lievens and E.F. Sinar (2003), 'Measuring attraction to organizations', *Educational and Psychological Measurement*, **63**, 986–1001.

Hornsby, J.S. and D.F. Kuratko (1990), 'Human resource management in small business: Critical issues for the 1990s', *Journal of Small Business Management*, **28**, 9–18.

Klaas, B., J. McClendon and T.W. Gainey (2000), 'Managing HR in the small and medium enterprise: The impact of professional employer organizations', *Entrepreneurship: Theory and Practice*, **25**, 107–24.

Lievens, F., C. Decaesteker, P. Coetsier and J. Geirnaert (2001), 'Organizational attractiveness for prospective applicants: A person–organization fit perspective', *Applied Psychology: An International Review*, **50**, 30–51.

Longenecker, J.G., C.W. Moore and J.W. Petty (1994), *Small Business Management: An Entrepreneurial Emphasis*, Cincinnati, OH: South Western.

McClelland, D.C. (1965), 'N achievement and entrepreneurship: A longitudinal study', *Journal of Personality and Social Psychology*, **1**, 389–92.

Mehta, S.N. (1996), 'Worker shortages continue to worry about a quarter of small businesses', *Wall Street Journal*, 27 June, pp. B-2.

Podsakoff, P.M., S.B MacKenzie, J-Y. Lee and N.P. Podsakoff (2003), 'Common method biases in behavioral research: A critical review of the literature and recommended remedies', *Journal of Applied Psychology*, **88**(5), 879–903.

Ranger-Moore, J. (1997), 'Bigger may be better, but is older wiser? Organizational age and size in the New York life insurance industry', *American Sociological Review*, **62**, 903–20.

Rentsch, J. and A. McEwen (2002), 'Comparing personality characteristics, values, and goals as antecedents of organizational attractiveness', *International Journal of Selection and Assessment*, **10**, 225–34.

Saucier, G. (1994), Mini-markers: A brief version of Goldberg's unipolar big-five markers', *Journal of Personality Assessment*, **63**, 506–16.

Schwoerer, E. and B. Rosen (1989), 'Effects of employment-at-will policies and compensation policies on corporate image and job pursuit intentions', *Journal of Applied Psychology*, **74**, 653–6.

Sexton, D.L. and N.B. Bowman (1986), 'Validation of a personality index: Comparative psychological characteristics analysis of female entrepreneurs, managers, entrepreneurship students and business students', in R. Ronstadt, J.A. Hornaday, R. Peterson and K.H. Vesper (eds), *Frontiers of Entrepreneurship Research*, Wellesley, MA: Babson College, pp. 40–51.

Stinchcombe, A.L. (1965), 'Social structure and organizations', in J.G. March (ed.), *Handbook of Organizations*, Chicago: Rand McNally, pp. 142–93.

Tansky, J.W. and R.L. Heneman (2006), *Human Resource Strategies for the High Growth Entrepreneurial Firm*, Greenwich, CT: Information Age Publishing.

Taylor, G.S. and M.C. Banks (1992), 'Entrepreneurs, small business executives, and large business executives: A comparison of the perceived importance of current business issues', *Journal of Small Business Management*, **30**, 24–40.

Turban, D.B. and D.W. Greening (1996), 'Corporate social performance and organizational attractiveness to prospective employees', *Academy of Management Journal*, **40**, 658–72.

Turban, D.B. and T.L. Keon (1993), 'Organizational attractiveness: An interactionist perspective', *Journal of Applied Psychology*, **78**(2), 184–93.

Turban, D.B., C. Lau, H. Ngo, I.H. Chow and S.X. Si (2001), 'Organizational attractiveness of firms in the People's Republic of China: A person–organization fit perspective', *Journal of Applied Psychology*, **86**, 194–206.

Weber, E. and R.A. Milliman (1997), 'Perceived risk attitudes: Relating risk perception to risky choice', *Management Science*, **43**(2), 123–44.

Williamson, I.O. (2000), 'Employer legitimacy and recruitment success in small businesses', *Entrepreneurship: Theory and Practice*, **25**, 27–42.

Williamson, I.O., D.M. Cable and H.E. Aldrich (2002), 'Smaller but not necessarily weaker: How small businesses can overcome barriers to recruitment', in J.A. Katz and T.M. Welbourne (eds), *Managing People in Entrepreneurial Organizations: Learning from the Merger of Entrepreneurship and Human Resource Management*, Amsterdam: JAI Press, pp. 83–106.

Zhao, H. and S.E. Seibert (2006), 'The big five personality dimensions and entrepreneurial status: A meta-analytical review', *Journal of Applied Psychology*, **91**(2), 259–71.

Zhao, H., S.E. Seibert and G.E. Hills (2005), 'The mediating role of self-efficacy in the development of entrepreneurial intentions', *Journal of Applied Psychology*, **90**(6), 1265–72.

18 The effect of small firms' recruitment practice portfolio composition on recruitment success

Ian Williamson and Jeffrey Robinson

Introduction

One of the most difficult but important goals for many small firms is to locate and hire new employees. A recent Conference Board survey of leaders of small and mid-size US firms found the scarcity of qualified employees to be the most often cited threat to business growth, and this was identified by almost 50 per cent of those surveyed (Muson, 2001). Consistent with these findings a UK Chartered Institute of Personnel and Development survey found over 40 per cent of small firms did not receive any applications for some vacancies (Anon, 2005). Yet, despite the importance of employee recruitment to the growth and success of small firms, there are still many questions about how small firms can effectively recruit a high-quality workforce. To date, the vast majority of the recruitment research has focused on large organizations (Barber et al., 1999; Williamson, 2000). However, because of their greater financial resources, social standing, and formalization of recruitment practices, large firms are likely to use different recruit methods than small firms (Barber et al., 1999). Thus, there are reasons why prior recruitment research based on large firms may not generalize to the case of small firms.

Past research examining small firm employee recruitment has often only focused on describing the types of practices used by small firms to hire employees (for example Barber, 1998; Barber et al., 1999; Marsden, 1994). In general extant research has found that small firms are likely to use different types of recruitment practices compared to large firms (Barber et al., 1999; Carroll et al., 1999; Carroll and Teo, 1996; Kotey and Sheridan, 2004; Saari et al., 1988; Tarnova, 2003; Wilkinson, 1999). There is also evidence of significant differences between how small firms of various sizes recruit employees. For example in their examination of the HRM practices utilized by Australian firms, Kotey and Sheridan (2004) reported that only 7 per cent of micro-sized small firms with fewer than five employees used newspaper advertisements to recruit for managerial or supervisory positions, compared to 28 per cent of firms with 5–19 employees and 55 per cent of firms with 20–199 employees. However, while there is evidence on the

361

types of practices utilized by small firms, very few studies examine the outcomes associated with using different types of practices (see for example, Heneman and Berkley, 1999). Thus, there is a need for research to examine the relationship between small firms' recruitment practices and their recruitment outcomes. In particular, given the evidence that firm size influences what types of practices firms use, it is important to understand whether certain types of recruitment practices are more or less effective for small firms of different sizes.

The purpose of this chapter is to advance our knowledge of small firm recruitment by examining the relationship between their recruitment practices and recruitment performance. In particular, we focus on the use of three categories of recruitment practices: informal practices (employee referrals); formal practices (newspaper advertisements); and brokers (use of temporary agencies). We examine how the simultaneous use of informal practices, formal practices and brokers, which we refer to as recruitment practice portfolios, influence two immediate recruitment outcomes: number of job applicants and time to fill positions. Our focus on immediate recruitment outcomes, as opposed to distal outcomes (such as post-hire performance, turnover or job satisfaction) is motivated by two factors. First, immediate recruitment outcomes can have large effects on the pay-off firms derive from their selection systems (Williams et al., 1993). For example the implementation of a sophisticated selection process is only likely to increase the quality of a firm's workforce if a large and talented pool of applicants can be attracted to go through the selection process. Second, several scholars have questioned the appropriateness of using data on firm recruitment practices to study post-hire outcomes (Barber et al., 1999; Werbel et al., 2001; Williams et al., 1993). Specifically, they point out that this approach ignores the important role that other HRM practices, such as compensation, training and performance management, have on employee behavior. Theoretically it is probable that recruitment practices will have stronger effects on proximal, as opposed to distal performance outcomes. Thus, our examination of immediate recruitment outcomes seems more likely to provide useful information about the consequences of firms' recruitment actions.

In this chapter, we define small firms as those employing 500 or fewer employees, which is consistent with the most common standard used by the US Small Business Administration (SBA) in most industries (SBA, 2007). This definition encompasses small firms without regard to their growth orientation or age. We do this, as effective recruitment is important to the performance and survival of all small businesses. In using this definition we acknowledge that there may be several significant structural and resource differences between micro-sized small firms and small firms with several hundred employees. As such, the use of HRM practices may vary greatly across small firms of various sizes (Kotey and Sheridan, 2004). Thus, in addition to examining how firm recruitment portfolios influence recruitment outcomes, our second goal is to explore how the size of small firms moderates this relationship. We believe that an examination of these issues has the potential to provide important insights for managers and owners of various types of small firms in their attempt to develop effective recruitment strategies.

Firm recruitment practice portfolio
Extant recruitment research has largely focused on three categories of recruitment practices used by firms to attract applicants: informal practices, formal practices and brokers. Informal practices refer to those based on the use of social ties to attract job applicants. This can include the referral of prospective applicants by family, friends or trusted employees (Taylor, 1994). Informal recruitment practices are widely used by organizations. For example, the National Organizations Study, a nationally representative sample of US employers, shows that 36.7 per cent frequently use employee referrals as a recruitment method (Kalleberg et al., 1996). The use of informal recruitment practices could enhance firm recruitment outcomes through at least two mechanisms. First, informal recruitment practices can increase the number of individuals who apply for jobs because referrals may expand firms' recruiting horizons and allow them to tap into pools of applicants that they would not otherwise identify (Breaugh and Mann, 1984; Fernandez and Weinberg, 1997). Second, informal practices may improve the quality of applicants, which decreases the time to fill vacant positions. Individuals tend to refer people like themselves and since the referring individual tends to have intimate knowledge of the organization and/or has survived prior screening processes, such homophily is likely to result in the referred applicants being a better fit than non-referred applicants (Fernandez et al., 2000). Furthermore, to the extent that an individual believes their reputation with other members of the firm will be affected by the quality of the people they refer, they will be motivated to refer only suitable applicants (Rees, 1966).

There has been consistent empirical evidence that informal practices are the primary means by which small firms recruit job applicants (Aldrich and Auster, 1986; Baker and Aldrich, 1994; Barber et al., 1999; Carroll and Teo, 1996; Kotey and Sheridan, 2004; Ram, 1999; Saari et al., 1988; Tanova, 2003; Wilkinson, 1999). One explanation for this finding is that informal recruitment practices tend to be inexpensive to implement, an important consideration for small firms that tend to have limited resources. Informal recruitment practices rely on the use of word-of-mouth to advertise job vacancies, thus they require minimal financial cost. Informal practices can also be implemented very quickly because they use existing channels and contacts and do not require specialized expertise in HRM to undertake (Carroll and Teo, 1996).

While there are several advantages to the use of informal practices by small firms, there are also potential shortcomings. The tendency for individuals to refer people who are similar to themselves means that there is a likelihood that informal practices will not reach prospective applicants who have different or novel skill sets (Tanova, 2003). This may be especially important if a position requires a unique set of qualifications or skills. The tendency for homophily in referrals also increases the potential for informal practices to reinforce existing race, gender or other demographic group imbalances within organizations, potentially reducing firm diversity and leaving firms open to accusations of indirect discrimination against disadvantaged groups (Carroll et al., 1999; Burton et al., 2002).

Formal recruitment practices refer to the use of asocial means to attract job applicants. This can include such things as help-wanted postings, newspaper advertisements, web-based recruitment or the use of recruitment brochures (Taylor, 1994). An advantage of formal practices is that the social network ties of entrepreneurs, managers or employees do not bound them. Thus, the use of formal recruitment practices is theorized to enhance firm recruitment outcomes by expanding the number and diversity of applicants for job vacancies. Tapping into a broader applicant pool may be particularly important for organizations attempting to grow or branch out into new domains (Williamson et al., 2002). However, while the use of formal practices may increase the diversity of a firm's applicant pool, one limitation of these types of practices is that, compared to informal practices, they can be more expensive to implement. For example, the cost of using formal recruitment and selection procedures (such as job ads, screen tests and so on) has been estimated to be 67 per cent higher than the use of employee-referral programs (Fernandez et al., 2000). The higher cost of formal practices may reduce small firms' adoption of these practices (Kotey and Sheridan, 2004), thus reducing the potential for small firms to realize the theorized benefits of formal practices.

The use of brokers refers to the practice of employers engaging third parties in the recruitment process. These parties may be institutions (such as schools, training institutes) or organizations (such as community or private sector temporary agencies) who assist managers by identifying potential employees. Broker-based methods allow employers to leverage the knowledge and social ties of others to enhance the breadth and depth of their information about the job market. First, broker methods expand the pool of potential job applicants beyond the employer's own personal social base (Burt, 1992). Second, broker ties provide 'reputation protection', as referrers will tend to pass on references for applicants that will not damage their own reputations (Fernandez et al., 2000). Third, if a prospective employer respects the broker, they can take greater confidence in the assumption that the candidate referred by the broker will be appropriate for their workplace. Fourth, brokers can give both the potential applicant and the employer information that might not be revealed through other screening processes. These points of leverage are similar to those offered by individual referrers; however, the type and scope of the contacts and the legitimacy passed on to potential applicants from the broker organizations make these methods qualitatively different from the informal methods described above.

There are some limitations to the use of brokers in the recruitment process. While employers can infer from the broker's screening methods or certification procedures the types of employees a broker is likely to recommend, brokers generally provide less intimate information about a potential candidate than the informal methods we describe above. Thus, this practice sacrifices depth of information for breadth of base. Secondly, it may not be that all brokers are appropriate for all firms. Brokers may specialize in sourcing employees for certain types of employment (for example, casual versus permanent employment), industries or occupations. Therefore, the use of a broker may depend on the nature of the job to be filled, the industry where the job is being filled or the specific occupation. Third, employers may spend significant amounts of time and/or money to establish and maintain an effective relationship with the brokers. For example, temporary employment agencies charge employers a premium for the employees they provide. Schools may not charge for referrals but there may be some expectation of employers participating in events promoted or hosted by the school.

In summary, while informal practices, formal practices and brokers each have shortcomings, there is evidence to suggest that their use may enhance small firms' recruitment outcomes. However, there is very little research examining how the use of these practices may actually influence immediate recruitment outcomes (Barber, 1998). What effect, if any, their use may have on the immediate recruitment outcomes of small firms is also unclear. Furthermore, we are unaware of research examining the simultaneous effect of these practices, as a set, on recruitment outcomes. Thus, the relative effectiveness for small firm recruitment of one type of practice compared to the other two is unknown. In order to shed light on these issues the first research question to be examined is: what is the effect of small firms' portfolio of recruitment practices on immediate recruitment outcomes?

Firm size and effectiveness of recruitment practices
Based on prior literature it is logical to predict that informal, formal and broker recruitment practices have the potential to enhance the recruitment outcomes of small firms. However, as stated above, small firms may vary considerably in their needs and capabilities. In particular, the size of a small firm may have an impact on their access to financial, human and social capital, which in turn may influence the ability of a small firm to effectively implement HRM practices. Thus the size of a small firm may play an important role in determining how effectively informal, formal or broker recruitment practices enhance firm recruitment outcomes.

In the case of informal recruitment practices, it is likely that these practices may be less effective for micro-sized small firms compared to small firms with several hundred employees. The effectiveness of an informal recruitment practice is linked to the nature and extent of a firm's manager and employee network ties. To the extent that a broad and diverse set of actors can be accessed through the firm's members' networks then this increases the probability that individuals with the desired skills can be recruited to the firm (Leung, 2001). The owners of micro-sized firms often utilize family or friendship ties to hire employees (Baker and Aldrich, 1994; Ram, 1999). As a result, the members of micro-sized small firms tend to have a high level of overlap in their network ties. The extensive use of referral practices in this type of setting may restrict micro-sized small firms' ability to access diverse sets of applicants, thus making it difficult to develop a large pool of applicants. This constraint may not be as severe for small firms with several hundred employees where there is a greater likelihood that organizational members come from different backgrounds, and as a result, do not share similar network ties outside the organization.

The benefits of formal recruitment practices may also increase as the size of a small firm increases. Individuals are not blank slates when they begin the recruitment process (Barber, 1998). In many situations prospective applicants already have pre-existing information about prospective employers. It is likely that this pre-existing information will anchor job seekers' reactions to small firms' formal recruitment advertisements, such that the more information individuals have about a firm the more likely they will respond favorably towards that firm's advertisements (Williamson et al., 2002). However, the smaller a firm, the less likely it is that prospective applicants will have information about that organization. This is because very small firms tend to lack the financial resources to invest in broad-scale marketing. In addition, the smaller the firm, the less likely it is to be part of a prospective job seeker's everyday experience because of lower media coverage, having a smaller customer base, and having smaller product and service distribution networks (Aldrich and Auster, 1986). Thus, due to lower levels of pre-existing information, prospective applicants may be less likely to respond to the formal job ads posted by micro-sized firms compared to small firms with several hundred employees (see also Cardon and Tarique, Chapter 17 this handbook). There are two exceptions to this: family-owned businesses and popular community firms. Both examples represent circumstances where the familiarity would attract prospective applicants via informal methods.

Finally, the size of a small firm may also play a role in shaping the effectiveness of brokers at increasing recruitment performance. Micro-sized firms may be less able to develop effective partnerships with brokers. Due to financial constraints it may be difficult for micro-sized firms to develop and retain ties with brokers for long periods of time. Furthermore, because very small firms tend to hire very few individuals it may be difficult for them to develop effective network ties with brokers that are high-volume sources of employees (Williamson et al., 2002). For example, micro-sized small firms may be less likely to form ongoing relationships with professors, university career office advisors or managers at temporary agencies due to the infrequency that they hire. As a result, brokers may be less able to identify prospective applicants who will fit with very small firms. This may lead to micro-sized firms receiving fewer applicants from brokers and applicants with a poor fit with the firm's needs.

In summary, there are several arguments suggesting that the effectiveness of small firms' recruitment practice portfolio will vary by their size. However, to date, we are unaware of any research examining this issue. Thus, based on the logic presented above we will explore the following research question: how does firm size affect the relationship between the use of informal, formal and broker recruitment practices and the immediate recruitment outcomes of small firms?

Design, methodology and approach
We examine these questions by utilizing data from the US Multi-City Study of Urban Inequality (MCSUI). The MCSUI contains telephone survey data from representatives of over 2500 small firms, defined as firms with fewer than 500 employees, in four United States metropolitan areas (Holzer et al., 2000). Survey respondents were firm owners, supervisors or personnel managers with the requirement that the respondent was responsible for hiring within the firm. Using this dataset we examined the relationship between the portfolio of informal, formal and brokered recruitment practices used by firms and two types of recruitment outcomes: total number of applicants for a job opening and time it took firms to fill a job opening. In addition, we examined how firm characteristics, such as size, shape the

effectiveness of recruitment practice portfolios. We conducted our analysis on all of the firms in the MCSUI database with 500 or fewer employees (according to the SBA definition). We eliminated 16 cases with missing data and were left with 2521 valid cases to analyze.

Independent variables: hiring methods and firm size
For our analyses we were interested in the hiring methods used by employers. To determine the type of hiring methods used by employers in the MCSUI, respondents were asked to 'Indicate if you used any of the following referral or recruiting methods to fill this position (the last position for which a firm hired)?' Responses were coded according to the type of method used. We used the recruitment strategies of newspaper advertisement and employee referrals as proxies for formal and informal methods, respectively. We then used school referrals and temporary agency referrals as the proxies for brokered recruitment strategies. We recoded the original variable to create four dummy variables representing informal, formal, school-broker and temporary agency-broker. We used the number of permanent employees as the indicator of the firm size.

Dependent variables
We used two different measures of recruitment effectiveness as dependent variables in our analysis. Both the number of applicants and the recruit time variables are common measures in HRM research (Barber, 1998). The 'time needed to hire last employee' was measured in weeks. We viewed any strategies associated with decreasing the time needed to fill a position as more effective than methods, which increased the time required to hire a new employee. The number of applicants is also a measure of the effectiveness of recruitment strategies because more applicants increase the chances that good candidates will be found (Barber, 1998; Taylor, 1994). The MCSUI asked respondents to reveal the number of applicants for the last hired job and we used this data to operationalize our variable.

Control variables
We used four control variables: industry, city, difficulty in finding qualified workers and the type of job.

For industry we used two-digit SIC designations provided in the MCSUI and we coded each of the firms in the dataset as manufacturing/construction, retail or service. We found that most of the firms in these data were categorized as service (49 per cent), followed by retail (27 per cent), manufacturing (22 per cent) and construction (2 per cent).

There are four cities in the MCSUI database: Boston, Detroit, Los Angeles and Atlanta. The original variable was a categorical variable. We created dummy variables for each of the cities in the dataset. When conducting analysis, Atlanta was the base category.

In terms of the difficulty finding qualified workers, MCSUI respondents were asked if it was easier, the same or more difficult to find qualified workers for the last hired position than five or ten years ago. While it may have been difficult for all respondents to accurately evaluate recruitment difficulty in the past, we believe this question provides important insight into managers' perceptions of the labor market within which they compete. This was a categorical variable that was coded 1 = easier, 2 = the same and 3 = difficult. The mean was 2.1, indicating that many of the respondents thought it was difficult.

The MCSUI was particularly concerned with jobs that did not require a college education. These are entry-level jobs that ostensibly anybody can get and that would mostly likely be sought locally. Jobs requiring college-level education can be sourced regionally and nationally. Only 8 per cent of the jobs in our dataset required college degrees.

Findings

In this study we were primarily concerned with examining two questions: (1) what is the effect of small firms' portfolio of recruitment practices on immediate recruitment outcomes? and (2) how does firm size affect the relationship between the use of informal, formal and broker recruitment practices and the immediate recruitment outcomes of small firms? To examine these issues we conducted two regression analyses. First we regressed the control variables, the main effects for the recruitment practice variables, and the firm size by recruitment practice interaction variables on the dependent variable which was number of job applicants. Second, we regressed the same set of predictors on the dependent variable time to fill position. Table 18.1 provides the means, standard deviations and correlations between the variables in the analyses.

Table 18.2 contains the results of the regression analyses. In it Model 1 shows the results for the number of job applicants variable. In terms of the control variables, industry, geographic location, perceived difficulty in finding employees, and the requirement of a college degree did not have significant effects on the number of applicants firms received for their last job posting. In addition, firm size did not have a significant main effect on the number of applicants. The results of Model 1 show that firm recruitment practices had both main and interactive effects on number of applicants. In terms of the main effects, informal recruitment practices had an insignificant main effect on the number of applicants. However, the use of formal recruitment practices had a significant positive effect on number of applicants. In the case of the broker variables, the use of school referrals

Table 18.1 Descriptive statistics and Pearson correlation co-efficients[a]

Variable	Mean	SD	1	2	3	4	5	6	7	8	9	10	11	12	13	14
1. Construction	.02	.15														
2. Retail	.27	.44	-.10													
3. Service	.49	.50	-.16	-.60												
4. Los Angeles	.29	.46	-.02	-.04	.00											
5. Boston	.26	.44	-.02	-.05	.03	-.38										
6. Detroit	.21	.41	.03	.06	-.01	-.33	-.31									
7. Difficulty finding qualified workers	2.10	.81	.04	.05	-.04	-.02	-.15	.12								
8. College degree required	.08	.27	.00	-.09	.14	-.03	.01	.05	-.05							
9. Firm size[b]	85.06	109.91	-.05	-.08	-.04	.06	-.02	-.01	-.08	.03						
10. Informal practices	.82	.38	-.03	.01	.01	-.02	.00	.02	.04	-.03	.18					
11. Formal practices	.47	.50	-.01	-.07	.07	-.06	.05	.13	.03	.03	.08	.10				
12. Use of school referrals	.20	.40	.00	-.03	-.03	.00	-.03	.06	.04	.04	.04	.05	.03			
13. Use of temporary agencies	.34	.47	.00	.00	.06	-.02	-.10	.15	.04	.06	.06	.14	.15	.12		
14. Time to fill position	2.96	5.08	-.02	-.09	.10	.00	.01	-.01	.05	.19	.01	.00	.08	.06	.04	
15. Number of job applicants	25.02	53.63	-.02	.01	-.03	.01	-.01	.02	-.04	.01	.16	.05	.22	.00	.08	0.07

Notes:

a. The results are based on 2521 observations. All correlations above the absolute value of .03 are significant at the $p < .05$ level.

b. Correlations calculated using natural log of firm size.

Table 18.2   Regression analyses predicting number of job applicants and time to fill the position

Predictors	Model 1[a] Number of job applicants[b]	Model 2[a] Time to fill position[c]
Control variables		
Construction	−0.01	−0.02
Retail	0.00	−0.05
Service	−0.05	0.04
Los Angeles	−0.01	−0.01
Boston	−0.03	0.00
Detroit	−0.02	−0.04
Difficulty finding qualified workers	−0.04	0.07*
College degree required	0.02	0.18*
Main effects		
Firm size	0.06	0.08
Informal practices	0.00	−0.02
Formal practices	0.20*	0.06*
Use of school referrals	0.05*	0.02
Use of temporary agencies	−0.02	0.05*
Interactive effects		
Size × Informal	0.03	−0.10*
Size × Formal	0.07*	0.03
Size × School	0.06*	−0.01
Size × Temporary agencies	−0.09*	0.00
Model R^2	.08*	.06*

Notes:
* $p<.05$.
[a]   Standardized coefficients (Beta) are shown.
[b]   N=2553.
[c]   N=2521.

had a significant positive main effect on number of applicants. However, the main effect for use of temporary services was not significant.

Our analyses also revealed several significant interactions between size and recruitment practice. First, there was a significant firm size by formal recruitment practice interaction. In order to interpret this result we plotted this interaction on number of applicants (see Figure 18.1). Consistent with the recommendations of Aiken and West (1991) we used the value of one standard deviation above and below the sample mean to represent high and low firm size, while use of formal recruitment practices was represented by a dichotomous variable (1 = firms used this practice or 0 = firms did not use this

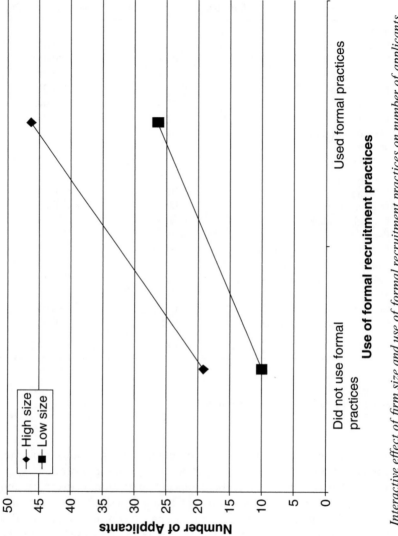

Figure 18.1   Interactive effect of firm size and use of formal recruitment practices on number of applicants

practice). As illustrated in Figure 18.1, the use of formal recruitment practices had a positive effect on the number of applicants for small and micro-sized small firms; however, this effect became stronger as firm size increased.

We also found a significant interaction between firm size and both the broker variables. Consistent with the procedures described above we used the value of one standard deviation above and below the sample mean to represent high and low firm size, while the use of each broker practice was represented by a dichotomous variable (1 = firms used this practice or 0 = firms did not use this practice).

As illustrated in Figure 18.2, the use of school referrals had no meaningful effect on the number of applicants for micro-sized firms. However, school referrals had a strong positive effect on number of applicants for small firms with several hundred employees. Interestingly we found the opposite outcome for the temporary agency interaction.

As illustrated in Figure 18.3, the use of temporary agencies had a positive effect on number of applicants for micro-sized small firms but a negative effect on the number of applicants for larger small firms. Taken together, the findings for the use of school and temporary agency brokers suggested that different types of brokers may be more or less effective at increasing applicant pool size for certain small firms.

In Table 18.2, Model 2 shows the results for the time to fill the position variable. In terms of the control variables, perceived difficulty in finding employees and the requirement of a college degree both had a significant positive effect on how long it took small firms to fill a position. Industry and geographic location were not significant predictors. In addition, firm size did not have a significant main effect on the time it took to fill the position. The results of Model 2 show that firm recruitment practices had both main and interactive effects on time to fill the position. In terms of the main effect, informal recruitment practices had an insignificant main effect on time to fill the position. However, the use of formal recruitment practices had a significant positive effect on time to fill, suggesting that it took small firms longer to fill job vacancies when they used formal recruitment practices. In the case of the broker variables, the use of school referrals had an insignificant main effect on time to fill the position. However, the use of temporary services had a positive significant effect on time to fill, such that using this practice increased the amount of time it took small firms to fill a job opening.

Our analyses also revealed one significant interactive effect. There was a significant interaction between firm size and informal recruitment practice. Following the procedures described above we plotted this interaction in order to interpret the finding. As illustrated in Figure 18.4, the use of informal recruitment practices had a positive effect on the time to fill a position

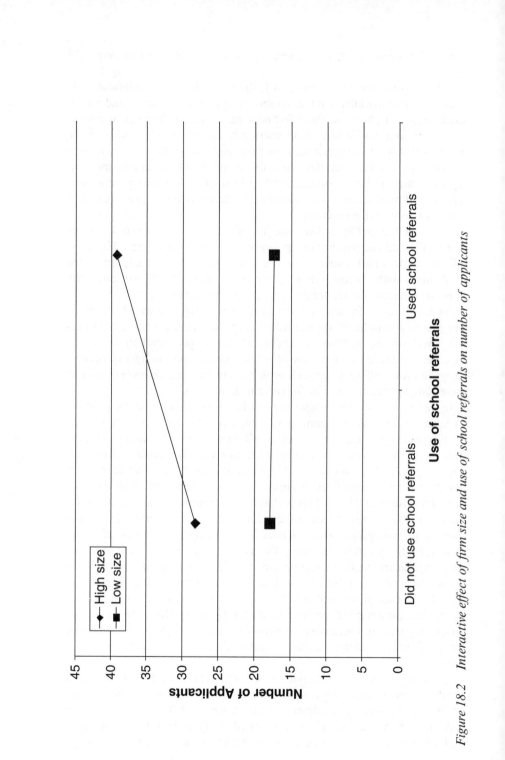

Figure 18.2   Interactive effect of firm size and use of school referrals on number of applicants

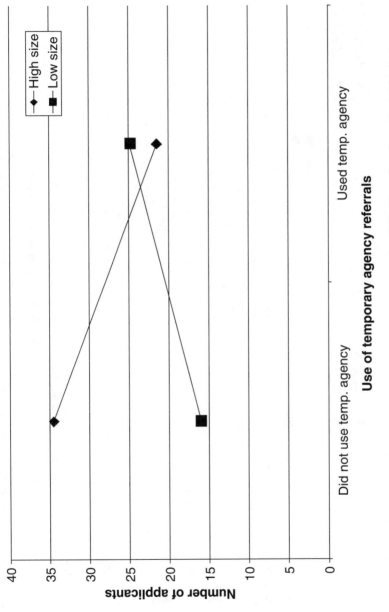

Use of temporary agency referrals

Figure 18.3   Interactive effect of firm size and use of temporary agency referrals on number of applicants

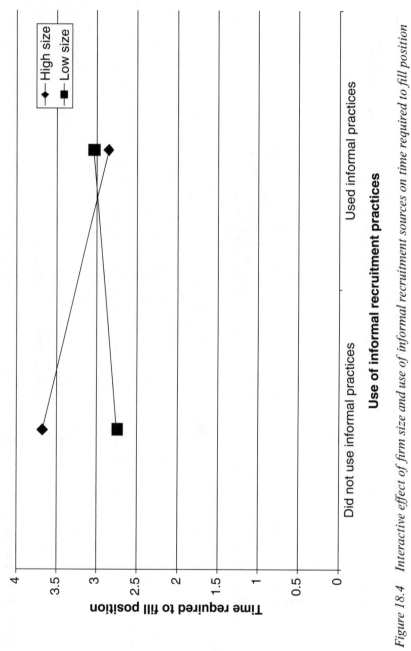

Figure 18.4 Interactive effect of firm size and use of informal recruitment sources on time required to fill position

for very small firms; however, this effect was negative for small firms with larger numbers of employees. This finding suggests that the use of informal recruitment practices was able to reduce the time it took small firms with several hundred employees to fill job openings, while the use of this practice actually increased the amount of time it took micro-sized firms to fill job vacancies.

Implications
Finding the appropriate workforce is one of the most difficult challenges for small businesses and this is an issue on which HRM researchers have been silent (Cardon and Stevens, 2004). Furthermore, there is little research on the effectiveness of various recruitment strategies for small firms. For this study, we went one step further toward understanding the dynamics of effective recruitment for small firms. We found that there were qualitative differences between the effectiveness of recruitment practices for micro-sized firms compared to small firms with several hundred employees. Our findings clearly illustrate that not all small firms are the same and that HRM in small firms is dynamic and cannot be portrayed by standardized descriptions. The effectiveness of recruitment methods is contingent on the size of the firm. With the variety of methods that can be used, which methods are the most effective and why? It is clear that the portfolio of methods – informal, formal and brokered – matter. By analyzing the use of these methods simultaneously we can see the relative effectiveness of one type of practice for small firm recruitment compared to the other two. Our findings indicate that a method may be effective for different reasons.

Formal recruitment methods
For the firms in our study, formal practices played a significant role in the recruitment portfolio. Our analysis demonstrated that the use of formal practices increased the number of job applicants for both small and micro-sized firms. This benefits employers in small firms because having more applicants raises the probability of better hires. Small firms with several hundred employees, however, seemed to benefit more from these methods than micro-sized. Why? One possible explanation for these findings is a legitimacy story. Firm size tends to influence the level of legitimacy firms receive, such that smaller firms tend to have lower levels of legitimacy, relative to large organizations (Williamson et al., 2002). Small firms with a number of employees will benefit from their reputation. Using formal methods reinforces their legitimacy in the labor market with potential employees. Micro-sized firms may be using formal methods to gain legitimacy in the labor market. Potential employees may be reluctant to apply for these jobs because they do not recognize these micro-sized firms. It should be noted

that the standardized coefficient for the main effect indicates that these formal practices have the largest effect within the portfolio of methods.

While formal methods increased the number of job applicants, the results were mixed for the time required to fill the position. In fact, formal methods increased the time to hire an employee. This finding makes some sense in the context of the timing of advertisement placement. Interestingly, size of the firm does not matter for formal methods.

Informal recruitment methods

The use of informal recruitment methods, such as employee referrals, was found to have no effect on the number of job applicants. However, we found that the use of these practices decreased the time required to fill a position for small firms with several hundred employees, while they increased the time required for micro-sized firms. Why does this work for larger small firms and not for the micro-sized firms? We believe the answer lies in the level of social capital present in the firm. Specifically, small firms with several hundred employees may have greater amounts of social capital than micro-sized firms. This may be due primarily to the larger number of employees and the greater diversity of their potential contacts. Some firms may also have provided incentives to their employees for good referrals and this could have led to quicker referral times. With all of the emphasis in the research on informal recruitment methods, why do micro-sized firms not see the same benefit? Micro-sized firms may have already used up their social capital to identify their current employees. Thus, it might have taken micro-sized firms longer to identify potential employees as current employees draw down on their social capital on behalf of the firm. While we believe that there is a social capital explanation, this is certainly an area that requires more research.

The use of brokered recruitment methods

The use of brokered recruitment methods, such as school and temporary agency referrals, also has mixed implications. The use of schools as brokers increased the number of job applicants for small firms with several hundred employees but did not have an effect on the applicant pool size of micro-sized small firms. One explanation for this finding could be that as small firms grow in size they may be better equipped to develop ongoing relationships with large providers of applicants, such as schools. In particular, as small firms grow they may have the resources to appoint an employee to act in a formal liaison role with the school. This may increase the likelihood that school administrators understand the needs of the firm, thus increasing the likelihood that administrators will channel prospective applicants towards the small firm. Furthermore, school counselors may view small firms with several hundred employees as more legitimate employers than micro-sized firms, which in turn may decrease their motivation to steer potential applicants to micro-sized firms.

Conversely, we found that the use of temporary agencies increased the pool of applicants for micro-sized small firms but decreased it for larger small firms. Micro-sized firms may have benefited from the use of temporary agencies because these brokers expanded the social capital of the company. As discussed above, micro-sized small firms may have limited network connections. As such, contracting with a temporary agency may have allowed micro-sized firms to leverage the connections of temporary agencies in order to expand the range of individuals that were aware of their job vacancies. Social capital may also explain why temporary agencies did not benefit larger small firms. It is possible that there was an overlap between the types of applicants temporary agencies could identify and the job seekers that larger small firms could identify using formal or informal practices. However, while our findings indicated that temporary services did not increase applicant pool size for larger small firms, we wonder if this practice resulted in firms hiring better employees. That is an empirical question for future research.

Taken together, these results suggest that in order to maximize applicant pool size, the composition of the small firm's recruitment practice portfolio should vary by its size. Interactions between size and the use of formal and both brokered methods were important indicators of the number of job applicants. These findings point us toward future areas for research. For example, why does the use of brokers play such different roles for the micro-sized firms versus small firms? Under what conditions might the role of brokers be enhanced for micro-sized firms? This is especially important when policy makers are seeking ways to assist small firms. Understanding the role and the effectiveness of brokers for these firms could be a means of supporting small firms.

Practical implications

Our findings point toward strategic implications for small firms. Since recruitment method can have a great influence on recruitment outcomes it is important for owners and managers of small firms to be deliberate in their choice of recruitment practices. When small firms with several hundred employees are trying to increase the size of their applicant pool the use of formal (such as newspaper ads) and school referrals can be very effective. Owners and managers of larger small firms should also be aware of the ability of employee referral programs to decrease the time it takes to fill a position. Thus, creating incentives for current employees to refer good potential employees may be a wise recruitment strategy.

The findings of our study suggest that the temporary agency may be a promising recruitment tool for micro-sized small firms when they want to increase the number of applicants. Micro-sized small firms that are entering a growth period may find this type of broker to be especially useful. However, it is important to note that managers should consider the cost associated with this strategy when determining the overall benefits of using temporary agencies.

References

Aiken, L.S. and S.G. West (1991), *Multiple Regression: Testing and Interpreting Interactions*, Newbury Park, CA: Sage Publications.
Aldrich, H.E. and E.R. Auster (1986), 'Even dwarfs started small: Liabilities of age and size and their strategic implications', in B.M. Stuart and L.L. Cummings (eds), *Research in Organizational Behavior*, Greenwich CT: JAI Press, pp. 165–98.
Anon (2005), 'Appropriate skills – the lifeblood of the small business community', *Education and Training*, **47**, 682–3.
Baker, T. and H.E. Aldrich (1994), 'Friends and strangers: Early hiring practices and idiosyncratic jobs', in W.D. Bygrave, S. Birley, N.C. Churchill, E. Gatewood, F. Hoy, R.H. Keeley and W.E. Wetzel (eds), *Frontiers of Entrepreneurship Research*, Wellesley, MA: Babson College, pp. 75–87.
Barber, A.E. (1998), *Recruiting Employees: Individual and Organizational Perspectives*, Thousand Oaks, CA: Sage Publications.
Barber, A.E., M.J. Wesson, Q.M. Roberson and M.S. Taylor (1999), 'A tale of two job markets: Organizational size and its effects on hiring practices and job search behavior', *Personnel Psychology*, **52**, 841–67.
Breaugh, J.A. and R.B. Mann (1984), 'Recruiting source effects: A test of two alternative explanations', *Journal of Occupational Psychology*, **57**, 261–67.
Burt, R.S. (1992), *Structural Holes: The Social Structure of Competition*, Cambridge, MA: Harvard University Press.
Burton, M.D., J.B. Sorensen and C. Beckman (2002), 'Coming from good stock: Career histories and new venture formation', in M. Loundsburry and M.J. Ventressca (eds), *Social Structure and Organizations Revisited*, London: Elsevier Science, pp. 229–62.
Cardon, M.S. and C.E. Stevens (2004), 'Managing human resources in small organizations: What do we know?', *Human Resources Management Review*, **14**, 295–323.
Carroll, G.R. and A.C. Teo (1996), 'On the social networks of managers', *Academy of Management Journal*, **39**(2), 421–40.
Carroll, M., M. Marchington, J. Earnshaw and S. Taylor (1999), 'Recruitment in small firms: Processes, methods and problems', *Employee Relations*, **21**(3), 236–50.
Fernandez, R.M. and N. Weinberg (1997), 'Shifting and sorting: Personal contacts and hiring in a retail bank', *American Sociological Review*, **6**, 883–902.
Fernandez, R.M., E.J. Castilla and P. Moore (2000), 'Social capital at work: Networks and employment at a phone center', *American Journal of Sociology*, **105**, 1288–356.
Heneman, H.G. and R.A. Berkley (1999), 'Applicant attraction practices and outcomes among small business', *Journal of Small Business Management*, **37**, 53–74.
Holzer, H., J. Kirschenman, P. Moss and C. Tilly (2000), *The Multi-City Study of Urban Inequality, 1992–1994: Atlanta, Boston, Detroit, and Los Angeles*, [Dataset], Inter-University Consortium for Political and Social Research.
Kalleberg, A.L., D. Knoke, P.V. Marsden and J.L. Spaeth (1996), *Organizations in America: Analyzing Their Structures and Human Resource Practices*, Thousand Oaks, CA: Sage.
Kotey, B. and A. Sheridan (2004), 'Changing HRM practices with firm growth', *Journal of Small Business and Enterprise Development*, **11**(4), 474–85.
Leung, H.K. (2001), 'Quality metrics for intranet applications', *Information and Management*, **38**(3), 137–52.

Marsden, P.C. (1994), 'The hiring process: Recruitment methods', *American Behavioral Scientist*, **27**, 979–91.

Muson, H. (2001), 'The people problem', *Across the Board*, **38**, 87–8.

Ram, M. (1999), 'Managing autonomy: Employment relations in small professional service firms', *International Small Business Journal*, **17**, 13–30.

Rees, A. (1966), 'Information networks in labor markets', *American Economic Review*, **56**, 559–66.

Saari, L.M., T.R. Johnson, S.D. McLaughlin and D.M. Zimmerle (1988), 'A survey of management training and education practices in US companies', *Personnel Psychology*, **41**, 731–43.

Small Business Administration (SBA) (2007), 'Specific FAQs', available at http://www.sba.gov/services/contractingopportunities/sizestandardstopics/faqs/index.html, downloaded on 30 January 2007.

Tanova, C. (2003), 'Firm size and recruitment: Staffing practices in small and large organizations in north Cyprus', *Career Development International*, **8**(2), 107–14.

Taylor, M.C. (1994), 'Impact of Affirmative Action on beneficiary groups: Evidence from the 1990 General Social Survey', *Basic and Applied Social Psychology*, **15**, 143–78.

Werbel, J.D., J. Landau and T.E. DeCarlo (2001), 'The relationship of pre-entry variables to early employment organizational commitment', *Journal of Personal Selling and Sales Management*, **16**(2), 25–36.

Wilkinson, A. (1999), 'Employment relations in SMEs', *Employee Relations*, **21**, 206–17.

Williams, C.R., C.E. Labig and T.H. Stone (1993), 'Recruitment sources and posthire outcomes for job applicants and new hires: A test of two hypotheses', *Journal of Applied Psychology*, **78**(2), 163–72.

Williamson, I.O. (2000), 'Employer legitimacy and recruitment success in small businesses', *Entrepreneurship: Theory and Practice*, **25**(1), 27–42.

Williamson, I.O., D.M. Cable and H.E. Aldrich (2002), 'Smaller but not necessarily weaker: How small businesses can overcome barriers to recruitment', in J.A. Katz and T.M. Welbourne (eds), *Advances in Entrepreneurship, Firm Emergence, and Firm Growth*, Greenwich, CT: JAI Press, pp. 83–106.

19 Would using the psychological contract increase entrepreneurial business development potential?
Deborah Blackman and Kevin Hindle

Introduction

In an Australian national newspaper in 2005 an entrepreneur complained that he could not find an appropriate employee for a certain job (Perrett, 2005). He was advised that his expectations were unrealistic and that he was likely to upset his new employees by taking far more than he was giving in terms of their personal expectations. The entrepreneur was not reflecting good human resource management (HRM) practices but he was also setting the stage for violation of the psychological contract.

As will be demonstrated in this chapter, this is not an isolated incident. Such a mismatch of expectations is common throughout small business operations, especially with respect to early stage firms (Massey et al., 2006). A study of the entrepreneurial literature demonstrates a shortage of research into the role of human resources in entrepreneurial businesses (Heneman et al., 2000; Katz et al., 2000) and that entrepreneurs mostly focus on human resources in terms of human capital (Florin et al., 2003; Zhang et al., 2003), not as a fundamental part of the success or failure of their enterprise.

In this chapter our focus is on the importance of relationships for successful entrepreneurship and their absence from the most often-used theoretical frameworks underpinning empirical work into the entrepreneurial development process (such as stage models). The lack of an appropriate theoretical model for understanding the nature of an entrepreneur's employment decision-making processes is promulgated and we then introduce the psychological contract and discuss why its well-developed theoretical tenets might form a useful addition to an entrepreneur's tool-kit. Although widely discussed in the HRM and organizational studies literature, the psychological contract is only rarely and peripherally discussed in the entrepreneurship literature. A significant contribution of this chapter is that entrepreneurs have strong, pre-conceived beliefs and values concerning their employees, which affects the nature of the psychological contract with their employees.

Consequently, our objective is first to identify and discuss the nature of the 'mismatch' between the dominant concerns of practising entrepreneurs and the principal interests and focuses of current entrepreneurship research with respect to the development of new ventures. Second, it is to explore the lack of HRM milestones in current stage models of the entrepreneurial process, while third it is to analyse, in light of existing theory, ways of implementing successful entrepreneurial relationships through the application of the psychological contract.

This is a theoretical argument linking two distinct areas of literature: entrepreneurial business development and the psychological contract, to create a substantive level theory (Creswell, 1994). Such theory building is often an important foundation for new theory development where researchers are still in the discovery phase and the relationship between different constructs is not yet defined (Judd et al., 1991; Sarantakos, 1998) especially in areas where the questions are unclear and the ideas are exploratory (Creswell, 1994). We intend to develop a research plan in order to develop middle-range level theory at the next research stage.

What is entrepreneurship?
Davidsson (2003) identified two main streams of entrepreneurial literature. In the first, entrepreneurship is about the discovery, evaluation and exploitation of opportunities (Shane and Venkataraman, 2000). This literature emphasizes entrepreneurship as a disequilibrium activity where opportunities are defined as 'situations in which new goods, services, raw materials, markets and organizing methods can be introduced through the formation of new means, ends, or means–ends relationship' (Eckhardt and Shane, 2003: p. 4). In the second stream, entrepreneurship is viewed as organizational or firm emergence (Gartner, 1993) where the evolutionary and dynamic aspects of entrepreneurship are crucial and the focus is on organizing activities in a Weickian sense.

Figure 19.1 represents two main dimensions distinguishing two streams of thought. Dimension 1 deals with actions involved in an entrepreneurial process and whether they are defined by creation and identification of new means and ends relationships or maximizing existing means and ends relationships. Dimension 2 is concerned with the context and whether it involves creation of new organizations or entrepreneurship taking place in an existing organizational context. 'A' is characterized by a venture whose essence is to be an innovative start-up that changes the competitive conditions within an industry and drives the market. 'B' includes start-ups that do not change underlying competitive conditions in an industry or the fundamental forces that drive the operation of an existing market, but fill gaps in an existing market by maximizing existing means and ends relationships.

Actions involved

	Creation of new means and ends relationships	Maximizing existing means and ends relationships
New organizations	(A) Change oriented venture creation	(B) Non-change oriented venture creation
Existing organizations	(C) Change oriented corporate venturing	(D) Traditional management

Context

Source: Klyver (2005).

Figure 19.1   Distinguishing the emergence and opportunity view of entrepreneurship

'C' includes creation or identification of new means and ends relationships exploited in an existing organizational context, involving an existing organization changing competitive market conditions by the introduction of new products, processes or production methods. 'C' represents the opportunity perspective and 'B' the emergence perspective. 'A' can be both, while 'D' is not entrepreneurship from either the opportunity or the emergence perspective, but merely traditional management.

One imperative common to 'A', 'B' and 'C' is a need to establish, develop and manage the relationships inside and outside the venture and this includes the employment relationship. Whilst it is often assumed that human resource issues for entrepreneurs will be constraining because they are about 'hard' processes and systems that hinder, rather than support a growing business (Kickul, 2001), the 'soft' side of human resources is increasingly seen to be fundamental to any business (Storey, 1994) including entrepreneurial ones. A study of the fundamental approaches to the nature of entrepreneurship in the entrepreneurship literature demonstrates a surprising lack of discussion about human resource management in general and the employment relationship in particular (Katz et al., 2000). Remarkably none of the most heavily used models of entrepreneurial development discuss this aspect.

How should we study the entrepreneur's employment decision?
The influential paper by Churchill and Lewis (1983) underpins many of the stage (or life cycle) models of entrepreneurial venture development that

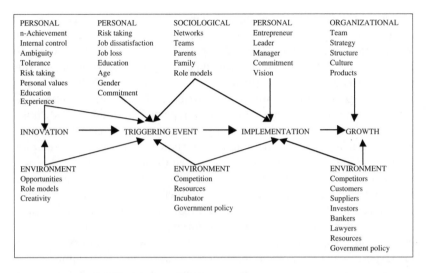

PERSONAL	PERSONAL	SOCIOLOGICAL	PERSONAL	ORGANIZATIONAL
n-Achievement	Risk taking	Networks	Entrepreneur	Team
Internal control	Job dissatisfaction	Teams	Leader	Strategy
Ambiguity	Job loss	Parents	Manager	Structure
Tolerance	Education	Family	Commitment	Culture
Risk taking	Age	Role models	Vision	Products
Personal values	Gender			
Education	Commitment			
Experience				

INNOVATION → TRIGGERING EVENT → IMPLEMENTATION → GROWTH

ENVIRONMENT	ENVIRONMENT	ENVIRONMENT
Opportunities	Competition	Competitors
Role models	Resources	Customers
Creativity	Incubator	Suppliers
	Government policy	Investors
		Bankers
		Lawyers
		Resources
		Government policy

Sources: Bygrave (1989) and Moore (1986).

Figure 19.2   Influences on entrepreneurial process through time

represent various 'typical' developmental stages that firms go through as they mature (for example Burns and Harrison, 1996; Gray, 1993; Greiner, 1972). An example of a stage model of entrepreneurial development is in Figure 19.2, which is a schematic illustration of the development of a 'typical' entrepreneurial venture.

The Moore–Bygrave framework posits four stages of the entrepreneurial process: innovation, triggering event, implementation and growth. It demonstrates that entrepreneurial decision-making and performance are simultaneously impacted by cognitive and environmental variables. In the cognitive domain, for example, the proportional importance of individual, sociological and organizational factors varies with respect to the stage of the process.

This typical stage-model reveals two failings. First, there is an unwarranted implicit presumption that growth is both a conscious and a desirable aim for every new venture. Second, the decision to hire an employee is a milestone conspicuous by its absence. Yet we know that growth is neither a universal objective nor a universal result in the entrepreneurial development process. Also entrepreneurial practitioners agree that the decision to hire an employee is a prominent milestone in the development trajectory of any venture.

A recent study demonstrates that amid the vast array of possible entrepreneurial developmental patterns there exist enough clustered similarities for various patterns to be worthy of generic classification: 'maturity and decline'; 'on a growth curve' and 'capped growth' (Massey et al., 2006). Whether a firm exhibited one or other pattern of development appeared to relate strongly to the attitude to growth held by the owner or manager; this position was also the consequence of a number of interrelated factors, including age and other demographic attributes. Massey et al. (2006) indicate that amongst the most commonly reported business-related 'milestones' or 'key events' was the employment of staff. All respondents were vociferous in highlighting the generic importance of this decision to employ someone. Often, the discussion that followed the identification of this particular milestone included details of the difficulties owner–managers were faced with regarding human resources in their firms. Especially problematic aspects included the burden of taking on new staff in terms of compliance and the inability to find appropriately trained staff. Anecdotal evidence also supports this view and it is hard to hold a conversation with any experienced entrepreneur without them stressing the vital importance of the decision to hire someone as a seminal event in the life of a new venture. Despite such evidence the decision to hire is strikingly absent from the stage-model approach. This absence is all the more remarkable, because an increase in employee numbers is considered a standard way of measuring the very growth that is at the heart of the stage-model approach. Moreover, growth in the number of employees (as a proxy for employment creation) is also identified as a desirable goal by most government agencies involved in supporting small and medium-sized enterprises (SMEs).

So why is it absent? We examined several theories currently in use in the entrepreneurial literature and considered their usefulness as a framework for structured investigation of early-stage entrepreneurial recruitment decisions. We considered theories on risk and return (Tobin, 1958); the capital asset pricing model (Sharpe, 1964), portfolio decision making (Banks et al., 2003; Samuelson, 1969), risk preferences of households (Jorion and Goetzmann, 1999), the presence of labour income (Merton, 1971) and multiple theoretical perspectives now finding currency in the area of 'Angel' investments (Wong and Ho, 2007). Unsurprisingly, mechanistic theories of risk and return did not encompass the complexities involved in making an interpersonal decision (whether or not it is regarded as an 'investment') such as hiring an employee. We considered trust, which is recognized within the entrepreneurship literature as a precondition for rational choice (Loasby, 1997), but any complexities attendant upon it are simply assumed away. What became clear was that, although there is a wide-ranging discussion of trust in the entrepreneurship literature (Clark and Payne, 1997; Dibben, 2000; Dubini and Aldrich, 1991; Harrison et al., 1997; Lewicki and Bunker, 1995, 1996; Ryan and Buchholtz, 2001), researchers have studied how different types and levels of trust relate to the criteria used by investors to establish their cooperation threshold (the point at which individuals decide to commit to an investment) but not in the context of the entrepreneurial employment decision. We turned then to consider context for the ways in which interpersonal contacts (and cognitions concerning them) are developed and applied and we contemplated social networks and social capital.

Recently, the entrepreneurship literature has highlighted the significance of 'social networks' and 'social capital' in the creation and growth of new ventures in order to clarify how ideas are developed and capitalized upon (Nahapiet and Ghoshal, 1998; Shane and Cable, 2002; Shane and Venkataraman, 2000; Zhang et al., 2003). When leveraged effectively social capital provides individuals with considerable resources to facilitate the identification, evaluation and exploitation of opportunities. Unfortunately, it seems either very difficult or somewhat artificial to try to use the concept of social capital or the wider concept of social networks as an effective framework for generic exploration of the early-stage employment decisions of entrepreneurs. Both theories, at this stage of their utilization in the entrepreneurship literature, identify the importance of the ideas but not the elements that drive them in terms of developing new employment relationships.

A consideration of the drivers in the employment decision led us to consider Ajzen's (2002) theory of planned behaviour, cited in the entrepreneurship literature for its potential to provide both a theoretical framework and operationalizable constructs for understanding the decision of individuals to make informal (angel) investments in entrepreneurial businesses (Maula et al., 2005; Wong and Ho, 2007). As recruitment is a form of investment decision by the entrepreneur (Mainprize and Hindle, 2005) it is possible that Ajzen's theory may provide a basis for the decision-making processes of entrepreneurs with respect to their early-stage employment decisions. This theory deconstructs human behaviour into three distinct but related belief elements: behavioural beliefs concerning the likely consequences of behaviour; normative beliefs concerning one's expectations of other people; and control beliefs concerning the presence of factors that may affect performance of the behaviour. Behavioural beliefs produce attitude towards the behaviour, normative beliefs produce a subjective norm, and control beliefs produce perceived behavioural control. The combination of attitude, subjective norm and perceived behavioural control forms a behavioural intention. When an adequate degree of actual control and opportunity is present, individuals will be able to act upon this intention and perform the behaviour.

We consider the second generic component of Ajzen's composite theory – normative beliefs concerning the entrepreneur's expectations – as applied to the specific area, decision-making concerning potential employees. The core concept of perceived behavioural control refers generally to people's expectations regarding their ability to perform a given behaviour (Ajzen, 2002). If, in thinking about entrepreneurial employment decision-making, one concentrates attention on what various parties to a contractual relationship expect of one another, this leads to a consideration of the theory of the psychological contract because of its focus upon the role of expectations and their impact upon emergent employee/employer relationships.

What is the psychological contract?
A psychological contract deals with implicit reciprocal promises and obligations in the workplace (Cullinane and Dundon, 2006; Guest, 1998; Rousseau, 1989; Winter and Jackson, 2006); it is 'the individual beliefs, shaped by the organization, regarding terms of an exchange agreement between individuals and the organization' (Rousseau, 1995: p. 9). It is a schema or mental model used to frame events within the workplace and make sense of the relationships within it (Rousseau, 1995). It differs from a formal contract in that it reflects the beliefs, ideals and values held by the individual, which lead to a set of unstated expectations about the workplace (Kickul, 2001; Roehling, 1997). Figure 19.3 demonstrates that commitment, relationships and trust are all going to affect the application of social processes within organizations and how individuals will perceive a critical incident. Individual expectations will be affected by, among other things, organizational culture/climate, HRM policy and practice, an individual's personal experience, and what potential alternatives are perceived as possible (Cullinane and Dundon, 2006; Guest, 1998; Winter and Jackson, 2006).

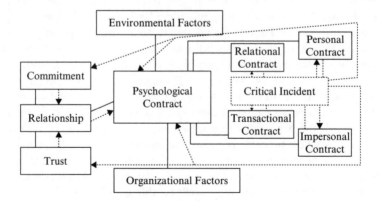

Source: Crossman (2004). Reproduced by kind permission of Dr Alf Crossman.

Figure 19.3   The psychological contract

In terms of early-stage entrepreneurial organizations, where there are likely to be close relationships between the founder/leader and the employees of the organization, closeness of contact will impact on both the psychological contract and consequently the potential effectiveness of the organization. Of the various types of contract that operate in Crossman's model (2004) it is likely that personal and relational contracts will have the most impact on how events are perceived by individuals in entrepreneurial (usually new or smaller) firms.

Breakdowns in the psychological contract tend to lead to a deterioration of trust relations and increased cynicism, and those 'are likely to make future strategic programs more difficult to implement' (Pate et al., 2000: p. 491). The state of the psychological contract helps explain the dynamics of the elements affecting the employment relationship and the likelihood of successfully utilizing or changing aspects of work (Rousseau, 1989). This could seriously impact upon the potential of a new business to achieve its desired outcomes.

The employment relationship is widely held to be an exchange relationship (Maguire, 2002) including subconscious and implicit elements (Spindler, 1994). The overall impact of the psychological contract is that employees develop a form of 'equity balancing' (Kickul, 2001); this is what Rousseau (1989) describes as a 'reciprocal exchange agreement'. There is an acceptance that 'if you do that, I will do this'. A breach of the contract can mean that because a promise has been broken employees may believe they do not need to work as effectively as before. In discussing the state of the psychological contract in small firms, Kickul (2001) concluded that there were five main factors affecting the contract and the way employees perceived it: autonomy and growth; benefits; rewards and opportunities; job security and work responsibilities; and work facilitation. These are areas that employees perceive as having been in some way agreed upon, and promises, albeit implicit, have been made. If these are not kept, a critical incident will result and lead to a breach. Guest (1998) indicated the causal nature of the relationship, showing that the 'content elements' (how the individual perceives the promises and the way they have been fulfilled) lead to the reactions that in turn lead to the employees' actual behaviours (Figure 19.4).

The psychological contract can be seen from the point of view of the employer as well as of the employee (Cullinane and Dundon, 2006; Guest, 2004). In an entrepreneurial context entrepreneurs could have a set of expectations, beliefs and ideals about their employees and this could lead to an unwritten set of agreements. This perspective may be beneficial when studying early-stage ventures because these enterprises are so heavily dependent upon their founders and leaders, and the difference between the

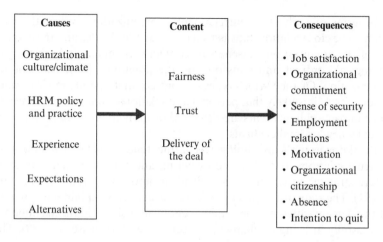

Source: Guest (1998).

Figure 19.4   Guest's model of the psychological contract

organization and the entrepreneur may be a blurred distinction. While Marks (2001) argues that, within the overall concept of the psychological contract there are many, multifarious, sub-contracts operating from the point of view of the employee, we argue that it is possible that diverse aspects of the psychological contract also apply and need to be considered with respect to the entrepreneur.

According to Maguire (2002) the relationship has expectations at three distinct levels (Figure 19.5), indicating what each party to the relationship will bring to the workplace. The transactional elements are usually overtly considered by all those entering a contract and focus upon 'specific monetary economic exchanges which are typically short-term' (D'Annunzio-Green and Francis, 2005: p. 328; see also Rousseau, 1995; Saunders and Thornhill, 2006). Such transactions are often (wrongly) seen to constitute the total of the relationship. This limited perception may pertain especially in the circumstances of small or developing enterprises that are often concentrating principally on short-term goals.

The other two levels depicted in the model may or may not be implicitly considered. At the heart of long-term successful relationships are career aspects which refer to an employee's expectation of how the employer will enable them to achieve their long-term career goals. In entrepreneurial ventures this can be a problem. Entrepreneurs may expect employees to stay with the company instead of leaving to take on new challenges; leaving is seen as disloyal instead of inevitable. The psychological contract provides a framework for understanding why people might leave and what can be

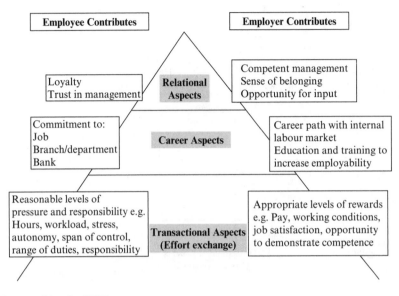

Source: Maguire (2002).

Figure 19.5   Three-tier model of the psychological contract

done to plan for such events or to enable employees to stay. For example, if the firm expands, the employees need to feel involved and not be left in their same roles with new people employed for the next stage of growth. Too often it is too late when growing firms consider the people aspects of change.

This then links into the third level in the Maguire model, the relational aspects. As can be expected from understanding the transactional and career aspects, these are about long-term emotional and development needs, not shorter term or merely instrumental job needs. Because the psychological contract represents a 'social exchange interaction' (Cullinane and Dundon, 2006: p. 119) a large element of its impact is based upon emotional expectations of one party upon the other (D'Annunzio-Green and Francis, 2005). It is here that trust becomes a very important part of the contract – especially as it will affect each party's perspective of the other elements of the contract. One of the things that high levels of trust can do is to reduce the apparent imbalance of power inherent in an employment contract; the imbalance is still there but the employee feels less threatened by it. However, once such a trust is breached, the psychological contract will be seriously threatened. In start-up businesses in particular, promises may be made and broken without enough thought for the longer-term ramifications of such behaviour.

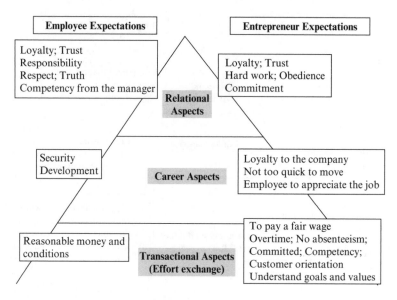

Source: Adapted from Maguire (2002).

Figure 19.6 Expectations in entrepreneurial relationships

What needs to be learnt from the above section is that if the employer reflects neither on whether their expectations are realistic, nor on the longer-term expectations of their employees, it is unlikely expectations will match from the outset of the relationship. Consequently Maguire's (2002) model could be more specific in terms of the mutual expectations held by those involved in an entrepreneurial employment relationship (Figure 19.6).

Given an entrepreneurial context, differences from established applications of psychological contract theory emerge from two main factors: the proximity between the parties in the relationship can lead to the development of personal rather than business relationships, and the strong sense of personal identity between the entrepreneur and their organization (where the entrepreneur may expect employees to feel the same way about the business as they do). Difficulties may also occur through the managerial incompetence of the entrepreneur leading to too little or too much supervision.

Consequences of poor psychological contracts

Poor psychological contracts lead to higher turnover, absenteeism and lower productivity and have a direct impact upon the bottom-line (Guest,

1998). It is important for those involved in employing others to be aware of the potential for problems to occur. In the specific case of an early-stage, entrepreneurial business we suggest that many problems emerge from unrealistic employer expectations. The way that success is measured, money is lent and entrepreneurs advised, means there is a tendency for employers to concentrate on the financial aspects of their enterprise and to expect employees to do the same. This is unrealistic. However enthusiastic employees may be, it is neither their company nor their risk. Figure 19.1 suggests all aspects of the implementation stage need 'managing'. However, it appears from the secondary data gathered from entrepreneurial cases (for example Massey et al., 2006; Perrett, 2005) that for many entrepreneurs the term 'manager' has a very structural and transactional connotation (Maguire, 2002). For them it relates to the control and organizational aspects of a relationship. Using the psychological contract as a basis for developing a way forward, means the entrepreneur might become aware that such arrangements are merely a small subset of the overall employment relationship. In particular, the issue of an employee's career ought to be considered. If entrepreneurs cannot offer future development, they must either expect to lose their employee and learn to consider themselves as a training ground, or they must change the way they recruit in order to attract those who will not want to leave. This may lead to the need to reconsider completely the profile of the types of employee that entrepreneurs wish to employ. This changed perspective will facilitate both an improved psychological contract and, potentially, a reduction in the overall risk profile of the venture.

Reduction of the risk
Entrepreneurs are attracted to challenge, not risk per se. While they do not fear risk-taking, good entrepreneurs seek to minimize it. However, the literature does not currently recognize the very real risks involved in employing someone in an early stage venture. This employment risk can be reduced through an understanding of the psychological contract. We can see this when Hindle and Gibson (2008) describe the employment of workers with a disability in a call centre. For the sake of seeing whether any performance differences distinguished employees with a disability from employees without a disability, it was hypothesized that workers with a disability would under-perform fully-able workers on several measures of employment performance. However, the only significant differences between workers without a disability and workers with a disability were in terms of length of employment and absenteeism. In these two areas the statistically significant and more positive performance belonged to workers with a disability. The differences can be explained by looking at the psychological

contract, although the researcher did not do this, and have potential implications in three areas for the entrepreneur.

1. Both employment duration (turnover) and absenteeism are consequences of poor psychological contracts.
2. Any reduction in either turnover or absenteeism will enable greater opportunities for a development of a more positive psychological contract on both sides.
3. Reduction in these elements should reduce the cost of labour and, therefore, the risk involved in developing an entrepreneurial venture.

The employer wants consistent work at a certain skill level and does not expect any particularly intense devotion to the company, whilst the disability-affected employees had historically had greater difficulty gaining employment and were predisposed to trust the current employer. Hence, it could be posited, in psychological contract terms, that, by being realistic about the skills actually required for a job, combined with due consideration for the employee and realistic expectations about how an employee will feel about the company, an entrepreneur can perform the employment task much better. Knowledge of the psychological contract could lead to reduced employment costs, less stress and reduced venture risk.

Conclusion
In this chapter we identified a mismatch between the concerns of practising entrepreneurs and the principal interests and focuses of current entrepreneurship research with respect to the entrepreneurial development of a new venture. We noted that the crucially important decision to employ others has been insufficiently explored and, currently, does not figure in any of the influential stage-models so often used as theoretical frameworks in entrepreneurship research. We also noted that the issues of implementing an entrepreneurial employment relationship are not well defined or discussed. At the least we need to reconsider the implementation section of Figure 19.2 and include the employee and the expectations of parties to the relationship. We posit that ideas about the psychological contract provide a way to develop better models of how to implement and develop a new entrepreneurial venture. At the very least, conscious and overt inclusion of the employment decision into any stage-model of the entrepreneurial development process will reflect the stages of growth more realistically. Reconsidering step models, to reflect the real complexities of developing employment relationships in early-stage ventures, can reduce the risk associated with entrepreneurial business development.

References

Ajzen, I. (2002), 'Perceived behavioral control, self-efficacy, locus of control and the theory of planned behaviour', *Journal of Applied Social Psychology*, **32**, 1–20.

Banks, J., R. Blundell and J.P. Smith (2003), 'Wealth portfolios in the UK and the US', in D. Wise (ed.), *Perspectives on the Economics of Aging*, Chicago: University of Chicago Press, pp. 205–46.

Burns, P. and J. Harrison (1996), 'Growth', in P. Burns and J. Dewhurst (eds), *Small Business and Entrepreneurship*, 2nd edn, Basingstoke: Macmillan.

Bygrave, W.D. (1989), 'The entrepreneurship paradigm (I): A philosophical look at its research methodologies', *Entrepreneurship: Theory and Practice*, **14**(1), 7–26.

Churchill, N.C. and V.L. Lewis (1983), 'The five stages of small business growth', *Harvard Business Review*, May–June, pp. 30–50.

Clark, M.C. and R.L. Payne (1997), 'The nature and structure of workers' trust in management', *Journal of Organisational Behaviour*, **18**, 205–24.

Creswell, J.W. (1994), *Research Design, Qualitative and Quantitative Aapproaches*, London: Routledge.

Crossman, A. (2004), 'Critical incidents and the dynamics of the psychological contract', *The Anahuac Journal*, **5**(1), 55–66.

Cullinane, N. and T. Dundon (2006), 'The psychological contract: A critical review', *International Journal of Management Reviews*, **8**(2), 113–29.

D'Annunzio-Green, N. and H. Francis (2005), 'Human resource development and the psychological contract: Great expectations or false hopes?', *Human Resource Development International*, **8**(3), 327–44.

Davidsson, P. (2003), 'The domain of entrepreneurship research: Some suggestions', in J. Katz and S. Shepherd (eds), *Advances in Entrepreneurship, Firm Emergence and Growth*, Greenwich: JAI Press, pp. 315–72.

Dibben, M.R. (2000), *Exploring Interpersonal Trust in the Entrepreneurial Venture*, London: MacMillan.

Dubini, P. and H. Aldrich (1991), 'Personal and extended networks are central to the entrepreneurial process', *Journal of Business Venturing*, **6**, 305–13.

Eckhardt, J.T. and S.A. Shane (2003), 'Opportunities and entrepreneurship', *Journal of Management*, **29**(3), 333–49.

Florin, J., M. Lubatkin and W. Schulze (2003), 'A social capital model of high-growth ventures', *Academy of Management Journal*, **46**(3), 374–84.

Gartner, W.B. (1993), 'Words lead to deeds: Towards an organizational emergence vocabulary', *Journal of Business Venturing*, **8**(3), 231–9.

Gray, C. (1993), 'Stages of growth and entrepreneurial career motivation', in F. Chittenden, M. Robertson and D. Watkins (eds), *Small Firms: Recession and Recovery*, London: Paul Chapman Publishing, pp. 149–59.

Greiner, L. (1972), 'Evolution and revolution as organizations grow', *Harvard Business Review*, July–Aug, pp. 37–46.

Guest, D. (1998), 'Is the psychological contract worth taking seriously?', *Journal of Organisational Behaviour*, **19**, 649–64.

Guest, D. (2004), 'The psychology of the employment relationship: An analysis based on the psychological contract', *Applied Psychology*, **53**, 541–55.

Harrison, R.T., M.R. Dibben and C.M. Mason (1997), 'The role of trust in the informal investor's investment decision: An exploratory analysis', *Entrepreneurship: Theory and Practice*, **22**(2), 63–81.

Heneman, R.L., J.W. Tansky and S.M. Camp (2000), 'Human resource practices in small and medium sized enterprises: Unanswered questions and future research perspectives', *Entrepreneurship: Theory and Practice*, Fall, **25**(1), 11–26.

Hindle, K. and B. Gibson (2008), 'Optimising employee ability in small firms: Employing people with a disability', *Small Enterprise Research*, **16**(1).

Jorion, P. and W.N. Goetzmann (1999), 'Global stock markets in the twentieth century', *Journal of Finance*, **54**(3), 953–80.

396 *International handbook of entrepreneurship and HRM*

Judd, C.M., E.R. Smith and L.H. Kidder (1991), *Research Methods in Social Relations*, 6th edn, Sydney: Harcourt Brace Jovanovich.
Katz, J.A., H.E. Aldrich, T.M. Welbourne and P.M. Williams (2000), 'Guest Editor's comments: Special issue on human resource management and the SME: Towards a new synthesis', *Entrepreneurship: Theory and Practice*, **25**(1), 7–10.
Kickul, J. (2001), 'Promises made, promises broken: An exploration of employee attraction and retention practices in small business', *Journal of Small Business Management*, **39**(4), 320–35.
Klyver, K. (2005), 'Entrepreneurship & social network development – a life cycle approach', unpublished PhD dissertation, University of Southern Denmark (publication pending).
Lewicki, R.J. and B.B. Bunker (1995), 'Trust in relationships: A model of trust development and decline', in B.B. Bunker and J.Z. Rubin (eds), *Conflict, Cooperation and Justice*, New York: Sage, pp. 133–73.
Lewicki, R.J. and B.B. Bunker (1996), 'Developing and maintaining trust in working relationships', in R.M. Kramer and T.R. Tyler (eds), *Trust in Organizations: Frontiers in Theory and Research*, Thousand Oaks, CA: Sage Publications, pp. 114–39.
Loasby, B.J. (1997), 'Authority and trust', paper presented at the Scottish Economic Society Conference, Stirling, April.
Maguire, H. (2002), 'Psychological contracts: Are they still relevant?', *Career Development International*, **7**(3), 167–80.
Mainprize, B. and K. Hindle (2005), 'Assessing the efficacy and standardization potential of five competing venture capital investment evaluation approaches', *Journal of Private Equity*, **9**(1), 6–21.
Marks, A. (2001), 'Developing a multiple foci conceptualization of the psychological contract', *Employee Relations*, **23**(5), 454–67.
Massey, C., K. Lewis, V. Warriner, C. Harris, D. Tweed, J. Cheyne and A. Cameron (2006), 'Exploring firm development in the context of New Zealand SMEs', *Small Enterprise Research*, **14**(1), 1–13.
Maula, M., E. Autio and P. Arenius (2005), 'What drives micro-angel investments? An examination of the determinants of family and non-family investments', *Small Business Economics*, **25**(5), 459–75.
Merton, R.C. (1971), 'Optimum consumption and portfolio rules in a continuous-time model', *Journal of Economic Theory*, **3**, 373–413.
Moore, C.F. (1986), 'Understanding entrepreneurial behaviour', in J.A. Pearce and R.B. Robinson Jr (eds), *Understanding Entrepreneurial Behaviour: Academy of Management Best Papers Proceedings*, Forty-sixth Annual Meeting of The Academy of Management.
Nahapiet, J. and S. Ghoshal (1998), 'Social capital, intellectual capital, and the organisational advantage', *Academy of Management Review*, **23**, 242–66.
Pate, J., G. Martin and H. Staines (2000), 'Exploring the relationship between psychological contracts and organizational change: A process model and case study evidence', *Strategic Change*, **9**(8), 481–93.
Perrett, J. (2005), 'Putting reputation before growth', *Business Network – The Age*, October, p. 6.
Roehling, M.V. (1997), 'The origins and early development of the psychological contract construct', *Journal of Management History*, **3**(2), 204–17.
Rousseau, D. (2001), 'Schema, promise and mutuality: The building blocks of the psychological contract', *Journal of Occupational and Organizational Psychology*, **74**, 511–41.
Rousseau, D.M. (1989), 'Psychological and implied contracts in organizations', *Employee Responsibilities and Rights Journal*, **2**(2), 121–39.
Rousseau, D.M. (1995), *Psychological Contracts in Organizations: Understanding Written and Unwritten Agreements*, London: Sage.
Ryan, L.V. and A.K. Buchholtz (2001), 'Trust, risk and shareholder decision making: An investor perspective on corporate governance', *Business Ethics Quarterly*, **11**(1), 177–93.
Samuelson, P. (1969), 'Lifetime portfolio selection by dynamic stochastic programming', *Review of Economics and Statistics*, **51**(3), 239–46.
Sarantakos, S. (1998), *Social Research*, 2nd edn, South Yarra: Macmillan Education Australia.

Saunders, M.N.K. and A. Thornhill (2006), 'Forced employment contract change and the psychological contract', *Employee Relations*, **28**(5), 449–67.

Shane, S. and D. Cable (2002), 'Network ties, reputation, and the finances of new ventures', *Management Science*, **48**(3), 364–81.

Shane, S. and S. Venkataraman (2000), 'The promise of entrepreneurship as a field of research', *Academy of Management Review*, **25**(1), 217–26.

Sharpe, W. (1964), 'Capital asset prices: A theory of market equilibrium under conditions of risk', *Journal of Finance*, **19**(3), 425–42.

Spindler, G.S. (1994), 'Psychological contracts in the workplace – a lawyer's view', *Human Resource Management*, **37**(1), 61–9.

Storey, D.J. (1994), *Understanding the Small Business Sector*, London: Routledge.

Tobin, J. (1958), 'Liquidity preference as behavior toward risk', *Review of Economic Studies*, **25**(2), 65–86.

Winter, R. and B. Jackson (2006), 'State of the psychological contract: Manager and employee perspectives within an Australian Credit Union', *Employee Relations*, **28**(5), 421–34.

Wong, P.K. and Y.P. Ho (2007), 'Characteristics and determinants of informal investment in Singapore', *Venture Capital*, **9**(1), 43–70.

Zhang, J., P.H. Soh and P.K. Wong (2003), 'Human capital, competitive intensity and entrepreneur's propensity to exploit social networks for resource acquisition', NUS Entrepreneurship Working Paper 2003/05.

20 Daily learning, job design and problem-solving in SMEs
Grahame Boocock, Kevin Daniels, Jane Glover and Julie Holland

Introduction

The emergence of innovative firms is the cornerstone of a competitive industrial society. Innovative firms are involved in the creation, development and introduction of new products and services, or new procedures or processes, for the benefit of one or more of the stakeholders in an organization (Birchall et al., 1996) and such firms raise the threshold of technology and create the potential for increased productivity (Huntsman and Hoban, 1980). In the US, smaller firms have generally been more effective contributors than large players in enhancing innovation (Bygrave and Timmons, 1992; Almus and Nerlinger, 1999), although it is important to keep a sense of perspective. Innovation in capital-intensive industries tends be located in large firms. However, the pace of economic and technical change in an increasingly global marketplace is breaking down established patterns of business and trade, creating opportunities for even the smallest and newest firms to enter overseas markets – these are the 'born global firms' or 'instant internationals' (McDougall and Oviatt, 2000).

Opportunities for rapid expansion are available to entrepreneurial firms that seek to create wealth by meeting genuine needs in the marketplace (Becherer and Maurer, 1999). The ability to solve customers' problems underpins small firm growth in a knowledge-driven global economy. Beaver (2002: p. 74, Example 5.4.) summarizes the principal strategic imperatives for growth as: concentrate on industries facing substantial technological or regulatory changes, especially those in the early, high-growth stages of evolution; differentiate products or services in ways that are meaningful to customers; seek to dominate the market segments in which the firm competes; emphasize innovation; and secure organic growth through flexibility and opportunism that builds on existing organizational strengths.

There are many ways to achieve growth yet the majority of smaller firms concentrate on survival and independence (Beaver, 2002; Curran, 1999). This may stem from a reluctance of entrepreneurs and owner–managers to accept external advice and a strong commitment to autonomy (Vickerstaff and Parker, 1994). The founder(s) can exert a powerful influence on the firm's direction and development and many have no desire to expand the firm. Alternatively, the motivation to grow might be constrained by factors that stem from a firm's size in relation to other market participants – a lack of resources, fewer sources of information, competition from entrenched larger firms and so on (Buckley, 1989).

Growth in smaller firms is therefore influenced by a number of factors, including the characteristics of the entrepreneur, the firm, the strategy adopted and the external environment (Storey, 1994). Bridge et al. (2003) sum up the current state of knowledge as follows, 'Growth is likely to occur when a number of key factors in each category combine, although it is most unlikely that there is only one or a few combinations, and the combinations for success could change as the business develops and market circumstances alter' (p. 292).

This chapter is concerned mainly with smaller firms that seek to grow through innovation. Whichever route to growth is adopted, there is a need for human resource management (HRM) to address strategic and structural concerns from the early stages of a firm's development (Flamholtz, 1990). Chell (2001) describes HRM as the deployment of human resources to achieve organizational objectives, and she stresses the need for smaller firms to shift focus from practical 'personnel' issues (especially recruitment) to the broader concerns of managing change and innovation. It is rare for smaller firms to appoint a trained HR manager from outside the firm (Stokes, 2002) but, over time, HRM can 'make or break a business' (Kellog, 1997: p. 204).

The founder(s) of smaller firms tend to assume responsibility for all the major business functions at the outset, but the recruitment, retention, training and compensation of staff assume much greater importance after achieving a certain level of growth (Ardichvili et al., 1998). It can be difficult to recruit and retain good quality staff because the payment of market-based salary levels and associated financial benefits is beyond the reach of many smaller firms. In these circumstances, those with HRM responsibility have to emphasize that 'compensation' in smaller firms encompasses not only monetary remuneration, but also psychological rewards, recognition and learning opportunities (Nelson, 1994).

Training and development (T&D) is at the heart of HRM yet T&D opportunities are often perceived to be restricted in smaller firms. This perception might be false. While smaller firms rarely offer formal training programmes, they can react quickly and provide appropriate training when (say) new equipment is installed or when planning a move into new markets (Scott et al., 1996; Vickerstaff, 1992). In addition, and crucially, the extent of informal training and on-the-job support is often underestimated (Curran et al., 1997).

Informal training and knowledge transfer can also help to reduce the uncertainty faced by smaller firms compared to their larger counterparts. By making connections across a broad spectrum of external structures and social networks (Dalley and Hamilton, 2000; Down, 1999) and by relying on intuitive approaches and 'episodic knowledge' obtained from business networks (Coviello and Martin, 1999; Karagozoglu and Lindell, 1998), smaller firms can operate with a far greater degree of certainty. So much so that according to Gibb (1998) a key factor in success is: 'managing and developing the network of interdependency under conditions of (more or less) uncertainty' (p. 18).

In its broadest context, therefore, HRM can enable smaller firms to become more competitive by helping employees (individually or in groups) to keep in touch with developments in the market, learn new skills, acquire new knowledge, solve new problems and so on. HRM in smaller firms has to operate within a strategy that is typically highly contingent, resource-constrained and executed within a rapidly changing external environment (Chell, 2001). Nonetheless there is some evidence that HRM can assist such firms to secure growth, despite the challenge of adjusting to constant changes in internal and external conditions (Taylor et al., 2003).

A key concern of this chapter is how HRM can create the right environment for individual and group problem-solving. Job design is an important factor in establishing the conditions required for problem-solving yet this is a neglected area within smaller firms. The Job Demands-Control (-Support) [JDC(S)] model of job design, employee health and productivity (Karasek and Theorell, 1990) is the dominant model in this field. It proposes that autonomy over job tasks and work schedules promotes employee psychological health, physical health and productivity by enabling workers to engage in problem-solving to deal with work demands. In turn, enhanced problem-solving ability can improve innovation and productivity.

Described in these terms, the JDC(S) would seem to offer straightforward advice for those looking to improve problem-solving within smaller firms. However, for a number of reasons, it might prove difficult to apply the JDC(S) to small firms. For example, the characteristics of small firms often result in such high levels of job demands (for example, high work pace and role conflict) that employees are forced to 'multi-task'; this might stifle any opportunity for workers to exercise control over their work. Before considering the relevance of the JDC(S) for smaller firms, it is necessary to explore the model in more detail and also to examine the learning process within smaller firms.

The JDC(S) model

The original JDC model (Karasek, 1979) identified two crucial elements in the work situation: job demands and job control. 'Demands' are psychological demands such as high work pace, time pressures and difficult work. Job control refers not to the supervisory regime but to the extent of authority to make decisions concerning the job (often termed decision latitude). A social dimension was subsequently added (Karasek and Theorell, 1990) and social support is the level of helpful interaction with co-workers. The JDC model and modifications explain the relationship between job design and safety, health and performance measures (Holman and Wall, 2002).

Karasek's (1979) model suggested that enhanced job control would reduce stress but improve learning, whereas high job demands would increase both learning and stress levels. This led to the 'strain hypothesis' whereby a 'high strain' job, comprising high demands and low control, could (in extreme cases) lead to physical illness in workers. By contrast, a combination of high job demands allied to high control would result in increased learning and motivation for example: van der Doef and Maes, 1999. Extending the degree of control to workers thus acts as a buffer to the potentially negative effects of high job demands.

The adapted JDC(S) model holds that job control and social support combine to negate the psychologically harmful effects of job demands. While learning also stems from difficulties associated with job demands, the amended model again proposes a 'buffer' effect, namely that efforts to reduce isolation should moderate the negative impact of high job demands. The outcome is that high-demands, high-control, high-support jobs result in personal and organizational benefits; specifically in this context, employees learn how to perform their work more efficiently and the firm's performance improves.

The JDC(S) maintains that support and control, in particular, promote effective problem-solving to cope with work demands (Karasek and Theorell 1990; Parker et al., 2003; Wall et al., 2002). This has led many to suppose that statistical interactions between demands, support and control should predict a range of health and performance outcomes. Many studies have found limited support for interactions that predict health effects (for example, see reviews by de Jonge and Kompier, 1997; de Lange et al., 2003; Terry and Jimmieson, 1999). Other researchers (fewer in number) have investigated the influence of statistical interactions on performance and learning outcomes (van der Doef and Maes, 1999) and have tended to reveal evidence of the independent contributions of control, demands and support on performance and learning (Holman and Wall, 2002).

In the light of the developments described above, we thought it appropriate to flesh out the basic frameworks of the JDC and JDC(S) in relation to smaller firms. Figure 20.1 represents a simplified version of a very complex set of (inter)relationships but shows key issues and areas to be

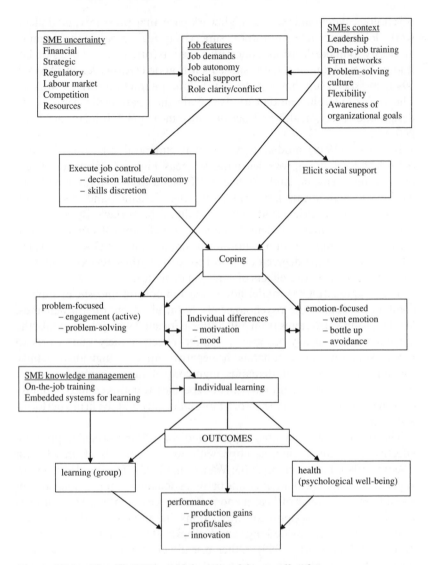

Figure 20.1   The JDC(S) model revisited for smaller firms

considered when applying the JDC(S) to the special contexts of smaller firms.

The basic thrust of the JDC(S) is that employees will execute job control or elicit social support as a means of coping with job demands (de Jonge and Dormann, 2002). Individuals can use control/support to engage in problem-solving (problem-focused coping). Alternatively, they may seek to deal with emotions or avoid a problem (Folkman and Lazarus, 1980), hence emotion-focused coping might involve, for example, taking an unscheduled break or talking to friends at work. Coping is a dynamic phenomenon and it has been demonstrated that different coping combinations have different effects over different time periods (Daniels and Harris, 2005). The 'temporal' aspect of the model is taken up later.

Control is associated with problem-focused coping in the JDC(S) although there is some evidence that it can also be used for other forms of coping (Daniels and Harris, 2005); support might be elicited for problem-focused or emotion-focused coping (Karasek and Theorell, 1990). Some studies indicate that control and support might enable and bolster problem-focused coping (de Rijk et al., 1998; Ito and Brotheridge, 2003). However, other studies suggest that control and support can sometimes accentuate the harmful effects of job demands and stressors (Buunk and Hoorens, 1992; Kaufman and Beehr, 1986; Mullarkey et al., 1997; Sargent and Terry, 1998). The implication is that control and support might facilitate less effective, or even harmful, coping patterns in certain circumstances. However, what these circumstances are remains largely unexplored.

The outcomes of changes implemented within this complex set of relationships are changes in group learning, performance indicators and the health of the workforce. The net outcomes will hopefully be positive, although any benefits might be outweighed in some cases by the impact of harmful or ineffective coping strategies. It also has to be acknowledged that it might be very difficult to identify the (multiple) outcomes that stem from changes in job design or to state with any assurance that (say) improvements in performance indicators are caused by specific changes in job design.

The analysis of the JDC(S) becomes even more problematic when additional factors are built into the model. For instance, some researchers have found that individual differences might operate as a third moderator in conjunction with control/support and demands (these may include internal locus of control (Daniels and Guppy, 1994) or self-efficacy (Parker and Sprigg, 1999)). There is also growing recognition that the model needs to be refined to incorporate greater specificity (see, Wall et al., 1996; de Jonge and Dormann, 2002). This is based on the notion that coping resources provided by control and support need to match the specific demands of the job for any benefits to be derived, for example emotional support from co-workers can counter adverse emotional demands at work (de Jonge and Dormann, 2006).

Returning to the 'temporal' theme, the JDC(S) implies that sustained problem-focused coping is related to better psychological well-being and performance. The beneficial effects of problem-solving enabled by control and support are thought to build cumulatively over time, as workers learn progressively better solutions to problems encountered at work (Karasek and Theorell, 1990). This view has been confirmed by most tests of the JDC(S) that assess stable levels of control, support and demands, and also by studies indicating that stable levels of job control are associated with subsequent measures of coping success (Elfering et al., 2005). Indicators of well-being and performance seem to be positively associated with the frequent use of problem-focused coping.

The JDC(S) also implies that support is beneficial to well-being, because it enables emotion-focused coping. If this coping mechanism is maintained over several days, however, the impact on work performance might be negative. By way of illustration, expressing emotions to others may be considered inappropriate in work settings (Ashforth and Humphrey, 1995) and in turn this may hinder the individual from receiving positive feedback about their own competence or achieving social goals (Daniels et al., 2004). Despite these caveats, occasional use of emotion-focused and/or avoidance strategies (through job control or social support) might give workers the chance to reflect on how they solve problems, thus enhancing learning and well-being (Kolb et al., 1974).

As suggested earlier, the relationships shown in Figure 20.1 have to be treated with caution, as it is extremely difficult to identify the additive or interactive effects of demands and control (van der Doef and Maes, 1999).

Studies of the JDC(S) model have been conducted in many firms, although not smaller ones. This is an important omission, as problem-solving is of critical importance for innovative small firms. A need exists to explore whether (and how) greater contextual specificity can be obtained when applying the JDC(S) to such firms. Prior to doing this we discuss conventional learning theories and their application to smaller firms because learning and problem-solving are important elements in the JDC(S).

Learning in smaller firms

Given the increased competitive pressures and the development of globalization, learning is important for small firms and multinationals alike (Easterby-Smith et al., 1998). However, research into organizational learning and knowledge creation focuses primarily on the experience and practice of large firms (see, for example, De Gues, 1998; Nonaka et al., 2000). Conclusions reached in the context of large firms may be inappropriate for smaller firms (Anderson and Boocock, 2002; Lane, 1994; Hill and Stewart, 2000).

The capacity to learn is one of the fundamental attributes of individuals yet much of this learning is unsystematic and randomly experienced. Most theorists follow Argyris and Schon (1978) in suggesting that learning embraces cognition (thought, insight or detection) and action (behaviour or correction), and maintain that learning occurs when concepts, frameworks and capabilities are created or re-developed in the light of knowledge new to the individual learner (Buckley and Carter, 2000; Chell, 2001). Learning thus encompasses training and development and also the reformulation of an individual's underlying assumptions and values.

The minimal level of learning is surface learning, which has immediate utility but lacks any longer-term or developmental implications (Cope and Watts, 2000). The next level occurs when behaviour is modified incrementally to rectify detected errors in a specific situation; this is known as single loop or adaptive learning (Senge, 1990). By contrast, generative or double-loop learning occurs where individuals reflect on, and question, their underlying values and perceptions. This level of learning implies 'stepping back from the thick of it' and undertaking critical reflectivity to promote more fundamental change (Cope and Watts, 2000).

Whatever the level of individual learning, it is 'context dependent' and the learning process is iterative and often unconscious. Over time, individuals are likely to acquire and develop both explicit (mainly technical) and implicit (or 'taken for granted', tacit) knowledge (Nonaka et al., 1998). The latter tends to be acquired through practice and revealed through application (Nonaka et al., 2000). Employees tend to utilize both tacit and explicit forms of knowledge when solving problems. Such knowledge might be obtained either within the workplace or externally – when other stakeholders and those involved within the value chain (customers, suppliers, professional advisors and so on) provide important opportunities for learning.

Moving from individual learning, the concept of organizational learning is perhaps even more complex and multi-dimensional. It is based on the premise that a firm, as a separate entity, is capable of collective thinking through 'theory-in-use', in other words, an unwritten body of knowledge that stems from learned, problem-solving behaviour (Prahalad and Bettis, 1996). Learning by individuals is obviously a prerequisite for organizational learning (Probst and Buchel, 1997), yet such learning may be lost if it is not shared and embedded in organizational systems, structures, strategies and routines (Crossan and Inkpen, 1994).

In applying learning theories to smaller firms, it should be evident that the experience, personality and goals of the entrepreneur(s) or owner–manager(s) exert a major influence on learning (Caird, 1993; Scase and Goffee, 1987). Whatever the influence exerted by the principal decision maker(s), formal skills development is rarely conducted (Lange et al., 2000). Informal, work-based learning is prevalent, as flexibility and adaptability are more important than explicitly formulated job descriptions and skill specifications (Anderson and Boocock, 2002; Rae and Carswell, 2000). The transmission of tacit knowledge through ad hoc and/or 'hands on' training is critical (Hendry et al., 1991), while the importance of social learning and networks was stressed earlier.

The value of generative learning for smaller firms may thus be called into question, as most communication is oral and informal, and the smaller firm is likely to be managed in a 'social' way. Adaptive learning is likely to be the norm (Dalley and Hamilton, 2000; Tsang, 1997). Anderson and Boocock (2002) argue that an apparently haphazard approach to knowledge acquisition and sharing may be quite logical because smaller firms have to respond quickly to opportunities arising from trading experience.

Applying the JDC(S) model to smaller firms

In broad terms, we argue that a wider understanding of control and support mechanisms in the context of smaller firms can lead to enhanced understanding of job design, learning and productivity. However, there are a number of specific questions in applying the model to smaller firms:

1.   What organizational factors might mean that the JDC(S) model has to be amended for smaller firms?
2.   Likewise, what characteristics of smaller firms' operating environments suggest that the JDC(S) model has to be adapted for such firms?
3.   What kind of temporal factors might characterize the relationships between problem-solving, or other activities, and learning in smaller firms; and, how do contextual factors influence these temporal factors?
4.   What are the links between the measures (formal or informal) used to gauge firm performance and changes in job design aimed at (say) the promotion of learning and problem-solving?

The analysis draws on the literature from a number of academic disciplines, as well as an intensive study (Glover et al., 2006) of learning and innovation that examined the activities of over 115 employees in 15 firms – see Table 20.1 for more details of participants.

While the usual UK and EU definition of a small firm is below 50 employees, it will be noted that the sample includes three firms employing in excess of that figure. The sample firms illustrate not only the heterogeneity within the SME population, but also the fact that the cut-off point between small and medium-sized firms is somewhat artificial. In the study, employment conditions differed between the two medical research firms and also between the training broker and the manufacturing firm, even though all four firms are classed as small. On the other hand, the two specialist manufacturers (employing 37 and 62 people respectively) had

Table 20.1 Participant and firm details

	Company age (yrs)	Total employed	Number of participants in the study
Specialist Manufacturer 1	22	37	9
Training Broker	3	12	6
Medical Research 1	6	12	7
Web Design 1	5	5	5
Manufacturing	24	41	9
Promotions 1	26	67	24
Hospitality	2	100	17
Software Developer 1	13	25	7
Consultancy	3	10	5
Recruitment Agency	17	15	8
Specialist Manufacturer 2	Over 100	61	10
Promotions 2	1	3	3
Software Developer 2	5	5	4
Web Design 2	5	3	2
Medical Research 2	3	3	3

very similar characteristics, even though one is classed as small and the other as medium-sized. Both had active R&D departments, a large proportion of skilled workers and short production runs. The firm engaged in hospitality is the largest in the sample yet the workers in that firm tended to operate in small units. In this chapter and reporting relevant details of our study, therefore, we tend to refer to smaller firms as the unit of analysis.

The 15 firms in the study were all based in Leicestershire in the UK; they included five 'spin-outs' from the three Leicestershire universities. On average, the firms had been trading for 16 years, with the oldest trading for over 100 years and the youngest for just one year. The average size of the 15 firms was 26 employees. The key criterion for inclusion in the study was that the firm was proactive in pursuing innovation (defined broadly) (Birchall et al., 1996).

Previous research in similar fields (such as T&D in smaller firms) has tended to utilize cross-sectional, quantitatively-based methods (for example, Curran et al., 1997). However, postal surveys have traditionally achieved poor response rates (Johnson et al., 1999) and crucially, they provide limited scope for analysis of subtle learning processes (Wong et al., 1997). Case studies have been more successful in capturing the reactive, dynamic and context-specific learning processes in smaller firms (Hill and

Stewart, 2000) yet it has proved difficult to manipulate variables and apply case study findings to the wider small firm population (Gill and Johnson, 1997).

The methodology used in the study started from the premise that learning is a dynamic phenomenon, hence the research instruments were designed to capture incremental learning as it happened. Job characteristics also have dynamic components (Daniels, 2006). The ways in which employees deal with work demands, adjust their learning processes and preserve their well-being can change on an hourly basis. It was therefore necessary to collect data over a sustained period of time.

Each participant completed a paper questionnaire at the start of the exercise, providing background information on well-being, job characteristics, organizational climate and learning. This was followed shortly after by an electronic diary exercise that monitored participants over a one-week period. A series of questions was repeated four times per day through normal working hours; employees were prompted by bleeps on palmtop computers. The questions covered areas such as demands at work for that day, mood ratings and the management of problems. The 117 participants supplied 1648 responses in the electronic diaries. The employees were involved in a range of activities, including production, research and development, marketing and administration. Two interviews with managing directors or other senior managers (just before and then some time after the diary week) supplemented the data gathered from the employees' questionnaires and electronic diaries. The data were collected between November 2005 and May 2006. Using Figure 20.1 as the frame of reference, points 1 to 4 above are now examined in turn, although there is some overlap between the various questions/topics.

Organizational factors in smaller firms
The academic literature tends to confirm the basic thrust of the JDC(S) model, namely that job control and social support combine to negate the psychologically harmful effects of job demands, and that learning stems from resolving the difficulties associated with job demands. However, some evidence indicates that executing work control and eliciting support can be used to regulate the emotional impact of job demands, or even promote avoidance behaviours that may be antithetical to learning (Daniels and Harris, 2005). Such concerns are amplified within the small firm context. Factors associated with the psychological climate within smaller firms (notably the extent to which innovation and personal decision-making are supported) are not taken into consideration, hence a number of factors, individually or in combination, might prevent individual learning becoming collective.

Smaller firms are characterized by diversity, hence job features within such firms will vary. We discovered considerable variation in problems encountered per hour across the 15 firms; those firms with an experienced and/or skilled workforce reported a lower incidence of problems, probably because the employees had come across similar problems before. Role conflict was an important job feature, as employees coped with a multitude of tasks. High levels of role conflict would be expected to have negative consequences, and we found role conflict to be high amongst these firms. Although role conflict may have had adverse effects elsewhere within the firm, it was not related directly to other variables such as learning and mood.

Smaller firms are also characterized by personalized, informal management styles and less rigid organizational structures (Wilkinson, 1999). This might suggest that employees enjoy a greater degree of job control, but the image of the small firm as a 'happy ship' or place of harmony with all workers sharing the same goals has been questioned over recent years (Wilkinson, 1999).

The strong influence of the founder(s) on learning within smaller firms (Storey, 1994) might prevent employees from exercising job control. The need for dominance and an internal 'locus of control', and the predilection for intuitive rather than formally rational thinking that characterizes managers in smaller firms, could inhibit the processes of knowledge acquisition and diffusion (Caird, 1993). In situations where employees have restricted autonomy, the JDC(S) suggests that there will be a negative impact on both individual and collective learning. Our study revealed that autonomy was generally not as high as might have been anticipated under the 'happy ship' image of smaller firms. However, where higher autonomy was present, this was linked to higher learning, provided that role clarity was high.

Employees can also deal with job demands by eliciting social support. Work-based learning is the norm in smaller firms and the transmission of tacit knowledge is critical, especially where employees are multi-skilled. The social environment and the extent to which staff help each other to solve problems are crucial factors. Despite the relatively low level of autonomy, our study confirmed that a high level of support exists within smaller firms; this was a key factor in the promotion of learning.

A detailed examination of the data revealed relatively low scores for autonomy, compared to those for role clarity and support. It was interesting to follow through these data into the coping mechanisms used by employees. We discovered that employees were more likely to change work processes (execute job control) to solve problems rather than avoid problems or manage their emotions. The study also revealed that changing work schedules to disengage from problems could reduce anxiety and enhance learning; short breaks away from work allowed time for reflection and refocusing.

Talking to others (eliciting social support) was used more frequently to solve problems rather than avoidance or managing emotions.

Individual differences can also exert an influence on job design, in conjunction with control/support and demands (Daniels and Guppy, 1994; Parker and Sprigg, 1999). In our study, positive moods and motivation were usually strong, and this translated into higher levels of learning. Likewise, the level of negative mood was generally low, and where morale was low this was sometimes linked to stress caused by external factors.

The impact of changes in individual learning can be seen in various outcomes – for example, group learning, performance indicators and the health of the workforce. The difficulties of measuring and separating these outcomes were discussed earlier. Nonetheless, our study revealed that innovation levels were high (compared to other firms where this research methodology had been employed by members of this research team), and there was also evidence that changes in job design had led to further improvements in levels of innovation.

We argue that specific organizational factors affecting smaller firms should be incorporated into the JDC(S) and hence suggest that the control and support mechanisms used in large firms might not be appropriate. Diversity is an inherent characteristic of smaller firms, and successful firms combine multiple factors in various ways at different times. Likewise the level of individual learning is context-dependent. This emphasis on context creates problems in making any general recommendations for good practice in job design or for targeting assistance at potential high-growth firms. Despite these caveats, some general observations can be put forward on the basis of the findings from the study and the academic literature.

First and foremost, the data tended to confirm the JDC(S) model; that is high-demands, high-control, high-support jobs yield organizational and personal benefits, although the way in which these factors combined appears to be complex. The level of learning across firms was generally sound and there was evidence of consistent acquisition of knowledge over the working week. Two key factors (support at work and job autonomy) facilitated active learning, and people did not need much encouragement to attempt to solve complex work problems. However, the study did identify changes in job design that could provide learning opportunities and enable more effective problem-solving, notably the encouragement of team-based problem-solving.

Role clarity seemed to aid the execution of job control (although any formalization of roles should not hamper an individual's capacity to use job autonomy to solve problems). Clarity can be enhanced when employees are made aware of organizational goals – this was not always the case, despite the flatter organizational structures in the 15 firms. Role conflict was found to be high, but not linked directly to the variables examined. Further investigation of this factor may be important for managerial policy or practice within smaller firms.

Characteristics of smaller firms' operating environments
The JDC(S) does not address the specific contexts in which smaller firms operate and hence does not take into account how external factors may shape links between problem-solving, job design and learning. For instance the uncertainty brought about by financial, regulatory, labour market and technological factors may all influence the impact of job design on learning (Wall et al., 2002). Smaller firms are also constrained by their size in relation to other market participants, which means they have to cope with fewer resources and competition from entrenched larger firms, for example.

These constraints could contribute to increased job demands and/or adversely impact on the mood and motivation of the workforce. In our study negative mood was particularly severe in a start-up company and a young company under pressure to meet the demands of a venture capital investor. In such cases, increased job control would be beneficial (Wall et al., 2002), but the pressing need to generate cash must surely restrict autonomy. These pressures may also reduce the willingness of employees to seek social support, and cause them to bottle up emotions.

Smaller firms have to exploit the advantage of flexibility in responding to opportunities, yet the ways in which knowledge is gathered to underpin problem-focused coping may also be constrained by a lack of resources. However, insufficient funds to (say) undertake a methodical approach to knowledge-gathering through market research need not necessarily result in a failure to maximize the outcomes specified in Figure 20.1. The importance of episodic knowledge obtained from business networks was stressed earlier, especially through contacts with suppliers, customers and other stakeholders. Those responsible for HRM in smaller firms should seek to maximize opportunities that stem from customer feedback and/or testing the boundaries of existing markets (Hendry et al., 1991). Knowledge acquired by individuals from such networks has then to be shared and embedded in a firm's 'theory-in-use' (group learning).

Job design in smaller firms therefore has to be informed by careful consideration of how external pressures influence the levels of support and control. Failure to take account of such pressures may have a detrimental impact on problem-solving and learning.

Temporal factors
Learning and problem-solving are dynamic phenomena. Problem-solving, supported by appropriate levels of control and support, may have to take

place over a sustained period before it has an influence on learning. In addition, the effects of problem-solving on learning could also decay quickly. Innovative, growth-oriented SMEs thrive by responding quickly as market opportunities arise, hence it is critical to find the 'right' combination of factors that maximizes problem-solving at a particular time.

Flexible organizational structures enable smaller firms to get close to their customers and reduce environmental uncertainty. Kirby (2003) argues that they use teams with varying levels of skills and experience to generate new products or services and secure the required speed to market and stresses that autonomy is also required to encourage curiosity and innovation (see Amit et al., 2000). Autonomy allows individuals and teams the time to reflect and to question existing values and perceptions, and this process of generative learning could bring longer-term benefits to the firm (Cope and Watts, 2000).

Any consideration of the 'right combination' of job control, support and other factors depends on the operational demands faced by a firm. We estimated the problem-solving cycle for each study participant, which is the maximum time frame over which problem-solving could be expected to influence product or service delivery. These cycles ranged from one day (service providers where customers' problems have to be sorted out at once) to over a year (the design and manufacture of bespoke equipment in high-technology markets). Large firms also face a range of problem-solving cycles, but they tend to adopt a longer-term perspective to structural change as sizeable resources are committed to a project (Anderson and Boocock, 2002).

It will be appreciated that temporal factors and task demands mean that HRM in smaller firms demands flexibility and foresight in establishing the kind of job positions required (Kellog, 1997) and also in designing T&D activities to provide the skills judged to be necessary both now and in future. This cannot be a precise exercise. Likewise, the formation of different groups for different purposes might be 'more chaotic than orderly . . . [within] a recurring non-identical process, punctuated by alternating periods of stability and instability' (Katz, 1993: p. 100). Finally, those with responsibility for HRM in smaller firms may need to use different time frames than their counterparts in large firms when judging the impact of any changes in job design – an issue taken up in the following section.

Measures used to gauge firm performance
The measures used to judge success in smaller firms will depend to a large extent on the goals/motivations of the founder(s) or principal decision makers. The firms in our study aspired to more than mere survival and/or independence, and their goals included: increases in sales, profit and

market share; enhanced levels of R&D and product development; intangible improvements in sharing of knowledge, empowerment of employees amongst others.

Whatever goals are pursued, it is essential that any changes implemented should be assessed against the specific aspects of firm performance where improvements are sought. Those responsible for monitoring the outcomes that stem from those changes will utilize a number of formal and/or informal indicators. It has to be recognized that the achievement of some targets will depend heavily on enhanced learning and problem-solving, while others may be strongly linked to external factors such as the state of the economy. The constraints facing smaller firms should also be borne in mind, so for example: learning might be taking place, but a firm could be held back by insufficient finance to invest in new machinery.

Even if suitable indicators can be identified, our study revealed that smaller firms found it almost impossible to track the (multiple) outcomes that stem from changes in job design. This is not surprising. It would also be a bold assertion that any improvements in learning or innovation could be linked directly to changes in job design. For instance, the loss of a large contract will have a major impact on the profits of a small firm (Curran, 1999). Methodological concerns of this nature are not unique to studies in this field; for example, those measuring the impact of small firm loan guarantee schemes have struggled to achieve any degree of precision (see Gudger, 1998).

Conclusions and practical implications for HRM in smaller firms

In exploring how the dominant model of job design, employee health and productivity could be adapted for smaller firms, this chapter has addressed a significant gap in the literature. The JDC(S) highlights many of the factors that contribute to positive outcomes for smaller firms and the wider economy. The ideal scenario for HRM practice in such firms would be to create a virtuous circle whereby incremental improvements in job design would enhance problem-solving, learning and innovation. These changes would assist smaller firms to acquire new knowledge that, in turn, would generate ideas and hence new products. However, it is not easy to translate the principles embodied in Figure 20.1 into definite guidance for firms seeking to leverage improvements in job design, problem-solving and learning.

The sheer number of factors to be taken into account, the complexity of the relationships between the different elements, and the issues involved in measuring and monitoring outcomes illustrate the problems in applying the JDC(S) approach to smaller firms. The optimal levels and best combination of factors (such as job demands, job control, social support, formalization) to achieve the goals of a small firm will almost certainly depend on factors unique to that firm's internal and external context, and this combination has to be adjusted to meet the situation prevailing at any one time.

HRM in smaller firms is thus highly contingent; it reflects the diversity within this sector and differing skills requirements within firms. There is some evidence that HRM can assist such firms to secure growth but, with limited resources at their disposal, it is imperative that smaller firms identify areas where gains can easily be made. The literature from a range of academic disciplines (and our study) suggests that relatively modest adjustments in job design could enable the majority of smaller firms to enhance well-being, learning, motivation and performance.

Smaller firms should aim to create an environment where job support and control are high. This should be allied to a problem-solving ethos. The level of job formalization should allow clarity of individual and organizational goals, without prescribing too heavily how to do a job. Such an approach should encourage learning and innovation, and hence facilitate the necessary flexibility to grasp opportunities.

Our study revealed that support from others at work and the autonomy to make decisions about work schedules and work processes were critical factors for higher levels of learning and also organizational performance. People tend to engage in problem-solving more than any other coping strategy. Most people do not need an invitation to attempt to solve problems – what they need is the organizational infrastructure to assist them in this process. Higher levels of motivation were associated with autonomy, especially the ability to disengage from problems. Limited and short-term breaks from work allowed time for reflection and refocusing (and possibly encouraged generative learning).

Our study confirmed that employees in smaller firms undertake a range of activities and engage with large numbers of people. An innovative, growth-oriented firm needs entrepreneur(s) and/or senior manager(s) with the capacity to meet unexpected challenges and to respond quickly to opportunities. Such firms also need employees with the ability to act under pressure, solve problems and think strategically (Hendry et al., 1991).

The analysis above can be translated into a number of specific recommendations to improve work design and problem-solving processes. They are as follows.

1. Job features – gather baseline data on where autonomy, clarity and support might be improved and in what ways.
2. Organizational design and structure – clarify reporting relationships, establish parameters for individual autonomy and investigate the

extent to which employees are able to solve their own problems; this will assist in succession planning.

3. Knowledge exchanges – establish intra-organizational exchanges and strengthen links with external networks; these maximize opportunities for acquiring knowledge that supports individuals and groups in their problem-solving activities. (From a policy perspective, inter-organizational exchanges can create communities of practice that can support smaller firms in their problem-solving activities.)

4. T&D – design T&D activities that recognize explicitly that employees learn on the job and adapt their know-how to the contingencies encountered.

5. Learning culture – promote an environment in which individuals take responsibility for solving their own problems and help others to do so. Associated with this is the implementation of procedures that reward team and individual success in solving problems, but do not punish failures.

6. 'Life-cycle' issues – recognize that heavy problem-solving demands (linked to high levels of anxiety and hence detrimental to psychological health) are likely to be prevalent during the early stages of the business life cycle. (Policy makers should also recognize that early-stage firms might require additional assistance.)

7. Temporal factors – judge the success or otherwise of any changes in job design over an appropriate time frame. For example, most changes might be implemented in response to immediate customer needs, while a one-off strategic review might involve reflective (generative) learning.

References

Almus, M. and E.A. Nerlinger (1999), 'Growth of new technology-based firms: Which factors matter?', *Small Business Economics*, **13**(2), 141–5.

Amit, R.H., K. Brigham and G.D. Markman (2000), 'Entrepreneurial management as strategy', in G.D. Meyer and K.A. Heppard (eds), *Entrepreneurship as Strategy: Competing on the Entrepreneurial Edge*, Thousand Oaks, CA: Sage Publications.

Anderson, V.A. and J.G. Boocock (2002), 'Learning to manage and managing to learn: The internationalisation of small organizations', *Human Resource Management Journal*, **12**(3), 5–24.

Ardichvili, A., P.D. Cardozo, B. Harmon, R.N. Reynolds and M.L. Williams (1998), 'The new venture growth: Functional differentiation and the need for human resource development interventions', *Human Resource Development*, **9**, 55–70.

Argyris, C. and D. Schon (1978), *Organisational Learning*, Reading, MA: Addison-Wesley.

Ashforth, B.E. and R.H. Humphrey (1995), 'Emotion in the workplace: A reappraisal', *Human Relations*, **48**, 97–125.

Beaver, G. (2002), *Small Business, Entrepreneurship and Enterprise Development*, Harlow, UK: Prentice Hall.

Becherer, R.C. and J.G. Maurer (1999), 'The proactive personality disposition and entrepreneurial behaviour among small company presidents', *Journal of Small Business Management*, **37**(1), 28–36.

Birchall, D.W., J.J. Chanaron and K. Soderquist (1996), 'Managing innovation in SMEs: A comparison of companies in the UK, France and Portugal', *International Journal of Technology Management*, **12**(3), 291–305.

Bridge, S., K. O'Neill and S. Cromie (2003), *Understanding Enterprise, Entrepreneurship and Small Businesses*, 2nd edn, Basingstoke, UK: Palgrave MacMillan.

Buckley, P.J. (1989), 'Foreign direct investment by small and medium-sized enterprises: The theoretical background', *Small Business Economics*, **1**, 89–100.

Buckley, P.J. and M.J. Carter (2000), 'Knowledge management in global technology markets: Applying theory to practice', *Long Range Planning*, **33**(1), 55–71.

Buunk, B.P. and V. Hoorens (1992), 'Social support and stress: The role of social comparison and social exchange processes', *British Journal of Clinical Psychology*, **31**, 445–57.

Bygrave, W.D. and J.A. Timmons (1992), *Venture Capital at the Crossroads*, Boston, Massachusetts: Harvard Business School Press.

Caird, S.P. (1993), 'What do psychological tests suggest about entrepreneurs?', *Journal of Managerial Psychology*, **8**(6), 11–20.

Chell, E. (2001), *Entrepreneurship: Globalization, Innovation and Development*, London: Thompson Learning.

Cope, J. and G. Watts (2000), 'Learning by doing – an exploration of experience, critical incidents and reflection in entrepreneurial learning', *International Journal of Entrepreneurial Behaviour and Research*, **6**(3), 104–24.

Coviello, N. and K. Martin (1999), 'Internationalization of service SMEs: An integrated perspective from the engineering consulting sector', *Journal of International Marketing*, **7**(4), 42–66.

Crossan, M. and A. Inkpen (1994), 'Promise and reality of learning through alliances', *The International Executive*, **6**(3), 263–73.

Curran, J. (1999), 'What is small business policy in the UK for? Evaluating and assessing small business policies', *International Small Business Journal*, **18**(3), 36–50.

Curran, J. and R.A. Blackburn (2001), *Researching the Small Enterprise*, London: Sage Publications.

Curran, J., R. Blackburn, J. Kitching and J. North (1997), 'Small firms and workforce training: Some results, analysis and policy implications from a national survey', in M. Ram, D. Deakins and D. Smallbone (eds), *Small Firms: Enterprising Futures*, London: Paul Chapman Publishing, pp. 90–101.

Dalley, J. and B. Hamilton (2000), 'Knowledge, context and learning in the small business', *International Small Business Journal*, **18**(3), 51–9.

Daniels, K. (2006), 'Rethinking job characteristics in work stress research', *Human Relations*, **59**, 267–90.

Daniels, K. and A. Guppy (1994), 'Occupational stress, social support, job control and psychological well-being', *Human Relations*, **47**, 1523–44.

Daniels, K. and C. Harris (2005), 'A daily diary study of coping in the context of the job demands–control–support model', *Journal of Vocational Behaviour*, **66**, 219–37.

Daniels, K., C. Harris and R.B. Briner (2004), 'Linking work conditions to unpleasant affect: Cognition, categorisation and goals', *Journal of Occupational and Organizational Psychology*, **77**, 343–64.

de Gues, A. (1998), 'Planning as learning', *Harvard Business Review*, **2**, 70–75.

de Jonge, J. and C. Dormann (2002), 'The DISC model: Demand induced strain compensation mechanisms in job stress', in M.F. Dollard, H.R. Winefield and A.H. Winefield (eds), *Occupational Stress in the Service Professions*, London: Taylor and Francis, pp. 43–74.

de Jonge, J. and C. Dormann (2006), 'Stressors, resources, and strain at work: A longitudinal test of the triple match principle', *Journal of Applied Psychology*, **91**(6), 1359–74.

de Jonge, J. and M.A.J. Kompier (1997), 'A critical examination of the demand–control–support model from a work psychological perspective', *International Journal of Stress Management*, **4**, 235–58.

de Lange, A.H., T.W. Taris, M.A.J. Kompier, I.R.D. Houtman and P.M. Bongers (2003), ' "The very best of the millennium": Longitudinal research and the demand–control–(support) model', *Journal of Occupational Health Psychology*, **8**, 282–305.

de Rijk, A.E., P. Le Blanc, W. Schaufeli and J. de Jonge (1998), 'Active coping and need for control as moderators of the job–demand–control model: Effects on burnout', *Journal of Occupational and Organizational Psychology*, **71**, 1–18.

Down, S. (1999), 'Owner-manager learning in small firms', *Journal of Small Business and Enterprise Development*, **6**(3), 267–80.

Easterby-Smith, M., R. Snell and S. Gerhardi (1998), 'Organisational learning: Diverging communities of practice?', *Management Learning*, **29**(1), 5–20.

Elfering, A., S. Grebner, N.K. Semmer, D. Kaiser-Freiburghaus, S. Lauper-Del Ponte and I. Witschi (2005), 'Chronic job stressors and job control: Effects of event-related coping success and well-being', *Journal of Occupational and Organizational Psychology*, **78**, 237–52.

Flamholtz, E. (1990), 'Toward a holistic model of organizational effectiveness and organizational development at different stages of growth', *Human Resource Development Quarterly*, **1**(2), 109–27.

Folkman, S. and R.S. Lazarus (1980), 'An analysis of coping in a middle-aged community sample', *Journal of Health and Social Behaviour*, **21**, 219–39.

Gibb, A.A. (1998), 'Small firms training and competitiveness: Building upon the small business as a learning organisation', *International Small Business Journal*, **15**(3), 13-29.

Gill, J. and P. Johnson (1997), *Research Methodology for Managers*, London: Paul Chapman.

Glover, J.L., J.G. Boocock, K.J. Daniels and J. Holland (2006), 'Innovation as it happens: Daily learning, problem solving and organisational learning in SMEs', Report produced for East Midlands Development Agency – EMDA, May 2006.

Gudger, M. (1998), *Credit Guarantees: An Assessment of The State of Knowledge and New Avenues of Research*, Rome: Food and Agriculture Organization of the UN.

Hendry, C., A. Jones, M. Arthur and A. Pettigrew (1991), *Human Resource Management in Small to Medium Sized Enterprises*, Centre for Corporate Strategy and Change, Research Paper, No. 88, Warwick Business School.

Hill, R. and J. Stewart (2000), 'Human resource development in small organizations', *Journal of European Industrial Training*, **24**(2/3/4), 105–17.

Holman, D.J. and T.D. Wall (2002), 'Work characteristics, learning-related outcomes, and strain: A test of competing direct effects, mediated, and moderated models', *Journal of Occupational Health Psychology*, **7**, 283–301.

Huntsman, B. and J.P. Hoban (1980), 'Investment in new enterprises: Empirical observations on risk, return, and market structure', *Financial Management*, Summer, pp. 44–51.

Ito, J.K. and C.M. Brotheridge (2003), 'Resources, coping strategies, and emotional exhaustion: A conservation of resources perspective', *Journal of Vocational Behaviour*, **63**, 490–509.

Johnson, P.S., C. Conway and P. Kattuman (1999), 'Small business growth in the short run', *Small Business Economics*, **12**, 103–12.

Karagozoglu, N. and M. Lindell (1998), 'Internationalization of small and medium sized technology-based firms: An exploratory study', *Journal of Small Business Management*, **36**(1), 44–59.

Karasek, R.A. (1979), 'Job demands, job decision latitude, and mental strain: Implications for job redesign', *Administrative Science Quarterly*, **24**, 285–308.

Karasek, R.A. and T. Theorell (1990), *Healthy Work*, New York: Basic Books.

Katz, J.A. (1993), 'The dynamics of organizational emergence: A contemporary group formation perspective', *Entrepreneurship Theory and Practice*, **17**(2), 97–101.

Kaufman, G.M. and T.A. Beehr (1986), 'Interactions between job stressors and social support – some counterintuitive results', *Journal of Applied Psychology*, **71**, 522–6.

Kellog, L. (1997) 'The critical link between business and organisation', in S. Birley and D. Muzyka (eds), *Mastering Entrepreneurship*, London: Pearson Education, pp. 204–5.

Kirby, D.A. (2003), *Entrepreneurship*, London: McGraw-Hill.

Kolb, D.A., I.M. Rubin and J.M. McIntyre (1974), *Organizational Psychology: An Experiential Approach*, Englewood Woods Cliffs, NJ: Prentice Hall.

Lane, D. (1994), 'People management in small and medium sized enterprises', *Issues in People Management*, **8**, London: Institute of Personnel and Development.

Lange, T., M. Ottens and A. Taylor (2000), 'SMEs and barriers to skills development: A Scottish perspective', *Journal of European Industrial Training*, **24**(1), 5–11.
McDougall, P.P. and B.M. Oviatt (2000), 'International entrepreneurship: The intersection of two research paths', *Academy of Management Journal*, **43**(5), 902–6.
Mullarkey, S., P.R. Jackson, T.D. Wall, J.R. Wilson and S.M. Grey-Taylor (1997), 'The impact of technology characteristics and job control on worker mental health', *Journal of Organizational Behaviour*, **18**, 471–89.
Nelson, B. (1994), *1001 Ways to Reward Employees*, New York: Workman Publishing.
Nonaka, I., P. Reinmoeller and D. Senoo (1998), 'The ART of knowledge: Systems to capitalize on market knowledge', *European Management Journal*, **16**(6), 673–84.
Nonaka, I., R. Toyama and J. Konno (2000), 'SEKI, Ba and leadership: A unified model of dynamic knowledge creation', *Long Range Planning*, **33**(1), 5–34.
Parker, S.K. and C.A. Sprigg (1999), 'Minimizing strain and maximizing learning: The role of job demands, job control, and proactive personality', *Journal of Applied Psychology*, **84**, 925–39.
Parker, S.K., N. Turner and M.A. Griffin (2003), 'Designing healthy work', in D.A. Hofmann and L.E. Tetrick (eds), *Occupational Health and Safety: A Multilevel Perspective*, San Francisco: Jossey-Bass.
Prahalad, C.K. and R. Bettis (1996), 'The dominant logic: A new linkage between diversity and performance', in K. Starkey (ed.), *How Organisations Learn*, London: Thompson Business Press, pp. 100–19.
Probst, G. and B. Buchel (1997), *Organisational Learning: The Competitive Advantage of the Future*, Hemel Hempstead: Prentice Hall.
Rae, D. and H. Carswell (2000), 'Using a life story approach in researching entrepreneurial learning: The development of a conceptual model and its implications in the design of learning experiences', *Education + Training*, **42**(4/5), 220–28.
Reid, M. and H. Barrington (1999), *Training Interventions*, London: CIPD.
Sargent, L.D. and D.J. Terry (1998), 'The effects of work control and job demands on employee adjustment and work performance', *Journal of Occupational and Organizational Psychology*, **71**, 219–36.
Scase, R. and R. Goffee (1987), *The Real World of the Small Business Owner*, London: Croom Helm.
Scott, P., B. Jones, A. Bramley and B. Bolton (1996), 'Enhancing technology and skills in small and medium sized manufacturing firms: Problems and prospects', *International Small Business Journal*, **14**(3), 85–99.
Senge, P.M. (1990), 'The leader's new work: Building learning organizations', *Sloan Management Review*, **32**(1), pp. 7–23.
Stokes, D. (2002), *Small Business Management*, London: Thomson Learning.
Storey, D.J. (1994), *Understanding the Small Business Sector*, London: Routledge.
Taylor, S., S. Shaw and C. Atkinson (2003), 'Human resource management: Managing people in smaller organizations', in O. Jones and F. Tilley (eds), *Competitive Advantage in SMEs*, Chichester: Wiley, pp. 87–104.
Terry, D.J. and N.L. Jimmieson (1999), 'Work control and employee well-being: A decade review', in C.L. Cooper and I.T. Robertson (eds), *International Review of Industrial and Organizational Psychology*, Chichester: Wiley, pp. 95–148.
Tsang, E.W.K. (1997), 'Organisational learning and the learning organisation: A dichotomy between descriptive and prescriptive research', *Human Relations*, **50**(1), 73–89.
van der Doef, M. and S. Maes (1999), 'The job demand–control (–support) model and psychological well-being', *Work and Stress*, **13**, 87–114.
Vickerstaff, S. (1992), 'The training needs of small firms', *Human Resource Management Journal*, **2**(3), 1–15.
Vickerstaff, S. and K. Parker (1994), 'Helping small firms: The contribution of TECs and LECs', *International Small Business Journal*, **13**(4), 56–72.
Wall, T.D., J.L. Cordery and C.W. Clegg (2002), 'Empowerment, performance, and operational uncertainty: A theoretical integration', *Applied Psychology: An International Review*, **51**, 146–69.

Wall, T.D., P.R. Jackson, S. Mullarkey and S. Parker (1996), 'The demands-control model of job strain: A more specific test', *Journal of Occupational and Organizational Psychology*, **69**, 153–66.

Wilkinson, A. (1999), 'Employment relations in SMEs', *Employee Relations*, **21**(3), 206–17.

Wong, C., N. Marshall, N. Alderman and A. Thwaites (1997), 'Management training in small and medium sized enterprises: Methodological and conceptual issues', *International Journal of Human Resource Management*, **8**(1), 44–65.

21 Encouraging skills acquisition in SMEs
David Devins

Introduction

The purpose of this chapter is to explore the nature of skills acquisition in small and medium-sized enterprises (SMEs) in the context of UK public policy seeking to encourage such activity in these enterprises. HRM comprises a wide range of activities and approaches as demonstrated by a wealth of writers such as Garavan et al. (1995), Stewart and McGoldrick (1996), Harrison (1997), Bratton and Gold (1999). However, the analysis in this chapter will focus on issues associated with skills acquisition both on behalf of the small firm entrepreneur and their employees, providing two examples of public sector intervention in the UK, which has sought to encourage skills acquisition through investment in training and development in smaller organizations. The nature of the challenges facing policy planners as they strive to develop an employer-led training and education infrastructure, a priority of the current UK government, will also be highlighted.

Why should we be interested in HRM in small, entrepreneurial organizations? In answer to this question the latest statistics (SBS, 2006) report that out of an estimated 4.3 million businesses in the UK, 99.3 per cent of them employ fewer than 50 people, they account for about 50 per cent of the 22 million people employed in the UK and almost 40 per cent of the total turnover. Furthermore, it is argued that SMEs are not merely scaled down versions of larger organizations (Penrose, 1959) and that the majority of HRM literature derives from larger organizations (Harrison, 1997). There is a clear need to explore and understand HRM practices in the SME context more generally and with specific reference to skills acquisition.

Skills and SME growth

Different commentators attribute different, albeit related meanings to skills. For example, skills can be seen in terms of social attributes, general education, training, qualifications and technical skills (Ashton and Green, 1996). Others refer to components of skill such as 'technical', 'behavioural' and 'cognitive' (Buchanan et al., 2004) or differentiate skills in terms of human capital (Becker, 1964), or skill in the job (Braverman, 1974). The relationship between skills and qualifications is particularly relevant as qualifications are seen as the most common measure of skills in the economy (Leitch, 2006), not only in the UK but elsewhere. However, it cannot be taken for granted that someone who possesses a 'skill' has a certifying qualification, neither can it be taken for granted that someone who has a qualification has the necessary skill to work in a particular industry, occupation or job.

The development of a well-motivated, highly skilled workforce is a key determinant of a firm being able to remain competitive (Hodgetts and Kuratko, 2001; Longenecker et al., 2000). Hornsby and Kuratko (2003) draw attention to key HRM practices (or more precisely the lack of them) in terms of ineffective recruitment, poor or non-existent training and weak performance appraisal as underlying causes of the failure of small, entrepreneurial firms. Furthermore effective HRM practices have been shown to be an integral part of the success of smaller businesses. For example Marlow and Patton (1993) argue that the effective management of HR is the key to survival for smaller ventures, whilst at the same time they recognize that in few SMEs is forward planning in terms of employment undertaken, even when moving into new markets and expansion, despite these being frequently cited as organizational goals.

Training is a key mechanism to support skills acquisition. Several studies report a positive relationship between training and growth in terms of productivity and turnover (Betcherman et al., 1997) and employment growth (Cosh et al., 2000) for example. However, the evidence suggests that training alone is not sufficient and it has to be part of a bundle of HRM activities, which together make a positive contribution to firm performance (Huselid, 1995; Storey, 2002).

SMEs, particularly the smallest, are notoriously weak in terms of HRM infrastructure and investment in training and development. The problem lies in the fact that smaller firms are relatively and absolutely less likely to provide external training than larger enterprises to all grades of workers (Devins and Johnson, 2003; Hendry et al., 1991; Johnson, 1999; Kitching and Blackburn, 2002). They are also much less likely to employ a HRM professional in the business or to develop and manage systems and processes to encourage human resource development (HRD) (Curran et al., 1997).

This generalized view of HRM activity in the small business context is often accompanied by outsiders such as policy makers and consultants desiring to systematize and formalize practices in an attempt to encourage or 'improve' HRD activity. However, these approaches often fail to relate to the interests of the small firm or manager as the underlying principles fail to connect with the existing small business operating environment (Down, 1999; Hill and Stewart, 1999; Ram, 2000). Further exploration of the small business learning environment goes some way to explaining why decontextualized concepts often fail to connect with the world of the small business.

For many owners, managers and employees in smaller organizations, skills acquisition is inextricably linked to the performance of work activities, solving problems and grasping new opportunities as they arise (Gibb, 1997). Much skills acquisition occurs naturally in a non-contrived manner as part of an everyday process that moves the organization in a direction that meets the desires and interests of the manager and workforce. Learning is largely informal or incidental, driven by the desires of those involved and seldom reliant on formal or structured training. Sometimes employees and particularly owners or managers create deliberate attempts to experiment in acquiring new knowledge but more often than not skills development is the by-product of a business process rather than the focus of the process itself.

Policy analysis has suggested that interventions tend to be formal and driven by supply-side considerations (PIU, 2001). The rhetoric of employer-led learning (Leitch, 2006) has some way to go before it connects with the world of the smaller business. Fundamental changes to the system are required if the multidisciplinary and holistic approach often required by smaller businesses is to be delivered in a way which addresses barriers such as cost and loss of productive time in the workplace. Storey (2004) sums up the challenge – if government seeks to enhance skills in smaller businesses through training it cannot use the same procedure and incentives for large firms and expect them to be equally effective.

In response to the need for intervention to encourage skills acquisition in SMEs, on the supply side some innovative responses have been developed. In the UK a number of these initiatives have been funded through non-mainstream mechanisms such as the European Social Fund. Sometimes intervention is based on seeking to meet the needs of employers whilst at other times it is aimed at encouraging employers to change their approaches to skills acquisition. In this chapter two such projects are used to further explore skills acquisition in the SME context.

The case study projects and research methodology
The case studies provide an illustration of the aims, approach and emerging impacts of two publicly funded interventions in the UK. These are referred to as the People and Technology Project (PAT) and the Developing Manager Skills Project (DMS).

The aim of the PAT project was to encourage learning in SMEs through resourcing a learning centre and developing closer links between local businesses and Higher Education and Further Education providers on three industrial estates in the East Midlands. The three industrial estates featured in the PAT project were home to about 150 SMEs (employing fewer than 200 people) operating in traditional – predominantly textiles, engineering and printing – sectors of the economy. A survey of 90 businesses operating on the industrial estates was conducted to explore the impact of the project on local businesses. Seventy-seven businesses participated in the survey, which represented an exceedingly high response rate of 85.5 per cent. About 40 per cent of these were micro businesses (employing fewer than 10 people) or SMEs employing between 11 and 50 people, with the remaining 20 per cent employing over 50 people. About 40 per cent of the businesses were 'growth oriented' and reported an expectation of business growth in the next 12 months.

The PAT project sought to widen learning in the workforce, and a structured questionnaire was used to generate data on the individual learners' experiences of the intervention. This questionnaire was delivered through the learning centres and returned in a reply paid envelope. One hundred and ninety three learners were engaged in learning through the project; 56 of these (29 per cent) returned questionnaires. The PAT case study provides an insight into the intervention process and some of its key outcomes in terms of skills acquisition and the development of HRM.

The DMS intervention sought to put the needs and interests of the small business at the forefront of training and development activity. The aim of the DMS programme was to work with small business managers to support problem-solving, business planning and associated skills development. The project resourced a business coach to work with a limited number of local small organizations in order to enhance their management capability overall as well as developing the skills of individual managers and their workforce.

DMS was a relatively small-scale programme engaging 35 local businesses employing between six and 56 employees drawn predominantly from the traditionally strong, although declining, engineering sector. Twenty-five of these businesses contributed to the research process over a period of up to three years. The focus of the intervention was placed on the owner–manager or management team, with the business coach delivering the intervention. The research methodology consisted of on-site visits and face-to-face interviews using a semi-structured discussion guide conducted with owner–managers every three months over the period of the intervention (up to three years). Qualitative data was collected from the business coaches every six months to triangulate data and to encourage reflective learning in an effort to improve the intervention process.

Example 1: the people and technology project (PAT)
The intervention model developed to pursue the initiative had three distinctive features:

- An Employee Led Development (ELD) philosophy
- An animateur
- The development of a learning centre

Underpinning the project as a whole was the desire to enable employees of smaller organizations to (re)engage in their own development, using ICT. This was seen to be appropriate as a means of involving people in addressing the challenges and opportunities which arise from ICT developments, therein supporting the wider aspirations of the individual and promoting company and estate development. Underpinning the project was an ELD philosophy. Such a philosophy promotes learning through the workplace but that is driven by the employee him/herself. Learning is undertaken on a voluntary basis and takes place mainly in the individual's own time.

On each industrial estate an animateur was responsible for the local management of the project, working with a local College of Further Education (FE), the University and the target SMEs in each area. It was envisaged at the outset of the project that the animateur would have a variety of roles, including acting as a champion for the PAT project and coordinating training on each of the industrial estates. This role of 'champion' was deemed crucial for the success of the project. That overcame the fact that, as with training and development activities per se, there is a relatively low take-up of ICT within SMEs, especially when they are drawn (as is the case in this project) from traditional industries such as engineering and textiles.

The animateur was responsible for encouraging, engaging and motivating individuals to participate at the learning centre, and spent a significant amount of time undertaking these activities.

The surveys provide an indication of the progress and impact of the intervention although the small sample sizes compromise the robustness of the findings. Whilst the survey of employers operating on the industrial estates achieved an excellent response rate, relatively few employers had actually used the learning centre at the time of the survey. Of the 14 SMEs who had used the centre the vast majority (over 90 per cent) reported that the training had been useful or very useful in supporting their employees' access to new technology, career development, increased motivation and ability to 'do their jobs'.

The findings from the survey of individual beneficiaries should also be treated with caution given the relatively low number of respondents (N = 56). Nevertheless the survey suggests that the intervention had met with some success in encouraging accredited learning, with almost 90 per cent of respondents achieving a qualification. Nearly three-quarters reported that the experience had provided relevant work-related skills and work-related ideas and the majority of respondents reported that they would like to continue studying in the learning centre. However, 60 per cent of the learners were drawn from supervisory/management or administrative occupations, with less than 5 per cent drawn from manual occupations, raising questions associated with the ability of ELD as enacted through the intervention to widen learning opportunities throughout the workforce (Devins et al., 2001).

In order to provide further insights into the impact of the intervention, qualitative research with selected companies was undertaken. The findings emerging from one of the participating companies reveal the value of the local learning centre to skills acquisition within one entrepreneurial small business.

This company had actively supported the development of the intervention, as in the words of the MD it 'dovetailed very well with what we wanted to achieve', particularly in the context of IT training. Operating in the print sector meant that as an organization 'We've undergone and will continue to undergo massive technological change . . . we've become highly reliant on IT.'

Take-up of the training in-house was actively encouraged and the opportunity was presented to all employees across the whole company. Administrative staff took the greatest advantage of the opportunity to acquire new skills; however, the MD reported that the real successes 'have been from people on the shop floor . . . where it's given people new skills . . . confidence and it's given them increased opportunity'.

Take-up was promoted by the fact that office staff, who were said to work up to a ten-hour day, were given time in that working day to attend the learning centre. However, hourly paid staff were required to make use of the centre in their own time without any financial support from the company.

The dropout rate, or rather the failure to progress, was one concern of this MD:

> I am a little bit disappointed with the dropout rate . . . for instance, some people basically they did the CLAIT and stayed with that, that's all that they want and they've not wanted to carry on, progress on . . . I think it is largely down to the relevance that they see in their own jobs.

The CLAIT he refers to is Computer Literacy and Information Technology and is the most popular UK information technology qualification. Individual learners were drawn from a variety of occupations and the following examples provide an indication of their learning activities and progression.

John, a warehouse operative had no formal qualification in IT or related subjects but had a computer at home and was comfortable using it. On leaving school he studied to improve his basic employability skills but did not complete the course. Participation in the learning centre started with

CLAIT; 'to prove what I know', which was completed in six weeks and then saw progression to ECDL (European Computer Driving Licence, a global standard in end-user computer skills). Attending the learning centre on a weekly basis and in his own time, the ECDL course was completed in approximately five months. The opportunity to progress on to graphic design courses was offered by the company and he pursued this opportunity for further development.

Sarah, a receptionist, had previously taken a one-day beginner and a two-day intermediate course on word processing at the company's behest. In-house training, in this and other employment, had been undertaken in a range of subjects (such as telephone techniques, train the trainer, buyer's course, fire fighter's course) but no formal qualification had been sought. With the advent of the learning centre, CLAIT was offered, undertaken and a certificate gained. Progression from CLAIT to ECDL did not take place, but there was an intention to start a further course. Sarah also undertook proprietary software training (QUARK and Photoshop) on a Wednesday evening, courtesy of the company.

Mary, a management accountant, had recently been promoted to the position from accounts clerk. She had formal qualifications and training in accounting but little experience with IT. With the open invitation to attend the learning centre, CLAIT was undertaken and followed by the ECDL course. The appointment of a new tutor encouraged her to progress on to further accredited IT training at a higher level.

The intervention galvanized this company into further skills development activity. Further training and initiatives concerned the development of a Mac-based learning centre in the company. Moreover, following the exposure to ELD through the intervention, the company adopted an Employee Led Development style approach to individual development.

Example 2: developing manager skills (DMS) programme
The DMS intervention was based primarily on the services provided by a coach who worked with the SME owner–manager to encourage development business. The coach 'tuned into' the issues that were important to small organization managers, and used them as a means to develop individual skills and organizational capability. The coach had the flexibility to work with individuals (such as owner–managers, directors, key staff) and teams (including management teams, production teams and administrative teams) in the business and was not tied to the delivery of one approach or a bundle of discrete HRM practices. Three business coaches (BCs) were recruited to deliver the programme that was funded for three years.

In the initial stages of the programme the BCs sought to establish relationships with small organizations in the locality. The evaluation research identified three approaches characterizing the way they 'tuned into' the specific requirements of the smaller organization managers:

1. A 'visioning' process generally involving the management team in the development of a vision for the company and the development of an action plan detailing projects to help achieve the vision.
2. A 'problem centred' process that was based on the identification, and subsequent tackling of key issues of concern to the manager or management team.
3. A 'sounding board' process that was based on relatively unstructured discussion of issues of concern to the manager of the small organization.

Regardless of the approach, the BC adopted an inclusive stance drawing organizational members into the coaching process. The three general approaches were not mutually exclusive so the BC could adopt a particular approach at a given point in time depending on the client interests, needs or preferences. It became clear that there was no right or wrong approach, instead BCs had to be aware of and adapt to the responses from those within the organization.

The visioning approach involved the manager and the management team in a collective development process. The BC facilitated the management team to determine what was needed to move from the present position to that outlined in a 'vision' and to construct an action plan with milestones and responsibilities to enable this to happen. A typical summary of the outcome of this approach was provided by one manager who noted:

> We now have a list of goals (for example increased turnover and profit) and a set of actions to help to meet the goals . . . for example we need to increase the number of enquiries, reduce costs and identify new product opportunities . . . we are all thinking about what we need to do to achieve these goals and taking ideas forward' (Manager, Equipment installation and servicing company, employing 16 people).

The problem-centred approach involved the BC facilitating the identification of key issues or business priorities, analysis (largely through discussion) and the drawing up of lists of issues, problems or opportunities. These were prioritized and the BC could provide further inputs (such as analysis, alternative models or knowledge) to help with addressing the identified problems. In some instances the BCs became involved in specific activities and offered 'hands-on support' for specific issues rather than simply teasing out solutions with the managers. The problem-centred approach was often the focus for specific activity and the BC and managers directed their resources into specific areas. For example, managers were able to point to tangible outcomes – such as: 'We have a new incentive system; I have had personal coaching'.

With the sounding board approach it became apparent that greater understanding of the DMS process emerged through implementation of the programme. This unstructured approach was largely dependent on the manager having an agenda s/he wished to pursue with the BC. In response the BC drew on their experience and knowledge to provide their view of the 'problems or opportunities' raised by the manager. The BCs reported that the sessions 'meandered' and could have been 'unproductive' in the sense that the outcomes were neither tangible nor measurable. However, the managers often suggested that they 'felt right' and were 'useful' but struggled to identify specific benefits although they remained committed to the DMS process. For example:

> It is useful to have someone who is not involved in the business to bounce ideas off . . . he puts a point of view across that is different . . . it gets you to analyse things in a different manner . . . tends to be well meaning and constructive not critical' (Managing Director, Engineering Services company, employing 25).

> The coach never tells us . . . he always says have 'you thought about' not 'I think you should do' (Co-owner, Jewellery Manufacturer and Retailer, employing 19).

> The BC has given me an appreciation of what needs to be done and what I am able to do. He has helped me focus on what I need to address meetings, delegation, leadership, planning . . . helped me to set goals. I still have problems making the time to do these things as just so much is happening . . . the BC is encouraging me to take a strategic look at the company . . . it has taken some time to recognize that change is an ongoing process and to realize that it is not a one-time event' (Co-owner-manager, Computer Software company, employing 45).

In most cases the development of the relationship between the coach and the small business manager formed the cornerstone of subsequent development activity in the business. Some of this activity was related to the development of HRM processes and activities but crucially all was grounded in the challenges and opportunities the business faced at that time.

A wide range of HRD-related activities were implemented in the SMEs as a direct or indirect result of working with the business coach. The development of technical and business activity (such as marketing, development of IT systems, information analysis, change associated with production processes, development of financial systems and analysis and administration and ISO 9000) often led to an identification and servicing of skills needs amongst the workforce as well as generic management skills such as planning and coordinating change. These activities resulted in changes that were unique to each small organization. In the majority of companies an increased awareness of external training and development opportunities meant that active engagement followed. The provision of workshops and networking events associated with DMS was a key factor in this change. One attendee reported:

> I learnt from the other MDs . . . we have all got our own problems and if you listen to them and how they got round them, then you learn different ways of dealing with your own problems (Owner manager, Engineering fabrication company, employing 12).

DMS also stimulated manager involvement in more structured training activity provided through the local training and education infrastructure. Two MDs attended courses run by local universities. The MD of another company attended a 10-week course on business development that was run by a local training provider. The DMS process led to the HRD needs of other staff being linked to the development needs of the business and steps taken to source appropriate support. The ability to link HRD to specific goals of the company highlighted the need for such training and development activity. For example, in one company the need for product training for their tele-sales team was recognized as was further sales training for their sales people. Three other companies noted the need for improved IT skills and pursued structured offerings from local Further Education colleges with varying degrees of success. The BCs drew other managers into the support network more widely and promoted the use of other publicly funded initiatives based on an understanding of the current situation of the manager and the business. Several managers and their staff attended quasi-structured events to encourage the acquisition of marketing and planning skills for example. Consequently the value of the intervention became more widespread as these services become relevant and suited to the business context.

Some implications for entrepreneurs and policy planners
At the outset of the interventions many of the participating businesses reflected the stereotypical view of SMEs in terms of their reluctance to pursue external training to support the development of skills, their lack of professional HRM representation and systems to manage HRM processes. Most of the businesses had been established for a number of years and were operating in declining industries. All the SMEs participating in the DMS project were engaged precisely because intermediaries identified them as being 'poor trainers'. Despite of this the research provides an insight into the variety of often informal HRM practices existing in SMEs. In common with the findings of Hornsby and Kuratko (2003) none of the SMEs

participating in either the DMS or PAT interventions could be described as having developed an integrated set of strategic practices to support HRD, and the specific approaches to HRM activity remained some way short of the sustained, integrated, strategic approach which underpins conceptions of what constitutes HRM more generally (Garavan et al., 1995; Harrison, 1997; Stewart and McGoldrick, 1996).

However, the experience of participating in the interventions encouraged some changes in the HRM and skills acquisition practices adopted in these SMEs. Whilst the two interventions illustrated in this chapter are very different in nature, they both provided a 'shock' from the external environment which caused managers to consider existing practice and, in the case of many of the participating businesses, this led to the initiation of new or extended HRM practices to meet the needs of the changing organization. In both instances, the interventions provided fledgling foundations for a more systematic approach to planning and HRM which is seen to be an important characteristic of growth-oriented businesses. There was some evidence to support the views of others such as Marlow (2000) of an emergent approach to strategy formulation, encouraged through public sector intervention, and this was reflected to varying degrees in the way in which skills acquisition was approached.

The design and implementation of the intervention clearly had an impact on its performance. The DMS approach was grounded in a proactive approach to encouraging the development of smaller organizations and the subsequent identification of skills requirements associated with identified business requirements. The proactive approach had three key benefits in terms of encouraging skills acquisition in SMEs. First, it helped to overcome the gap between what is reported as being important by managers of SMEs in terms of the training and development of the workforce and what is practised by the managers of the organization (Duberley and Walley, 1995). Second, it made any action in terms of skills acquisition directly relevant to the business and consequently of value to the business. Subsequently the approach to skills development was sensitive and 'tuned into' the circumstances of the SME, overcoming many of the problems associated with HRM interventions identified by others (Hill and Stewart, 1999; Ram, 2000). Third, it was not uncommon for the DMS coach (and to a lesser extent the PAT animateur) to act in a role akin to an outsourced personnel professional, providing ideas and advice and championing HRD and change within the SME, thus overcoming one of the factors (at least for the duration of the intervention) constraining training in SMEs (Curran et al., 1997; Vickerstaff and Parker, 1995).

In contrast to the non-prescriptive approach underpinning DMS, the PAT intervention illustrated some of the problems of being wedded to (at least at the design stage) a particular model associated with encouraging wider skills acquisition in the workforce, ELD. The experience highlighted the tension between the supply and demand for training. On the supply side is an approach that seeks to broaden out training amongst the workforce more generally and to overcome inequalities in its distribution, while on the demand side employers want training to meet their own current business interests. ELD acted as a framework and provided financial incentives for participating organizations to enable their employees to engage in a wide range of training and development activities. However, the concept of encouraging wide-ranging learning opportunities, which lies at the heart of ELD, did not sit easily with the majority of SMEs on the industrial estates or the training providers who did not wish to provide a wide range of courses through the small-scale local learning centres. Consequently the wider non-vocational skills development activity envisaged by ELD did not materialize. The orientation of the intervention developed over time as SMEs 'bent' the intervention model with the acquiescence of those on the supply side to reflect an employer-led approach to skills acquisition focused on satisfying business needs.

The analysis of these programmes clearly shows that the animateur (PAT) and the coach (DMS) had a key role to play in the success or otherwise of each intervention. The experience of implementing both interventions provides further evidence of the guarded response that many smaller business managers have towards external interventions that seek to influence internal HRM practices and skills acquisition. Both the coaches and the animateurs had to overcome considerable resistance or scepticism on behalf of the small business managers regarding their offerings (Curran et al., 1997). In spite of being free at the point of delivery, delivered on-site and by an intermediary who was responsive, getting owners to be involved was a challenge. It required considerable effort on behalf of the coach or animateur to allay the concerns of the owner–managers, convince them of potential benefits and ultimately to get the organization to participate in the intervention. The time required to engage small business people, to develop an understanding of their organization and to influence practice in their business should not be underestimated. The research underpinning the intervention highlighted the need for sufficient time and space for the coach to develop a robust relationship with the small business manager (Barrett, 2006). This enabled them to facilitate drivers of skills acquisition activity and facilitate internal training and development activity and the use of external training providers where it was in the interests of the business. The applied, timely and experiential learning provided through the coaching process was highly valued by many of the owner–managers (see also Burgoyne and Hodgson, 1983) participating in the intervention although not by the supply-side funders of the intervention who were impatient with the time it took to establish the relationship and who wished to see accredited learning outcomes emerging. Furthermore, in spite of considerable effort to provide accessible and flexible training, the provision through Further and Higher Education providers still fell some way short of the expectations of some SMEs and their employees. This provides an insight into the institutional and structural challenges that lie ahead for those tasked with developing an employer-led training system that connects with the interests of SMEs and supports the growth of entrepreneurial organizations.

References
Ashton, D. and F. Green (1996), *Education, Training and the Global Economy*, Aldershot, UK and Brookfield, US: Edward Elgar.
Becker, G.S. (1964), *Human Capital*, New York: Columbia Press.
Barrett, R. (2006), 'Small business learning through mentoring: Evaluating a project', *Education + Training*, **48**(8/9), 614–26.
Betcherman, G., N. Leckie and K. McMullen (1997), 'Developing skills in the Canadian workplace', *CPRN Study No W02*, Ottawa: Renouf Publishing.
Bratton, J. and J. Gold (1999), *Human Resource Management: Theory and Practice*, 2nd edn, Basingstoke: Macmillan Business.
Braverman, H. (1974), *Labour and Monopoly Capital*, New York: Monthly Review Press.
Buchanan, J., I. Watson and C. Briggs (2004), 'Skill and the renewal of labour', in C. Warhurst, I. Grugulis and E. Keep (eds), *The Skills that Matter*, London: Palgrave, pp. 186–206.
Burgoyne, J. and V. Hodgson (1983), 'Natural learning and managerial action: A phenomenological study in a field setting', *Journal of Management Studies*, **20**(3), 87–99.
Cosh, A., A. Hughes and M. Weeks (2000), 'The relationship between training and employment growth in small and medium enterprises', *Department for Education and Employment Research Report RR 245*.
Cosh, A., A. Hughes, A. Bullock and M. Potton (2003), 'The relationship between training and business performance', *Department for Education and Employment Research Report RR 454*.
Curran, J., R. Blackburn, J. Kitching and J. North (1997), 'Small firms and workforce training: some results, analysis and policy implications', in M. Ram, D. Deakins and D. Smallbone (eds), *Small Firms: Enterprising Futures*, London: Paul Chapman Publishing, pp. 90–101.
Devins, D. and S. Johnson (2003), 'Training and development activities in SMEs: Some findings from an evaluation of the ESF Objective 4 Programme in Britain', *International Small Business Journal*, **21**(2), pp. 213–28.
Devins, D., V. Smith and R. Holden (2001), 'Creating learning industrial estates: Addressing lifelong learning in SMEs', *Journal of Research in Post-Compulsory Education*, **6**(2), 205–21.
Down, S. (1999), 'Owner–manager learning in small firms', *Journal of Small Business and Enterprise Development*, **6**(3), 267–78.
Duberley, J.P. and P. Walley (1995), 'Assessing the adoption of HRM by small and medium-sized manufacturing organizations', *The International Journal of Human Resource Management*, **6**(4), 891–909.
Garavan, T.N., P. Costine and N. Heraty (1995), 'The emergence of strategic human resource development', *Journal of European Industrial Training*, **19**(10), 4–10.
Gibb, A. (1997), 'Small firms training and competitiveness: Building upon the small business as a learning organisation', *International Small Business Journal*, **15**(3), 13–29.
Harrison, R. (1997), *Employee Development*, London: Institute of Personnel Development.

Hill, R. and J. Stewart (1999), 'Human resource development in small organizations', *Human Resource Development International*, **2**(2), 103–23.

Hodgetts, R.M. and D.F. Kuratko (2001), *Effective Small Business Management*, 6th edn, Fort Worth, Texas: Dryden Press.

Hornsby, J.S. and D.F. Kuratko (2003), 'Human resource management in US small businesses: A replication and extension', *Journal of Developmental Entrepreneurship*, **8**(1), 73–91.

Huselid, M.A. (1995), 'The impact of human resource management practices on turnover, productivity, and corporate financial performance', *Academy of Management Journal*, **38**(3), 635–72.

Johnson, S. (1999), 'Skills issues for small and medium sized enterprises', *Skills Task Force Research Paper No 13*, Sheffield: DfEE.

Kitching, J. and R. Blackburn (2002), 'The nature of training and the motivation to train in small firms', *Department for Education and Skills Research Report RR 330*.

Leitch, S. (2006), 'Skills in the UK: The Long Term Challenge. Interim Report December 2005, Available at http://www.hm-treasury.gov.uk (accessed September 2006).

Longenecker, J.G., C.W. Moore and J.W. Petty (2000), *Small Business Management*, 11th edn, Cincinnati, OH: South Western.

Marlow, S. (2000), 'Investigating the use of emergent strategic human resource management activity in the small firm', *Journal of Small Business and Enterprise Development*, **7**(2), 135–48.

Marlow, S. and D. Patton (1993), 'Managing the employment relationship in the small firm: Possibilities for human resource management', *International Small Business Journal*, **11**(4), 57–64.

Penrose, E. (1959), *The Theory of the Growth of the Firm*, Oxford: Oxford University Press.

PIU (2001), *In Demand: Adult Skills in the 21st Century*, A Performance and Innovation Unit Report (December), London: Cabinet Office.

Ram, M. (2000), 'Investors in People in small firms: Case study evidence from the business services sector', *Personnel Review*, **29**(1), 69–91.

Small Business Service (SBS) (2006), 'Small and Medium Sized Enterprise Statistics 2005', available at http://www.sbs.gov.uk/sbsgov/ (accessed September 2006).

Stewart, J. and J. McGoldrick (1996), *Human Resource Development: Perspectives, Strategies and Practice*, London: Pitman.

Storey, D.J. (2002), 'Education, training and development policies and practices in medium and small sized enterprises in the UK: Do they really influence small firm performance?', *Omega*, **30**(4), 249–64.

Storey, D. (2004), 'Exploring the link, among small firms, between management training and firm performance: A comparison between the UK and other OECD countries', *International Journal of Human Resource Management*, **15**(1), 112–30.

Vickerstaff, S. and K.T. Parker (1995), 'Helping small firms: The contribution of TECs and LECs', *International Small Business Journal*, **13**(4), 56–72.

22 Training and development: practices, definitions and desires
Scott Taylor

Introduction

As this collection makes clear, research into the intersection of human resource management (HRM) and entrepreneurship is increasing rapidly in volume and variety. The aim of this chapter is to draw together selected evidence and key theory developed in one of the four key tasks of HRM: the provision and management of training and development. As a research field, I suggest that two areas of activity are clearly identifiable: first, the management of training and development in 'entrepreneurial' firms; and second, the provision of training and development to encourage entrepreneurial activity. In reviewing two papers that provide exemplary contributions to these areas, I further suggest that we have a considerable amount of evidence relating to managerial/employee practices in entrepreneurial organizations and on policy interventions to train entrepreneurs, but that little progress has been made in understanding any causal configurations within this aspect of HRM and entrepreneurship (a key stated aim of much of the work in this area).

In the final section of the chapter potential future research directions are purposed that might address this issue through theory development and clearer definition of the phenomenon being studied.

This approach contrasts with calls to collect ever more data on managerial practices or policy initiatives (such as Curran and Storey, 2002). While it is important to understand managerial perspectives and the impact of expensive public policy interventions, it is also crucial that we examine what goes on inside and around the complex social entity of the organization (Edwards et al., 2006). HRM is more than simply setting up managerial policies in the workplace (Marlow, 2003) or adhering to prescriptive models (Taylor, 2004), and policy interventions must also be subject to interpretive analysis for meaning or reception within organizations.

Taking the time to develop more robust theoretical frameworks to underpin empirically informed analysis of the intersection of HRM and entrepreneurship would provide a counterbalance to research that assumes engagement with training and development must be founded on the pursuit of organizational success (Heyes and Stuart, 1998; Storey and Westhead,

1997). Formal learning guided by educational institutions, learning by doing (such as 'sitting with Nellie' in the UK), learning by using, and learning by interacting have all been proposed as paths to improved financial performance, increased innovation, increased motivation and reduced employee turnover. However, as is emphasized in this chapter, there is a tendency towards abstracted empiricism in this approach, with an emphasis on the structural conditions of training and development and a lack of acknowledgement of the complex social negotiation that training and development are always situated within (Edwards et al., 2006).

Two separate paths
In surveying these two areas of scholarship contributing to an understanding of the intersection of HRM, training and entrepreneurship, what is most visible is assessment and analysis of training and development practices in smaller (often implicitly entrepreneurial) firms. This agenda is pursued through either an assessment of the impact of training and development on productivity, performance or innovation (Freel, 2005) or an analysis of the social organization of managing training. A substantial amount of literature has been generated around the theme of management education and development and the contention that managers in smaller companies are less likely to be given the opportunity to participate in either educational (for example, certificated, leading to a formal qualification) or developmental (for example, uncertificated) programmes. This literature is largely driven by a concern with assessing 'value for money' of state-funded training (Storey and Westhead, 1997). There are numerous attempts to quantify the effect of management development on firm performance (Storey, 2004; Storey and Westhead, 1997) and examples in the UK include the frequent assessment of state-funded initiatives such as Investors-in-People (Fraser, 2003), training loans (Fraser et al., 2002) or the University for Industry (Matlay and Hyland, 1999). While in this literature there is an acknowledgement that desire for growth cannot be read off directly from company size (that is, not all small firms wish to grow – see Storey and Westhead, 1997), government training policies and many academics (for example, Fuller-Love, 2006) continue to imply that more or better training will lead to growth and higher levels of entrepreneurial activity (Cosh et al., 2000).

The second path leading to the intersection of training and entrepreneurship is based on understanding training for entrepreneurs or entrepreneurship education. As might be expected, entrepreneurship education has been embraced most enthusiastically in the US; but it is also present in many other countries, particularly in undergraduate education (Henry et al., 2003). Katz (2003) notes historical precedents for this dating back to the mid-nineteenth century, but documents the most significant expansion in the 1980s. Despite received wisdom telling us that entrepreneurs are born, not made, academics working in this area argue that entrepreneurship is a discipline which can be taught and learned (Kuratko, 2005). Indeed debate has moved to addressing the questions of what should be taught and how, from whether the subject should be present in management education at all. We are told that pedagogy and content of an entrepreneurship programme can and should differ from mainstream management and business education (Solomon et al., 2002). Yet educators have been criticized for paying insufficient attention to the personal or social development of entrepreneurs as well as the ethical nature of the activity (Béchard and Grégoire, 2005).

These two pathways will be pursued further in the next section of the chapter. However, it is important to note that this chapter is not and does not aim to be a comprehensive review of literature in this area. A considerable number of journal articles and state-sponsored reports are already available, providing full overviews of published work in various countries, and assessing the empirical evidence in detail. Such reviews are immensely valuable in demonstrating the breadth and depth of work in analysing the intersection of training, HRM and entrepreneurship; however, my purpose in this chapter is to indicate the potential for theoretical development and it is with this in mind that the studies to be reviewed were chosen.

Training and development in small entrepreneurial firms

It is often stated that managers and employees in small firms are less likely to engage in training and development when compared with their counterparts in large organizations. Research supporting this claim tends to take a formal definition of the issue under examination. Storey (2004) for example tells us that management training must be in a group, provided by an external organization such as a college or university and be funded, at least in part, by the organization. If any of these criteria are not met then the activity is not formal training or development. The narrowness of this definition is clearly oriented towards allowing researchers to operationalize management education in a questionnaire format, and to enable quantitative analysis of data. This echoes the approach in other types of research where large-scale quantitative datasets are used to provide standardized and easily processed responses as a basis for statistical analysis that can be claimed to be based on representative data (see McCarthy, 1994) on this approach to IR research. However, any sense of meaning in the data is missing, particularly in relation to the social context. As McCarthy (1994) notes of industrial relations research, there is a danger that a lack of 'imaginative insights with practical consequences' (p. 321) results from too great a focus on monitoring-style data collection that is designed to enable computer-aided correlation tests on groups of variables.

Another problem emerges through the use of criteria for inclusion in a study. Only companies that employ fewer than 500 people are included in Storey's research although he acknowledges that 250 could also have been a valid cut-off point. This is a remarkably fuzzy boundary, yet it accurately reflects the variety of definitions in use by policy makers and researchers in small firm research more generally. It raises the question of whether this is a coherent research area at a very basic level, if we could be thinking about an organization staffed by 10 people and a company that employs 450 as belonging to the same 'small' category. The managerial challenges and demands, and hence the need for formal management training, in a firm made up of almost 500 people will surely be quite different from those facing the owner–manager of, say, a small independent shop. This combi- · nation of a very narrow definition of training and a very broad criterion for inclusion, which I suggest is typical of the dominant form of research in this area, does not inspire confidence in the robustness of the general conclusions drawn from them.

The situation is further complicated by the possibility that training and development may not be present in smaller organizations because provision is inappropriate (Thomson and Gray, 1999). This would support one of the explanations suggested by Storey and Westhead (1997) for the difference between large and small organizations in this area; market failure. These authors argue that training and development is not relevant to those working in smaller companies, and that therefore the gap between take-up in large and small firms is not surprising. While the argument that man-agement education tends to exclude organizational contexts other than large or private sector firms has some merit, it is surely simplistic to claim that market failure lies at the root of lower levels of engagement? Such an explanation neglects all activities and dynamics within and around the firms, and given that management education and knowledge are inherently political or politicized (see Clegg and Palmer, 1996) we might conclude once again we are left with a very thin explanation.

It would be foolish not to recognize the involvement of governments and taxpayers in the provision of management development to smaller and entrepreneurial organizations. The level of funding is surprisingly high, and in the UK there is a remarkable turnover of state and quasi-governmental organizations with a remit in this area. This leads to further questions as to whether or not funds are being well managed. However, the narrow approach of allocating blame to either managers or training providers for the lack of formal engagement of very small firms in training, especially when the subject under study is so broadly defined, does little to further our understanding of this area of HRM in practice or theory, in entrepreneurial firms or anywhere else.

Training and development for entrepreneurship

When we look at this path of thinking we can see a similarity to that identified above. That is, much of the debate around training and development for entrepreneurship is framed by a series of economic claims or issues. Smaller entrepreneurial companies are suggested, claimed or assumed to generate new jobs, to be increasing their overall share of economic activity and to be replacing larger organizations as the key institutional site for economic development (Henry et al., 2003). From this perspective the only significant research question is whether to attempt interventions to further increase the importance of the sector.

Henry et al. (2003) provide an exemplary contribution in this area. A comprehensive review of both sides of the debate, pro and anti, takes the authors to the conclusion that 'governments do intervene and . . . various types of interventions exist' (p. 6). They further note that considerable sums of 'taxpayers' money' are spent on efforts in this policy area (unfortunately without being more precise than that). This also provides a rationale for researching the question of whether such interventions work.

These authors analyse eight training programmes (interventions) from five European countries, drawing on documentary data and interviews with programme providers and funders, constructing themes that emerged from their interview structuring and respondents. From their data a long series of policy recommendations and best practice guidelines are constructed, all based on the assumption that intervention is inherently worthwhile.

This assumption can be challenged by the evidence present in Ram et al. (2001) to indicate that becoming an entrepreneur may not be such a smooth process. They focus on the experience of working in small, ethnic minority owned companies noting that such companies are assumed to be vehicles of upward mobility for both owners and employees, and that employees are assumed to be in training for entrepreneurial activity of their own in the future. Their analysis strongly challenges this, noting the vulnerable labour market position of many employees in this sector and the family dynamics that shape decisions. The Ram et al. (2001) paper is significant for the present discussion in a number of ways. It first illustrates the importance of research methods. In this research, owners and employees are observed and interviewed and this provides a rounded understanding of how entrepreneurs are trained or developed (or not, as proved to be the case in many of the organizations studied). Second, they emphasize that the purpose of smaller companies is not necessarily to train or develop more entrepreneurs, or even to train or develop anyone. The working conditions of the particular sector under study (catering) are certainly significant, in that they tend to be harsher than other sectors, yet the core point remains valid – smaller companies will not necessarily be ideal contexts in which to develop entrepreneurial skills or traits. Finally, their exemplary study also indicates the need to analyse training and development for/in entrepreneurship in social and societal contexts. Disembodied or deracinated studies of education and training that take no account of human or social capital, domestic setting or the sectoral, physical or institutional locations of organizations will only ever be able to provide thin description or abstracted empiricism instead of analysis or insight.

In finishing this section it is worth noting that the idea of the job-generating, successful entrepreneurial economy can be explored in more depth and detail whilst retaining a focus on policy. Parker (2001), for example, picks apart the commonly made claims that small firms generate a disproportionate number of new jobs, that small firms are innovative or progressive, and that economies with a higher proportion of small firms have lower unemployment and higher industrial competitiveness. Using secondary analysis of large datasets, Parker's analysis comprehensively challenges all of these widely accepted claims, and ultimately suggests that there is little evidence to justify state policies that target smaller companies. It may be that this is the question scholars should be asking in relation to both training for entrepreneurship and training in entrepreneurial organizations – whether in fact the category and the characteristics often associated with 'it' are mythical.

Future directions

In the final section of this chapter my aim is to synthesize my arguments with the intent of positively indicating potentially fruitful future research directions in this area. My summary of what we might take from a different understanding of published work explores the problematics of the concepts in use and suggests some future research directions.

There is no doubt that we now have a breadth and depth of published work that takes the management of people in smaller companies as a focus, leading Ram and Edwards (2003) to contend that research into managerial and employee behaviour in smaller companies is an 'exemplar of analytical advance [where] research has made empirical and analytical progress' (p. 719). Our understanding of HRM and training in particular is considerably deeper now than it was two decades ago. However, it would be rash to think that we can take this achievement to mean that there is little more to be done.

In the previous two sections I briefly indicated ways in which the dominant mode of research in these areas is problematic, through review of exemplary contributions to understanding training and development in smaller companies. My intention was not to suggest that either of the papers I examined were 'bad' research, instead I wished to question the approach to data collection and analysis in its claims to truth, in its assumptions and epistemologies.

The volume of data in this area is increasing steadily, particularly through collection of questionnaire-based information from managerial respondents. Despite authors frequently emphasizing their recognition of the small-firm context 'as making a difference', it remains the case that theoretical concepts and prescriptive norms of good practice are being imported from studies conducted with the larger organization in mind (Taylor, 2004). A considerable amount of research energy is being expended on a category of organization that is simultaneously defined with precision yet is vague and almost meaninglessly broad. While there are commonalities to the experience of work and management in any form of organization, it is also the case that smaller organizations produce and are subject to specific conditions that would enable alternative perspectives to be taken. If such perspectives can be grounded in robust data and analysis, particularly data collected from multiple respondents, then they could inform the analysis of larger organizations and lead towards a more complete understanding of the economy as a whole. To achieve this, however, I would suggest that the notion of size must be explored in considerably more depth, to emphasize that it is not a fixed category that has little effect on, for example, training and development.

Similarly, the pursuit of understanding in the area of training for working in small firms, and in particular the notion of training for entrepreneurial activity, provides us with a clear sense of the progress that can be made. Both data and theory enable us to examine practice and policy from a more informed perspective. Alongside the issues noted above in relation to researching training in small firms, there is an additional difficulty with taking this programme of research forward. That difficulty resides in the concept of 'entrepreneurship'. Much of the research in this field is founded on an embedded notion of entrepreneurship that does not allow for critical examination of the assumptions and effects of encouraging people towards an entrepreneurial personality or entrepreneurial attitude towards their work and/or careers.

While suggesting that the two key terms underpinning debate and scholarship in the field of training and development in small or growth firms, size and entrepreneurship, are under-developed conceptually, I do not suggest previous research was flawed or not worthwhile. All I am arguing is that closer examination of how these terms are used could help to avoid abstracted empiricism and a-theoretical generic recommendations for organizational and educational practice. Approaches like that are unlikely to take us beyond descriptions of current practice or foster critical thinking and learning.

Organizational size, for example, has a long and complex conceptual history, rarely acknowledged in contemporary small firm research. After providing the independent variable for numerous studies of organization and management in the 1950s and 1960s, the notion became less fashionable. The early dominant conception, defined by number of personnel, was refined through the addition of input, output and other materialist approaches (Slater, 1985). However, the notion of size in use today remains largely a-conceptual, as can be seen from the definitions used within the training and development literature (Gray and Mabey, 2005). Firms are treated as objects, so that we lose the sense of small firms as 'diffuse, quarrelsome and fissile' (Bechhofer and Elliott, 1978: p. 84) social contexts. In addition the ambiguous structural and ideological position that smaller organizations and managers in growing firms occupy is reduced to uniformity (Burrows and Curran, 1989). This pragmatic methodological approach also encourages scholars to exclude 'large firm theory' from their analyses (Ram, 1994) to the detriment of both areas.

One possibility here would be to take the social and institutional context of entrepreneurial activity into consideration. Edwards et al. (2006) note that the majority of research on small firms has been driven by a desire to understand the entrepreneur and the nature of entrepreneurship – an aim that is not in itself mistaken, but one that tends to exclude the social negotiation of employment relations and the wider social embeddedness of the firm among other institutions. These authors propose a form of institutional analysis that focuses on the meaning of embeddedness in relation to context (Edwards et al., 2006: p. 718). They outline six major external influences or structural conditions that they suggest will influence the negotiation of employment relations within smaller organizations. It would be relatively straightforward to apply this theoretical framework to understanding training and development in entrepreneurial organizations, either as an aspect of employment relations or in its own right. In particular, exploration of how managerial activity varies according to changing structural conditions offers fruitful new ways of understanding what goes on inside entrepreneurial firms.

Similarly entrepreneurship is an increasingly contested concept. As chapters in this collection make clear its definition draws on contributions from numerous directions. Yet little of this complexity is acknowledged in research on training for entrepreneurship. Two recent comprehensive reviews (Katz, 2003; Kuratko, 2005) present conceptions of entrepreneurship that begin and end with functionalist approaches. Kuratko (2005) for example suggests that entrepreneurship is central to the maintenance of market economies, providing new firms, ideas and growth. Further, he argues that a clearly identifiable entrepreneurial perspective underpins the economic strength of the US, as well as influencing cultural development by encouraging immigrants to enter the economic mainstream. Two areas are emphasized when considering theories of entrepreneurship: personality and structural conditions for example. However, as Jones and Spicer (2005) observe, 30 years of investigation into 'the entrepreneurial character' has yielded little beyond acknowledgement that no one can really say what 'it' is. In addition, they note that analysis of the structural factors contributing to 'it' generates a chaotic list of externalities that emphasize the space or lack at the centre.

Hence one possibility is to consider Jones and Spicer's (2005) suggestion that the long search for positive attributes to define the entrepreneur will always be akin to searching for mythical animals like the heffalump. Drawing on psychoanalytical theory, these authors argue that the difficulty does not lie with the methods used or the volume of research (as they note, empirical evidence is plentiful in this area). Instead they say that our lack of definition of the entrepreneur is indicative of the nature of the thing itself. In other words, if we see the progress of entrepreneurship research and its 'failure' to identify positive traits or actions as a finding, then we can begin to think about entrepreneurship in other, more creative and perhaps more fruitful ways.

For Jones and Spicer (2005), entrepreneurship and the search for an entrepreneurial character has only provided paradoxical, contradictory and incomplete images telling us something important about the subject. We are left with a narrative that constructs 'being an entrepreneur' and 'entrepreneurship' as desirable objects, which are mobilized to enlist people into contemporary economic structures and to define what is desirable. Entrepreneurship thus becomes something mysterious, never to be achieved, and that is central to its discursive success. Their conclusion is that entrepreneurship is in fact a desire rather than a bundle of essential character traits or structural initiatives. This provides a fresh way of thinking about entrepreneurship in an educational context.

This possibility re-opens the notion of entrepreneurship in a number of interesting ways. First, it casts doubt on the ability of management educators to construct training or educational programmes that develop entrepreneurship. In particular it challenges those who claim to provide training or development that will make employees or students more entrepreneurial in action or character. Instead, perhaps we would be better to see such training and development as part of the process of constructing entrepreneurship as a desirable condition that encourages students to engage with broader societal expectations. This might especially be the case for undergraduates in a business school context where they are expected to learn practical skills that will enable them to contribute positively towards the economy.

In addition, an approach to researching the intersection of training and entrepreneurship informed by this and other recent contributions to the debate about the nature of entrepreneurship (see Armstrong, 2001; Grey, 1998) provides the theoretical means to explore the formation of entrepreneurs and entrepreneurship in a number of different training or educational contexts. Moving away from the notion of traits or transactional skills and towards exploring how agency and discourse interact could provide new insights into how and why training for entrepreneurship remains so popular, despite repeated questions as to its value or use.

Moreover, as Jones and Spicer (2005) hint, in attempting to understand the frames that a powerful discourse such as enterprise places around subject positions we can come to a greater understanding of structures as well as subjectivity and agency. Training for entrepreneurship and associated policy structures tends to take the notion of enterprise or the entrepreneur as understood, as undeniably good things that all should naturally aspire to. In the current context when so much of management and organization theory is devoted to questioning economic rationality and individualism, it is surely time to analyse the structural conditions of training for entrepreneurs in such a way that we can question their bases.

For training and development the application or adoption of these or related frameworks might see new developments in three areas. First, scholars would seek to explain more clearly the negotiation of training and development in firms that are highly constrained by lack of financial resources. It is often noted that owners of smaller organizations close to start-up can neglect or reject a more formalized approach to HRM, yet little is known as to why this approach is taken or what forms of pressure colleagues might apply in order to protect their own development. Second, the 'mixed embeddedness' approach sketched by Edwards et al. (2006) has an obvious potential application to the assessment of the interplay between firm independence or 'disembeddedness' from structural conditions and engagement with training and development. Third, this approach would allow researchers to frame comparative analysis of levels of engagement in entrepreneurial firms with formal structures of training and development themselves. This would have the additional potential of bringing training and development structures such as skills-based development, further and higher education or good practice guidelines into the framework that Edwards et al. (2006) outline.

This final possibility is the ultimate aim of this chapter. Training has long been the 'Cinderella' of both HRM and the managerial activity of people management. Yet it is, as I have argued in this chapter, a significant aspect of how governments engage with entrepreneurship and entrepreneurial firms – whether measured in terms of financial commitment or in terms of how influential the language is as a framing discourse. Despite this, research into training and development either in entrepreneurial firms or for entrepreneurship appears to be at something of a crossroads. I have suggested that if we wish this particular intersection to be larger or recognized then there are theoretical signposts, particularly from recent contributions to the psychoanalytics of organization or institutional theory. It is surely time to draw on such frameworks rather than simply collecting ever more data on specific policy initiatives or suggesting yet another version of the entrepreneurial personality.

References

Armstrong, P. (2001), 'Science, enterprise and profit: Ideology in the knowledge driven economy', *Economy and Society*, **30**(4), 524–52.
Béchard, J.P. and D. Grégoire (2005), 'Entrepreneurship education research revisited: The case of higher education', *Academy of Management Learning and Education*, **4**(1), 22–43.
Bechhofer, F. and B. Elliott (1978), 'The voice of small business and the politics of survival', *Sociological Review*, **26**, 57–88.
Burrows, R. and J. Curran (1989), 'Sociological research and service sector small businesses: Some conceptual considerations', *Work, Employment and Society*, **3**(4), 527–39.
Clegg, S. and G. Palmer (eds) (1996), *The Politics of Management Knowledge*, London: Sage.
Cosh, A., N. Cox and A. Hughes (2000), *The Relationship between Training and Employment Growth in Small and Medium Enterprises*, Department for Education and Employment (UK) Research Report 245.
Curran, J. and D. Storey (2002), 'Small business policy in the United Kingdom: The inheritance of the Small Business Service and implications for its future effectiveness', *Environment and Planning C: Government and Policy*, **20**(2), 163–78.
Edwards, P., M. Ram, S. Gupta and C. Tsai (2006), 'The structuring of working relationships in small firms: Towards a formal framework', *Organization*, **13**(5), 701–24.
Fraser, S. (2003), 'The impact of Investors in People on small business growth: Who benefits?', *Environment and Planning C: Government and Policy*, **21**, 793–812.
Fraser, S., D. Storey, J. Frankish and R. Roberts (2002), 'The relationship between training and small business performance: An analysis of the Barclays Bank small firms training loan scheme', *Environment and Planning C: Government and Policy*, **20**, 211–34.
Freel, M. (2005), 'Patterns of innovation and skills in small firms', *Technovation*, **25**, 123–34.
Fuller-Love, N. (2006), 'Management development in small firms', *International Journal of Management Reviews*, **8**(3), 175–90.
Gray, C. and C. Mabey (2005), 'Management development: Key differences between small and large businesses in Europe', *International Small Business Journal*, **23**(5), 467–85.
Grey, C. (1998), *Enterprise and Culture*, London: Routledge.
Henry, C., F. Hill and C. Leitch (2003), *Entrepreneurship Education and Training: The Issue of Effectiveness*, Aldershot: Ashgate.
Heyes, J. and M. Stuart (1998), 'Bargaining for skills: Trade unions and training at the workplace', *British Journal of Industrial Relations*, **36**(3), 459–67.
Jones, C. and A. Spicer (2005), 'The sublime object of entrepreneurship', *Organization*, **12**(2), 223–46.
Katz, J. (2003), 'The chronology and intellectual trajectory of American entrepreneurship education', *Journal of Business Venturing*, **18**(2), 283–300.

Kuratko, D. (2005), 'The emergence of entrepreneurship education: Developments, trends and challenges', *Entrepreneurship: Theory and Practice*, **29**(5), 577–97.

Marlow, S. (2003), 'Formality and informality in employment relations', *Environment and Planning C: Government and Policy*, **21**, 531–47.

Matlay, H. and T. Hyland (1999), 'Small firms and the University for Industry: An appraisal', *Educational Studies*, **25**(3), 253–67.

McCarthy, W. (1994), 'Of hats and cattle: Or the limits of macro-survey research in industrial relations', *Industrial Relations Journal*, **25**, 315–22.

Parker, R. (2001), 'The myth of the entrepreneurial economy: Employment and innovation in small firms', *Work, Employment and Society*, **15**(2), 373–84.

Ram, M. (1994), *Managing to Survive: Working Lives in Small Firms*, Oxford: Blackwell.

Ram, M. and P. Edwards (2003), 'Praising Caesar not burying him', *Work, Employment and Society*, **17**(4), 719–30.

Ram, M., T. Abbas, B. Sanghera, G. Barlow and T. Jones (2001), 'Apprentice entrepreneurs? Ethnic minority workers in the independent restaurant sector', *Work, Employment and Society*, **15**(2), 353–72.

Slater, R. (1985), 'Organizational size and differentiation', in S. Bacharach and S. Mitchell (eds), *Research in the Sociology of Organizations vol. 4*, Greenwich, CT: JAI Press, pp. 127–80.

Solomon, G., S. Duffy and A. Tarabishy (2002), 'The state of entrepreneurship education in the United States', *International Journal of Entrepreneurship Education*, **1**(1), 65–86.

Storey, D. (2004), 'Exploring the link, among small firms, between management training and firm performance: A comparison between the UK and other OECD countries', *International Journal of Human Resource Management*, **15**(1), 112–30.

Storey, D. and P. Westhead (1997), 'Management training and small firm performance: Why is the link so weak?', *International Small Business Journal*, **14**(4), 13–24.

Taylor, S. (2004), 'HRM in small firms: Hunting the Snark?', in S. Marlow, D. Patton and M. Ram (eds), *Managing Labour in Small Firms*, London: Routledge, pp. 18–42.

Thomson, A. and C. Gray (1999), 'Determinants of management development in small businesses', *Journal of Small Business and Enterprise Development*, **6**(3), 113–27.

23 The maturation of entrepreneurial careers

David M. Kaplan and Jerome A. Katz

Introduction

Career theory tends to focus on white-collar workers in established organizations (Thomas, 1996). As a result, there is not a strong theoretical underpinning for the careers of entrepreneurs (Dyer, 1994; Katz, 1994; Rae, 2005). Even recent theoretical advances such as the protean (Hall, 1996), boundaryless (Arthur and Rousseau, 1996; DeFillipi and Arthur, 1994) and emergent (Bloch, 2005) careers, which focus on personal empowerment and direction, still conceptualize the individual as an employee. And while employees within an organization can operate entrepreneurially (Dess et al., 2003), they are not technically entrepreneurs in the sense that they do not create organizations (Gartner, 1988). Consequently, there is a need to adapt or develop new theories to accommodate those individuals who start their careers outside existing organizational structures and constraints.

While entrepreneurs may begin their careers outside established organizations, they are not free of organizational influences. The emerging organizations that entrepreneurs create will exert an influence on the individual's career development in a way that the organization does not influence traditional careers. Because an entrepreneur is the founder of the organization he or she will tend to have greater levels of accountability and responsibility than non-entrepreneurial counterparts with the same level of career experience. From the beginning the success or failure of the enterprise is in the hands of the entrepreneur, which is very different from what most people experience in the first week of their job.

This represents just one example of where existing career theory falls short of explaining the complexities of entrepreneurial careers. However, traditional theories do provide important starting points for developing a useful framework for understanding entrepreneurial careers. In addition to looking at how an emerging organization shapes an entrepreneur's career, there are two additional aspects of the entrepreneurial career that will be addressed in this chapter. First, what is the path that most entrepreneurs experience in their career? This details how an entrepreneur matures or progresses through various career stages, each with their own issues and challenges. Second, why do people pursue an entrepreneurial career and how do they experience it? This makes it necessary to consider variations between types of entrepreneurs. While both these issues have been previously studied for entrepreneurs, with Katz (1994) focusing on types and Dyer (1994) developing paths, both issues and theories will be examined simultaneously in this chapter. In doing so, a flexible framework of entrepreneurial careers that relies upon traditionally separate areas of career theory is developed in this chapter.

Careers, career paths and entrepreneurs

Individuals experience their careers through a series of stages that begin with some type of exploration and end with disengagement (Dalton et al., 1977; Schein, 1978). While Schein (1978) outlined nine distinct career stages, in this chapter we will focus on the four-stage model suggested by Dalton et al. There are several reasons for using this four-stage model rather than Schein's nine. The first is parsimony, which facilitates a clearer and more concise discussion of entrepreneurial careers. Second, the nine stages have overlapping age ranges. This makes it difficult to draw clear distinctions, and there is also research suggesting that such age linkages to career stages may not hold (Dowd and Kaplan, 2005), especially for those individuals who embark on a second career, as is the case for some entrepreneurs. Finally, the four-stage model is frequently used in discussions about careers in general (Mathis and Jackson, 2006; Noe, 2005) while it has also been used in entrepreneurship research (Dyer, 1994). In Table 23.1 the four-stage model as developed by Dalton et al. is outlined, and we show how it relates to the Schein and Dyer conceptualizations.

In addition to the nine stages of careers outlined by Schein, the real contribution of his approach was to include the organizational cone

Table 23.1   Alternative stage conceptualizations for career theories

Dalton et al. (1977)	Schein (1978)	Dyer (1994)
1. Exploration	1. Growth, fantasy, exploration	1. Socialization
2. Establishment	2. Entry into the world of work	2. Early career
	3. Basic training	
	4. Full membership, early career	
3. Maintenance	5. Full membership, mid-career	3. Mid-career
	6. Mid-career crisis	
	7. Late career (in non-leadership role or leadership role)	
4. Disengagement	8. Decline and disengagement	4. Late career
	9. Retirement	

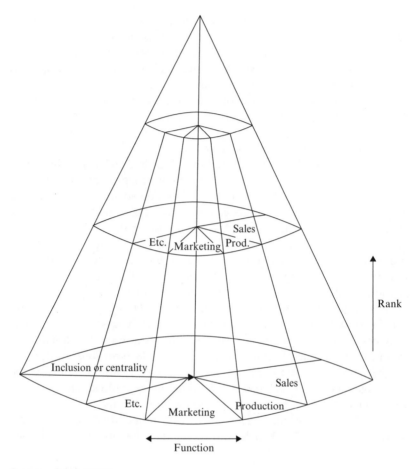

Source: Schein (1971).

Figure 23.1   Schein's organizational cone

conceptualization (see Figure 23.1), which operationalizes the variables of hierarchy, centrality and function as explanatory variables in a career. Hierarchy identified the total level or power available to the person, while function described the type of work the individual was performing (for example, sales, production). As such, hierarchy and function represent relatively structural elements of one's career, whereas centrality was more cultural. Specifically, centrality was the term to describe the individual's position relative to the core of the profession. For example, a dentist practicing dentistry is close to the core. Whereas a dentist managing a dental plan is farther removed from the core, and a dentist like Winfield Dunn, who served as Governor of Tennessee (1971–1975), would be almost totally removed from the core, although still legally licensed as a dentist.

Another challenge when discussing career theory for entrepreneurs is the fact that there are different types of entrepreneur. These differences have important implications for the career decisions that a person will make. It is therefore possible for entrepreneurs to diverge in the career paths they take. Two important dimensions along which entrepreneurs can be differentiated include the level of multiplicity (in regard to creating organizations) and the career anchor of the entrepreneur.

The multiplicity of entrepreneurial behavior (Katz, 1994) was originally conceived as a continuous variable, but subsequent research by Westhead and colleagues (Westhead and Wright, 1998, 1999; Ucbasaran et al., 2003; Westhead et al., 2005) on entrepreneurs with multiple firms has made a strong case for dichotomizing the construct.

So for example, if someone has only engaged in one entrepreneurial endeavor, he or she can be classified as a novice entrepreneur (Westhead and Wright, 1998). Once someone has crossed the threshold of starting a second organization there is no distinction between starting a second or a fortieth enterprise. The only factor that differentiates habitual entrepreneurs is how they have chosen to go about creating the multiple ventures. For example, individuals who retain control in their initial or previous venture while creating a new one are known as portfolio entrepreneurs as opposed to those who leave behind their old organization and start anew; they are known as serial entrepreneurs (Westhead et al., 2005). While the novice entrepreneur is a relatively straightforward fit to career models, serial and portfolio entrepreneurs pose additional challenges. For example, how should the multiple organizational roles and previous career experiences of the portfolio entrepreneur be factored into evaluations of entrepreneurial choice and capability? Or if serial entrepreneurs move from one start-up to the next, do their careers ever mature? These questions are not directly addressed or easily answered using conventional career theory, although new approaches are beginning to model such potentially complex work lives (see for example Moen, 2005).

In addition to the multiplicity of entrepreneurial careers, how a career is anchored may also influence an individual's career development. According to Schein (1978; 1996) a career anchor reflects the values, talents and motives of the individual. Katz (1994) originally focused attention on the two anchors most clearly related to entrepreneurship – the autonomy/freedom and entrepreneurial/creative anchors. Since that time, however, research has shown that one other anchor can operate in entrepreneurial groups, this is known as the security/stability anchor (Feldman and Bolino, 2000).

Individuals with an autonomy/freedom anchor are motivated by a desire for independence. As a general rule, they want to be free of organizational constraints and are attracted to entrepreneurship by the opportunity to be their own boss. As Katz (1994) noted, this anchor is a close fit with the model of the small business owner from traditional entrepreneurship research (Carland et al., 1984; Smith, 1967).

Despite its name someone with an entrepreneurial/creative anchor does not have to be an entrepreneur. Schein reported the anchor in employed designers as well as a smattering of individuals in diverse fields. These are people who enjoy the process of innovation and creation. Katz (1994) identified this group as potentially analogous to the entrepreneurs in traditional entrepreneurship studies, but also noted that there were several problems with the correspondence of the two classifications.

The Feldman and Bolino (2000) finding of a security/stability anchor provides another explanation for entrepreneurial behavior. People with a security/stability anchor create an organization because it maximizes their ability to ensure that they will be financially independent and able to sustain that through their own effort, rather than through dependencies on an organization controlled by others. These individuals share the autonomy interest of those with the autonomy/freedom career anchor, but are also driven to higher levels of achievement, similar to those with an entrepreneurial/creative anchor. In many ways, this group fills the gap between the two anchors, or the two extremes of the small business owner and the high-growth entrepreneur, which was first identified by Smith (1967) and linked to Schein's model by Katz (1994).

Finally, there remains a question as to the fixedness of the stages of the entrepreneurial career. This issue of sequence is perhaps the most distinctive one differentiating the application of career theory to the entrepreneurship literature. Traditional career theorists have conceptualized the career process using a linear stage model. However, the 'new career theory' approach (Bloch, 2005) posited a non-linear process, while a similar argument is evident in entrepreneurial careers research. So for example, Dyer (1994) acknowledged stage sequences but made possible stage simultaneity and overlap. This contrasted with Katz's (1994) argument that stages could come in a variety of orders.

One reason for this non-linearity can be attributed to the fact that the entrepreneur is creating, rather than being a member of, an organization. As such, the organization's success or failure has the ability to either enhance or impede the entrepreneur's career development. If the organization is very successful, this may require that the entrepreneur advance more quickly in his or her career than would otherwise be desirable. As a result of the organization's success, the entrepreneur is more likely to have to take on additional tasks and responsibilities, particularly in the area of management, before he or she may feel fully competent. This is different from the employee in an existing organization who is promoted or transferred into a position for which he or she is not fully qualified. Conversely, if an entrepreneurial organization fails to grow or fails, then the entrepreneur is not likely to get the opportunity to experience or develop the skills associated with subsequent career stages. As a result, his or her career could stall or even end. By comparison, while a downsizing event has negative implications on an individual's career, it is much easier for that individual to move to another organization and continue in his or her career than it is to create and nurture a new organization as the entrepreneur would need to do.

Entrepreneurial careers

Stage 1: exploration
The first stage of the Dalton and Schein models is called Exploration, and this label also serves those pursuing entrepreneurial careers. Individuals start at this stage when they consciously intend to become an entrepreneur. While intentionality is not necessarily the first phase of an entrepreneurial or emerging organization (Katz and Gartner, 1998), it is a requirement for the entrepreneurial career. This results from the fact that a career depends on how a person identifies and experiences his or her life (Townsend, 1999). So until people identify themselves as entrepreneurial they will not experience their careers that way, even if they engage in similar activities.

For entrepreneurs and non-entrepreneurs, the main focus is learning about business and how one fits into it, although this process is more environmental than organizational for the entrepreneur. For example, instead of socialization within an organization, the burgeoning entrepreneur is learning such processes as getting financial backing and legal compliance. Instead of learning how to take direction, the entrepreneur needs to deal with the challenges of either working alone or how to be someone's boss, depending on the business model. In fact, the specific skills the potential entrepreneur needs to develop have been standardized into an educational curriculum standard in the USA by the Consortium for Entrepreneurship Education (2004), with another parallel effort underway in Europe as part of the ENTREVA/EDULEARN/ENTLEARN projects (European Commission, 2004; Hytti et al., 2004; Hytti et al., 2002).

The amount of time that someone stays in the exploration stage is highly dependent on the success of the entrepreneurial search. Research around this idea has focused on the concept of gestation times for a business (Katz, 1990; Reynolds and Miller, 1992; Reynolds, 1997). This can be a source of frustration for some individuals, especially if the search for a viable opportunity, needed skills, or resources is not successful, causing the career of the entrepreneur-to-be to stagnate. Conversely, if the entrepreneurial effort is extremely successful then the individual may be forced to mature in his or her career to handle the additional complexities of actually starting an organization before being ready either socio-emotionally or technically.

Although this is the first stage of an entrepreneurial career, it is not entirely clear that all entrepreneurs participate in it. This possibility occurs with security/stability anchored entrepreneurs. One reason for this is the fact that the security/stability anchored entrepreneur may not realize or identify that he or she is an entrepreneur. This situation could easily occur for someone who never intended to become an entrepreneur but had an avocation or hobby that became marketable or became an entrepreneur by necessity (due to losing a job) rather than desire (Cooper and Dunkelberg, 1986). Another possibility is that these individuals chose the franchisee path to entrepreneurship (Shane and Spell, 1998). As a result they are fitted into a larger organization, even if they are technically their own boss, and therefore do not experience the same issues and problems as those who develop an organization from scratch.

Stage 2: establishment
Simply put, compared to non-entrepreneurs at the beginning of their careers, entrepreneurs will typically have more power and handle a greater variety of organizational functions. This is perhaps most evident at the very beginning of the actual entry process – in what would typically be called the early career or establishment stage. For non-entrepreneurs, this would be when the individual learns about their self, job and how to function within an organization. A person at this career stage typically enters the organization at the lower levels of the hierarchy, faces high levels of supervision or oversight, and is probably limited to one functional area. As these employees become acculturated and demonstrate their technical expertise they will be given expanded areas of responsibility – either functional or hierarchical. Along this path, they may participate in training and career development activities to help them handle increasing levels of accountability and responsibility. Their progress tends to be monitored so no one is given more responsibility than they can handle. As a result, the career development for most employees is consistent and predictable.

This contrasts strongly with the entrepreneurial career that lacks predictability from the outset. In creating a new firm, the entrepreneur *is* the organization. In the modal case of the one-person firm (Katz, 1984; Schreiner and Woller, 2003) hierarchical totality results. The natural consequence of this is that the entrepreneur lacks the supervision, the gradation of assignment and responsibility, and the opportunities for immediate and frequent feedback, coaching and training. It describes the very fundamental way in which entrepreneurs are socially isolated, even when part of a broader social network support (Chrisman, 1999; Ruef et al., 2003; Sullivan, 2000).

This has two consequences for the entrepreneur. First, they may lack additional socializing influences including the skills to operate in or inter- act optimally with those in a hierarchical system (Krueger and Brazeal, 1994; Sullivan, 2000). Second, they shoulder financial, career and social risk. Even when there are other investors or partners, the entrepreneur holds a high degree of personal responsibility for the firm and from day one, which may be weeks or months before any sales occur. In other words, the entrepreneurial career operates without a social safety net from day one (Cunningham and Lischeron, 1991) and this may explain, in part, the enduring finding of high levels of anxiety or Type A behavior among a group who generally report high levels of job satisfaction (Eden, 1975; Miner, 2000).

The consequence of hierarchical totality from the firm's beginning is that there is less chance of the entrepreneur gaining feedback or support, thus limiting organizational and personal learning. As a result, one would expect higher rates of failure for an entrepreneur's first business, especially when operated as a one-person enterprise. Research on the volatility of new firms in general bears out this prediction (Bruderl et al., 1992; Carroll and Mosakowski, 1987; Phillips and Kirchoff, 1989).

Exacerbating this problem is the other consequence of hierarchical total- ity – functional totality. In the one-person firm all functions are carried out by that one person (Katz, 1992). Even with the addition of partners, employees or subcontractors, research suggests that the entrepreneur still performs multiple roles (Erikson, 2003; Sadler-Smith et al., 2003). Given what has been learned about entrepreneurial competencies (Chandler and Hanks, 1994; Mitchell et al., 2000) it is clear that few entrepreneurs are equally adept at all required roles, although most have one or two roles in which they excel, which is the individual-level equivalent of the Katz and Kahn (1978) leading subsystem idea (Katz and Peters, 2001). Even where an entrepreneur is expert in a few areas, the number, variety and lack of internal supports for the roles and behaviors needed to make a firm suc- cessful place enormous stress on the individual, limiting opportunities for learning by the entrepreneur and the firm (Politis, 2005; Rae, 2002; Rae and Carswell, 2001).

Not all entrepreneurs will respond the same way at the establishment stage. We can envision a spectrum with the security/stability anchored entrepreneur at one end and the autonomy/freedom entrepreneur at the other. In both cases, the cause is the associated level of control within the organization. To the security/stability anchored entrepreneur, the early stage firm, with uncertainty in the customer base, skill level, and virtually all processes, will seem daunting and stressful. This is the career stage where these individuals least enjoy being entrepreneurs. By comparison the autonomy/freedom anchored entrepreneur would be more likely to derive a high level of happiness at the establishment stage. These individuals wanted to become entrepreneurs so they could get away from formal procedures and supervision. Thus life is better from the perspective of being the boss, as opposed to the subordinate, which is a role that the autonomy/freedom anchored entrepreneur would chose to avoid. In fact, it would only be in the case of unexpectedly successful start-up that these entrepreneurs might begin to feel stress, because they would need to hire more employees, or even a manager, to help cope with the larger-than-expected flow of business.

Stage 3: maintenance–rejuvenation

Dalton's third stage, Maintenance, poses an interesting challenge to stage modeling. One area in which Schein's nine-stage model offers a particular advantage is in stage seven, where the individual might have different career experiences depending on whether or not they pursue a leadership role. Dalton has no corresponding factor.

At this stage there is really a fundamental choice for the entrepreneur. The choice is between the desire to rest on his/her laurels and aim for maintaining the firm or to take new risks and kick-start a new entrepreneurial endeavor. Thus Rejuvenation is added to the title of this stage to reflect this choice.

Entrepreneurial effort has clearly led to a business being created. This is the period where the organization can benefit from greater standardization and profitability. Individuals enter this stage after the organization has matured to the desired level of structure, complexity or market position and the entrepreneur has either mastered the managerial tasks necessary to run the organization or learned to delegate them. An important distinction in this stage is the desired level of organization. Of course the entrepreneur may continue to grow the firm; however, those pursuing a maintenance approach would not be expected to make any fundamental changes to the organizational design or culture. This allows for variety in the types of firms and careers that exist in this stage and in how individuals respond to it.

While someone with an entrepreneurial/creative anchor may be satisfied with the economic returns of the organization, the lack of fundamental change or challenge may eventually lead to dissatisfaction. In order to avert stagnation, these entrepreneurs are most likely to take steps to mitigate it and they would be inclined toward efforts at rejuvenation, meaning that they will be looking for new opportunities to create or exploit. As a result, entrepreneurial/creative individuals are likely to become habitual entrepreneurs. Further, given that their dissatisfaction is based on the lack of change or challenge and not in the existing organization, they are more likely to pursue portfolio/parallel entrepreneurship rather than a serial path.

The maintenance-rejuvenation stage can pose very different outcomes for autonomy/freedom anchored entrepreneurs. Where the business is successful in financial and emotional returns to the entrepreneur, maintenance is the order of the day. Rejuvenation becomes likely when the entrepreneur lets the first organization grow to a level at which they are no longer comfortable. Its very size or complexity may make its management/operation less rewarding as a career choice. For such entrepreneurs, there are two general options to rejuvenate it – restructuring the existing organization to bring it back to a smaller, more manageable form, or creating a new organization where they plan to do a better job of limiting growth to a manageable size. By recapturing the essence of the early days of the first firm, these approaches become a form of rejuvenation, although it may actually be more of a chance to go back to old ways of working, rather than pioneering new ways.

For those who elect the rejuvenation stage, it is important to note that the career of a serial or portfolio entrepreneur goes through a rejuvenation instead of a second beginning. At the most basic, the individual is still an entrepreneur. There is no change in identity, which would foster the creation of a new career. And perhaps more importantly, the entrepreneur has already experienced the establishment stage. Much of what made the exploration stage important is the initial investigation of the unknown and the associated learning of how to create a business. Habitual entrepreneurs (whether serial or portfolio), because they have already created an organization, know what is involved in building a business. Further, they have most likely learned from experiences, both successes and mistakes. As a result, the way or reason someone would build a business the second time around is likely to be different from how he or she did it the first time (Westhead et al., 2005; Wright et al., 1997). Consequently, it is necessary to conceptualize such a process occurring within its own career stage. However, because the development that occurs during this stage is dependent on prior experiences and learning it is difficult to develop propositions that fully encompass all habitual entrepreneurs.

Stage 4: disengagement–destination
While Dalton talks of a final stage in which individuals distance themselves from the world of work – the disengagement stage – entrepreneurs often have a different experience. Disengagement is traditionally described in

terms of one's withdrawal from work, engaging in retirement, and finding a new balance, with work at most a minor part of the whole life. How an entrepreneur withdraws can be significantly different. For many of these older entrepreneurs, the preference is to never retire, preferring what is popularly known as the 'feet first' exit strategy (Aronoff, 1998). This approach is likely to be most strongly true for autonomy anchored entrepreneurs, who will often equate leaving the business with leaving the one situation in which they feel in control. Because of such distinctions, a useful addition to the nomenclature for this stage is Destination.

Amongst the self-employed is a higher percentage of individuals aged 65 years and more than those in the regular workforce (Bruce et al., 2000).

A key, but often overlooked, factor in the decision to pursue the destination stage is an economic one. Katz and Green (2007) report on the nature of business closures in the USA categorizing nine outcomes, as shown in Figure 23.2. They estimate that over four million firms go through changes in ownership or existence, reflecting the destination stage. While some of the forms are self-explanatory, other such as a 'pass-off' occur when a firm is given as a gift to family, friends or workers, usually because

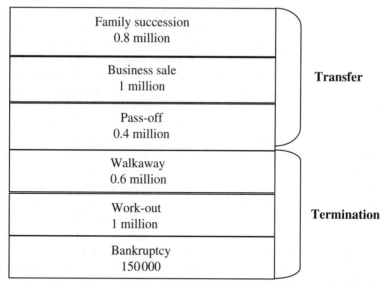

Source:　Adapted from Katz and Green (2007, p. 584).

Figure 23.2　Forms of firm destinations

the firm does not have the revenue or profits to make it saleable. A 'walk-away' occurs when the entrepreneur meets all obligations and simply closes the firm and walks away, while a 'work-out' is when, at the time of closure, the entrepreneur still owes money to debtors, and typically they take on salaried work to pay these off.

Some of these destinations offer ongoing financial security to the entre-preneur from the firm's sale or revenues. However, others reflect situations where the entrepreneur will not receive any financial gain once they leave the firm, and in some cases, they will be required to undertake additional work. While the focus in much of the entrepreneurial literature is on the sale of a firm, its transfer to the family or IPOs, the reality is that an equally typical destination for an entrepreneur is one of little return, and potential additional work (Ronstadt, 1986). This financial dimension, and its effect on the nature of the destination stage, has been severely under-represented in both the career and the entrepreneurship literature. In effect, financial outcomes for a firm may have a stronger influence on destination stage activities than career anchors or other factors.

Where a transition or termination is possible, there is a particular concern because of the unique relationship an entrepreneur has had with the organization in terms of its success and identity (Wasserman, 2003). Among the issues needing to be addressed is how to structure the organ-ization so that the entrepreneur can 'let go'. This is especially true for those with an autonomy/freedom career anchor, but can also be the case for those with other anchors if the entrepreneur has been in denial as to his or her capabilities and therefore has not prepared a successor. Further complica-tions can occur if the succession takes place within the entrepreneur's family (see for example, Bjuggren and Sund, 2001; Flamholtz, 1986). So while parallels can be drawn on this issue between the disengagement stage and the destination stage, the context of entrepreneurship places increased importance and complexity on the issue of succession.

Both the entrepreneurial/creativity anchored and the security/stability anchored entrepreneurs are more likely to take steps ahead of time to arrange for a controlled changeover of the firm. These are the types of people most likely to prepare for a succession within the family or the sale of the firm, since both approaches permit an ongoing revenue stream for the founding entrepreneur. When this works, the remaining problem is one of a loss of control over the source of the income.

Creativity/entrepreneurial anchored entrepreneurs are more likely to see the sale or succession of a firm as an opportunity to undertake new forms of work, while security/stability anchored founders may have trouble shift-ing their focus from the firm they can no longer control to the alternatives where they can take control of their lives.

Research implications
While career stage has been alluded to in many articles on entrepreneurship, rarely has the actual sequence of stages for entrepreneurial careers been described. For example, Carroll and Mosakowski (1987) discussed movements into and out of self-employment, but used a linear career sequence. Rae (2005) considered mid-career transitions to entrepreneurship, and even espoused a non-linear approach to entrepreneurial careers, following a concept by Bloch (2005), but failed to explain the types of stages or activities that might occur within stages.

While much of the model presented above is based on research, little of the model itself has been tested. The ideas of number of stages, age–stage linkages, stage fixedness, requisite variables and entrepreneurial type have far to go to be considered stable concepts. For example, while there have been hundreds of studies using Schein's career anchors, relatively few of those have included entrepreneurs in the samples, leaving even this basic sort of work to future researchers.

Moreover, while some core concepts such as hierarchical totality and functional totality make sense from both theoretical and practical perspectives, it can be just that 'obvious' sort of belief that is most in need of confirmation before going onto more complex model validation issues.

One shortcoming of the model, which is shared by career theories in general, is a failure to accommodate part-time activities. The Panel Study of Entrepreneurial Dynamics (Davis and Aldrich, 2004) suggests that about a quarter of the entrepreneurs in the USA are only self-employed on a part-time basis and they are pursuing entrepreneurial careers as well as waged or salaried ones. Reconciling different career stages in different jobs, as well as managing the role demands and conflicts of competing jobs, represents a whole other area of research to be undertaken. While models like the one presented here are more open than the traditional linear theories of career to the prospect of multiple simultaneous jobs, the actual work to assess multiple jobs and types of employment status remains to be seen.

Along these same lines, as e-commerce electronic-based opportunities for entrepreneurship – such as selling through eBay – become more readily available and widespread (Katz et al., 2003), the number of people who derive considerable satisfaction and significant income from part-time electronic entrepreneurship will increase. This situation alone will increase the need for career counseling theories, which can account for part-time entrepreneurship when counseling people engaged in full-time waged or salaried jobs. The underlying research still needs to be done.

This chapter maps Katz's concept of entrepreneurial multiplicity to the better developed model of habitual entrepreneurship developed by Westhead and colleagues, but it remains for the two approaches to be cross-validated.

This chapter also furthers the de-linearization of career theory, more closely following the initiative of the new career theorists to embrace emergent forms of process, rather than strict sequential orderings. While readily accepted today, that acceptance springs deeply from the current *zeitgeist*. While dismissing the idea of non-linear career 'paths' was intellectually unfounded ten years ago, its immediate acceptance today is on no stronger an intellectual basis. It is a subject that should be explored empirically.

The model in this chapter took on the simplified and more widely accepted four-stage approach of Dalton and colleagues but it was also evident that the four-stage approach is an over-simplification at least with the maintenance-rejuvenation stage, where Schein's model accommodates both approaches through its consideration of late career individuals with and without leadership positions. The approach used in this chapter was, in effect, to combine two potential outcomes in Stage 3 (maintenance-rejuvenation) and Stage 4 (disengagement-destination). This suggests a potential way to structure a career stage model strong inference test (Platt, 1964). Obviously, the proposed career stage model for entrepreneurs is also in need of stage testing, as are those two joint stages in particular.

Practical implications

The entire area of entrepreneurial careers is underplayed in the pedagogical and support systems for potential and practicing entrepreneurs. Part of this comes from the limited amount of material on entrepreneurial careers, and the variety of the material, which in the absence of a simple-to-understand theory, becomes hard to fit together. Efforts such as ours in this chapter but perhaps even more so, full models such as Dyer's (1994), might help provide the framework to help integrate and use the disparate ideas comprising entrepreneurial career theory.

There are several areas where such an application could be made.

- Given the power of entrepreneurial type to help shape one's approach to firm creation and management, giving prospective entrepreneurs a career anchors scale, with counseling, could help them find an approach to firm creation and management which is optimally compatible with their personal style.
- Helping those who have jumped into entrepreneurship because of immediate pressures or opportunities, rather than taking a planned, sequential approach, could benefit from knowing what the other steps or stages in entrepreneurship are. Knowing this might help them to cover areas that could become personal or organizational liabilities. It may also help to improve the level of competence of the entrepreneur *in situ*.

- The suggestion of the destination stage research mentioned above and the numbers in Figure 23.2 suggest that perhaps as many as two million US entrepreneurs may be reaching the end of an entrepreneurial career in a less than optimal way – from both a personal satisfaction and an economic benefit standpoint. As a point of entry for support networks, and as a way to help better manage the stresses for individuals and institution caused by financial losses, the destination stage is a topic ready for more in-depth consideration.
- Entrepreneurship education tends to treat careers in a linear fashion for students, even when the typical entrepreneurship class may have students who already run a business (and sometimes not even their first business), as well as those considering becoming an entrepreneur. Accepting the non-linear career theory approach may help reformulate the basic structure of entrepreneurship classes. The simple effort to vary teaching to accommodate those with firms already and those who have not yet 'taken the plunge' could make an immediate and major difference in learning effectiveness.
- Along the same lines, developing career counseling approaches that can accommodate part-time forms of entrepreneurship – whether on eBay or from a local stand run on weekends – would be a benefit for student counseling, career counseling of adults and children, as well as therapists seeking to master the full range of work-related outlets for clients.

The list above is suggestive rather than exhaustive, but points to the obvious need to convert the existing research into actions in our classrooms, offices and counseling centers.

Conclusion

This chapter makes some valuable contributions. Most immediately, it provides an update to the Schein–Katz model for explaining entrepreneurial careers, incorporating new research on relevant career anchors, habitual entrepreneurship, and the growing literature on non-linear career dynamics. We also extend the Schein–Katz model, providing a more in-depth consideration of issues of hierarchy, function and multiplicity, which should help researchers improve their use of these variables. We offer, on the surface, a simplification of the entrepreneurial career model, moving it from Schein's nine-stage approach to Dalton's four – stage one, but also bringing up the shortcomings of the four-stage model by identifying contingency outcomes at the maintenance and disengagement stages. This leaves the two competing stage theories in a heightened state of disequilibrium, and will hopefully lead to inference tests to resolve the number and nature of career stages for entrepreneurs as well as others.

In doing all of the above we have provided empirically-grounded concepts and actionable ideas for researchers and counselors interested in entrepreneurial careers, non-linear career dynamics and attitudinal or personological typologies in service of career theory. It is an area in which the best research and practice is yet to be done.

References

Aronoff, C. (1998), 'Megatrends in family business', *Family Business Review*, **11**, 181–5.
Arthur, M.B. and D.M. Rousseau (eds) (1996), *The Boundaryless Career: A New Employment Principle for a New Organizational Era*, New York, NY and Oxford, UK: Oxford University Press.
Bjuggren, P.O. and L.G. Sund (2001), 'Strategic decision making in intergenerational successions of small and medium-size family-owned businesses', *Family Business Review*, **14**, 11–23.
Bloch, S. (2005), 'Complexity, chaos, and nonlinear dynamics: A new perspective on career development theory', *The Career Development Quarterly*, **53**, 194–207.
Bruce, D., D. Holtz-Eakin and J. Quinn (2000), *Self-Employment and Labor Market Transitions at Older Ages*, Boston, MA: Center for Retirement Research at Boston College, www.escholarship.bc.edu/cgi/viewcontent.cgi?article=1032andcontext=retirement_papers.
Bruderl, J., P. Preisendorfer and R. Zeigler (1992), 'Survival chances of newly founded business organizations', *American Sociological Review*, **57**, 227–42.
Carland, J.W., F. Hoy, W.R. Boulton and J.C. Carland (1984), 'Differentiating entrepreneurs from small business owners: A conceptualization', *Academy of Management Review*, **9**, 354–9.
Carroll, G. and E. Mosakowski (1987), 'The career dynamics of self-employment', *Administrative Science Quarterly*, **32**, 570–89.
Chandler, G.N. and S.H. Hanks (1994). 'Founder competence, the environment, and venture performance', *Entrepreneurship: Theory and Practice*, **18**(3), 77–89.
Chrisman, J.J. (1999), 'The influence of outsider-generated knowledge resources on venture creation', *Journal of Small Business Management*, **37**, 42–58.
Consortium for Entrepreneurship Education (2004), *The National Content Standards for Entrepreneurship Education*, Columbus, OH: Consortium for Entrepreneurship Education, www.entre-ed.org/Standards_Toolkit/, (accessed 1 July, 2006)>.
Cooper, A.C. and W.C. Dunkelberg (1986), 'Entrepreneurship and paths to business ownership', *Strategic Management Journal*, **7**(1), 53–69.
Cunningham, J.B. and J. Lischeron (1991), 'Defining entrepreneurship', *Journal of Small Business Management*, **29**, 45–67.
Dalton, G.W., P.H. Thompson and R.C. Price (1977), 'The four stages of professional careers: A new look at performance by professionals', *Organizational Dynamics*, **6**, 19–42.
Davis, A.E. and H.E. Aldrich (2004). 'Work participation history', in W.B. Gartner, K.G. Shaver, N.M. Carter and P.D. Reynolds (eds), *Handbook of Entrepreneurial Dynamics: The Process of Business Creation*, Thousand Oaks, CA: Sage Publications, pp. 115–28.
DeFillippi, R.J. and M.B. Arthur (1994), 'The boundaryless career: A competency-based perspective', *Journal of Organizational Behavior*, **15**, 307–24.
Dess, G., R. Ireland, S. Zahra, S. Floyd, J. Janney and P. Lane (2003), 'Emerging issues in corporate entrepreneurship', *Journal of Management*, **29**(3), 351–78.
Dowd, K.O. and D.M. Kaplan (2005), 'The career life of academics: Boundaried or boundaryless?', *Human Relations*, **58**, 699–721.
Dyer, W.G., Jr (1994), 'Toward a theory of entrepreneurial careers', *Entrepreneurship: Theory and Practice*, **19**, 7–22.
Eden, D. (1975), 'Organizational membership vs. self-employment: Another blow to the American dream', *Organizational Behavior and Human Performance*, **13**, 79–94.

Erikson, T. (2003), 'Towards a taxonomy of entrepreneurial learning experiences among potential entrepreneurs', *Journal of Small Business and Enterprise Development*, **10**, 106–12.

European Commission (2004), *Helping to Create an Entrepreneurial Culture: A Guide on Good Practices in Promoting Entrepreneurial Attitudes and Skills Through Education*, Luxembourg: Office for Official Publications of the European Communities.

Feldman, D.C. and M.C. Bolino (2000), 'Career patterns of the self-employed: Career motivations and career outcomes', *Journal of Small Business Management*, **38**, 53–67.

Flamholtz, E.G. (1986), *How to Make the Transition from an Entrepreneurship to a Professionally Managed Firm*, San Francisco: Jossey-Bass.

Gartner, W.B. (1988), ' "Who is an entrepreneur?" is the wrong question', *American Journal of Small Business*, **12**, 11–32.

Hall, D.T. (1996), 'Protean careers of the 21st century', *The Academy of Management Executive*, **10**, 8–16.

Hytti, U., P. Kuopusjärvi and the Entreva-Project Team (2004), *Evaluating and Measuring Entrepreneurship and Enterprise Education: Methods, Tools and Practices*, Small Business Institute, Business Research and Development Centre, Turku School of Economics and Business Administration.

Hytti, U., P. Kuopusjärvi, I. Vento-Vierikko, A. Schneeberger, C. Stampfl, C. O'Gorman, H. Hulaas, J. Cotton and K. Hermann (2002), *State-of-Art of Enterprise Education in Europe*, Turku, Finland: Small Business Institute, Turku School of Economics and Business Administration.

Katz, D. and R.L. Kahn (1978), *The Social Psychology of Organizations*, 2nd edn, New York: John Wiley and Sons.

Katz, J.A. (1984), 'One person organizations: A resource for researchers and practitioners', *American Journal of Small Business*, **8**(3), 24–30.

Katz, J.A. (1990), 'Longitudinal analysis of self-employment follow-through', *Entrepreneurship and Regional Development*, **2**(1), 15–26.

Katz, J.A. (1992), 'A psychosocial cognitive model of employment status choice', *Entrepreneurship: Theory and Practice*, **17**(1), 29–37.

Katz, J.A. (1994), 'Modelling entrepreneurial career progressions: Concepts and considerations', *Entrepreneurship: Theory and Practice*, **19**, 23–40.

Katz, J.A. and W.B. Gartner (1998), 'Properties of emerging organizations', *Academy of Management Review*, **13**, 429–41.

Katz, J.A. and R.P. Green (2007), *Entrepreneurial Small Business*, Burr Ridge, IL: McGraw Hill.

Katz, J.A. and S. Peters (2001), 'Understanding the entrepreneur in the growth process of SMEs', *The International Journal of Entrepreneurship and Innovation Management*, **1**(3/4), 366–80.

Katz, J.A., S.R. Safranski and O. Khan (2003), 'Virtual instant global entrepreneurship: Cybermediation for born international service firms', *Journal of International Entrepreneurship*, **1**, 43–57.

Krueger, N. and D. Brazeal (1994), 'Entrepreneurial potential and potential entrepreneurs', *Entrepreneurship: Theory and Practice*, **18**, 91–104.

Mathis, R.L. and J.H. Jackson (2006), *Human Resource Management*, 11th edn, Mason, OH: Thomson-Southwestern.

Miner, J.B. (2000), 'Testing a psychological typology of entrepreneurship using business founders', *Journal of Applied Behavioral Science*, **36**, 43–69.

Mitchell, R.K., B. Smith, K.W. Seawright and E.A. Morse (2000), 'Cross-cultural cognitions and the venture creation decision', *Academy of Management Journal*, **43**(5), 974–93.

Moen, P. (2005), 'Beyond the career mystique: Time in, time out, and second acts', *Sociological Forum*, **20**, 189–208.

Noe, R.A. (2005), *Employee Training and Development*, 3rd edn, St. Louis: McGraw-Hill Irwin.

Phillips, B.D. and B.A. Kirchhoff (1989), 'Formation, growth, and survival: Small firm dynamics in the US economy', *Small Business Economics*, **1**, 65–74.

Platt, J.R. (1964), 'Strong inference', *Science*, **16**, 347–53.

Politis, D. (2005), 'The process of entrepreneurial learning: A conceptual framework', *Entrepreneurship: Theory and Practice*, **29**, 399–424.

Rae, D. (2002), 'Entrepreneurial emergence: A narrative study of entrepreneurial learning in independently owned media businesses', *The International Journal of Entrepreneurship and Innovation*, **3**, 53–9.

Rae, D. (2005), 'Mid-career entrepreneurial learning', *Education+Training*, **47**, 562–74.

Rae, D. and M. Carswell (2001), 'Towards a conceptual understanding of entrepreneurial learning', *Journal of Small Business and Enterprise Development*, **8**, 150–58.

Reynolds, P.D. (1997), 'Who starts new firms? Preliminary explorations of firms-in-gestation', *Small Business Economics*, **9**, 449–62.

Reynolds, P.D. and B. Miller (1992), 'New firm gestation: Conception, birth, and implications for research', *Journal of Business Venturing*, **7**, 1–14.

Ronstadt, R. (1986), 'Exit, stage left: Why entrepreneurs end their entrepreneurial careers before retirement', *Journal of Business Venturing*, **1**, 323–38.

Ruef, M., H.E. Aldrich and N. Carter (2003), 'The structure of organizational grounding teams: Homophily, strong ties, and isolation among US Entrepreneurs', *American Sociological Review*, **68**(2), 195–222.

Sadler-Smith, E., Y. Hampson, I. Chaton and B. Badger (2003), 'Managerial behavior, entrepreneurial style, and small business performance', *Journal of Small Business Management*, **41**, 47–67.

Schein, E.H. (1971), 'The individual, the organization, and the career: A conceptual scheme', *Journal of Applied Behavioral Science*, **7**, 401–26.

Schein, E.H. (1978), *Career Dynamics: Matching Individual and Organizational Needs*, Reading, MA: Addison-Wesley.

Schein, E.H. (1996), 'Career anchors revisited: Implications for career development in the 21st century', *Academy of Management Executive*, **10**, 80–88.

Schreiner, M. and G. Woller (2003), 'Microenterprise development programs in the United States and in the developing world', *World Development*, **31**, 1567–80.

Shane, S. and C. Spell (1998), 'Factors for new franchise success', *Sloan Management Review*, **39**, 43–50.

Smith, N.R. (1967), *The Entrepreneur and His Firm*, East Lansing, MI: Bureau of Business and Economic Research, MSU.

Sullivan, R. (2000), 'Entrepreneurial learning and mentoring', *International Journal of Entrepreneurial Behaviour and Research*, **6**, 160–75.

Thomas, R.J. (1996), 'Blue-collar careers: Meaning and choice in a world of constraints', in M. Arthur, D.T. Hall and B.S. Lawrence (eds), *Handbook of Career Theory*, Cambridge, UK: Cambridge University Press, pp. 354–79.

Townsend, E. (1999), 'Enabling occupation in the 21st century: Making good intentions a reality', *Australian Occupational Therapy Journal*, **46**, 147–59.

Ucbasaran, D., M. Wright, P. Westhead and L. Busenitz (2003), 'The impact of entrepreneurial experience on opportunity identification and exploitation: Habitual and novice entrepreneurs', in J.A. Katz and D. Shepherd (eds), *Advances in Entrepreneurship, Firm Emergence and Growth*, **6**, Greenwich, CT: JAI Press, pp. 231–63.

Wasserman, N. (2003), 'Founder-CEO succession and the paradox of entrepreneurial success', *Organization Science*, **14**, 149–73.

Westhead, P. and M. Wright (1998), 'Novice, serial, and portfolio founders: Are they different?', *Journal of Business Venturing*, **13**, 173–204.

Westhead, P. and M. Wright (1999), 'Contributions of novice, portfolio and serial founders located in rural and urban areas', *Regional Studies*, **33**, 157–73.

Westhead, P., D. Ucbasaran and M. Wright (2005), 'Experience and cognition: Do novice, serial, and portfolio entrepreneurs differ?', *International Small Business Journal*, **23**, 72–98.

Wright, M., K. Robbie and C. Ennew (1997), 'Serial entrepreneurs', *British Journal of Management*, **8**, 251–68.

24 Intention to quit: evidence from managers and professionals in small and medium-sized enterprises
Terry H. Wagar and James D. Grant

Introduction

Although there is a considerable amount of literature examining both intention to quit one's job and actual quit behaviour, most of the research has been carried out at the individual level of analysis. Researchers are now placing considerable attention on the association between human resource management (HRM) practices and the performance of the firm (Bae and Lawler, 2000; Wood, 1999; Wright et al., 2005), aspects of employee voice (Colvin, 2003), and organizational downsizing and restructuring (Cameron, 1994; Chadwick et al., 2004; Freeman, 1999; Littler and Innes, 2003). In this chapter we examine these issues and investigate their impact on the intention of small business managers and professionals to quit their job. This has important implications for continued and sustained growth in SMEs.

Literature review

Employee turnover

There is substantial literature (in excess of 1500 studies) on turnover in the organizational sciences, with the primary focus on individual-level predictors of turnover. While researchers looking at individual-level predictors generally acknowledge the distinction between voluntary and involuntary turnover, many organization-level turnover studies collapse 'voluntary' and 'involuntary' turnover into a single category (Shaw et al., 1998). Quitting or voluntary turnover refers to an individual employee's decision to leave an organization, whereas involuntary turnover, variously termed termination, discharge or dismissal represents an employer's decision to end the employment relationship.

High quit rates have been of particular interest in the literature because of a number of associated direct and indirect costs. Direct costs can raise labour costs (Batt et al., 2002) through replacement and training costs. Indirect costs result when turnover undermines organizational performance (Huselid, 1995) and are revealed by outcomes that include lowered productivity and loss of customer loyalty.

Voluntary turnover is thought to be affected by the attractiveness of staying in a current job and the relative availability of employment alternatives (Shaw et al., 1998). Most researchers have found a significant association between quitting or intention to quit, and attitudinal measures of job satisfaction and organizational commitment (Hanisch, 2002; Hulin et al., 1985). Furthermore, Hanisch (2002) suggests that while thinking about quitting may or may not translate into quitting, it may also translate into alternative withdrawal behaviours such as absenteeism, lateness, playing on the computer, frequent breaks, and chatting with co-workers, among other avoidance behaviours.

While various practices and activities can be used to make the firm a more (or less) attractive place to work, the availability of alternative employment is not directly controlled by the organization. Consequently, in this chapter the focus is on the impact of management practices that may play a part in making the small or medium-sized business a more (or less) attractive workplace. Specifically the focus is on high commitment/involvement HRM practices, employee voice and organizational cost-cutting measures.

Human resource management in SMEs
In a review of the literature on human resource management (HRM) practices in SMEs, Heneman et al. (2000) note that scant research attention is given to studying human resource management in SMEs. They also identify the high costs to small firms associated with poor selection decisions, the importance of human resource 'bundles' or systems of practices, and the need to examine how SMEs in countries other than the United States manage their human resources. Although there has been a dramatic increase in the number of articles examining the link between HRM and performance of the firm (Combs et al., 2006; Wall et al., 2004; Wood, 1999), there are relatively few studies exploring this linkage using data from SMEs (Sels et al., 2006). An exception is Carlson et al. (2006) who investigated the relationship between HRM and sales growth performance using data from 168 family-owned businesses. They found that HRM practices were more important for high sales growth firms (compared with SMEs with low sales growth).

Small business practitioners regularly comment on the importance of attracting and retaining quality employees; Carlson et al. (2006) note that family-owned SMEs identify the inability to attract and retain non-family executives as a significant barrier to business success and growth, while Baker and Aldrich (1999) underscore the importance of employee retention as a critical issue in managing a small firm. Way (2002) asserts that gaining access to superior employees is a source of competitive advantage for small firms as they are often more labour-intensive than larger organizations and other sources of competitive advantage are often limited. Still, few studies have specifically investigated employee retention in SMEs.

Way (2002) examined the use of high performance work systems (HPWS) in small American firms with fewer than 100 employees. He found that HPWS were associated with lower voluntary turnover in addition to being related to lower turnover overall and higher perceived productivity. He concluded that voluntary turnover (the loss of an employee who the firm would prefer to retain) is potentially very important for small businesses and the use of HPWS may be the key to sustainable competitive advantage in the small business sector.

Sels et al. (2006) in a study of small businesses in Belgium investigated the mediating effect of voluntary turnover (and productivity) on the link between HRM and firm performance. They found a negative but non-significant relationship between HRM and voluntary turnover. The authors indicated that there was a severe labour shortage at the time of the survey, leading to high labour mobility. They noted that retention efforts by smaller firms may have had little impact on keeping employees because most SMEs cannot compete with larger businesses when it comes to terms and conditions of employment.

Using data from 151 individuals employed in small businesses, Kickul (2001) had participants consider the psychological contract that existed between them and their employer and evaluate the extent to which the employer had fulfilled the promises made to them. The results indicated that intention to leave the employer was greater if the employer was perceived to have breached promises relating to autonomy and growth (for instance, providing meaningful work or the freedom to be creative) or rewards and opportunities (for example, opportunities for promotion and advancement or pay and bonuses tied to performance). This study is similar to ours in that the unit of analysis was the individual rather than the establishment or firm.

We must emphasize that HRM in small firms may differ noticeably compared with larger organizations, with the use of 'formal' human resource practices being far less common in small businesses (Kotey and Slade, 2005) and perhaps viewed as unnecessary (MacMahon and Murphy, 1999). In designing our study, we build on a model developed by Batt et al. (2002) to examine the relationship between intention to quit and three variables: (1) human resource management, (2) employee voice at the workplace, and (3) organizational cost cutting (each of which is discussed in more detail below).

Human resource management issues

According to Barney (1991, 1995), the resource-based view of the firm suggests that employers can create competitive advantage by means of a highly productive workforce – a valuable source of competitive advantage because it cannot be copied quickly, is hard to imitate, and is somewhat specific to the climate or environment of the organization. Effective human resource management allows an organization to attract, keep and develop higher quality employees that are a relatively rare resource (Koch and McGrath, 1996; Pfeffer and Veiga, 1999; Way, 2002).

In light of the focus on human resource management 'systems' or 'bundles' of human resource management practices (Becker and Gerhart, 1996; Huselid and Becker, 1996) and the importance of 'high-involvement work practices' (Bae and Lawler, 2000), this study examines whether a high-involvement HRM strategy is related with an employee's intention to quit a job. The use of a bundle of practices is consistent with Heneman et al.'s (2000) review of HRM issues for SMEs, and Way (2002) and Sels et al. (2006) who acknowledged the importance of HRM systems in their research. In addition, there is evidence (Rogg et al., 2001) that organizational climate may be an important factor affecting workplace performance.

Recent research focusing on commitment-enhancing or high performance work systems has shown that both specific human resource management practices (Batt et al., 2002) and coherent sets, or clusters, of human resource practices (Arthur, 1994; Huselid, 1995) lead to lower turnover. For instance, firm-specific training (Miller and Mulvey, 1991) and higher pay (Delery et al., 2000; Shaw et al., 1998), as well as satisfaction with promotion opportunities, job security and pay (Griffeth and Hom, 2001) have been shown to lead to lower turnover.

Studies of team participation have frequently considered teams only as part of a cluster of practices (Arthur, 1994; Huselid, 1995). However, the relationship between enriched jobs (for example, autonomy, variety and ability to complete a whole task) and higher job satisfaction and lower turnover is well established (Griffeth and Hom, 2001), suggesting that teams must have real discretion to affect conditions at work (Batt et al., 2002).

Shaw et al. (1998) argue that research on the determinants of turnover at the organizational level is almost non-existent. Their examination of the effects of HR management practices in the trucking industry focused on inducements and investments including compensation and benefits packages, job stability and tenure, training opportunities and voice mechanisms (specifically unionization), as well as practices that would tend to increase the expected contributions of employees including employee monitoring and other noxious working conditions such as time on the road. Shaw et al. (1998) found that quit rates increased with electronic monitoring and time on the road and decreased with better pay and benefits.

Shaw et al. (2005) attempted to unravel the 'black box dynamics' of the relationship among organizational turnover, HRM practices and organizational performance. They found that voluntary turnover was negatively related to measures of workforce performance including productivity and safety, and that there was modest support for the finding that these measures of workforce performance mediated the relationship between voluntary turnover and financial performance. Moreover, the negative effects of voluntary turnover on workforce performance were attenuated as turnover rates increased. That is, the negative effects on workforce performance were felt more acutely as the voluntary turnover rate increased.

Employee voice
Representation by a union may give employees a greater voice at the workplace. Turnover in heavily unionized industries and among unionized workers has been shown to be significantly lower than in non-unionized settings (Batt et al., 2002; Delery et al., 2000). While many researchers have argued that this is largely due to union monopoly bargaining power ensuring higher wages, Freeman and Medoff (1984) suggested that unions also establish 'voice' mechanisms. They based their suggestion on Hirschman's (1970) theoretical framework that proposed that workers express dissatisfaction through either exit or voice. Hirschman defined voice as any attempt to change unsatisfactory work conditions. Since non-unionized workers generally do not have access to the voice mechanisms found in a unionized setting, they are more likely to exit in response to workplace dissatisfaction. However, it can be argued that the balance between voice and exit may be influenced by the evolving design of work and human resource practices (Batt et al., 2002). Furthermore, Delery et al. (2000) questioned whether union voice mechanisms were still as effective in influencing quits in the 1990s.

While grievance procedures are well established in unionized organizations, a number of employers are now adopting formal dispute resolution procedures for their non-union workforce (Batt et al., 2002; Colvin, 2003). Some research has shown that, among organizations that have similar voice mechanisms available, greater usage of these mechanisms may lead to higher quit rates (Lewin and Peterson, 1999). However, Olson-Buchanan and Boswell (2002) found that more loyal employees may prefer and use less formal methods to voice discontent and that the use of less formal voice methods was associated with less job search activity and lower intent to quit.

Organizational cost-cutting and job security
Cameron (1994) identifies three downsizing strategies – workforce reduction, work redesign and systematic change. Workforce reduction, which is the most common strategy, is characterized by the use of such programmes

as attrition, early retirement or voluntary severance, layoffs or terminations. Workforce reduction strategies are often band-aid measures, which do not address strategic issues confronting employers.

Work redesign, a more medium-term strategy, is concerned not simply with reducing the number of employees but entails a critical assessment of whether specific functions, products, and/or services need to be changed or eliminated. Work redesign may include eliminating functions, groups or divisions, reducing bureaucracy, and redesigning tasks and/or jobs.

The final strategy identified by Cameron, systematic change, is a long-term approach in which the organization's culture and the attitudes and values of employees are altered so that they are congruent with the goals of reducing costs and improving quality. The systematic change strategy takes considerable time and involves major commitment of resources. Employers who focus on achieving short-term profit or budget goals rarely see the systematic change strategy as an attractive alternative to workforce reduction.

Batt et al. (2002) have suggested that the use of organizational cost-cutting and restructuring has introduced labour market competition inside organizations, resulting in the contradictory practices of commitment enhancement on the one hand, and contingent staffing and pay on the other. For instance, while contingent and part-time workers might be used to insulate core employees from job loss, firms often use contingent staffing to cut costs. Hence, an organization's restructuring efforts may, however inadvertently, signal to employees that job security commitments have been withdrawn because future cost-cutting may lead to greater use of contingent staffing. Greater use of contingent pay may also increase employee uncertainty by increasing compensation variability without a compensating wage increase for the additional risk. In such a case, the more skilled employees may be expected to consider employment alternatives. Our concern in this chapter is intention to quit, which we argue is related to firm-level management practices, specifically HRM, employee voice and cost-cutting measures. In the next section we outline our data methodology and results. Although we measure intention to quit (rather than actual turnover), Breukelen et al. (2004) found behavioural intentions to be the best predictor of turnover after controlling for the effects of job satisfaction, organizational commitment, age, and tenure for which we also control.

Method

Data collection
Our data were collected by means of a mail survey to business school alumni of a Canadian university. The mailing list was provided by the

Alumni Office of the university. Other researchers have also used university alumni as their sample (Feuille and Chachere, 1995). While we received responses from just under 1000 graduates (for a response rate of 28 per cent), we excluded respondents who were not currently employed, those working in the public sector, and those employed in organizations with 500 or more employees. In addition, missing data on our variables also reduced the number of useable responses. As a result, the findings presented in this chapter are based on 351 responses.

Dependent variable
Our interest was in the retention of small business employees, with a particular focus on the factors associated with intention to quit (in other words, voluntary turnover behaviour). We measured our dependent variable by having respondents indicate whether they intended to quit their job over the next two years using a 6-point scale (1 = definitely no and 6 = definitely yes that the individual intended to quit his or her job).

Although we measure intention to quit (rather than actual turnover), Breukelen et al. (2004) found behavioural intentions to be the best predictor of turnover after the effects of job satisfaction, organizational commitment, age and tenure were controlled for.

Independent variables
As noted previously, we were influenced by the model of quit behaviour developed by Batt et al. (2002), who hypothesized that employee quit rates may be influenced by a high commitment/involvement human resource management strategy, employee voice, and organizational cost-cutting practices (such as downsizing and restructuring). The current research on high commitment human resource management focuses on human resource management 'systems' or 'bundles' of practices rather than on examining the impact of any one practice (Becker and Gerhart, 1996; Huang, 2000; Sels et al., 2006; Wood, 1999). We measured a high-involvement HRM strategy using 14 items adapted from Bae and Lawler (2000), with each of the items measured on a six-point scale (1 = strongly disagree and 6 = strongly agree). The various items addressed issues relating to employee training, employee empowerment, selective staffing and performance-based compensation. Sample items included: 'the organization places a high priority on training, the organization gives employees an opportunity to use personal initiative, and the organization is very selective when hiring new employees'. The Cronbach's coefficient alpha for the scale was 0.91.

In examining aspects of employee voice, there is an emerging body of work indicating that the presence of a grievance procedure to address employee disputes or complaints may also be associated with reduced employee quits (Batt et al., 2002). The presence of a grievance procedure was dummy-coded (1 = presence; 0 = absence). We hypothesized that the presence of a grievance procedure would be related with a reduced intention to quit.

While we also asked participants to indicate whether they were members of a trade union, we do not include this measure in the chapter because we limit our analysis to respondents from the private sector that are in a professional or managerial capacity. Under Canadian labour laws, individuals in management positions or in certain professional roles are generally not permitted to have union representation. Such restrictions on union representation are not as limiting in the non-profit and government sectors.

There is a developing body of research on organizational cost-cutting practices (Batt et al., 2002; Freeman, 1999; Littler and Innes, 2003). We measured organizational cost-cutting using a five-item scale which addressed the extent to which the employer engaged in contracting out of work, cutting planned capital investment, using across-the-board cutbacks, outsourcing of work, and using contingent workers. Each of these items was measured on a six-point scale, with one indicating that the organization did not use the practice in question over the past two years and six representing a substantial use of the practice. The organizational cost-cutting scale had a Cronbach's coefficient alpha of 0.78. We expected that organizational cost-cutting would be associated with a greater intention to quit.

Receiving little research attention is the relationship between the performance of the company and an employee's intention to quit. In SMEs this would be important, impacting on perceptions of job security. We measured company performance using a four-item scale. We relied on subjective measures of performance (productivity, product or service quality, operating efficiency and customer or client satisfaction), with each item being measured on a six-point scale (1 = very low to 6 = very high). We relied on research suggesting that subjective measures of performance are correlated with more objective measures (Wall et al., 2004). The Cronbach's coefficient alpha for the scale was 0.83. We hypothesized that an employee's intention to quit would be less if the organization was performing well.

Control variables

A number of variables were also entered into the statistical model to control for other factors that may be associated with an employee's intention to quit his or her job. The control variables included the employee's age in years, sex (1 = male; 0 = female), whether the respondent had a graduate degree (1 = yes; 0 = no), whether the individual was employed in a management position (1 = yes; 0 = no), the industry sector of the respondent's employer (1 = manufacturing; 0 = service sector), and the size of the employer (measured by the natural logarithm of the number of employees). Previous research (Delery et al., 2000; Griffeth and Hom, 2001; Shaw et al., 1998; Shaw et al., 2005) has pointed to the need to control for such variables.

Results

Descriptive statistics
Descriptive statistics for the independent and control variables are presented in Table 24.1. About 64 per cent of the respondents were male and the average age of the respondents was just over 37 years. Slightly under one-quarter (22 per cent) of participants had a graduate degree, and 33 per cent were business owners or senior managers. In terms of industry sector of the employer, 17 per cent of the participants were employed in manufacturing and 83 per cent in service-related businesses. Approximately 38 per cent of the respondents were employed in organizations with 25 or fewer employees and a further 33 per cent were in businesses with 26 to 100 employees. About 36 per cent of the firms had a grievance procedure.

With respect to the use of a high-involvement HRM strategy, the mean score for this scale was 3.90 (out of a maximum of 6). In examining this finding, it appears that while a number of employers were making positive attempts to manage human resources effectively and focus on employee well-being, there was considerable variation among organizations. In terms of organizational cost-cutting practices, the mean score was 2.87 (out of a maximum of 6), suggesting modest use of such practices by employers. The

Table 24.1   Descriptive statistics

Variable	Mean	Standard deviation
High involvement HRM	3.9	0.97
Grievance procedure	0.36	0.48
Organizational cost-cutting	2.49	1.08
Employer performance	4.33	0.90
Employee gender	0.64	0.48
Manufacturing sector	0.17	0.38
Number of employees (Nat'l log)	3.78	1.36
Graduate degree	0.22	0.41
Manager	0.35	0.48
Employee age	37.44	8.53

Table 24.2   Intention to quit

Score	Number	Per cent
1	150	42.8
2	69	19.7
3	35	10.0
4	47	13.4
5	22	6.3
6	28	8.0

average score on the employer performance scale was 4.33, indicating moderately good performance.

Considering an employee's intention to quit his or her job (see Table 24.2), 27.7 per cent of participants indicated that they intended to quit their job over the next two years (as measured by a score of four or more on the six-point scale).

Factors associated with intention to quit

We estimate two models (using OLS regression) to examine the relationship between intention to quit and the independent variables. In the first model (Column 1 of Table 24.3), we include only the independent variables, while the control variables are added in the second model (Column 2 of Table 24.3).

A high-involvement HRM strategy is negatively related ($p < .05$) with intention to quit. Similarly, more positive employer performance is associated ($p < .01$) with a lower score on the intention to quit scale. These findings suggest that human resource management strategy and the perceived success of the business may be important factors when considering employee quit behaviour. These findings are relatively stable even after the control variables were entered into the model.

With reference to organizational cost-cutting, the coefficient on this variable is both positive and significant ($p < .05$) in both models. In other words, intention to quit increases when an employer engages in major cost-cutting or restructuring efforts.

The results pertaining to employee voice are less clear. In both models, the coefficient on the employee voice measure (that is, the presence of a grievance procedure to address employment-related issues) is negative but not statistically significant.

For the most part, the control variables (including the employee's sex, the sector in which the employee worked, the employee's position in the organization, and the size of the employee's organization) are not related to

Table 24.3   OLS regression results

Variable	Model 1	Model 2
High involvement HRM	−0.522***	−0.508***
	(0.106)	(0.103)
Organizational cost-cutting	0.149***	0.147***
	(0.073)	(0.073)
Grievance procedure	−0.212	−0.137
	(0.169)	(0.168)
Employer performance	−0.334***	−0.350***
	(0.112)	(0.109)
Employee gender		−0.025
		(0.162)
Manufacturing sector		−0.149
		(0.200)
Number of employees (Nat'l log)		−0.006
		(0.060)
Graduate degree		0.467**
		(0.186)
Manager		−0.107
		(0.167)
Employee age		−0.049 ***
		(0.009)
Constant	5.628***	7.440***
	(0.465)	(0.603)
F-Test	27.381***	15.338***
R^2	0.240	0.311
Change in R^2		0.071
N	351	351

Notes: *$p < .10$; **$p < .05$; ***$p < .01$.

intention to quit. However, intention to quit is strongly associated ($p < .01$) with employee age. As expected, older workers are less likely to report that they plan to quit their job, when compared to younger employees. Not surprisingly, employee age is very strongly correlated with employee work experience (as measured by years of service) and when we run additional models with years of service instead of employee age, the results are very similar.

There is also evidence that intention to quit is significantly related ($p < .05$) to the completion of a graduate degree. Our results suggest that small business employees with a graduate degree (such as an MBA) are more likely to quit their job (as measured by intention to quit).

Supplemental analysis

Recent research by Rogg et al. (2001) underscores the importance of workplace climate in the human resource management literature. While we measured workplace climate in our survey, we did not include this scale in our initial OLS results because it was highly correlated with the high-involvement HRM strategy scale. We measured workplace climate using a six-item scale adapted from Dastmalchian et al. (1991), with the measures addressing such issues as the prompt settlement of employee disputes, whether the conditions of employment are fair, and the exchange of information between the employer and employees. The items were measured using the anchors 1 = strongly disagree and 6 = strongly agree. The workplace climate scale had a Cronbach's coefficient alpha of 0.93.

When we re-estimate our OLS regression models using workplace climate instead of high-involvement HRM strategy, the results indicate that workplace climate is strongly and negatively associated ($p < .01$) with intention to quit (in both the full and reduced models). In other words, as the score on the workplace climate increases (more positive climate), intention to quit is reduced.

Conclusion

In this chapter we examined whether intention to quit was associated with human resource management, employee voice, and organizational cost-cutting using a sample of graduates from a Canadian university. Overall, fewer than 28 per cent of respondents indicated an intention to quit their job over the next two years.

The results suggest that organizations using a high-involvement human resource strategy are more attractive to employees and thus fewer workers intend to quit such employers. This finding supports previous research (Delery et al., 2000; Batt et al., 2002; Guthrie, 2001; Shaw et al., 1998; Way, 2002) indicating a relationship between human resource management and quit rates. Our measure of a high-involvement HRM strategy follows Bae and Lawler (2000) and combines or 'bundles' items addressing employee training, employee empowerment, selective staffing and performance-based compensation. It may be that SMEs with more high involvement HRM systems are better able to select quality employees, retain such individuals, and improve the quality of work of poorer workers.

Although a high-involvement HRM strategy is important to employee retention, the findings also demonstrate the significance of the workplace climate. Rogg et al. (2001) found that organizational climate was an important predictor of customer satisfaction and mediated the relationship between human resource practices and customer satisfaction. Our findings are particularly relevant to small firms who may see improving workplace climate as a more viable strategy than substantial investment in human resource management – Sels et al. (2006) concluded that while HRM intensity is positively related to productivity, one must also consider the cost increases associated with HRM intensity. Further attention to the role of workplace climate as a mediating variable is called for.

Our finding that intention to quit was negatively related with employer performance was not surprising. One would expect a preference on the part of employees to work for a successful organization. Unfortunately, we did not measure the extent to which respondents were compensated based on company performance or whether the participants had an equity interest in the organization. These issues clearly deserve future research attention.

Although there was some evidence that intention to quit was negatively associated with the presence of a grievance system to address employee complaints and workplace issues, this finding was not significant in the OLS regressions. One might expect that a formal dispute resolution procedure would encourage employees to use a voice rather than exit approach. However, the structure and features of grievance procedures vary considerably and research suggests that while a number of organizations are implementing non-union grievance procedures, they are often used by a relatively small number of employees (Colvin, 2003). There is a need for additional work on dispute resolution in SMEs.

While the 1990s were also known as the 'downsizing decade', the past few years have seen a decline in the use of massive employment cutbacks and greater attention to careful managing of the restructuring process (Freeman, 1999; Littler and Innes, 2003). We found that organizational cost-cutting (characterized by such practices as contracting out of work, using across-the-board cutbacks, and increasing the use of contingent workers) was associated with a greater intention to quit. Pfeffer and Veiga (1999) discuss the importance of job security for employers seeking to become high-performance work organizations – quite simply, lower employer commitment to job security encourages employees to look around for alternative employment and is in conflict with a high-involvement HRM strategy. Again, the bulk of the research on workplace restructuring has been directed toward larger organizations and we know very little about SMEs and restructuring.

It was not surprising that older workers reported that they were less likely to quit their job (Griffeth and Hom, 2001). However, while we expected female respondents to be more likely to indicate an intention to quit their job, we did not find a significant relationship between quit intention and sex of the respondent. There is considerable evidence to suggest that both women's intent to leave and actual leaving are based on different reasons than those for men. For instance, non-work factors (Dalton et al., 1997) such as co-worker intent to leave (Weisberg and Kirschenbaum, 1993), valued social relationships (Russ and McNeilly, 1995), household duties and family illness (Sicherman, 1996) have all been found to be predictors of women leaving their job. Alternatively, men have a greater tendency to cite work-related reasons for leaving, including the availability of on-the-job training and long-term career opportunities (Sicherman, 1996). While men typically hold higher positions in their organizations, it seems that less-educated women in lower positions tend to leave their jobs more frequently than their male counterparts. In our study the women were highly educated and consequently, their exit behaviour may be different when compared to less-educated women. Again, there is a need for additional research on the quit behaviour of highly educated women in SMEs.

Overall our findings suggest that investment in people is very important. However, investing in a high-involvement HRM strategy is a long-term and potentially expensive commitment on the part of the employer. Furthermore, there is some evidence that a high-involvement HRM strategy may not be appropriate or feasible for all employers. Although a growing body of research supports the proposition that investment in human resources is related to higher performance, Guthrie (2001) clearly points out that the cost of losing an employee is much higher in a high-involvement workplace because the organization has a much greater investment in the employee. Our sample was comprised of well-educated individuals and thus one would expect that the cost of replacing such employees may be much greater than for less-skilled workers. From a practical perspective, employers should consider developing policies and strategies with the goals of attracting and retaining high quality employees but recognize that the importance of employee retention may vary from business to business.

Our study identified a number of variables associated with intention to quit by managers and professionals working in small and medium-sized businesses, but we can see several opportunities for future research. For instance, it would be helpful to know whether the results generalize to employees without a university education and to workers in other countries. In addition, there is need for considerably more work on the relationship between quit behaviour and HRM strategy, and the potential mediating role of workplace climate. Moreover, actually tracking individuals over time would allow researchers to investigate actual quit behaviour, rather than intention to quit (although there is some research suggesting that the two measures are clearly correlated). Finally, and consistent with survey research, we acknowledge potential concerns relating to common method variance and non-response bias.

While dysfunctional turnover is costly to large businesses, it can be argued that losing quality employees may be particularly harmful to smaller firms who can rely on one or a handful of key people. In addition, smaller firms may have more difficulty attracting good employees to replace those individuals leaving the business (see Chapters 17 and 18 by Cardon and Tarique and Williamson and Robinson in this handbook).

In terms of practical implications, our study addresses the issue of functional and dysfunctional turnover and helps identify those variables associated with the retention of managers. Although employee retention may be important in many organizations, there is little guidance for what needs to be done in SMEs to retain key staff.

References

Arthur, J. (1994), 'Effects of human resource systems on manufacturing performance and turnover', *Academy of Management Journal*, **37**, 670–87.
Bae, J. and J. Lawler (2000), 'Organizational and HRM strategies in Korea: Impact on firm performance in an emerging economy', *Academy of Management Journal*, **43**, 502–18.
Baker, T. and H. Aldrich (1999), 'The trouble with gurus: Responses to dependence and the emergence of employment practices in entrepreneurial firms', *Frontiers of Entrepreneurship Research*, Wellesley, MA: Babson College for Entrepreneurial Studies.
Barney, J. (1991), 'Firm resources and sustained competitive advantage', *Journal of Management*, **17**, 99–120.
Barney, J. (1995), 'Looking inside for competitive advantage', *Academy of Management Executive*, **9**, 49–61.
Batt, R., A. Colvin and J. Keefe (2002), 'Employee voice, human resource practices, and quit rates: Evidence from the telecommunications industry', *Industrial and Labor Relations Review*, **55**, 573–94.
Becker, B. and B. Gerhart (1996), 'The impact of human resource management on organizational performance', *Academy of Management Journal*, **39**, 779–801.
Breukelen, W., R. Vlist and H. Steensma (2004), 'Voluntary employee turnover: Combining variables from the "traditional" turnover literature with the theory of planned behavior', *Journal of Organizational Behavior*, **25**(7), 893–914.
Cameron, K. (1994), 'Strategies for successful organizational downsizing', *Human Resource Management*, **33**, 189–211.
Carlson, D., N. Upton and S. Seaman (2006), 'The impact of human resource practices and compensation design on performance: An analysis of family-owned SMEs', *Journal of Small Business Management*, **44**, 531–43.
Chadwick, C., L. Hunter and S. Walston (2004), 'Effects of downsizing practices on the performance of hospitals', *Strategic Management Journal*, **25**, 405–27.
Colvin, A. (2003), 'Institutional pressures, human resource strategies, and the rise of nonunion dispute resolution procedures', *Industrial and Labor Relations Review*, **56**, 375–92.
Combs, J., Y. Liu, A. Hall and D. Ketchen (2006), 'How much do high-performance work practices matter? A meta-analysis of their effects on organizational performance', *Personnel Psychology*, **59**, 501–28.
Dalton, D., J. Hill and R. Ramsay (1997), 'Women as managers and partners: Context-specific predictors of turnover in international public accounting firms', *Auditing*, **16**, 29–50.
Dastmalchian, A., P. Blyton and R. Adamson (1991), *The Climate of Workplace Relations*, London: Routledge.
Delery, J., N. Gupta, J. Shaw, D. Jenkins and M. Ganster (2000), 'Unionization, compensation, and voice effects on quits and retention', *Industrial Relations*, **39**, 625–45.
Feuille, P. and D. Chachere (1995), 'Looking fair or being fair: Remedial voice procedures in nonunion workplaces', *Journal of Management*, **21**, 27–42.
Freeman, R. and J. Medoff (1984), *What Do Unions Do*, New York: Basic Books.

Freeman, S. (1999), 'The gestalt of organizational downsizing: Downsizing strategies as packages of change', *Human Relations*, **52**, 1505–41.

Griffeth, R. and P. Hom (2001), *Retaining Valued Employees*, Thousand Oaks, CA: Sage Publications.

Guthrie, J. (2001), 'High involvement work practices, turnover and productivity: Evidence from New Zealand', *Academy of Management Journal*, Reading, MA: Addison-Wesley.

Hanisch, K. (2002), 'The timing of thinking about quitting: The effect on job attitudes and behaviors', in M. Koslowsky and M. Krausz (eds), *Voluntary Employee Withdrawal*, New York: Kluwer Academic / Plenum Publisher, pp. 193–211.

Heneman, R., J. Tansky and S. Camp (2000), 'Human resource management practices in small and medium-sized enterprises: Unanswered questions and future research perspectives', *Entrepreneurship: Theory and Practice*, **25**, 11–26.

Hirschman, A. (1970), *Exit, Voice, and Loyalty*, Cambridge, MA: Harvard University Press.

Huang, T. (2000), 'Are the human resource practices of effective firms distinctly different from those of poorly performing ones? Evidence from Taiwanese enterprises', *International Journal of Human Resource Management*, **11**, 436–51.

Hulin, C., M. Roznowksi and D. Hachiya (1985), 'Alternative opportunities and withdrawal decisions: Empirical and theoretical discrepancies and an integration', *Psychological Bulletin*, **97**, 233–50.

Huselid, M. (1995), 'The impact of human resource management practices on turnover, productivity, and corporate financial performance', *Academy of Management Journal*, **38**, 635–72.

Huselid, M. and B. Becker (1996), 'Methodological issues in cross-sectional and panel estimates of the human resource–firm performance link', *Industrial Relations*, **35**, 400–22.

Kickul, J. (2001), 'Promises made, promises broken: An exploration of employee attraction and retention practices in small businesses', *Journal of Small Business Management*, **39**, 320–55.

Koch, M. and R. McGrath (1996), 'Improving labor productivity: Human resource management policies do matter', *Strategic Management Journal*, **17**, 335–54.

Kotey, B. and P. Slade (2005), 'Formal human resource management practices in small growing firms', *Journal of Small Business Management*, **43**, 16–40.

Lewin, D. and R. Peterson (1999), 'Behavioral outcomes of grievance activity', *Industrial Relations*, **38**, 554–76.

Littler, C. and P. Innes, (2003), 'Downsizing and deknowledging the firm', *Work, Employment and Society*, **17**, 73–100.

MacMahon, J. and E. Murphy (1999), 'Managerial effectiveness in small enterprises: Implications for HRD', *Journal of European Industrial Training*, **23**, 25–35.

Miller, P. and C. Mulvey (1991), 'Australian evidence on the exit/voice model of the labor market', *Industrial and Labor Relations Review*, **45**, 44–57.

Olson-Buchanan, J. and W. Boswell (2002), 'The role of employee loyalty and formality in voicing discontent', *Journal of Applied Psychology*, **87**(6), 1167–74.

Pfeffer, J. and J. Veiga (1999), 'Putting people first for organizational success', *The Academy of Management Executive*, **13**, 37–48.

Rogg, K., D. Schmidt, C. Shull and N. Schmidt (2001), 'Human resource practices, organizational climate, and customer satisfaction', *Journal of Management*, **27**, 431–9.

Russ, F. and K. McNeilly (1995), 'Links among satisfaction, commitment, and turnover intentions: The moderating effect of experience, gender, and performance', *Journal of Business Research*, **34**, 57–65.

Sels, L., S. De Winne, J. Delmotte, J. Maes, D. Faems and A. Forrier (2006), 'Linking HRM and small business performance: An examination of the impact of HRM intensity on the productivity and financial performance of small businesses', *Small Business Economics*, **26**, 83–101.

Shaw, J., N. Gupta and J. Delery (2005), 'Alternative conceptualizations of the relationship between voluntary turnover and organizational performance', *Academy of Management Journal*, **48**(1), 50–68.

Shaw, J., J. Delery, D. Jenkins and N. Gupta (1998), 'An organization-level analysis of voluntary and involuntary turnover', *Academy of Management Journal*, **41**, 511–25.

Sicherman, N. (1996), 'Gender differences in departures from a large firm', *Industrial and Labor Relations Review*, **49**, 484–95.
Wall, T., J. Michie, M. Patterson, S. Wood, M. Sheehan, C. Clegg and M. West (2004), 'On the validity of subjective measures of performance', *Personnel Psychology*, **57**, 95–118.
Way, S. (2002), 'High performance work systems and intermediate indicators of firm performance within the US small business sector', *Journal of Management*, **28**, 765–85.
Weisberg, J. and A. Kirschenbaum (1993), 'Gender and turnover: A re-examination of the impact of sex on intent and actual job changes', *Human Relations*, **46**, 987–98.
Wood, S. (1999), 'Human resource management and performance', *International Journal of Management Reviews*, **1**, 367–413.
Wright, P., T. Gardner, L. Moynihan and M. Allen (2005), 'The relationship between HR practices and firm performance: Examining causal order', *Personnel Psychology*, **58**, 409–46.

Index

Abbreviations used in the index:
HRM – human resources management
SMEs – small and medium-sized enterprises.

Titles of publications are shown in *italics*.